THECLA AND MEDIEVAL SAINTHOOD

Saint Thecla was one of the most prominent figures of early Christianity who provided a model of virginity and a role model for women in the early Church. She was the object of cult and of pilgrimage and her tale in the *Acts of Paul and Thecla* made a tremendous impact on later hagiographies of both female and male saints. This volume explores this impact on medieval hagiographical texts composed in Armenian, Coptic, Ethiopic, Greek, Irish, Latin, Persian, and Syriac. It investigates how they evoked and/or invoked Thecla and her tale in constructing the lives and story worlds of their chosen saints and offers detailed original readings of the lives of various heroines and heroes. The book adds further depth and nuance to our understanding of Thecla's popularity and the spread of her legend and cult.

GHAZZAL DABIRI is an Iranist who specializes in narratives of kingship, kinship, and sainthood. She received her PhD from UCLA and has held positions at various institutions including Columbia University and currently the University of Maryland. A Fulbright Scholar, she also held a European Research Council postdoctoral fellowship at Ghent University.

FLAVIA RUANI is a researcher at the Institut de recherche et d'histoire des textes, CNRS, Paris. She specializes in late antique and medieval Syriac Christianity, focusing on religious controversies, manuscript studies, hagiography, and the history of Manichaeism. She has translated into French the *Hymns against Heresies* by Ephrem the Syrian (2018).

THECLA AND MEDIEVAL SAINTHOOD

The Acts of Paul and Thecla
in Eastern and Western Hagiography

EDITED BY

GHAZZAL DABIRI

University of Maryland, College Park

FLAVIA RUANI

Institut de recherche et d'histoire des textes, CNRS, Paris

CAMBRIDGE
UNIVERSITY PRESS

Shaftesbury Road, Cambridge CB2 8EA, United Kingdom

One Liberty Plaza, 20th Floor, New York, NY 10006, USA

477 Williamstown Road, Port Melbourne, VIC 3207, Australia

314–321, 3rd Floor, Plot 3, Splendor Forum, Jasola District Centre, New Delhi – 110025, India

103 Penang Road, #05-06/07, Visioncrest Commercial, Singapore 238467

Cambridge University Press is part of Cambridge University Press & Assessment, a department of the University of Cambridge.

We share the University's mission to contribute to society through the pursuit of education, learning and research at the highest international levels of excellence.

www.cambridge.org
Information on this title: www.cambridge.org/9781009005050

DOI: 10.1017/9781009008631

© Cambridge University Press & Assessment 2022

This publication is in copyright. Subject to statutory exception and to the provisions of relevant collective licensing agreements, no reproduction of any part may take place without the written permission of Cambridge University Press & Assessment.

First published 2022
First paperback edition 2023

A catalogue record for this publication is available from the British Library

Library of Congress Cataloging-in-Publication data
NAMES: Dabiri, Ghazzal, 1975- editor. | Ruani, Flavia, editor.
TITLE: Thecla and Medieval sainthood : the Acts of Paul and Thecla in Eastern and Western hagiography / edited by Ghazzal Dabiri, University of Maryland, College Park; Flavia Ruani, Centre National de la Recherche Scientifique (CNRS), Paris.
DESCRIPTION: Cambridge : Cambridge University Press, 2022. | Includes bibliographical references and index.
IDENTIFIERS: LCCN 2021052187 (print) | LCCN 2021052188 (ebook) | ISBN 9781316519219 (hardback) | ISBN 9781009005050 (paperback) | ISBN 9781009008631 (epub)
SUBJECTS: LCSH: Christian hagiography–History and criticism. | Thecla, Saint. | Acts of Paul and Thecla. | BISAC: HISTORY / Ancient / General
CLASSIFICATION: LCC BX4662 .T49 2022 (print) | LCC BX4662 (ebook) | DDC 229/.925–dc23/eng/
20211213
LC record available at https://lccn.loc.gov/2021052187
LC ebook record available at https://lccn.loc.gov/2021052188

ISBN 978-1-316-51921-9 Hardback
ISBN 978-1-009-00505-0 Paperback

Cambridge University Press & Assessment has no responsibility for the persistence or accuracy of URLs for external or third-party internet websites referred to in this publication and does not guarantee that any content on such websites is, or will remain, accurate or appropriate.

Contents

List of Contributors	*page* vii
Acknowledgments	ix
List of Abbreviations	xi

Introduction   1
Ghazzal Dabiri

PART I AN ACT TO FOLLOW

1. A Cainite Invocation of Thecla? The Reception of the *Acts of Paul* in North Africa as Exemplified in Tertullian's *de Baptismo*   35
   Jeremy W. Barrier

2. Saint Thecla in Geʿez Hagiographical Literature: From Confessor to Martyr   61
   Damien Labadie

3. Versified Martyrs: The Reception of Thecla from the Latin West to Medieval Ireland   85
   Caitríona Ó Dochartaigh

4. The Reception of the *Acts of Thecla* in Armenia: Thecla as a Model of Representation for Holy Women in Ancient Armenian Literature   110
   Valentina Calzolari

5. Thecla beyond Thecla: Secondary Characters in Syriac Hagiography   142
   Flavia Ruani

6   Shifting the Poetics of Gender Ambiguity: The Coptic
    Naturalization of Thecla   175
    Arietta Papaconstantinou

PART II AN ACT TO SURPASS

7   Thecla, the First Cross-Dresser? The *Acts of Paul and
    Thecla* and the Lives of Byzantine Transvestite Saints   197
    Julie Van Pelt

8   From Diotima to Thecla and Beyond: Virginal Voice
    in the Lives of Helia and Constantina   233
    Virginia Burrus

9   Reception and Rejection: Thecla and the *Acts of Paul and
    Thecla* in the *Passion of Eugenia* and Other Latin Texts   256
    Klazina Staat

10 A Medieval Sufi Thecla? Female Civic and Spiritual
    Leadership in 'Attār's "Tale of the Virtuous Woman"
    and the *Life and Passion of Eugenia*   282
    Ghazzal Dabiri

Afterword: Thecla and the Power of an Open Story   318
    Kate Cooper

Appendix   329
Index   340

Contributors

JEREMY W. BARRIER is Professor of Biblical Literature at Heritage Christian University, Florence, Alabama. He is the author of several books, articles, and volumes concerning Thecla.

VIRGINIA BURRUS is the Bishop W. Earl Ledden Professor of Religion at Syracuse University. She is the author or coauthor of nine books, including *Ancient Christian Ecopoetics* (2019).

VALENTINA CALZOLARI is Professor of Armenian Studies at the University of Geneva and corresponding member of the Académie des Inscriptions et Belles-Lettres (Institut de France).

KATE COOPER is Professor of History at Royal Holloway, University of London. Her significant publications include *The Virgin and the Bride: Idealised Womanhood in Late Antiquity* (1996), *The Fall of the Roman Household* (2007), and *Band of Angels: The Forgotten World of Early Christian Women* (2013).

GHAZZAL DABIRI is an Iranist who specializes in narratives of kingship, kinship, and sainthood. She received her PhD from the University of California–Los Angeles and has held positions at various institutions including Columbia University and currently the University of Maryland.

DAMIEN LABADIE holds a PhD from the École pratique des hautes études (Paris) and is currently a researcher at the Centre National de la Recherche scientifique (CNRS) at the CIHAM institute in Lyon.

CAITRÍONA Ó DOCHARTAIGH is Lecturer in Early and Medieval Irish at University College Cork. Her research focuses on the devotional and apocryphal literature of medieval Ireland in both Latin and Irish.

ARIETTA PAPACONSTANTINOU is Associate Professor of Ancient History at the University of Reading and has published widely on the religious, linguistic, social, and economic aspects of the transition from Rome to the Caliphate in the eastern Mediterranean.

FLAVIA RUANI is a researcher at the Institut de recherche et d'histoire des textes, CNRS, Paris and specializes in late antique and medieval Syriac Christianity, including religious controversies and hagiography.

KLAZINA STAAT is Assistant Professor in Latin Language and Literature and Roman Cultural History at VU University Amsterdam. Her research focuses on late antique and early medieval Latin hagiography and travel literature.

JULIE VAN PELT is an FWO Flanders postdoctoral researcher at Ghent University. She specializes in late antique and early medieval Greek hagiography.

Acknowledgments

This volume, much like the impetus for late antique pilgrims to Saint Thecla's shrines, was born out of a series of group readings and discussions held at the Department of Literary Studies at Ghent University in Belgium. The focus of these meetings was on late antique Christian hagiographies and pagan and Jewish romances. These meetings and, thus, this volume would not have come to fruition without funding from the European Research Council (ERC). The ERC's interest in research that spans across time and space provided the resources for scholars working on different regional and textual traditions to come together and focus on popular tales and motifs found throughout the late antique and medieval periods across east and west. As such, I would like to express my appreciation for and gratitude to the ERC for their financial support for such endeavors and to Ghent University for the time and space to pursue these studies.

I would like to express my deepest gratitude to Flavia Ruani whose friendship, dedication, exuberant enthusiasm, and moral support made working on this volume a great pleasure. My thanks go to Koen De Temmerman, who brought a wonderful group together on his ERC project (no. 337344). My sincerest thanks go to Julie Van Pelt and Klazina Staat for their enthusiasm for the volume from its inception, for their lively and spirited discussions, and ultimately for agreeing to contribute to the volume. I would like to thank wholeheartedly the contributors of the volume for their enlightening chapters. I offer my gratitude to the anonymous reviewers at Cambridge University Press for taking the time to read the volume, offering their invaluable suggestions for improvement, and their overall support for the volume's publication. My sincere thanks go to the commissioning editor, Michael Sharp, and the editorial assistant, Katie Idle, for their expert guidance.

Above all, I thank my parents for their unwavering support and endless patience. The completion of this volume was made possible by their love and generosity. The encouragement of great siblings and friends also did wonders. As did Thecla's intercession at key moments.

Ghazzal Dabiri

Abbreviations

Arm.	Armenian
BHG	François Halkin, ed. *Bibliotheca Hagiographica Graeca.* Subsidia hagiographica 8a. Brussels, 1957; François Halkin, ed. *Novum Auctarium Bibliothecae Hagiographicae Graecae.* Subsidia hagiographica 65. Brussels: Société des Bollandistes, 1984.
BHL	*Bibliotheca Hagiographica Latina.* 3 vols. Brussels: Société des Bollandistes, 1898–1911; Henryk Fros, ed. *Bibliotheca hagiographica latina antiquae et mediae aetatis. Novum supplementum.* Brussels: Société des Bollandistes, 1896.
BHO	Paul Peeters, ed. *Bibliotheca Hagiographica Orientalis.* Subsidia hagiographica 10. Brussels: Société des Bollandistes, 1910.
CANT	Maurice Geerard, ed. *Clavis Apocryphorum Novi Testamenti.* Turnhout: Brepols, 1992.
CPG	Maurice Geerard and J. Noret, eds. *Clavis Patrum Graecorum.* 5 vols. Turnhout: Brepols, 1974–1987, 1998, 2003.
CPL	Eligius Dekkers, ed. *Clavis Patrum Latinorum.* 3rd ed. Turnhout: Brepols, 1995.
CSCO	Corpus Scriptorum Christianorum Orientalium
Gk.	Greek
PG	Jacques Paul Migne, ed. *Patrologia Graeca.* 161 vols. Paris: Garnier Fratres, 1857–1886.
PL	Jacques Paul Migne, ed. *Patrologia Latina.* 221 vols. Paris: Garnier Fratres, 1844–1864.
Syr.	Syriac
WUNT	Wissenschaftliche Untersuchungen zum Neuen Testament

Introduction

Ghazzal Dabiri*

It is an old, yet powerful story. A beautiful young woman falls in love, and try as they might, her disapproving family and friends fail to dissuade her from that love or keep her from her beloved. Persistent and uncompromising, the young woman disrupts the social order of her world, be it that of high school or high society. And by tale's end, either the lover and her beloved are integrated back into society or a new world order arises (uneasily sometimes) out of the ashes.

Perusing through a list of popular young adult novels, teen movies, and ancient romances, one may be struck by the sheer number of stories that follow this arc. The same story line was also popular in the late antique and medieval periods. A subset of the latter, however, follow a slightly different track. They detail the lives and trials of women who have fallen deeply and irrevocably in love with the transcendental, namely, the word of God, and some, even on pain of torture and death, claim Christ as their eternal bridegroom.

One of, if not the earliest extant tale to carve out this particular track is the *Acts of Thecla*, also commonly known as the *Acts of Paul and Thecla* (henceforth *APT*). Composed in the second century, the *Acts of Thecla* is a short, yet engrossing and complex tale within the larger apocryphal *Acts of Paul*. It is the story of a persistent, young, beautiful woman named Thecla who comes to love the word of God as spoken by the apostle Paul. She leaves her home, mother, and fiancé to learn more about the eternal rewards accorded to virgins. In her pursuit of Paul's teachings, she survives violent rejection by her mother, denial of baptism and her personhood by her beloved teacher,[1] sexual assault, trifling governors, and, miraculously,

---

* I would like to express my gratitude to Flavia Ruani and the anonymous reviewers for their careful reading of this introduction and for their insightful remarks and suggestions. I also would like to acknowledge the European Research Council (no. 337344) and Ghent University for their financial support.
[1] He claims to not know her when the nobleman, Alexander, makes clear his desire for Thecla.

two sadistic trials before finally emerging triumphant, having self-baptized with God's tacit approval to become an apostle in her own right.

Though the *Acts of Thecla* takes place in Iconium (modern-day Konya, Turkey),[2] Antioch (modern-day Antakya, Turkey), and, to a lesser extent, Seleucia (modern-day Sifilike, Turkey), the tale spread like wildfire throughout Christendom. It sparked the imaginations of bishops, church fathers, saints, emperors, hagiographers, and ordinary readers alike from as far west as medieval Ireland, as far east through the late antique Iranian world via the Church of the East to the borders of China, and as far south as North and East Africa. Wherever Christians trekked, so too did Thecla's story. Greatly cherished, the heroine and her tale inspired numerous cults as well as shrines to be built in her name.[3] Among the most important of the latter is the Hagia Thecla near Seleucia, which was a popular pilgrimage destination and a location where important personages such as Gregory of Nazianzus (d. 390), the Archbishop of Constantinople and one of the most influential Christian theologians, visited and for which the Byzantine emperor Zeno the Isaurian (d. 491) added a prominent church on a hillside nearby.[4] The tale's many admirers (and even some of its detractors)[5] heralded its heroine as Paul's disciple and as an apostle. They also celebrated her as a paradigmatic model of virginity, charismatic confessor, (proto-)martyr, leader, teacher, intercessor, and saint in a wide variety of literary and material productions.[6] As Jeremy Barrier and Damien Labadie point out in their respective contributions to this volume (Chapters 1 and 2),

---

[2] As a matter of interest, Konya is currently a major site of pilgrimage for Muslims and Sufis. Konya is the place where, centuries after Thecla made her first stand, the magisterial poet and Sufi, Rumi (1207–1273), found safe harbor from the invading Mongol armies and set up the famous Mevlevi school. One of his major influences is Farīd al-Dīn ʿAṭṭār (d. c. 1222), whose version of the "Tale of the Virtuous Woman" demonstrates many strong parallels with the *APT* and is the subject of my contribution in this volume (Chapter 10).

[3] For more on this, see the chapters in this volume; Davis, *The Cult of St. Thecla*, 2001; and the collected articles in Barrier et al. (eds.), *Thecla*, 2017.

[4] Davis, *The Cult of St. Thecla*, 2001: 4–5 and 36–80.

[5] On the shifting views of the tale throughout late antiquity, see Barrier, *The Acts of Paul and Thecla*, 2009: 25–26; and Klazina Staat's contribution in this volume (Chapter 9). An important point worth mentioning here is that, generally speaking, the Apocryphal Acts of the Apostles were accorded this status in large part because Christian groups deemed heretical made use of them in their teachings.

[6] Literary, here, is used in the sense of the formal aspects of the discourse of a specific linguistic, regional, and/or confessional literature as we have them in extant texts – manuscripts and other material objects. On this, in terms of the Apocryphal Acts, see Valantasis, "The Nuptial Chamber Revisited," 1997: 261–264. This includes the discourse that testifies to orality and oral transmission as well. In consideration of this latter approach, it should be noted that literary is not meant to evoke the older view, appropriately laid to rest in the last half of the twentieth century, that the formal aspects of written literature are of a higher, thus better, art form than oral literature or folk tales.

the *APT* might have been read as hagiography among women in North Africa (Barrier), who were claiming Thecla and her story as their justification for teaching and baptizing as soon as the late second and early third centuries, and, later, in East Africa (Labadie) as her story was transmitted along with other Martyr Acts. Moreover, as the chapters in this volume altogether highlight, she served as a preeminent model for later hagiographers of female and sometimes male saints in each of the aforementioned capacities and to varying degrees both directly and indirectly. Whether in their relationships, in moments of great peril, or in word, behavior, or deed, many female saints, as they are represented in hagiographies, are inspired to be like Thecla.

But who exactly was Thecla? According to the anonymous presbyter from Asia, who gathered and organized the stories of Paul and Thecla, she is a beautiful young woman from a prominent family who rises to prominence as a model of virginity and forbearance; she is someone who baptizes herself and is given a mandate to teach by Paul himself. More specifically, she is the daughter of Theocleia and, by the end of the first act, the ex-fiancée of Thamyris. Significantly, she was a "leading woman of the Iconians" (§ 4.1) before becoming the "handmaiden of God"(§ 4.12).[7] Scholars have noted that besides Paul, two other figures in the tale, namely, Falconilla and Queen Tryphaena, did exist.[8] However, there is little to support the historicity of Thecla herself or the events described in her tale, miracles aside.[9] It has been suggested that Thecla's legendary tale may be based on oral and written accounts of women or one woman, who may or may not have been named Thecla, who suffered through trials after encountering Paul and subscribing to his teachings. In any case, it is salient that throughout the pre-modern world, Thecla was widely considered a powerful and prominent symbol and model and that she was frequently evoked and invoked as such in a wide variety of cultural productions. It is quite likely, then, that she and her story were accepted as historical by those who heard or read her tale; made the long, arduous, and, especially for women, dangerous journey across the eastern and western Mediterranean world to visit her shrines; or evoked her as a model in their writings of later saints' Lives. It certainly is the sense one gets reading later works that refer to her. Nevertheless, just as her historicity remains an

---

[7] References to the *APT* are taken from Barrier, *The Acts of Paul and Thecla*, 2009.
[8] Ibid.: 11 and 23–24.
[9] The inclusion of figures and sites suggests that the authors of the Apocryphal Acts were not interested in facts but rather in "a historical fiction" relating the events of the apostles toward various ideological aims: ibid.: 10–12. See also, Barrier, "*The Acts of Paul and Thecla*," 2017.

open question, so too does the perception of her historicity throughout the pre-modern world.

The overarching aim of this volume, then, is to explore the extents to which late antique and medieval hagiographers evoked and/or invoked Thecla and her tale in constructing the lives and storyworlds of their chosen saints. Indeed, in the various hagiographical tales under study in this volume, Thecla is a model for saints who by turns are depicted as acts to follow for embodying various aspects of holiness – confessor, martyr, virgin, spiritual lover, leader, and teacher – of which, in circular fashion, Thecla is most emblematic.[10] Thus, with this aim, we hope to add further depth and nuance to our understanding of Thecla's popularity, the spread of her legend and cult, which studying female storytelling, shrines dedicated to her, and the shifting perspectives of the Church have afforded us heretofore. Here, then, it would behoove us to delve further into the *APT* before transitioning to an overview of the larger debates surrounding Thecla and her tale and the specifics of this volume.

The *Acts of Thecla*: A Tale of Reversals, Replacements, and Disruptions

According to the *Acts of Thecla*, Thecla's apostolic career begins soon after Paul enters Iconium. He is invited by Onesiphorus and his family – Thecla's neighbors – to teach in their home. Thecla, sitting by a window, hears Paul's teaching and is immediately enthralled. She remains riveted to her chair for three days and nights listening to him. Theocleia, distraught, sends for Thamyris to see if he can persuade Thecla to speak, eat, or just simply move since she has failed to do so. When his pleas also fall on deaf ears, Thamyris seethes, and his very public display of anger instigates a mob to arrest Paul. Later that night, Thecla steals away from her home so she can continue to listen to Paul's teaching. She bribes her own porter and the prison guards with her gold bracelets and some valuables she has taken

---

[10] Generally, saints have two, often overlapping, functions, namely, intercessor and as exemplar of/ embodying holiness – functions that Thecla fulfills. While most of the chapters focus on Thecla's holiness, the contributions by Caitríona Ó Dochartaigh (Chapter 3) and Klazina Staat (Chapter 9) in this volume illustrate how Thecla is invoked as an intercessor in Latin litanies for the dead and the bearing this may have had on later hagiographical works. On saints and sainthood, see, for instance, among many studies available, Brown, "The Rise and Function," 1971; Brown, *The Cult*, 1981; Brown, *Society and the Holy*, 1982; Brown, "The Saint as Exemplar," 1987; and the collected essays in Strickland (ed.), *Images of Medieval Sanctity*, 2007; Clarke and Claydon (eds.), *Saints and Sanctity*, 2011; and Meltzer and Elsner (eds.), *Saints*, 2011. See also the sources cited in the various chapters.

from her house. She spends the night listening to Paul teach, kissing his shackles. In the morning, seeing that Thecla is not home, her mother and household mourn for her as for the dead. Later, they find her at the prison with Paul and alert the governor who orders Paul to be flogged and driven from the city. Theocleia, enflamed with fury, also demands that her daughter be burned at the stake.[11] Tied to the stake, Thecla searches for her teacher but sees the Lord who takes on Paul's image. When the fire is lit, a great blaze breaks out, and God sends rain and hail to protect Thecla while it destroys many nearby.

Amazed by the turn of events, the governor releases Thecla who then sets out to find Paul. After a touching reunion with Paul and Onesiphorus and his family in a cave near Antioch, Thecla offers to cut her hair, but Paul tells her that she is beautiful and that she may not endure a second trial. She then asks him to baptize her so that she may be fortified, but he defers. In Antioch, Alexander, a nobleman, sees Thecla and is captivated by her beauty. He turns to Paul and asks him to whom does she belong. Paul claims not to know her. Alexander then grabs Thecla, who, in defense of herself, declares herself to be a leading woman of the Iconians and so is not to be touched. She then rips Alexander's clothes and knocks his crown off his head. Enraged, Alexander arranges and pays for her trial with the proconsul. While awaiting trial, Thecla is taken under the protection of Queen Tryphaena, a relative of the emperor and whose daughter, Falconilla, had recently passed away. In mourning, Tryphaena asks Thecla to pray for her daughter's soul. After Thecla does, Tryphaena dreams of her daughter who is now in heaven. Later, at the trial, Alexander releases a series of wild animals among which a lioness emerges to protect Thecla from the other beasts. Then, a pool of savage seals is brought out, and Thecla sees it as her opportunity to be baptized. She jumps into the pool in the name of Jesus. Fiery lightning strikes. The seals are struck dead as a cloud covers Thecla's nude body. After miraculously surviving another onslaught, this time by bulls whose genitals are enflamed and which causes Queen Tryphaena to faint, the proconsul calls a halt to the trial in his fear that the queen may have passed away. Though she has not, the proconsul, nonetheless awed, asks who Thecla is. This time, she

---

[11] Thecla's mother Theocleia is apparently powerful enough to demand that her daughter be put to trial by the city's governor when she refuses to marry her fiancé. Kate Cooper and James Corke-Webster, "Conversion, Conflict," 2014, in a short, but all the same exquisite article address the detrimental effects that Thecla's actions (rejection of social status, financial security, and cultural values, especially reproductive choices) caused and that, thus, call for a more sympathetic reading of Thecla's mother.

declares that she is the handmaiden of God. She is released and, after fashioning a male cloak for herself, she sets out for Myra to find Paul with her new followers, which includes witnesses at her trial and Queen Tryphaena and her household, in tow. She informs Paul of her baptism, and when she also informs him of her intent to return to Iconium, he tells her to go and teach. In Iconium, she finds her mother and offers herself and wealth to her, both of which her mother, in her turn, silently refuses. Then, she sets out for Seleucia where she remains teaching until her dying day.

What emerges from even a summary of the events is that the tale is one of progression – a housebound, silent young woman from a leading family of Iconium becomes a vocal handmaiden of God who travels and teaches. Nevertheless, it is also clear that, intratextually, Thecla's story is one of continual "reversals and replacements."[12] It maintains a delicate equilibrium between opposing tensions. For instance, as much as it is about emotional and physical brutality, it is also about companionship and love: for the loss of her mother, her teacher, and family wealth, Thecla gains a benefactor, protector, and adoptive mother in the powerful Queen Tryphaena whom she turns into her disciple. In a symbolically charged moment, Thecla bribes her porter and Paul's prison guard with a silver mirror and her gold bracelets respectively, giving up the trappings of her status and familial wealth, to be able to sit at Paul's feet to listen to his teachings. By tale's end, however, Thecla is in the position to offer money and herself as a daughter to her mother, who may have lost her status with Thecla's dismissal of her engagement. And while Thecla was silent and unresponsive to her mother's pleas in the beginning, her mother at the end is silent and unresponsive to her daughter. Thecla also receives divine solace, which appears in the shape of Paul's face, when she searches for her teacher among the crowd at her first trial and cannot find him. Though tortured and denied baptism by her beloved teacher, she takes baptism for herself with God's tacit approval, and as a result Paul gives her permission to teach on her own. Meanwhile, though Paul and Thecla preach and adhere to sexual continence, the tale also promotes the Christian family in its depiction of Onesiphorus and the aid he and his family give to Paul at the risk of losing their own wealth and status.[13] Moreover, Thecla is both

[12] Lipsett, *Desiring Conversion*, 2011: 78.
[13] In ibid.: 64, B. Diane Lipsett makes the astute observation that inasmuch as the *APT* disrupts the social order (marriage and reproduction), it also affirms it by the tale's two frames – in the first frame, Onesiphorus and his family are Thecla's neighbors who invite Paul into their home where he preaches, and his words reach Thecla through her window. And in the second frame, when Thecla

desiring (following Paul to learn more about the word of God) and its reverse, desired (the object of love – Thamyris – and lust – Alexander),[14] as the tale illustrates the potential damages of being both the subject and object of desire.[15] And, finally, if Alexander, at the beginning of the second act, asks Paul if he knows to whom Thecla belongs, and she responds with her social status, by the end of her trial, the awed proconsul directly asks Thecla who she is, and she declares that she belongs to (is a servant of) God.

The most significant reversal, however, is to be found at the level of the greater text; in a story dedicated to Paul's apostolic mission, for the duration of two acts, Thecla is the primary focus. Put in other terms, Thecla is the protagonist of her own tale, her own apostolic calling and mission, in a work that is otherwise centered around Paul. Just as remarkable is the fact that Paul is largely absent from Thecla's tale, albeit his presence is greatly felt throughout in Thecla's desire to be with and follow him and in her choice to follow his teaching even to (near) death. It should come as little surprise, then, that the tale, which, as noted above, is sometimes referred to as the *Acts of Thecla* by ancient, medieval, and modern authors and scholars alike, was detached from the larger *Acts of Paul* and circulated separately and widely. The situation was replicated in the last few decades of the twentieth century when the *Acts of Thecla* garnered much scholarly interest among feminist scholars who sought to reclaim the role women played in the development of early Christianity. From thence forward, the *Acts of Thecla* was catapulted into the limelight, nearly rivaling Thecla's popularity in the late antique and medieval periods.

Indeed, both the *APT* and the attention it received throughout the late antique and medieval periods have been the subjects of a vast trove of studies, with each scholar breaking new ground while building on the seminal works of their peers and predecessors. Thecla and her tale have been analyzed from multiple perspectives.[16] On the historical front,

---

survives her first trial; she seeks out Paul, at which point Onesiphorus' son finds Thecla and brings her to the cave, in which Paul and the rest of Onesiphorus' family are breaking bread, to join them happily.

[14] For more on Thecla as subject and object of desire and the ensuing gender ambiguities of the text, see ibid.: 54–85.

[15] Though, it might be more precise to state that it is desire sought and thwarted that defines Thecla's relationships with Paul, Thamyris, and Alexander and that leads to her trials.

[16] See Bremmer, "Bibliography," 2017. For a comprehensive overview of these studies, especially against the backdrop of the history of gender, religious, and cultural studies in the West, see Davis, "From Women's Piety," 2015.

Stephen Davis, in an impressive study, has looked at the establishment and spread of Thecla's cult across Eurasia and North Africa.[17] Sever J. Voicu has traced the popularity of Thecla and her tale into the most eastern parts of the Iranian world.[18] Valentina Calzolari similarly has dedicated multiple studies to the establishment of Christianity in relation to the cult of Thecla in Armenia.[19] On the social front, scholars have read Thecla's tale to shed light on the lives of women. For instance, in their groundbreaking works, Stevan L. Davies, Dennis R. MacDonald, and Virginia Burrus have explored different aspects of women's autonomy in early Christianity – including virginity as a form of freedom from conservative social constraints – with the premise that women were not only the intended audiences but also the tellers of the *APT* and other Apocryphal Acts.[20] In this regard, these scholars have taken part, to varying degrees, in the debates surrounding the complex, overlapping roles oral and written transmission may have played in the compiling and composition of the Apocryphal Acts more broadly.[21] On the other hand, Kate Cooper, in her seminal study, notes that the representation of the overlapping spheres of the private and public lives of men and women (a stable home makes for a stable society) were upended in the *APT* and other apocryphal tales.[22] Accordingly, the *APT* was one of the many Christian texts to introduce a different moral language, one that through encouraging virginity challenged married Roman women's identity, both Christian and pagan, in various ways, including the promotion of the ideal chaste wife for men.[23] In contrast, noting the growing power and influence of the figure of Thecla in the Church, Susan E. Hylen argues that the *APT* offers a nuanced, highly complex representation of women in early Christianity whereby women achieved leadership by upholding the standards of modesty.[24] Meanwhile, Maud Burnett McInerney, taking her cue from earlier studies on virginity, argues that in medieval Europe, the virgin body staged and channeled aggressive masculine desire and reigned it in for the sake of "'normal' heterosexual communities" while, for women, virgin bodies

---

[17] Davis, *The Cult of St. Thecla*, 2001.   [18] Voicu, "Thecla," 2017.
[19] See the footnotes in her contribution to this volume (Chapter 4) for the relevant bibliography.
[20] Davies, *The Revolt*, 1980; MacDonald, *The Legend*, 1983; and Burrus, *Chastity as Autonomy*, 1987.
[21] For an overview of the sources and main arguments, see Davis, *The Cult of St. Thecla*, 2001: 8–18. Barrier, *The Acts of Paul and Thecla*, 2009: 30–47, sees a weaker link between the oral tradition and *APT*.
[22] Cooper, *The Virgin and the Bride*, 1996.   [23] Ibid.: 14.   [24] Hylen, *A Modest Apostle*, 2015.

became "sites upon which female communities were founded in life and in texts" with the *APT* as a popular vehicle.[25]

The *Acts of Paul* too has benefited from a wide array of studies in connection with other Apocryphal Acts. Though comparative studies between the Apocryphal Acts and the ancient novels (on which see below) had begun by the early twentieth century,[26] much of the initial studies on the Apocryphal Acts themselves centered on manuscript studies – putting the pieces of the texts together – and philological questions that eventually gave way to broader interests such as linguistic and literary dependence – which Apocryphal Act depended on the others and by how much and, thus, which of the Apocryphal Acts came first. With the rise of intertextual studies, the conversation shifted from questions regarding primacy and dependence toward the dynamic relationship between the apocryphal and canonical Acts, possible oral versions in circulation, and the synoptic gospels.[27] Simultaneous to intertextual studies, and largely driven by the efforts of François Bovon and Jan N. Bremmer, has been the study of the Apocryphal Acts as social documents that offer a window onto various aspects of late antique life and the ideological interests of their authors.[28]

However, the discourse that has given the most shape to studies on the *Acts of Thecla* is the possible relationship that exists between it and the ancient Greek novels.[29] For indeed, the relationship between the *Acts of Thecla* and the ancient Greek novels is ultimately one of reversal at the intertextual level. As is well known, the heroines in the ancient Greek novels, like Thecla, are torn from their beloveds and families and face multiple obstacles to preserve their chastity, including sexual assault and forced marriages, as they travel about hoping to return home and be reunited with their loved ones. However, Thecla's beloved is the word of God as spoken by Paul. In other words, even if, as many have argued, she desires to be with Paul and is torn from him, that desire is framed around learning (first act) and receiving baptism (second act). As such, though she

---

[25] McInerney, *Eloquent Virgins*, 2003.
[26] For an overview, see Aubin, "Reversing Romance?," 1998.
[27] A prime example is the collection of essays in Stoops (ed.), *The Apocryphal Acts*, 1997.
[28] For a brief overview of the field, see Bovon, "Preface," 1999. For a synopsis of Bovon's various contributions to the field, see Bovon, "The Corpus Christianorum Series," 2012. For illuminating studies on the social world of Christians represented by the Apocryphal Acts, see, for instance, the collected essays in Bremmer (ed.), *The Apocryphal Acts of John*, 1995; Bremmer (ed.), *The Apocryphal Acts*, 1996; Bovon (ed.), *The Apocryphal Acts*, 1999; and Bremmer (ed.), *The Apocryphal Acts of Andrew*, 2000.
[29] For the most recent example, see McLarty, *Thecla's Devotion*, 2018. These sorts of analyses are not limited to the *APT* alone. The Acts of the Apostles and Jewish romances have also been studied in this way. See below.

is reunited with Paul (and twice no less) and her mother, she finally takes her leave of them as she does of her own fiancé. And, if we understand the cloak that she fashions for herself as that of the philosopher's as McInerney does, she also departs metaphorically cloaked in God's word, which she, in turn, imparts to others.[30]

Though it is difficult to pin down exact dates for the ancient Greek novels, modern scholarship places them between the second and fourth century, which would make the earliest of them coeval with the *Acts of Thecla*. It is generally acknowledged, furthermore, that the *Acts of Thecla*, and much of Christian literary production from the first to the fourth centuries, were written, copied, or edited by authors who illustrate the same literary training (rhetoric, argumentation, imitation, and use of allusion) and belonged to the same cultural milieu as those of the ancient Greek novels. In other words, their authors not only read the same works and received similar training, they also likely competed for the same audiences.[31] When viewed altogether, however, the reversals, the tension in opposition, exhibited in the *Acts of Thecla* and the growing number of hagiographical tales of female saints that follow a similar arc, on the one hand, and the ancient Greek novels, on the other, illustrate two different responses to the immense socio-religious upheavals underway that were sparked by the growth of Christianity. This is the conclusion to which both Judith Perkins and Kate Cooper have come in their own close readings of these texts; the relationship between them is an inverse one. In other words, while paying attention respectively to pain/suffering and constructions of gender, Perkins and Cooper have illustrated that the motifs of travel, adventure, love at first sight, displacement, chastity and fidelity, and threats to both work differently in the *APT* and Apocryphal Acts, on the one hand, and the romance novels, on the other. The latter affirm older social norms and the former work to disrupt them to create new, specifically Christian ones.[32]

Taking a look at social disruption in the *Acts of Thecla*, two different trajectories are pursued by our two protagonists, which reverberate

---

[30] McInerney, *Eloquent Virgins*, 2003: 41–43.

[31] For a concise overview, see Barrier, *The Acts of Paul and Thecla*, 2009: 1–21. See also Perkins, "This World or Another?," 1997; and Stoops, "The *Acts of Peter*," 1997: 61–65.

[32] Perkins, *The Suffering Self*, 1995. Cooper, *The Virgin and the Bride*, 1996: 55, in her much-discussed line, reads the tensions in the *APT* and the other Apocryphal Acts thusly: "The challenge by the apostle to the householder is the urgent message of these narratives, and it is essentially a conflict *between men*." Though she makes this observation against reading the Apocryphal Acts as being written by and for communities of continent women, her general point that these tales are about authority and the social order is pertinent.

throughout later hagiographies of female saints quite broadly. For, much like Thecla, "the sanctity of the large majority of women commemorated in Byzantine hagiography is associated with a man who makes female holiness possible either as a torturer or as a spiritual father"[33] (though Thecla's own mother plays no small role in the *APT*). In fact, many tales either follow or reverse the *APT*'s specific dynamics between apostle/teacher and disciple. Turning our attention to the *APT*, at the start, the apostle Paul enters the city of Iconium continuously (seemingly without pause for breath) teaching the word of the Lord. Soon after, he is invited into the home of Onesiphorus, who has been waiting for him at the town's entrance, to continue that teaching. There, Paul carries on, offering beatitudes on God's word as it concerns self-control and resurrection: "'Blessed are those,' he states, 'who have kept the flesh chaste, for they will be a temple of God .... Blessed are they who are set apart from this world, for they will be well pleasing to God'" (§ 3.5). Unbeknownst to either Paul or his host, Thecla, the girl next door, hears these words. They resound so powerfully within her that she immediately gives up all aspects of her life. By doing so, she disrupts what we can only assume to be a peaceful moment in her home life and city. But that was hardly her intent; it was Paul's. For, even if he were unaware of Thecla at this particular juncture, many Iconians, including women, were visiting Onesiphorus' home to listen to Paul's teaching.

Indeed, Paul travels throughout the Greco-Roman world with the intent to proselytize. And he continues to do so in city after city, never deterred by the threats of or actual physical harm he receives at the hands of citizens and their leaders, until his martyrdom ends his mission. Thecla, meanwhile, is so enthralled by what Paul is teaching, specifically abstinence, that in the beginning she moves toward her new life intending only to hear more. Thus, Thecla's life is upended and changed by circumstances of her own making, certainly, but not by initial intention. In Iconium, it is Thecla's mother and fiancé who demand that the troublemakers, Paul and Thecla, be put to public trial for rejecting marriage and, thus, childbirth – essentially, their way of life; one that was actively promoted by the imperial family and Roman moral laws.[34] In other words, it is her family's despair and the disruption in their private and public lives that catapult Thecla

---

[33] Constantinou, "Performing Gender," 2014: 32.
[34] The household and then the city were microcosms of the Roman Empire. For the privileges and status, as a matter of law, accorded to married elite men and women with children, see Hylen, *A Modest Apostle*, 2015: 18–42.

into the public arena. In the beginning, then, Thecla is too young and inexperienced, perhaps, to be aware of the full ramifications of her actions until they have come to pass, especially since she embodies the virtues – namely, chastity and self-control[35] – that while highly valued by her pagan society, also make her an appropriate disciple to Paul.[36]

Thecla, however, does more than disrupt the social order and project a different metanarrative than coeval romances with her conversion.[37] She disrupts Paul's plans – or more aptly lack thereof – for her with her steadfastness. Once she has survived her first trial, she seeks out Paul (who was driven from Iconium after he was flogged). She asks to accompany him. And he refuses with what many have noted is a hollow sounding excuse: she is beautiful, and she might find that she will act cowardly should she be forced to endure another trial.[38] When she insists that she will not, especially if she receives the seal of baptism, he tells her to be patient for she will receive the water (§ 3.25).[39] We neither know if Paul's words meant that he had foreseen her baptism or that he was shrugging her off. Scholarly opinion largely falls on the latter. Regardless, as has been noted previously and as Jeremy Barrier explores in new ways in his contribution to this volume (Chapter 1), Paul's later acceptance of her self-baptism and permission to let her teach the word of God, in another intertextual reversal, runs contrary to what is attributed to him in the New Testament, where he declares women to not even be fit for speaking out loud in church, (1 Cor 14:35) much less teaching or giving baptism. This is, of course, the very issue Tertullian (b. c. 155) famously pointed out since he knew of women doing both, using Thecla as their model.

---

[35] On the importance of both concepts in the Roman empire, see Cooper, *The Virgin and the Bride*, 1996: 1–19.

[36] Thecla, at the window, adamantly listening to Paul, and not eating and moving has been typically read as desire (love at first hearing) and as the heroine displaying the well-known symptoms of love sickness. Hylen, *A Modest Apostle*, 2015: 74–75, reads her refusal to move from her spot at the window to join other virgins entering into Onesiphorus' home to listen to Paul as part of the social reality that the story assumes, namely, that women were not confined to the home and that "her modest position at the window conveys her indisputable honor."

[37] Burrus in her article, "Mimicking Virgins," 2005: 55, makes an intriguing suggestion that bears quoting here: "Indeed, it may be that the less-than-subtle subversions of the Apocryphal Acts, when read comparatively, do not so much invert as simplify and intensify certain aspects of the pagan romances' already ambivalent views of *eros* and *gamos*, city and empire – or, conversely, that the pagan romances complicate and render more ambiguous the strident social critique already conveyed by the Apocryphal Acts."

[38] Barrier, *The Acts of Paul and Thecla*, 2009: 9–10, sees this as more in keeping with ancient Greek novels which see their protagonists, the lovers, separated on more than one occasion until final reunion.

[39] Barrier, *The Acts of Paul and Thecla*, 2009.

The Tale of Reversal Continues: *Imitatio Theclae* or Stories of Imitation and Emulation

Reversals and the social disruptions that confessional and spiritual conversions bring about for the individual and their family and community also permeate a large number of late antique and medieval hagiographies of female saints. So do perceptions of female saints as virgins and martyrs with a cause, intercessors, confessors, teachers, and leaders. And, as this volume aims to highlight in detail, many draw from Thecla's tale to do so. It is, thus, surprising that apart from the notable work by Scott F. Johnson, which looks at the later *Life and Miracles of Thecla* as an "erudite paraphrase" of the *APT*,[40] and by Davis, which examines many of the intimate connections between the *APT* and the *Life and Passion of Eugenia*,[41] there remain few works that systematically study the reception of the *Acts of Thecla* or study the work as an important intertext for a wide variety of hagiographical narratives. This, even as many studies overwhelmingly acknowledge Thecla's ubiquitous popularity in a wide variety of contexts.

In this volume, thus, Valentina Calzolari (Chapter 4) demonstrates that the protagonists of several foundational texts for Armenian Christianity embody four different paradigms of holiness associated with Thecla, namely, virgin, preacher, patron saint, and apostle. One such heroine is Rhipsime (Arm. Hṙipʻsimē) who, according to the *History* attributed to Agathangelos, becomes the instrument by which all of Armenia converts to Christianity as a martyred virgin. And it is precisely, as Calzolari demonstrates, Thecla's struggles with Alexander that Rhipsime's tale follows, namely, through the saint's personal and physically violent struggle with the pagan king of Armenia who was trying, unsuccessfully, to bed her. Another heroine, Sanduxt, and her teacher, Thaddaeus, trace Thecla's and Paul's respective apostolic paths. However, it is Sanduxt's conversion of a powerful royal patron, Zarmanduxt, that Calzolari argues parallels closely the *APT*. Except, the former's career as preacher is ended rather quickly; in this case, by the saint's father (rather than mother as in the *APT* in a prime example of intertextual reversal) who orders her and her teacher's execution.

---

[40] Johnson, *The Life and Miracles*, 2006.
[41] Davis, "Crossed Texts, Crossed Sex," 2002. The story is also known as the *Life and Martyrdom of Eugenia*, *Life of Eugenia*, or *Passion of Eugenia*.

Flavia Ruani, in her contribution (Chapter 5), looks at the ways in which four Syriac hagiographies not only model their protagonists on Thecla but also their secondary characters on those of the *APT*. In the *Martyrdom of Febronia*, for instance, the women who take on motherly roles similar to Queen Tryphaena (but in different respects) invoke Thecla as a model of endurance for Febronia as she faces a gruesome trial that is similarly staged as the one Queen Tryphaena witnesses. Interestingly, the *Life of John of Tella* is one of two texts that reverse the roles of parallel secondary characters. Indeed, the hagiographer of the *Life of John of Tella* notes the influence Thecla's tale had on John as a young man before becoming bishop. But, as Ruani points out, the role of Thecla's mother and fiancé is revised as supportive mother and friend. Arietta Papaconstantinou (Chapter 6), meanwhile, illustrates not a reversal in relationships but a reconfiguration of the multifaceted relationship between Paul and Thecla as a threesome between Paese and his sister Thecla and his business partner Paul in the Coptic *Martyrdom of Paese and Thecla*. The holy threesome, she argues, becomes an eschatological love triangle that adopts the language of brotherly love among monks.

Jeremy Barrier (Chapter 1) addresses directly the very fact that women were reading the *APT*, as a hagiographical text in North Africa, and were taking Thecla as a model for teaching and administering (or not) baptism. As Barrier argues, at the heart of Tertullian's disgruntlement with these developments is the possible threat to the disruption of the authority of the North African churches that these practices entailed. Damien Labadie (Chapter 2), meanwhile, recounts the various ways in which medieval Ethiopic hagiographies invoke Thecla as a perfect confessor and martyr, even though she was never martyred and despite the fact that Ethiopian Christians were never ruled by a polytheist and, hence, were never persecuted.[42] Then, Labadie illustrates the extents to which the Ethiopic text *Epistle of Pelagia* draws from Thecla's trials, especially in its depiction of torture and its ambiguous end. More than the specific acts of torture themselves, it is Thecla's behavior (her steadfastness) at her trials on which various hagiographers center their attention, as in the cases of the aforementioned Ethiopic *Epistle of Pelagia* and the Syriac *Martyrdom of Bassus and Susanna*. In the latter, as Ruani highlights, the hagiographer pauses from his narration to inform us that while persecuted, Susanna takes up the images of Thecla and Febronia, bringing to bear a larger hagiographical

---

[42] Christianity, as Labadie points out in Chapter 2, was introduced in the fourth century upon the conversion of Ethiopia's ruler, 'Ezānā.

tradition. Caitríona Ó Dochartaigh, in her contribution (Chapter 3), traces Thecla's literary itinerary throughout the Latin-speaking west, including litanies for the dead, to account for her appearance as a model martyr and apostle in medieval Irish poems and *menologia*.

Here, we turn our attention to those tales that not only imitate Thecla but also emulate (surpass in their imitation of) her. In Chapter 8, Virginia Burrus traces the development of virginal voice in late antiquity. She highlights the fact that in his *Symposium*, Methodius of Olympus (250–311) upends two central questions posed by Plato's *Symposium* and the ancient Greek novel, *Leucippe and Clitophon*, namely, who gets to speak and to dictate the nature of the conversation on desire. He accomplishes this by giving Thecla pride of place in a debate on virginity. Burrus then notes how debating virgins surpass their model Thecla in their quite vocal defense and advocacy of chastity in the *Life of Helia* and the *Life of Constantina*, respectively.

As noted above, it is well established that the *APT* is prominently evoked in the *Life and Passion of Eugenia* – the heroine is inspired to lead a life of continence after reading Thecla's tale, and she even takes on Paul's apostolic track in the second half of the narrative as she teaches and converts women inside their homes. As I highlight in my contribution (Chapter 10), the *Life and Passion of Eugenia* and a medieval Persian mystical tale of an anonymous virtuous woman composed in verse, which contains strong parallels to both the *APT* and Eugenia's story, pick up the thread of leadership and powerful patronage just at the moment when Thecla gains both, but her tale ends. Much like Thecla, the personal decisions of Eugenia and the virtuous woman have profound consequences for their respective families and cities. Except in these later cases, both Eugenia and the virtuous woman surpass Thecla as they both become the active instruments by which their entire communities convert. In Chapter 9, Klazina Staat demonstrates that in two Latin recensions of the *Life and Passion of Eugenia*, the heroine also surpasses Thecla but in her superb rhetorical skills. One peculiar aspect that she explores in relation to the changing reception of the *APT* among church fathers is that the later recension has removed all specific references to the *APT*. As Staat argues, audiences would have recognized Thecla and the *APT* as models nonetheless since she remained a popular figure throughout the Latin-speaking west and Paul's beatitudes, as delivered in the *APT* (see above), remain largely intact.

Julie Van Pelt (Chapter 7) analyzes various allusions to the *APT*, including the marshalling of clustered motifs, across Greek and

Italo-Greek hagiographies in a bid to understand how Thecla is evoked as a model broadly and to question whether she is evoked specifically as a model for cross-dressing saints. Van Pelt, in her contribution, thus, reverses course and asks readers to reexamine carefully the notion, prevalent in modern scholarship, that Thecla is the paradigmatic model for female transvestite saints. She argues, instead, that more nuanced readings illustrate that while the tales of transvestite saints do recall Thecla in multiple concrete ways, they do so less in terms of cross-dressing and more so in other aspects of Thecla's life. In other words, though transvestite saints may imitate Thecla in other respects, they certainly surpass her in terms of disguise of identity and gender. She then proposes the *Acts of Xanthippe and Polyxena*, the *Life and Miracles of Thecla*, and the *Life of Eusebia called Xenê* as important intermediary steps both in the later interpretation of Thecla as a cross-dresser and in the development of this theme across a wide variety of later hagiographies in the Greek-speaking world.

The questions that may arise at this juncture for some readers are the following: How can we be certain that the Thecla invoked in the aforementioned texts is our Thecla, especially considering that many later saints bear her name? Relatedly, are the tales centering on Thecla's namesakes, as in the Coptic *Martyrdom of Paese and Thecla*, enough to justify the claim that the *APT*'s Thecla is the model? And, by what criteria may we judge motifs as having been drawn specifically from our Thecla's tale, given the popularity of motifs such as fidelity to chastity and cross-dressing and their ubiquitous diffusion throughout oral and written texts?

In response, it should be noted first that there is good reason, generally speaking, to presume that hagiographers had direct access to the *APT*; namely, the fact that much of "the lost apocryphal acts have been recovered from hagiographic sources."[43] And indeed, Ruani and Labadie (Chapters 5 and 2, respectively), point out that the *APT* specifically circulated in manuscript collections of Lives of female saints including the ones they have chosen for study, while Calzolari notes that the tale circulated in manuscripts of homilies. On the one hand, then, the circulation of the Apocryphal Acts in manuscript compendia further confirms the argument that the *APT* and the other Apocryphal Acts were accessible inasmuch as they formed part of the important web of texts that simultaneously belonged and contributed to the making of Greco-Roman culture and eastern and western Christianity together with the Old and New

---

[43] Bovon, "Byzantine Witnesses," 1999: 88.

Testaments, canonical Acts, Greek and Jewish novels, philosophical and theological treatises, and later hagiographies.⁴⁴ On the other hand, this may suggest that the Apocryphal Acts were indeed read as hagiography and served further to connect the one group of texts to the other. As noted above, the former is the track Barrier follows as he argues that Tertullian did have direct access to the *Acts of Paul and Thecla*; in other words, Tertullian was not basing his opinions solely on the fact that women were claiming Thecla as their model for teaching and baptizing. Tertullian *and* the women were intimately familiar with the tale.

Second, the contributors were not presented with any prerequisite criteria for their selections. This was done so as not to heavily favor one or a few hagiographical texts or generic types, motifs, or techniques (which will be addressed below). Indeed, to have done otherwise would have risked a smaller pool of texts certainly, but it also would have come at the expense of studying the rich variety of techniques that were used throughout the late antique and medieval periods generally and that are employed in the texts under study here and that give them layered depth. Nevertheless, even without such prerequisite criteria, the contributors have grappled with these challenging questions in similar ways as they detail the stronger and weaker ties and parallels to the *APT*.

In setting out to demonstrate that Thecla and the *APT* are used as models in the hagiographical texts under study here, the contributors trace the importance and itinerary of the *APT* within the cultural spheres of their linguistic traditions. By doing so, they establish the reputation, ubiquity, and popularity of Thecla and/or the *APT* specifically and primarily within the literary sphere (Papaconstantinou [Chapter 6] and Staat [Chapter 9] also delve into material culture). Each contributor, next, carefully sifts through the tales to highlight the various techniques with which hagiographers use to situate Thecla and her tale as models for their chosen saint. These techniques include but are not limited to invoking Thecla directly by name though not for its own sake but in order to specifically highlight certain characteristics a protagonist needs at moments similarly structured to the *APT*, marshalling hallmark motifs of the *APT* that cluster at similar moments (such as bribing guards with personal valuables and kissing the shackles of an imprisoned teacher within the

---

⁴⁴ In other words, the theory of intertextuality first outlined by Julia Kristeva (b. 1941) and refined and reevaluated by her many followers. See also discussion further below. On Jewish novels and romances, see Wills, *The Jewish Novel*, 2015 and for a general discussion, from a comparative perspective, see the collected essays in Ramelli and Perkins (eds.), *Early Christian and Jewish Narrative*, 2015.

broader motif of devotion to teacher), retracing specific elements of the *APT*'s plot, staging similar scenes, alluding to the *APT* through phrasing and imagery, depicting similar relationships and dynamics among various characters, and imitating and emulating Thecla's characteristics and multifaceted career, including but not limited to when and how protagonists disrupt their family life and the social order through spiritual or confessional conversion. These techniques make up an important part of the hagiographer's practice. Lastly, it should almost go without stating that inasmuch as hagiographers were interested in Thecla as a model to imitate or to surpass, they were not interested in copying every facet of Thecla's character or moment in the *Acts of Thecla*. Even a brief glance at the texts under discussion here immediately obviate that notion. Yet the obvious point is raised here since it is clear that the *APT* was an older, authoritative, and much beloved tale.[45] Appropriating older, authoritative works was one of several important ways to address contemporary or individual concerns; a technique, perhaps the most important for our discussion, that is widely acknowledged as an immensely popular one throughout the pre-modern period. As the individual chapters in this volume illustrate, the *APT* is evoked in the hagiographies under study to detail contemporary interests and concerns regarding holiness, conversion, preservation of chastity, female voice, education, teaching, leadership, and communal identity formation (the latter is addressed below). This, in addition to the fact that the chapters demonstrate hagiographers' use of multiple techniques in a variety of combinations and at many points in their respective narratives.

Though none of the chapters address oral transmission specifically, it is worth mentioning here because it was a prominent means by which the *APT* circulated. Much of what is outlined above holds even if we are to assume that the references to the *APT* come from oral versions of the tale in circulation.[46] Indeed, as each contributor demonstrates, the number and specificity of the references to the *APT*, all of which are drawn out by

---

[45] Even if the *APT*'s reception among the church fathers fluctuated, by and large, Thecla remained a preeminent model. And, in their choice to model certain aspects of the *APT* or Thecla in their own productions illustrates that the hagiographers considered the text an authoritative one.

[46] The possible oral background to motifs and tales and the confluence between oral and written circulation lies just beyond the scope of this volume. For the debates about the oral background to and circulation of the *APT*, I refer the reader to the sources listed in n. 20 and n. 21. For an excellent analysis of the complexities involving the overlaps between oral and written texts, memory, and the circulation of motifs as it relates to the Apocryphal Acts generally and the *Acts of Peter* specifically, see Thomas, "The 'Prehistory,'" 1999. On the circulation of biblical texts and the Apocryphal Acts in oral and written forms simultaneously as well as the connections between motifs, see Narro, "The Cloud of Thecla," 2019: 102.

paying attention to the various techniques the hagiographers employ, make it immaterial whether these references were drawn from the tale as it was heard and memorized or as it was held directly in hand.[47] Along similar lines, it should be noted that other motifs and texts in oral and written circulation, including those that make direct and indirect references to Thecla and her tale, are undoubtedly also represented in many of the hagiographical tales analyzed in this volume. In fact, hagiographies are highly complex and layered, and to treat them as otherwise does them a great disservice. Our contributors, sensitive to such issues, present these motifs and texts when they crop up and address them directly. Thus, they add another dimension to our understanding of the popularity of the *APT*. Here, then, we turn to the aims of our volume.

The Aims of the Volume

This volume offers, for the first time, a collection of essays that explores the reception of the figure of Thecla and the *APT* as models in medieval (broadly defined from the fourth–twelfth century) hagiographical texts composed in Armenian, Coptic, Ethiopic, Greek, Irish, Latin, Persian, and Syriac.[48] The authors, who were selected either for their erudite studies on Thecla and her legend in other respects and/or for their expertise in relation to their studies of lives and tales of (female) saints, illustrate the extents to which the *APT* is deployed as an important intertext; they highlight when hagiographers implicitly and/or explicitly refer to Thecla and her tale using a variety of techniques. They, thus, offer original, detailed readings of the lives of various heroines and heroes from different traditions and types of texts that draw from Thecla's tale. In doing so, the volume positions itself on a rather broad map. In fact, inasmuch as no criteria were offered to contributors in terms of techniques, no effort was made to streamline the studies toward one particular theme, motif, language, or region. This was done to avoid unintentionally reaffirming early modern scholarship's misleading view that linguistic and

---

[47] Without tripping into the rabbit-hole, it might be worth noting that if we presume a prominent role for orality, the specificities exhibited in the later hagiographies with reference to the *APT* would suggest a similar dynamic between the fluidity and stability seen in written texts (as witnessed in manuscript copies) within and across various linguistic and literary traditions.

[48] This volume is envisioned as a conversation starter as there are many other important linguistic traditions, such as Arabic, that would add further depth and dimension to our understanding of the reception of Thecla in medieval hagiographies. As circumstances beyond our control, in addition to limitations of time and space, precluded us from representing these traditions here, we hope the conversation will be taken up by others.

regional boundaries are strictly impermeable or offering skewed views of Thecla and the *APT* as models. Furthermore, it also follows the growing number of studies that have resuscitated interest in apocryphal and canonical Acts and hagiographical works as social documents that help paint more detailed pictures of the worlds from which they emerged,[49] the views and interests of their writers, and the literary history of a given tradition (engagement with other texts and traditions and the practice of that engagement). In essence, then, rather than reading these texts simply for the facts or their historicity, the chapters in this volume highlight the ideological, cultural, and religious concerns of their writers and, by extension, their audiences by outlining the richly varied techniques they used to deploy the *APT* as a model.

The volume also follows those studies that over the past few decades have taken a broad, open understanding of hagiography, namely, as portraits of holy exemplary living, as edifying tales.[50] Thus, under the large umbrella of hagiography are now included different kinds of texts such as poems, *menologia*, short tales, dialogues, spiritual romances, passions, and histories that feature portraits of saints, all of which are considered and represented in this volume. This broadening of generic considerations arose out of a gradual shift in perspective that has taken place over the last few decades, namely, that the strict delineations between generic boundaries are more reflective of early modern scholarship's views and less so of pre-modern standards. We certainly must pay attention to when ancient and medieval writers signal participation in one genre or another, for instance, by title headings (Lives and histories among others). Nevertheless, such considerations should not eclipse the fact that premodern writers were not always as fastidious in adhering to generic considerations as early modern scholars would have liked. Indeed, to have followed this latter path would have meant sacrificing medieval Irish poetry and a medieval Persian mystical tale composed in verse, which not only invoke and evoke Thecla respectively but also adopt (even if partially) the generic stance of hagiographies. Even Tertullian's *de Baptismo* (*On Baptism*) would have been excluded even though as it stands, it is the earliest text extant that testifies to the fact that the *APT* was being read as hagiography almost soon after it was compiled. In fact, if we take this a

---

[49] Brock and Harvey, "Introduction," 1987: 3.
[50] This may even include *menologia* that circulated with homilies, apocryphal and canonical Acts, and hagiographical tales which were brought together for church readings. On this, see Bovon, "Byzantine Witnesses," 1999: 88–91. For an overview of this development as it relates to hagiography, see Rapp, "The Origins," 2010 and the sources therein.

step further to consider sub-genres, even passions are not necessarily solely concerned with Thecla as a model of forbearance and fortitude on pain of death. As a few of the chapters illustrate, histories can elide easily into passion (Rhipsime), and passions, in turn, can be the dénouement of a spiritual romance (*Martyrdom of Paese and Thecla*), which can be expounded upon in dialogues (*Life of Helia*) all while using the multifaceted figure of Thecla and her equally complex tale as models. We may count, then, such blending and blurring of genres and sub-genres as yet another ubiquitous technique in the pre-modern world that the texts under study here employ.

Like the *APT*, the hagiographies under discussion here were also retold, written down, and translated into Greek, Latin, Armenian, Georgian, Syriac, Coptic, Ethiopic, Slavonic, and Arabic to name but a few of the most prominent languages; thus, adding another complex layer to the study of these texts. As varied as the linguistic and literary traditions to which these texts belong, the underlying meaning – edifying tales on how to live a moral life, even if it means going against the familial and social grain so to speak[51] – remains fairly firm. However, the social worlds of each text (not to mention linguistic tradition) differs from one generation to the next and from one era to the other. And even within a given generation or linguistic community, no two copies of a text are exactly alike. In some cases, even, the most popular plot outlines and thematic motifs[52] were reconstituted to create new (fictional) Lives of (female) saints. In other cases, the texts underwent major and sometimes only minor tinkering in each new manuscript copy. In other cases still, copies of these tales and other similar stories were placed together, sometimes along with the *APT*, into manuscript compendia, as noted above. Some of these compendia were compiled even according to a particular theme, such as martyrdoms as in the Ethiopic case, and, thus, highlight the different ways the iterations of a tale engaged with the *APT* and other hagiographical texts.

The choice, then, to study the ways in which Thecla is evoked in later hagiographical texts or, more precisely, reception, lies precisely in its usefulness as a means of discerning how audiences – which include writers – make meaning out of older and contemporaneous texts while

---

[51] For more see, Rapp, "Storytelling," 1998.
[52] By which I mean those motifs most commonly associated with a particular theme such as desire, suffering, cross-dressing, wealth distribution, and interpersonal relationships among others.

determining possible audience expectations.[53] Reception allows us to bridge the gaps in the intervening centuries between multiple texts (and even copies of texts) that were oftentimes separated across vast, even inhospitable terrains, yet belong to a greater tradition[54] and draw from the same pool of narratives and motifs. Reception, then, helps us understand the author's practice across two axes, the vertical – the creative deployment of older texts or their reiterations in later ones – but also the horizontal – how contemporary texts offer their own unique perspectives on similar social concerns.

In terms of this volume, reception is particularly useful since it helps us better appreciate the authors of the texts under discussion here as avid, devoted readers of the *APT*[55] inasmuch as our authors were admirers of the historical saints whose lives they recounted. As such, they blended the boundaries between the life of Thecla and that of their chosen saints, historical or fictional, to varying degrees depending on their particular aims. This is similar to today's fan fiction – the rewriting of a beloved story or film with one's own interests in mind.[56] In other words, hagiographers mined a multifaceted, well-known, and complex text for different resources to weigh-in on specific interests and concerns. Some, as noted above, were interested in Thecla as an apostle, others as a chaste virgin, charismatic confessor, leader, martyr, intercessor, or teacher or some

---

[53] Jauss, *Toward an Aesthetic*, 1982.

[54] Here, it is useful to turn to Charles Martindale, "Reception," 2010: 298, who notes that "[t]he etymology of 'tradition,' for example, from the Latin *tradere* suggests a – usually benign – handing down of material from the past to the present. 'Reception,' by contrast ... operates with a different temporality, involving the *active* participation of readers (including readers who are themselves creative artists) in a two-way process, backward as well as forward, in which the present and the past are in dialogue with each other." See also Martindale and Thomas (eds.), *Classics*, 2006; Martindale, "Introduction," 2006; and Pollman, "How to Do Things," 2008.

[55] On the readers of the Apocryphal Acts, among many examples see, for instance, Nasrallah, "'She Became,'" 1999; Stoops, "The *Acts of Peter*," 1997; and MacDonald, "Is there a Privileged Reader?," 1995.

[56] The popular 1995 film *Clueless*, written and directed by Amy Heckerling (b. 1954) and starring Alicia Silverstone (b. 1976) and Paul Rudd (b. 1969), is a particularly illuminating example in this regard. A comedy and recently labeled New Classic, *Clueless* follows the trials and tribulations of a beautiful, precocious yet naïve young woman who belongs to the upper echelons of Hollywood society as she learns to navigate the perils and joys of high school, city life (or at least San Fernando Valley) outside her sheltered and secluded home in Beverly Hills, and dating (which includes an episode of sexual assault) as she comes to realize she has fallen in love with a handsome college student, a slightly older and comparatively more worldly young man who orbits the outer edges of her social world and guides her as she tears down her social world and builds it up again in a new way. *Clueless* is a modern retelling of Jane Austen's (1775–1817) classic novel, *Emma*, and thus belongs to the category of young adult films highlighted at the beginning.

combination thereof, but rarely all at once, to construct the Lives of their saints as model acts to follow for their own audiences.

Here, then, we are confronted with two overlapping trajectories: hagiographers were first readers, and hagiographies, as noted above, are edifying, exemplary works. Though discussions related to matters regarding authorial interest, ideal and real audience, and audience expectation lie beyond the scope of this volume, these issues do linger in the background of the chapters in this volume.[57] For indeed, as edifying, exemplary tales, hagiographies necessarily target a broad, non-specialist audience; those who are interested in certain topics but may not be reading necessarily dense theological treatises. Ideally, this audience is well-read – those in the upper echelons of society – or well-informed – those, whatever their literacy and social background, who would hear these tales recited and were, thus, familiar with them.[58] They would need to be in order to recognize references to other texts and (hopefully) understand the underlying message(s). As such, they would have been the same audiences and reciters of the *APT* itself.[59] Moreover, they would have been reading or reciting them in a variety of public and private contexts, including but not limited to while on pilgrimage or in a monastery or convent as the *Martyrdom of Febronia* indicates. And, as a number of our contributors speak of intertextuality, and a number of the techniques by which scholars within and without this volume understand intertextuality have been highlighted, a few words on its theory are especially pertinent before delving into the point at which the aforementioned two trajectories overlap or, more aptly, intersect.[60]

As such, we should recall first that intertextuality seeks to understand the techniques by which authors make meaning out of a vast network of oral and written texts; texts that crisscross one another in many ways.[61] The result is that the new text, then, becomes a part of this dense network, informing in its turn the larger cultural milieu. Second, intertextuality too

---

[57] For an insightful discussion, see Rapp, "Author, Audience, Text," 2015.
[58] This also crosses the gender divide as noted in the studies cited above.
[59] As many have remarked, the famous and much-cited travel journal written by Egeria (fl. fourth century), a female pilgrim who visited Thecla's shrine in Seleucia on her way back from Jerusalem, offers a fascinating (and tantalizing) glimpse into the practice of reading and hearing the *APT*. On this pilgrim and her journal, see McGowan and Bradshaw (eds. and trans.), *The Pilgrimage of Egeria*, 2018. On her tale as it relates to readings and recitations of the *APT*, see Johnson, *The Life and Miracles*, 2006: 1–4.
[60] Davis, "Crossed Sex, Crossed Texts," 2002, explores the intertextuality of the *APT* and the *Life and Passion of Eugenia*.
[61] For an insightful overview of the theory of intertextuality and its application to the Apocryphal Acts, see Matthews, "*Apocryphal* Intertextual Activities," 1997.

attempts to address the author as audience as well. Thus, authorial interest is the node at which reception theory and intertextuality intersect for hagiography. For indeed, as much as texts come from and are then a part of a dense network, hagiographers were as much a part of the same audience as the reader/listener they, in turn, targeted. The hagiographers' interests, in other words, are informed by that of the greater community, and when they promote, subvert, or highlight a particular outlook or ideological bent they do so by making use of a shared discourse – all that is or can be expressed at a particular moment and place.[62] They, thus, anticipate audience expectation that largely coincides with their own. In other words, hagiographers use popular techniques to refer to other texts; this accords with audience expectation, which parallels a hagiographer's own experience as a reader; they, thus, further contribute to audience expectation as writers (intertextuality) to make new meaning out of – address specific concerns of interest to them – by using older, authoritative and/or contemporary texts (reception); as such, they meet audience expectation in yet another fashion.

Taking this a step further, using and, its converse, recognizing references to familiar tales, over time and across numerous texts, builds an identity that simultaneously transcends and situates the reader within a specific linguistic, regional, and cultural context. In terms related to our purposes, this resembles the universalism and localism of Christianity. As such, considering reception and intertextuality from these multiple and complex angles helps illustrate, for instance, why it may have been important for medieval Ethiopian and Irish writers to promote Thecla as a martyr even though she miraculously survived her trials, and neither community was suffering from such fatal persecutions. As has been frequently noted, passions were integral to the formation of early Christian communal identity.[63] The promotion, then, of one of the most well-known and beloved figures of early Christianity as a martyr in one's own terms and language was likely intended to intensify the sense of belonging to the greater Christian community across time and space while reinforcing the bonds of the local community. While doing so, hagiographers directly but, more often, indirectly subsume all the Lives that privilege Thecla as the preeminent female (near) martyr. The Ethiopian and Irish cases thus are

---

[62] This is a short paraphrasing of Jan Blommaert's theory on social discourse. For more, see Blommaert, *Discourse*, 2005: 120 in particular.
[63] For more on this, see Boyarin, *Dying for God*, 1999; the collected essays in Leemans (ed.), *More than a Memory*, 2005; and Moralee, "State Power, Hagiography," 2021.

edifying and meet audience expectation (how to act as a Christian under pressure – Thecla as proto female-martyr) while ensuring the longevity of such expectations as they create, at least in the Ethiopic case, new models from which later hagiographers may draw.

Even as each chapter stands independently on its own – for its particular concerns for a certain time, place, writer, and community – when viewed altogether, they shed light on how various communities understood and in turn made meaning out of the *APT* and, more broadly speaking, their own societies. They highlight what it meant for a saint to be presented as a model to be followed who, in turn, followed an older, authoritative one; it is participation in saintly living on multiple levels, across time, within a well-established tradition. Ultimately, by approaching these texts diachronically and synchronically, the volume, as a whole, sets out to paint a more detailed and nuanced portrait of the *APT* as a foundational text of not just Christianity but also of Christian literary output across east and west.[64]

Given all these factors, especially the blurring of different kinds of boundaries, the volume is not divided by regional, epochal, generic, or linguistic considerations. There is a case to be made that the contributions by Barrier (Chapter 1), Staat (Chapter 9), Labadie (Chapter 2), and Ó Dochartaigh (Chapter 3) should be grouped together for their emphasis on the oftentimes profound impact that the *APT* had on transforming society and its perceptions; for Barrier and Staat examine the perceptions of church fathers and, as outlined above, Labadie and Ó Dochartaigh deal with complicated questions of representation. However, since the volume's emphasis is on tracing the complex ways in which Thecla and her legend live on in other texts, a different course is called for. Indeed, for just as *imitatio Christi* is the practice of following Christ and is a large feature of Lives and Martyrdoms of male saints, the hagiographies under study here demonstrate an equivalent *imitatio Theclae*.[65] Therefore, the chapters are grouped based on the extents to which the protagonists of the texts imitate or imitate and surpass Thecla as their model. Part I, "An Act to Follow" (Chapters 1–6), is devoted to contributions by Jeremy Barrier, Damien Labadie, Caitríona Ó Dochartaigh, Valentina Calzolari, Flavia Ruani, and Arietta Papaconstantinou since they illustrate the extents to which Thecla

---

[64] For a transversal study of sainthood, see the volume by Meltzer and Elsner (eds.), *Saints*, 2011.
[65] On Thecla's perceived "madness" in the way she follows Paul and turns toward an ascetic life as an example of *imitatio Christi*, see Narro, "The Cloud of Thecla," 2019: 106. The chain of imitation thus proceeds from Christ to Thecla to the later saints featured in this volume.

and, in the case of Ruani's and Papaconstantinou's chapters, her companions were models to be imitated. It is fitting that the volume begins with Barrier's discussion of the famous passages in Tertullian's *de Baptismo*, which, as noted throughout, shines light on the fact that women were reading the *APT* and using it as a model for their own lives as well as for the roles they adopted in their community relatively soon after the composition of the text. But also because it responds to a pressing issue that permeates the volume as a whole – access to the *APT* – by addressing directly the question of whether Tertullian had the *APT* in hand as he repudiated both the presbyter who compiled the *APT* and the women who were teaching and baptizing based on it. While Labadie's chapter discusses Thecla's importance in the development of Ethiopic hagiographical literature, it follows Barrier's contribution since it illustrates how the *APT* was similarly read as hagiography, except, in this case, Thecla is evoked not as a teacher or baptizer but as a martyr and confessor. Despite the vast distances (physical and cultural) separating medieval Ethiopia and Ireland, Ó Dochartaigh's contribution follows Labadie's chapter since it also explores how Thecla was celebrated as a model apostle and martyr, with implications for communal and cross-regional ties, and since Thecla appears in versified calendrical notices in both traditions to do so. Which brings us around to Calzolari's and Ruani's respective chapters. Though Ruani's chapter focuses on secondary characters who follow their *APT* counterparts either positively or negatively, Calzolari's and Ruani's chapters illustrate, like Labadie's and Ó Dochartaigh's contributions, how Thecla was perceived and celebrated as a martyr (more often), virgin, apostle, ascetic, and preacher in Armenian and Syriac hagiographic literature. Papaconstantinou's chapter, as a study in reconfigured relationships, follows Ruani's contribution and rounds out this group of chapters. It also serves as a transitional essay of sorts since, in reimagining the relationship between Paul and Thecla as an eschatological love triangle between Paese and Paul and Thecla, the *Martyrdom of Paese and Thecla* surpasses the *APT* as a completed passion and one in which this Thecla and Paul, at least, are finally reunited in heaven.

The remaining four chapters, which are grouped under the heading, "An Act to Surpass" (Part II), investigate heroines who emulate Thecla in various ways. Part II begins with Van Pelt's chapter for its thought-provoking analysis of the ways in which later hagiographers understood Thecla as a cross-dresser or, more aptly, not. In the texts she studies, the holy heroines imitate their model Thecla in various respects but surpass her in terms of cross-dressing. Thus, her chapter also serves as a transition.

Burrus' contribution follows next since it illustrates that Thecla played a prominent role in the development of female voice and the debate on desire and chastity from antiquity throughout the Latin-speaking west, but it also demonstrates that later writers were interested in pushing female agency, their vociferousness, beyond Thecla. This leads us to Staat's contribution, which maps the highs and lows of the *APT*'s reception among the church fathers and throughout the Latin-speaking west. Similar to Burrus' contribution, the chapters by Staat and my own, which follows hence, focus on the interest of the writer of the *Life and Passion of Eugenia* to surpass the boundaries of female rhetorical abilities and leadership imposed by the *APT*'s abrupt end of Thecla's tale – just as its heroine gains both. In an Afterward that rounds up secondary scholarship's attempt to locate Thecla and her tale and the meaning(s) they held for different communities, Kate Cooper pens her thoughts about Thecla's popularity across time and space.

It is our sincere hope that readers – whether their interest is in the literary and social history of early Christianity across east and west, Christian and Islamic narratives of sainthood, comparative studies generally, or the literary afterlives of Thecla and the *APT* – will find something fruitful within each contribution but especially in the volume as a whole. We also hope that it serves as a stepping-stone for further forays into the social, historical, and theological aspects of the hagiographies under discussion here and, especially, as a conversation starter for addressing Thecla and the *APT* as prominent models for other hagiographical narratives and their protagonists and in other linguistic traditions.

Bibliography

Aubin, Melissa. "Reversing Romance? *The Acts of Thecla* and the Ancient Novel." In *Ancient Fiction and Early Christian Narrative*, edited by Ronald F. Hock, J. Bradley Chance, and Judith Perkins. Society of Biblical Literature Symposium Series 6. Atlanta: Scholars Press, 1998: 257–272.

Barrier, Jeremy W. *The Acts of Paul and Thecla: A Critical Introduction and Commentary*. WUNT 2.270. Tübingen: Mohr Siebeck, 2009.

"*The Acts of Paul and Thecla*: The Historiographical Context." In *Thecla: Paul's Disciple and Saint in the East and the West*, edited by Jeremy W. Barrier, Jan N. Bremmer, T. Nicklas, and A. Puig i Tàrrech. Studies on Early Christian Apocrypha 12. Leuven: Peeters, 2017: 327–350.

Barrier, Jeremy W., Jan N. Bremmer, T. Niklas, and A. Puig i Tàrrech, eds. *Thecla: Paul's Disciple and Saint in the East and West*. Studies in Early Christian Apocrypha 12. Leuven: Peeters, 2017.

Blommaert, Jan. *Discourse: A Critical Introduction: Key Topics in Sociolinguistics.* Cambridge: Cambridge University Press, 2005.
Bovon, François. "Byzantine Witnesses for the Apocryphal Acts of the Apostles." In *The Apocryphal Acts of the Apostles: Harvard Divinity School Studies*, edited by François Bovon, Ann Graham Brock, and Christopher R. Matthews. Cambridge, MA: Harvard University Press, 1999: 87–100.
"Preface." In *The Apocryphal Acts of the Apostles: Harvard Divinity School Studies*, edited by François Bovon, Ann Graham Brock, and Christopher R. Matthews. Cambridge, MA: Harvard University Press, 1999: xv–xx.
"The Corpus Christianorum Series Apocryphorum and the Association pour l'étude de la littérature apocryphe chrétienne." *Early Christianity* 3 (2012): 137–143.
Bovon, François, Ann Graham Brock, and Christopher R. Matthews, eds. *The Apocryphal Acts of the Apostles: Harvard Divinity School Studies.* Cambridge, MA: Harvard University Press, 1999.
Boyarin, Daniel. *Dying for God: Martyrdom and the Making of Christianity and Judaism.* Stanford: Stanford University Press, 1999.
Bremmer, Jan N., ed. *The Apocryphal Acts of John.* Studies on the Apocryphal Acts of the Apostles 1. Kampen: Kok Pharos, 1995.
ed. *The Apocryphal Acts of Paul and Thecla.* Studies on the Apocryphal Acts of the Apostles 2. Kampen: Kok Pharos, 1996.
ed. *The Apocryphal Acts of Andrew.* Leuven: Peeters, 2000.
"Bibliography of Thecla." In *Thecla: Paul's Disciple and Saint in the East and West*, edited by Jeremy W. Barrier, Jan N. Bremmer, T. Niklas, and A. Puig i Tàrrech. Leuven: Peeters, 2017: 279–285.
Brock, Sebastian P., and Susan Ashbrook Harvey. "Introduction." In *Holy Women of the Syrian Orient*, edited and translated by Sebastian P. Brock and Susan Ashbrook Harvey. Berkeley: University of California Press, 1987.
Brown, Peter. "The Rise and Function of the Holy Man in Late Antiquity." *The Journal of Roman Studies* 61 (1971): 80–101.
The Cult of the Saint. Chicago: University of Chicago Press, 1981.
Society and the Holy in Late Antiquity. Berkeley: University of California Press, 1982.
"The Saint as Exemplar in Late Antiquity." In *Saints and Virtues*, edited by John S. Hawley. Berkeley: University of California Press, 1987: 3–14.
Burrus, Virginia. *Chastity as Autonomy: Women in the Stories of Apocryphal Acts.* Studies in Women and Religion 23. Lewiston: Edwin Mellen Press, 1987.
"Mimicking Virgins: Colonial Ambivalence and Ancient Romance." *Arethusa* 38, no. 1 (2005): 49–88.
Clarke, Peter D., and Tony Claydon, eds. *Saints and Sanctity.* Studies in Church History 47. Woodbridge: Boydell Press, 2011.
Constantinou, Stavroula. "Performing Gender in Lay Saints' Lives." *Byzantine and Modern Greek Studies* 38, no. 1 (2014): 24–32.
Cooper, Kate. *The Virgin and the Bride: Idealized Womanhood in Late Antiquity.* Cambridge, MA: Harvard University Press, 1996.

Cooper, Kate, and James Corke-Webster. "Conversion, Conflict, and the Drama of Social Reproduction: Narratives of Filial Resistance in Early Christianity and Modern Britain." In *Conversion and Initiation in Antiquity: Shifting Identities-Creating Change*, edited by Birgitte Secher Bøgh. Frankfurt am Main; New York: Peter Lang, 2014: 169–183.

Davies, Stevan L. *The Revolt of the Widows: The Social World of the Apocryphal Acts*. Carbondale: Southern Illinois University Press, 1980.

Davis, Stephen J. *The Cult of St. Thecla: A Tradition of Women's Piety in Late Antiquity*. Oxford Early Christian Studies. Oxford; New York: Oxford University Press, 2001.

——— "Crossed Texts, Crossed Sex: Intertextuality and Gender in Early Christian Legends of Holy Women Disguised as Men." *Journal of Early Christian Studies* 10, no. 1 (2002): 1–36.

——— "From Women's Piety to Male Devotion: Gender Studies, the *Acts of Paul and Thecla*, and the Evidence of an Arabic Manuscript." *Harvard Theological Review* 108, no. 4 (2015): 579–593.

Hylen, Susan E. *A Modest Apostle: Thecla and the History of Women in the Early Church*. New York: Oxford University Press, 2015.

Jauss, Hans. *Toward an Aesthetic of Reception*, translated by Timothy Bahti. Theory and History of Literature 2. Minneapolis: University of Minnesota Press, 1982.

Johnson, Scott F. *The Life and Miracles of Thekla: A Literary Study*. Washington, DC: Center for Hellenic Studies, Trustees for Harvard University, 2006.

Leemans, Johan, ed. *More Than a Memory: The Discourse of Martyrdom and the Construction of Christian Identity in the History of Christianity*. Annua Nuntia Lovaniensia 51. Leuven; Dudley: Peeters, 2005.

Lipsett, B. Diane. *Desiring Conversion: Hermas, Thecla, Asenneth*. Oxford: Oxford University Press, 2011.

MacDonald, Dennis, R. *The Legend and the Apostle: The Battle for Paul in Story and Cannon*. Philadelphia: Westminster, 1983.

——— "Is There a Privileged Reader? A Case from the Apocryphal Acts." *Semeia* 71 (1995): 29–44.

Martindale, Charles. "Introduction: Thinking through Reception." In *Classics and the Uses of Reception*, edited by Charles Martindale and Richard F. Thomas. Malden; Oxford: Blackwell, 2006: 1–13.

——— "Reception." In *A Companion to the Classical Tradition*, edited by Craig W. Kallendorf. Malden: Wiley-Blackwell, 2010: 297–311.

Martindale, Charles, and Richard F. Thomas, eds. *Classics and the Uses of Reception*. Malden; Oxford: Blackwell, 2006.

Matthews, Christopher R. "*Apocryphal* Intertextual Activities: A Reframing of Harold W. Attridge's 'Intertextuality in the *Acts of Thomas*.'" In *The Apocryphal Acts of the Apostles in Intertextual Perspectives*, edited by Robert F. Stoops. Semeia 80. Atlanta: Scholars Press, 1997: 125–136.

Meltzer, Françoise, and Jaś Elsner, eds. *Saints: Faith without Borders*. Chicago: University of Chicago Press, 2011.

McGowan, Anne, and Paul F. Bradshaw, eds. and trans. *The Pilgrimage of Egeria: A New Translation of the Itinerarium Egeriae with Introduction and Commentary*. Collegeville: Liturgical Press, 2018.

McInerney, Maud Burnett. *Eloquent Virgins: From Thecla to Joan of Arc: The New Middle Ages*. New York: Palgrave Macmillan, 2003.

McLarty, Jane D. *Thecla's Devotion: Narrative and Emotion in Late Antiquity*. Cambridge: James Clark & Co., 2018.

Moralee, Jason. "State Power, Hagiography, and the Social Shape of the Past: Re-reading the *Gesta Martyrum Romanorum*." In *Narrating Power and Authority in Late Antique and Medieval Hagiography across East and West*, edited by Ghazzal Dabiri. Fabulae 1. Turnhout: Brepols, 2021: 153–164.

Nasrallah, Laura S. "'She Became What the Words Signified': The Greek *Acts of Andrew*'s Construction of the Reader-Disciple." In *The Apocryphal Acts of the Apostles: Harvard Divinity Studies*, edited by François Bovon, Ann Graham Brock, and Christopher R. Matthews. Cambridge, MA: Harvard University Press, 1999: 233–258.

Narro, Ángel. "The Cloud of Thecla and the Construction of Her Character as a Virgin (παρθένος), Martyr (μάρτυς) and Apostle (ἀπόστολος)." *Collectanea Christiana Orientalia* 16 (2009): 129–199.

Perkins, Judith. *The Suffering Self: Pain and Narrative Representation in the Early Christian Era*. London: Routledge, 1995.

"This World or Another? The Intertextuality of the Greek Romances, the Apocryphal Acts, and Apuleius' *Metamorphoses*." In *The Apocryphal Acts of the Apostles in Intertextual Perspectives*, edited by Robert F. Stoops. Semeia 80. Atlanta: Scholars Press, 1997: 247–260.

Pollmann, Karla. "How to Do Things with Augustine: Patristics and Reception Theory." *Church Studies* 5 (2008): 31–41.

Ramelli, Ilaria, and Judith Perkins, eds. *Early Christian and Jewish Narrative: The Role of Religion in Shaping Narrative Forms*. WUNT 348. Tübingen: Mohr Siebeck, 2015.

Rapp, Claudia. "Storytelling as Spiritual Communication in Early Greek Hagiography: The Use of Diegesis." *Journal of Early Christian Studies* 6, no. 3 (Fall 1998): 431–488.

"The Origins of Hagiography and the Literature of Early Monasticism: Purpose and Genre Between Tradition and Innovation." In *Unclassical Traditions: Volume I: Alternative to the Classical Past in Late Antiquity*, edited by Christopher Kelly, Richard Flower, and Michael Stuart Williams. Cambridge: Cambridge University Press, 2010: 119–130.

"Author, Audience, Text and Saint: Two Modes of Early Byzantine Hagiography." *Scandinavian Journal of Byzantine and Modern Greek Studies* 1 (2015): 111–130.

Stoops, Robert F. "The *Acts of Peter* in Intertextual Contexts." In *The Apocryphal Acts of the Apostles in Intertextual Perspectives*, edited by Robert F. Stoops. Semeia 80. Atlanta: Scholars Press, 1997: 57–84.

ed. *The Apocryphal Acts of the Apostles in Intertextual Perspectives*. Semeia 80. Atlanta: Scholars Press, 1997.

Strickland, Debra Higgs, ed. *Images of Medieval Sanctity: Essays in Honour of Gary Dickson*. Leiden: Brill, 2007.

Thomas, Christine M. "The 'Prehistory' of the *Acts of Peter*." In *The Apocryphal Acts of the Apostles: Harvard Divinity School Studies*, edited by François Bovon, Ann Graham Brock, and Christopher R. Matthews. Cambridge, MA: Harvard University Press, 1999: 39–62.

Valantasis, Richard. "The Nuptial Chamber Revisited: The Acts of Thomas and Cultural Intertextuality." In *The Apocryphal Acts of the Apostles in Intertextual Perspectives*, edited by Robert F. Stoops. Semeia 80. Atlanta: Scholars Press, 1997: 261–276.

Voicu, Sever J. "Thecla in the Christian East." In *Thecla: Paul's Disciple and Saint in the East and West*, edited by Jeremy W. Barrier, Jan N. Bremmer, T. Niklas, and A. Puig i Tàrrech. Studies on Early Christian Apocrypha 12. Leuven: Peeters, 2017: 47–68.

Wills, Lawrence M. *The Jewish Novel in the Ancient World: Myth and Poetics*. Eugene: Wipf and Stock, 2015.

PART I

An Act to Follow

CHAPTER I

A Cainite Invocation of Thecla?
The Reception of the Acts of Paul in North Africa as Exemplified in Tertullian's de Baptismo

Jeremy W. Barrier*

Introduction and *Apologia*

Sometime between 196 and 206, Tertullian (b. c. 155), a Christian living and writing in Carthage, North Africa, wrote a homily entitled *de Baptismo*.[1] This work is probably best known for a reference to the acrostic ΙΧΘΥΣ (i.e., Ιησου Χριστος Θεου [or Θεος] Υιος Σωτηρ, "Jesus Christ God Son Savior") that is translated as "fish" and was popularly used as an early Christian symbol. However, the primary thrust of the homily seems to be Tertullian's defense of baptism directed against a woman, whom he calls a female viper from a Cainite sect,[2] who is preaching, teaching, and denying the practice. My interest in *de Baptismo* is connected to a minor argument of Tertullian where he denounces the *Acts of Paul* (Lat., *Acta Pauli*) as part of his denunciation of the female adversary. Therefore, the purpose of this chapter is to critically examine the reception of Thecla as a female described within a known literary work, *Acta Pauli*, within Tertullian's *de Baptismo*.

Before conducting this examination, a brief discussion of several broad concerns might be helpful. I realize the scope of the entire volume is to examine the *literary* reception of Thecla within *late antique* and *early medieval hagiography*. The italicized words, of course, point to the specific areas that I wish to reflect upon briefly as they pertain to my topic. First, after a cursory reading of *de Baptismo*, one will quickly note that an explicit

---

* This chapter is an expansion of a presentation I gave at the 2006 Annual Meeting of the Society of Biblical Literature, Washington, DC, as a part of the "Christian Apocrypha" section. The presentation was entitled "Tertullian and the *Acts of Thecla* or *Paul*? Readership of the Ancient Christian Novel and the Invocation of Thecline and Pauline Authority." I appreciate David Brakke, Ed Gallagher, and the editors for reading an earlier form of this essay and offering helpful feedback.
[1] Latin text and English translation taken from Evans (ed. and trans.), *Tertullian's Homily*, 1964. See also the edition edited by Borleffs (ed.), *Tertulliani Opera*, 1954.
[2] Evans (ed. and trans.), *Tertullian's Homily*, 1964: 4. See also Borleffs (ed.), *Tertulliani Opera*, 1954: 291.

"literary" reference to the *Acts of Paul* can hardly be found. Tertullian does not make a citation from any part of what we know of as the *Acts of Paul* nor specifically to the section within it that is known as the *Acts of Paul and Thecla*. Nevertheless, we may be able to justify our inquiry if we content ourselves by looking for "allusions" and "echoes" in the text.[3] Tertullian is seemingly aware (at most) of a text, or, at the least, he has heard rumors of the story as told within a text. However, to say that he is appreciative of its literary, martyrological, or hagiographical value might be an overstatement.

This leads to my second point: one would be hard-pressed to argue that Tertullian is living within the *late antique* (to say nothing of "early medieval") period. As best can be determined, while Tertullian is alive throughout most of the first half of the second century, this writing still precedes the reign of Diocletian (r. 284–305) by nearly three quarters of a century.[4] We are dealing with a mention of a literary work that could be thought to be too early for the scope of this volume.

Third, I would be remiss if I failed to mention that hagiography is often thought of as a "later" phenomenon that may be observed within the late antique, byzantine, and early medieval period (and beyond).[5] Nevertheless, this is where a loophole may be exploited in order to consider Tertullian's opinions on Thecla within the context of this volume. Granted that we are essentially one century removed from Eusebius of Caesarea's (d. 339) lost work, *An Assembly of Ancient Martyrs*, and two centuries earlier than the *vita* written by Athanasius (d. 373) to honor Antony, my approach is similar to that argued by Ghazzal Dabiri, in the Introduction to this volume, that we address hagiographies in the broader sense.[6] This is where we might gain traction.

The place of this essay could be described as a terminus a quo for investigations of hagiographical references pertaining to Thecla. In other words, this would be the historical "origins" for thinking about the *literary reception of Thecla* that grows and flourishes within late antiquity and the early medieval period. Thus, from a certain point of view, this is the beginning of a phenomenon of thinking of Thecla within the framework of hagiography.

---

[3] See Hays, *Echoes of Scripture*, 1989; and Hays, *The Conversion*, 2005.
[4] Diocletian's reign can represent the "beginning" of late antiquity. See Eder, "Late Antiquity," 2005.
[5] On hagiography, see Georgios, "Acta Sanctorum," 2001; Wyrwa, "Hagiography," 2004; Talbot, "Hagiography," 2008; Rühle, "Hagiographie," 1986; and Thurston, "Saints and Martyrs (Christian)," 1920.
[6] Talbot, "Hagiography," 2008: 862–863.

If, then, we are to examine the reception of the *Acts of Paul* as a form of hagiography within the churches of North Africa (as will be done shortly), this leads to acknowledging several factors. The honoring of "saint" Thecla in this region should be thought of as an already important part of church life as Tertullian inadvertently proves.[7] Tertullian appears to be aware of *the* Thecla, as noted above, and associates her with an *Acta* – possibly the *Acts of Paul* – which deals with her teaching and baptizing. In his denunciation of (1) the writer of the *Acts*, for claiming that Thecla teaches, and (2) a Cainite female teaching, he is obviously threatened by communities who appeal to Thecla. This detail is highlighted here again due to the fact that Tertullian's reference to Thecla has become standard in discussions of the dating and reception of the *Acts of Paul*, however, scholars are not questioning his knowledge of Thecla of Iconium.

I am aware that the textual evidence, relatively speaking, is considered "strong" for this time period, but I am trying to indicate that no manuscripts of the *Acts of Paul* exist near to the time of its composition.[8] In regard to the evidence that remains of the *Acts of Paul*, there is a Greek, third-century manuscript containing 3 Corinthians (i.e., *Bodmer Papyrus X*), three Greek papyri fragments from the third to fifth centuries, and the Coptic "Heidelberg" papyrus from the fifth–sixth century.[9] Thus, the evidence that does remain clearly fits within a time period where the veneration of saints and the production of hagiography have significantly increased, and Thecla, more than many saints, has reached the peak of her popularity.[10] To go along with these thoughts, we also know that the *Acts of Paul and Thecla* does seem to represent a prototype and exemplar *martyrion* similar to the *martyrion* of Perpetua and Felicitas. This appears to represent a sort of "origins" for hagiography.[11] As an example, many of the descriptive elements that loosely fit within hagiography (i.e., *passiones*, *vitae*, miracle stories, emphasis upon asceticism and virginity, the praise of missionary efforts, and so forth) are clearly present

---

[7] MacMullen, *The Second Church*, 2009.
[8] Hurtado, *The Earliest Christian Manuscripts*, 2006: 228–229; Roberts, "The Acts of Paul and Thecla," 1950: 27.
[9] One should begin with Geerard (ed.), "Acta Pauli," 1992, then consult the following titles: Testuz, *Papyrus Bodmer X–XI*, 1959; Mackay, "Observations," 1979; Mackay, "Content and Style," 1986; Roberts, "The Acts of Paul and Thecla," 1950; Schmidt (ed. and trans.), *Acta Pauli*, 1904; Schmidt (ed. and trans.), *Acta Pauli*, 1905; and Schmidt and Schubart (eds. and trans.), *PRAXEIS PAULOU*, 1936.
[10] See Davis, *The Cult of St. Thecla*, 2001; and Johnson, *The Life and Miracles*, 2006.
[11] Talbot, "Hagiography," 2008: 863.

here; and again, as indicated by Tertullian, this is a source of inspiration and veneration by the early Christians within North Africa.

Therefore, *if* no early manuscripts exist and *if* the *Acts of Paul and Thecla* is a text within a tradition of hagiographical production, then one cannot help but wonder if and to what extent the text might have been altered. While serious *Formgeschichte Untersuchungen* have been conducted on the *Acts of Paul and Thecla*, I am not quite sure we can reduce the text down to any earlier forms without offering an uncomfortable degree of speculation.[12] In the same way that Hippolyte Delehaye was able to present a reduced version of Procopius from his surrounding legends, a similar reduction cannot be accomplished in this case.[13] In other words, as best as can be determined by the manuscript history, the text of the *Acts of Paul and Thecla* that we have today should be considered stable and, thus, represents a hagiography at a very early date. Therefore, for the purposes of this volume, I offer this brief discussion for the inclusion of a piece focused upon Tertullian's interest in Thecla and suggest that this early hagiography might suit the context of this volume well as a beginning point for inquiring into her literary reception in later hagiographies.

Having made these comments above, I now backtrack to an important question; namely, what is Tertullian reading and what does he know about Thecla and the text that "speaks" of her, the *Acts of Paul*? To answer this question, another component will be added into the mix. In addition to his opposition to Thecla and the *Acts of Paul*, Tertullian seems to be aware of another group he opposes that he identifies as "Cainites" while also possibly alluding to a second group, known as "Ophites." Both groups may have been two branches of early Christian Gnosticism[14] whose locations and origins are not known with certainty.[15] At a minimum, he

---

[12] See Jensen, *Thekla – die Apostolin*, 1995; MacDonald, *The Legend*, 1983; Davies, *The Revolt*, 1980; and Burrus, *Chastity as Autonomy*, 1987.

[13] Delehaye, *Les Légendes grecques*, 1909; and Delehaye, *Cinq leçons*, 1934. See also the comment of Conybeare, *Myth, Magic*, 1910: 348: "In his scholarly work, *Les Légendes Hagiographiques*, Father Hippolyte Delehaye, S.J. (Brussels, 1905), has a chapter entitled 'The *Dossier* of a Saint,' in which he shows how the brief and true account given by Eusebius of a martyr named Procopius, who suffered under Diocletian, was added to and recast by the professional compilers of Acts of Saints until it was no longer recognizable. All the stages by which the acts of this saint were exaggerated and falsified lie before us in the different manuscripts; and, if we had not got Eusebius' succinct and sober narrative of his trial and execution, we could hardly venture to affirm that Procopius was a historical personage at all, and not rather a creation of the mythoplastic imagination of hagiographers."

[14] On Gnosticism and the sustaining utility of the term, see Brakke, *The Gnostics*, 2010.

[15] For descriptions of Cainites and Ophites, see Irenaeus, *Adversus Haereses* 1.30–31 (henceforth *Haer.*); Clement, *Stromata* 7.17; Pseudo-Tertullian, *Adversus omnes haereses* 2; Pseudo-Hippolytus, *Refutatio omnium haeresium* 2.5 and 8.13; Origen, *Contra Celsum* 3.13; Epiphanius, *Panarion*

is familiar with a particular concept as something worthy of his opposition, namely, a Cainite female teaching and denying baptism. In fact, a "literary analysis" could be made on how Tertullian weaves his understanding of the "Ophites" [Gk., ὄφις, "snake"] as a group into his theology by making a play on words as he compares the group to asps, vipers, basilisks, and even the serpent in Genesis 3, all of which may have been important Ophite symbols that he connects to the Cainite female. At any rate, the reason for adding Tertullian's mention of Cainites and the possible allusion to Ophites has to do with the fact that Tertullian is clearly opposing the "Cainite viper" while also opposing Thecla's example. In other words, we could equally ask: Is Tertullian reading Cainite/Ophite texts and the *Acts of Paul (and Thecla)* or does he mention them only as a rhetorical invention drawn from contemporary situations in North Africa?

If a conservative assessment is made of *de Baptismo*, as will be done later within this chapter, it is not immediately apparent that Tertullian is reading either the *Acts of Paul (and Thecla)* or texts from Cainites or Ophites. Thus, while it would be presumptuous to make the conclusions before the evidence has been examined, I do offer this information to suggest that the aforementioned points may be the two opposite poles between which a conclusion will likely fall. Stated differently, on one end of the spectrum, Tertullian is reading "Cainite" texts such as the *Gospel of Judas*, or – more cautiously – on the other end of the spectrum, he is not reading them but is aware of North African churches who are reading and/or using concepts from these texts.[16] Of course, in mentioning "Cainite" texts, I refer here to the only text that has been identified directly with the Cainites: namely, the *Gospel of Judas*. Having been brought to light as

---

38.1.5 (henceforth *Pan.*); Filaster, *Diversarum Hereseon Liber* 2.34; Jerome, *Indiculus de haeresibus* 8; Augustine, *De haeresibus ad Quodvultdeum* 18; and Theodoret, *Haereticarum fabularum Compendium* 1.15. See also Bareille, "Cainites," 1904; and Bardy, "Cainites," 1953. See the notes in Irenaeus for comments on Ophites and Cainites, *Haer.* 1.31 in Unger (trans.), *St. Irenaeus of Lyons*, 1992: 268. See also Cross and Livingston (eds.), "Cainites," 2005, where they note that "[t]he mention of Cain in the NT (1 Jn. 3. 12, Jude 11–19) suggests a very early, perhaps, pre-Christian, origin of the sect." See Meyer, *The Gospel of Judas*, 2011: 13. For a quick overview of Ophites, see Cross and Livingston (eds.), "Ophites," 2005. It further should be noted that the reality of groups called "Cainites," "Barbeloites," or "Ophites" is highly questionable and is thought by some to be "purely a heresiological invention:" Turner, "The Place of the *Gospel of Judas*," 2008: 194. See also Brakke, *The Gnostics*, 2010: 29–51; and Rasimus, *Paradise Reconsidered*, 2014: 9–61.

[16] Our knowledge of the Cainites and the *Gospel of Judas* is limited. For Cainites and/or Ophites as a sect of Gnosticism, see n. 15. On the *Gospel of Judas* as an authority text for the Cainites, see first the primary source of Irenaeus, *Haer.* 1.31. As an introduction to the subject, see Gathercole, *The Gospel of Judas*, 2007, and most recently, Gathercole, "Das Judasevangelium," 2018; Kasser et al., *The Gospel of Judas*, 2008; Kasser and Wurst, *The Gospel of Judas*, 2007; and further extensive discussion in Scopello (ed.), *The Gospel of Judas*, 2008.

recently as 2006, the mid-second century Gnostic text called the *Gospel of Judas* is a text sharing an affinity for Seth with other similar Gnostic texts, such as the *Apocryphon of John*, *Apocalypse of Adam*, *Gospel of the Egyptians* (i.e., *The Holy Book of the Great Invisible Spirit*), or *Zostrianos*, but has prompted the most controversy by generating new discussions of the role of Judas in the betrayal of Jesus.[17]

At any rate, my point is that the beginning of a discussion of the literary reception of Thecla in hagiography, while early on the timetable, could (and possibly should) begin here and might be corroborated indirectly by an assessment of Tertullian's utilization of other figures (and texts) that he opposes. With such thoughts in mind, a deeper investigation into Tertullian's *de Baptismo* could prove stimulating, especially if we critique it with a view to (1) see how well his insights on Thecla match up with the *Acts of Paul* and (2) consider how his allusions to Ophites and mention of Cainites match up with a possible Cainite text, the newly discovered *Gospel of Judas*.

Putting Together Tertullian's *de Baptismo*, the *Acts of Paul*, and the *Gospel of Judas*

Tertullian states in *Bapt.* 1.2–3:

> a certain female viper from the Cainite sect, who recently spent some time here, carried off a good number with her exceptionally pestilential doctrine, making a particular point of demolishing baptism. Evidently in this according to nature: for vipers and asps as a rule, and even basilisks, frequent dry and waterless places. But we, being little fishes, as Jesus Christ is our great Fish, begin our life in the water, and only while we abide in the water are we safe and sound. Thus it was that that portent of a woman, who had no right to teach even correctly, knew very well how to kill the little fishes by taking them out of the water.[18]

---

[17] For further discussion on Sethianism within the *Gospel of Judas*, see first Schröter, "The Figure of Seth," 2017; and also Turner, "The Place of the *Gospel of Judas*," 2008. In general, Sethianism is known as a "mainstream" or "classical" version of Gnosticism that emphasizes the role of Seth as providing the incorruptible "seed" to humanity from Barbelo (i.e., the ultimate divine being) and is best attested in six of the (thirteen) Nag Hammadi codices that contain texts such as the *Apocryphon of John*, the *Trimorphic Protennoia*, or the *Holy Book of the Great Invisible Spirit*. However, in recent scholarship, the designation "Sethian Gnosticism" is being brought into question as a misnomer that has been advanced and propagated in the last half century, largely due to Hans-Martin Schenke. (See Schenke, "Das sethianische System," 1974).

[18] Tertullian, *de Baptismo* 1: Evans (ed. and trans.), *Tertullian's Homily*, 1964: 4–5. See also Borleffs (ed.), *Tertulliani Opera*, 1954: 291–292.

While I shall return to this citation soon, it would behoove us now to notice that Tertullian is beginning his defense of the practice of baptism by making it clear that he is refuting a woman who is apparently associated with a Cainite sect (or possibly an Ophite sect) in North Africa and is denying the practice of baptism.[19] Further, the problem is not only her doctrine but the fact that she is "undermining the faith" (*Bapt.* 2) by "carrying off" the laity.

Moving further along into the homily, near the end, in *Bapt.* 17, Tertullian refers to another early Christian text, the *Acts of Paul*. In particular, he seems to have a precise section of the *Acts of Paul* in mind: the *Acts of Paul and Thecla*. His reason for mentioning this text is not a commendation to read the text but rather a criticism of it. He seems to find the text offensive as it seems to lend support and legitimacy to his female opponent who is looking to it to justify female authority within churches to preach, teach, or determine the appropriateness of baptism. Tertullian writes:

> But the impudence of that woman who assumed the right to teach is evidently not going to arrogate to her the right to baptize as well – unless perhaps some new serpent appears, like that original one, so that as that woman abolished baptism, some other should of her own authority confer it. But if certain Acts of Paul, which are falsely so named, claim the example of Thecla for allowing women to teach and to baptize, let men know that in Asia the presbyter who compiled that document, thinking to add of his own to Paul's reputation, was found out, and though he professed he had done it for love of Paul, was deposed from his position. How could we believe that Paul should give a female power to teach and to baptize, when he did not allow a woman even to learn by her own right? Let them keep silence, he says, and ask their husbands at home.[20]

Is Tertullian reading the *Acta Pauli*? As he indicates, the *Acts of Paul* was written by a presbyter living in Asia and had apparently made its way as far as North Africa. From what we know today, the text recounts the many adventures of Paul in his travels throughout Asia, Greece, Macedonia, Turkey, Palestine, Syria, and Italy and, in this regard, is similar to the Acts of the Apostles. In particular, in one section entitled the *Acts of Paul and Thecla*, Paul travels with a female companion by the name of Thecla. As the story unfolds, Paul refuses to permit her to teach with him, yet God essentially sets her apart; he saves her miraculously from two violent

---

[19] I shall deal with the textual problems associated with "Cainite" at a later point.
[20] Tertullian, *de Baptismo* 17, ll. 22–29.

martyrdoms and then allows her to baptize herself and further to go out on her own as a missionary preaching and teaching others. Tertullian is annoyed and offended by this bold impertinence. In *Bapt.* 1.3, he seems to be drawing on 1 Tim 2:12 ("I do not permit a woman to teach or to assume authority over a man") when he criticizes his female opponent in stating that she has no right to teach at all. Then, here in *Bapt.* 17, he encapsulates his thoughts on Thecla with a reference to the misplaced impudence of the woman in Genesis 3:1 and concludes with a citation from Paul from 1 Cor 14:35, "Let them keep silence ... and ask their husbands at home."

As we see from these two excerpts in *Bapt.* 1 and 17, Tertullian is a reader of what is now known as "canonical" Scripture (e.g., 1 Timothy and 1 Corinthians). Beyond this, it would seem that he and others in his communities are also reading other Christian narratives, in particular the *Acts of Paul*, and possibly even Cainite or Ophite texts. It is the reading of the latter that now focuses my thoughts.

For the better part of the past century, scholars have had sufficient access to most of the *Acts of Paul* and specifically to the *Acts of Paul and Thecla*. Yet, only since 2006 have scholars had the opportunity to read what is thought of as a "Cainite" text (and the only one of its kind of which we are aware). I am referring to the most famous, supposed "Cainite" text: the *Gospel of Judas*. This is important for our discussion since Irenaeus (130–202), bishop of Lyon, helped connect a text entitled the *Gospel of Judas* to a group who identified with Cain.[21] Therefore, scholars can now read what heresiologists wrote about Cainites (e.g., Irenaeus in *Against the Heresies* or Tertullian's *de Baptismo*), then compare it to writings of the Cainites themselves (e.g., *Gospel of Judas*) and, from this comparison, make an evaluation of the various data.

While many of the details of Irenaeus' life are unclear, especially in regard to his life in Gaul, we do know that he was living in Lyon, France when he wrote the five-volume work *Against the Heresies*.[22] In books 1 and 2, he begins by establishing and identifying many of the various groups and tenets of faith within so-called Gnostic factions. Most pertinent to this discussion are his comments in chapter 31 concerning one particular sect. Irenaeus states:

---

[21] One should note that Irenaeus probably did not mention the name of the group explicitly (e.g., "Cainites"), but the connection of Irenaeus' words with the group comes two centuries later from Epiphanius of Salamis (d. 403), who is reading Irenaeus. See Gathercole, "Das Judasevangelium," 2018: 28.

[22] See Payton, *Irenaeus*, 2012; Grant, *Irenaeus of Lyons*, 1997; and Behr, *Irenaeus of Lyons*, 2013.

Others, again, say that Cain comes from the Supreme Authority on high. They confess that Esau, Core, the Sodomites, and all such persons are their relatives. And so they indeed were attacked by the Maker; but none of them were injured; for Wisdom snatched to herself from them whatever they possessed that was proper to herself. Also Judas, the traitor, they say, had exact knowledge of these things, and since he alone knew the truth better than the other apostles, he accomplished the mystery of betrayal. Through him all things in heaven and on earth were destroyed. This fiction they adduce, and call it the Gospel of Judas.[23]

In this passage, Irenaeus points to the *Gospel of Judas* as a primary source for the Cainites' understanding of God and religious practice.[24] Since the discovery, re-discovery, and publication(s) of the *Gospel of Judas*,[25] scholars are now able to test Irenaeus' claim that the Cainites were using it to support their religious claims.[26] The excitement of such an opportunity is difficult to put into words. Therefore, when Tertullian mentions a Cainite woman who is teaching, preaching, and denying baptism, and then suggests that she is drawing on Thecla and the *Acta Pauli* for authoritative support, now that we have the *Gospel of Judas*, we can at least test whether or not this scenario is possible.

Indeed, the recently discovered *Gospel of Judas* affords scholars the opportunity to determine if this is the same text that Irenaeus had heard about and, further, whether or not Irenaeus' descriptions of "Cainites" are accurate. The first examinations have resulted in only modest conclusions.[27] Most notably, the high moral standards described in the *Gospel of Judas* do not meld well with the descriptions of loose morality amongst the Cainites reported by Irenaeus and elaborated upon by Epiphanius and other late-antique heresiographers. At best, Garry Trompf is able to "square" the *Gospel of Judas* with the comments of Jude and Irenaeus by concluding that this Cainite sect must have used the *Gospel of Judas* only to champion the primary ideas of their group, but they could never have authored it.[28] The factual discrepancies between Irenaeus' account of the Gnostics who used the *Gospel of Judas* and the text of the *Gospel of Judas* itself are simply too great. Two examples will make this point clear. First, while according to Irenaeus, Cain seems to be the key figure within the

---

[23] Irenaeus, *Haer.* 1.31: Unger (trans.), *St. Irenaeus of Lyons*, 1992: 102–103. See also Rousseau and Doutreleau (eds. and trans.), *Irénée de Lyon*, 1979: 2, 386–389.
[24] For more on the Cainites, see n. 15 and n. 16. It is doubtful that Irenaeus used the term "Cainites."
[25] Kasser and Wurst, *The Gospel of Judas*, 2007. Subsequent updated translations of various sections based on unpublished fragments may be found in Robinson, "An Update," 2011.
[26] See Trompf, "The Epistle of Jude," 2010. [27] See Scopello (ed.), *The Gospel of Judas*, 2008.
[28] Trompf, "The Epistle of Jude," 2010: 575–578.

cosmology of this Gnostic sect; nevertheless, he is never mentioned within the *Gospel of Judas*.[29] Second, Irenaeus seems to think this group to be loose in their social legislation of morality. However, a reading of the *Gospel of Judas* would imply just the opposite; they are quite rigid in the governance of morality within their group, while their apparent opponents within the Great Church are represented as quite immoral (e.g., *Gospel of Judas* 38–39). While some are ready to completely dismiss the heresiographers' categories of Barbeloites, Cainites, and Ophites as "purely a heresiological invention," I would like to examine this issue a little further.[30] Therefore, in spite of these differences between Irenaeus' account and the evidence of the *Gospel of Judas*, if we were to grant some legitimacy to Irenaeus' claims, then what might be determined when attention is turned to Tertullian and his mention of the *Acts of Paul*, Thecla, and Cainites? After all, the fact that Tertullian addresses his female adversary in North Africa as part of an existing Cainite sect does give me pause in dismissing this group as merely a rhetorical invention.

Baptism within the *Gospel of Judas* and the *Acts of Paul*

To probe this issue further, the discussion may be narrowed down to a specific examination of one particular concern, namely, baptism. By doing so, we may be able to deal with a concrete issue that is addressed in the *Gospel of Judas*, the *Acts of Paul*, and also within Tertullian's homily *On Baptism*. All three texts seem to affirm the practice of the ritual of baptism.[31] It should be noted here that an outlier in this discussion are the comments of Irenaeus. He does not address directly baptism amongst the Cainites, unless one believes that the statement, "they hold that they cannot be saved except they pass through all things," (*Haer.* 1.31.2) might be a reference that would include baptism.[32] (cf. Epiphanius,

---

[29] Unfortunately, the recent translations of the additional fragments of the *Gospel of Judas* have not added anything to this issue. Again, see Robinson, "An Update," 2011. Ehrman, *The Lost Gospel*, 2008: 62–65, thinks it is possible that the text says more about Cain, but too many of the pages have been lost to acknowledge this with certainty.

[30] Turner, "The Place of the *Gospel of Judas*," 2008: 194.

[31] While there is a strong polemic against the "sacrificial theology of the so-called apostolic churches at the turn to the third century," which includes the rituals of baptism and the eucharist, the text nonetheless appears to be quite in line with Sethian Gnostic practices and with "obvious Sethian features:" Turner, "The Place of *the Gospel of Judas*," 2008: 228–229. This would have included ritual baptisms.

[32] See brief comment in Unger (trans.), *St. Irenaeus of Lyons*, 1992: 268 n. 3. This citation most certainly refers to their "immoral" activities to defy the creator god. See Trompf, "The Epistle of Jude," 2010: 575–581.

Pan. 1.38.1.6) Nevertheless, I tend to agree with Trompf's conclusion (mentioned above) that Irenaeus indeed may be considered a vaguely reliable source concerning the *Gospel of Judas*, even if this requires us to understand that the Cainites were "unable or not prepared to see the inconsistency between their own view and the moral tenor of the Judas gospel."[33] In other words, Irenaeus' silence on the subject is probably not sufficient reason (1) to think that he had no knowledge or opinion on their ritual activities when they gather as a community or (2) to prohibit my advancing of the following comparison of texts.

In examining baptism, one is immediately struck by the apparent incompatibility of the aforementioned three texts. For instance, Tertullian, who is attempting to refute the teaching and practices of a Gnostic, Cainite woman, offers up a condemnation of Thecla and the entire *Acts of Paul*: a text that is obviously not known to be influenced by Gnostics.[34] Would a Cainite woman be using the *Acts of Paul*? To further aggravate this discrepancy, from what we know of early Gnostic practices, many Gnostics did practice the rite of immersion; especially as demonstrated within those Gnostic texts that have come to be associated with the figure of Seth.[35] However, Tertullian suggests that this Cainite woman is opposing baptism. It could be that Tertullian is mixing different concerns from his opponents and making a sort of collage of them and their ideas. Yet, his homily does imply that Thecla is being heralded within certain, and among them Gnostic, communities as a heroine worthy of emulation. This promotion of Thecla seems like a concrete reality for one or more communities with which Tertullian is familiar. Otherwise, there would be no reason for Tertullian to even bring up Thecla as an example to be condemned. One must assume that Thecla's authority is a reality within his community and the community of his opponents in order for his argument to hold any weight. In other words, it would seem that his statement could be taken as reflecting a historical reality of Christian North Africa. One may even view the cult of Thecla's immense growth in popularity in this region in later centuries as proof of this reality.[36]

---

[33] Ibid.: 581. No support for baptism is even alluded to in the Nag Hammadi text, the Coptic *Apocalypse of Paul*, if one were to (speculatively) equate it with the *Ascension of Paul* as mentioned by Epiphanius (cf. *Pan.* 1.38.2.5).

[34] I think it is safe to say that the tenets of faith that are described within Marcionism, the Nag Hammadi codices, or other texts of gnosis did not significantly influence the thought world of the author of the *Acts of Paul*.

[35] Schenke, "The Phenomenon," 1980.

[36] See Davis, *The Cult of St. Thecla*, 2001. See also Arietta Papaconstantinou's contribution in this volume (Chapter 6).

If this is the case, then I am missing something. Tertullian seems to demonstrate a lack of clear information concerning the "female viper." In other words, why would a Cainite (i.e., a branch of immersion-practicing Gnosticism) *withhold* the ritual of baptism while using a text about Thecla that *affirms* baptism? Ernest Evans resolves the difficulty by cautioning the readers that

> [i]t is possible to make too much of this woman's importance. Christian institutions continually call for explanation or even defense: and a wise preacher conciliates attention by reference to current interests, however temporary and insignificant.[37]

In other words, Tertullian's mention of a Cainite woman opposing baptism might be a rhetorical technique used in the homily and perhaps should not be taken too seriously. If we follow Evans on this point, then we are assuming that Tertullian actually knows very little about his opponents, what they are reading, or even exactly what they are doing. However, this is precisely what I am attempting to do: determine if his knowledge may be taken seriously, especially in regard to baptism.

Despite the problems that emerge,[38] a comparison with other Gnostic texts is not out of line here considering that the *Gospel of Judas* appears to be a text with cosmological affinities to the *Apocryphon of John* and other texts that emphasize the roles of Barbelo, Saklas, Seth, etc. Is there anything in Gnostic literature that tells us about baptismal rites?[39] The answer is "yes." To address what is known of Gnostic baptism, we may turn to Hans-Martin Schenke, who wrote a foundational essay entitled "The Phenomenon and Significance of Gnostic Sethianism."[40] In the section entitled "Cultic Practice in Sethianism,"[41] Schenke illustrates that baptism was one of two major sacraments of these Gnostics.

Indeed, in several Gnostic texts, baptism is referred to as "taking off the body of the flesh," (*Gospel of the Egyptians*) alluding to an earlier deutero-Pauline tractate on baptism, entitled Colossians.[42] (in particular Col 2:11–15) Other, similar metaphoric expressions, such as "taking off the body of the flesh," can also be found that deal with ascensions to heaven or

---

[37] Evans (ed. and trans.), *Tertullian's Homily*, 1964: xi.
[38] I refer to the discussions of others concerning this matter. See Ehrman, "Christianity Turned," 2007; Ehrman, *The Lost Gospel of Judas*, 2008; DeConick, *Thirteenth Apostle*, 2009; Robinson, "The Relationship," 2008; Meyer, *Judas*, 2007; and Robinson, *Secrets of Judas*, 2007. See especially Emmel, "The Presuppositions," 2008; and Turner, "The Place of the *Gospel of Judas*," 2008.
[39] On Gnostic rites, see Pearson, *Gnosticism and Christianity*, 2004: 207; and Schenke, "The Phenomenon," 1980: 602–607. Again, see also Turner, "The Place of the *Gospel of Judas*," 2008.
[40] Schenke, "The Phenomenon," 1980.   [41] Ibid.: 602–607.   [42] Ibid.: 603–605.

moving out of darkness and into the light. Reading the *Gospel of Judas*, one is immediately drawn to Judas' question on leaves 55–56, "'What will those who have been baptized in your name do?' Jesus said, 'Truly I say [to you], this baptism [in] my name …'" Unfortunately, the manuscript breaks off there. When the text resumes in 56.11, Jesus is speaking of sacrifices being made to Saklas, leading one to assume that the Great Church sacrificial baptisms are being equated with human sacrifice offered to Saklas. As is stated in the text, "Truly [I] say to you, Judas,[12] [those who] offer sacrifices to[13] Saklas [*as if a*] god [*speaks*][14] [*in him*][15] …" It is unclear from the fragmented text how Jesus intends the readers to think of baptism (ⲐⲰⲔⲘ in Coptic, meaning *to wash* or *baptize*).[43] John Turner suggests that these lines should be read with a generally "hostile stance toward the practice of ordinary Christian baptism in Jesus' name (55,22–56,1)."[44] Yet, while it is inferred that the author detests the ritual, namely, the baptismal practices of "l'Église chrétienne," it can also be inferred that Sethian Gnostic baptism is subtly supported through a discussion in 42.5–23.[45] Thus, one should note that the hostile response has more to do with baptism in *Jesus' name* than to the ritual of baptism itself. The implication from the *Gospel of Judas* is that Jesus is teaching Judas that baptisms in the name of the Christ are misguided and, further, are sacrificial offerings to Saklas and his human, corruptible body. In other words, they are in vain.[46] On the other hand, the implications of the *Gospel of Judas* are that these Gnostics practice a baptismal ritual (e.g., *Gospel of Judas* 42.5–23), and there is no clear reason to think that this text would differ from other similar Gnostic texts that also affirm the practice. Nevertheless, with such practices being "assumed" by the implied author and readers of the text, subsequently, this would make the *Gospel of Judas* what might be thought of as an "insider's text." At any rate, to summarize my main points here, the practice of baptism is explicitly addressed in the *Gospel of Judas*. Beyond this, Jesus seems to direct his polemic "against the baptismal practice of the proto-orthodox Christian church," especially in regard to its (human) sacrificial theology that is supported by the symbolic rituals of the eucharist and baptism. Meanwhile, Gnostic baptismal rituals are implicitly affirmed.[47]

---

[43] See Crum, *A Coptic Dictionary*, 2005; or Kasser and Wurst, *The Gospel of Judas*, 2007: 367.
[44] Turner, "The Place of the *Gospel of Judas*," 2008: 213.   [45] Pouderon, "Judas," 2008: 90.
[46] Gathercole, "Das Judasevangelism," 2018: 38.
[47] Thomassen, "Is Judas Really the Hero?" 2008: 165–166. See also Pouderon, "Judas," 2008: 90–92; and Painchaud, "Polemical Aspects," 2008, all of which are within Scopello (ed.), *The Gospel of Judas*, 2008.

Up to this point, the evidence suggests the *Acts of Paul* and the *Gospel of Judas* both affirm baptism. This leaves us to unravel Tertullian's comments. Are his remarks directed at a Cainite woman historically valid or are they merely rhetoric? As we have ascertained, Tertullian is making a defense of baptism against a Cainite woman who rejects baptism and is apparently addressing the portion of the *Acts of Paul* that deals with Thecla.[48] Several options exist to deal with this dilemma:

(1) Tertullian is not refuting a Cainite sect at all. In fact, in the quote above by Evans, the Latin word for Cain, *caina*, is not found in any manuscripts of *de Baptismo*. Based on two passages in Jerome (*Epistle* 82 and *Adv. Vigilantium*), Adolf von Harnack surmised that the words *canina* or *Gaiana* as found in the twelfth-century manuscript *Codex Trecensis 523* and the fifteenth-century compilation of codices by Martin Mesnart, respectively, must have been misspellings for *Caina*. Ernest Evans agrees with Harnack that *de caina haeresi* is the correct reading.[49] However, he acknowledges that the reference may have been toward Cynics living in Carthage at the time, and the word *canina* (an adjective meaning dog) may have been a play on words in reference to Cynics. In other words, an original reading of *canina*, rather than *caina*, could be possible. Indeed, if we consult Apuleius (c. 125–170), *Florida* ii.14, we learn that, in second-century Carthage, the Cynic philosopher Crates consummated his marriage to his young bride Hipparche in the arena before a crowd to demonstrate a rejection of the social mores and values of their society. In sum, since there is no clear textual evidence in the manuscripts to suggest that Tertullian knows of the Cainite "heresy," maybe he just called this woman "a dog" to compare her implicitly to Hipparche? If this is the case, then Tertullian is not reading a Cainite text. Therefore, reconciling *de Baptismo*'s understanding of Cainite doctrine with the Gnostic texts is not necessary since we can just assume that Tertullian did not mention Cainites at all, and he is calling the woman a "dog." However, to come to this conclusion, one must reject the learned insight of both Evans and Harnack.

(2) If we agree with Harnack's and Evans' reconstruction of the text, Tertullian does call his opponents a Cainite sect, but his assessment is

---

[48] Porter and Heath, *The Lost Gospel of Judas*, 2007: 44–45, make reference to the overlap of Cainites and the *Gospel of Judas* but overlook the fact that the *Gospel of Judas* upholds rather than denies baptism to its readers.

[49] Evans (ed. and trans.), *Tertullian's Homily*, 1964: 47.

inaccurate. He is mistaken. They are not truly Cainites. His (1) mention of Cainites, (2) the utilization of a woman attempting to subvert baptism and claim authority, and (3) the condemnation of the *Acts of Paul* along with Thecla are all rhetorical devices to aid his homily. This may be possible, but it still does not deal with the fact that a historical situation must have developed to prompt Tertullian's tractate. Thus, to dismiss the specific details within the homily would be negligent from a methodological point of view.

(3) Again, if we agree with Harnack's and Evans' reconstruction of the text (i.e., Tertullian did mean *caina*, "Cainite" and not *canina*, "dog"), Tertullian does refer to a Cainite sect and he knows what he is talking about. They are a Cainite sect, but the Cainites are more diverse than what we previously knew of them and some of them abolished the physical ritual of baptism. Going back to the textual problem, Evans bases his establishment of the text on the fact that Jerome (d. 420) in *Adv. Vigilantium* also reads this as *caina* (Cainite). In this case, Jerome is probably basing his knowledge on his reading of Tertullian, and we can assume Tertullian did write "Caina." This is coupled with the calling of the Cainite woman a "serpent," which, as has been noted already, is probably a reference to the Ophites. The Ophites were a branch of Gnostics, as mentioned by Irenaeus, who used the serpent as a symbol. If this reference is correct, then Evans seems to have understood that the Cainites were a sub-sect of the Ophites and thus takes this as evidence that the text should read *Cainite*. The problem with this interpretation is that it is not at all certain that the Cainites are a subset of the Ophites. Evans seems to be assuming that the paragraph on the "Cainites" in Irenaeus' *Adversus Haereses* is an extension of the previous chapter on the Ophites and further deduces that the Cainites are a branch of Ophites.[50] If we follow this logic, then Tertullian must have been referring to the Ophites here, and consequently he could have been alluding to the woman as an Ophite and also calling her a Cainite. In spite of the fact that Cainites are not likely to be considered a branch of the Ophites, this reasoning seems fair.

The most likely inference to draw from this is that Tertullian is not certain of the beliefs of his opponents other than that they represent some form of Gnosticism. He does not seem to have a clear understanding of the

---

[50] Evans (ed. and trans.), *Tertullian's Homily*, 1964: 47.

difference between an Ophite or a Cainite. Either way, having found the *Gospel of Judas* helps us realize that the issues of the early Church are more complicated than we knew before discovering such significant primary sources.

In my assessment, I think Tertullian is aware of a group being led by a Cainite woman. Further, his references to her as a serpent in *Bapt.* 1.2–3 and 17 is an allusion to the Ophites. On the other hand, it seems to me that Tertullian is ill informed about the details of the faith of the Cainites. If this is the case, then why would a Cainite sect be withholding baptism? Especially when the evidence that does remain of so-called Cainite Gnostics (i.e., *Gospel of Judas*) supports the fact that they performed the ritual of baptism upon their proselytes. Maybe Tertullian is aware that there is some branch of Gnosticism that is preventing people from immersing their followers, possibly a branch of Cainites that do not immerse. Nonetheless, the evidence suggests that Tertullian has grouped several sects together and is using this situation as an opportunity to write a treatise on baptism. Further, while he may be aware of their existence, I do not think Tertullian's homily indicates necessarily that he had read Cainite or Ophite texts prior to the time of this writing.

Tertullian's Underlying Issue

If Tertullian is not using Cainite or Ophite texts, what might be said of the *Acts of Paul*? On a first examination, the data seems to indicate that Tertullian is not reading the *Acts of Paul* either. Tertullian is aware of the *Acts of Paul* and some of the content regarding Thecla (maybe more), but what he says about it does not closely reflect the actual content of the document. It is true that Tertullian is primarily concerned with refuting the right of a woman to teach and administer baptism. However, the *Acts of Paul* affirms baptism, and it is not a Gnostic text. Neither does the *Acts* report that Thecla is administering baptism to anyone. Once again, at this point, it would seem that Tertullian is not reading Gnostic texts or the *Acts of Paul*. Before making a final conclusion, several other facets need to be considered that might provide evidence to the contrary.

The usual discussion of Tertullian's comments concerning the *Acts of Paul and Thecla* tend to center on the accuracy of Tertullian's assessment that Thecla was giving authorization to baptize (i.e., "claim the example of Thecla for allowing women to teach and to baptize," *Bapt.* 17.5). The discussion tends to move from Tertullian's comments on the *Acta Pauli* and the mention of Thecla to a search regarding whether or not there is any evidence of Thecla baptizing or giving authorization to others to baptize within the *Acts of Paul and Thecla*.[51] Of course, Thecla baptizes no one after her commission from Paul in § 4.16 nor does she commission anyone else. The discussion then moves back to Thecla's supposed self-baptism and whether or not the Spirit baptized her, God baptized her, or she baptized herself as related in passage 4.9,15. These results are variously interpreted due primarily to the fact that a "self"-baptism is considered highly unusual.[52] The evidence seems to indicate that Tertullian is not reading the *Acts of Paul and Thecla* closely or at all.

To take this discussion in a new direction, a closer look at Tertullian's comments in *de Baptismo* 13–14 might prove helpful. In chapter 13, Tertullian repudiates his critics by reminding them that

> there has been imposed a law of baptizing, and its form prescribed: "Go," he says, "teach the nations, baptizing them in the Name of the Father and the Son and the Holy Spirit." When this law was associated with that [well known] pronouncement, "Except a man have been born again of water and the Holy Spirit he shall not enter into the kingdom of heaven," faith was put under obligation to the necessity of baptism.[53]

Tertullian moves from this (1) "great commission" of the Lord to baptize in Matt 28:19–20 and (2) authorization to baptize by the Spirit (John 3:5) to the immediate fulfillment of the command by the apostle Paul who is subsequently baptized (Acts 9:6; 22:10). The implications of Tertullian's argument are that the pronouncement from Jesus to "go" and baptize (Matt 28:19–20) was the establishment of this ritual practice, even to be obeyed by the likes of apostles, namely, the apostle Paul. Subsequently, the implications are that this process has continued down through the ages and ultimately has come down to North Africa. Therefore, anyone teaching that baptism is not essential is breaking with this tradition that goes back to Jesus.

At this point, Tertullian shifts his argument to discuss Paul's statement in 1 Cor 1:14–17:

> I thank God that I baptized none of you except Crispus and Gaius, so that no one can say that you were baptized in my name. (I did baptize also the household of Stephanas; beyond that, I do not know whether I baptized anyone else.) For Christ did not send me to baptize but to proclaim the gospel.

---

[51] Rordorf, "Tertullien," 1990: 475–484. See page 481 in particular.
[52] See my discussion in *The Acts of Paul and Thecla*, 2009: 160–164; and Dunn, "The *Acts of Paul*," 1996: 66–67.
[53] Evans (ed. and trans.), *Tertullian's Homily*, 1964: 30–31.

After this passage, a detailed analysis ensues in chapter 14 concerning Paul and why he would have said this in Corinth. He begins by saying "[m]oreover they have something to say about the apostle himself," immediately addressing an attack against Paul. Tertullian's stream of consciousness runs as follows: God commissioned the apostles to baptize. The Holy Spirit divinely authorized the commission. The ritual practice for believers was initiated. Even the apostle Paul was compelled to obey the command. Then did Paul stop the ritual in Corinth (1:14–17)? At least, Tertullian's opponents seem to think so. Tertullian's opponents have deduced from Paul's comment that the passing on of the ritual of baptism is unnecessary. The implications are that if one is given the commission and authority to teach, then they have the authority to *decide* if baptism is relevant or not. In other words, accordingly, Paul has taken upon himself the authority to decide when he will and will not baptize anyone.

Tertullian opposes this. Tertullian's defense centers on Paul's claim in 1 Cor 1:14–17 that he did not come to Corinth to baptize but to teach and concludes his argument on Paul by stating:

> On this account the apostle, a lover of peace, so as not to seem to claim everything himself, said he was not sent to baptize but to preach. For preaching comes first, baptizing later, when preaching has proceeded. *But I suppose one who had permission to preach had also permission to baptize.*[54]

Tertullian has just reinforced his arguments for baptism by using a passage from 1 Corinthians, conjured up possibly by a dissenting interlocutor, where Paul states plainly that he did not come to baptize. Tertullian has made the reasonable deduction that if one has the authority to teach, then he or she has the authority to decide if baptism is necessary or not.

Thus, it seems the interest by Tertullian in *de Baptismo* is probably centered upon who baptized Thecla in the *Acts of Paul and Thecla* or whether or not she was authorized by others to baptize. The theological matter, according to Tertullian, is composed of interpreting texts such as Matt 28:19–20, 1 Cor 1:14–17, and possibly specific passages within the *Acts of Paul and Thecla*. For instance, the last conversation between Paul and Thecla in the *Acts of Paul* (§ 4.16) may have been important for Tertullian. In this passage, immediately after her baptism, Thecla finds Paul and says to him:

> "I have received baptism, O Paul; for he who worked with you for the gospel has worked with me also for baptism." And Paul, taking her, led her

---

[54] Tertullian, *de Baptismo* 14; emphasis added.

to the house of Hermias and heard everything from her . . . . And Thecla rose up and said to Paul, "I am going to Iconium." Paul answered, "Go, teach the word of God."

This passage is significant. At this point, Paul has clearly given a directive with authority to "Go, teach the word of God" reminiscent of the statement made by Jesus to his disciples in Matthew 28:19 (and quoted by Tertullian in *Bapt.* 13). Tertullian is certainly playing with both texts. Tertullian has just argued that if one is authorized to teach, then they are authorized to baptize, *yet this should not be interpreted to mean that they have the authority to withhold baptism.* Apparently, Tertullian's opponents interpreted 1 Cor. 1:14–17 in this manner.

Why is withholding of baptism a problem for Tertullian? The primary issue at hand is authority. Tertullian might be concerned that the "Asian presbyter," who authored the *Acts of Paul*, is drawing from a tradition, whether oral or written, that suggests that Paul has directly supported and empowered a woman to teach, and subsequently this gives her the right to either baptize or not baptize. This version of apostolic tradition, in other words, gives her a sort of apostolic authority. Tertullian's rhetoric against the presbyter and the *Acts of Paul* suggests that the presbyter's writing must have been regarded as an authentic representation of Paul's activities in Lycaonia by many within the communities of faith in North Africa. In other words, the *Acts of Paul* was being perceived as authoritative for North African Christian communities. This would make the *Acts of Paul*, and specifically Thecla, a threat to Tertullian and to the system of authority within the local church there. This turbulent situation is reflected in *de Baptismo* 17, which might help clarify the issue at hand. He begins the chapter as follows:

> To round off our slight treatment of this subject it remains for me to advise you of the rules to be observed in giving and receiving baptism. The supreme right of giving it belongs to the high priest, which is the bishop: after him, to the presbyters and deacons, yet not without commission from the bishop, on account of the Church's dignity: for when this is safe, peace is safe. Except for that, even laymen have the right.

Tertullian concedes that "even laymen" have the right to administer baptism, knowing that the Lord's disciples were not bishops, presbyters, or deacons. However, he then highlights the thrust of his argument.[55] He states, "[o]pposition to the episcopate is the mother of schisms." Indeed,

---

[55] Jensen, "Baptismal Rites," 2005.

breaking outside of the authorized hierarchy for baptizing is not advisable, nor should it be considered standard practice.[56] Tertullian continues by pointing out that it is a problem when women are willing to "arrogate to themselves" the function of a bishop and the right to baptize or not baptize. The issue at stake here is whether or not the Cainite woman has the authority to teach. If so, according to Tertullian's earlier reasoning, then she has the authority to administer (or not administer) baptism.

The Cainite woman is apparently acting with some form of authority, either ceded to her by a faith community or otherwise. Tertullian writes "but the impudence of that woman who assumed the right to teach is evidently not going to arrogate to her the right to baptize as well" (*Bapt.* 17.4). If she is acting with a community sanctioned authority, then Tertullian may be aware of his obvious limitations in restricting the ability of this woman to teach. Yet, if he can break the chain of reasoning that suggests that because she can teach, she also has the authority to baptize or not, then the role of baptism can be preserved and protected. The problem with the *Acts of Paul* is not necessarily that Thecla has baptized herself or not. The problem is rather that Paul has sanctioned her to teach, thus, in effect, she has been authorized to choose to baptize or not baptize. *Paul's own words* in 1 Cor 1:14–17 support this interpretation. The startling fact for Tertullian in the quoted passage of the *Acts of Paul and Thecla* is not merely that "God himself baptizes her," but rather that the Holy Spirit has sanctioned the rite, and the apostle Paul has commissioned it.[57] In other words, the *Acts of Paul and Thecla* offers an alternative trajectory that does not necessitate a bishop, presbyter, or deacon for administering baptism. This threatens the chain of authority being passed down as a tradition all the way from Jesus to the current bishops. This is a direct threat to Tertullian, who is resisting a supposed Pauline tradition that supports the teaching and preaching of Thecla and, more importantly, that undermines the hierarchy of the church, the traditions of the church, and the legitimacy of the episcopacy.

Interpreting *Bapt.* 13–17 in this fashion suggests that Tertullian seems to be quite aware of the content of the *Acts of Paul and Thecla* and, in particular, of passage 4.16. Tertullian's citation of Matt 28:19–20 and subsequent argumentation imply that there is a witty "dialogue" of sorts going back and forth on how to interpret these commissioning texts in light of the current situation in the North African context. In conclusion,

---

[56] Tertullian, *de Baptismo* 17.   [57] Dunn, "The *Acts of Paul*," 1996: 67.

if my assessment of *de Baptismo* 17 is correct, then we can assume that Tertullian is indeed reading the *Acts of Paul*.

Conclusion

From my investigation of *de Baptismo*, the evidence is not clear whether or not Tertullian is reading Gnostic texts, whether Cainite, Ophite, or otherwise. Unfortunately, the evidence does not seem strong enough to make any conclusions. Looking solely at the example of baptism in the *Gospel of Judas*, as best can be determined, the Gnostics who read these texts practiced immersion. Yet Tertullian opposes a Cainite who seems to be withholding baptism. The reasons for withholding are far from certain when reading Tertullian's *de Baptismo*. Thus, while questions still seem to linger over the association between *de Baptismo* with either Cainites or specifically the *Gospel of Judas*, we move on to the second concern that does seem to shift the discussion slightly. Is Tertullian reading the *Acts of Paul*? There are no clear citations from the *Acts of Paul* in Tertullian's *de Baptismo*, at least no citations from the extant version of the *Acts of Paul*. Further, one of the more reliable sections of the *Acts of Paul* is the portion that deals with Thecla, the *Acts of Paul and Thecla*, and this is most certainly not cited by Tertullian. If not a citation, then is there evidence for an allusion or an echo? From reading his remarks about Thecla in *Bapt.* 13–17, I think the evidence is sufficient to suggest Tertullian is dialoguing and engaging with specific content from the *Acts of Paul*. Specifically, there is an allusion to *Acts of Paul* § 4.16 that details Thecla's baptism. From this evidence, I think it is fair to suggest that Tertullian is reading the *Acts of Paul*. Beyond this, I think it should be considered certain that some communities outside of Tertullian's community of faith in North Africa at this time are also reading the text. The underlying issue behind Tertullian's discussion is whether or not one who is commissioned to teach also has the authority to baptize (or the authority to deny baptism). Tertullian supports his rationale by quoting 1 Cor 1:14–17. It is precisely after his discussion of these matters in *Bapt.* 13–14 that Tertullian not only attacks his opponents' reading of the "great commission" coming from the lips of Paul and is spoken to Thecla in the *Acts of Paul*, "Go, teach the word of God," but he attacks the entire text, the entire Pauline trajectory exemplified in the *Acts of Paul*, and even its author, the Asian presbyter. The underlying thoughts of this section of *de Baptismo* most certainly assume a knowledge of Thecla and specific events that unfold within the *Acts of Paul*. It possibly even acknowledges that as Matt 28:19–20 was the great commission for the earliest disciples who were men, this commissioning by God, via Paul in the *Acts of Paul*, may have been thought by the Cainite woman's community to be the great commission for the earliest disciples who were women.

Last, but not least, maybe the more significant point that needs to be acknowledged here is that Tertullian provides evidence that Thecla has become a source of inspiration within the churches of North Africa and is directly impacting the ritual practices of the churches. The evidence indicates that the *Acts of Paul* was being read and was inspiring followers to higher levels of faith and praxis, and, finally, it was leading to a burgeoning of activity especially amongst women in the churches of North Africa. From Tertullian's *de Baptismo*, we are able to affirm the reading of the *Acts of Paul* as an early use of hagiography within the communities of faith. In particular, I think we can feel comfortable in suggesting that Tertullian is reading portions of the *Acts of Paul*. The ensuing implication is that other churches – especially those that he is critiquing – are reading portions of the story of Thecla that could be categorized as *vitae* and *passiones*. Most importantly, this is intriguing for how it is impacting the ritual practices of their communities (i.e., baptismal rituals, or even the commissioning of women, like Thecla, who are praised for "missionary efforts"). Hopefully, this glimpse will provide some insight into a phenomenon that only continued to grow and flourished over the following centuries.

Bibliography

Bardy, Gustave. "Cainites." In *Dictionnaire d'histoire et de géographie ecclésiastiques*. Paris: Letouzey et Ané, 1953: 11: 226–228.

Bareille, Georges. "Cainites." In *Dictionnaire de théologie catholique*. Paris: Letouzey et Ané, 1904: 2.2: 1307–1309.

Barrier, Jeremy W. *The Acts of Paul and Thecla: A Critical Introduction and Commentary*. WUNT 2.270. Tübingen: Mohr Siebeck, 2009.

Behr, John. *Irenaeus of Lyons: Identifying Christianity*. Oxford: Oxford University Press, 2013.

Borleffs, Jan William Philip, ed. *Tertulliani Opera: Pars I*, edited by Eligius Dekkers, Jan William Philip Borleffs, R. Willems, F. Refoulé, G. F. Diercks, and E. Kroymann. Corpus Christianorum. Turnhout: Typographi Brepols Editores Pontificii, 1954.

Brakke, David. *The Gnostics: Myth, Ritual, and Diversity in Early Christianity*. Cambridge, MA: Harvard University Press, 2010.

Burrus, Virginia. *Chastity as Autonomy: Women in the Stories of Apocryphal Acts.* Queenston: Mellen, 1987.
Conybeare, Fred Cornwallis. *Myth, Magic, and Morals: A Study of Christian Origins.* 2nd ed. London: Watts & Co, 1910.
Cross, L., and E. A. Livingston, eds. "Cainites." In *The Oxford Dictionary of the Christian Church.* Oxford: Oxford University Press, 2005: 215.
"Ophites." In *The Oxford Dictionary of the Christian Church.* Oxford: Oxford University Press, 2005: 984.
Crum, Walter E. *A Coptic Dictionary,* edited by James M. Robinson. Ancient Language Resource. Portland: Wipf and Stock, 2005.
Davies, Stevan L. *The Revolt of the Widows: The Social World of the Apocryphal Acts.* London: Feffer and Simmons, 1980.
Davis, Stephen J. *The Cult of St. Thecla: A Tradition of Women's Piety in Late Antiquity.* Oxford: Oxford University Press, 2001.
DeConick, April D. *Thirteenth Apostle: What the Gospel of Judas Really Says.* Rev. ed. London: Continuum, 2009.
Delehaye, Hippolyte. *Les Légendes Hagiographiques.* Brussels: Société des Bollandistes, 1905.
Les Légendes grecques des saints militaires. Paris: Picard, 1909.
Cinq leçons sur la méthode hagiographique. Brussels: Société des Bollandistes, 1934.
Dunn, Peter Wallace. "The *Acts of Paul* and the Pauline Legacy in the Second Century." PhD diss., Queen's College, University of Cambridge, 1996.
Eder, Walter. "Late Antiquity: I. The Historical Period." In *Brill's New Pauly-Antiquity, Vol. 7*, edited by Helmuth Schneider and Hubert Cancik. Leiden: Brill, 2005: 260–261.
Ehrman, Bart D. "Christianity Turned on Its Head: The Alternative Vision of the Gospel of Judas." In *The Gospel of Judas.* Washington, DC: National Geographic, 2007: 77–102.
The Lost Gospel of Judas Iscariot: A New Look at Betrayer and Betrayed. Oxford: Oxford University Press, 2008.
Emmel, Stephen. "The Presuppositions and the Purpose of the Gospel of Judas." In *The Gospel of Judas in Context: Proceedings of the First International Conference on the Gospel of Judas,* edited by Madeleine Scopello. Nag Hammadi and Manichaean Studies 62. Leiden: Brill, 2008: 33–40.
Evans, Ernest, ed. and trans. *Tertullian's Homily on Baptism: The Text Edited with an Introduction, Translation and Commentary.* London: SPCK, 1964.
Gathercole, Simon J. *The Gospel of Judas: Rewriting Early Christianity.* Oxford; Toronto: Oxford University Press, 2007.
"Das Judasevangelium." *Zeitschrift für Neues Testament* 21.41 (2018): 25–41.
Geerard, Maurice, ed. "Acta Pauli." In *Clavis Apocryphorum Novi Testamenti.* Corpus Christianorum. Turnhout: Brepols, 1992.
Georgios, Makris. "Acta Sanctorum." In *Brill's New Pauly-Antiquity, Vol. 1*, edited by Helmuth Schneider and Hubert Cancik. Leiden: Brill, 2001: 119–120.
Grant, Robert M. *Irenaeus of Lyons.* London; New York: Routledge, 1997.

Hays, Richard. *Echoes of Scripture in the Letters of Paul*. New Haven; London: Yale University Press, 1989.
    The Conversion of the Imagination: Paul as Interpreter of Israel's Scripture. Grand Rapids: Eerdmans, 2005.
Hurtado, Larry W. *The Earliest Christian Manuscripts: Manuscripts and Christian Origins*. Grand Rapids; Cambridge: Eerdmans, 2006.
Jensen, Anne. *Thekla – die Apostolin: Ein apokrypher Text neu entdeckt: Übersetzt und kommentiert*. Freiburg; Basel; Wien: Herder, 1995.
Jensen, Robin M. "Baptismal Rites and Architecture." In *A People's History of Christianity: Volume 2, Late Ancient Christianity*, edited by Virginia Burrus. Minneapolis: Fortress, 2005: 123–124.
Johnson, Scott F. *The Life and Miracles of Thekla: A Literary Study*. Washington, DC: Center for Hellenic Studies, 2006.
Kasser, Rodolphe, Marvin W. Meyer, Gregor Wurst, François Gaudard, and Bart D. Ehrman, eds. *The Gospel of Judas*. Washington, DC: National Geographic: 2008.
Kasser, Rodolphe, and Gregor Wurst. *The Gospel of Judas Together with the Letter of Peter to Philip, James, and a Book of Allogenes from Codex Tchacos*. Washington, DC: National Geographic, 2007.
MacDonald, Dennis R. *The Legend and the Apostle: The Battle for Paul in Story and Canon*. Philadelphia: Westminster, 1983.
Mackay, Thomas W. "Observations on P. Bodmer X (Apocryphal Correspondence between Paul and the Corinthian Saints)." In *Papyrologica Bruxellensia 18: Actes du XVe Congrès International de Papyrologie*. Brussels: Fondation Egyptologique Reine Elisabeth, 1979: 3.119–128.
    "Content and Style in Two Pseudo-Pauline Epistles (3 Corinthians and the Epistle to the Laodiceans)." In *Apocryphal Writings and Latter-Day Saints*, edited by C. Wilfred Griggs and Noel B. Reynolds. Salt Lake City: Brigham Young University, 1986: 215–240.
MacMullen, Ramsay. *The Second Church: Popular Christianity, A.D. 200–400*. Writings from the Greco-Roman World Supplement Series 1. Atlanta: Society of Biblical Literature, 2009.
Meyer, Marvin W. *Judas: The Definitive Collection of Gospels and Legends about the Infamous Apostle of Jesus*. New York: HarperOne, 2007.
    The Gospel of Judas: On a Night with Judas Iscariot. Eugene: Cascade Books, 2011.
Painchaud, Louis. "Polemical Aspects of the Gospel of Judas." In *The Gospel of Judas in Context: Proceedings of the First International Conference on the Gospel of Judas*, edited by Madeleine Scopello. Nag Hammadi and Manichaean Studies 62. Leiden: Brill, 2008: 171–186.
Payton, James R. Jr. *Irenaeus on the Christian Faith: A Condensation of Against Heresies*. Cambridge: James Clarke & Co., 2012.
Pearson, Birger. *Gnosticism and Christianity in Roman and Coptic Egypt*. New York: T & T Clark International, 2004.

Porter, Stanley E., and Gordon L. Heath. *The Lost Gospel of Judas: Separating Fact from Fiction.* Grand Rapids: Eerdmans, 2007.

Pouderon, Bernard. "Judas, l'homme double. Recherches sur les archétypes du disciple qui trahit Jésus dans l'Évangile de Judas." In *The Gospel of Judas in Context: Proceedings of the First International Conference on the Gospel of Judas*, edited by Madeleine Scopello. Nag Hammadi and Manichaean Studies 62. Leiden: Brill, 2008: 81–96.

Rasimus, Tuomas. *Paradise Reconsidered in Gnostic Mythmaking: Rethinking Sethianism in Light of the Ophite Evidence.* Nag Hammadi and Manichaean Studies 68. Leiden; Boston: Brill, 2014.

Roberts, Colin H. "The Acts of Paul and Thecla." In *The Antinoopolis Papyri Part 1.* London: Egyptian Exploration Society, 1950: 26–28.

Robinson, Gesine Schenke. "The Relationship of the *Gospel of Judas* to the New Testament and to Sethianism: Appended by a New English Translation of the *Gospel of Judas*." *Journal of Coptic Studies* 10 (2008): 63–98.

"An Update on the *Gospel of Judas* (after Additional Fragments Resurfaced)." *Zeitschrift für die neutestamentliche Wissenschaft* 102, no. 1 (2011): 110–129.

Robinson, James M. *Secrets of Judas: The Story of the Misunderstood Disciple and His Lost Gospel.* New York: HarperOne, 2007.

Rordorf, Willy. "Tertullien et les Actes de Paul (à propos de *bapt.* 17,5)." In *Hommage à René Braun. 2. Autour de Tertullian.* Nice: Association Publications de la Faculté des Lettres et Sciences Humaines de Nice, 1990: 153–160. Reprint, *Lex Orandi-Lex Credendi: Gesammelte Aufsätze zum 60. Geburtstag.* Paradosis 36. Freiburg: Universitätsverlag Freiburg Schweiz, 1993: 475–484.

Rousseau, Adelin, and Louis Doutreleau, eds. and trans. *Irénée de Lyon, Contre les hérésies Livre I, Édition Critique.* Sources chrétiennes 264. Paris: Éditions du Cerf, 1979.

Rühle, O. "Hagiographie." In *Die Religion in Geschichte und Gegenwart*, edited by Wilfried Werbeck. Tübingen: Mohr Siebeck, 1986: 3: 26–28.

Schenke, Hans-Martin. "Das sethianische System nach den Nag-Hammadi-Handschriften." In *Studia Coptica*, edited by Peter Nagel. Berliner byzantinistische Arbeiten 45. Berlin: Akademie, 1974: 165–172. Reprint, *Der Same Seths. Hans-Martin Schenkes Kleine Schriften zu Gnosis, Koptologie und Neuem Testament*, edited by G. Schenke-Robinson and U.-K. Plüsch. Nag Hammadi and Manichaean Studies 78. Leiden; Boston: Brill, 2012: 285–292.

"The Phenomenon and Significance of Gnostic Sethianism." In *The Rediscovery of Gnosticism: Proceedings at the Conference at Yale, March 1978, II Sethian Gnosticism*, edited by Bentley Layton. Leiden: Brill, 1980: 588–616.

Schmidt, Carl, ed. and trans. *Acta Pauli aus der Heidelberger koptischen Papyrushandschrift.* Leipzig: J. C. Hinrichs, 1904.

Acta Pauli aus der Heidelberger koptischen Papyrushandschrift Nr. 1: Tafelband. Leipzig: J. C. Hinrichs, 1904.

Acta Pauli aus der Heidelberger koptischen Papyrushandschrift: Zusätze zur ersten Ausgabe. Leipzig: J. C. Hinrichs, 1905.

Schmidt, Carl, and Wilhelm Schubart, eds. and trans. *PRAXEIS PAULOU: Acta Pauli nach dem Papyrus der Hamburger Staats und Universitäts-Bibliothek*. Veröffentlichungen aus der Hamburger Staats- und Universitäts-Bibliothek 2. Glückstadt; Hamburg: J. J. Augustin, 1936.

Schröter, Jens. "The Figure of Seth in Jewish and Early Christian Writings: Was there a 'Sethian Gnosticism?'" In *The Other Side: Apocryphal Perspectives on Ancient Christian "Orthodoxies,"* edited by Tobias Nicklas, Candida R. Moss, Christopher Tuckett, and Joseph Verheyden. Novum Testamentum et Orbis Antiquus/Studien zur Umwelt des Neuen Testaments 117. Göttingen: Vandenhoeck & Ruprecht, 2017: 135–148.

Scopello, Madeleine, ed. *The Gospel of Judas in Context: Proceedings of the First International Conference on the Gospel of Judas*. Nag Hammadi and Manichaean Studies 62. Leiden: Brill, 2008.

Talbot, Alice-Mary. "Hagiography." In *The Oxford Handbook of Byzantine Studies*, edited by Elizabeth Jeffreys with John Haldon and Robin Cormack. New York; Oxford: Oxford University Press, 2008: 862–871.

Testuz, M. *Papyrus Bodmer X–XI. X: Correspondance apocryphe des Corinthiens et de l'apôtre Paul. XI: Onzième Ode Salomon. XII: Fragment d'un Hymne liturgique*. Cologne; Geneva: Bibliotheca Bodmeriana, 1959.

Thomassen, Einar. "Is Judas Really the Hero of the Gospel of Judas?" In *The Gospel of Judas in Context: Proceedings of the First International Conference on the Gospel of Judas*, edited by Madeleine Scopello. Nag Hammadi and Manichaean Studies 62. Leiden: Brill, 2008: 155–170.

Trompf, Garry W. "The Epistle of Jude, Irenaeus, and the Gospel of Judas." *Biblica* 91, no. 4 (2010): 555–582.

Thurston, Herbert. "Saints and Martyrs (Christian)." In *Encyclopedia of Religion and Ethics*, edited by James Hastings. Edinburgh: T. & T. Clark, 1920: 11: 51–59.

Turner, John D. "The Place of the *Gospel of Judas* in Sethian Tradition." In *The Gospel of Judas in Context: Proceedings of the First International Conference on the Gospel of Judas*, edited by Madeleine Scopello. Nag Hammadi and Manichaean Studies 62. Leiden: Brill, 2008: 187–237.

Unger, Dominic J., trans. with revisions by John J. Dillon. *St. Irenaeus of Lyons: Against the Heresies*. Ancient Christian Writers 55. New York: Newman, 1992.

Wyrwa, Dietmar. "Hagiography." In *Brill's New Pauly-Antiquity, Vol. 5*, edited by Helmuth Schneider and Hubert Cancik. Leiden: Brill, 2004: 1095–1096.

CHAPTER 2

Saint Thecla in Geʿez Hagiographical Literature
From Confessor to Martyr

Damien Labadie

Looking briefly at the index of E. A. Wallis Budge's translation of the *Senkessār* (*Synaxarium*),[1] the official Ethiopic book of saints, one notices many Theclas in Geʿez (i.e., classical Ethiopic) hagiographical texts. At least eight different female saints bear that name:

(1) Thecla of Iconium, Paul's disciple.[2]
(2) Thecla and her four companions, martyred in Persia.[3] The story of this martyrdom is known under the specific Geʿez title of *Gadla Ṭēqalā* (*The Contendings of Thecla*). This account is also preserved in Greek and Syriac.[4]
(3) Thecla, a martyr, described as a "virgin" and a "bride of Christ."[5]
(4) Thecla and her brother Abbā 'Ēsi of Ashmunayn.[6]
(5) Thecla and Mugi of Qayrāqus (Qarāqos, in Lower Egypt), martyred in Alexandria.[7]
(6) The nun Thecla and the soldier Agabus, martyred by the governor Lulianus (Julian?).[8]
(7) Thecla, some martyr, commemorated with Paula.[9]

---

[1] Budge (trans.), *The Book of Saints*, 1928.   [2] Ibid.: 94–95, 597, 1152–1154.
[3] Ibid.: 566–567. See also Caraffa, "Tecla, Mariamne, Marta," 1969.
[4] For the Syriac version (*BHO* 1157), see Assemani (ed. and trans.), *Acta martyrum*, 1748: 123–127; and Bedjan (ed.), *Acta martyrum*, 1892: 308–313. For an English translation of this Syriac account, see Brock and Harvey (trans.), *Holy Women*, 1998: 78–81. See Flavia Ruani's contribution in this volume (Chapter 5) on the role of secondary characters in this text. For the Greek version (*BHG* 3417), see Delehaye (ed.), *Synaxarium Ecclesiae Constantinopolitanae*, 1902: 739–742.
[5] Budge (trans.), *The Book of Saints*, 1928: 84. These attributes may refer to Thecla of Iconium, but it remains doubtful.
[6] Ibid.: 344–348.   [7] Ibid.: 1156–1157. See Sauget, "Tecla (Theclah)," 1969.   [8] Ibid.: 1253.
[9] Ibid.: 870. It is interesting to note that this Thecla is associated with a female saint named Paula. Would this be an altered recollection of Thecla of Iconium and Saint Paul? Unfortunately, we have no further information about these two female saints mentioned in the *Synaxarium*.

(8) Another Thecla, about whom nothing is said, commemorated with Gabra 'Iyāsus.[10]

Despite this wealth of homonymous saints, Thecla of Iconium is easily recognizable, as she is generally signaled by the honorary title "Thecla the Apostolic" (*Ṭēqalā ḥawāryāwit*) in most Ge'ez texts that refer to her.[11] Though not as famous as in the Coptic tradition, Saint Thecla is still an important figure in Ethiopic hagiographical literature. Ethiopians cherish and venerate her among the major saintly Christian figures, as her Life is told and commemorated in the *Synaxarium* and in one original Ge'ez production, the *Maṣḥafa Ṭēqalā* (*Book of Thecla*).

But, looking briefly at this list, one realizes that none of these Theclas is Ethiopian. It may seem paradoxical that such an extensive collection of saints' Lives like the Ethiopic *Synaxarium* does not record, among all these different Theclas, a single Ethiopian saint bearing that name. More importantly, in the above list, most of the Theclas referred to are Egyptian saints, with the exception of Thecla and her four companions who are Persian martyrs. Consequently, a first problem that we are confronted with when studying Ge'ez hagiographical literature is that it is mainly translated literature, at least, as far as antique and late antique saints are concerned. Indeed, a great proportion of saints' Lives or Acts, as they are preserved in Ethiopic hagiographical collections, are translations of Greek and, above all, Arabic sources. Therefore, martyrdom stories in Ge'ez literature concern mostly non-Ethiopian saints. A second issue lies in the fact that the Lives and Acts of genuine Ethiopian saints are limited to the story of medieval monks, such as 'Iyasus Mo'a (1214–1294) or Takla Hāymānot (b. 1215), whose biographies were written from the fourteenth century onwards.[12] This is due in part to the fact that there is no such thing as martyrdom stories narrating the sufferings and death of early Ethiopian saints since Ethiopian Christians never lived under the rule of a pagan monarch.[13] Actually, Christianity was introduced in Ethiopia as soon as its

---

[10] Ibid.: 1138. The Thecla referred to might be Paul's companion since, according to Guidi (ed. and trans.), *Le synaxaire éthiopien*, 1911: 360–370, she is also commemorated together with Gabra 'Iyasus on the 20th of the month of *Ḥamlē*.

[11] For example, see Guidi (ed. and trans.), *Le synaxaire éthiopien*, 1911: 405.

[12] See Cerulli, *Storia*, 1956: 93–100.

[13] This assertion needs qualifying since some medieval monks, like Baṣalota Mikā'ēl (fl. fourteenth century), 'Ewosṭātēwos or 'Anorēwos (fl. fourteenth century), were depicted like martyrs in their biographies. Though they do not suffer death as martyrs, they are usually described as such since the king persecuted them on account of their unorthodox teaching. Having bravely endured the king's iniquitous rule, these monks were celebrated by their followers as martyrs. See Derat, *Le domaine*, 2003: 137–171.

ruler, ʿĒzānā (d. 356), converted.[14] A third issue is that these Geʿez Lives of holy monks are only interested in male characters. Among all these monastic Lives, only three recount the story of holy nuns: Krestos Śemrā, who lived in the fifteenth century, and Walatta Pēṭros and Feqerta Krestos, who both lived in the seventeenth century.[15] Unfortunately, the Lives of these nuns are of little use for the study of the cult of Thecla in Ethiopia, especially when one is interested in earlier periods. To put it briefly, unlike the Armenian tradition that can boast noteworthy martyrs like Rhipsime (Arm. Hṙipʿsimē) or Sanduxt,[16] there is no record of such female holy martyrs specifically in Ethiopian traditions and literature. As a consequence, it remains rather difficult to assess the impact of Thecla on Ethiopian sainthood in late antiquity.

From this point of view, the very nature and limited scope of Geʿez literature do not enable us to paint a reliable picture of the history of the reception of the figure of Saint Thecla in Ethiopia in late antiquity and the medieval period. Yet, by analyzing the few Geʿez texts that mention Thecla, we will try to delineate the main literary characteristics that are peculiar to this holy figure. We will especially focus on her characterization as a martyr in Geʿez hagiographical texts. In fact, Thecla appears as an ambiguous and elusive character as far as the theme of martyrdom is concerned. This ambiguity arises from the fact that, though she never died a martyr, she is generally viewed as a perfect martyr in Geʿez texts. This is typified in the *Book of Thecla* in which Thecla is never designated as a martyr in the story, although it has been transmitted in a collection of martyrdom stories. How can we account for this state of affairs? In this study, we will try to highlight how this ambiguous status is dealt with in Geʿez literature and evaluate the importance of this female saint in Geʿez hagiographical and, especially, martyrological literary *corpora*.

Thecla in the Ethiopic *Synaxarium*: The "Crown of Confessors"

The *Senkessār*, or Ethiopic *Synaxarium*, is a collection of hagiographical texts that commemorates saints and martyrs.[17] It is specifically designed for liturgical reading. Consequently, the texts are generally short (mere notices as a matter of fact) and are ordered according to the liturgical

---

[14] On king ʿĒzānā, see Hahn, "Ezana," 2005.
[15] See Böll, "Holy Women," 2003: 37–39; and Mecca, "Women in Ethiopic Hagiography," 2009.
[16] See Calzolari, "The Legend of St. Thecla," 2017.
[17] On the *Senkessār* or Ethiopic *Synaxarium*, see first Colin, "Le synaxaire éthiopien," 1988. See also Colin and Bausi, "Sənkəssar," 2010.

calendar of the whole year. Known in two main recensions, the Ethiopic *Synaxarium* was translated from the Arabic *Synaxarium* of the Coptic Church in the fifteenth century at the earliest.[18] One major innovation of the *Senkessār*, compared with older collections like the *Gadla samā ʿtāt*, is the insertion of hagiographical notices dealing with Ethiopian saints.[19]

Thecla's story is told in the notice of the 25th of the month of *Ḥamlē*.[20] On the whole, the story of "Thecla the Apostolic," contained in the Ethiopic *Synaxarium*, appears as rather close to the Greek and Eastern versions of her Acts. Though extremely condensed, the account follows closely the general plot of the *Acts of Paul and Thecla*. For instance, like in the *Acts of Paul and Thecla*, the action takes place in Iconium (*Qonyā* in Geʿez) where Paul teaches in prison; a love scene occurs in Antioch (with the minor difference, though, that it is the governor of Antioch who falls in love with Thecla rather than the nobleman Alexander);[21] and the female saint returns to Iconium and converts her parents to Christianity (here, too, with an important difference since in the Greek, Latin, and Eastern versions, she tries unsuccessfully to convert her mother). Two features seem quite unique to the *Senkessār*. On the one hand, it is Thecla's father (unnamed in the story) who denounces his own daughter to the governors of Iconium. The presence and role of Thecla's father in the *Synaxarium* story are specific additions. Thus, it stands apart from both the Geʿez *Book of Thecla* and the Greek, Latin, and Eastern versions of the *Acts of Paul and Thecla*, in which there is no mention of a father, and it is Thecla's mother who accuses her daughter. On the other, the governors of Iconium, who receive the father's complaint, are called Dimās (Demas) and ʾArmogānos (Hermogenes). They are therefore identified with the two characters who collaborate with the governor of Iconium in view of arresting the apostle Paul.[22]

---

[18] See the manuscripts listed by Colin, "Le synaxaire éthiopien," 1988: 288–294. Because of its close ecclesiastical links with the patriarchate of Alexandria – the head of the Ethiopian Church was nominated by the bishop of Alexandria up to 1948 – the Ethiopian Church adopted some of the liturgical usages and religious literature of the Coptic Church.

[19] See ibid.: 312. These Ethiopian saints' Lives are attested only in the second recension, also known as the "Vulgate," which was elaborated on in the second half of the sixteenth century.

[20] The eleventh month of the Ethiopian calendar. It runs from the 8th of July to the 6th of August. The text was edited and translated in French: Guidi (ed. and trans.), *Le synaxaire éthiopien*, 1911: 405–408.

[21] It should be noted though that the "governor" (*mak^wannen*) of Antioch is not named in the *Synaxarium* and that he takes on the features of the nobleman Alexander mentioned in the other versions of the *Acts of Paul and Thecla*.

[22] See Guidi (ed. and trans.), *Le synaxaire éthiopien*, 1911: 405. The reasons why these changes were made are not at all clear. Be they deliberate or accidental, these kinds of rewritings are frequent in hagiographical texts. See Goullet, *Écriture et réécriture*, 2005: 107–199.

Though the trial of Thecla in the *Senkessār* does not radically differ from the plot of the *Acts of Paul and Thecla*, as it is known and transmitted in the other linguistic traditions, two features of the *Synaxarium* text deserve special notice. First, the text ends with an interesting remark regarding the sanctuary of Saint Thecla in Sengār in Lower Egypt.[23] According to the author of the *Senkessār*, Saint Thecla's relics are housed in this sanctuary and are renowned for their miraculous powers.[24] This short digression thus illustrates the prestige of this Egyptian *locus sanctus*, which the author praises as a major site of pilgrimage. Consequently, the purpose of the text is not only to remind readers and listeners of Thecla's saintly life but also to encourage devotional practices; in particular, going on a pilgrimage to the holy place of Sengār. Nevertheless, as one remembers that the Ethiopic *Synaxarium* is a translation of the Arabic *Synaxarium* of the Copts, the mention of this sanctuary is not a specific feature of the Ge'ez text but should be viewed in the context of Egyptian religious practices.

Secondly, what is noteworthy is the insertion of a *salām*, a short panegyric in verse praising the qualities and virtues of the saint, which is appended at the end of Thecla's story. The *salām* (meaning "peace" but usually used as a term of address to greet someone) always follows each commemorative notice of the Ethiopic *Synaxarium*. The *salām* is also especially frequent at the end of the saints' Lives, where all the virtuous deeds of the saint are summed up and praised in a poetic fashion. According to Denis Nosnitsin, the *salām* "summarizes the account and exposes, in poetic mode, the essence of the saint's spiritual deeds, stressing the most peculiar episodes of the saint's life."[25] In the case of Thecla, her *salām* insists on her miraculous survival through her trial and her absolute renunciation of earthly life. The whole text runs as follows:

> I say hail to Thecla the Apostolic,
> whom the Lord made powerful!
> The lions did not injure her and the blazing fire did not burn her.
> When she believed in the doctrine of righteousness as Paul told her,
> She left her parents and cast aside her treasures.[26]

---

[23] About this sanctuary, see Timm, *Das christlich-koptische Ägypten*, 1991: 2359–2361. About the cult of Thecla in Egypt, see Davis, *The Cult of St. Thecla*, 2009: 83–194. This sanctuary of Sengār or Sinjār (Arabic سنجار, Coptic ⲡϭⲉⲛⲕⲉⲣⲓ) is also mentioned in the parallel text contained in the Copto-Arabic *Synaxarium*. See Basset (ed. and trans.), *Le synaxaire arabe jacobite*, 1923: 683.
[24] See Guidi (ed. and trans.), *Le synaxaire éthiopien*, 1911: 405.
[25] Nosnitsin, "Sälam," 2010. See Caitríona Ó Dochartaigh's contribution in this volume (Chapter 3) for a discussion on Thecla in versified notices in medieval Irish calendars.
[26] See Guidi (ed. and trans.), *Le synaxaire éthiopien*, 1911: 407, l. 14–408, l. 3. In this chapter, all translations are mine and are based on the Ge'ez original.

Another *salām* in honor of the saint is to be found in the *Synaxarium* for the 20th of Ḥamlē.[27] This short poem, which does not depend on a preceding hagiographical narrative, also underlines the ascetic calling of Thecla and the miracles that surrounded her trial:

> Hail to Thecla who, for the sake of righteousness, was not saddened to have her hair, stretching from her head to toes, cut off,
> for she accepted Paul's epistle as good news.
> The governor failed, in both his attempts,
> to have her torn apart by the lions' tooth and consumed by the flame.[28]

The Ethiopic *Synaxarium* thus exemplifies how the life and trial of saint Thecla can be framed in a liturgical setting. The briefness of the account, specially designed for church reading at the occasion of the liturgical commemoration (*tazkār*)[29] of the saint, coupled with the recitation of the *salām*, gives a peculiarly Ethiopian flavor to this short version of the *Acts of Paul and Thecla*. Indeed, these Geʿez *salāms* represent one major Ethiopian innovation since they do not appear in the Copto-Arabic *Synaxarium* and were incorporated in the Geʿez *Synaxarium* in the process of translation. Moreover, the allusion to the sanctuary of Sengār in Egypt as a famous pilgrimage destination perfectly fits with the general purpose of this text, namely, promoting the cult and veneration of saint Thecla.

More interestingly, however, Thecla is not designated as a "martyr" (*samāʿet*) but as a "confessor" (*taʾamāni*) in the *Synaxarium*. Near the end of the story, it is thus written: "When her fight was over, she found rest in peace and received the crown of preachers and confessors in the Kingdom of heaven."[30] According to the redactor of the *Synaxarium*, Thecla is not a martyr since she did not die because of ill treatment; she died a natural death and reached the end of her life "in peace" (*ba-salām*). Nevertheless, because she survived many trials and tortures, she is rightly honored as a confessor, that is, someone who suffered persecution but survived throughout. Though not a martyr, Thecla has received the crown of confessors and accordingly deserves to be venerated as such. Thus, the Ethiopic *Synaxarium* unambiguously conveys the image of Thecla as a confessor. However, other Geʿez texts, like the *Book of Thecla*, prove much more

---

[27] See ibid.: 368. A few other but unrelated saints, such as Theodore, Theoctistus, and Gabra 'Iyasus, are commemorated on this day.
[28] Ibid.: 368, ll. 12–17.
[29] Regarding the *tazkār*, the commemorative feast for a dead person, see Alehegne, "Täzkar," 2010.
[30] Guidi (ed. and trans.), *Le synaxaire éthiopien*, 1911: 407, ll. 10–11.

ambiguous and seem reluctant to present such a praiseworthy character as a mere confessor.

An Unlabeled Martyr: Thecla in the *Maṣḥafa Ṭēqalā* or *Book of Thecla*

Recounting the story of her life, companionship with Saint Paul, and final trial, the *Maṣḥafa Ṭēqalā* (*Book of Thecla*) is an abridged and modified version of the famous apocryphal *Acts of Paul and Thecla*.[31] Though the plot of the *Book of Thecla* follows, on the whole, that of the Greek *Acts of Paul and Thecla*, it evinces many noteworthy peculiarities that make it stand apart from all the other ancient versions.

The *Book of Thecla* has been transmitted within an Ethiopic medieval collection of Martyr Acts, the *Gadla samāʿtāt* (*The Contendings of the Martyrs*).[32] This vast hagiographical collection, preserved in at least 34 manuscripts,[33] contains about 140 texts, less than one-third of which has been studied or edited to date. Belonging to various literary genres (Lives, Acts, martyrdoms, collections of miracles, homilies, etc.), these Geʿez hagiographical texts deal mostly with biblical, Eastern, and Egyptian martyrs who are venerated and commemorated in the Ethiopian Church.[34] The oldest extant texts that are part of this collection were translated chiefly from Arabic and from the thirteenth century onwards.[35] The importance of the *Book of Thecla* cannot be understated since it is certainly the oldest witness of a Geʿez translation of the apocryphal *Acts of Paul and Thecla*.

In the various manuscripts of the *Gadla samāʿtāt*, the *Book of Thecla* is read and commemorated on the 27th of *Maskaram*, the first month of the Ethiopian calendar.[36] The *Book of Thecla* is contained in the following manuscripts:

(1) London, British Library, Or. 687–688 (eighteenth century), fol. 49r–51v[37]

---

[31] For a general introduction to this work, see Barrier, *The Acts of Paul and Thecla*, 2009: 1–62; and Schneemelcher (ed.), *Neutestamentliche Apokryphen*, 1989: 194–214 and 216–224. All references to the Greek *Acts of Paul and Thecla* (*APT*) will be drawn from the Barrier edition unless otherwise stated.

[32] On this collection, see Bausi, "Gädlä sämaʿətat," 2005; and Bausi (ed. and trans.), *La versione etiopica*, 2002: 1–18.

[33] For a list, see Bausi (ed. and trans.), *La versione etiopica*, 2002: 3–7.

[34] A few examples that may be mentioned are the following: John the Baptist, Stephen the protomartyr, the martyrs of Najran, Pantaleon, Cyriacus and her mother Julitta, and Menas.

[35] See Cerulli, *Storia*, 1956: 68–70. [36] From the 11th of September to the 10th of October.

[37] Number 258 in Wright, *Catalogue*, 1877: 169–170.

(2) London, British Library, Or. 689 (fifteenth century), fol. 31r–34r[38]
(3) Monastery of Abbā Sayfa Mikāʿēl (Eritrea), Ethiopian Manuscript Microfilm Library (EMML) microfilm 1479 (1459/1460), fol. 55v–59v[39]
(4) Monastery of Dabra Ḥayq ʾEsṭifānos (Ethiopia), EMML mf. 1766 (fourteenth/fifteenth century), fol. 57r–63v[40]
(5) Wallo province (Ethiopia), EMML mf. 6951 (fifteenth century; not yet cataloged)[41]
(6) The *Gadla samāʿtāt* of Dabra Libānos in Eritrea (fifteenth century; not yet cataloged)[42]

In 1901, Edgar J. Goodspeed published an edition of the Geʿez text based on the two London manuscripts mentioned above, namely, BL Or. 687–688 and BL Or. 689.[43] More accurately, he edited BL Or. 689 (called manuscript A) and collected the variant readings of the BL Or. 687–688 (called manuscript B) in the footnotes.[44] He also provided an English translation and detailed commentaries in his footnotes. He asserts cautiously, following Theodore Nöldeke's suggestion, that the *Book of Thecla* was translated from Arabic.[45]

In the text edited by Goodspeed, the narrative opens with the preaching of Paul in Macedonia, which the author of the *Book of Thecla* seems to understand as a city.[46] There he meets a certain Tāmerēnos[47] who greets

---

[38] Number 253 in ibid.: 159–161. [39] Getatchew Haile, *A Catalogue*, 1979: 593–598.
[40] Getatchew Haile and Macomber, *A Catalogue*, 1981: 235–236.
[41] Bausi (ed. and trans.), *La versione etiopica*, 2002: 29.
[42] On this manuscript and its contents, see Bausi, "Su alcuni manoscritti," 1997: 23–32.
[43] Goodspeed (ed. and trans.), "The Book of Thekla," 1901. The Geʿez text is on pp. 71–85 and the English translation on pp. 86–95.
[44] Ibid.: 69.
[45] Actually, this is the case with most of the Lives contained in the *Gadla samāʿtāt*. See Bausi, "Su alcuni manoscritti," 1997: 15–18. For an example of a Geʿez hagiographical text of the *Gadla samāʿtāt* translated from Arabic, see Labadie (ed. and trans.), "Une version éthiopienne," 2015. An Arabic version of the *Acts of Paul and Thecla* was recently edited and translated by Davis (ed. and trans.), "An Arabic *Acts*," 2017. This Arabic version follows the plot lines of the Greek, Coptic, and Syriac accounts and differs markedly from the Geʿez *Book of Thecla*. Though the *Book of Thecla* was certainly translated from Arabic, its *Vorlage* cannot be related to the version edited by Davis since it represents a wholly different recension. For a list of manuscripts preserving an Arabic version of the *Acts of Paul and Thecla*, see Graf, *Geschichte*, 1944: 514; and Davis (ed. and trans.), "An Arabic *Acts*," 2017: 108. On the Arabic tradition, see also Proverbio, "Apocrypha Arabica," 1997.
[46] As the other versions of the *Acts of Paul and Thecla* locate the story in Asia Minor, the Ethiopic text unexpectedly locates it in መቄድንያ፡ (Macedonia) and all the other places found in the other versions (Iconium, Lystra, Antioch …) have disappeared. The only other place mentioned in the Geʿez text is Thessalonica (ተሰሎንቄ፡).
[47] This Tāmerēnos (ታምሬኖስ፡) plays the same role as that of Onesiphorus in the other versions of the *Acts of Paul and Thecla*. The Ethiopic name is obviously a corruption, through the Arabic, of the

him and invites him to preach in his house. Paul then delivers a sermon full of biblical quotations and recollections.[48] The Gospel of Matthew seems to be of particular relevance for the *Book of Thecla*. Indeed, a negative form of the so-called Golden Rule ("Do to others what you want them to do to you" Matt 7:12) appears.[49] Significantly for our purposes, it is noteworthy that the first part of Paul's homily is based on the Beatitudes of Matt 5:3–12.[50] Here, Paul delivers no less than thirteen Beatitudes on the model of the evangelical narrative, using the Ethiopic expression *beḍuʿān ʾella* (blessed are those who . . .):

> Blessed are those who believe in their heart in the Son of God .... Blessed are those who are now hungry and thirsty .... Blessed are those who make peace and reconcile one with another .... Blessed are those who are persecuted for the sake of righteousness.[51]

Paul's sermon places particular emphasis on abstinence and inveighs against any sexual intercourse. This encratic tendency is visible in the thirteenth and last of Paul's beatitude: "Blessed is the woman who does not marry and forsakes this world, and the virgin who does not marry and remains unmarried[52] while she declares to the Lord that the one who marries is part of the Gehenna."[53]

Further on, Paul concludes his sermon by defending the superiority of celibacy and widowhood over marriage. This final and lengthy exhortation, largely based on 1 Corinthians 7, reveals how important this subject was in the eyes of the anonymous author:

Greek Θάμυρις. The two figures of Onesiphorus and Thamyris have thus been merged in the Geʿez tradition.

[48] Goodspeed (ed. and trans.), "The Book of Thekla," 1901: 71–75 (86–88 for his translation).

[49] "And what you do not want others to do to you, do not do to others." Ibid.: 74, ll. 12–13: ወዘኢትፈቅዱ፡ ይግበሩ፡ ለክሙ፡ ሰብእ፡ አንትሙ፡ ኢትግበሩ፡ ለባዕድ፤. In an article published in 1935, George Brockwell King, "The 'Negative' Golden Rule," 1935: 59–60, drew attention to this negative form of the Golden Rule in the *Book of Thecla*. Although we do not agree with his assumption that this is due to an Indian influence, we regard the parallel he found in the Laws of King Alfred the Great (849–899) as quite compelling.

[50] See *APT* § 3.6. The same pattern is found in the other versions of the *Acts of Paul and Thecla* but in a much shorter form, though the number of Beatitudes is roughly the same. See, for example, Vouaux (ed. and trans.), *Les Actes*, 1913: 154–159, for the Greek; von Gebhardt (ed.), *Die lateinische Übersetzungen*, 1902: 12–17, for the Latin; Wright (ed. and trans.), *Apocryphal Acts*, 1871: 131–133, for the Syriac; Calzolari (ed. and trans.), *Apocrypha Armeniaca I*, 2017: 246–257, for the Armenian; and Davis (ed. and trans.), "An Arabic Acts," 2017: 116–117, for the Arabic.

[51] Goodspeed (ed. and trans.), "The Book of Thekla," 1901: 71, l. 4–72, l. 5: ብፁዓን፡ አለ፡ የአምኑ፡ በልቦሙ፡ በወልደ፡ አግዚአብሐር፡ [. . .] ብፁዓን፡ አለ፡ ይአዜ፡ ይርኅቡ፡ ወይጸምኡ፡ [. . .] ብፁዓን፡ አለ፡ ያስተሳለሙ፡ ወያስተኻንኑ፡ [. . .] ብፁዓን፡ አለ፡ ይሰደዱ፡ በእንተ፡ ጽድቅ፡. We reproduce exactly manuscript A, with its orthographical peculiarities, as edited by Goodspeed.

[52] Cf. 1 Cor 7:38.   [53] Goodspeed (ed. and trans.), "The Book of Thekla," 1901: 72, ll. 9–12.

> Now, do not marry anyone you may find and do not covet another's wife. If her husband happens to die, she shall remain unmarried and shall not get married. But if she cannot restrain herself without a husband, she shall marry one for it is better to marry than to fornicate. How could you possibly fornicate since you are the Lord's body and the Lord's body is yours? Therefore, do not make the Lord's body like the body of a harlot because, when a man has intercourse with a woman, they become one flesh. So, do not have intercourse with a harlot and whoever marries a harlot, his judgement will be death in Gehenna. Hand your souls over to Jesus Christ, the Son of God, for whoever commits his soul before the Lord will inherit the Kingdom of heaven.[54]

Thecla, who is described as Tāmerēnos' beloved (*feqert*), is carefully listening to Paul's lecture from the window of her house, located opposite Paul's abode. Aroused by the apostle's preaching, she decides to meet him at night several times so as to listen to his teaching. But Thecla's mother, having found out that her daughter has had many secret interviews with the apostle, brings her back home and summons Tāmerēnos. She informs him that Thecla has converted to Paul's encratic teaching and will no longer marry him. Paul is then brought to the local governor (*mak^{w}annen*)[55] to whom Tāmerēnos declares:

> This man who has come into our land has perverted our wives and many other women. After listening to his instructions, they divorced their spouses and the husbands even divorced their wives. Virgins, hearing his voice, also followed him and refused to marry.[56]

The governor orders that Paul be tortured and burnt, but the apostle survives miraculously.[57] As for Thecla, she is also sent to the stake by the governor at the behest of Thecla's own mother who had previously cursed her daughter in a passionate speech.[58] But an unexpected miracle occurs when she throws herself into the blaze:

> She entered this fire making the sign of Christ.[59] But at that moment the fire fled from her and rain fell from the sky and extinguished this fire.

---

[54] Ibid.: 74, l. 14–75, l. 5.   [55] The word can also mean "judge."
[56] Goodspeed (ed. and trans.), "The Book of Thekla," 1901: 77, l. 17–78, l. 1.
[57] Ibid.: 78 (90 for his translation). This episode is unique to the Ge'ez version.
[58] Ibid.: 79 (91 for his translation). This dialogue between Thecla and her mother before the first trial is not reported in the other versions. According to these other accounts, Saint Thecla is immediately brought to the judge after her visit to Paul. Compare especially Goodspeed (ed. and trans.), "The Book of Thekla," 1901: 76–77; and Vouaux (ed. and trans.), *Les Actes*, 1913: 182–187.
[59] Literally, "sealing (herself) with the sign of Christ" (ኀቲማ፡ [...] በማኅተመ፡ ክርስቶስ፤).

Thunder crashed and deafened the governor's ear because he had devised evil plans against the servants of God. His ear festered, putrefied and became deaf. Thecla went out from the middle of the fire while nobody stopped her.[60]

As soon as Thecla emerges from the fire, she is rejected by her mother and is abandoned in a burial vault (?)[61] in the city. There she meets a woman who owed her a thousand dinars.[62] Thecla, in a compassionate move, cancels all her debts.[63] Following this short episode, the Ge'ez text narrates the meeting of Thecla and one of Paul's disciples (*rade'*), whom Thecla meets by chance in the city. The disciple, whose name is not mentioned, leads Thecla to the place where Paul has been staying. As the two joyously meet, Thecla swears to Paul that she wants to become the handmaid of God (*'amata 'egzi'abḥēr*) and to lead a life of abstinence and celibacy. As a token of her commitment, she begs Paul to cut her hair and gird her, which he does quite reluctantly.[64] Afterwards, they both travel to Thessalonica. Thecla's mother, saddened by her daughter's conversion and full commitment to an apostolic life, goes to see another governor so as to ask him to judge and chastise her unruly daughter. Thecla is summoned by the governor who has her cast into a den of bears and lions:

> They took her and threw her into a den of bears and lions.[65] When they came to the door of that den of bears and lions, she spread out her hands again as she was accustomed to doing and she signed herself[66] with the sign of the cross. In front of its door, she signed[67] in the name of Jesus, the Son of God: "I will go in today with the help of the Holy Spirit." Because of this, she was rejoicing. It seemed to those who brought her that those beasts were about to devour her. But when the beasts saw her, they stood up and bowed down. They started to lick her and to roll at her feet.[68]

---

[60] Ibid.: 80, ll. 3–9.
[61] The Ge'ez word ንዋስ: in manuscript A (or ቅዋስ: in B) is uncertain. It is nowhere to be found in Ge'ez dictionaries. We follow Goodspeed's conjecture, which is probably based on a comparison with the other versions, in which it is told that Paul is hidden in a vault or tomb (*APT* § 3.23). See, for example, the Greek μνημεῖον, the Latin *monumentum*, or the Syriac *bēt 'ālmā* in Vouaux (ed. and trans.), *Les Actes*, 1913: 188–189; von Gebhardt (ed.), *Die lateinische Übersetzungen*, 1902: 60–61; and Wright (ed.), *Apocryphal Acts*, 1871: 146, respectively.
[62] This passage is unique to the Ge'ez version. See Goodspeed (ed. and trans.), "The Book of Thekla," 1901: 80–81 and 92.
[63] Ibid.: 80–81 (92 for his translation). [64] Ibid.: 80–82 (92–93 for his translation).
[65] Contrary to the other versions of the *Acts of Paul and Thecla*, the presence of ferocious seals is not mentioned in the Ge'ez account of this second trial.
[66] Literally, "she sealed herself" (ተተመት፡ ርእሳ፡). [67] Literally, "she sealed" (ተተመት፡).
[68] Goodspeed (ed. and trans.), "The Book of Thekla," 1901: 83, ll. 5–13.

Thecla, while staying among the beasts, says a prayer in praise of God for the life and salvation he has granted her.[69] The governor, unaware of Thecla's miraculous survival, orders that her bones be buried in the hope that the mysterious plague that "torments him" (*yeqaśśefo*) might definitively cease. As the governor discovers that Thecla is safe and sound, he humbly beseeches her to cure his torment and the wounded ear of the other governor. Thecla, however, first requires the presence of Paul. The apostle Paul comes and cures the two governors of whom it is stated, "both lived by the might of Jesus-Christ" (*wa-ḥaywu kelʾēhomu ba-ḥayla ʾIyasus Kerestos*).[70]

Compared with the Greek, Syriac, or Latin versions of the *Acts of Paul and Thecla*, the *Book of Thecla* is noteworthy for its brevity. Of particular relevance is the absence of the story of Paul and Thecla in Antioch of Pisidia where Alexander becomes enamored of Paul's companion.[71] The *Book of Thecla* simply notes that Paul and Thecla went to the city of Thessalonica, which here seems to be a substitute for Antioch. Then, the story of the second trial of Thecla in the Ethiopic text loosely follows this short allusion, and it is not clear at all whether her trial happened in Thessalonica or not. Among the other abridgements, we should mention the reunion between Paul and Thecla after her first trial.[72] Whereas the ancient versions describe a dramatic and joyful meeting followed by a meal, the *Book of Thecla* simply reports, in Thecla's own words, her escape from the fire. Furthermore, the place names are very few in the *Book of Thecla* (Macedonia and Thessalonica are the only places mentioned), and many characters are omitted as, for instance, Paul's traitors, namely, Demas and Hermogenes.[73] Since the Antioch episode is omitted, the names of Tryphaena and Alexander are absent from the Geʿez narrative. Closely related to this feature is the general paucity of proper names for the different characters mentioned in the Ethiopic narrative. As a matter of fact, Thecla's mother, the two governors, and Paul's disciple are anonymous. One possible reason for these omissions would lie in the scribe's inability to correctly transcribe the proper nouns. Indeed, all the proper nouns in the *Book of Thecla* are heavily corrupted and hardly recognizable.[74] We can assume that the scribe, faced with so many cumbersome

---

[69] Ibid.: 83–84 (94–95 for his translation).   [70] Ibid.: 84–85 (95 for his translation).
[71] *APT* § 4.1.
[72] Goodspeed (ed. and trans.), "The Book of Thekla," 1901: 80–81 (see 92–93 for his translation and especially 92 n. k).
[73] Ibid.: 171–175.   [74] Ibid.: 86 n. b and c.

nouns, would rather omit these words instead of transcribing them erroneously.

Finally, the Ethiopic *Book of Thecla* exhibits special features as far as the martyr status of Thecla is concerned. Indeed, the text seems to put great emphasis on the near-martyrological aspect of Thecla, and secondarily Paul, at the expense of her ascetic and apostolic calling. First, the lack of interest in her apostolic calling is striking; there is no indication that the female saint converted her family or the inhabitants of her native city on her return, which is in contrast to the *Synaxarium* (see above). The *Book of Thecla*, concluding with the account of her trial and salvation, thus presents this part of Thecla's life as the climax of her saintly destiny. Second, this Geʿez version adds many more details about Paul's sufferings, thus enhancing the martyrological dimension of this text. Whereas the other ancient versions tersely indicate that Paul was flogged,[75] the Geʿez text is unique in presenting a detailed account of the torture which Paul had to endure. Confronted with Paul's obstinacy, the governor declares:

> "Take him and bind him upside down! Put a crown of brass on his head and burn him with pitch, sulphur and the chaff of the threshing floor!" They did as they were told but they were not able to burn Paul with their fire because the Holy Spirit was upon him. The governor marveled and said: "That the fire cannot burn him is a miraculous thing! Cast him out of our city, take his remaining ashes and bring them forth, saying: These are the remaining ashes of Paul, whom we have burnt and utterly cast forth."[76]

Finally, it is worth remembering that the Ethiopic *Book of Thecla* has been transmitted in a collection of martyrdom stories, the *Gadla samāʿtāt* (*The Contendings of the Martyrs*). As a consequence, Thecla was viewed, among Ethiopian Christians, as a martyr figure. Read alongside the accounts of other famous martyrs, the *Acts of Paul and Thecla* was expected to be for its Ethiopian readers, first and foremost, a story of martyrdom and suffering. Yet this martyrological dimension, sustained by both internal and external criteria, is somewhat counterbalanced by the fact that nowhere in the text is Thecla labeled a "martyr" (*samāʿet*). This discrepancy reveals how ambiguous the figure of Thecla is in Geʿez hagiography. Though never named a "martyr" in the *Book of Thecla*, she is presented as though she

---

[75] *APT* § 3.21. See, for example, Vouaux (ed. and trans.), *Les Actes*, 1913: 184–185 (φραγελλώσας); von Gebhardt (ed.), *Die lateinische Übersetzungen*, 1902: 54–55 (*flagellatum*); Wright (ed. and trans.), *Apocryphal Acts*, 1871: 145 (*naggdūhy*); Davis (ed. and trans.), "An Arabic Acts," 2017: 123 (*yujallidūhu*); and Calzolari (ed. and trans.), *Apocrypha Armeniaca I*, 2017: 305 (*harkaneł*).
[76] Goodspeed (ed. and trans.), "The Book of Thekla," 1901: 78, ll. 8–15.

were a fully-fledged martyr, whose story was written and copied alongside other martyrdom stories, all included in the Ethiopic *Gadla samāʿtāt*. Thus, although the trials she went through could rightly grant her the status of a perfect martyr, she cannot be named that way since, technically, she did not die a martyr but ended her life peacefully as the Ethiopic *Synaxarium* asserts. Because of this paradoxical situation, Thecla appears in the *Book of Thecla* as a genuine female martyr without ever being called a "martyr." She remains an unlabeled martyr.

The *Epistle of Pelagia*: Thecla as a Model for an Undying Martyr

Apart from the *Synaxarium* and the *Book of Thecla*, which deal directly with Saint Thecla, two other hagiographical Geʿez texts make reference to her. The first of these texts is the *Epistle of Pelagia* (BHO 890), an apocryphal text that is attested in Geʿez only.[77] According to this short text, preserved in some manuscripts of the *Gadla samāʿtāt*, the apostle Paul visits Caesarea in Palestine and preaches the Gospel. Expelled from the city because of his missionary activity, he flees to the surrounding mountains, where he meets a huge lion. The lion asks him to teach him the Gospel and to receive baptism. Paul then returns to Caesarea, brings a dead man to life, and converts many people, including the king's daughter Pelagia. Following Paul's exhortation to renounce marriage and worldly pleasures, Pelagia is sentenced to death in the theater together with Paul. As Paul is led into the theater, a lion is unleashed. But this lion is the same as the one that he had baptized earlier in the mountains. Instead of devouring Paul, the lion prays with him and praises God. The astonished king decides to let Paul and the beast go. As for Pelagia, she is ordered to be cast into a burning brass cow. But, before she can enter it, a pouring rain suddenly extinguishes the fire. Nevertheless, Pelagia still decides to go in, and her husband, appalled by this, commits suicide. The story abruptly ends here and states nothing more about Pelagia.

This martyrdom story appears to be based on two sources. First, the *Passion of Pelagia of Tarsus* (BHG 1480) seems to be a possible source for the *Epistle of Pelagia* as Goodspeed correctly noted.[78] In the *Passion of*

---

[77] Also *CANT* 211.IV. The text was edited and translated into English by Goodspeed (ed. and trans.), "The Epistle of Pelagia," 1904. He used three London manuscripts: BL Or. 686 (fifteenth century), BL Or. 687–688 (eighteenth century), and BL Or. 689 (eighteenth century). His translation was reprinted in Schmidt (ed. and trans.), *Acta Pauli*, 1905: XXI–XXV.

[78] See Goodspeed (ed. and trans.), "The Epistle of Pelagia," 1904: 96–97. On Pelagia of Tarsus, see Sauget, "Pelagia di Tarso," 1968; and Delehaye, *Les légendes hagiographiques*, 1927: 191–192. For

Pelagia of Tarsus, the female protagonist is baptized by the fugitive bishop Clinon. Then she dedicates herself to a life of poverty and celibacy. Her lover, Diocletian's (244–311) son, commits suicide as soon as he learns what Pelagia has done. Diocletian, failing to force the young Christian woman to apostatize, has her thrown in a burning brazen bull. This story offers a few interesting parallels with the *Epistle of Pelagia*. First, Clinon is a wandering character like the apostle Paul who baptizes a young and noble pagan girl. Secondly, the female convert refuses to marry her fiancé who, in both martyrdom stories, commits suicide. Finally, the use of a scalding brazen bull, as an instrument of torture, is shared by both stories.

However, another probable source for the *Epistle of Pelagia* is a particular recension of the *Acts of Paul and Thecla*. As a matter of fact, both accounts share the same general plot.[79] The apostle Paul converts a young noble woman who then refuses to live a marital life. This sudden change leads to her conviction and final trial. More striking is the reference to, in both stories, a sudden rain that extinguishes a fire, which is used as a means of execution, and a burning bull. But, more importantly, the episode of the baptized lion, though absent in the *Acts of Paul and Thecla*, is directly drawn from a peculiar passage of the *Acts of Paul* in Ephesus that has been preserved in a Coptic papyrus deposited in the Staats- und Universitäts-Bibliothek of Hamburg.[80] In the fragmentary Coptic text, it is told that Paul, being condemned *ad bestias* in the stadium of Ephesus, recognizes the lion that he had baptized earlier. As other beasts are unleashed into the stadium so as to kill Paul and the talking lion, suddenly a hailstorm breaks out and frightens the beasts. Then, Paul leaves the stadium and embarks on a boat bound for Macedonia. As for the lion, it is said that he returns to the mountains where he lives. This last allusion provides a significant parallel to the *Epistle of Pelagia* since it is reported that Paul met the lion in the "mountain" (*dabr*) after fleeing from Caesarea. The dependency of the Ge'ez text on this *Vorlage* could also be conjectured on the basis of a translation error. Indeed, the Ethiopic text does not explicitly state that the

---

the Greek, see Usener (ed.), *Legenden*, 1879: 17–28; and Delehaye (ed.), *Synaxarium Ecclesiae Constantinopolitanae*, 1902: 118–119.

[79] See Schmidt (ed. and trans.), *Acta Pauli*, 1905: XXVI–XXIX, who draws many relevant parallels between the *Epistle of Pelagia* and the *Acts of Paul*.

[80] Schmidt and Schubart (eds. and trans.), *PRAXEIS PAULOU*, 1936: 22–45. A German translation of this episode is printed in Schneemelcher (ed.), *Neutestamentliche Apokryphen*, 1989: 230. For a useful and detailed commentary, see Schneemelcher, "Der getaufte Löwe," 1964. This strange episode was already known to ancient authors like Jerome, *De Viris Illustribus* 7, Hippolytus, *In Danielem* 3.29; Commodian, *Carmen Apologeticum* 627–628; and Nicephoros Callistos, *Historia ecclesiastica* 2.25.

lion was baptized but was "received in the great[81] of the Christians" (*westa ʿabiya kerestiyān*).[82] Although it seems difficult to explain the enigmatic form of the Geʿez passage, the word "great" is probably to be understood as meaning here "baptism." It could be either the result of a scribal corruption or a deliberate attempt by a later copyist to substitute "baptism" for the vague word "great" since he might have viewed this act of baptizing as highly unorthodox.[83] Whatever the reason for such a change might be, it remains certain that the Geʿez *Epistle of Pelagia* offers an invaluable parallel to the *Acts of Paul* in Ephesus. To sum up, the *Epistle of Pelagia* is probably dependent on three previous hagiographical and apocryphal works, that is, the *Passion of Pelagia of Tarsus*, the *Acts of Paul and Thecla*, and the Coptic *Acts of Paul* in Ephesus.

Additionally, three further pieces of literary evidence reveal not only that the *Epistle of Pelagia* was partly based on the *Acts of Paul and Thecla* but also that the character of Pelagia has been fashioned and modeled on the figure of Saint Thecla. In the *Epistle of Pelagia*, after the lion episode, Paul resurrects a dead man and addresses and teaches the crowd about the power of faith.[84] Recalling biblical *exempla*, such as Rahab, Daniel, Ezekiel, Elijah, or Joseph, Paul tells how these men and women were saved by God in perilous circumstances thanks to their unflinching faith. Among all these *exempla*, only one is not of biblical origin and concerns precisely Saint Thecla. She is praised by Paul as an example of a faithful servant of God, who saved her twice from a certain death, thus alluding to her two trials in the *Acts of Paul and Thecla*: "See how Thecla, by her faith, was saved from the fire and the mouth of the lions."[85] Though Pelagia is not directly associated with Thecla in this passage, it is worth observing that Thecla is the only non-biblical figure to be mentioned in this sermon. She is presented to the crowd, and especially to the women who were listening to Paul, as a model to be followed and imitated. Among these women stood Pelagia, who immediately converted after hearing the apostle's preaching and exhortation.

---

[81] The adjective "great" (*ʿabiy*) is here used absolutely, without a dependent noun.
[82] See Goodspeed (ed. and trans.), "The Epistle of Pelagia," 1904: 100.
[83] Goodspeed assumes that the Arabic translator, reading the Coptic original, read ⲚⲞϬ (*noč*, "great") instead of ⲰⲘⲤ (*ōms*, "baptism"). This mistake might account for the strange Ethiopic rendering, which was based on a faulty Arabic original. See ibid.: 105 n. 2. However, the two words do not look alike, and his explanation remains doubtful since we do not have a Coptic or Arabic parallel that could substantiate it.
[84] Ibid.: 101–103 (106–107 for his translation). [85] Ibid.: 101, ll. 11–12.

Another startling passage deserves to be commented on. As Paul is brought before the king to account for his troublesome activities in Caesarea, the king addresses him with these ominous words:

> The king met Paul and said to him: "Behold, you are perverting all our people and everyone, once he has listened to your exhortation,[86] leaves this world. The man divorces his wife and the wife even divorces her husband. Now you shall pay for all that you did to that Thecla." He ordered them to send Paul to prison and they did as the king commanded.[87]

Surprisingly, the name Pelagia has been replaced here by that of Thecla! The BL Or. 686 and BL Or. 687–688 manuscripts have the "Thecla" (*Ṭēqālā*) reading, whereas the BL Or. 689 manuscript has the consistent reading "Pelagia" (*Pilāgyā*).[88] This anomalous reading can be explained in two ways. First, the author, availing himself of some recension of the *Acts of Paul and Thecla*, directly copied a passage from this source text and forgot to change "Thecla" into "Pelagia." We may likewise assume that Pelagia, in the scribe's or author's mind, was viewed as so close to Thecla that both characters were confused and mixed up when he copied or wrote the *Epistle of Pelagia*. Anyway, this *lapsus calami*, about which we cannot state confidently that it is original even though it is preserved in the oldest manuscript, is surely no coincidence. In this particular passage of the *Epistle of Pelagia*, Thecla is unintentionally identified with Pelagia, thus revealing how the latter is regarded as a copy or a substitute of the former.

A third argument can be put forward. There is an interesting parallel to be drawn between Pelagia and Saint Thecla as far as their respective final trials are concerned. Pelagia's end appears as rather startling since it is not at all clear whether she died or not. Although a miraculous rain extinguished the molten brass cow, she nevertheless goes into it:

> And they brought also that cow of brass and they started to throw her into it. But at that moment rain fell and put it out. However, she was determined to go in. When the man[89] saw her determination to go in, he took a sword and let his face fall upon it and died for Pelagia's beauty was wonderful and she neither considered her beauty nor regarded this transient world.[90]

The end of the text offers an enigmatic conclusion. Did Pelagia die or not? On the one hand, it seems so for it is told that she despises her beauty and

---

[86] Or "rebuke," "reproach" (ተግሣጽ፡).
[87] Goodspeed (ed. and trans.), "The Epistle of Pelagia," 1904: 103, ll. 7–12.
[88] See Ibid.: 103 n. 26 and 107 n. 2.   [89] Pelagia's fiancé.
[90] Goodspeed (ed. and trans.), "The Epistle of Pelagia," 1904: 104, ll. 12–16.

this fleeting world. It is as though she were ready to leave this earthly life; it is the reason why she seems eager to go into the cow. On the other, is it really conceivable that she could suffer martyrdom and death in this brass cow, when the fire was extinguished by a heavy rain? We can conjecture that this ambiguous end might be a deliberate attempt to draw a parallel between Pelagia and Thecla since the latter's final trial includes two bulls whose genitalia are scorched to enrage them. Pelagia longs for death and, like Thecla, she survives her final trial. Though she earnestly wishes to die as a martyr, Pelagia, similarly to Thecla in the *Book of Thecla*, appears as an ambiguous martyr whose very death is not at all mentioned at the end of the story. Thus, Pelagia appears on the threshold of martyrdom; while she is characterized by all the attributes of a holy female martyr, she nevertheless escapes death and, consequently, cannot receive the crown of martyrdom. Therefore, it seems that Thecla was, in the Ethiopian literary tradition, famous enough so as to be the source and model for Pelagia and another female saint like her; one whose character and story appears as an original creation in the corpus of Geʿez hagiographical literature.

An Inspiring Martyr: The Figure of Thecla in the Geʿez *Martyrdom of Cyrus and John*

Whereas the *Synaxarium*, the *Book of Thecla*, and the *Epistle of Pelagia* do not openly assert that Thecla is a fully-fledged martyr, it is worth noting that the Geʿez *Martyrdom of Cyrus, John, Their Mother, and Three Virgins* (*BHG* 469–471)[91] claims Thecla as a genuine martyr. The story, preserved in Greek, Latin, Arabic, and Geʿez sources, tells of the martyrdom of a group of Alexandrian Christians who were tortured at the time of Diocletian's imperial rule. Living in Antioch but hailing from Alexandria, these Christians are arrested by Diocletian who then sends them to Alexandria so that they may be judged and sentenced by the local governor. After their brutal deaths, their relics were kept hidden in Alexandria until Bishop Cyril (412–444) transferred the holy remains to a new sanctuary in Menuthis (today Abukir in northern Egypt). In one of

---

[91] See Caraffa, "Ciro e Giovanni," 1964. The story was probably written in the seventh century, at a time when the Coptic sanctuary of Menuthis reached international fame and prestige. See Delehaye, "Les saints d'Aboukir," 1911. Sophronius of Jerusalem (560–638) wrote a famous collection of miracle stories, the *Miracles of Cyrus and John*, related to the relics of Cyrus and John in the sanctuary of Menuthis (*BHG* 477–479). See Gascou (ed. and trans.), *Sophrone de Jérusalem*, 2006.

the Ge'ez versions of the story, contained in the Ethiopic *Synaxarium*,[92] saint Cyrus (*'Abāqir*) recalls Thecla's trial as a way of encouraging and strengthening the three Alexandrian virgins in the face of their impending deaths: "Likewise, saint Cyrus was revealing to them and telling them what torments befell saint Thecla the Apostolic."[93] However, this allusion to Thecla is not specific to this passage in Ge'ez. The Copto-Arabic *Synaxarium*, from which the Ethiopic *Synaxarium* was translated, also refers to Thecla when Cyrus addresses the young virgins and presents Paul's female companion as a model to follow. Actually, the Ge'ez is a faithful rendering of the Arabic.[94]

The *Gadla samā'tāt* preserves a richer and longer form of the story, including saint Cyrus' energetic plea to the three virgins. Indeed, the Ge'ez *Acts of Cyrus and John*, a translation from the Arabic that remains unedited, offers a more explicit reference to Thecla when it comes to Cyrus' address. This time, both Cyrus and John speak and remind their listeners of the heroic behavior of Saint Thecla who should be regarded as a model and an example in a time of persecution and torture. According to the London manuscript BL Or. 687–688,[95] Cyrus and John deliver the following message:

> Cyrus and John were encouraging them and saying to them: "Remember the might of our Lord, who says in the pure and holy Gospel: Do not fear those who will kill your body. They have no power over your souls."[96] And he said: "His name be blessed in the holy Gospel for the one who endures the ignominy of the wicked in this world will be saved and rescued. Be like saint Thecla who was led into martyrdom in the middle of virgins and who became a martyr for the name of our Lord Christ and found eternal rest for him."[97]

This exhortation is specially designed for virgins since Thecla, according to the above account, was martyred among other virgins. This passage is an allusion to the *Acts of Paul and Thecla*. Indeed, in the Greek *Acts*, when Thecla is sentenced to burning, the governor of Iconium demands that the other women, who were instructed by Paul, attend Thecla's trial in the

---

[92] Colin (ed. and trans.), *Le synaxaire éthiopien*, 1992: 494–495. The Ge'ez account is based on the version transmitted in the Arabic *Synaxarium*. See Basset (ed. and trans.), *Le synaxaire arabe jacobite*, 1915: 796–797.
[93] Colin (ed. and trans.), *Le synaxaire éthiopien*, 1992: 494, ll. 21–23.
[94] See Basset (ed. and trans.), *Le synaxaire arabe jacobite*, 1915: 797, for the Arabic text and his French translation.
[95] Number 45 in Wright, *Catalogue*, 1877: 170.   [96] Matt 10:28.
[97] BL Or. 687–688, fol. 226r.

theater so that they may be scared and, we may conjecture, renounce their abstemious way of life.[98] In some Latin recensions, the governor explicitly demands that the other virgins come and see Thecla's execution.[99] During her trial, Thecla is thus being looked at and encouraged by the other young virgins who are sitting in the theater. Therefore, according to the author of the Ethiopic *Acts of Cyrus and John*, as Thecla was a source of inspiration for the virgins who attended her trial in Iconium, she must also be contemplated as a model and a source of inspiration for the three Alexandrian virgins who were awaiting a fatal condemnation.

Finally, it should be emphasized that the *Acts of Cyrus and John*, both in the *Synaxarium* and the *Gadla samāʿtāt*, is the only Geʿez text that unambiguously presents Thecla as a "martyr" (*samāʿet*). Since both versions were translated from Arabic in the fourteenth and fifteenth centuries, this mention of Thecla is certainly not an original addition belonging to the Geʿez version but comes from Egyptian Arabic sources. The allusion to Thecla is not reflected in the final martyrdom of the three virgins. Indeed, Cyrus, John, and the virgins are all crucified and then beheaded without mention of Thecla either directly or indirectly.[100] Neither is Paul alluded to as a model for male martyrs such as Cyrus and John. It seems, therefore, that this passing mention of Thecla is incidental and represents a rather vague memory of Thecla as a perfect martyr. Nevertheless, the *Acts of Cyrus and John* is a precious testimony since it clears up Thecla's ambiguous status by describing her as a genuine martyr.

Conclusion

This brief survey of the figure of Thecla the "Apostolic" has revealed that the saint was fairly famous in classical Ethiopic literature. Especially noteworthy is the *Book of Thecla* (*Maṣḥafa Ṭēqalā*), the Geʿez version of the *Acts of Paul and Thecla*. Transmitted as part of a collection of martyrdom stories, the *Book of Thecla* was read alongside other hagiographical texts and enjoyed wide circulation in Ethiopian monastic circles during the medieval period. Therefore, it was not considered as an apocryphal work but as a hagiographical text in its own right. It also indicates that Thecla's life was primarily understood and received as a martyrdom story in the

---

[98] Pervo (trans.), *The Acts of Paul*, 2014: § 3.20. See also Vouaux (ed. and trans.), *Les Actes*, 1913: 184–185.
[99] von Gebhardt (ed.), *Die lateinische Übersetzungen*, 1902: 53.
[100] See BL Or. 687–688, fol. 226r–v.

Ethiopian tradition. This is confirmed by the literary testimonies of the liturgical *salāms*, the *Epistle of Pelagia*, and the *Martyrdom of Cyrus and John*, in which Thecla is generally alluded to as a model of female martyrdom.

As we saw, however, Thecla's status as a martyr is fraught with ambiguity in Geʿez hagiographical texts. The way she is described varies greatly from one text to another. Whereas the *Synaxarium* presents her as a "confessor" (*taʾamāni*), the *Book of Thecla*, transmitted as part of a collection of martyrdom stories, puts great emphasis on certain martyrological aspects without ever labeling her a "martyr." As for the *Epistle of Pelagia*, Thecla is taken as a model for the female protagonist, even in the description of her ultimate trial. Like Thecla, Pelagia appears as an ambivalent figure, presented as a fully-fledged martyr but one who does not die during her trial. Finally, the Geʿez *Acts of Cyrus and John*, unlike the other texts, explicitly states that Thecla is a perfect martyr who deserves to be imitated by three young virgins. Hence, in Geʿez literature, Thecla appears to be a fluid and elusive figure whose status varies greatly from one text to another. This unsettled status results from her very own peculiar story in which she weathers excruciating tortures but never dies as a martyr. This ambiguity is perfectly reflected in the Arabic version of the *Acts of Paul and Thecla*, in which the female saint is straightforwardly described as a "martyr-confessor" (*šahīda muʿtarifa*).[101] Likewise, the Ethiopic literary tradition, wavering between "confessor" and "martyr," evinces the same ambiguity regarding this female saint and her dual role.

Bibliography

Alehegne, Mersha. "Täzkar." In *Encyclopaedia Aethiopica*. Wiesbaden: Harrassowitz, 2010: IV: 881–882.

Assemani, Stephanus Evodius, ed. and trans. *Acta martyrum orientalium et occidentalium*. Vol. 1. Rome: Typis Josephi Collini, 1748.

Barrier, Jeremy W. *The Acts of Paul and Thecla: A Critical Introduction and Commentary*. WUNT 2.270. Tübingen: Mohr Siebeck, 2009.

Basset, René, ed. and trans. *Le synaxaire arabe jacobite. Les mois de Ṭoubeh et d'Amchir*. Patrologia orientalis 11.5. Paris: Firmin-Didot, Fribourg-en-Brisgau, and B. Herder, 1915.

⎯⎯⎯ ed. and trans. *Le synaxaire arabe jacobite. Les mois de Baounah, Abib, Mésoré et jours complémentaires*. Patrologia orientalis 17.3. Paris: Firmin-Didot, 1923.

---

[101] See Davis (ed. and trans.), "An Arabic *Acts*," 2017: 136 and 151.

Bausi, Alessandro. "Su alcuni manoscritti presso comunità monastiche dell'Eritrea. Parte terza." *Rassegna di studi etiopici* 41 (1997): 13–56.
 ed. and trans. *La versione etiopica degli Acta Phileae nel Gadla samā'tāt*. Naples: Istituto universitario orientale, 2002.
 "Gädlä sämaᶜətat." In *Encyclopaedia Aethiopica*. Wiesbaden: Harrassowitz, 2005: III: 644–646.
Bedjan, Paul, ed. *Acta martyrum et sanctorum*. Vol. II. Paris; Leipzig: Otto Harrassowitz, 1892.
Brock, Sebastian, and Susan Ashbrook Harvey, trans. *Holy Women of the Syrian Orient*. Berkeley; Los Angeles; London: University of California Press, 1998.
Brockwell King, George. "The 'Negative' Golden Rule: Additional Note." *The Journal of Religion* 15, no. 1 (1935): 59–62.
Böll, Verena. "Holy Women in Ethiopia." In *Saints, Biographies and History in Africa*, edited by Bertrand Hirsh and Manfred Kropp. Frankfurt am Main: Peter Lang, 2003: 31–45.
Budge, Ernest Alfred Wallis, trans. *The Book of Saints of the Ethiopian Church*. 4 vols. Cambridge: Cambridge University Press, 1928.
Calzolari, Valentina, ed. and trans. *Apocrypha Armeniaca I: Acta Pauli et Theclae, Prodigia Theclae, Martyrium Pauli*. Corpus Christianorum Series Apocryphorum 20. Turnhout: Brepols, 2017.
 "The Legend of St. Thecla in the Armenian Tradition: From Asia Minor to Tarrogona through Armenia." In *Thecla: Paul's Disciple and Saint in the East and West*, edited by Jeremy W. Barrier, Jan N. Bremmer, T. Nicklas, and A. Puig i Tàrrech. Studies on Early Christian Apocrypha 12. Leuven: Peeters, 2017: 285–305.
Caraffa, Filippo. "Ciro e Giovanni." In *Bibliotheca Sanctorum*. Rome: Istituto Giovanni XXIII nella Pontificia Università Lateranense, 1964: IV: 2–4.
 "Tecla, Mariamne, Marta, Maria e Amai." In *Bibliotheca Sanctorum*. Rome: Istituto Giovanni XXIII nella Pontificia Università Lateranense, 1969: XII: 184.
Cerulli, Enrico. *Storia della letteratura etiopica*. Milan: Nuova Accademia Editrice, 1956.
Colin, Gérard. "Le synaxaire éthiopien. État de la question." *Analecta Bollandiana* 106 (1988): 273–317.
 ed. and trans. *Le synaxaire éthiopien. Mois de Yakkatit*. Patrologia orientalis 45.3. Turnhout: Brepols, 1992.
Colin, Gérard, and Alessandro Bausi. "Sənkəssar." In *Encyclopaedia Aethiopica*. Wiesbaden: Harrassowitz, 2010: IV: 621–623.
Davis, Stephen J. *The Cult of St. Thecla: A Tradition of Women's Piety in Late Antiquity*. Oxford Early Christian Studies. Oxford; New York: Oxford University Press, 2009.
 ed. and trans. "An Arabic *Acts of Paul and Thecla*: Text and Translation, with Introduction and Critical Commentary." In *Thecla: Paul's Disciple and Saint in the East and West*, edited by Jeremy W. Barrier, Jan N. Bremmer, T.

Nicklas, and A. Puig i Tàrrech. Studies on Early Christian Apocrypha 12. Leuven: Peeters, 2017: 106–151.
Delehaye, Hippolyte, ed. *Synaxarium Ecclesiae Constantinopolitanae, Propylaeum ad Acta Sanctorum Novembris*. Brussels: Société des Bollandistes, 1902.
"Les saints d'Aboukir." *Analecta Bollandiana* 30 (1911): 448–450.
Les légendes hagiographiques. 3rd ed. Brussels: Société des Bollandistes, 1927.
Derat, Marie-Laure. *Le domaine des rois éthiopiens (1270–1527). Espace, pouvoir et monachisme*. Paris: Publications de la Sorbonne, 2003.
Gascou, Jean, ed. and trans. *Sophrone de Jérusalem. Miracles des saints Cyr et Jean (BHG I 477–479)*. Paris: De Boccard, 2006.
von Gebhardt, Otto, ed. *Die lateinischen Übersetzungen der Acta Pauli et Theclae*. Texte und Untersuchungen 22.2. Leipzig: J. C. Hinrichs, 1902.
Getatchew Haile. *A Catalogue of Ethiopian Manuscripts Microfilmed for the Ethiopian Manuscript Microfilm Library, Addis Ababa and for the Hill Monastic Manuscript Library, Collegeville*. Vol. IV. Project Numbers: 1101–1500. Collegeville: Hill Monastic Manuscript Library, St. John's University, 1979.
Getatchew Haile, and William F. Macomber. *A Catalogue of Ethiopian Manuscripts Microfilmed for the Ethiopian Manuscript Microfilm Library, Addis Ababa and for the Hill Monastic Manuscript Library, Collegeville*. Vol. V. Project Numbers: 1501–2000. Collegeville: Hill Monastic Manuscript Library, St. John's University, 1981.
Goodspeed, Edgar J., ed. and trans. "The Book of Thekla." *The American Journal of Semitic Languages and Literatures* 17 (1901): 65–95.
——— ed. and trans. "The Epistle of Pelagia." *The American Journal of Semitic Languages and Literatures* 20 (1904): 95–108.
Goullet, Monique. *Écriture et réécriture hagiographiques. Essai sur les réécritures de Vies de saints dans l'Occident latin médiéval (VIIIe–XIIIe s.)*. Hagiologia 4. Turnhout: Brepols, 2005.
Graf, Georg. *Geschichte der christlichen arabischen Literatur*. Vol. I. Studi e testi 118. Vatican City: Bibliotheca Apostolica Vaticana, 1944.
Guidi, Ignazio, ed. and trans. *Le synaxaire éthiopien. Le mois de hamlê*. Patrologia Orientalis 7.3. Paris: Firmin-Didot, Fribourg-en-Brisgau, and B. Herder, 1911.
Hahn, Wolfgang. "Ezana." In *Encyclopaedia Aethiopica*. Wiesbaden: Harrassowitz, 2005: II: 478–480.
Labadie, Damien, ed. and trans. "Une version éthiopienne des Actes apocryphes du protomartyr Étienne. Édition, traduction et commentaire du manuscrit BnF d'Abbadie 110 (f. 81r–88r)." *Le Muséon* 128 (2015): 415–472.
Mecca, Selamawit. "Women in Ethiopic Hagiography." In *Proceedings of the 16th International Conference of Ethiopian Studies*, edited by Svein Ege, Harald Aspen, B. Teferra, and S. Bekele. Trondheim: NTNU-trykk, 2009: 1365–1374.
Nosnitsin, Denis. "Sälam." In *Encyclopaedia Aethiopica*. Wiesbaden: Harrassowitz, 2010: IV: 484.

Pervo, Richard I., trans. *The Acts of Paul: A New Translation with Introduction and Commentary*. Cambridge: James Clarke & Co., 2014.

Proverbio, Delio Vania. "*Apocrypha Arabica*. Le recensioni arabe degli *Acta Pauli et Theclae*." In *Scritti in memoria di Emilio Teza*, edited by Delio Vania Proverbio. Miscellanea Marciana 12. Venice: Biblioteca nazionale marciana, 1997: 171–186.

Sauget, Joseph-Marie. "Pelagia di Tarso." In *Bibliotheca sanctorum*. Rome: Istituto Giovanni XXIII nella Pontificia Università Lateranense, 1968: X: 440–441.

"Tecla (Theclah) e Mugi (Mūǧī)." In *Bibliotheca Sanctorum*. Rome: Istituto Giovanni XXIII nella Pontificia Università Lateranense, 1969: XII: 184–185.

Schmidt, Carl, ed. and trans. *Acta Pauli, Übersetzung, Untersuchungen und Koptischer Text*. 2nd ed. Leipzig: J. C. Hinrichs, 1905.

Schmidt, Carl, and Wilhelm Schubart, eds. and trans. *PRAXEIS PAULOU: Acta Pauli nach dem Payrus der Hamburger Staats- und Universitäts-Bibliothek*. Veröffentlichungen aus der Hamburger Staats- und Universitäts-Bibliothek 2. Glückstadt; Hamburg: J. J. Augustin, 1936.

Schneemelcher, Wilhelm. "Der getaufte Löwe in den Acta Pauli." In *Mullus: Festschrift Theodor Klauser*, edited by Alfred Stuiber and Alfred Hermann. Jahrbuch für Antike und Christentum Ergänzungsband 1. Münster: Aschendorff, 1964: 316–326.

ed. *Neutestamentliche Apokryphen*. Vol. II. Tübingen: Mohr Siebeck, 1989.

Timm, Stefan. *Das christlich-koptische Ägypten in arabischer Zeit*. Vol. V. Wiesbaden: Ludwig Reichert Verlag, 1991.

Usener, Hermann, ed. *Legenden der heiligen Pelagia*. Bonn: A. Marcus, 1879.

Vouaux, Léon, ed. and trans. *Les Actes de Paul et ses lettres apocryphes*. Paris: Letouzey et Ané, 1913.

Wright, William, ed. and trans. *Apocryphal Acts of the Apostles: Edited from Syriac Manuscripts in the British Museum and Other Libraries*. Vol. I: The Syriac Texts. London: Williams and Norgate, 1871.

Catalogue of the Ethiopic Manuscripts in the British Museum. London: British Museum, 1877.

CHAPTER 3

Versified Martyrs
The Reception of Thecla from the Latin West to Medieval Ireland

Caitríona Ó Dochartaigh

A remarkable feature of medieval Irish hagiography is that some of the earliest extant vernacular texts in the corpus survive in verse form. *Amra Choluim Chille*, an elegiac composition in honor of Saint Colum Cille (Columba), may contain elements composed shortly after his death in 597. This poetic lament is not only an early attestation of the veneration of native saints in medieval Ireland but may also be one of the earliest surviving poems in the Irish language.[1] The metrical hymn *Génair Pátraic* ("Patrick was born"), ascribed to his contemporary Fiacc of Sleaty (d. late fifth century), attempts a condensed hagiography, giving an abbreviated account of the life and deeds of Saint Patrick (fl. fifth century).[2] The last in this trio of Ireland's patron saints, Saint Brigit (supposedly fifth century), chief amongst Ireland's virgin saints despite her dubious historicity, is the focus of two surviving early medieval Irish verse compositions. The works with the initia *Brigit bé bithmaith*[3] ("Brigit ever excellent woman") and *Ní car Brigit búadach bith*[4] ("Victorious Brigit loved not the world") are styled hymns in the surviving manuscripts but adhere to the exigencies of medieval Irish syllabic poetry. The former text, which is ascribed to Saint Ultán (d. 657) inter alia and which may date to the seventh century, attains a particularly high level of stylistic artistry in the verses calling on Brigit's protection; being described by one of its

---

[1] Bernard and Atkinson (eds. and trans.), *The Irish Liber Hymnorum*, 1898: vol. 1, 162–183 (trans. vol. 2, 53–80); Stokes, "The Bodleian Amra Choluimb Chille," 1899; Clancy and Markús, *Iona*, 1995: 96–128; and Henry (ed.), *Amra Choluim Chille*, 2006. Cf. Ó Riain, *A Dictionary*, 2011: 213. More recently, Bisagni, *Amrae Coluimb Chille*, 2019, has argued for a later date for the poem.
[2] Bernard and Atkinson (eds. and trans.), *The Irish Liber Hymnorum*, 1898: vol. 1, 96–104 (trans. vol. 2, 31–35); and Stokes and Strachan (eds.), *Thesaurus palaeohibernicus*, 1903: vol. 2, 307–321. Cf. Ó Riain, *A Dictionary*, 2011: 529.
[3] Bernard and Atkinson (eds. and trans.), *The Irish Liber Hymnorum*, 1898: vol. 1, 107–111 (trans. vol. 2, 37–39); and Stokes and Strachan (eds.), *Thesaurus palaeohibernicus*, 1903: vol. 2, 323–326.
[4] Bernard and Atkinson (eds. and trans.), *The Irish Liber Hymnorum*, 1898: vol. 1, 112–128 (trans. vol. 2, 40–46); and Stokes and Strachan (eds.), *Thesaurus palaeohibernicus*, 1903: vol. 2, 327–349.

editors as "the only one of the Irish hymns which shows high poetic art."[5] The latter composition, *Ní car Brigit búadach bith* ("Victorious Brigit loved not the world"), which is ascribed to Saint Brocán, is a versified enumeration of Brigit's miracles with a close relationship to the earliest Latin hagiographical tradition.

These texts in honor of Brigit highlight the persistent challenge of relating fluid medieval nomenclature to the terminology of modern literary criticism. The aforementioned compositions are generally referred to as hymns primarily because later scribes who added rubrics, glosses, and prefaces categorized them in that fashion; however, there is no musical notation in the manuscripts nor any other indication of melody or liturgical context. Judging the texts on form, it is clear that they are versified, with end rhyme, syllable count, alliteration, and other ornamentation; but as was alluded to above, that does not always classify such works as poetry. To call a text poetry is after all an aesthetic evaluation and not necessarily a description of form. This challenge of categorization is amplified in religious texts where medieval sacred language, as in many cultures, employs rhetorical figures that are typical of oral style, such as parallelism and antithesis, rhythmic clausulae, rhyme, and alliteration. In some cases, such texts may be elevated to the category of poetry, in others they might be best described as stylized prose. The modern preconceptions inherent in the term genre should be avoided; form and function were often of greater concern to the medieval audience. It is worth bearing in mind that the primary function of these works was not aesthetic appeal but to obtain the intercession of these saintly figures. As a result, one must think creatively and latterly about both genre and the related question of form when searching for the traces of a saint's cult across texts that are both formally and linguistically diverse. Such an approach is particularly necessary the further one ventures from the center of any such cult, where disparate fragments may be the only evidence that remains; particularly in the case of female saints. Therefore, within this context of versified hagiography and poems in praise of saints, it is perhaps less surprising that the scant references to Thecla in medieval Irish sources are principally poetic in nature.

Versified Martyrology

The earliest Irish allusion to Thecla's story survives in a ninth-century verse composition entitled *Félire Óengusso* (*The Calendar/Martyrology of Oengus*). Despite the nomenclature, this work is not a typical martyrology; rather, the

---

[5] Stokes and Strachan (eds.), *Thesaurus palaeohibernicus*, 1903: vol. 2, xxxviii.

author has used the theme of saints' feast days to structure his poem. In addition to being employed as a work of reference on the saints and their feast days, *Félire Óengusso*, as is made quite clear in the epilogue to the martyrology, is to be recited in its entirety[6] and is intended for private devotion and not liturgical celebration.[7] Therefore, the days of the year supply a structure and order to the list of saints, but they do not define the function of the work. *Félire Óengusso* consists of a prologue of 85 stanzas, a core-poem of 365 stanzas (one for each day of the year), and an epilogue of 141 stanzas. The numerous glosses and scholia, which were added to the text with the passage of time, as well as the multiple extant manuscripts bear witness to the wide dissemination of the martyrology. Each stanza within the text contains four lines, written in a strict meter of six syllables per line. The limitations imposed by the meter and the difficulty of finding multiple ways of expressing the fact that on a certain day a certain saint is celebrated result in a repetitive style in the main body of the text. However, the prologue and epilogue (or second prologue, as it is entitled in the manuscripts) display greater poetic artistry. As part of the prologue, Oengus (d. 824) enumerates the terrible trials that the martyrs have endured for their faith. Their suffering is rewarded with salvation and everlasting life just as salvation and the kingdom of God are promised to those who follow their example.[8] Our author is also keenly aware that the form that he has chosen, one stanza for each day, entails the exclusion of innumerable saints and martyrs. Only the most renowned can be included:

De mílib ammórsin	That abundance of thousands,
ammuir mbrígach mbúansin,	that mighty everlasting sea:
ní tucsam dind línsin	we have only given, out of that company,
acht ríga na slúagsin.[9]	the kings of those multitudes.

At the same time, Oengus seems to regret that many had to be excluded:

Ní dermat na díchell	Whoever is not mentioned,
in cháich nád ro thuirmed,	it is not through forgetfulness or neglect,
acht cuimbrigud indsce,	but rather a shortening of speech skilfully
fo soas do chuibded.[10]	adjusted.

Given the constrained choices that the form of the work imposed, it is all the more remarkable that space is found to include Thecla in the epilogue.

---

[6] Stokes (ed. and trans.), *Félire Óengusso*, 1905: 272, epilogue ll. 165–168.
[7] Ibid.: 272–273, epilogue ll. 165–204. [8] Ibid.: 20, prologue ll. 69–72 and 77–80.
[9] Carey, *King of Mysteries*, 1998: 211. Cf. Stokes (ed. and trans.), *Félire Óengusso*, 1905: 265, ll. 29–32.
[10] Carey, *King of Mysteries*, 1998: 214. Cf. Stokes (ed. and trans.), *Félire Óengusso*, 1905: 269, ll. 121–124.

There, she is inserted in a long sequence of stanzas composed principally of references to occasions when biblical characters were saved from mortal danger through divine intervention. Thecla's salvation in the amphitheater of Antioch is recalled between stanzas referring to Isaac and Jacob:[11]

Rom-sóerae, á Íssu,	May you save me, Jesus,
lat nóebu tan tíastae,	with your saints when you come,
amail sóersai Teclam[12]	as you saved Thecla
de ginol na bíastae.[13]	from the jaws of the beast.

This litany-like sequence does not adhere slavishly to biblical chronology; the majority of the characters invoked are from the Old Testament, but at the conclusion of this enumeration, we find one Continental and two Irish saints.[14] The sole reference to the New Testament Gospels is to the apostle Peter being saved from drowning (Matt 14:22–33). An emphasis on the deeds of apostles is also evident in the two non-canonical episodes cited, both of which are associated with the apostle John. In the first, he is saved from poison[15] and, in the second, from a cauldron of burning oil.[16] There is also an allusion to the canonical account of the imprisonment of Paul and Peter (Acts 16:19–34 and 12:1–12).

The invocation of Thecla in the epilogue of the calendar is, however, not the only reference to her as a saint in *Félire Óengusso*. Her feast days are also recalled in the main body of the text; in the last line of the stanza for February 22,[17] there is a brief mention of Thecla after Saints Peter and Laurence: "with Thecla's radiant feast" (*la féil tóidlig Teclae*).[18] On

---

[11] Stokes (ed. and trans.), *Félire Óengusso*, 1905: 285, ll. 469–472. On Thecla's similar appearance in Ethiopic calendars and in verse, see Damien Labadie's contribution in this volume (Chapter 2).

[12] Note that the personal name is declined here; the majority of the manuscripts of *Félire Óengusso* supply the accusative form *Teclam* here, but one manuscript supplies *Tecla* and another *Declam*: see Stokes (ed. and trans.), *Félire Óengusso*, 1905: 285.

[13] Cf. Stokes' translation: "Mayst Thou save me, O Jesus, with Thy saints when they come, as Thou savedst Thekla from the maw of the monster:" ibid.: 285, ll. 469–472.

[14] Ibid.: 288, St. Martin ll. 547–548, St. Patrick ll. 551–552, and St. Kevin ll. 555–556.

[15] Stokes (ed. and trans.), *Félire Óengusso*, 1905: 285, ll. 479–480: *amail sóersai Ióain / de neim inna nathrach* ("as you saved John from the poison of the serpent"). Cf. Elliott (trans.), *The Apocryphal New Testament*, 1993: 'The Acts of John,' 303–349 at 343–345; and McNamara, *The Apocrypha*, 1984: 95–99.

[16] Stokes (ed. and trans.), *Félire Óengusso*, 1905: 287, ll. 539–540: *amail sóersai Ióain / assin dabaig thened* ("as you saved John from the fiery cauldron"). Cf. James (trans.), *The Apocryphal New Testament*, 1924: 265.

[17] Thecla of Iconium is also celebrated in the *Martyrologium Hieronymianum* on February 22 and November 17, as well as September 12, 23, and 24 and December 20 and 21. In this influential calendar, she is first in the entry for September 23, her principal feast day in the west: de Rossi and Duchesne (eds.), *Martyrologium Hieronymianum*, 1894: *AS* LXXXII November, part II. Cf. also Delehaye, *Commentarius perpetuus*, 1931: *AS* XXIV November 11, part II.

[18] Stokes (ed. and trans.), *Félire Óengusso*, 1905: 62.

November 17, half a stanza is devoted to her with an ambiguous reference to her "triumph/victory:"[19]

Celebair féil Teclae,	Celebrate Thecla's feast:
is íar mbúaid dorochair	after triumph she has fallen

Reference to triumph in a context such as this usually implies martyrdom, and it may indicate that there was merely fragmentary acquaintance with the details of her story in medieval Ireland. Glossators in two of the manuscripts of *Félire Óengusso*,[20] who deemed it necessary to add a short explanatory note beside her name, also seemed to be under the impression that she died a martyr (*.i. uirgo et martir*).[21] Confusion regarding the outcome of Thecla's travails, however, is not unusual in Insular sources as is demonstrated by the works of the Anglo-Saxon writer Aldhelm (639–709), Abbot of Malmesbury, an accomplished Latin scholar and stylist.[22] A third reference to Thecla in the main body of *Félire Óengusso* at June 1 exhorts devotees to "Give heed to Thecla's feast" (*Oid menmain féil Teclae*).[23] In this instance, however, it is unclear if Thecla of Iconium is intended since other medieval sources record the martyrdom of one Thecla of Antioch and her companions as a group on that day. The challenge in assessing the impact of Thecla of Iconium's cult is the profusion of Theclas in medieval martyrologies, only a few of whom are recorded in hagiographic tradition.[24] The fame of Saint Thecla spawned many other namesakes. In some cases, the alternative Theclas appear to be founded on veneration of the virgin of Iconium, which then became localized as is probably the case with the Antiochian martyr. Given the paucity of evidence for the putative Thecla of Antioch, she may well have grown out of the confusion surrounding the attempted martyrdom of the virgin of Iconium in the amphitheater of Antioch.

The complexity surrounding the distinction between the various Saint Theclas means there is no way to ascertain whether the poet of *Félire Óengusso* was even aware that the figure commemorated on June 1 may not

---

[19] Ibid.: 235. [20] Oxford, Bodleian Library, MSS Rawlinson B 505 and Laud 610.
[21] Stokes (ed. and trans.), *Félire Óengusso*, 1905: 242.
[22] See Franc, "The Cult of Saint Thecla," 2004: 45, and discussion below.
[23] Stokes (ed. and trans.), *Félire Óengusso*, 1905: 138. A Saint Thecla is also commemorated on June 1 in the ninth-century Karlsruhe Calendar: Schneiders, "The Irish Calendar in the Karlsruhe Bede," 1989: 52.
[24] The *Bibliotheca sanctorum* lists at least three further Theclas in addition to Thecla of Antioch (feast day June 1): Thecla of Adrumeto (Lat. Hadrumetum, modern Sousse, Tunisia; feast day August 30), Thecla of Aquileia (September 3), and Thecla of Rome (March 26). For the cult of Thecla in Rome see Cooper, "A Saint in Exile," 1995. References are also extant to a Thecla of Gaza, a Thecla of Alexandria, and a couple of further African Theclas, inter alia: Caraffa and Morelli (eds.), *Bibliotheca sanctorum*, 1961–1970: vol. 12, col. 174.

be one and the same as the Thecla referred to earlier in his composition. This question is further complicated by an explanatory gloss to this stanza in one of the manuscripts,[25] which underlines the confusion between Thecla of Iconium and Thecla the martyr of Antioch: "She was a virgin and crowned as a martyr" (*.i. uirgo fuit et martyrio coronata est*).[26] A further reference to Thecla in the *Félire Óengusso* glosses occurs in another manuscript[27] in a note with regard to the feast day of Saint Agnes on January 21: "Agnes, Thecla, and Mary, the mother of the Lord, are the three most excellent virgins among the virgins of the Scriptures" (*Agna et Tecla et Maria mater Domini, tres uirgines ex[c]elsisimae sunt inter uirgines Scribturae* [*sic*]). The exalted company in which Thecla is included here may initially seem unusual, but this triple association does occur in other medieval contexts where the reference is clearly to Saint Thecla of Iconium.[28] The inclusion of two, or possibly three, references to Thecla of Iconium in the main body of the *Félire*, in addition to the highly significant reference in the epilogue, point to a not insignificant cult of the virgin proto-martyr in ninth-century Ireland.[29]

As has already been underlined, the metrical form of *Félire Óengusso* restricts entries to one rhyming verse per day. Therefore, instead of the extensive lists extant in many medieval calendars, the *Félire* can only accommodate four saints per day at the most, demonstrating that Thecla was a significant figure to the poet. It would appear, however, based on the ambiguity evident in the later glosses added to the text in many manuscripts, that her cult may have waned in Ireland by the twelfth century, when the majority of the commentary was compiled.[30] It has been

---

[25] Dublin, University College Dublin Library, MS A7.
[26] Stokes (ed. and trans.), *Félire Óengusso*, 1905: 144.
[27] Oxford, Bodleian Library, MS Rawlinson B 512.
[28] Stokes (ed. and trans.), *Félire Óengusso*, 1905: 50. The association of Thecla with Agnes and the Virgin Mary is not unique to this glossator. Sulpicius Severus in his dialogues on the virtues of Saint Martin recounts how these three appeared together, on a number of occasions, to the saint in his cell. See Fontaine and Dupré (eds.), *Sulpice Sévère*, 2006: Bk 2.13.5; and *PL* 20.210. Cf. Franc, "The Cult of Saint Thecla," 2004: 44; and Vouaux (ed. and trans.), *Les Actes*, 1913: 54. Bishop Maximus of Turin (b. 380) in a fifth-century sermon on the feast of Saint Agnes also makes a connection between the manner in which both Agnes and Thecla were miraculously saved from flames, cf. *PL* 17.704. Note also that Bede in the poem on virginity discussed below refers to both Agnes and Thecla of Iconium.
[29] Other early female continental saints are also included in the *Félire*: Agatha (February 5, June 5?), Euphemia (July 11, September 17), Agnes (January 21), Cecilia (September 1, November 22), Juliana (February 16), Lucy (February 6), and Perpetua (March 7).
[30] This hypothesis is supported by the later Gorman's martyrology (1166–1174) where Thecla is commemorated only once on September 23: *Tecla oengel alimm / for oebnemh co hebhinn* ("white Tecla whom I entreat [and who dwells] delightfully in beautiful heaven"): Stokes (ed. and trans.), *Félire hUí Gormáin*, 1895: 182.

demonstrated that both *Félire Óengusso* and its sister text, the *Martyrology of Tallaght*,[31] were compiled between the years 829–833 at a monastery in Tallaght, now a suburb of Dublin.[32] Despite the fact that both texts were drawing on the same sources and were composed in the same place, the *Martyrology of Tallaght* curiously does not share any dates for Saint Thecla with *Félire Óengusso*. The former, which is in Latin, not versified, and more expansive, supplies an abundant alternative sequence of dates, with reference to a Thecla in nine separate entries.[33] The earliest surviving Irish calendar now in Karlsruhe's Badische Landesbibliothek provides a third important contemporary source of evidence. The compact ninth-century calendar, which is thought to have been compiled in Ireland and has survived alongside a collection of Bede's (d. 735) writings, commemorates Thecla on two separate dates.[34] The first of these entries on June 1 is the feast day of the shadowy Thecla of Antioch commemorated on the same date in *Félire Óengusso*, and the second entry on November 18 differs by only one day from another entry in that martyrology. The references to Thecla in *Félire Óengusso*, the *Martyrology of Tallaght*, and the Karlsruhe Calendar certainly demonstrate that a cult of the proto-martyr existed in ninth-century Ireland but do not tell us how much of her narrative was known to the communities who celebrated her feast days. The allusion to a beast in the *Félire Óengusso* epilogue, quoted above, suggests some familiarity with the events in the arena in Antioch, but it is difficult to assess the extent of that familiarity. In the absence of more substantial narrative details, literary form and context are the only common features to pursue. Thecla's association with other saintly figures may also be of assistance in tracing the lines of transmission that carried her fame from the Mediterranean to the Atlantic seaboard. In that regard, we can now turn to the second medieval Irish versified text with reference to Thecla.

Vernacular Biblical Verse Narrative

Saltair na Rann (*The Psalter of the Quatrains/Stanzas*) is a versified account of the Bible narrative from Genesis to Revelation that also includes much

---

[31] Best and Lawlor (eds.), *The Martyrology of Tallaght*, 1931.
[32] Ó Riain, "The Tallaght Martyrologies," 1990; and Ó Riain, *Feastdays of the Saints*, 2006: 97.
[33] April 11, May 10, August 11, September 1, September 12, September 23, October 18, December 20, and December 21; of these it shares the following dates with the *Martyrologium Hieronymianum* for Thecla: September 12, September 23, December 20, and December 21.
[34] Schneiders, "The Irish Calendar in the Karlsruhe Bede," 1989: 52 (June 1) and 63 (November 18). For the importance of this Calendar, see Ó Riain, "The Early Ninth-Century Karlsruhe Irish Calendar," 2021.

apocryphal material.[35] It is a remarkably long text of 162 poems, which amount to 8,393 lines in all, although the original composition is thought to have contained only 150 poems in order to mirror the structure of the Psalter. Thus, a scribal note at the end of the 150th poem states that we have come to the end of the body of the Psalter of the Quatrains (*corp saltrach na rann*). The length of individual poems within the work varies considerably. In a passage on the six ages of the world, the poet supplied a calculation of the timespan between the birth of Christ and a devastating cattle-plague (ll. 2333–2344). On the assumption that the poet was writing around the time of the plague in question, the *Saltair* is commonly assumed to have been written in the year 988 or shortly thereafter. It is a work of considerable learning, with particular emphasis on biblical history and the chronology of the world from its creation to Judgment Day. The work shares its major theme with *Félire Óengusso*, namely, that of time. The *Félire* is concerned with documenting the order in which the saints departed this life for "cloudy heaven"[36] as encapsulated in the calendar year, however, the concept behind *Saltair na Rann* is far more ambitious. The intention was to create a work that encompasses all of time, not just the past but the future as well, so that God's plan for the world is laid out clearly in a series of interconnected poems. The audience for such a work, however, is not altogether clear; there is no rubric or other indication that the work was intended for private devotion or any other liturgical function. Any text that contains meditation on Scripture is of course devotional to some degree, but the main function of the text does not appear to be spiritual reflection. The question that poses itself is why create a verse narrative on biblical history when the Bible itself tells the story? The answer must be that the author wished to create a vernacular summary of the Bible in verse.

A summary of biblical history would have had considerable didactic merit, especially one in the native language of the majority of the medieval Irish populace. The principal themes of the work and the message that all of history is a progression to a point in time when salvation or damnation will be determined seem particularly suitable for a general audience. The inexorable progression of biblical history toward its conclusion is reiterated throughout: the Old Testament is a preliminary to the New, prefiguring the coming of Christ. The New Testament, in turn, is a promise of salvation, and Judgment Day is the end of time. Such an ambitious work

---

[35] Stokes (ed.), *The Saltair na rann*, 1883.
[36] Stokes (ed. and trans.), *Félire Óengusso*, 1905: 28, prologue ll. 277–280.

must have been created by a culture with an intense interest in biblical scholarship and especially in the Old Testament since the majority of the composition is devoted to the latter. The Old Testament narrative concludes with the Historical Books at poem 134. After which comes a poem on the Lord's great deeds with some reference to the major prophets. Following this are two poems (136, 137) on the wonders of creation, with particular emphasis on the natural world, animals, and plants. The next poem, 138, is structured somewhat like a litany with a sequence in which examples of divine aid to significant figures are invoked. The majority of the episodes cited come from the Old Testament. Toward the end of the poem, however, we find the following verse (ll. 7409–7412):

Rí saer Teclai ṅdíascaig ṅdil	King who saved dear, blameless Thecla
ona bíastaib béldergaib,	from the animals with bloody mouths,
isint anfabrocht for ruth	and the paralytic, immediately,
ba hadbalbocht dind fuatluch.	who was very miserable, from the bed.[37]

In the first half of this stanza, the reference to Thecla here is presumably, as in *Félire Óengusso*, to the animals in the arena at her second trial in Antioch; the only difference with *Félire Óengusso* is that the beasts are plural here rather than singular. The plurality of animals may be referring not simply to the lioness but to the other lions, bears, sealions, etc., which figure in the episode. The latter half of this stanza seems to refer to the miracle in which Christ heals the paralytic in Saint Matthew's Gospel (Matt 9:2–7).[38] As the present author has argued elsewhere, however, citing the healing of a paralytic in the same verse as Thecla may be motivated by some acquaintance with her reputation for healing and, in particular, the miraculous cure of a paralytic child.[39] If, on the other hand, the reference here is a random invocation of an episode from the Gospels, it disturbs the biblical chronology that poem 138 follows relatively faithfully.

The dominance of Old Testament figures in poem 138 reflects the themes of *Saltair na Rann* more generally with significant emphasis on the

---

[37] Ó Dochartaigh, "Poems 138–41," 2013: 307. An alternative translation supplied by David Greene can be found at www.dias.ie/wp-content/uploads/2011/03/canto131-140.pdf: "The King saved dear blameless Thecla from the red-mouthed beasts, and (saved) the paralyzed man, who was very miserable, immediately from his couch."

[38] The poorly attested form *fúatlach* may correspond to *lectus* (couch, bed) in the Vulgate. This instance is only one of three attestations supplied by the *Dictionary of the Irish Language*, in one of which *fúatlach* glosses the Latin word *grabatus* (couch, camp-bed, pallet). See Marstrander et al. (eds.), *Dictionary of the Irish Language*, 1913–1976.

[39] Ó Dochartaigh, "A Cult of Saint Thecla," 2015: 324–326. For the account of the child's healing, see Kaestli and Rordorf (eds. and trans.), "La fin de la vie de Thècle," 2014: v.

heroic characters of the Pentateuch and the Historical Books. It is remarkable that only two Gospel episodes are cited in poem 138, that is, Peter being saved from drowning while walking on water[40] and an ambiguous reference to Mary Magdalene.[41] The remaining four New Testament incidents recalled in the poem all come from the Acts of the Apostles, both canonical and apocryphal. Remarkably, these are the only instances in the whole work of 8,392 lines in which the Acts of the Apostles figure. Equally significant is the fact that the two apostolic examples of divine intervention invoked, namely, Peter's escape from prison (Acts 12:6–11) and Paul and Silas also being liberated (Acts 16:25–27), are exactly the same as in *Félire Óengusso*.[42] The apocryphal episodes are when John is saved from poisoning and the burning cauldron of oil[43] and Thecla in the arena as cited above. As with *Félire Óengusso*, Thecla is included in an apostolic and not a hagiographic context, suggesting that the Irish compilers of these texts were drawing on sources in which she was treated as a quasi-biblical figure as well as an early saint.

The most striking feature, however, which these two medieval Irish witnesses share, is the form in which they were composed, that is, syllabic verse. Perhaps it should not surprise us, however, that Thecla appears in versified form in these Irish texts since she is associated with poetry in earlier continental Christian sources also. In particular, she figures regularly in a genre of text in praise of virginity in which the virtues of continence are elucidated and the triumph of the virgin-saints celebrated. This literary genre in praise of prominent early Christian female virgins and martyrs is usually in versified form, but examples in rhythmic prose also survive. In conjunction with analyzing Thecla's place within this textual tradition, it may be useful to present an overview of the development of the genre in both Greek and Latin sources.

Poetry in Praise of Virginity

The earliest evidence for the development of the genre of texts extolling virginity, in which Thecla will play such a prominent role, is in the

---

[40] Matt 14: 28–31. Stokes (ed.), *The Saltair na rann*, 1883: 108, ll. 7393–7396.

[41] Stokes (ed.), *The Saltair na rann*, 1883: 109, ll. 7405–7408. This unique reference to Mary Magdalene in *Saltair na Rann* "turning away from sin" could refer to the penitent woman washing Christ's feet, Lk 7: 36–50.

[42] Paul only figures twice in *Saltair na Rann*, here and in a list of the apostles at line 7585: Stokes (ed.), *The Saltair na rann*, 1883: 111.

[43] Cf. n. 26 and n. 27. Ó Dochartaigh, "Poems 138–41," 2013: 306: *Rí ro sáer Eoin bai tan / triana gnim ṅgleóir ṅgleglan, / di gae gona ind nemi glais / ocus dind olai amnais* ("King who saved John once by his pure, luminous deed, from the piercing spear of the green poison and from the cruel oil"). See Stokes (ed.), *The Saltair na rann*, 1883: 109, ll. 7401–7404.

writings of the church father, Bishop Methodius of Olympus in Lycia (southern Turkey today), who is believed to have been martyred in the last great persecution of Christians in 311. Methodius evidently received a high standard of Classical education, and his writings are framed in the Hellenistic philosophical tradition. Plato's works exercised a particular influence on his thought, and, in Methodius' surviving texts, Christianity is envisaged as the logical completion of the Platonic ideal. Although Methodius is known to have written many philosophical and theological tracts in Greek, most have only survived in fragmentary form or in Slavonic sources. The only work of his which has survived intact in its original Greek is a long tract on virginity entitled the "Symposium, or on Virginity" (*Symposion he peri hagneias*).[44] The title *Symposium* is a conscious reference to Plato's work on which the elegant and rhythmic style is modeled. In this case, the *Symposium* or "Banquet" is a festive meal shared by ten illustrious virgins in the garden of Arete (virtue). Each virgin in turn proclaims a discourse beginning with a quotation from the Bible before going on to extol Christian virginity. In this declamatory form, the virgins reject Eros and praise Parthenia as the perfect ideal of Christian chastity and in the process introduce many fundamentals of Christian doctrine. At the end of the work, there is an eleventh discourse by Arete herself where the philosophical tone alters and the dialogue comes to a close with a hymn of praise to Christ the bridegroom. Not alone does Thecla proclaim the eighth discourse, but, at the close, she is chosen by Arete to lead the virgins in song because "she has been your leader and has shone more magnificently than the rest."[45] Thecla then leads the others in singing a marriage hymn to Christ in twenty-four poetic strophes with a refrain chanted by the virginal chorus.[46] In the fourth strophe, Thecla declares how she has escaped from the wiles of the devil and has "braved fire and flame and the ravenous assaults of wild beasts."[47] Methodius, in assigning this hymn to Thecla, is placing her at the head of the choir of virgins singing couplets in praise of chastity. Léon

---

[44] Musurillo and Debidour (eds.), *Méthode d'Olympe*, 1963: Discourse 8, 200–261 and 310–321; Musurillo (trans.), *St. Methodius*, 1958: Logos 8, 104–130 and 151–157; and *PG* 18.27–220, at 140. The work is also sometimes referred to under its Latin title *Symposion seu convivium virginum*. On this work, see also Virginia Burrus' contribution (Chapter 8) in the present volume.
[45] Musurillo (trans), *St. Methodius*, 1958: 151. Cf. Musurillo and Debidour (eds.), *Méthode d'Olympe*, 1963: 309.
[46] In commenting on the text, Musurillo (trans.), *St. Methodius*, 1958: 236, noted that "in form the hymn is an acrostic of twenty-four stanzas with a refrain in the manner of the ancient *cantus responsorius* of the Western Church, in which the solo voice of the precentor sings the stanzas or strophes, with the rest of the congregation repeating a regular response or refrain."
[47] Musurillo (trans.), *St. Methodius*, 1958: 152. Cf. Musurillo and Debidour (eds.), *Méthode d'Olympe*, 1963: 313; and Roberts and Donaldson (eds.), *The Ante-Nicene Fathers*, 1868–1872: vol. 6, Discourse 11, chs. 1 and 2.

Vouaux, writing at the beginning of the twentieth century, suggested that the status that Methodius afforded Thecla is evidence that as early as the late third or early fourth century, the story of Thecla had detached itself from the apocryphal narrative and was developing an independent status.[48] In this context, it appears that poetry in praise of virginity may have been a significant vehicle for the transmission of her fame.

The genre that Methodius promulgated was picked up by another Christian writer of great talent with a thorough appreciation of the Hellenistic tradition, namely, Bishop Gregory of Nazianzus (d. 390) in ancient Cappadocia (central Turkey today). Gregory is undoubtedly most famous as Archbishop of Constantinople, close friend of Saint Basil (330–379), and defender of Catholic orthodoxy against the Arian heresy. In contrast to Methodius, a great number of Gregory's writings have survived, including his influential theological tracts and eloquent orations. Gregory was also an accomplished poet and, according to his admiring student Jerome (d. 420), supposedly composed many thousands of verses.[49] His classical training and cultured intellect are evident in the polished and delicate style of his poetry. Among the works that survive is a tract, sometimes styled a hymn, in praise of virginity that opens with an exhortation to virgins to glorify Christ their bridegroom.[50] It is not only the concept behind this encomium, thought to have been written around 363, which is indebted to Methodius, but also certain lines in the work echo the earlier composition. While praising the many virtues of chastity, Gregory urges virgins to follow the example of Thecla who voluntarily accepted her torments but was saved from both flame and beasts. In later writings, he returns to the exemplary status of Thecla in urging all virgins to follow her whom God protected from fire and the fury of the beasts.[51]

In Western Christendom, another staunch defender of orthodoxy against Arianism, Ambrose of Milan (d. 397), also cited the example given by Thecla in a number of works.[52] His most detailed treatment of Thecla as a paradigm of chastity is, however, in a work entitled *De virginibus*

---

[48] Vouaux (ed. and trans.), *Les Actes*, 1913: 34.
[49] Jerome, *De viris illustribus* 117. Cf. Tuilier and Bady (eds.), *Saint Grégoire de Nazianze*, 2004.
[50] Gregory of Nazianzus, *Poemata Moralia* Sectio II: *PG* 37.593.
[51] Gregory of Nazianzus, *Contra Julianum* 1, Oratio IV (LXIX): *PG* 35.589. Gregory may have developed his interest in Thecla during the time he spent in contemplation at the center of her cult in Seleucia.
[52] Ambrose of Milan, *Ad Simplicianum* ep. xxxvii, 36: Faller and Zelzer (eds.), *Ambrosius*, 1968–1996 (at 1968): vol. 1, 61; and *PL* 16.1139. Ambrose of Milan, *Ad Vercellensem ecclesiam* ep. lxiii, 34: Faller and Zelzer (eds.), *Ambrosius*, 1968–1996 (at 1982): vol. 3, 253 and *PL* 16.1250. In the former epistle, Thecla is once again associated with Agnes.

(*Concerning Virgins*) written around the year 377.⁵³ This long treatise written in rhetorical, rhythmic style is organized in three books and is dedicated to his sister Marcellina who also had chosen the religious life. The influence of Ambrose's Hellenistic education is evident in the polished classical Latin and the textual allusions to earlier works. At the beginning of the first book, the child martyr Agnes is held up as a model of virginity who displayed exemplary courage and fortitude despite the terrors she faced. Further on in the treatise in the second book, a section is devoted to the example of the Virgin Mary and Saint Thecla:

> Let, then, holy Mary instruct you in the discipline of life, and Thecla teach you how to be offered, for she, avoiding nuptial intercourse, and condemned through her husband's rage, changed even the disposition of wild beasts by their reverence for virginity. For being made ready for the wild beasts, when avoiding the gaze of men, she offered her vital parts to a fierce lion, and caused those who had turned away their immodest looks to turn them back modestly. The beast was to be seen lying on the ground, licking her feet, showing without a sound that it could not injure the sacred body of the virgin. So the beast reverenced his prey, and forgetful of his own nature, put on that nature which men had lost.⁵⁴

It has been asserted that the emphasis on Thecla in Ambrose's writings is evidence that a Latin version of the *Acts of Paul and Thecla* must have been circulating in fourth-century Northern Italy.⁵⁵ Although it is possible that a Latin version of Thecla's narrative was available by then, Ambrose, unusually for a Western bishop, had good Greek and his acquaintance with Greek texts is undoubtedly the inspiration for his treatise on virginity. Ambrose was also an admirer of the writings of Saint Basil and other Eastern Christian thinkers from whom his interest in Thecla may have sprung. Crucially, Thecla also appears to have been particularly venerated in late antique Milan, the seat of Ambrose's episcopacy, since the basilica in the city was dedicated to her in the fifth century.⁵⁶

Saint Ambrose as well as being a formidable theologian is also famed for composing hymns, and he is often credited with bringing the Eastern

---

⁵³ de Romestin (trans.), *St. Ambrose*, 1896: 843–905; and *PL* 16.198–244. Also often referred to by the longer title *De virginibus ad Marcellinam sororem suam*; not to be confused with his later treatise *De virginitate* which may be a response to criticism of the earlier work.

⁵⁴ Ergo sancta Maria disciplinam vitae informet, Thecla doccat immolari: quae copulam fugiens nuptialem, et sponsi furore damnata, naturam etiam bestiarum virginitatis veneratione mutavit. Namque parata ad feras, cum aspectus quoque declinaret virorum, ac vitalia ipsa sævo offerret leoni, fecit ut qui impudicos detulerant oculos; pudicos referrent: de Romestin (trans.), *St. Ambrose*, 1896: 878; and *PL* 16.223, Bk 2, ch. 3, § 19–20.

⁵⁵ Rordorf, "Sainte Thècle," 1984: 77.   ⁵⁶ Ibid.: 78.

innovation of hymn singing to the West.⁵⁷ The influence and status of his writings served to disseminate the genre of panegyrics on virginity throughout Western Christendom and inspired others such as Augustine (354–430) to write on the same subject.⁵⁸ Evidence of this influence is even felt in Anglo-Saxon England, particularly in the writings of Aldhelm, already mentioned above. The classical education that Aldhelm received at Canterbury made him a pioneer of Latin verse and metrics in medieval England. One of his most famous works is a tract composed in two versions entitled *De virginitate* (*Concerning Virginity*) whose title and theme deliberately echo Ambrose's work.⁵⁹ Aldhelm wrote an initial prose version around the year 705 for the community of nuns of Barking and their Abbess Hildelith (fl. eighth century). The reaction of the convent residents to the erudite content and the elaborate style was so positive that he composed a second poetic version of the text in Latin hexameters. As with his patristic models, Aldhelm employs allegory to create elaborate imagery portraying chastity as one of the highest of Christian virtues. Some doubt has been expressed, however, with regard to the extent of his knowledge of Thecla's story: for example, in the prose version, no mention is made of her death, but, in the poetic account, Thecla is martyred in the arena.⁶⁰

Aldhelm's near contemporary and that other great scholar of Anglo-Saxon England, Bede, was also inspired by the theme of virginity. As part of his monumental and celebrated work on the history of Christianity in England, *Historia ecclesiastica*, he included a poem in praise of virgins. The poem is inspired by Aethelthryth (636–679), Abbess of Ely, who had managed to maintain a vow of perpetual chastity despite being married twice. In praising Aethelthryth's continence, Bede recalls the example of prominent virgin saints and martyrs of the early Church. He opens his sequence with verses in praise of the Virgin Mary and then proceeds to list six illustrious virgins according to the form of their martyrdom or persecution: Agatha and Eulalia, who were scorched by flames, and Agnes and Cecilia, who laughed at swords. In the midst of this illustrious company is

---

⁵⁷ Cf. Fontaine and Charlet (eds.), *Ambroise de Milan*, 1992.
⁵⁸ Augustine, *De sancta virginitate*, where Thecla is again lauded as an example to all virgins. See Walsh (ed. and trans.), *Augustine*, 2001: 130–131; and *PL* 40.422. For a comprehensive list of references to Thecla in patristic writing, see Vouaux (ed. and trans.), *Les Actes*, 1913.
⁵⁹ Ehwald (ed.), *Aldhelmi opera*, 1919: 226–323; Lapidge and Herren (trans.), *Aldhelm*, 1979: 113 (§ xlvi); and Gwara (ed.), *Aldhelmi Malmesbiriensis Prosa*, 2001: vol. 2, 312, l. 61.
⁶⁰ Franc, "The Cult of Saint Thecla," 2004: 45.

a verse in praise of Thecla and Euphemia who overcame wild beasts: "The lofty soul of chaste Thecla overcomes the wild beasts, chaste holy Euphemia overcomes the wild beasts."[61]

The Anglo-Saxon and Patristic evidence combined demonstrate that citing Thecla in a poetic context is not unusual and, furthermore, that such versified evocations of the proto-martyr may have played a significant role in disseminating her fame. Returning to the Irish material, however, in addition to a common metrical form, the other striking similarity between the verses in *Saltair na Rann* and *Félire Óengusso* is the formula in which they are framed. The extracts from the Irish texts examined above are structured in prayer-like litanies in which the supplicant asks to be saved in the manner in which biblical and saintly figures, including Thecla, were saved. This ancient devotional motif, often referred to by the Latin title *Libera . . . sicut liberasti* ("Save/free . . . as you saved/freed") or a similar wording, was later integrated into the *Commendatio animae*, the Roman Catholic rite for the "commendation of the soul" at the moment of death.

Rites for the Dying

The history and development of the *Commendatio animae* as a set text is complex and imperfectly understood. It is not until the period of the Catholic Counterreformation that the details of the rite are proscribed definitively. At that point, when the *Libera* exhortations are allotted their final place in the body of the *Commendatio animae*, Thecla is included in the sequence.[62] Therefore, for almost four centuries, all Roman Catholics globally heard Thecla's name pronounced as death approached and the last rites were administered. In the wake of the second Vatican Council in the 1960s, however, a series of liturgical reforms replaced the sacrament of Extreme Unction with the less elaborate Anointing of the Sick. Thus, the *Commendatio animae*, including the invocation of Thecla's heroism, was superseded, and she lost her place in the liturgy. The impetus for her original inclusion in the *Commendatio animae* is also difficult to account for because reference to Saint Thecla is otherwise quite rare in the history

---

[61] Casta feras superat mentis pro culmine Tecla, / Euphemia sacra casta feras superat. Colgrave and Mynors (eds. and trans.), *Bede*, 1969: Bk 4, ch. 20. Cf. Quentin, *Les martyrologes historiques*, 1969: 93; and *PL* 94.1052. Thecla is also included in Bede's martyrology under September 23, her traditional feast day in the Western Church.

[62] Schönfelder (ed.), *Liturgische Bibliothek*, 1904: vol. 1, 38–41; and Hennig, "Quelques notes," 1964: 21–27.

of the *Libera* prayer up to that point.[63] It is evidently a testament to the strength of her cult in the sixteenth century that her name was included in the fundamental rite for the dying. There may be a further explanation for her inclusion in a mortuary rite that demonstrates that the choice may not be as arbitrary as it initially appears. Jacques le Goff in his seminal work on the birth of Purgatory underlines the importance of a passage in the *Acts of Paul and Thecla* in which prayers are said for a young girl who has died.[64] The queen Tryphaena asks Thecla to pray for her dead daughter Falconilla who appeared to her in a dream and spoke to her: "Mother, thou shalt have in my place the stranger, the desolate Thecla, that she may pray for me and I be translated to the place of the just."[65] Thecla then, at the request of Tryphaena, prays for the eternal salvation of Falconilla's soul in the following manner: "Thou God of heaven, Son of the Most High, grant to her according to her wish, that her daughter Falconilla may live forever."[66] This short episode is crucial in attributing to Saint Thecla the power to intercede on behalf of the dead and to ensure that their souls are "translated to the place of the just." Thecla's proven efficacy in such intercessions would make her a powerful advocate in the eyes of the faithful at the moment of death and of the commendation of the soul.

This being the case, however, one would expect more premodern evidence of her inclusion in funeral rites or rites for the dying, but the only extant medieval evidence, known to the present author, of Thecla invoked in a funerary rite is the Rheinau Sacramentary.[67] The place of compilation of the Rheinau sacramentary is uncertain. A number of Frankish saints are named in the martyrology, including two references to saints from Nivelles, which is located in present-day Belgium. This led earlier scholars to suggest a Belgian provenance for the work. Modern researchers, however, tend to take the view that this simply points to northern influence in the text and that it was most probably compiled in Switzerland. The editors of the sacramentary laid particular emphasis on the Irish elements in the text and on Irish influence in the area of Lake

---

[63] Only three references to Thecla survive in the *Libera me* formula in the pre-modern period. In addition to the Rheinau Sacramentary and the *Oratio Cypriani* discussed here, an eleventh-century manuscript also contains a prayer invoking her in this manner: Magistretti (ed.), *Manuale Ambrosianum*, 1904–1905: vol. 1, 83–93. It is also worth remarking that in the fourth-century composition by Gregory of Nazianzus cited above (*Poemata Moralia*, Sectio II), Thecla's miraculous liberation is associated closely with that of Jonah from the whale and Susannah from false accusations; paradigms of salvation which are evoked often in the *Libera me* texts.
[64] le Goff, *Un autre Moyen Âge*, 1999: 835.
[65] Schneemelcher (ed.), *New Testament Apocrypha*, 1992: 244.
[66] Ibid. On the *Commendatio animae*, see also Klazina Staat's contribution in this volume (Chapter 9).
[67] Hänggi and Schönherr (eds.), *Sacramentarium Rhenaugiense*, 1970.

Constance in the early medieval period. The strongest Irish influence is discernible in the Sacramentary's calendar, which appears to have a local Irish-influenced abbreviated martyrology at its core.[68] The editors also believed that the manuscript was compiled within the sphere of the St. Gallen and Reichenau *scriptoria*, two monasteries with Irish connections.[69] They argued that of these two centers, Reichenau is the most likely home of the Sacramentary, which must have been subsequently transferred to Rheinau soon after that monastery was founded in the ninth century.

Significantly for this study, in the Rheinau Sacramentary, Thecla is included in a sequence of names all framed in the *Libera . . . sicut liberasti* liturgical formula. The Rheinau manuscript[70] is part of a collection of eighth-century sacramentaries in which an important development in the final rites has been noted.[71] The rites for the sick, which in earlier sacramentaries or missals were found among prayers for clerical visits, are now placed before the last rites in order to create a continuous sequence from illness and death to burial.[72] This development shifts the emphasis in the rites for the sick from healing and physical health to a purification of the soul and a penitential preparation for death.[73] The most significant innovation and the defining characteristic of these rituals, however, is the development of a separation rite. This new rite takes the form of a communal aid to the dying in the struggle to free the immortal soul from the mortal body. The rite is focused on a series of prayers that would later develop to become the *Commendatio animae*. Within this newly adopted ritual, a series of "Save me" (*Libera . . . sicut liberasti*) invocations is included, prefaced by another prayer. Therefore, the text is often referred to by the opening word *Proficiscere* ("Depart"):

> Depart Christian soul from this world in the name of God the almighty Father, who created you. Lord, free the soul of this your servant, as you freed Peter and Paul from prison. Free the soul of this your servant, as you saved Thecla from the three torments; thus may you deign to free the soul of this man and grant that it may reside with you in the heavenly good.[74]

---

[68] Ibid.: 49.
[69] Ibid.: 58. Cf. also Moreton, *The Eighth-Century Gelasian Sacramentary*, 1976: 186.
[70] Zürich, Zentralbibliothek, MS Rh. 30 (dated 795–800); and Gamber, *Codices liturgici Latini antiquiores*, 1968: 802.
[71] Moreton, *The Eighth-Century Gelasian Sacramentary*, 1976. Cf. Bourque, *Étude*, 1949–1958. In some works, the eighth-century Gelasian sacramentaries are also referred to by the terms *Gelasiana mixta* or *Junggelasiana*.
[72] The liturgical reforms of the 1960s and 1970s were thus a reversal of this development.
[73] Paxton, *Christianizing Death*, 1990: 109.
[74] Proficiscere anima christiana de hoc mundo in nomine dei patris omnipotentis, qui te creauit .... Libera domine animam serui tui illius, sicut liberasti petrum et paulum de carceribus. Libera animam serui tui illius, sicut liberasti theglam de tribus tormentis, sic liberare digneris animam

As in the case of both *Saltair na Rann* and *Félire Óengusso*, Thecla is closely associated here with Saints Peter and Paul's imprisonment, although her own torments are not specified. These three individuals are the only non–Old Testament figures invoked in the Rheinau ritual and come toward the end of a long list of patriarchs and prophets. The Gellone Sacramentary,[75] which is very closely related to the Rheinau text, finishes a similar group of invocations with Peter and Paul but does not include Thecla. Therefore, demonstrating that her place in this prayer-formula has not yet solidified at this early stage in the development of the *Libera* text.

Rhythmic Prayers and Devotional Litanies

At much the same period as the Rheinau Sacramentary was being compiled, two very long Latin devotional texts or prayers, with no connection to funerary rites but including a sequence similar to that of the "Save me ... as you saved" formula, were in circulation. Both of these curious texts are ascribed to a Saint Cyprian of Antioch, who, according to the legendary accounts that survive, was a magician who converted to Christianity, but the details of his life are quite fanciful. Therefore, there is reason to believe that he is an invention based on the model of the more famous Saint Cyprian of Carthage (d. 258).[76] Moreover, the two stylized prayers that are ascribed to him, the *Orationes Cypriani*, contain marked exorcism overtones.[77] The earliest manuscripts, in which the Latin text of the *Orationes Cypriani* survives, date from the eighth century.[78] However, the first editor of the prayers demonstrated that these manuscripts derive from a common archetype of the seventh century or earlier.[79] In addition, he pointed to certain linguistic and stylistic features of the texts that indicate a Gallican origin.[80] Having considered these factors in conjunction, he concluded that the Latin version of the poems was written in the early fifth century in Southern Gaul. He then suggested that the author

---

hominis istius et tecum habitare in bonis caelestibus concede: Hänggi and Schönherr (eds.), *Sacramentarium Rhenaugiense*, 1970: 272.

[75] Paris, Bibliothèque nationale de France, MS Latinus 12048 (dated 790–800).

[76] Cabrol and Leclercq (eds.), *Dictionnaire*, 1907–1953: s.v. "*Oratio Cypriani*," cols 2326–2327; and von Hartel (ed.), *S. Thasci Caecili Cypriani*, 1868.

[77] Cabrol and Leclercq (eds.), *Dictionnaire*, 1907–1953: s.v. "*Oratio Cypriani*," col. 2331; Cf. also Ntedika, *L'évocation*, 1971: 76. For exorcism rituals in Christian liturgy and tradition, see Chave-Mahir, "Medieval Exorcism," 2016; and Twelftree, *In the Name of Jesus*, 2007.

[78] Cabrol and Leclercq (eds.), *Dictionnaire*, 1907–1953: s.v. "Défunts," cols 430–440; Lundberg, *La typologie baptismale*, 1942: 59–60; and Ntedika, *L'évocation*, 1971: 76.

[79] von Harnack, *Drei wenig beachtete*, 1899: 30.   [80] Ibid.: 29.

may have been the Gallican Cyprian who composed a poetic version of the Heptateuch.[81] After this Cyprian's death, his prayers may have been attributed to the legendary magician from Antioch on the basis of confusion between the names. It cannot be proved definitively that it was the Gallican Cyprian who compiled the *Orationes Cypriani*, however, since very little is known of his life. It is, at any rate, widely accepted that the prayers, in their Latin form, were written in fifth-century Gaul.[82] Whoever the compiler was, it is presumed that he was modeling his Latin prayers on a Greek text of the *Orationes Cypriani* since several earlier Greek versions are extant.[83] The Greek archetype is believed to date from about the year 300[84] and was probably composed in Eastern Mediterranean Christian circles from whence it was widely disseminated; late medieval versions of the prayers exist in Arabic, Ethiopic, and Syriac.[85]

Toward the end of the first of the Latin prayers ascribed to Cyprian, we find the following exhortation:

> Help us, as (you helped) the apostles in chains, Thecla in the flames, Paul in persecutions, Peter in the waves. You who sit over the seven thrones at the right hand of the Father, look upon us and free us from the destruction of eternal death.[86]

Thecla is once more referred to here in close association with the imprisonment of the apostles, with Paul, and with Peter walking on water. The second Pseudo-Cyprian prayer also includes a short invocation of Thecla: "Save me from the midst of this age, as you saved Thecla from the midst of the amphitheatre" (Liberes me de medio saeculi huius, sicut liberasti Teclam de medio amphitheatre).[87] Moreover, in the second prayer, notwithstanding the long list of names invoked, she is the only New Testament–era figure included in the list of "Save me" invocations, underlining the special status she is afforded in these texts. The *Orationes*

---

[81] Ibid.: 23.
[82] Ntedika, *L'évocation*, 1971: 76; Salmon et al. (eds.), *Testimonia orationis christianae antiquioris*, 1977: xvi–xvii. But see Martimort, "L'ordo commendationis animae," 1948: 150 n. 8, who proposes a fourth-century date for the Latin texts.
[83] Cf. Schermann, "Die griechischen Kyprianosgebete," 1903.   [84] Ntedika, *L'évocation*, 1971: 76.
[85] Cabrol and Leclercq (eds.), *Dictionnaire*, 1907–1953: s.v. "Oratio Cypriani," cols 2331–2332; and Basset, *Les prières*, 1896.
[86] Assiste nobis, sicut apostolis in vinculis, Theclae in ignibus, Paulo in persecutionibus, Petro in fluctibus. Qui sedes super septem thronos ad dexteram Patris, respice nos et libera nos de aeternae mortis interitu: Cabrol and Leclercq (eds.), *Dictionnaire*, 1907–1953: s.v. "Oratio Cypriani," col. 2332; and von Hartel (ed.), *S. Thasci Caecili Cypriani*, 1868: 145.
[87] Cabrol and Leclercq (eds.), *Dictionnaire*, 1907–1953: s.v "Oratio Cypriani," cols 2332–2334; and von Hartel (ed.), *S. Thasci Caecili Cypriani*, 1868: 146–148; and *PL* 101.567–569.

Cypriani are the most widely disseminated of any early medieval text that employs the *Libera* formula, and they represent a significant development in the history of this devotional motif. No other prayer containing this formula is found in so many languages and in so many medieval manuscripts and, wherever the *Orationes Cypriani* were copied or translated, Thecla traveled with them.

In medieval Western Europe, the second prayer with the reference to Thecla in the amphitheater proved to be more popular than the first and was particularly widespread in Carolingian collections of prayers known commonly as *Libelli precum* ("Booklets of Prayers").[88] One of the most influential Insular examples of this type of prayer book is Pseudo-Alcuin's compilation of services for feast days (*Officia per ferias*).[89] There is also evidence that Aldhelm was influenced by the works of the Gallican Cyprian.[90] Moreover, there is a poem in the margin of the *Martyrology of Tallaght* that refers to the feast day of Saint Cyprian,[91] and a Cyprian is commemorated in the main body of the martyrology on April 15, but it does not specify which Cyprian is intended.[92] The reference in the marginal poem indicates a devotion to a Saint Cyprian in early ninth-century Tallaght, but it does not follow that either of the *Orationes Cypriani* were known in medieval Ireland. Nevertheless, the close similarity of the "Save me" formulae employed in *Félire Óengusso*, *Saltair na Rann*, the Rheinau Sacramentary, and the *Orationes Cypriani*, in conjunction with the coincidence of apostolic figures and episodes grouped together, point to a prayer similar to the Latin examples cited above as the source underlying the Irish texts.

There is, however, a third text, ascribed to Saint Cyprian of Antioch, associated both geographically and chronologically with the aforementioned two prayers and which is probably also the work of the Gaulish Cyprian. The *Caena Cypriani* ("Cyprian's Supper/Dinner") is often preserved in medieval manuscripts alongside the two *Orationes Cypriani* and is particularly closely connected with the second prayer. It is a long and eclectic Latin poem, best described as a litany crossed with a list of banquet

---

[88] Salmon et al. (eds.), *Testimonia orationis christianae antiquioris*, 1977: xvii n. 8.
[89] *PL* 101.567–569.
[90] Cf. Ehwald (ed.), *Aldhelmi opera*, 1919: 544; and Franc, "The Cult of Saint Thecla," 2004: 44.
[91] Best and Lawlor (eds.), *The Martyrology of Tallaght*, 1931: x.
[92] Saint Cyprians are commemorated in two other places in the martyrology, April 12 and September 14, but in these cases, it is clear that they are not Saint Cyprian of Antioch.

invitees, structured around an extensive versified enumeration of biblical figures coupled with scriptural allusions. Both its title and prandial setting recall Methodius' *Symposium*, except that instead of an arcane philosophical discussion of chastity amongst the dinner guests, we are presented with exhaustive lists of those attending the feast accompanied by peculiar descriptions of the dishes served. Scattered throughout the curious enumeration of names and allusions to biblical episodes are no less than eleven references to Thecla, each of which refers to a different episode from the account of her life. The events referred to are not simply the standard images of the arena or the attempt to burn her alive, although these are included, but there is also reference inter alia to her listening to Paul at the window, Tryphanea crying, and Onesiphorus waiting attentively for Paul.[93] Moreover, there are also four allusions to episodes in the ancient *Acts of Paul* that are not connected with Thecla and that do not make their way into the later medieval Western narratives about her. Therefore, the author of the *Caena* knew many details from the Apocryphal Acts that makes this eccentric text a unique witness for the existence of some version of the *Acts of Paul and Thecla* in fifth-century Western Europe. In addition, this long versified creation makes no reference to any other episode or figure from the Acts of the Apostles, whether apocryphal or otherwise, and, as has been highlighted by a number of scholars, the poet seems to treat the *Acts of Paul* as canonical.[94]

Leaving aside the extent of familiarity with the *Acts of Paul and Thecla* in Western Europe,[95] the evidence assembled here demonstrates the multifarious sources in which elements of Thecla's story were disseminated. It also highlights the significance and evidential value of less obviously hagiographic or apocryphal texts as precious indications of the strength of the influence of her narrative. Sometimes, devotional texts, poems, prayers, hymns, and versified litanies supply valuable attestations to her popularity when other evidence is lacking. As for the Irish references to Thecla in *Félire Óengusso* and *Saltair na Rann* they testify, at the very least, to a far North-Western echo of the association of Thecla with verse.

---

[93] Vouaux (ed. and trans.), *Les Actes*, 1913: 51–52.
[94] Rordorf, "Sainte Thècle," 1984: 78; von Harnack, *Drei wenig beachtete*, 1899: 18; and Vouaux (ed. and trans.), *Les Actes*, 1913: 51–52. von Harnack, *Drei wenig beachtete*, 1899: 33, who edited the *Orationes Cypriani*, also argued that the influence of the apocryphal *Acts of Paul* is discernable in the prayers.
[95] For the possible circulation of elements of the *Acts* in medieval Ireland, see McNamara, *The Apocrypha*, 1984: 113 § 92; and Ó Dochartaigh, "A Cult of Saint Thecla," 2015.

Bibliography

Basset, René. *Les prières de S. Cyprien et de Théophile*. Les Apocryphes éthiopiens 6. Paris: Librairie de l'art indépendant, 1896.
Bernard, John Henry, and Robert Atkinson, eds. and trans. *The Irish Liber Hymnorum*. 2 vols. Henry Bradshaw Society 13–14. London: Henry Bradshaw Society, 1898.
Best, Richard I., and Hugh J. Lawlor, eds. *The Martyrology of Tallaght from the Book of Leinster and MS 5100-4 in the Royal Library, Brussels*. Henry Bradshaw Society 68. London: Harrison, 1931.
Bisagni, Jacopo, ed. and trans. *Amrae Coluimb Chille: A Critical Edition*. Dublin: Dublin Institute for Advanced Studies, 2019.
Bourque, Emmanuel. *Étude sur les sacramentaires romains*. 3 vols. Laval; Vatican City: Tipografia poliglotta vaticana, 1949–1958.
Cabrol, Fernand, and Henri Leclercq, eds. *Dictionnaire d'archéologie chrétienne et de liturgie*. Paris: Letouzey et Ané, 1907–1953.
Caraffa, Filippo, and Giuseppe Morelli, eds. *Bibliotheca sanctorum*. 12 vols. Rome: Istituto Giovanni XXIII nella Pontificia Università Lateranense, 1961–1970. Reprint, 1998.
Carey, John. *King of Mysteries: Early Irish Religious Writings*. Dublin: Four Courts Press, 1998.
Chave-Mahir, Florence. "Medieval Exorcism: Liturgical and Hagiographical Sources." In *Understanding Medieval Liturgy: Essays in Interpretation*, edited by Helen Gittos and Sarah Hamilton. Burlington: Ashgate, 2016: 159–175.
Clancy, Thomas Owen, and Gilbert Márkus, eds. *Iona: The Earliest Poetry of a Celtic Monastery*. Edinburgh: Edinburgh University Press, 1995.
Colgrave, Bertram, and R. A. B. Mynors, eds. and trans. *Bede: Historia ecclesiastica gentis Anglorum*. Oxford Medieval Texts. Oxford: Clarendon Press, 1969.
Cooper, Kate. "A Saint in Exile: The Early Medieval Thecla at Rome and Meriamlick." *Hagiographica* 2 (1995): 1–24.
Delehaye, Hippolyte. *Commentarius perpetuus in Martyrologium Hieronynianum ad recensionem H. Quenti*. In *Acta Sanctorum* XXIV. Brussels: Société des Bollandistes, 1931: November 11, part II.
Ehwald, Rudolf, ed. *Aldhelmi opera*. Monumenta Germaniae Historica, Auctores Antiquissimi 15. Berlin: Weidmann, 1919.
Elliott, James K., trans. *The Apocryphal New Testament: A Collection of Apocryphal Christian Literature in an English Translation Based on M. R. James*. Oxford: Oxford University Press, 1993. Reprint, 2005.
Faller, Otto, and Michaela Zelzer, eds. *Ambrosius: Epistulae et acta*. Corpus Scriptorum Ecclesiasticorum Latinorum 82/1–4. Vienna: Verlag der Österreichischen Akademie der Wissenschaften, 1968–1996.
Fontaine, Jacques, and Jean-Louis Charlet, eds. *Ambroise de Milan: Hymnes*. Paris: Les Éditions du Cerf, 1992.
Fontaine, Jacques, and Nicole Dupré, eds. *Sulpice Sévère, Gallus. Dialogues sur les 'Vertus' de saint Martin*. Sources Chrétiennes 510. Paris: Les Éditions du Cerf, 2006.

Franc, Catherine. "The Cult of Saint Thecla in Anglo-Saxon England: The Problem of Aldhelm's Sources." *Bulletin of the John Rylands Library* 86, no. 2 (2004): 39–54.

Gamber, Klaus. *Codices liturgici latini antiquiores*. Spicilegii Friburgensis subsidia 1. Freiburg: Universitätsverlag Freiburg Schweiz, 1968.

le Goff, Jacques. *Un autre Moyen Âge*. Paris: Gallimard, 1999.

Greene, David. "Saltair na Rann." *Dublin Institute for Advanced Studies (DIAS)*, March 10, 2020. www.dias.ie/celt/celt-publications-2/celt-saltair-na-rann/.

Gwara, Scott, ed. *Aldhelmi Malmesbiriensis Prosa de virginitate cum glosa latina atquea Anglosaxonica*. Corpus Christianorum, Series Latina 124, 124A. 2 vols. Turnhout: Brepols, 2001.

Hänggi, Anton, and Alfons Schönherr, eds. *Sacramentarium Rhenaugiense*. Spicilegium Friburgense 15. Fribourg: Universitätsverlag, 1970.

Harnack, Adolf von. *Drei wenig beachtete cyprianische Schriften und die Acta Pauli*. Texte und Untersuchungen 19.3, N.F. 4.3. Leipzig: J. C. Hinrichs, 1899.

Hartel, Wilhelm von, ed. *S. Thasci Caecili Cypriani opera omnia*. Corpus Scriptorum Ecclesiasticorum Latinorum 3, pt. 3. Vienna: C. Geroldi, 1868.

Hennig, John. "Quelques notes sur la mention de sainte Thècle dans la *Commendatio animae*." *Nuovo Didaskaleion* 14 (1964): 21–27.

Henry, Patrick L., ed. *Amra Choluim Chille: Dallán's Elegy for Columba*. Belfast: Colmcille, 2006.

James, Montague R. *The Apocryphal New Testament*. Oxford: Clarendon Press, 1924.

Kaestli, Jean-Daniel, and Willy Rordorf, eds. and trans. "La fin de la vie de Thècle dans les manuscrits des Actes de Paul et Thècle. Édition des textes additionnels." *Apocrypha* 25 (2014): 9–101.

Lapidge, Michael, and Michael Herren, trans. *Aldhelm: The Prose Works*. Cambridge: D. S. Brewer, 1979.

Lundberg, Per I. *La typologie baptismale dans l'ancienne Église*. Uppsala: Alfred Lorentz, 1942.

Magistretti, Marco, ed. *Manuale Ambrosianum: Ex codice saec. XI olim in usum canonicae Vallis Travaliae*. 3 vols. Milan: U Hoepli, 1904–1905.

Marstrander, Carl S., et al., eds. *Dictionary of the Irish Language Based Mainly on Old and Middle Irish Materials*. 15 vols. Dublin: Royal Irish Academy, 1913–1976. Reprint, Compact edition, E. G. Quin, ed. 1984 and online edition, 2007 and 2019.

Martimort, Aimé-Georges. "L'ordo commendationis animae." *La Maison Dieu* 15 (1948): 143–160.

McNamara, Martin. *The Apocrypha of the Irish Church*. Dublin: Dublin Institute for Advanced Studies, 1984.

Moreton, Bernard. *The Eighth-Century Gelasian Sacramentary*. Oxford: Oxford University Press, 1976.

Musurillo, Herbert, trans. *St. Methodius: The Symposium, A Treatise on Chastity*. London: Longmans, Green and Co., 1958.

Musurillo, Herbert, and Victor-Henry Debidour, eds. *Méthode d'Olympe: Le Banquet*. Sources Chrétiennes 95. Paris: Les Éditions du Cerf, 1963.
Ntedika, Joseph. *L'évocation de l'au-delà dans la prière pour les morts*. Recherches africaines de théologie 2. Louvain: Nauwelaerts, 1971.
Ó Dochartaigh, Caitríona. "Poems 138–41 in Saltair na Rann." In *Saltair saíochta, sanasaíochta agus seanchais: A Festschrift for Gearóid Mac Eoin*, edited by Dónal Ó Baoill, Donncha Ó hAodha, and Nollaig Ó Muraíle. Dublin: Four Courts Press, 2013: 297–310.
——— "A Cult of Saint Thecla in Early Medieval Ireland?" In *Sacred Histories: A Festschrift for Máire Herbert*, edited by John Carey, Kevin Murray, and Caitríona Ó Dochartaigh. Dublin: Four Courts Press, 2015: 311–332.
Ó Riain, Pádraig. "The Tallaght Martyrologies, Redated." *Cambrian Medieval Celtic Studies* 20 (Winter 1990): 21–38.
——— *Feastdays of the Saints: A History of Irish Martyrologies*. Subsidia Hagiographica 86. Brussels: Société des Bollandistes, 2006.
——— *A Dictionary of Irish Saints*. Dublin: Four Courts Press, 2011.
——— "The Early Ninth-Century Karlsruhe Irish Calendar of Saints." *Peritia* 32 (2021): 181–195.
Paxton, Frederick S. *Christianizing Death: The Creation of a Ritual Process in Early Medieval Europe*. Ithaca; London: Cornell University Press, 1990.
Quentin, Henri. *Les martyrologes historiques du Moyen Âge: Étude sur la formation du martyrologe romain*. Aalen: Scientia, 1969.
Roberts, Alexander, and James Donaldson, eds. *The Ante-Nicene Fathers: Translations of the Writings of the Fathers down to A.D. 325*. 24 vols. Edinburgh: T&T Clark, 1868–1872.
Romestin, H. de, trans. *St. Ambrose: Selected Works and Letters*. Select Library of the Nicene and Post-Nicene Fathers of the Christian Church 10. Oxford: Christian Literature Publishing Company, 1896.
Rordorf, Willy. "Sainte Thècle dans la tradition hagiographique occidentale." *Augustinianum* 24, nos. 1–2 (1984): 73–81.
Rossi, Giovanni B. de, and Louis Duchesne, eds. *Martyrologium Hieronymianum*. In *Acta Sanctorum* LXXXII. Brussels: Société des Bollandistes, 1894: November, part II. Reprint, 1971.
Salmon, Pierre, Carolus Coebergh, and Pierre de Puniet, eds. *Testimonia orationis christianae antiquioris*. Corpus Christianorum Continuatio Mediaevalis 47. Turnhout: Brepols, 1977.
Schermann, Theodor. "Die griechischen Kyprianosgebete." *Oriens Christianus* 3 (1903): 303–323.
Schneemelcher, Wilhelm, ed. *New Testament Apocrypha*. Tübingen: J. C. B. Mohr, 1989. English edition, R. McL. Wilson, ed. 2 vols. Cambridge: James Clarke & Co., 1992.
Schneiders, Marc. "The Irish Calendar in the Karlsruhe Bede." *Archiv für Liturgiewissenschaft* 31 (1989): 33–78.
Schönfelder, Albert, ed. *Liturgische Bibliothek*. Paderborn: Ferdinand Schoeningh, 1904.

Stokes, Whitley, ed. *The Saltair na rann: A Collection of Early Middle Irish Poems*. Mediaeval and Modern Series 1.3. Oxford: Clarendon Press, 1883.

———. ed. and trans. *Félire hUí Gormáin: The Martyrology of Gorman*. Henry Bradshaw Society 9. London: Harrison, 1895.

———. ed. "The Bodleian Amra Choluimb Chille." *Revue Celtique* 20 (1899): 31–55, 132–183, 248–289, and 400–437.

———. ed. and trans. *Félire Óengusso Céli Dé: The Martyrology of Oengus the Culdee*. Henry Bradshaw Society 29. London: Harrison, 1905.

Stokes, Whitley, and John Strachan, eds. *Thesaurus palaeohibernicus: A Collection of Old-Irish Glosses, Scholia, Prose and Verse*. 2 vols. Cambridge: Cambridge University Press, 1903.

Tuilier, André, and Guillaume Bady, eds. *Saint Grégoire de Nazianze: Œuvres Poétiques*. Paris: Les Belles Lettres, 2004.

Twelftree, Graham H. *In the Name of Jesus: Exorcism among Early Christians*. Grand Rapids: Baker Academic, 2007.

Vouaux, Léon, ed. and trans. *Les Actes de Paul et ses lettres apocryphes*. Paris: Letouzey et Ané, 1913.

Walsh, Patrick G., ed. and trans. *Augustine: De bono coniugali, De sancta uirginitate*. Oxford Christian Texts. Oxford: Clarendon Press, 2001.

CHAPTER 4

The Reception of the Acts of Thecla *in Armenia*
Thecla as a Model of Representation for Holy Women in Ancient Armenian Literature

Valentina Calzolari*

The figure of Thecla has played an important role in the development of Lives of female saints, and this is no less the case in the Armenian tradition. Indeed, research into the diffusion of her cult and her legend in Armenia has allowed us to identify several pertinent documents that range from the fifth to the fourteenth century.

It is important to emphasize that Saint Thecla, as represented in her apocryphal *Acts*, soon became popular in Armenian literature. Her success is demonstrated by the fact that already in the fifth century, her tale inspired the representation of two female saints in two separate works. Both works, significantly, are originally composed in Armenian and are associated with two pivotal moments in the history of Armenian Christianity. The first is Agathangelos' *History*, which traces the conversion of Armenia, and the second is the *Martyrdom of Thaddaeus and Sanduxt*, which recounts the apostolic origin of the Armenian Church. In addition, Thecla herself is the protagonist of a fifth-century Armenian historiographic work, the *History of Armenia* (*Buzandaran Patmut'iwnk'* or "Epic Stories"), by Faustus of Byzantium (fl. fifth century), for which one may suppose a different model, namely, the Greek *Miracles of Thecla*, which is attributed to Basil of Seleucia (d. c. 468).[1]

The female characters featured in the aforementioned works embody three models of holy women, which are equivalent to three paradigms of holiness associated with Thecla in the ancient Christian East and West: the holy virgin, the holy preacher, and, less frequently, the patron saint of Nicene religious orthodoxy. The model of Thecla as holy apostle is also found in an Armenian hagiographic text (probably of Greek origin): the *Martyrdom of Saint Photine*, which will be analyzed in this chapter along

---

* The author would like to thank Flavia Ruani and Ghazzal Dabiri for their careful translation of this article from French.
[1] Dagron (ed. and trans.), *Vie et Miracles*, 1978.

with the aforementioned *History* by Agathangelos, *Martyrdom of Thaddaeus and Sanduxt*, and *History of Armenia* by Faustus of Byzantium.[2]

The results of our research, which center on the Armenians' devotion to Thecla, have been published elsewhere.[3] For the purposes of this current volume, then, we will offer a summary of these results, and, in response to the aims of this volume and to the desiderata of its editors, we will focus on the texts that promoted the spread and facilitated the reception of Thecla's legend in Armenian literature. Thus, we will begin with the Armenian translation of the Syriac version of the Greek *Acts of Thecla*.

The Armenian Translation of the Syriac *Acts of Thecla*

The Armenian translation of the Syriac *Acts of Thecla* is situated within the formative period of Armenian literature, specifically the first half of the fifth century, and it testifies to a general interest in Syriac literature. In this regard, it should be recalled that Armenian literature was born in the early fifth century immediately after the creation of the alphabet by Maštocʻ (d. 439).[4] It is in the primarily Syriac-speaking cities of Amida, Edessa, and Samosata that Armenians organized trips to find a system of writing capable of reproducing the sounds of their language. The main goal was to develop an instrument for writing down the Bible in Armenian in order to complete the evangelization of the country that formally had begun a century before.[5] Equipped with their newly created and perfected letters, Maštocʻ and his collaborators, during several expeditions, were able to quickly translate the Bible and several works composed by the fathers of the Greek and Syrian Orthodox Church. In

---

[2] The later Armenian tradition (eleventh-twelfth century?) also includes the translation of two Byzantine writings that make Thecla the protagonist of a series of episodes and miracles in which she heals, preaches, and converts several people in Seleucia. The Armenian translations combined are known as the *Prodigies of Thecla* (different from the *Miracles of Thecla* by pseudo-Basil of Seleucia). These Byzantine texts fit in the cycle of additional works preserved in the Greek manuscripts of the *Acts of Thecla*. They testify to the development of the final sections of the Greek *Acts of Thecla* and of the evolution of the legend of the saint beyond the *Acts*. See Calzolari (ed. and trans.), *Apocrypha Armeniaca I*, 2017: 109–132; text and translation, 427–485; on the Greek text, see Kaestli and Rordorf (eds. and trans.), "La fin de la vie de Thècle," 2013.
[3] Calzolari (ed. and trans.), *Apocrypha Armeniaca I*, 2017.
[4] From here on, for the transliteration of Armenian proper names and words, we adopt the system of the *Revue des Études Arméniennes* (system Hübschmann-Meillet-Benveniste). For a brief presentation of Maštocʻ and his activities, see Calzolari, "Mesrop (Maštocʻ)," 2011.
[5] The Armenian kingdom officially adopted Christianity as the state religion at the beginning of the fourth century under the rule of King Tiridates the Great and as a consequence of the activity of St. Gregory the Illuminator (d. 328). The traditional date of the conversion of Armenia is 301, but the most likely date is 314. Cf. Ananian, "La data," 1961, followed by Garsoïan, *L'Église arménienne*, 1999: 2 n. 3.

addition to the texts of the church fathers, the first wave of translations of Greek and Syriac texts into Armenian also included apocryphal works. The *Acts of Thecla*, which was already circulating independently from the larger *Acts of Paul*, was among these texts.

As is well known, in the Syriac tradition, the *Acts of Thecla* entered a collection of lives of women, known as the *Book of Women*, which was composed in the sixth century and which contains the Lives of Ruth, Esther, Susanna, and Judith among others.[6] In the Armenian tradition, there is no equivalent to the Syriac *Book of Women*. In most cases, the Armenian *Acts of Thecla* was transmitted in collections of homilies called *čaṙəntir* (chosen discourses), which preserve many Apocryphal Acts of the apostles as well as other kinds of texts.[7] The popularity of the Armenian version of the *Acts of Thecla* is attested in the large number of extant manuscripts (twenty-seven). It is indeed a considerable amount, especially if we compare it to the smaller number of manuscripts (fifteen) that preserve the *Martyrdom of Paul*, namely, the final section of the apocryphal *Acts of Paul*.[8] The Armenian version faithfully follows the Syriac text – it reproduces all the variances of the Syriac with respect to the Greek. The hypothesis of F. C. Conybeare, who considered the Armenian version to be based on a lost Syriac text, one that he hypothesized is closer to the Greek, is now obsolete.[9] Nevertheless, the fact remains that the Armenian version is an important witness for the establishment of the critical edition of the Syriac text (it is a desideratum in the field of Syriac studies).[10]

In the next section, we will turn to the figure of Saint Hṙip'simē who plays a crucial role in the conversion of Armenia in the *History* by Agathangelos and who is modeled on the figure of Thecla as a holy virgin in the *APT*.

---

[6] On the manuscript tradition of the Syriac text, see Calzolari (ed. and trans.), *Apocrypha armeniaca I*, 2017: 179–181 (edited and unedited manuscripts, based on the information provided by Alain Desreumaux and Claude Détienne to the present author in personal communications, as well as the following catalogue: Brock and van Rompay, *Catalogue*, 2014). On the reception of the *Acts of Thecla* and the *Book of Women*, see Burris, "The Reception," 2010.

[7] On the manuscript tradition of the Armenian text, see Calzolari (ed. and trans.), *Acta Armeniaca I*, 2017: 192–223.

[8] On the Armenian manuscript tradition of the *Martyrdom of Paul*, cf. Calzolari (ed. and trans.), *Apocrypha Armeniaca I*, 2017: 524–545. For a brief introduction to the Greek *Acts of Paul*, see Rordorf, "Actes de Paul," 1997.

[9] Conybeare (ed. and trans.), *The Apology*, 1894: 59. Translations of the *Acts of Thecla* are taken from the latter, with adjustments according to my new critical edition of the Armenian text: Calzolari (ed. and trans.), *Apocrypha armeniaca I*, 2017: 231–409.

[10] Calzolari (ed. and trans.), *Apocrypha Armeniaca I*, 2017: 178–181. The only available edition of the Syriac text is Wright (ed. and trans.), *Apocryphal Acts*, 1871.

The Paradigm of the Holy Virgin and the Figure of Saint Hṙip'simē in Agathangelos' *History* as an Epigone of Thecla

There is no need to dwell, in this volume, on the features of Thecla as a holy virgin, nor on the priority given in the *Acts of Thecla* to female figures. This is an aspect that has attracted the attention of the scholarly community since the 1930s.[11] In the 1980s, various academic works, inspired by gender studies, emphasized the transgressive aspect of Thecla's character in the *Acts of Thecla* in which we see the girl from Iconium oppose her family, her fiancé, and the laws of her city in order to defend her chastity in accordance with the precepts of Paul.

This choice of chastity, which can be considered as a choice of autonomy in relation to the family and the city, has been interpreted differently by historians of Christianity. For some scholars, especially Virginia Burrus in her early works, the chastity stories of the Apocryphal Acts, and first of all the *Acts of Thecla*, may be read as a reflection of a sociocultural reality; in particular, they may be considered as sources testifying to the existence of contexts of female emancipation in early Christianity.[12] For others, on the contrary, these stories of chastity are a literary revival of narrative models and *topoi* already exploited in the ancient Greek novel. Among the most well-known advocates of this latter interpretation is Peter Brown,[13] followed by Kate Cooper.[14] Since there

---

[11] Söder, *Die apokryphe Apostelgeschichten*, 1932, thought that the text, inspired by the Greek Hellenistic novel, was essentially meant for a female readership. On the relation between Greek novels and apocryphal literature, see already Rohde, *Der griechische Roman*, 1876; and von Dobschütz, "Der Roman," 1902. On the *Acts of Thecla* and the Greek novel, see more recently Aubin, "Reversing Romance?," 1998; Calef, "Thecla 'Tried and True,'" 2006; Corsaro, "Elementi romanzeschi," 1995; and Perkins, *The Suffering Self*, 1995: 41–76.

[12] See Burrus, "Chastity as Autonomy," 1986; Burrus, *Chastity as Autonomy*, 1987; Davies, *The Revolt of the Widows*, 1980; MacDonald, *The Legend and the Apostle*, 1983; and MacDonald, "The Role of Women," 1984. Chastity has long been a focus of these types of stories and drawn the attention of contemporary scholars with opinions evolving over the past few decades. However, it is not our aim here to give an exhaustive state-of-the-art on the question. On the evolution of the feminist interpretation of the *Acts of Thecla*, see Vander Stichele and Penner, *Contextualizing Gender*, 2009: 142–146, who especially stress a shift in Burrus' positions (cf. Burrus, "Mimicking Virgins," 2005). For a helpful overview of these developments, see the more recent Davis, "From Women's Piety," 2015. See also the following footnotes and Ghazzal Dabiri's Introduction to this volume.

[13] Brown, *The Body and Society*, 1988: 153. The passage in question and, more generally, the interpretation proposed by Brown have been analyzed and criticized by Matthews, "Thinking of Thecla," 2001, who follows the feminist approach and considers the Apocryphal Acts as witnesses to the role of women in the history of Early Christianity.

[14] See Cooper, *The Virgin and the Bride*, 1996: 55. Cooper's positions were then criticized by Kraemer, *Unreliable Witnesses*, 2011: 150. Kraemer insists on the value of the *Acts of Thecla* as a

are now summary publications to which we can refer,[15] we will state here that whatever its origin and whatever it may teach us about the context of the production and circulation of the text,[16] the importance of female virginity in the *Acts of Thecla* is without a doubt an essential feature of the representation of the saint.

It is worth noting here that the patristic tradition from the fourth century onwards imposed an emphasis on the figure of the virgin and relegated the figure of the female preacher to the background, especially with regards to Thecla. In fourth-century Greco-Latin literature, the "transgressive" figure gave way to the exemplary figure of the holy virgin who became a model of conduct to follow.[17] Thus, Methodius of Olympus (250–311) makes of Thecla a new Socrates; one who is responsible for explaining that virginity is the privileged condition with which to recapture humanity's original purity and to be close to God. In fact, it is to her that he awards the prize of victory for having given the most eloquent speech on the theme of virginity during a competition among holy women.[18] Gregory of Nyssa (d. 378) also reminds us that his sister, Macrina, had secretly adopted the name of Thecla by taking the saint of Iconium as a model.[19]

As is well-known, from the fourth century onwards, chastity and virginity became the ideal for Christian perfection. Furthermore, suffering

---

witness to the existence of groups of women who baptized and preached. It should be recalled that already Tertullian, in his treatise *On Baptism* 17.5 had evoked groups of women who, taking Thecla as a model, claimed for themselves the right to baptize: Refoulé (ed.), *Tertullien*, 1952. Cf. Hilhorst, "Tertullian," 1996; Rordorf, "Tertullien," 1990; Davies, "Women, Tertullian," 1986. See also Jeremy Barrier's contribution in this volume (Chapter 1).

[15] For a summary of these perspectives, see Barrier, "*The Acts of Paul and Thecla*," 2017: 342–349; Davis, "From Women's Piety," 2015; and Vander Stichele and Penner, *Contextualizing Gender*, 2009. See also Calzolari, "Les *Actes*," 2015, with a focus on the Armenian tradition.

[16] Scholars are now divided between those who deny their value as sources for the existence of female Christian communities or women's emancipation currents in early Christianity (see, for instance, Boughton, "From Pious Legend," 1991; Dunn, "Women's Liberation," 1993; and Ng, "*Acts of Paul and Thecla*," 2004) and those who, on the contrary, believe in this possibility (see, for instance, Matthews, "Thinking of Thecla," 2001; and Kraemer, *Unreliable Witnesses*, 2011).

[17] On this theme in Latin hagiography, see Klazina Staat's contribution in this volume (Chapter 9).

[18] Musurillo and Debidour (eds.), *Méthode d'Olympe*, 1963: XI § 284, at 308–309. At the end of the *Symposium*, Thecla sings, together with her other nine companions, the hymn of virginity addressed to Christ, the fiancé of the Church and of the virgins. See also Virginia Burrus' contribution in this volume (Chapter 8).

[19] Maraval (ed.), *Grégoire de Nysse*, 1971: 146–148; and see Albrecht, *Das Leben*, 1986. In patristic literature, Thecla is presented as the model for other holy women too. For example, Eustochium in Jerome or Syncletica in Pseudo-Athanasius. See Jerome, *Letter 22 to Eustochium* 41: Hilberg (ed.), *Sancti Eusebii Hieronymi Epistulae*, 1996: 209; and Pseudo-Athanasius, *Life of Saint Syncletica*: PG 28.1489 CD. On the figure of Thecla in the patristic tradition, see Hayne, "Thecla and the Church Fathers," 1994.

in the defense of chastity was valorized as a form of physical endurance, in fighting for the faith, comparable to martyrdom.[20] Chaste and virginal men and women were considered equal to the angels (which is commonly referred to as the *isangelia* of the virgins), and their condition was compared to that of the protoplasts (as in when God created man in his image and likeness).[21] The defense of this special bond with God can go as far as (the acceptance of) death – as in the case of Thecla who is condemned to death, although she miraculously escapes twice.[22]

The figure of the holy woman, who resists martyrdom for the defense of her virginity, becomes significant in the history of the conversion of Armenia as recounted by the historian Agathangelos. Agathangelos' *History* contains a section that relates the story of the arrival of Roman Christian virgins in Armenia and their subsequent deaths on the orders of the Armenian King Tiridates IV (298–330).[23] As we shall see, this martyrdom is invested with a soteriological value that involves Armenia as a whole. It is in this section that we find an important intertextual parallel with the *Acts of Thecla*, namely, in the representation of the struggle of the holy virgin against a man who threatens her chastity and her decision to remain a virgin. Now, we will turn to a discussion of Saint Hṙipʿsimē as the epigone of Saint Thecla in Agathangelos' *History*.

Modern scholarship dates the *History*, attributed to Agathangelos, to the second half of the fifth century.[24] The text at our disposal is not the oldest

---

[20] On virginity and continence in the late Jewish traditions and in the first Christian centuries, see Angelidi, "Virginité ascétique," 2006; Beatrice, "Continenza," 1976; Consolino, "La sessualità," 2006; Coyne Kelly, *Performing Virginity*, 2000: ch. 2; Elm, *Virgins of God*, 1994; and Sfameni Gasparro, *Enkrateia*, 1984.

[21] As Aline Rousselle, *Porneia*, 1983: 13, states, virginity is a "privileged means of exclusive encounter" with God. On the *topos* of the *isangelia* of the virgins in ascetical literature, see inter alia Muehlberger, "Ambivalence about the Angelic Life," 2008; and Muehlberger, *Angels in Late Ancient Christianity*, 2013; Sfameni Gasparro, *Enkrateia*, 1984: *passim*; Lane Fox, *Pagans and Christians*, 1986: 347–388. Among the ancient sources, see inter alia Methodius of Olympus, *Symposium* 1.2–4: Musurillo and Debidour (eds.), *Méthode d'Olympe*, 1963: 56–65. The theme of the *isangelia* and of the intimacy (ὁμιλία) with God, to which only the virgins can have access on earth, is also developed by John Chrysostom (d. 407) in *De Virginitate*: Musurillo (ed.), *Jean Chrysostome*, 1966: 44 and n. 3. On virginity and proximity to God, see also Streete, "Buying the Stairway to Heaven," 2006.

[22] The first time for breaking off her engagement with Thamyris, to whom she had been promised in marriage, and a second time for resisting the aggression of Alexander, a noble of Antioch. Although in this second case, the charge is as a "profaner of the temple of god" for having thrown down the crown of Alexander which is decorated with the image of the emperor. Her resistance is as the virgin who fights for the preservation of her purity (§ 26, cf. § 28).

[23] Toumanoff, "The Third-Century Arsacids," 1969: 233–281.

[24] See Thomson (trans.), *Agathangelos*, 1976: LXXXIX–XC. Edition: Tēr-Mkrtčʿean and Kanayeancʿ (eds.), *Agathange*, 1909. This edition was copied in Thomson (trans.), *Agathangelos*, 1976. Translations of the *History* used in this chapter are taken from the latter.

History but rather a more recent compilation comprising different sections in which it is difficult to distinguish between the contribution of oral and/ or written sources and between the different strata of the redaction.[25] The *History*, as it stands, is the result of the efforts of an editor whose identity remains unknown. Indeed, Agathangelos is a fictitious name of Greek origin (the one who announces the good, the good messenger) that was chosen by the Armenian compiler. In the prologue and in the epilogue, Agathangelos claims to have been a contemporary of the recounted facts and to have written on the orders of King Tiridates the Great who adopted Christianity as the official religion of the kingdom.[26] This is an expedient yet common rhetorical device in antiquity that confers authenticity and truth on a narrative.

As just noted, the *History* is the result of a compilation of sections of different origin. Nevertheless, it is equally true that the resulting work unifies the sections such that each is in its proper place, reflecting Agathangelos' overall aims. As early as 1942, Paul Peeters wrote:

> Whether the editor of Agathangelos' [book] operated on pre-existing narratives, or whether he himself fabricated, through plagiarism, counterfeits or otherwise, the pieces assembled in his rhapsody, the following pieces: the actions of Tiridates, the Acts of S. Gregory and the novel of St. Hṙip'simē were shaped to fit into each other and thus create the illusion that they belong to the same cycle and form the vicissitudes of a tragedy marching towards the same denouement.[27]

These "vicissitudes," which tend toward the same denouement, refer to the differing circumstances that saw the Armenian kingdom embrace Christianity as a state religion and that, for Agathangelos, respond to God's intended purpose for the Armenians.[28]

At the heart of the country's conversion, as Agathangelos describes it, are two holy figures: Gregory, the Illuminator of Armenia, and Saint Hṙip'simē, the main figure among a group of Roman virgins whose

---

[25] For a summary of the various recensions and versions of the *History of Armenia*, see Winkler, "Our Present Knowledge," 1980; and Thomson (trans.), *The Lives of Saint Gregory*, 2010.

[26] See n. 5.

[27] Cf. Peeters, "S. Grégoire l'Illuminateur," 1942: 102–103: "Que le rédacteur [du livre] d'*Agathange* ait opéré sur des récits préexistants, ou qu'il ait fabriqué lui-même à coup de plagiats, de contrefaçons ou autrement, les pièces assemblées dans sa rhapsodie, ces pièces: la geste de Tiridate, les Actes de S. Grégoire et le roman de Ste Hripsimé ont été façonnés pour s'emboîter les uns dans les autres et créer ainsi l'illusion qu'ils appartiennent au même cycle et forment comme les péripéties d'un drame marchant vers le même dénouement."

[28] On Agathangelos' theological and providential vision of history, see Mahé, "Entre Moïse et Mahomet," 1992; and Calzolari, "La citation du Ps 78 [77]," 2003–2004.

martyrdom is considered fundamental for the conversion of the Armenian kingdom.[29]

According to the text, Hṙipʻsimē fled Rome along with the superior of her convent, Gayianē, and other companions to escape Diocletian (244–311) who wanted to marry her. Note that Agathangelos presents Diocletian as the "Enemy" (Arm. *tʻšnami*) – an epithet traditionally reserved for Satan[30] – who endangers the virgins' vow of chastity and the foundations of the whole Church together:

> But when the pious women saw the hidden arrows of the enemy [cf. Eph 6:6], who is accustomed to shoot secretly at the saints who love Christ, they found that the emperor (had become) a vessel of evil [cf. Jer 51:34], and that just as in the garden he had used the snake as a vehicle for causing the forgetting of the commandments, entering into the foolish ear of the first woman [cf. Gen 3], so here too he had used the lawless emperor as a mask through which he could fight with the church built by God. (§ 141)

This passage illustrates that the figure of Hṙipʻsimē is built on the basis of the model of Thecla (a discussion of which follows momentarily) but also, contrarily, on that of Eve who constitutes the anti-type of the Roman virgin.[31] For indeed, contrary to Eve, Hṙipʻsimē does not allow herself to be seduced by the promises of the Enemy. The association between the defense of virginity and the defense of the Church against the threats of the Enemy is further reinforced in other passages of the work, which present the virginal body as a "temple of God" and make the virgin a metaphor for the Church.[32]

---

[29] On Hṙipʻsimē, see Ananian, "Ripsima, Gaiana," 1968: 206; Mahé, "Hṙipʻsimē," 2008; Pogossian, "Women," 2003: 358–363; and Pogossian, "Female Asceticism," 2012. We should recall here that the historicity of Hṙipʻsimē and her companions was denied, for example, by the Bollandists. For others, on the contrary, the virgins really existed; they would have originally come not from Rome but from a Roman province closer to Armenia and could have been victims of the persecution of Maximinus Daia (c. 311–312), which raged in Roman Armenia according to Eusebius, *Ecclesiastical History* 9.8.2: Bardy (ed.), *Eusèbe de Césarée*, 1986: 57.

[30] On the qualification of the Devil as "Enemy," see Calzolari, "La version arménienne," 2000: 167–168.

[31] We should note that this typology is centered on the valorization of virginity: out of the virginal body of Mary the redeemer of humankind was to be born; the virginal body of Hṙipʻsimē and her companions had to prepare the conversion and the redemption of the Armenians. On the Eve-Hṙipʻsimē typology and, in parallel, the Eve-Mary typology in the Armenian tradition, see Calzolari, "Les récits apocryphes," 2011: 571–574; and Calzolari, "Mary and Eve," 2019.

[32] We analyzed this passage in Calzolari, "Le sang," 2011. See also Calzolari (ed. and trans.), *Apocrypha Armeniaca I*, 2017: 53–68. This image can allude to the *Acts of Thecla* § 5: "Blessed are they that keep themselves chaste, because they shall be called the temple of God." Conybeare's translation with adjustments. It is a *topos* of ancient Christian literature; we find it for example in the *Acts of Thomas* 1.12: Lipsius and Bonnet (eds.), *Acta apostolorum apocrypha*, 1903: 116–117; Origen, *Against Celsus* 4.26: Marcovich (ed.), *Origens, Contra Celsum*, 2001: 239–240; Basil of Ancyra, *On*

During their flight, Hṙipʻsimē, Gayianē, and their companions arrive in Armenia and stay there assuming, wrongly, that they have found safe shelter. Having learned that Hṙipʻsimē ran away, Diocletian correctly assumes that she is in Armenia. He writes to King Tiridates, his ally, and asks him to look for and send her back to him. Toward the end of the letter, he adds an unexpected concession: if Tiridates should, in his turn, succumb to the virgin's charms, Diocletian grants him the favor of keeping her in the name of their friendship.

As Diocletian has anticipated, Tiridates also falls in love with Hṙipʻsimē. However, Tiridates falls in love with her based on the tales of her legendary beauty, long before having seen her (§ 165). This second threat is apparently a more serious one for Tiridates too decides to take her as his wife (§ 166) and to make her the Queen of Armenia (§ 173). Tiridates has her brought to the royal chambers of his palace (§ 178). While the king enters the room, a crowd outside sings wedding songs and dances (§ 180). But Hṙipʻsimē refuses the king's proposal. Instead of becoming Queen of Armenia, she prefers to remain faithful to her heavenly spouse, namely, Christ.[33] In this regard, it must be emphasized that in several passages, we find the nuptial metaphor of the virgin fiancée of Christ,[34] which is a frequent *topos* of Christian literature, inspired by the parable of the wise and foolish virgins of Matthew 25:1–10 as well as the Song of Songs.

Hṙipʻsimē's struggle for the preservation of her virginity is successful, so much so that it leads to her death. Her martyrdom is followed by that of her superior who had encouraged her and her other companions, as well, to resist the advances of the king. The girl's resistance against Tiridates is not only presented in the figurative sense: Hṙipʻsimē must indeed protect herself from the physical aggression of the king with whom she verbally

---

Virginity 27: *PG* 30.725B; Eusebius of Emesa, *On Virginity* 25.27: Buytaert (ed.), *Eusèbe d'Émèse*, 1953: 192 and 194, and Eusebius of Emesa, *Homily 6 On the Martyrs* 24: Buytaert (ed.), *Eusèbe d'Émèse*, 1953: 166–168; *Life of Saint Melania* 19: Gorce (ed.), *Vie de sainte Mélanie*, 1962: 182; and Ps.-Basil, *On Virginity* 2.41: Amand de Mendieta and Moons (eds.), "Une curieuse homélie grecque inédite," 1953. On the virgins' bodies as representing the "body of the Church," cf. Clark, *Reading Renunciation*, 1999: 259–329; Coyne Kelly, *Performing Virginity*, 2000: 41–42; and MacDonald, *Early Christian Women*, 1996: 242–243. On the body of the virgin as a metaphor for the Church, see Cameron, "Virginity as Metaphor," 1989. See also Wehn, "'Blessed are the Bodies,'" 2000.

[33] On the symbolism of engagement and marriage, which is based on 2 Cor 11:2 and on Eph 5:27 (concerning the spiritual wedding between Christ and the Church), see Brown, *The Body and Society*, 1988: 259 and 275–276. The expression "fiancée of Christ" constitutes a *leitmotiv* of ascetic and patristic literature.

[34] See, for example, § 149 (on the virgins and the "divine fiancé") and § 174 (on the virgins' love and desire for Christ).

wrestles for a whole day and night (§ 191). At the end of the second assault, however, Hṙipʿsimē physically wrestles the king, leaving him on the ground, naked, and ashamed with his royal diadem thrown to the floor. The emphasis of the text on the physical endurance of the "maiden" (Arm. *aŀjik*) against Tiridates, who is known for his legendary titanic strength,[35] should be read as an emphasis of God's support for his protégée and, at the same time, for his Church.

It is important to note that, in order to portray Hṙipʿsimē at the most crucial moment of her struggle in the defense of her chastity, Agathangelos draws inspiration from a famous episode of the *Acts of Thecla*. The episode in question recounts Thecla's struggle against Alexander, a noble of the city of Antioch, who falls in love with Thecla and assaults her at the entrance of the city, when she rejects his advances. The parallel between the two texts is clear as can be seen in the following passages, beginning with the excerpt from Agathangelos' *History*:

> The maiden (*scil.* Hṙipʿsimē) was strengthened by the Holy Spirit; she struck him, chased him and overcame him; she wore the king out, weakened him and felled him. She stripped the king naked of his clothes; she tore his robes and threw away his royal diadem, leaving him covered with shame. (§ 191)

This is modeled after the following episode in the *Acts of Thecla*:

> And straightway she attacked Alexander and rent his raiment, and tore off the golden crown with the image of Caesar,[36] which he had on his head, and dashed it to the ground, and left him naked, stripped and full of shame. (§ 26)

The parallel between Thecla and Hṙipʿsimē allows us to precisely identify the paradigm of the victorious virgin and, simultaneously, the exalted status of Hṙipʿsimē for Agathangelos. Hṙipʿsimē indeed merges two figures: (1) that of Thecla when she defends her virginity, enjoying a burst of "virile" force,[37] and, in having God's support, (2) a cohort of female

---

[35] In Agathangelos, Tiridates is compared, in terms of his strength, to the eponymous hero of the Armenians, Hayk, a hero belonging to the primordial race of giants (§ 767, cf. § 123, 202, 249).

[36] In Armenian, *kayserakerp* is an adjective composed of *kayser*, the genitive form of *kaysr* "emperor," the vowel *-a-* typical of compound words, and the noun *kerp* "form, manner, image, figure." The Armenian adjective is a translation of the Syriac expression *d-ṣlmʾ d-qsr* (*varia lectio*) "in the image of the emperor" (absent in Greek). See Wright (ed.), *Apocryphal Acts*, 1871: 150 n. b.

[37] The theme of the masculinization of women, especially of the virgin and the martyr, constitutes a well-known *topos* in Christian literature, which is also present in the *Acts of Thecla* (§ 25–26). On this theme, see, for example, Aspegren, *The Male Woman*, 1990; Castelli, "'I Will Make Mary Man,'" 1991; Cobb, *Dying to Be Men*, 2008; Cooper, "The Bride of Christ," 2013; Marjanen,

characters from the Old Testament who, before her, obtained divine assistance. This latter also overlaps with the figure of Thecla. The god invoked by Hṙipʻsimē in her prayers is the God of Sarah, Rebecca, Susanna, Yael, and Deborah (§ 170 and § 179).[38] Unlike Thecla, Hṙipʻsimē finds death in martyrdom for she had been called to another mission, namely, to bring the Armenians close to God through her sacrifice.

Indeed, in the *History*, the martyrdom of the virgins has serious consequences for the king and Armenians. The king and the kingdom of Armenia are in a situation of "deep distress" (§ 213). Tiridates undergoes a metamorphosis; he is transformed into a boar and the entire royal household is "afflicted with torments" while a "terrible ruin fell upon the country" (§ 213). The metamorphosis of the king, which is reminiscent of a *topos* in ancient Greek and Latin literature,[39] can be interpreted by different criteria that are not mutually exclusive. First, the wild boar is likely an allusion to the animal symbolizing the war god of Armenian Mazdeism, Vahagn, which also echoes the metamorphosis of the impious king Nebuchadnezzar (605–562 BCE) mentioned in Daniel 4.[40] At the same time, the transformation from the human condition to the brute one of animals also may be read as an allusion to pagans, who are often compared to the brute status of animals in Christian apologetic literature.[41] The metamorphosis, charged with this multilayered set of symbolisms, constitutes the punishment of the king, who is guilty of having profaned the bodies of the virgins that were considered as "God's temples." Moreover, the king will be unable to return to his human appearance until he provides the martyrs with a proper burial and personally contributes to the construction of a chapel over their remains. It is only after having completed these tasks in honor of the virgins that he is able to shed his

---

"Male Women Martyrs," 2009; and Vogt, "'Becoming Male,'" 1991. This *topos* is also attested in the Jewish tradition: Boyarin, *Dying for God*, 1999: 75–81.

[38] It is the same God who saved Noah and Abraham, who parted the Red Sea, and who fed the Jews in the desert and who rescued Jonas and Daniel and the three Hebrews from the furnace (§ 170 and 179): the story of Hṙipʻsimē merges with the one of the covenant.

[39] It suffices for us to recall here Ovid's (43 BCE–17/18 CE) *Metamorphoses* or Apuleius' (c. 125–170) *Metamorphoses*.

[40] On the wild boar as symbol of Vahagn, the god of war and bravery in the Mazdean religion, see Garsoïan, "The Iranian Substratum," 1982; and Garsoïan, "Les éléments iraniens," 1997: 27–33. The Mazdean religious symbol is ridiculed in the passages where Agathangelos uses the Armenian word *xoz* "pig, pork" rather than *varaz* "boar."

[41] See, for instance, in the same book of Agathangelos, passage 66 in which Gregory compares the king Tiridates and the other Armenians, still heathens, to "horses or mules, since there is no wisdom in them" and qualifies them as "less intelligent than an ox or donkey since you have not recognised your Fashioner" (see Ps 31:9, Is 1:3).

boar's skin. Indeed, at the very moment when the respect due to the sacred bodies of the virgins is given, the body of the profaning king passes from the inhuman (the animal) to the human and finds, with its human semblance, a soft skin like that of a newborn child (§ 773). The healing of the king, which is described as a new birth, corresponds to that of the Armenian people; it prefigures the "new and wonderful birth" that, in the second part of the work, Tiridates, his army, his household, and a multitude of Armenians receive by the water of baptism in the Euphrates (§ 830). The *martyria* that shelter the bodies of the virgins become sites of intercession for the Armenians. As Gregory explains to the Armenians: "Their bodies and their bones are temples of God in your midst for in no other way can you reconcile God with yourselves and approach God, except by the intercession of their prayers" (§ 564, see § 241).

The martyrdom of the virgin Hṙip'simē is explicitly presented by Agathangelos as the sacrifice necessary to "bring (the Armenians) near to God" (§ 720). As Gregory explains to the king, while he is still a boar, and to the other members of his court gathered around him, the bloodshed has a soteriological value that invests all Armenians:[42]

> And these martyrs (*scil.* Hṙip'simē and her companions) through his mercy will be for you a strong fortress and mighty tower, your advocates by intercession, your strengtheners by the shedding of their blood, and by their martyrdom they will bring you near to God. (§ 720)

This passage parallels the following part of Gregory's speech to the king:

> So now, on account of the death of these blessed saints, whose blood was poured on your land and who became worthy of divine grace and were sacrificed, therefore you have been visited and this land of Armenia has been heeded. (§ 249)

This soteriology is closely linked to the primordial purity of the virginal body, the "temple of God," and to the salvific power of which martyrs are bearers not only for themselves individually but also for others collectively.[43] It is interesting to note that in this section of the *History*, the valorization of Hṙip'simē's role as a virgin martyr is fundamental to the sequence of events that relate the journey of Armenians to God. This valorization is realized by the very fact that the figure of Thecla is

---

[42] Thomson, *The Teaching*, 1970.
[43] On the collective soteriological value of martyrdom, see, for example, Streete, "Women as Sources," 1999.

superimposed on that of Hřipʻsimē and by the evocation of key passages in the *Acts of Thecla* in the defense of chastity.

The close connection between Thecla and Hřipʻsimē and the latter's role as an agent of conversion for Armenians (through her death) are evoked in the following passage of Agathangelos' *History*:

> By their intercession you (*scil*. Armenians) will be reconciled with God according to the instruction of the companion apostle to these apostles of yours, the great Paul. (§ 572)

In this passage, Gregory makes of Hřipʻsimē and her sisters the "apostles" of the Armenians and the companions of Paul's apostolate. The association of the virgin apostles with Paul, indeed, can be read as another reference to the *Acts of Thecla*. In fact, at the end of the *Acts of Thecla*, Thecla receives from Paul her mission to preach (§ 41), which she precisely does in Seleucia after trying in vain to convert her mother in Iconium (§ 43).[44] Nevertheless, unlike Thecla, it is not through the "word of God" and preaching but through the shedding of blood that Hřipʻsimē is confirmed in her role as "apostle."

The role of the female saint as holy preacher, diminished in Agathangelos, is on the contrary emphasized in the *Martyrdom of Thaddaeus and Sanduxt*. In this text, to which we turn momentarily, we see Sanduxt, the disciple of the apostle Thaddaeus, participate in the conversion of Armenians through her speeches and charitable works. Several passages allow us to suppose that the author of this *Martyrdom* knew the *Acts of Thecla* and that he was inspired by them to not only compose this work but also to draw the portrait of Thaddaeus' young disciple, Sanduxt.

The Paradigm of the Holy Preacher, Modeled on Thecla, in the *Martyrdom of Thaddaeus and Sanduxt*

The *Martyrdom of Thaddaeus and Sanduxt* (*BHO* 1145) is an apocryphal Armenian text that describes the circumstances surrounding the preaching and martyrdom of Thaddaeus (presented as an apostolic figure) in Armenia.[45] The origin of the text is controversial. Scholars have vacillated between the hypothesis of a translation (from Greek or Syriac) and that of

---

[44] See, for example, Jensen, *Thekla – Die Apostolin*, 1995.
[45] The text is edited in Ališan (ed.), *Sopʻerkʻ haykakankʻ*, 1853: 9–58; French translation in Calzolari (trans.), *Les apôtres*, 2011: 51–88. The English translation by Malan (trans.), *The Life and Times*, 1868: 66–98, is used throughout this article.

a text written directly in Armenian; we concur with the latter.[46] As will be illustrated in the following paragraphs, the author knew earlier apocryphal sources, which he used in his account.

The text opens with a brief summary of the *Teaching of Addai* which relates the journey of Thaddaeus to Edessa to the court of King Abgar (fl. first century) (§ 2–3).[47] After his stay in Osrohene, the text describes the arrival of the apostle in Armenia (§ 4). The attention is quickly focused on a female figure, namely, the king's daughter, Sanduxt, who goes to Thaddaeus at night to listen to his preaching (§ 5). After hearing the Gospel, the girl adheres to Thaddaeus' teaching and immediately receives baptism (§ 5). With this gesture, she breaks with the Mazdean religion, which is the religion of her father, the king, who is also a guardian of the religion. This disobedience to both her father and the official religion of the kingdom comes at a great cost to her: her father sentences her to death (§ 23). Since her conversion is the source of the king's wrath, he also sentences the apostle to death.

At this juncture, we pause for a moment to consider the points of contact between the *Acts of Thecla* and the *Martyrdom of Thaddaeus and Sanduxt*. Indeed, there are many comparisons to be made between the two texts. Here, we will summarize these comparisons and the results of more detailed analyses that were published elsewhere.[48]

We may notice several, general features that the two texts share in common. We may break these down into the following categories: the meeting between the apostle and disciple, the conversion of a royal woman, the torture of a saint on two separate occasions, and the presence of protective animals during the trials. In the *Acts of Thecla*, for instance, Thecla "went and sat at the feet of Paul and ... with great joy kissed the feet and the chains which bound the feet and hands of Paul" (§ 18), which is similar to when Sanduxt "threw herself at his [*scil.* of Thaddaeus] holy feet, embracing them with tears" (§ 5). It is interesting to note that the

---

[46] The theological vision of the history of the Armenian people as the "chosen people," which the *Martyrdom of Thaddaeus* shares with ancient Armenian historiography, represents an argument in support of the hypothesis that the text was originally written in Armenian: Calzolari (trans.), *Les apôtres*, 2011: 43–44.
[47] The *Teaching of Addai* was translated into Armenian from Syriac in the first half of the fifth century (*BHO* 24 and *BHO* 9): Calzolari (trans.), *Les apôtres*, 2011: 32–41. The *Martyrdom of Thaddaeus* presupposes the superposition of the figure of Addai, protagonist of the *Teaching*, and that of Thaddaeus, already attested in Eusebius of Caesarea, *Ecclesiastical History* 1.13: Bardy (ed.), *Eusèbe de Césarée*, 1986: 40–45.
[48] Calzolari, "Les Actes," 2015. See also Calzolari (ed. and trans.), *Apocrypha Armeniaca I*, 2017: 69–80.

same situation described in the *Acts of Thecla* is found in another passage of the *Martyrdom of Thaddaeus*, but in reverse. It is now Thaddaeus who kisses the chains of Sanduxt ("... and coming to Sandukht, he kissed her chains" § 7). Moreover, St. Sanduxt falls to the ground in tears and kisses Thaddaeus' feet ("Sandukht ... fell on her face, and with tears kissing the Apostle's feet, said..." § 12). This parallel, however, is not conclusive: it is indeed a recurring *topos* also present, to cite one example, in the *Martyrdom of Matthew* § 6 in which Bishop Plato and other members of the clergy fall to the ground before the apostle and kiss his feet. More conclusive is the parallelism described in the following lines.

In passages 27–31 of the *Acts of Thecla*, Thecla is brought under the protection of a woman of royal stock – a close relative of the emperor – named Tryphaena ("And there was there a certain lady of a royal house and rich, Tryphaena by name, whose daughter had died" § 27; see also § 36 "for the Lady Tryphaena... is the Caesar's kinswoman..."). After having escaped martyrdom, Thecla converts her and her entire household ("And the Lady Tryphaena believed and many of her handmaidens" § 39) after having preached "all the commands of God" (§ 39). In the *Martyrdom of Thaddaeus*, among the converted, there is also a woman of royal lineage, named Zarmanduxt. As Tryphaena and her maids are converted by Thecla, so Zarmanduxt and her household are converted by Sanduxt ("Then a woman of rank, by name Zarmantukht, who was related to the king, believed with all her house" § 20). Nevertheless, the excerpt in the *Martyrdom of Thaddaeus* is shorter and does not provide more information about the relationship between Zarmanduxt and Sanduxt.

Turning our attention to the trials, like Thecla (*Acts of Thecla* § 22, see also § 28), Sanduxt (*Martyrdom of Thaddaeus* § 17, see also § 23) is condemned twice to martyrdom. Moreover, contrary to the classic scheme of the apocryphal accounts of martyrdom, in both works it is the young girl, not the apostle, who is condemned first.[49] In both works, the two saints are condemned to death by fire first and then are miraculously saved. However, the details of the miracles differ between the two texts.[50] Thus, in the *Acts of Thecla*, the flames are extinguished by a cloud of dew, hail,

---

[49] In the *Acts of Thecla* § 21, Paul is defeated and exiled from Iconium while Thecla is condemned to death. In the second part of the text, which is set in the city of Antioch, Paul disappears, and Thecla remains the sole protagonist of the episode whose central element is that she is condemned to death. In the same way, in the *Martyrdom of Thaddaeus* § 17, it is Sanduxt who is condemned for provoking the rage of the king, her father; Thaddaeus will be condemned at a later moment.

[50] In other apocryphal texts, too, the ordeal by fire is avoided by a miracle. For example, see the *Martyrdom of Matthew* § 19 in which fire is transformed into dew.

and violent rain accompanied by a loud noise; these extraordinary manifestations cause the death of the spectators:

> and a roaring sound went forth from the earth, and a cloud of dew cast a shadow over her, and hail and heavy rain was poured down upon the earth. And many people who sat and saw were destroyed; and the fire was quenched and Thecla was saved.[51] (§ 22)

In the *Martyrdom of Thaddaeus*, the martyrdom of Sanduxt is first avoided by an earthquake and a miraculous light which cause the death of the executioners. Moreover, the chains by which Sanduxt is tied are loosed and the girl is freed.[52] All this follows a manifestation of the divine voice that reassures her (§ 17). In the *Acts of Thecla*, too, Thecla is freed from her chains, although the details here differ as well:

> but the flame of the fire arose and burned the bonds with which the feet of Thecla were bound; and Thecla stood up, leapt up and remained in front of the bulls, as if no harm had happened at all to her, and as if she had not been bound at all by the feet.[53] (§ 35)

One also observes that, in the *Martyrdom of Thaddaeus*, the apostle is also condemned to death twice (§ 28 and § 31). Moreover, like Thecla and Sanduxt, he is first sentenced to death by fire. Martyrdom, furthermore, is prevented by a violent wind which manifests itself under miraculous circumstances; the wind is mixed with a cloud of dew which falls on the furnace in which Thaddaeus should have burned. The miracle causes the end of the "wicked heathens" rather than the death of the apostle. We thus find the same *topos* of the *Acts of Thecla* (§ 22).

In the *Martyrdom of Thaddaeus*, Thaddaeus must face wild beasts before the trial by fire (§ 28). This episode closely parallels the *Acts of Thecla*; in particular, the episode of the second trial in Antioch where a lioness is released into the arena to attack the saint (§ 28). However, instead of attacking her, the lioness begins to lick Thecla's feet while protecting her from the other beasts that subsequently have been released: "And they let loose upon her a great lioness … The lioness came and began to lick Thecla" (§ 28).[54] Similarly, in the *Martyrdom of Thaddaeus*, two lions are released to attack the apostle, but they do not:

---

[51] Conybeare's translation with adjustments.
[52] The broken chains theme is also found in the episode of Ephesus in *Acts of Paul* § 9.19. See also the *Martyrdom of Thaddaeus* § 28.
[53] Conybeare's translation with adjustments. [54] Ibid.

Then they let into it two lions; but these went and, crouching at the feet of the holy Apostle, licked his shoes, and howled, fawning. The Saint then prayed, and his bonds were loosened;[55] and making a sign to the lions, they each retired to his own place.[56] (§ 28)

Now that we have addressed the various points of contact that plead in favor of the hypothesis that the *Acts of Thecla* is one of the sources of the *Martyrdom of Thaddaeus*,[57] let us turn to a more telling example, namely, the portrait of Sanduxt, to examine how much it may have been influenced by the model of Thecla.

From the start, the work pays special attention to the figure of Sanduxt. At baptism, a light appears on her face as a sign of election (§ 5). After baptism, Sanduxt assumes more and more significance as the story progresses. Her most important role is evident, for example, when the text grants her the privilege of pronouncing the first profession of faith in God the Creator (§ 16). Her profession of faith occurs during a dialogue with her father who, as we have mentioned, represents both political power and the ancestral religion of Mazdean Armenia as king. The obstinacy of Sanduxt, who persists in rejecting the deities of the kingdom, is at the origin of the anger of the father-king. Thus, like Thecla – but also Maximilla in the *Acts of Andrew*, Mygdonia and queen Tertia in the *Acts of Thomas*, Nicanora in the *Acts of Philip*, and Xanthippe in the *Acts of Peter* to name a few – Sanduxt fits into a classical narratological schema of apocryphal literature and, more broadly, of hagiographic literature developed especially in the stories of martyrdom. According to this scheme, a woman belonging to a notable family is converted and provokes the anger of a man, normally the husband or the fiancé, who embodies a leading institutional role. Anger is linked to the choice of chastity adopted by the woman who, following her conversion, moves away from her spouse and chooses chastity.[58] Sanduxt, however, incurs her father's wrath. As a result, the king, according to the classic scheme of martyrdom narratives, holds the apostle responsible for misleading his daughter and, thus, condemns the apostle to death.

---

[55] The chains that are loosened evokes a similar miracle that took place during the torture of Sanduxt (*Martyrdom of Thaddaeus* § 17) and of Thecla (*Acts of Thecla* § 35).
[56] We will not repeat here the analyses of the passages in both texts that mention the baptism of the two saints, albeit in different circumstances (denied baptism, in the case of Thecla, allowed baptism, for Sanduxt). The reader, rather, is referred to Calzolari, "Les *Actes*," 2015: 400–401.
[57] This hypothesis was already proposed by Akinean, "Researches," 1970.
[58] Tissot, "Encratisme," 1981.

The example of Sanduxt, however, presents features that distinguish her from the aforementioned. In the *Martyrdom of Thaddaeus*, in fact, conflict is not provoked by choosing to live a chaste life. To be sure, Sanduxt is often described by the traditional epithet of "virgin" (Arm. *koys*) as in the following passage: "keep this Sandukht, who is yet a spotless maid [lit. virgin]" (§ 13, 23, 26, 27, and *passim*). Nevertheless, her death sentence is provoked by her vociferous opposition to the gods and morals of her father and kingdom, of which he is the ruler, rather than by her choice of chastity in her responses to her father. Indeed, Sanduxt contrasts earthly fatherhood on the one hand and heavenly and spiritual fatherhood on the other. She recognizes the Lord or even the apostle who raised her in the faith as father, rather than her biological father (§ 12, see also § 14 and § 22). In other passages, Sanduxt addresses the Lord by acknowledging him as "father and creator" (§ 17) while the Lord acknowledges Sanduxt as "daughter" (§ 17 and § 7) just as Thaddaeus refers to Sanduxt as "sister," "daughter," or "daughter of the heavenly King" (§ 14, § 12, and *passim*).

As a counterpoint to Sanduxt's denial of Sanatruk's paternity are the passages that refer to Sanatruk's paternal love and piety. At first, he wishes to spare his daughter out of "his fatherly feelings of pity for her whom he loved so much, and that made him weep bitterly" (§ 11). Faced with her denial ("Deniest thou me, and lovest thou that deceiver?"), Sanatruk orders Sanduxt to turn from her stubborn thoughts, threatening to kill her with a nasty death in case she does not follow his injunction (§ 16). Sanatruk's threats do not move Sanduxt. She instead responds by confirming her faithfulness to God, the creator, whom she came to know through Thaddaeus. She also professes her faith in the "Lord, the Maker of heaven and earth, and the only Son of God, with the Holy Ghost Who comes from them [. . .] He is the Lord of lords and King of kings; he is the light and the life of all creatures" (§ 16).[59]

On the eve of her death, Sanduxt's initiation is accomplished (§ 23). She can now assist the apostle in his activity: indeed, we see her preach, comfort, take care of her companions and martyrs, and, also, like an apostle, she performs miracles and converts many souls:

---

[59] Cf. also Sanduxt's following reply to her father, who asks her: "'Who is He Whom thou callest God and Father?' Sandukht answered, 'God. God is He Who made all things out of nothing, and established all things made by the Word of His mouth; but your deceived mind and your darkened imagination have forsaken God your Maker, Who made and established you out of nothing. And ye worship the ghosts of dead men that neither see nor hear, that are akin to devils, that doom to perdition your darkened minds, and make you the children of hell. And now ye have to go into outer darkness with your leader Satan, where there is weeping of eyes and gnashing of teeth" (§ 16).

> She then comforted all the believers, feeding them with bread, and covering them with raiment, allowing them to be in want of nothing; and she preached the Word of Life, and converted many through the signs and miracles which she wrought. (§ 19)

Sanatruk accuses his daughter as someone who "deceives most of them" (§ 20); words that accentuate and emphasize her active role. Before her first condemnation, she is seen exhorting her companions in the faith with a loud voice, repeating formulas that are uttered elsewhere by the apostle or by God himself ("Then raising her voice, she said rejoicing, to her companions in the faith, 'Stand fast, brethren, and be strong in Christ...'" § 15). A passage from the *Martyrdom of Thaddaeus*, moreover, mentions Sanduxt's compassion towards her companions in the faith:

> And when it was night, a heavenly light spread all over them; when the holy maiden Sandukht sent to her own home, unknown to her father, to fetch from thence fine linen cloth; and taking her sainted companions in the faith, she wound their bodies and kissed them, saying: "Blessed are ye, brethren and sisters, who have been made worthy of the heavenly joy. Remember me, your handmaid." Then she buried them near to her own palace, taking care that no one in the royal hall should be made aware of it. (§ 11)

The passages cited above illustrate that it is not the model of Thecla as a virgin that was followed by the author of the *Martyrdom of Thaddaeus* for his portrait of Sanduxt, but rather that of Thecla as an apostle as she appears in the final section of the *Acts of Thecla*.

The *Martyrdom of Photine*

Now, we will turn our attention to an Armenian hagiographic text, the *Martyrdom of Saint Photine* (the Samaritan woman of John 4:1–42), since it also depicts a holy apostle modeled on Thecla as a female apostle. The complete title of the work is the *Martyrdom of the Holy Samaritan Woman Photine, which Is Something Luminous* (*BHO* 992).[60] The date of redaction is not known, and extensive studies to clarify its origin have not been undertaken to date.[61] Despite these unresolved issues, its existence in

---

[60] The text was edited for the first time in Ališan, *Vark' ew vkayabanut'iwnk'*, 1874: 503–505, on the basis of one manuscript from Venice (not specified). The text has been reedited more recently, with a French translation, on the basis of manuscripts Arm. 116 and 178 held in the Bibliothèque nationale de France, in Outtier (ed.), "La sainte samaritaine," 1998: 204–208 (which does not specify the possible dating of the Armenian text nor its origin).

[61] It would be worth comparing it systematically to the Greek *Passion* edited in Halkin and Festugière (eds. and trans.), *Dix textes inédits*, 1984: 94–103 (with French translation).

Armenian remains an interesting testimony to the reception of Thecla in Armenia. Indeed, this text lends itself to various considerations relevant for our purposes. It contains several details that establish unique connections between Thecla and Photine. These details are absent from John's account but also from the Greek *Passion* preserved in Koutloumous' *Imperial Menology* (*BHG* 1541g).[62]

Let us recall here that in John 4:39–42, the Samaritan woman believed in the Messiah and, by her example and testimony, converted other Samaritans in her city. The Armenian *Martyrdom* states that the conversion of the other inhabitants of the city took place thanks to the preaching of the Gospel by the saint whom Christ himself "sent as a female apostle, before the apostles, to preach [his] coming."[63] She then became a companion of the apostle Paul himself. Indeed, after receiving baptism and taking the name of Photine, the Samaritan woman, described as "follower of apostles," became a disciple of Peter and Paul; she went with them to Rome where she continued to teach. Like them, she too was condemned to death by the emperor Nero (37–68).[64]

The link between the woman and the apostles, especially Paul, presupposes a possible association with Thecla. This parallel becomes explicit at the trial. Thrown into the fire (like Thecla in the first trial), she addresses the apostles Peter and Paul by shouting and begs them "to help her by prayer, like Blessed Thecla in the past, whom the fire did not approach nor the fangs of the ferocious beasts." This is an explicit reference to the *Acts of Thecla* § 22 and § 33. The protection is granted to her: "Indeed, this arm which had been extended on the cross protected her as well as the prayer of Saint Paul. The same grace of the Holy Spirit took Saint Photine under his shadow."[65]

Thanks to this protection, Photine resists the effects of her gruesome torture and survives. The emperor then orders that she be thrown into a deep and dark jail where there are venomous snakes and reptiles.[66] In the jail, Photine receives a miraculous vision – God himself appears to her, accompanied by the two apostles,[67] and restores sight to her eyes, which had been gouged out during the trial. She survives another three years in the pit before dying. Her relics were later deposited in a suitable place from where, according to a frequent *topos* of hagiographic literature, they

---

[62] See n. 61.   [63] Translations of this text are mine.
[64] According to the Greek *Passion* § 2, after the martyrdom of Peter and Paul, Photine goes to Carthage where she converts many people before being condemned to death by Nero.
[65] Outtier (ed.), "La sainte samaritaine," 1998: 208, 47–49.
[66] The detail of the pit is also found in the Greek *Passion* § 5.   [67] Cf. Greek *Passion* § 5.

continued to provide "healings of the eyes and illuminations by the intercession of the saint."⁶⁸

After having presented stories that are inspired, implicitly or explicitly, by the *Acts of Thecla* to draw the portrait of female figures, it is interesting to conclude with a work in which Thecla intervenes as the protagonist: the *History of Armenia* by Faustus of Byzantium. In this case, the author is not inspired by the *Acts of Thecla* but by the *Miracles* composed by pseudo-Basil of Seleucia.⁶⁹

Thecla, Patroness of Nicene Orthodoxy, in the *History of Armenia* by Faustus of Byzantium: The *Miracles of Thecla* by Pseudo-Basil as a Source

The *History of Armenia* by Faustus of Byzantium, or *Buzandaran Patmut'iwnk'*, deals with Armenian history in the fourth century.⁷⁰ In this period, the Armenian Church was confronted with questions about religious orthodoxy that agitated the Christian East, especially after the Council of Nicaea (325), whose canons it had adopted. The religious policy of the kingdom was conditioned inter alia by the requirement of loyalty that the kings of Armenia necessarily owed to the Roman emperors.⁷¹ This question became complex when the emperors followed Arian tendencies, which the Armenian Church had always condemned strongly.⁷² The *History of Armenia* by Faustus is centered around three topics: (a) the organization of the primitive Church of Armenia and the history of its first patriarchs, (b) the history of the Armenian Arsacid kings (12–428), and (c) the history of the noble Armenian family, the Mamikonians. Its exploration of these three narrative veins is indicative of the context that animated Armenia in the fourth century. Moreover, it shows the clear alignment of its author to the doctrinal positions followed by the Church, from which the Armenian kings of the time seem to have deviated. Now, the character of Thecla is at the heart of a section of book IV that depicts the Armenian Catholicos Nersēs (353–373) as the main champion of Nicene orthodoxy against Valens (328–378), the Arian emperor.⁷³

---

⁶⁸ Outtier (ed.), "La sainte samaritaine," 1998: 210, 78–79.   ⁶⁹ See n. 2.
⁷⁰ Patkanean (ed.), *P'awstosi Buzandac'woy Patmut'iwn Hayoc'*, 1883. The English translation in Garsoïan (trans.), *The Epic Histories*, 1989, is used throughout this chapter.
⁷¹ Garsoïan, "Politique ou orthodoxie?," 1967.
⁷² On the Armenian Church in the fourth century, see Garsoïan, *L'Église arménienne*, 1999; and Garsoïan, "Politique ou orthodoxie?," 1967.
⁷³ The whole section on Nersēs lends itself to other considerations, especially the fact that it takes some elements from the hagiographical legend of Basil that Faustus attributes to Nersēs, in his rewriting of the story. On this, see Calzolari, "De sainte Thècle à Anahit," 1997; and Calzolari (ed.

In this section, Thecla herself is one of the characters (IV, 10). As such, she enters into the story of the most significant events of Armenian history and of the Eastern Roman Empire in the fourth century. According to the author's perspective, these events revolve around the defense of Nicene orthodoxy. The death of the Arian emperor Valens, which occurred during a disastrous battle against the Goths at Adrianople, is presented by Faustus as divine punishment for his deviation from orthodoxy toward the Arian heresy. According to the Armenian historian, the emperor was indeed killed not on the battlefield but by two military saints, namely, St. Sergius and St. Theodore.[74]

It is possible to consider the episode of Valens' death in Faustus as an Armenian variant of a *topos* preserved in different forms in Eastern literature, namely, that of the death of the impious emperor; a *topos* that was especially deployed with regard to the emperor Julian (331–363).[75] However, the Armenian variant presents a *hapax*. According to Faustus' text, the death of Valens is decided during a meeting of apostles and saints who gathered at the sanctuary of Thecla to deliberate the matter and were received and welcomed by Thecla (Tʻekł) in person:

> And the holy lady Tʻekł went to meet them adorned in such brilliance that radiance like light seemed to emanate from her. They greeted each other, and the lady Tʻekł said to them: "Welcome, dear friends and laborers of Christ." (IV, 10)

According to Faustus, a sophist happened to be traveling to the capital to meet the emperor. He decided to spend the night in the sanctuary of Thecla and came upon the meeting where the plan was being hatched. He also happened to be present at the reunion of the saints on the day after the murder of the emperor, when the news of Valens' death was communicated. The sophist is an important figure to understand from which source Faustus possibly drew this image of Thecla as patroness of Christendom struggling against the Arian enemy.

In general, the analysis of the passage makes it possible to formulate the hypothesis that the author of the Armenian narrative was able to draw inspiration from the *Miracles of Thecla* by pseudo-Basil of Seleucia.[76] This

---

and trans.), *Apocrypha Armeniaca I*, 2017: 89–91. On the figure of Nersēs, see Garsoïan, "'*Quidam Narseus?*," 1969.

[74] See Peeters, "Un miracle," 1921.
[75] See Calzolari, "De sainte Thècle à Anahit," 1997; and Calzolari (ed. and trans.), *Apocrypha Armeniaca I*, 2017: 87–89.
[76] Calzolari, "De sainte Thècle à Anahit," 1997.

work recalls the practices of incubation associated with Thecla's cult in Seleucia (*Miracles* 12, 17–19, 23–24, 38–39, and *passim*),[77] a practice presupposed by the Armenian narrative. The work also makes Thecla a new Athena with a weakness for men of letters and sophists (*Miracles* 3, 37–39, 41, and *passim*).[78] Moreover, in the *Miracles* we find, for the first time in Greek literature, the portrait of Thecla as a saint opposing the Arians. Furthermore, we find in the text that the Nicene Creed, inscribed on the walls of her sanctuary at Seleucia, is protected by the hand of the saint. In this way, Thecla becomes the guarantor of the inviolability of the canons of Nicaea. *Miracle* 10, in fact, recounts the vain attempt of the Arian bishop of Seleucia, Symposios (c. 370–380), to destroy the inscription. After several useless attempts, the emissary "who waged war against the godly letters fell off his ladder, broke his bones, and all at once paid the penalty for his audacity."[79] As for Bishop Symposios, he has to face the facts: he recognizes the inviolable nature of the inscription and the doctrine it conveys and adheres to the dogma of the consubstantial Trinity:

> Immediately at that moment, having exchanged his false opinion, Symposios pronounced, breathed forth, confessed, publicly and visibly proclaimed, and was teaching the very formula [of the inscribed creed] which he had formerly attacked: the consubstantial Trinity.[80]

As the text states, "the undefiled and immaculate hand of the virgin was clearly protecting and guarding those letters like imperial seals."[81] The saint, a patroness of orthodoxy, intervenes *in personam* to protect the letters against enemies. If we cannot speak of a phenomenon of intertextuality, it is nevertheless clear that Faustus grants Thecla the same active role in the punishment of the Arian emperor by making her personally involved in the core events. The cycle of the miracles of Thecla, which abounds with multiple variants especially in the Greek tradition, is thus enriched by a new, Armenian, and unprecedented episode.

Finally, it is interesting to observe that this episode of Christian history – the death of Valens – specifically the variant written by Faustus, enjoyed longevity in the medieval Armenian reception. Indeed, in the *History of*

---

[77] Dagron (ed. and trans.), *Vie et Miracles*, 1978: 103–105; and Johnson, *The Life and Miracles*, 2006: 172–175. On the diffusion of the cult of Thecla in Asia Minor, see also Davis, *The Cult of St. Thecla*, 2001.
[78] Dagron (ed. and trans.), *Vie et Miracles*, 1978: 82 and 84–85.
[79] A full English translation of the *Miracles of Thecla* is not available; we follow the translation of *Miracle* 10 in Johnson, *The Life and Miracles*, 2006: 136.
[80] Ibid.   [81] Ibid.

Arcruni (IV, 2) by Tʿovma Arcruni (fl. ninth-tenth century) and his successors, the death of the emir of Azerbaijan Muhammad al-Afšīn (d. 901) is interpreted as the result of divine punishment for the misfortunes that befell Armenia. It is explicitly compared to the death of Valens and the exceptional circumstances associated with the appearance of Thecla:

> There he met with vengeance for the evils he had inflicted on Armenia. God did not spare him, but smote him with a painful ulcer through a holy angel – as once [he smote] the emperor Valens through the valiant martyrs of Christ by the vision of Saint Thecla, as the historian Biwzand has accurately expounded to us.[82]

This is one of the few passages of the *History of Armenia* by Faustus that is mentioned by later sources,[83] which demonstrates that this episode and the image of Thecla that it conveys were consolidated in the memory of Armenian historiographers over the centuries.

Conclusion

The texts presented above are witnesses to the legend of Thecla's success in the Armenian literary tradition. As we have seen, the figure of the saint of Iconium, with the peculiarities that characterize her in the apocryphal *Acts*, influenced the representation of holy women (Sanduxt and Hṙipʿsimē), women whom the early Armenian historiographical and apocryphal tradition associates with two fundamental stages of the Christianization of Armenia. First, Thecla serves as a model of female sanctity along three important lines, namely, as holy virgin, teacher, and apostle. Second, as the venerated first proto-martyr, she serves as a model for the first female martyrs in the history of Armenian Christianity, respectively, in the apostolic age (Sanduxt) and at the time of the foundation of the first official Church of Armenia (Hṙipʿsimē). It is also important to note that the Armenian tradition not only borrowed elements from the apocryphal and hagiographic traditions of Thecla, but it also helped to create new ones. In particular, it contributed to the development of the legend of the saint by adding a new episode to the cycle of miracles that have been attributed to her. This new miracle is linked to a turning point in the Christian history of the whole Empire – the struggle against heresy – and

---

[82] Patkanean (ed.), *Tʿovma Arcruni*, 1887: 275. The English translation by Thomson (trans.), *Thomas Artsruni*, 1985: 338, is used here.

[83] Garsoïan (trans.), *The Epic Histories*, 1989: 4–5.

lies within a section of a text that presents the fight against the enemies of orthodoxy as a struggle in which a patriarch of the Armenian Church stands out. The shifts and changes made to this section help to make of Thecla a holy protector of orthodoxy and its defenders, especially the Armenian champion. In general, it is fascinating to think that the varied ways in which the features of Thecla's legend are referred to helped shape the Armenian tradition. In other words, they helped Armenians to rethink their history on the model of one of the earliest Christian female figures from the Greek world through the mediation of Syria.

Bibliography

Akinean, Nersēs. "Researches in Armenian literature: *The Martyrdom of Saint Thaddaeus and the Virgin Sanduxt* and the *Canons of Thaddaeus.*" *Handēs Amsōreay* 83 (1969): 399–426 and 84 (1970): 1–34 (in Armenian).

Albrecht, Ruth. *Das Leben der heiligen Makrina auf dem Hintergrund der Thecla-Traditionen: Studien zu den Ursprüngen des weiblichen Mönchtums im 4. Jahrhundert in Kleinasien.* Forschungen zur Kirchen- und Dogmengeschichte 38. Göttingen: Vandenhoeck & Ruprecht, 1986.

Ališan, Łewond, ed. *Sop'erk' Haykakank' [Armenian Writings].* Vol. 8. Venice: Mekhitarian Press, 1853.

——— ed. *Vark' ew vkayabanut'iwnk' srboc' hatəntir k'ałealk' i čaṙəntrac' [Saints' Lives and Martyrdoms: Anthology Gathered from the čaṙəntir.* 2 vols. Venice: Mekhitarian Press, 1874.

Amand de Mendieta, David, and Matthieu-Charles Moons, eds. "Une curieuse homélie grecque inédite sur la virginité adressée aux pères de famille." *Revue bénédictine* 63 (1953): 18–69.

Ananian, Paolo. "La data e le circonstanze della consecrazione di S. Gregorio Illuminatore." *Le Muséon* 74 (1961): 43–73 and 317–360.

"Ripsima, Gaiana e compagne, sante, martiri in Armenia." In *Bibliotheca Sanctorum*. Rome: Città Nuova editrice, 1968: 11: 206–212.

Angelidi, Christine. "Virginité ascétique: Choix, contraintes et imaginaire (4ème–7ème siècles)." In *Comportamenti e immaginario della sessualità nell'Alto Medioevo*. Atti delle settimane di studio della Fondazione Centro Italiano di Studi sull'Alto medioevo 53. Spoleto: Fondazione CISAM, 2006: 675–695.

Aspegren, Kerstin. *The Male Woman: A Feminine Ideal in the Early Church*. Acta Universitatis Upsaliensis/Uppsala Women's Studies 4. Uppsala; Stockholm: Almqvist and Wiksell International, 1990.

Aubin, Melissa. "Reversing Romance? *The Acts of Thecla* and the Ancient Novel." In *Ancient Fiction and Early Christian Narrative*, edited by Ronald F. Hock, J. Bradley Chance, and Judith Perkins. Society of Biblical Literature Symposium Series 6. Atlanta: Scholars Press, 1998: 257–272.

Bardy, Gustave, ed. *Eusèbe de Césarée, Histoire ecclésiastique et les Martyrs de Palestine*. Sources chrétiennes 31. Paris: Les Éditions du Cerf, 1952. 4th ed., 1986.

Barrier, Jeremy. "*The Acts of Paul and Thecla*: The Historiographical Context." In *Thecla: Paul's Disciple and Saint in the East and West*, edited by Jeremy W. Barrier, Jan N. Bremmer, T. Nicklas, and A. Puig i Tàrrech. Studies in Early Christian Apocrypha 12. Leuven: Peeters, 2017: 327–350.

Beatrice, Pier Francesco. "Continenza e matrimonio nel cristianesimo primitivo." In *Etica sessuale e matrimonio nel cristianesimo delle origini*, edited by Raniero Cantalamessa. Milan: Vita e Pensiero, 1976: 3–68.

Boughton, Lynne C. "From Pious Legend to Feminist Fantasy: Distinguishing Hagiographical License from Apostolic Practice in the *Acts of Paul/Acts of Thecla*." *The Journal of Religion* 71 (1991): 362–383.

Boyarin, Daniel. *Dying for God: Martyrdom and the Making of Christianity and Judaism*. Stanford: Stanford University Press, 1999.

Brock, Sebastian P., and Luke van Rompay. *Catalogue of the Syriac Manuscripts and Fragments in the Library of Deir al-Surian, Wadi al-Natrun (Egypt)*. Orientalia Lovaniensia Analecta 227. Leuven; Paris; Walpole: Peeters, 2014.

Brown, Peter. *The Body and Society: Men, Women and Sexual Renunciation in Early Christianity*. New York: Columbia University Press, 1988.

Burris, Catherine. "The Reception of the *Acts of Thecla* in Syriac Christianity: Translation, Collection, and Reception." PhD diss., University of North Carolina, Chapel Hill, 2010.

Burrus, Virginia. "Chastity as Autonomy: Women in the Stories of the Apocryphal Acts." *Semeia* 38 (1986): 101–117.

Chastity as Autonomy: Women in the Stories of the Apocryphal Acts. San Francisco: Winston & Seabury, 1987.

"Mimicking Virgins: Colonial Ambivalence and the Ancient Romance." *Arethusa* 38, no. 1 (2005): 49–88.

Buytaert, Éligius M., ed. *Eusèbe d'Émèse, Discours conservés en latin*. Vol. 1. Spicilegium Sacrum Lovaniense 26. Louvain: Peeters, 1953.

Calef, Susan A. "Thecla 'Tried and True' and the Inversion of Romance." In *A Feminist Companion to the New Testament Apocrypha*, edited by Amy-Jill Levine and Marya M. Robbins. London: T&T Clark, 2006: 163–185.

Calzolari, Valentina. "De sainte Thècle à Anahit: Une hypothèse d'interprétation du récit de la mort de l'empereur Valens dans les *Buzandaran Patmut'iwnk'*." In *Armenian Perspectives: 10th Anniversary Conference of the Association Internationale des Études Arméniennes. SOAS, London*, edited by Nicholas Awde. Richmond; Surrey: Curzon Press, 1997: 39–49, 371–377.

"La version arménienne du *Martyre d'André*." In *The Apocryphal Acts of Andrew*, edited by Jan N. Bremmer. Studies in Early Christian Apocrypha 5. Louvain: Peeters, 2000: 149–185.

"La citation du Ps 78 [77], 5–8 dans l'épilogue de l'*Histoire de l'Arménie d'Agathange*." *Revue des Études Arméniennes* 29 (2003–2004): 9–27.

"Mesrop (Maštoc')." In *Reallexikon für Antike und Christentum*. Vol. 24. Stuttgart: Anton Hiersemann Verlag, 2011: 749–758.

"Le sang des femmes et le plan de Dieu. Réflexions à partir de l'historiographie arménienne ancienne (Ve siècle ap. J.-C.)." In *Victimes au féminin*, edited by Francesca Prescendi, Agnès A. Nagy, Marc Kolakowski, and Aurore Schwab. L'Equinoxe. Genève: Georg, 2011: 178–194.

"Les récits apocryphes de l'enfance dans la tradition arménienne." In *Infancy Gospels: Stories and Identities*, edited by Claire Clivaz, Andreas Dettwiler, L. Devillers, and E. Norelli, with the collaboration of B. Bertho. WUNT 281. Tübingen: Mohr Siebeck, 2011: 560–587.

trans. *Les apôtres Thaddée et Barthélemy. Aux origines du christianisme arménien*. Apocryphes 13. Turnhout: Brepols, 2011.

"Les *Actes de Paul et Thècle* et le *Martyre de Thaddée et Sanduxt arméniens*: Phénomènes d'intertextualité et rôle des femmes." *Le Muséon* 128 (2015): 381–414.

"The legend of St. Thecla in the Armenian tradition: From Asia Minor to Tarragona through Armenia." In *Thecla: Paul's Disciple and Saint in the East and West*, edited by Jeremy W. Barrier, Jan N. Bremmer, T. Nicklas, and A. Puig i Tàrrech. Studies in Early Christian Apocrypha 12. Leuven: Peeters, 2017: 285–305.

ed. and trans. *Apocrypha armeniaca I: Acta Pauli et Theclae, Prodigia Theclae, Martyrium Pauli*. Corpus Christianorum. Series Apocryhorum 20. Turnhout: Brepols, 2017.

"Mary and Eve: The Permanence of the First Mother in Armenian Apocryphal Infancy Gospel." In *Pregnancy and Childbirth in the Premodern World: European and Middle Eastern Cultures from Late Antiquity to the Renaissance*, edited by Costanza Gislon Dopfel, A. Foscati, and Ch. Burnett. Cursor 36. Turnout: Brepols, 2019: 193–212.

Cameron, Averil. "Virginity as Metaphor: Women and Rhetoric of Early Christianity." In *History as Text: The Writing of Ancient History*, edited by Averil Cameron. London: Duckworth, 1989: 184–205. Reprint, Chapel Hill: North Carolina University Press, 1990.

Castelli, Elizabeth. "'I Will Make Mary Man:' Pieties of the Body and Gender: Transformation of Christian Women in Late Antiquity." In *Body Guards: The Cultural Politics of Gender Ambiguity*, edited by Julia Epstein and Kristina Straub. New York; London: Routledge, 1991: 29–49.

Clark, Elizabeth A. *Reading Renunciation: Asceticism and Scripture in Early Christianity*. Princeton: Princeton University Press, 1999.

Cobb, L. Stephanie. *Dying To Be Men: Gender and Language in Early Christian Martyr Texts*. New York: Columbia University Press, 2008.

Consolino, Franca E. "La sessualità nella tradizione patristica." In *Comportamenti e immaginario della sessualità nell'Alto Medioevo*. Atti delle settimane di studio della Fondazione Centro Italiano di Studi sull'Alto medioevo 53. Spoleto: Fondazione CISAM, 2006: 85–134.

Conybeare, Frederick C., ed. and trans. *The Apology and Acts of Apollonius and Other Monuments of Early Christianity*. London: Swan Sonnenschein & Co., 1894.

Cooper, Kate. "Apostles, Ascetic Women, and Questions of Audience: New Reflections on the Rhetoric of Gender in the Apocryphal Acts." In *Society of Biblical Literature Seminar Papers 31*, edited by Eugene H. Lovering Jr. Atlanta: Scholars Press, 1992: 147–153.

The Virgin and the Bride: Idealized Womanhood in Late Antiquity. Cambridge, MA; London: Harvard University Press, 1996.

"The Bride of Christ, the 'Male Woman,' and the Female Reader in Late Antiquity." In *The Oxford Handbook of Women and Gender in Medieval Europe*, edited by Judith Bennet and Ruth Karras. Oxford: Oxford University Press, 2013: 529–544.

Corsaro, Francesco. "Elementi romanzeschi e aretalogia negli *Atti* apocrifi *di Paolo e Tecla*. Codici e strutture formali." In *La narrativa cristiana antica. Codici narrativi, strutture formali, schemi retorici: XXIII Incontro di studiosi dell'antichità cristiana. Roma, 5–7 maggio 1994*, edited by Salvatore Pricoco, P. Siniscalco, and G. Dareggi. Studia Ephemeridis Augustinianum 50. Rome: Institutum Patristicum Augustinianum, 1995: 77–90.

Coyne Kelly, Kathleen. *Performing Virginity and Testing Chastity in the Middle Ages*. London; New York: Routledge, 2000.

Dagron, Gilbert, ed. and trans. *Vie et Miracles de sainte Thècle. Texte grec, traduction et commentaire par Gilbert Dagron avec la collaboration de M. Dupré La Tour*. Subsidia Hagiographica 62. Brussels: Société des Bollandistes, 1978.

Davies, Stevan L. *The Revolt of the Widows: The Social World of the Apocryphal Acts*. Carbondale: Southern Illinois University Press, 1980.

"Women, Tertullian and the Acts of Paul." *Semeia* 38 (1986): 139–143.

Davis, Stephen J. *The Cult of St. Thecla: A Tradition of Women's Piety in Late Antiquity*. Oxford Early Christian Studies. Oxford: Oxford University Press, 2001.

"From Women's Piety to Male Devotion: Gender Studies, *The Acts of Paul and Thecla* and the Evidence of an Arabic Manuscript." *Harvard Theological Review* 108, no. 4 (2015): 579–593.

Dobschütz, Ernst von. "Der Roman in der alt-christlichen Literatur." *Deutsche Rundschau* 111 (1902): 87–106.

Dunn, Peter. "Women's Liberation, the *Acts of Paul* and Other Apocryphal Acts of the Apostles: A Review of Some Recent Interpreters." *Apocrypha* 4 (1993): 245–261.

Elm, Susan. *Virgins of God: The Making of Ascetism in Late Antiquity*. Oxford: Clarendon Press, 1994.

Garsoïan, Nina G. "Politique ou orthodoxie? L'Arménie au quatrième siècle." *Revue des Études Arméniennes* 4 (1967): 297–320. Reprint, Nina G. Garsoïan, *Armenia between Byzantium and the Sasanians*. Collected Studies. London: Variorum Reprints, 1985, no. IV.

"'*Quidam Narseus?*' A Note on the Mission of St. Nersēs the Great." In *Armeniaca. Mélanges d'études arméniennes*. Venice: Île de Saint-Lazare, 1969.

"The Iranian Substratum of the 'Agat'angelos Cycle.'" In *East of Byzantium: Syria and Armenia in the Formative Period*, edited by Nina G. Garsoïan, Th. F. Matthews, and R. W. Thomson. Washington, DC: Dumbarton Oaks, Center for Byzantine Studies, 1982: 153–164. Reprint, Nina G. Garsoïan, *Armenia between Byzantium and the Sasanians*. Collected Studies. London: Variorum Reprints, 1985, no. XII.

trans. *The Epic Histories Attributed to P'awstos Buzand (Buzandaran Patmut'iwnk')*. Harvard Armenian Texts and Studies 8. Cambridge, MA: Harvard University Press, 1989.

"Les éléments iraniens dans l'Arménie paléochrétienne." In *Des Parthes au Califat: Quatre leçons sur la formation de l'identité arménienne*, edited by Nina G. Garsoïan and Jean-Pierre Mahé. Travaux et mémoires du Centre de recherche d'histoire et civilisation de Byzance. Monographies 10. Paris: De Boccard, 1997: 9–37.

L'Église arménienne et le grand schisme d'Orient. CSCO 574. Subsidia 100. Louvain: Peeters, 1999.

Gorce, Denys, ed. *Vie de sainte Mélanie*. Sources chrétiennes 90. Paris: Les Éditions du Cerf, 1962.

Halkin, François, and André-Jean Festugière, eds. and trans. *Dix textes inédits tirés du Ménologe impérial de Koutloumous*. Cahiers d'orientalisme 8. Geneva: Patrick Cramer, 1984.

Hayne, Léonie. "Thecla and the Church Fathers." *Vigiliae Christianae* 48 (1994): 209–218.

Hilberg, Isidor, ed. *Sancti Eusebii Hieronymi Epistulae*. Corpus Scriptorum Ecclesiasticorum Latinorum 54. Vienna: Verlag der Österreichischen Akademie der Wissenschaften, 1996.

Hilhorst, Anthony. "Tertullian on the *Acts of Paul*." In *The Apocryphal Acts of Paul and Thecla*, edited by Jan N. Bremmer. Studies on the Apocryphal Acts of the Apostles 2. Kampen: Kok Pharos, 1996: 150–163.

Jensen, Anne. *Thecla – Die Apostolin. Ein apokrypher Text neu entdeckt*. Frauen – Kultur – Geschichte 3. Freiburg; Basel; Vienna: Herder, 1995.

Johnson, Scott F. *The Life and Miracles of Thekla: A Literary Study*. Hellenic Studies 13. Washington, DC: Center for Hellenic Studies, 2006.

Kaestli, Jean-Daniel, and Willy Rordorf, eds. and trans. "La fin de la vie de Thècle dans les manuscrits des *Actes de Paul et Thècle*. Édition des textes additionnels." *Apocrypha* 25 (2014): 9–101.

Kraemer, Ross S. *Unreliable Witnesses: Religion, Gender, and History in the Greco-Roman Mediterranean*. Oxford; New York: Oxford University Press, 2011.

Lane Fox, Robin. *Pagans and Christians*. Harmondsworth: Alfred A. Knopf, 1986.

Lipsius, Richard A., and Max Bonnet, eds. *Acta apostolorum apocrypha*. Vol. II.2. Leipzig: Hermann Mendelssohn, 1903. Reprint, Hildesheim: Olms 1959.

MacDonald, Dennis R. *The Legend and the Apostle: The Battle for Paul in Story and Canon*. Philadelphia: Westminster, 1983.

"The Role of Women in the Production of the Apocryphal Acts of the Apostles." *The Iliff Review* 41 (1984): 21–38.

MacDonald, Margaret Y. *Early Christian Women and Pagan Opinion: The Power of the Hysterical Woman.* Cambridge: Cambridge University Press, 1996.

Mahé, Jean-Pierre. "Entre Moïse et Mahomet: réflexions sur l'historiographie arménienne." *Revue des Études Arméniennes* 23 (1992): 121–153.

"Hŕip'simē 'jetée de la mort vers la vie.'" In *Hypermachos: Studien zu Byzantinistik, Armenologie und Georgistik. Festschrift für Werner Seibt zum 65. Geburtstag*, edited by Christos Stavrakos, A.-K. Wassiliou, and M. K. Krikorian. Wiesbaden: Harrassowitz, 2008: 235–241.

Malan, Solomon C., trans. *The Life and Times of S. Gregory the Illuminator the Founder and Patron Saint of the Armenian Church.* London; Oxford; Cambridge: Rivingtons, 1868.

Maraval, Pierre, ed. *Grégoire de Nysse, Vie de sainte Macrine.* Sources chrétiennes 178. Paris: Les Éditions du Cerf, 1971.

Marcovich, Miroslav, ed. *Origenes, Contra Celsum Libri VIII.* Vigiliae Christianae, Supplements 54. Leiden; Boston: Brill, 2001.

Marjanen, Antti. "Male Women Martyrs: The Function of Gender-Transformation Language in Early Christian Martyrdom Accounts." In *Metamorphoses: Resurrection, Body and Transformative Practices in Early Christianity*, edited by Turid K. Seim and J. Økland. Berlin: De Gruyter, 2009: 231–247.

Matthews, Shelly. "Thinking of Thecla: Issues in Feminist Historiography." *Journal of Feminist Studies in Religion* 17, no. 2 (Fall 2001): 39–55.

Muehlberger, Ellen. "Ambivalence about the Angelic Life." *Journal of Early Christian Studies* 16 (2008): 447–478.

Angels in Late Ancient Christianity. Oxford: Oxford University Press, 2013.

Musurillo, Herbert, ed. *Jean Chrysostome, La virginité.* Sources chrétiennes 125. Paris: Les Éditions du Cerf, 1966.

Musurillo, Herbert, and Victor-Henri Debidour, eds. *Méthode d'Olympe, Le Banquet.* Sources chrétiennes 95. Paris: Les Éditions du Cerf, 1963.

Ng, E. Y. L. "*Acts of Paul and Thecla*: Women's Stories and Precedent?" *Journal of Theological Studies* 55 (2004): 1–29.

Outtier, Bernard, ed. "La sainte samaritaine chez les Arméniens." In *Études sémitiques et samaritaines offertes à Jean Margain*, edited by Christian-Bernard Amphoux, A. Frey, and U. Schattner-Rieser. Histoire du texte biblique 4. Lausanne: Zèbre, 1998: 203–212.

Patkanean, Kʻerovbē, ed. *Pʻawstosi Buzandacʻwoy Patmutʻiwn Hayocʻ.* St. Petersburg: Imperial Academy of Sciences, 1883. Reprint, Delmar: Caravan Books, 1984.

Tʻovma Arcruni, Patmutʻiwn tann Arcruneacʻ. St. Petersburg: Skoroxodov, 1887. Reprint, Tiflis 1917 and Delmar, Delmar: Caravan Books, 1991.

Peeters, Paul. "Un miracle des SS. Serge et Théodore et la *Vie de S. Basile*, dans Fauste de Byzance." *Analecta Bollandiana* 39 (1921): 65–88.

"S. Grégoire l'Illuminateur dans le calendrier lapidaire de Naples." *Analecta Bollandiana* 60 (1942): 91–130.

Perkins, Judith. *The Suffering Self: Pain and Narrative Representation in the Early Christian Era.* 2nd ed. London: Routledge, 1995. Reprint, 2002.

Pogossian, Zaruhi. "Women at the Beginning of Christianity in Armenia." *Orientalia Christiana Periodica* 69 (2003): 355–380.

"Female Asceticism in Early Medieval Armenia." *Le Muséon* 125 (2012): 169–213.

Refoulé, François, ed. *Tertullien, Traité du baptême.* Sources chrétiennes 35. Paris: Les Éditions du Cerf, 1952.

Rohde, E. *Der griechische Roman und seine Vorläufer.* Leipzig, 1876. 3rd ed., 1914; Reprint, Hildesheim; New York, 1974.

Rordorf, Willy. "Tertullien et les Actes de Paul (à propos de *bapt.* 17,5)." In *Hommage à René Braun. 2. Autour de Tertullien*, edited by Jean Granarolo. Publications de la Faculté des Lettres et Sciences humaines de Nice 56. Paris, 1990: 151–160. Reprint, *Lex Orandi-Lex Credendi: Gesammelte Aufsätze zum 60. Geburtstag.* Paradosis 36. Freiburg: Universitätsverlag Freiburg Schweiz, 1993: 475–484.

"Actes de Paul." In *Écrits apocryphes chrétiens*, edited by François Bovon and Pierre Geoltrain. Bibliothèque de la Pléiade 442. Paris: Gallimard, 1997: 1115–1177.

Roussele, Aline. *Porneia. De la maîtrise du corps à la privation sensorielle. IIe–IVe siècles de l'ère chrétienne.* Paris: PUF, 1983.

Sfameni Gasparro, Giulia. *Enkrateia e antropologia. Le motivazioni protologiche della verginità nel cristianesimo dei primi secoli e nello gnosticismo.* Studia Ephemeridis "Augustinianum" 20. Rome: Institutum Patristicum Augustinianum, 1984.

Söder, Rosa. *Die apokryphe Apostelgeschichten und die romanhafte Literatur der Antike.* Würzburger Studien zur Altertumswissenschaft 3. Stuttgart: Kohlhammer, 1932. Reprint, Darmstadt: Wissenschaftliche Buchges, 1969.

Streete, Gail C. "Women as Sources of Redemption and Knowledge in Early Christian Traditions." In *Women & Christian Origins*, edited by Ross S. Kraemer and Mary Rose D'Angelo. New York; Oxford: Oxford University Press, 1999: 330–354.

"Buying the Stairway to Heaven: Perpetua and Thecla as Early Christian Heroines." In *A Feminist Companion to the New Testament Apocrypha*, edited by Amy-Jill Levine and Maria M. Robbins. London: T&T Clark, 2006: 186–205.

Redeemed Bodies: Women Martyrs in Early Christianity. Louisville: Westminster John Knox, 2009.

Tēr-Mkrtčʻean, G., and S. Kanayeancʻ, eds. *Agatʻangełay Patmutʻiwn Hayocʻ.* Tbilisi: Mnacʻakan Martiroseancʻ, 1909. Reprint, Delmar: Caravan, 1980.

Thomson, Robert W., trans. *Agathangelos, History of the Armenians.* Albany: State University of New York Press, 1976.

trans. *Thomas Artsruni, History of the House of the Artsrunik*. Detroit: Wayne State University, 1985.
The Teaching of Saint Gregory: An Early Armenian Catechism. Cambridge, MA: Harvard University Press, 1970. Rev. ed., New York: St. Vladimir's Seminary Press, 2001.
trans. *The Lives of Saint Gregory: Translated with Introduction and Commentary, by R. W. Thomson*. Ann Arbor: Caravan, 2010.
Tissot, Yves. "Encratisme et Actes apocryphes." In *Les Actes apocryphes des Apôtres: Christianisme et monde païen*, edited by François Bovon. Publications de la Faculté de Théologie de l'Université de Genève 4. Geneva: Labor et Fides, 1981: 109–119.
Toumanoff, C. "The Third-Century Arsacids: A Chronological and Genealogical Commentary." *Revue des Études Arméniennes* 6 (1969): 233–281.
Vander Stichele, Caroline, and Todd Penner. *Contextualizing Gender in Early Christian Discourse: Thinking beyond Thecla*. New York; London: T&T Clark, 2009.
Vogt, Kari. "'Becoming Male:' A Gnostic and Early Christian Metaphor." In *The Image of God and Gender Models in Judaeo-Christian Tradition*, edited by Kari E. Børresen. Oslo: Solum Forlag, 1991. 2nd ed., Minneapolis: Fortress, 1995.
Wehn, Beate. "'Blessed are the Bodies of Those Who Are Virgins:' Reflections on the Image of Paul in the Acts of Thecla." *Journal for the Study of the New Testament* 79 (2000): 149–164.
Winkler, Gabriele. "Our Present Knowledge of the *History of Agat'angełos* and Its Oriental Versions." *Revue des Études Arméniennes* 14 (1980): 125–141.
Wright, William, ed. and trans. *Apocryphal Acts of the Apostles: Edited from Syriac Manuscripts in the British Museum and Other Libraries*. Vol. 1: The Syriac Texts. London: Williams & Norgate, 1871.

CHAPTER 5

Thecla beyond Thecla
Secondary Characters in Syriac Hagiography

Flavia Ruani*

Secondary characters can be quite extraordinary. Who among us, as readers of modern literature, can forget Sancho Panza? Banquo? Or Count Vronsky? Even if these characters are technically secondary compared to Don Quixote, Macbeth, and Anna Karenina, their personalities and actions are just as memorable. And, more importantly, without their presence and interactions with the protagonists, the latter would just not be who they are.

There is no reason to assume that this would be any different for ancient literature and their audiences. One may imagine that audiences, from across the social spectrum, were attracted to popular and widespread stories that were read in public contexts and on a regular basis. And like us, our ancient counterparts would have been just as fond of the characters from their favorite tales. As such, this chapter investigates the impact of the ancient Christian "best-seller" the *Acts of Paul and Thecla* (henceforth *APT*). However, not as it concerns the *APT*'s main protagonist, Thecla, but rather, precisely, its secondary characters. It argues that the secondary characters of several Syriac late antique hagiographies, namely, the *Martyrdom of Febronia* (*BHO* 302), the *Martyrdom of Bassus and Susanna* (*BHO* 174), the *Life of John of Tella* (*BHO* 524), and the *Martyrdom of Thecla and Her Companions* (*BHO* 1157), are modeled after those of the *APT*. By analyzing these case studies, this chapter illustrates that secondary characters intervene at precise moments in the plot to reinforce the protagonists as "second Theclas."

Indeed, as we will see, the secondary characters of the aforementioned tales take on the characteristics of Thecla's cohorts – in words, actions, and

---

* My sincere thanks go to the European Research Council (ERC, Grant Agreement 337344, project *Novel Saints: Ancient Novelistic Heroism in the Hagiography of Late Antiquity and the Early Middle Ages*, Ghent University) for funding this research. I am grateful to Ghazzal Dabiri for her invaluable suggestions.

personality – in multiple ways but always in key moments that directly concern the protagonists. In this way, they contribute to the notion that the protagonists are sound imitators of Thecla. In other words, even if in a subordinated role, these secondary characters participate in the construction of the psychological profile and the saintly portrait of the protagonists. From this vantage point, it becomes salient that secondary characters are actively deployed to further solidify the connection of their tales to the *APT* and likewise their protagonists' literary and saintly lineage to Thecla, the famous female saint of Christian tradition. Thus, secondary characters assure that Thecla and her tale live on in later texts in different yet meaningful ways, while simultaneously imbuing the new texts with the authority of an older and much beloved tale.

Put differently, hagiographers constructed a variety of secondary characters modeled on the *APT* for their own edifying stories. Such indirect intertextual references, in turn, may have played on the mechanics of the ancient reader's memory: late antique audiences, like us, must have been able to recognize the roles of various secondary characters. They then would have grasped the correlations with the secondary characters of the *APT*. This would implicitly activate, in their minds, the hagiographers' intended connection with Thecla and her story, a connection that serves to underscore hagiographers' various goals.

Secondary Characters: An Indirect, Reinforcing, and Flexible Form of Reception

There is no doubt that the *APT* was a popular text for Syriac Christians. The reception of Thecla and the *APT* in Syriac Christianity has become the object of scholarly attention in recent years, mainly thanks to Catherine Burris' works. She has traced and analyzed three *forms of reception*, namely, translation, collection, and composition. More specifically, she has detailed (1) the translation of the *APT* from Greek into Syriac, which entails significant variants that are ideologically charged;[1] (2) the circulation of the Syriac *APT* in manuscripts and above all its insertion in the so-called *Book of Women*, a collection of narratives portraying biblical female figures among whom Thecla is included;[2] and (3) the direct

---

[1] Burris, "The Reception," 2010: ch. 3. The translation can be dated to the late fourth-early fifth century (ibid.: 45), and there are convincing arguments to be made that it was not only adapted to a specifically Syriac audience but also oriented to an assimilation of Thecla's story to the biblical Book of Daniel (ibid.: 60–68).

[2] Ibid.: ch. 5.

reference to Thecla in homiletic, poetic, and hagiographical literature.[3] This latter form singles out the moments in Syriac literature when Thecla is explicitly mentioned. Burris examines such references to Thecla to better perceive her role as a model of different kinds of holiness, namely, martyr, ascetic, and confessor among others, that the various authors and their texts intend to promote.[4] If the presence of Thecla seems to have been exhaustively surveyed and discussed at different levels and in multiple manifestations of Syriac culture (literature, manuscripts, cult, liturgy), what remains to be addressed is the impact that her story might have had on the composition of Syriac hagiography as another mode of reception in addition to the aforementioned. Looking at secondary characters is a first step in this direction.

It should be mentioned here that scholars certainly have noticed that the *APT* has been used as a model for various types of *peripheral* characters we encounter in late antique hagiography at large: a prominent example is the prison or house guard. In a number of texts, heroines bribe prison guards, so that they may enter the cell of an authoritative figure who is preaching, or house guards, so that they may escape and fulfill their Christian vocation, which is how and why, respectively, Thecla leaves her home and makes her way into Paul's cell at night (§ 3.18).[5] Another is the members of the protagonists' household, who, upon hearing that the latter has left home to follow a Christian life, weep as if they are mourning the death of their loved one. An example of this type has been noted by Stephen Davis: he highlights the striking parallelism between the behavior of Thecla's household in the *APT* and that of Eugenia's in the latter's fifth-century tale:

> And they wept bitterly, Thamyris missing his betrothed, Theocleia her child, the maidservants their mistress. (*APT* § 3.10)

> For her parents were mourning for their daughter; and her brothers for their sister; and her servants for their mistress. (*Life of Eugenia* § 8)[6]

---

[3] Ibid.: ch. 4.
[4] See also Burris and Van Rompay, "Thecla in Syriac Christianity," 2002; and Burris and Van Rompay, "Some Further Notes," 2009. Sever J. Voicu, "Thecla," 2017, for his part, has rounded out this line of inquiry by exploring the figure of Thecla in Syriac cultic and liturgical traditions.
[5] For example, the Italo-Greek *Martyrdom of the Brothers of Lentini* and the *Martyrdom of Agatha*. See Julie Van Pelt's contribution in this volume (Chapter 7) for more.
[6] Davis, *The Cult of St. Thecla*, 2001: 143–144. This very turn of phrase, however, also appears in later Byzantine hagiographical texts that seem to lack any connection with Thecla; they thus may attest to a gradually independent circulation of this specific phrasing. For more on this, see Chapter 7.

Davis also remarks in passing an aspect of the *Life of Eugenia* with respect to the *APT* that is pertinent to our present discussion and, thus, deserves some exploration here. He observes that "the connection to Thecla" in the *Life of Eugenia* is established a first time when the saint reads Thecla's story, which prompts her to imitate the virgin of Iconium and choose an ascetic Christian life. "The connection to Thecla," he continues, "is *reinforced* later; when the author describes the reaction of Eugenia's household upon discovering her absence, he borrows a phrasing reminiscent of the *Acts of Paul and Thecla*."[7] In other words, Davis draws a hermeneutical trajectory that may reveal useful: the link with Thecla can be assured both by an explicit reference to the heroine *and* by an implicit and broader reminiscence that involves other aspects of the story, including bystanders.[8] The latter's function is one of reinforcement, of strengthening an already intended or existing connection. Thus, whenever the link to Thecla's story is established in a later text, due to the fact that she is explicitly evoked by name, it is methodologically safe to explore whether there are other hints that a text deploys Thecla and the *APT* as models in other ways.

In consideration of time and space, and as noted above, the present chapter will focus on the secondary characters of four Syriac texts written between the fifth and the seventh century in which Thecla is already explicitly mentioned as a model for the protagonists: the *Martyrdom of Febronia*, the *Martyrdom of Bassus and Susanna*, the *Life of John of Tella*, and the *Martyrdom of Thecla and Her Companions*.[9] We will examine, thus, how and to what extents characters surrounding Thecla also serve as models for those surrounding the saints of the aforementioned hagiographies and to what possible aims. Surprisingly, whereas in all these hagiographical narratives the protagonists take over Thecla's saintly features, when it comes to secondary characters there seems to be a more flexible attitude in imitating the model. The first two texts certainly do follow the *APT* (as in the case of the *Life of Eugenia* quoted above). The latter two, on the contrary, while still using it, appear to drastically deviate from it, operating in contrasting imitation.

---

[7] Ibid. Emphasis mine.
[8] On the rhetorical connection between Thecla and Eugenia, see Klazina Staat's contribution to this volume (Chapter 9).
[9] For the purposes of this chapter, our corpus is thus selected (with one exception) based on the texts, identified by Catherine Burris, which mention Thecla directly. The analyses provided here might be useful for examining other Syriac hagiographical texts in which Thecla is *not* directly evoked.

Before delving into our analyses, a final methodological clarification is in order here: we must be careful not to draw conclusions about a text solely based on literary parallelisms, especially since modern scholarship has quite amply demonstrated that hagiographical writings rely on various authenticating strategies in constructing saints and their worlds, including historicity.[10] Nevertheless, focusing on intertextuality (parallelisms, modeling characters, etc.) – the goal of this chapter – is but one of several fruitful ways of better appreciating certain nuances of a text, including its appropriation of an authoritative source in multiple, concrete ways. In this regard, it is important to note that the manuscript traditions of the *Life of John of Tella* and *Martyrdom of Thecla and Her Companions* provide a historical anchoring for this intertextuality; both texts circulated together with the *APT* in some hagiographical collections.[11]

Corresponding Imitation 1: Thomais, a Second Tryphaena in the *Martyrdom of Febronia*

The *Martyrdom of Febronia* was composed in the late sixth to early seventh century and gained popularity in the Syriac world and beyond as it was soon translated into Greek and Latin.[12] Part of its vast success is due to the singular fact that claiming to be the author is a woman named Thomais who is also a character in the narrative; she is the second-in-charge after the abbess.[13] The story centers on Febronia and takes place in Nisibis, a city in the eastern regions of the Roman Empire, during the reign of the emperor Diocletian (r. 284–305). Febronia is an extremely beautiful girl who lives in a convent of fifty nuns under the guidance of the abbess Bryene. Febronia distinguishes herself in many ways; she is wise, knowledgeable about the Scriptures, and a gifted teacher. And she is quickly able to make

---

[10] See Turner, *Truthfulness*, 2012.
[11] The former is found, among other witnesses, in the manuscript London, British Library, Add. 12174, at fol. 152r–165v (story no. 17), which also contains the story of Thecla (fol. 445r–448r, story no. 76) and which was copied in 1196 for the monastery of Mor Barṣaumo, near Melitene, at the instigation of the Syrian Orthodox Patriarch Michael Rabbo (d. 1199); the latter is transmitted in four manuscripts, including the manuscript Berlin, Staatsbibliothek zu Berlin – Preussischer Kulturbesitz, syr. 75 (Sachau 222) copied in Alqoš in 1881 (the *Martyrdom* is the story no. 38 at fol. 546r–548r), which also contains the *APT* (story no. 40, fol. 559v–570r). The *Martyrdom of Febronia* and the *Martyrdom of Bassus and Susanna* did not circulate in the same manuscripts as the *APT*, as far as I know, yet further research on the places of production and circulation of the individual manuscript traditions may pinpoint areas and epochs of contact among them that would contribute to our understanding of their intertextual link.
[12] See Saint-Laurent, "Images de femmes," 2012: 214–219. See also Kaplan, "Une hôtesse," 2011.
[13] On this, see Jullien, "Le monachisme," 2010: esp. 80–81.

a noble widow named Hieira her disciple. One day, the Roman army enters Nisibis for the sole purpose of persecuting Christians. All the nuns of the convent hide away with the exception of Febronia, Bryene, and Thomais. The three are determined to resist the assailants. The soldiers, however, take hold of Febronia, and she is publicly put on trial. When she refuses the pagan judge's offer for her to marry his nephew, who is also the commander-in-chief, she is repeatedly and cruelly tortured – she is beaten and burned, and her body is stretched and combed with iron nails as she undergoes other bodily mutilations – until she is finally beheaded. Her body is carried back to the convent, and, after a procession attended by a great crowd, she is buried in a holy spot with all due honors and respect. Though a bishop builds a shrine in her honor on another site in the city, miracles occur at the site where she is interred.

Thecla is mentioned explicitly at the turning point in the narrative, namely, when Febronia is about to be taken away from the convent to her public trial. She is invoked by Bryene as a model of endurance for Febronia in her prayer to God:

> Bryene then stretched out her hands towards heaven and said in a loud voice, "Lord Jesus Christ, who appeared to your servant Thekla in the guise of Paul, turn toward this poor girl at the time of her contest."[14]

Burris interprets this reference as a demonstration of the fact that in the text Thecla serves as "an exemplar, high-status model to be followed" and a "template for proper religious behavior."[15] However, she comments further:

> Thecla's name does not appear again, and the details of Febronia's life do not resemble Thecla's beyond references to both being beautiful. Febronia has neither hostile pagan mother nor fiancé, does not travel, and is emphatically not saved from her trials or from pain.[16]

Whereas this remark cannot be contested as such, there are arguably other, more indirect allusions to Thecla and her story in this martyrdom account. For example, if Febronia is modeled upon Thecla when it comes to her trial, one could suggest that she also takes on the role of Paul. Similar to the *APT*, the *Martyrdom* highlights that Febronia makes of Hieria her proselyte due to her teaching. More significantly, she accomplishes this without being seen, thus reminding us of how Thecla was converted

---

[14] Brock and Harvey (trans.), *Holy Women*, 1998: 163.   [15] Burris, "The Reception," 2010: 104.
[16] Ibid.: 103.

without seeing Paul: she was sitting by a window in her home when she heard Paul's teaching.[17]

In addition to the characterization of the protagonist, other characters' actions evoke Thecla's story. To illustrate this point, we turn our attention back to the tale's critical juncture, namely, Bryene's invocation that occurs at the convent after the last dialogue between Febronia, Bryene, and Thomais but before Febronia is brought to the tribunal. It is a very moving scene, as the reader understands that this is the last time that the three of them will be together.[18]

It has been suggested convincingly that throughout the entire narrative, Bryene forms a motherly bond with Febronia instead of the spiritual one that usually forms between abbess and nun.[19] If Bryene assumes the role of mother, one may wonder who then is Thomais to Febronia? Upon a first reading, it appears that the motherly figure is simply doubled: both Bryene and Thomais call Febronia their "daughter," and Febronia takes leave of both by calling them "mothers."[20] Yet, rather than duplicating the same maternal figure, it seems, on the contrary, that Bryene and Thomais embody two different maternal attitudes altogether, at least with respect to the trial. And it is precisely the intertextual reference with Thecla and her narrative, under the same circumstance, that helps reveal these nuances. Indeed, when the soldiers take Febronia away, Bryene says that she "will stay in the convent in mourning," whereas Thomais makes the promise: "As the Lord lives, my daughter Febronia, I will put on a laywoman's dress and come to see your contest."[21] Her resoluteness is a direct challenge to the Roman soldiers since it violates their order that no

---

[17] Indeed, Febronia is a sort of "second Paul" when she is described as teaching without being seen and thus attracting Hieria's curiosity: "Bryene instructed Febronia to sit behind a curtain and read from there. She never saw any worldly finery and did not know what a man's face looked like. But she was the subject of much talk throughout the entire town – people spoke of her learning, beauty, humility, and gentleness. When Hieria, who had been married to a senator, heard all this, she was fired by divine love and became very eager to see Febronia:" Brock and Harvey (trans.), *Holy Women*, 1998: 155. This is not unique to Febronia, as other saintly heroines like Eugenia, for example (see Chapter 7), are modeled both upon Thecla and Paul at different moments in the narrative and for different purposes.

[18] This evokes Tryphaena too who mourns for her daughter Falconilla and fears for her "adopted daughter" Thecla at the moment of her trial (*APT* § 4.3–4) in a reverse scenario where instead of two "mothers" and a "daughter" we have one mother and two "daughters." I thank Ghazzal Dabiri for this insight.

[19] Harvey, "Sacred Bonding," 1996: 46–48.

[20] Brock and Harvey (trans.), *Holy Women*, 1998: 163.   [21] Ibid.

one is to accompany Febronia to her trial.[22] Hence, the necessity of wearing a disguise: "Thomais put on laywoman's clothing and went out to watch the spectacle of the contest, as did all those lay women who used to come to the convent on Fridays to listen to the Scriptures."[23] Ancient readers, familiar with the *APT*, likely would have heeded the invitation to compare Thomais' actions with those of Tryphaena, the lay noble lady who took Thecla under her protection and who stood in the theater to watch her protégée suffer bodily tortures (§ 4.2–14).[24]

The invitation to read the two women similarly is especially salient when we take into account two important aspects: the first is the personality trait the two women share in common and demonstrate on similar occasions. The second is the focal point of the narration. As for the former, Thomais and Tryphaena are protectors; they both refuse to let Febronia/Thecla be dragged away by the soldiers. Let us consider first the relevant passages in the *APT*:

> Queen Tryphaena did not let go her hold on Thecla, but was taking her by the hand, and going (with her) . . . . And the young men came and took Thecla away from the hands of queen Tryphaena, and led her into the theatre to throw her to the beasts.[25]

This echoes the image of Bryene and Thomais who "clung to Febronia" to the point that the latter says: "I beg you, mothers, send me on my way with blessings and pray for me. Let me go now."[26] In terms of the focal point, it is striking that as Thomais and Tryphaena bear witness to their respective protégées' trials, the narrators temporarily suspend the accounts of the torture. Both dramatically redirect the focus from the tortured saint in the arena to the protective maternal figure standing among the spectators. Thomais and Tryphaena are portrayed as having identical reactions. Here, the parallelism between the two scenes is palpable, so to speak, at the level of wording. In this regard, it is valid only if we consider that it is the Syriac version of the *APT* that the author of the *Martyrdom of Febronia* used since the original Greek presents a different phrasing:

---

[22] Ibid.: 162: "The women asked the soldiers to take them off to the 'contest' as well, so that Febronia should not be left all by herself . . . . But the soldiers replied, 'We have not been instructed to bring you as well before the judge's tribunal, only Febronia on her own.'"
[23] Ibid.
[24] On the figure of Tryphaena, see Misset-van de Weg, "A Wealthy Woman," 1996, as well as other references mentioned in Barrier, *The Acts of Paul and Thecla*, 2009: 144–145 n. 11.
[25] Wright (ed. and trans.), *Apocryphal Acts*, 1871: vol. 2, 134–135.
[26] Brock and Harvey (trans.), *Holy Women*, 1998: 162–163.

Syriac *APT*	*Martyrdom of Febronia* § 25
And queen Tryphaena, who was standing by the door of the theatre, **fainted, was cast down and fell** (ܘܢܦܠܬ ܗܘܬ ܐܩܠܝܢܘܣ ܠܘܬ ܬܪܥܐ), because she thought that Thecla was dead. And her slaves saw that she had fainted and fallen down, they broke out into wailing, and rent their garments and say: "The queen is dead."[27]	When Thomais saw the terrible things that were happening to Febronia, **she fainted, falling on the ground** (ܘܢܦܠܬ ܗܘܬ ܥܠ ܐܪܥܐ ܠܘܬ) at Hieria's feet. Hieria herself cried out with a loud voice, "Alas, Febronia, my sister, alas my lady and my teacher. Today we have been deprived of your instruction, and not just yours, but also that of the lady Thomais, for here she is dead as well."[28]

Moving further along in the narrative, we continue to see other parallels: at the announcement of Queen Tryphaena's death, the governor interrupts the games. Jeremy Barrier notes that as the events in the arena come to a halt, "it is almost as if time freezes as the situation now centers on the death of the queen."[29] This description is applicable to the *Martyrdom of Febronia*, as well, for events are halted too when Thomais faints: Febronia asks for some water and demands to see Hieria, even though it is to no avail. Both texts further proceed in parallel as Tryphaena and Thomais are no longer the focusees of the narrative. Moreover, the reader will discover only later that, in both cases, it was a false alarm and that the two women did not actually die. Instead, both narratives train their respective focuses back on to the protagonists. Both Thecla and Febronia are asked a series of questions and, in their responses, they both demonstrate that the trials did not interfere with the preservation of their chastity or with their loyalty to their heavenly betrothed, Christ.[30] Ultimately, then, not only is Febronia like Thecla in the arena, but Thomais reacts to the horrors of torture by collapsing exactly as Tryphaena does, and the entire scene seems to be modeled on the one depicted in the *APT*.

---

[27] Wright (ed. and trans.), *Apocryphal Acts*, 1871: vol. 2, 139 (slightly modified in a more literal rendering to make the parallel wording with the *Martyrdom of Febronia* apparent). The Greek *APT* reads: "But Tryphaena lost consciousness, while standing alongside the arena upon the sideboard of the theater, so that the female slaves said, 'Queen Tryphaena is dead.'" See *APT* § 4.11 in Barrier, *The Acts of Paul and Thecla*, 2009: 168. For a commentary on this passage, see ibid.: 168–170.
[28] Brock and Harvey (trans.), *Holy Women*, 1998: 166–167 (slightly modified).
[29] Barrier, *The Acts of Paul and Thecla*, 2009: 170.
[30] For the *APT*, see Wright (ed. and trans.), *Apocryphal Acts*, 1871: vol. 2, 140. For the *Martyrdom of Febronia*, see Brock and Harvey (trans.), *Holy Women*, 1998: 168.

This does not mean, of course, that Thecla and her story are the only models for this hagiographical text. In a dialogue between Febronia and Bryene that takes place before the Roman soldiers break into the convent, the text mentions other martyrdoms that should be considered as fruitful intertextual material to explore. These references highlight exemplary mother-daughter relationships, but more than that, they are superlative portrayals of the bond linking Febronia and Bryene, especially in times of hardship, such as a trial:

> Remember the wrestlers who went before you, who underwent a glorious martyrdom, receiving a crown of victory from the heavenly ringmaster of the fight. These people were not just men, but they include women and children as well; remember the glorious martyrdoms of Lewbe and Leonida: Lewbe was crowned at her death by the sword, Leonida by burning. Remember the girl Eutropia, who, at the age of twelve, was martyred along with her mother for the sake of our Lord's name. Weren't you always amazed and filled with wonder at Eutropia's submissiveness and endurance? When the judge gave orders that arrows be shot in her direction in order to make her run away frightened by the arrows, she heard her mother call out, "Don't run away, Eutropia my daughter," and clasping her hands behind her back she did not run away; instead she was hit by an arrow and fell down dead on the ground. She showed complete obedience to her mother's command. Was it not her perseverance and obedience that you always admired? She was just an unschooled girl, whereas you have actually been teaching others.[31]

And, indeed, Febronia will echo these words when, just before being led away, she addresses Bryene as a second Eutropia, a daughter obedient to her mother's command:

> I have never transgressed your commandments, so now I will not do so or be neglectful of your admonition. Rather, let the peoples see and be astounded, let them congratulate the aged Bryene and say, "Truly this is a plant belonging to Bryene."[32]

Interestingly enough, the text references other stories (i.e., the martyrdoms of Lewbe and Eutropia) as they are known through textual sources.[33] Indeed, earlier in the narrative, the readers are informed that exemplary

---

[31] Brock and Harvey (trans.), *Holy Women*, 1998: 160–161.   [32] Ibid.: 163.
[33] In ibid.: 160 n. 25, the translators identify the martyrdom of Lewbe, Leonida, Eutropia, and her mother Leonis with the Greek text *BHG* 2322 edited by Halkin (ed.), "La passion grecque," 1958. It is a martyrdom that also took place in Nisibis during Diocletian's reign; see Fiey, *Nisibe*, 1977: 20. This is also referenced in Brock and Ashbrook Harvey (trans.), *Holy Women*, 1998: 160 n. 25.

accounts are read out loud to the sisters for instructional/spiritual purposes:

> Bryene was a disciple of Platonia, who had also been a deaconess before her, and she kept the traditions and rule handed down to her by Platonia right up to the end. It has been Platonia's practice not to let the sisters do any work at all on Fridays; instead they used to gather in the place for prayer and celebrate the Office of Matins. Then, from dawn to the third hour Platonia used to take a book and read to them. After the Office of the Third Hour she would give the book to Bryene and tell her to read to the sisters until vespers. When Bryene took over as head of the convent, she continued this practice.[34]

It is within this practice – listening and reading out loud – that Febronia becomes familiarized with the stories of Thecla and other female martyrs.[35] Incidentally, the different settings notwithstanding, this resembles the activities the late fourth-century pilgrim Egeria describes upon arriving at Thecla's shrine near Tarsus: "When I had arrived in the Name of God, prayer was made at the memorial, and the whole of the acts of saint Thecla having been read, I gave endless thanks to Christ our God."[36]

As we draw our discussion on the *Martyrdom of Febronia* to a close, it bears reiterating that the text appears to be fairly explicit in highlighting the literary sources upon which it models its own characters and episodes. The narrative itself signals the presence of such models by offering them an appropriate context. From this, we can make two major observations.

The first refers to a common practice of late antique and medieval hagiographers: the recourse to not just one but multiple source-models. Indeed, certain scenes, characteristics, and narrative techniques are drawn from different texts to emphasize what the hagiographer deems exemplary and when and among which types of relationships. For example, the

---

[34] Ibid.: 154.
[35] Bryene passes on to Febronia the task of reading to the other sisters: "On Fridays, when all the sisters were gathered in the place of prayer, Bryene used to tell Febronia to read the divine words to them." Ibid.: 155. The "divine words" primarily designate the Scriptures, but one can imagine that they may also refer to other edifying texts, such as Lives of saints, since the context described with reference to Platonia mentions "a book" to be read after the prayer. This is described in other Syriac sources, like John of Ephesus and Martyrius Sahdona, who report that on specific times of the day, monks or nuns would read the Scriptures but also the commentaries of Christian writers and hagiographical texts. See Binggeli, "Les collections," 2012: 69, with further reference to Palmer, *Monk and Mason*, 1970: 82 and Debié, "Livres et monastères," 2010: 137–139. See also Jullien, "Le monachisme féminin," 2010: 82; and, for the practice of reading saints' stories to public audiences, Durmaz, "Hearing Sanctity," 2021. The colophon of one of the manuscripts transmitting the Syriac *APT* datable to the sixth century suggests that the text was read among a community of nuns, see Burris and Van Rompay, "Thecla in Syriac Christianity," 2002: 227.
[36] McClure and Feltoe (eds. and trans.), *The Pilgrimage of Etheria*, 1919: 43.

analysis above demonstrates that there were at least two literary models the hagiographer of Febronia considered important for constructing the portraits of the martyr and her "mothers," each one serving a precise role. While Lewbe, Leonida, and Eutropia and her mother are evoked to represent the relationship that the author wants to create between the protagonist and Bryene, Thecla seems to be the exemplar specifically of forbearance when being tortured, and the *APT* is the model for the trial scene. Thomais' reaction, which echoes Tryphaena's, reinforces the intended connection with Thecla. Moreover, the fainting episode at the trial stresses the cruelty of the torture to which both protagonists are subjected and, by contrast, emphasizes the valiant endurance of the saint.

The second observation is that whenever the text directly names one of these models, it is as if a spotlight is shone on them. In other words, it invites the audience to dig deeper into the fabric of the interwoven references regarding that same model; references that are implicitly present elsewhere in the text and that involve multiple characters. It is following this textual invitation that we turn to a discussion of the *Martyrdom of Bassus and Susanna* in the section below, even if the very mention of Thecla needs to be assessed as a preliminary issue.

Corresponding Imitation 2: Abuzard the Predator in the *Martyrdom of Bassus and Susanna*

The *Martyrdom of Bassus and Susanna*, which was probably composed after the middle of the seventh century, is in metrical prose (*memra*) and consists of 741 verses.[37] The story takes place during the reign of Shapur II (309–379) and centers on twelve-year-old twins, Bassus and Susanna, who are the children of Abuzard, the Zoroastrian governor of Beth Zabdai, a region situated within the Persian Empire at the border with the Roman Empire. When their father is absent, the two children are converted to Christianity by a captive named Stephen and are then baptized by Longinus, a hermit who lives in a mountain nearby. Upon his return, Abuzard organizes a feast and asks his son Bassus to sacrifice to the gods; Bassus refuses and escapes together with his sister and Stephen into the

---

[37] This *terminus post quem* is determined by the earlier date envisaged for the composition of another martyrdom account, the *History of 'Abda da-Mšiḥa*, on which the *Martyrdom of Bassus and Susanna* is supposedly based. For the approximate date of the *History of 'Abda da-Mšiḥa*, see Butts and Gross (eds.), *The History of the "Slave of Christ,"* 2016: 34–36; and for the dependence of the *Martyrdom of Bassus and Susanna* on it, see ibid.: 39–40 n. 120; Fiey, *Nisibe*, 1977: 169; and Fiey, *Saints syriaques*, 2004: 52.

mountain; the furious Abuzard chases them and, in a crescendo of cruelty and suspense, kills Stephen, Susanna, Longinus, and, finally, Bassus, one after the other, with his sword before he is burnt to death in divine punishment.[38]

This story shares many features with other accounts of Syriac martyrdoms that take place within the territories of the Sassanian Empire and are carried out by Zoroastrians. These stories are usually referred to collectively in Syriac scholarship as the Persian Martyr Acts.[39] More specifically, it has been noted that the *Martyrdom of Bassus and Susanna* is similar in its themes and structure to those narratives recounting the story of children martyred by their fathers, such as the *Martyrdom of ʿAbda da-Mšiḥa*, the *Martyrdom of Behnam and Sarah*, and the *Martyrdom of Saba Pirgušnasp*.[40] Nevertheless, if we look at the text itself, we find a unique, explicit intertextual reference, which, as a matter of fact, is a double reference. The reference appears when the twins are fleeing across the mountain: after a while, Susanna's feet are bleeding, and she cannot continue further. Interrupting the flight would mean death, and the narrator describes Susanna's attitude about her predicament in the following terms:

> Chaste and modest, dressed up in strength and valiance, she took on the image (*dmuta*) of Thecla and Febronia![41]

The editor and French translator, Jean-Baptiste Chabot, understands these two references as relating to two female saints, who, like Susanna, are martyred in Persia: one is the Febronia of the text we analyzed above, who died in 304, and the other is a virgin named Thecla who was murdered with her companions around 346 and whose account was written down.[42] Our interest here is not to critique the latter identification; rather, we would suggest a different interpretation and argue that the Thecla in

---

[38] The text is edited by Bedjan (ed.), *Acta Martyrum et Sanctorum* IV, 1894: 471–507, and reproduced by Chabot (ed.), *La légende de Mar Bassus*, 1893, accompanied by a French translation.

[39] Brock, *History of the Holy Mar Maʿin*, 2008: 77–84, offers a list of these texts. The *Martyrdom of Bassus and Susanna* is no. 42 in the list. On the scholarly construct of such a collection, see Becker, "The Invention," 2020.

[40] See Butts and Gross (eds. and trans.), *The History of the "Slave of Christ,"* 2016: 38–42; and Fiey, *Nisibe*, 1977: 167. Among those features, we may mention the protective role of the mothers, who act as confidants of the child martyrs, the meeting with a Christian monk, and the following sequence of events: conversion, baptism, confrontation with the father, persecution, and martyrdom. See also Mellon Saint-Laurent and Smith (eds. and trans.), *The History of Mar Behnam and Sarah*, 2018. I am currently preparing the edition and translation of the *Martyrdom of Saba Pirgušnasp*.

[41] My translation. Chabot (ed.), *La légende de Mar Bassus*, 1893: 34, vv. 459–460.

[42] Ibid.: 34 n. 1. The *Martyrdom of Thecla and Her Companions* will be discussed below.

question is the apostle of Iconium. There are several intra-textual pieces of evidence to support this hypothesis, and we claim that the text is best understood in light of this identification.

First, the order in which their names appear may not be casual but rather meaningful.[43] The author of the *Martyrdom of Bassus and Susanna* may have adopted the connection between Thecla of Iconium and Febronia (specifically her characterization as a martyr-to-be)[44] and added his protagonist Susanna, thus creating a chain of defiant female virgins who valiantly face torture and death. Thus, the sequence makes sense only if we identify Thecla with the protagonist of the *APT*, who is the one quoted in the Febronia account. The order, moreover, may be in fact symbolically charged; in the Syriac world, and more specifically in the East-Syrian tradition, to which the *Martyrdom of Bassus and Susanna* belongs, the idea of creating lists of exemplary figures linked by a symbolic thread is not uncommon. For instance, an East-Syrian hymn, *On the Saintly Women*, preserves a list of selected Old Testament, New Testament, and hagiographical female characters.[45] Interestingly for our purposes, Thecla, Febronia, and Susanna also appear in this hymn, whereas the Persian Thecla is not mentioned.[46] This illustrates that the three holy women were perceived as linked to one another in at least one other prominent instance.

Second, a number of details in the story point to a parallelism with the Thecla of the *APT*. Susanna is defined as the "handmaiden" (*amta*) of Christ, an epithet that also characterizes Thecla in multiple occasions in the Syriac *APT*.[47] Febronia too receives this title in her narrative,[48] but not the Persian Thecla. Certainly, this attribute is widely attested in late antique texts to characterize holy women, especially martyrs. Yet it is important to note that the list-like connection between the women would

---

[43] If we accept Chabot's identification, the order would not be chronological since Thecla's martyrdom should be placed in 346 and Febronia's in 304.
[44] He evidently knows Febronia's account for expressly naming her.
[45] See Fiey, "Une hymne nestorienne," 1966.
[46] Thecla is no. 31 on the list, Febronia no. 49, and Susanna no. 85. The hymn, difficult to date, is part of the liturgy of various offices: the tonsure of the nuns, the feast of certain holy women, and the commemoration of the Holy Virgin. (Ibid: 79)
[47] For the occurrences of the term in the Syriac *APT*, see Wright (ed. and trans.), *Apocryphal Acts*, 1871: vol. 1, 149, 155, 156, and 162, for the text, and vol. 2, 131, 135–136, 140, and 143, for the translation.
[48] Bedjan (ed.), *Acta Martyrum et Sanctorum* V, 1895: 593; and Brock and Harvey (trans.), *Holy Women*, 1998: 164: "Lysimachos addressed her, 'Tell me, young girl, what are you, slave or freeborn?' Febronia replied, 'Slave (*amta*).' 'Whose slave are you, then?' asked Lysimachos. 'Christ's,' replied Febronia."

be further strengthened for an informed audience if indeed Susanna's models are also well-known "handmaidens." And, in fact, the "handmaiden" designation, which also appears in ancient Greek novels, is established in the Christian milieu starting with the *APT*. The significance of this is that the "handmaiden" designation ties the condition of servitude to the preservation of chastity in trial contexts in the *APT* and later hagiographies (and ancient Greek novels).[49] Thecla, Febronia, and Susanna are indeed called handmaidens (*amta*) in such specific circumstances, in other words, when their virginity is stressed and their lives are threatened.

To the point, Thecla calls herself the "handmaiden of Christ" in the second part of her narrative, which takes place in Antioch. The frequency of its appearance increases especially when her purity is at stake and her trial is imminent:

> "Grant Thou a recompense to Tryphaena, because her soul has had compassion upon Thy handmaiden and she has kept me in purity;" "Behold Thy handmaiden, for lo, the shame of women is uncovered in me, and I stand in the midst of all this people. My Lord and my God, remember Thy handmaiden in this hour."[50]

Febronia, likewise, defines herself as a "slave of Christ" in reply to the first question that the judge asks her at the beginning of her trial before blackmailing her with the choice between marriage or death.[51] Susanna also is called a handmaiden of Christ just after the narrator defines her as chaste and modest. Furthermore, her brother Bassus addresses a prayer to God upon seeing that she is lying on the ground, unable to move:

> The valiant boy stepped up on the outskirts of the mountain, making a passionate supplication on her behalf: "God of the universe, come to the aid of your servant; do not abandon her in the hands of the wicked one, thirsting for her ruin!"[52]

It is worth noting that in the case of Thecla and Febronia, the epithet is always uttered by the protagonists themselves, it is a self-designation. As

---

[49] On this, see De Temmerman, "Noble Slaves," 2019.
[50] Wright (ed. and trans.), *Apocryphal Acts*, 1871: vol. 2, 135–136.
[51] What follows the first exchange of questions and answers quoted above is the following: "At that point Selenos … began to interrogate Febronia: '… You shall be wife to Lysimachos …. If, however, you resist my wishes and do not listen to my words, the gods know very well that you will not stay alive in my hands for another three hours. So reply as you wish." Brock and Harvey (trans.), *Holy Women*, 1998: 165.
[52] Chabot (ed.), *La légende de Mar Bassus*, 1893: 35, vv. 469–472.

we have just seen for Susanna, on the contrary, someone else, specifically her twin brother Bassus, calls her God's servant. Yet, instead of considering this a significant discrepancy or even an anomaly, we argue the possibility that here too it is a self-designation: it seems that the text promotes the model of Thecla and Febronia not only for the female protagonist, Susanna, but surprisingly for the male character, Bassus, too.

There is one, peculiar detail that supports a strong intertextual link between Thecla and Bassus. Somewhat curiously, we find this link in a variant ending of the *APT* attested in a few Greek manuscripts:[53] In order to help Thecla, who is living in a cave in Seleucia, flee from some impudent harassing physicians, God splits a rock in two and summons Thecla to enter it alive; the stone closes up without leaving any sign of the opening, and the men "were not able to seize the handmaiden of God."[54] In the *Martyrdom*, likewise, Bassus enters the cave of the hermit Longinus to escape his aggressor, his father. Upon Abuzard's arrival, God performs a miracle:

> The stone opened up from top to bottom and He ordered the boy to implant himself in the middle like a grain of wheat, and he sprouted up and germinated, and ascended to the top of the mountain like a palm-tree.[55]

Despite the similarities, however, this miracle does not prevent the martyrdom from taking place as a shepherd reports the presence of Bassus on top of the mountain and his father is able to see his wrath through. In any case, what is salient is that when Bassus calls Susanna the "handmaiden (*amta*) of God," he is also doing so for himself as much as for his sister. It is almost as if Susanna were a Thecla, and Bassus, Thecla's voice.[56] Thus,

---

[53] Further research is needed to assess whether and to what extent and through which historical channels of transmission, the author of the *Martyrdom of Bassus and Susanna* was familiar with this particular ending of the *APT*, which is not attested in Syriac as far as current research has been able to assess.

[54] See Kaestli and Rordorf (eds. and trans.), "La fin de la vie de Thècle," 2014, texts III and VI. We quote here the first one, in the French translation given in ibid.: 44, before the edited Greek text: "Et lorsqu'elle eut fini de dire amen, une voix se fit entendre du ciel, disant: 'N'aie pas peur, Thècle, car je suis avec toi, ma servante véritable. Regarde et vois le lieu qui s'est ouvert devant toi; c'est là en effet que tu auras ta demeure éternelle et c'est là que tu recevras la visite.' Alors la bienheureuse Thècle, ayant fixé son attention, vit que le rocher s'était ouvert assez pour qu'un homme pût entrer, et elle agit selon ce qui lui avait été dit; elle échappa noblement aux hommes impies et elle entra dans le rocher; et aussitôt le rocher se referma, si bien qu'il ne laissait paraître aucune jointure. Eux, à la vue de ce prodige extraordinaire, restèrent comme hors d'eux-mêmes et n'eurent pas la force de retenir la servante de Dieu; ils saisirent seulement son voile et ne purent qu'en déchirer un morceau." See also Monaca, "Tecla e la grotta," 2017.

[55] Chabot (ed.), *La légende de Mar Bassus*, 1893: 38, vv. 519–522.

[56] It is worth noting that on one occasion, Bassus too presents himself as the "slave of Jesus" ('*abda d-yešu*') in front of his father, who is full of anger when he discovers that his two children have

Susanna *and* Bassus together are a "second Thecla" or, more aptly, Thecla, as a model, is somewhat split between two characters. In any case, the point here is that she lives through both twins, blurring gender boundaries along the way.[57]

In fact, the case for gender blurring can be strengthened by looking at other aspects of the text. While Susanna is called "chaste and modest" and "strong and valiant" like Thecla and Febronia, Bassus takes on some features of Febronia as well, thus adding yet another layer (specifically characterization) to the doubling effect of twins (physical/genetic/gender). For example, like Febronia, Bassus rejoices at his upcoming martyrdom at the hands of his father, by equating it with a marriage banquet and a wedding feast.[58] It hardly needs mentioning that this is a theme that is usually associated with women who are typically depicted as the "bride of Christ" who reunite with their divine beloved at the moment of death. It also may be worth mentioning here that Bassus' death somewhat evokes Febronia's, since he is beheaded after bodily mutilation (specifically, his hands are cut off).[59]

Now, if, based on the analyses above, we assume that the text is referring to Thecla of Iconium and her story, the question that we may ask is this: Given that the text points to an intertextual relationship with the *APT* in terms of the protagonists, what else may we discern when we turn to the secondary characters? In this light, one detail stands out as striking: the emphatic and repetitive characterization of the father Abuzard as various beasts. As soon as it becomes clear that Abuzard is the antagonist of the tale (when he is infuriated that his children have converted to Christianity and resolves to kill them), the narrative characterizes him in the manner of beastly predators: a lion,[60] a cruel wolf ready to devour innocent lambs,[61] a cursed serpent,[62] a dragon,[63] a cursed hawk attacking a pure dove or swallow,[64] and an asp.[65] Many of these are famous biblical

---

converted to Christianity. See Chabot (ed.), *La légende de Mar Bassus*, 1893: 27, v. 362. Moreover, he is also defined as "chaste and pure:" ibid.: 38, v. 524.

[57] As we will see below, Thecla is a model for another holy man, John of Tella. For a similar gender switching in the Coptic reception of the *APT*, see Arietta Papaconstantinou's contribution in this volume (Chapter 6) and her discussion of the *Martyrdom of Paese and Thecla*.

[58] Chabot (ed.), *La légende de Mar Bassus*, 1893: 41–42, vv. 567–568. See also ibid.: 31, vv. 416, 420. For Febronia, see Brock and Harvey (trans.), *Holy Women*, 1998: 165: "I have a marriage chamber in heaven, not made with hands, and a wedding feast that will never come to an end has been prepared for me."

[59] Chabot (ed.), *La légende de Mar Bassus*, 1893: 44. [60] Ibid.: 27, 42.
[61] Ibid.: 27, 30, 32, and 34.   [62] Ibid.: 31, v. 421.   [63] Ibid.: 32, v. 428.
[64] Ibid.: 33, v. 446; 35, v. 473; 37, v. 499.   [65] Ibid.: 38, v. 517.

Thecla beyond Thecla 159

metaphors;⁶⁶ however, considering the *APT* as one of the textual models of this account, the reader is invited to recall the series of savage beasts unleashed against Thecla in the arena of Antioch: lions and lionesses, leopards, bears, seals, and "numerous beasts," and "more fearful beasts" (§ 4.8–10). The rhythm of Abuzard's pursuit, chasing one character after the other, parallels the many attempts to kill Thecla devised first by the judge and later by Alexander, especially as the latter unleashes one animal after the other. The analogy is complete: if Bassus and Susanna are modeled upon Thecla, then Abuzard assumes, here, not so much the role of the human antagonists of Thecla's story, but rather of her beastlike assailants.

Now that we have seen two cases of corresponding imitation, with the *Life of John of Tella*, we turn to a different mode of reception, namely, that of contrasting imitation of a source text. In other words, texts such as the *Life of John of Tella* still take the *APT* as their model, but rather than adhering to it, they seem to react to it by offering an opposite reading.⁶⁷

Contrasting Imitation 1: A Supporting Partner and an Accepting Mother in the *Life of John of Tella*

The *Life of John of Tella* stands out in the panorama of Syriac hagiography for its sophisticated literary style.⁶⁸ It was written by a monk named Elias shortly after the death of the titular character, John (538), bishop of Tella, the ancient Constantina, which was a city not far from Callinicum (present-day Raqqah) where he was born. John is a historical figure; he was one of the leaders of the Syrian Orthodox Church. He is most famous for helping the Syrian Orthodox Church maintain its hierarchy in the Syrian region, despite the persecutions by the Chalcedonians, after the eparchy of Severus, Patriarch of Antioch from 512 to 518.⁶⁹ The story of John is framed as a letter that Elias writes as an eyewitness to the vicissitudes of the bishop's life in reply to a request made by two spiritual brothers. The narrative is composed of two major parts and includes a long

---

⁶⁶ For the conversion of the Armenian Zoroastrian king into a boar after executing saint Hṙipʻsimē, and its significance as anti-Zoroastrian polemic among other aspects, see Valentina Calzolari's contribution to this volume (Chapter 4).
⁶⁷ For a similar mode in the reception of the Old Testament in early Christian ascetic literature, see Clark, *Reading Renunciation*, 1999: 134–136. Clark uses the expression "Changing Context" to designate the "dehistoricization and relocation" of biblical verses from their original context into new ones (reference provided in Burris, "The Reception," 2010: 96 n. 163).
⁶⁸ See Palmer, "Saints' Lives with a Difference," 1987; and Menze, *Justinian*, 2008: 229–235.
⁶⁹ See Andrade, "The Syriac *Life*," 2009; and Menze, "Yuḥannon of Tella," 2011.

preface. In the first part, Elias describes John's early life, how he discovered his ascetic vocation and became a monk before being elected as a bishop (from 483 to 519). The second focuses on the upheavals of his episcopal career, which is marked by his debates with religious opponents and his teachings and ordinations in Syria and Persia, until his incarceration and death.[70]

Thecla is mentioned in the first part of the tale. It is significant that she appears at a turning point in the life of the protagonist, namely, when John makes a firm decision to follow an ascetic life after failing a first time:

> And one day he took the book of the history of the blessed Thecla, who became the disciple of the blessed Apostle, and he was reading in it. Since he was a chosen vessel ... the love of Christ settled with fervor in his soul. And he immediately took (the book of) the blessed Apostle and he was reading in it diligently. And as soon as in truth he had become a disciple of the blessed Apostle, like the blessed Thecla, he built in his apartment a small upper room and spent there all his time.[71]

Reading Thecla's story is, thus, at the origin of a prompt resolution to abandon a worldly life as John was promised to be an officer of the Byzantine administration, following in the footsteps of his father. Instead, he chooses a life of radical asceticism. His experience is similar to Eugenia's as recounted in her *Life and Martyrdom*: as noted earlier, Eugenia too is inspired to radically change her life by reading the Thecla narrative whereupon she flees to a monastery.[72] John though does not physically leave his house or his family, but builds "a small upper room" at home in which he can isolate himself, abstain from eating and drinking wine, and practice severe ascetical exercises.[73]

Catherine Burris highlights the fact that the reference to Thecla is used to "explain [John's] withdrawal" from the world, "as precedent, even authority, for withdrawal to an upper room; John's withdrawal is presented

---

[70] This twofold, "well-considered" structure is highlighted by Palmer, "Saints' Lives with a Difference," 1987: 211, whereas a summary of the life is provided by the author himself in his preface: Brooks (ed.), *Vita Iohannis*, 1907: 34–37; and Ghanem, "The Biography," 1970: 44–46.

[71] The Syriac text can be found in Brooks (ed.), *Vita Iohannis*, 1907: 42–43; this English translation is provided by Burris and Van Rompay, "Some Further Notes," 2009: 340.

[72] See Burris and Van Rompay, "Some Further Notes," 2009: 340–341. On the reception of Thecla in this text, see also Klazina Staat's contribution in the present volume (Chapter 9).

[73] "He refrained from eating flesh and from drinking wine, and his meals the tutor would eat. From eventide to late in the evening he would eat only dry bread, and later he would take a taste of something once every two days .... The blessed one would stand and bend as doubled up like a hook with his hands bound behind him and the hair of his head would rest upon the ground. He would wait thus until deep in the evening. Then he would cast himself upon the ground and lie down for a little bit:" Translation by Burris, "The Reception," 2010: 99.

as an image or copy of this actual component of Thecla's story."[74] Yet she argues that this reference serves as a citation or an "elaboration, even ornamentation, of [Elias'] main themes," rather than an "explanation or exemplary modeling."[75] She states that it is "not presented as either uniquely authoritative or suitable for use as an exemplar, a blueprint to be followed by Christians."[76] In support of this particular way of using Thecla, which in her opinion stands in sheer contrast to the use observable in the *Martyrdom of Febronia*,[77] she adduces the fact that Thecla is just one of the ninety scriptural figures quoted in the text, none of which is given the prominent role of representing *the* authority for the entire narrative.[78] She further substantiates her claim by stating that even the reference to Thecla in the passage cited above does not stand alone. It is not sufficient in itself but is rather interwoven with an allusion to the biblical book of Daniel as far as it concerns the "upper room" (the Syriac word is the one used in Dan 6:10 [in the Syriac Bible, Dan 6:11] and not in the *APT*)[79] and his self-discipline, the description of which is reminiscent of Daniel's diet in Dan 1:5–16.[80] Moreover, Burris adds that the trajectory of Thecla's life to fulfill her discipleship toward Paul diverges from John's: Thecla leaves her room to follow the apostle, whereas John confines himself to it.[81]

While subscribing to this refined understanding of the reference to Thecla in this text, we suggest that the allusion to Thecla goes beyond the actual citation or her being marked as an early example of withdrawal from the world. We argue that her *tale* may have played a larger role in the

---

[74] Ibid.: 99. [75] Ibid.: 97. [76] Ibid.: 101. [77] Ibid.
[78] Ibid.: 96–101; at 97: "No single text, figure, or idea serves as sufficient, or even necessary, evidence of John's virtue and orthodoxy, and by their sheer volume, each citation becomes less notable, less authoritative, illustrative .... This multiplicity of citation, this illustrative deployment of episodes and figures, not only serves to make any one reference inessential, but also to allow for narrowly episodic claims of similarity, a citational modeling amounting to an inverted form of typological interpretation [namely, that John becomes a copy of the originals, rather than their fulfillments – my explanation]."
[79] Namely, *'ellita*; the Syriac *APT* mentions "a window near their roof" (*kawta d-qariba hwat l-garhon*).
[80] Burris, "The Reception," 2010: 100 (see also 63). Burris summarizes this literary practice as following: "The reference supporting one small aspect of John's praxis leads to the next, which supports another aspect of that practice, in a chain of references to episodes and details within them rather than to entire narratives. This mode of reception, of textual deployment, also allows Elias to introduce ideas not apparent in the cited original texts."
[81] Ibid. Burris draws these conclusions: "It is Elias' introduction of elements from Daniel's story into Thecla's linking an upper room with prayer and then moving on to dietary restrictions, that allows him to use Thecla and her 'window near the roof' to legitimate John's withdrawal and ascetic behavior."

way in which Elias recounts John's early life. In other words, the *APT* may have provided a literary template for John's calling (see below). Furthermore, we argue that the adoption of the *APT* as a template is in keeping with the aforementioned rhetorical style of the text, which is a product of the Hellenistic education of its author.

Scholars have remarked that the "polished and well-balanced preface"[82] was structured according to some well-known *topoi* of ancient biographical writing, such as the humility of the author and his recourse to authentication strategies.[83] It has also been suggested that the first part is a "*classically* hagiographic narrative of [John's] innate holiness and conversion,"[84] and that the second part shares several features with the literary tradition of the Christian martyr acts.[85] In other words, there are no doubts that the *Life of John* is a sophisticated literary text constructed according to previous literary models – a quality that is not necessarily always in contradiction with the historicity of the contents it relates. It just means that its author put his literary skills to great use and gathered his inspiration in constructing his narrative and his characters from a wider pool of textual sources, the *APT* being one of many.

In particular, the *APT* may have offered the author ideas about narrative sequences, roles, individual scenes, and secondary characters too. Indeed, the first part of the *Life of John*, in describing the events leading to his consecration, places the figures of John's mother and his tutor up front and center in addition to our protagonist. And which ancient reader of the *APT* could forget Thecla's mother and her fiancé and their roles in the events set in Iconium describing Thecla's conversion and in her trials?

In particular, the reaction of John's mother and tutor to his initial ascetic resolution bears some similarities with that of Thecla's family to her initial conversion. But first let us consider some of the similarities and differences between our respective protagonists. Like Thecla, John is the only child of a noble family whose patriarch is not present (his father, we are told, has passed away while in the *APT* Thecla's father is never mentioned).[86] As Thecla is noted for her great beauty, John is described as very handsome. He too is betrothed to a woman much like Thecla who

---

[82] Palmer, "Saints' Lives with a Difference," 1987: 209.
[83] See Ghanem, "The Biography," 1970: 120 n. 28. For more on these strategies in hagiography, see Turner, *Truthfulness*, 2012.
[84] Burris, "The Reception," 2010: 97. Emphasis mine.
[85] Palmer, "Saints' Lives with a Difference," 1987: 212.
[86] Despite the omission of this explicit information in the *APT*, Theocleia too is likely a widow. Cf. Vorster, "Construction of Culture," 2006: 108–109.

is betrothed to Thamyris, an important citizen of Iconium. Both Thecla and John pursue their new lifestyle to extreme degrees: when John retires to his upper room and abstains from food and drinking wine, he becomes emaciated. Thecla is completely absorbed by Paul's words, so much so that she refuses to move from her window for three days and three nights, not even to eat or drink and much to her mother's dismay (§ 3.8).[87] Unlike Thecla, though, from an early age, John had a private tutor who provided him with a solid education in Greek literature and philosophy. Turning our attention to the secondary characters, it is worth mentioning that unlike Thecla's mother, Theocleia, and her fiancé, Thamyris, John's tutor and mother are devoted Christians. John's mother remains a devout widow as she is described as "serving the Lord day and night in fasting and prayer, with great abstinence, tears, and suffering."[88] Yet, despite this discrepancy with the pagan mother of Thecla, John's mother represents, as much as her literary predecessor, the values of traditional society:

> Meanwhile his mother, of blessed memory, was concerned to educate her son in every good thing and in all honesty. She would not be for him a cause of scandal in any thing, nor would she be found a cause of disgraceful sin, the deed of the devil. Rather, she wished to see and rejoice in the good things that careful parents in right and justice do for their children in their proper time, according to the wonderful laws which the Creator has ordained for us . . . . In all conscience she betrothed him to a woman, and in gladness of heart prepared to make for him a great and expensive wedding feast.[89]

The hagiographer's tone is almost apologetic here, as if he were justifying the upcoming behavior of the mother by appealing to both civic customs and moral duties. Indeed, when John first flees from his home to the cell of a holy man, longing for a solution to his spiritual struggle, his mother reacts with anger and sorrow and refuses to accept his choice: "When his mother – out of her mind because her son had gone from her sight – knew where he had gone, she arose quickly with her servants and maidens and went after him" and brought him back home.[90] This is reminiscent of the

---

[87] For a commentary on this chapter of the *APT*, see Barrier, *The Acts of Paul and Thecla*, 2009: 89–91, where he highlights how a spiritual feeling manifested in fasting and abstinence is cast in erotic discourse.
[88] Ghanem, "The Biography," 1970: 49.
[89] On the figure of Theocleia in terms of a defense of such values, see Cooper and Cork-Webster, "Conversion, Conflict, and the Drama," 2015. See also Graham Brock, "Political Authority," 1999: 162, who highlights how the Syriac version of the *APT* presents an even stronger image of Theocleia as the guarantor of familial and social conventions.
[90] Ghanem, "The Biography," 1970: 51.

actions of Thecla's family after she leaves home to go visit Paul in prison: "And when her family and her betrothed sought for Thecla, as if she had been lost, they arose, going about and searching for her in the streets."[91] However, when they find her, instead of bringing her back home, they drag her in front of the proconsul together with Paul for judgment.

Before taking Thecla to trial, Theocleia tries to find an explanation for her daughter's unusual behavior, or even a way to bring it to an end, so does John's mother. Both mothers do not directly confront their children but summon instead the person who is closest to them: Theocleia calls for Thamyris, Thecla's fiancé ("But since she [Thecla] was not departing from that window, her mother sent for Thamyris" *APT* § 3.8), and John's mother for the tutor, who thus somehow plays the role of John's partner more than his official betrothed:

> And when his mother, of blessed memory, saw that the color of her son's face and the brightness of his youth had changed, she asked her tutor, "What sort of sign is this which I see in my son, that he looks sad so much?"[92]

The responses of Thamyris and the tutor are radically different. Whereas Thamyris adopts his mother-in-law's worries and tries to convince Thecla to stop staring at the window (§ 3.10), John's tutor immediately takes his pupil's side by lying to the mother, thus allowing John to continue his holy practices undisturbed: "To calm her, at least with a word, he said to her, 'Because he remains up until late at night reading.'"[93] The tutor is indeed connected to John by a special bond that excludes the mother, as underlined a bit earlier in the text: "And they made a pact with each other not to let his mother learn his thoughts or what he was doing."[94] Whereas the figures of the two mothers are parallel thus far, it seems that the tutor is constructed in correlation with the figure of Thamyris. However, this is the case only insofar as it concerns their role and initial function as someone close to the protagonist but not in terms of personality or spiritual and social values. The same happens eventually with John's mother. She is still like Theocleia on two separate occasions: first, when she realizes that her son's choice to become a monk will cause damage to her social status,[95] and second, when she mourns John as if he were dead

---

[91] Wright (ed. and trans.), *Apocryphal Acts*, 1871: vol. 2, 126.
[92] Ghanem, "The Biography," 1970: 53.   [93] Ibid.   [94] Ibid.: 52–53.
[95] Ibid.: 55: "But when his mother knew of these things [that John decided to be tonsured and become a monk], being a widow she was very sad, for then she would be bereft of both husband and heir: her son who was her consolation and the light of her eyes." This anxiety of social marginalization or decrease of social status connected to the departure of a child from home is

upon learning that he has fled to a monastery.[96] Yet she ultimately accepts John's choice, thereby drastically deviating from her counterpart, Theocleia, who instead condemns Thecla to the pyre (§ 3.20):[97]

> But finally – thanks to the divine grace which visited her also, because she was a true widow and had put her faith in God – she conformed her will to her son's will in everything.[98]

In conclusion, Thecla's narrative may not have been the authority for what concerns holy exemplarity or plot structure of the *Life of John* but may have provided a model for two characters, namely, the protagonist's mother and companion, the only two figures of Thecla's family who are present during her initial conversion. For indeed, his mother and tutor are also the only two people in close proximity to John throughout his early life, when he decides to pursue an ascetic life. Even if the sequences of the plot are not the same in the two texts, the roles and the behaviors attributed to those two figures are analogous, with the significant difference that in the *Life of John* they eventually depart from their apocryphal counterparts and become their antithetic doubles. We argue that the *Life of John* "saves" and "corrects," in literary terms, these two important figures by assigning them a positive role.

Though the question of historicity is beyond the scope of this chapter, the fact that the *Life of John of Tella* easily blends the basic facts of John's decision to pursue an ascetic life with elements from the *APT* bears some consideration. Indeed, all the events depicted in this narrative may well be historical, yet arranging them into a tale was a creative act that required literary skills. This is all the more pertinent when we consider the particular moments in a life for which there is hardly any historical evidence such as, for instance, the early years – infancy and childhood and relationships with parents, siblings, and extended family as well as the community. In the case of John of Tella, we possess historical evidence related to his ecclesiastical career – first and foremost, the writings of John himself, like

---

also what specifically worries Theocleia. On this, see Barrier, *The Acts of Paul and Thecla*, 2009: 95 n. 6, quoting Vorster, "Construction of Culture," 2006: 108.

[96] Ghanem, "The Biography," 1970: 55: "When his mother heard about this, she did what all mothers who are deprived of such excellent children would do: she responded with crying, sadness, and bewailing." This evokes the reaction of Thecla's household, mentioned at the beginning of this chapter, to her spiritual departure (*APT* § 3.10).

[97] On this portrayal of Theocleia as the persecutor of her own daughter, as a way of representing social and familial expectations, mentioned above, which also deal with late antique parental education, see Horn, "Suffering Children," 2006: 125–127.

[98] Ghanem, "The Biography," 1970: 55.

his *Canons* – but not his private life, such as the conversations he had with his mother at home as a young man.⁹⁹ For the later period, the biographer Elias deploys a variety of common techniques such as collecting, selecting, and arranging materials. To fill in the lacunae regarding the saint's early life, however, Elias must have woven his own version, supposedly based on interviews he conducted with John's mother and tutor, using other available sources, among which we may count literary sources.¹⁰⁰ Rather than being mutually exclusive, these techniques skirt each other at the edges, at the transitional period of adulthood. In other words, the questions with which the hagiographer Elias seemed to be preoccupied against the background of the epoch are these: Who was the saint as a child and a teenager? What was the relationship between sons and parents like back then? What were the popular literary conventions and texts in circulation and viewed as models for depicting that relationship? It is in this respect that the *APT*, among other texts, may have offered the author materials about narrative sequences and roles precisely during the period in John's life for which there is hardly any documentation, namely, his youth, and about the people surrounding him at this age, that is, John's mother and tutor. For the latter, there are no records (as far as we currently know) apart from this very text. When we discuss the behaviors lent to these two secondary characters by the hagiographer, we are not referring to their historical persons but to their literary constructions – the ways in which the author chose to present them, make them act, speak, and think to answer the aforementioned questions. There is no doubt that this authorial choice was quite likely to have been inspired by the socio-historical context of late antique Roman Syria – the likely reaction of an aristocratic family of this place and time to a son's choice to follow an ascetic life.¹⁰¹ This imagining is not mutually exclusive, however, with adopting other popular texts as models that highlight the various paths leading toward a saintly life. The fact that the *APT* is explicitly quoted in the *Life*, as recalled above, offers a solid clue in affirming not only that the author knew the text but also, as I suggest, that it was a literary antecedent with which the author engaged to write his version of John's life and construct his protagonist's early

---

⁹⁹ For the historical sources on John of Tella, see Andrade, "The Syriac *Life*," 2009; and Menze, "Yuḥannon of Tella," 2011.

¹⁰⁰ Andrade, "The Syriac *Life*," 2009: 203, considers these interviews as a convention of the hagiographical genre rather than a historical fact and argues that Elias was not as close to John of Tella as he claims in the course of the *Life*.

¹⁰¹ On this, see Vuolanto, "Choosing Asceticism," 2009; and Vuolanto, *Children and Asceticism*, 2015.

environment. Ultimately, John's mother and tutor could have really acted, spoken, and thought the way the text says they did, but this probability does not negate the author's choice to carve out their characters by indirectly modeling them on the *APT*.

Contrasting Imitation 2: Paul the Executioner in the *Martyrdom of Thecla and Her Companions*

Here, we now turn to our final text, the *Martyrdom of Thecla and Her Companions*, which also rewrites the roles of the *APT*'s secondary characters albeit more drastically than our previous example, the *Life of John*. The *Martyrdom of Thecla and Her Companions* is a short text that belongs to the corpus of the Persian Martyr Acts (see above).[102] Though it is difficult to precisely date the text within the period (fifth–seventh century) in which the majority of the Persian Martyr Acts were composed, the story takes place in 346, during the reign of Shapur II (309–379), in the Adiabene region – a territory in northern Mesopotamia that corresponds to the area surrounding present-day Erbil, near Mosul. The content is somewhat unique in Syriac martyrdom literature: the story recounts the execution of five pure, blessed women, namely, Thecla, Mary, Martha, Emmi, and an unnamed woman, who are "daughters of the covenant" (i.e., who belong to the Syriac urban ascetical movement).[103] What makes this tale exceptional is that they did not suffer martyrdom at the hands of the Zoroastrian king or his officials as is typical of the Persian Martyr Acts. Rather, they are executed by a Christian priest named Pawle, who, threatened by the loss of all his wealth, apostatizes and, much to the surprise of the Zoroastrian governor himself, consents to kill his religious sisters, before he is himself murdered.[104]

What may link this text to the success of Thecla and the *APT* in Syriac Christianity is onomastics. Catherine Burris and Lucas Van Rompay have highlighted the fact that namesakes are evidence of the popularity of the virgin of Iconium.[105] They have noticed that two women martyred in Persia (one of whom is our "daughter of the covenant") were named after her. They have further remarked that two other women bearing the same

---

[102] They are no. 25 in Brock's list. See also Fiey, *Saints syriaques*, 2004: 186, no. 438.
[103] On this movement, see Harvey, "Revisiting," 2005.
[104] Actually, other martyrdom accounts originating in the Persian Empire offer portraits of Christian apostates who are given the role of executioner. See, for example, the *Martyrdom of Badmo* and the *Martyrdom of Narsai*. I thank Annunziata Di Rienzo for these references.
[105] Burris and Van Rompay, "Thecla in Syriac Christianity," 2002: 233.

name are the mother and the sister of two protagonists of East-Syrian monasticism, the seventh-century Rabban Hormizd and the fourth-century Mar Awgin, respectively.[106] They conclude by stating that "Thecla seems to have been regarded as an appropriate name for women accompanying venerable men, after the example of Thecla, Paul's companion."[107]

In this regard, one cannot help but being struck by the name of the other prominent figure of this *Martyrdom*, namely, the apostate priest Pawle (ܦܘܠܐ), which strongly recalls the apostle's name (ܦܘܠܘܣ, *Pawlos*). We cannot confirm with any certainty whether or not this similarity is intentional. The text does not refer to Paul or the *APT* explicitly, even though it still draws on narrative parallels from the wider Christian tradition. For instance, Pawle is portrayed as a second Judas Iscariot, both in regards to his treason and to his final death by hanging.[108] But if the author of this text has intentionally alluded to the heroine of the *APT*, Thecla, and her co-protagonist, Paul – as suggested by the use of their names – then the author is completely reversing the relationship between them. In other words, the relationship between the co-protagonists, Paul and Thecla, has been likened to that between two lovers.[109] However, in this *Martyrdom*, Paul, through his Persian namesake Pawle, turns from spiritual guide and desired partner to become Thecla's executioner!

Still, as readers of the *APT*, we may advance two considerations for explaining this turnaround, grounded on a specific and possible reading of the *APT*. In what follows, we will offer some loose associations that are nevertheless worth exploring since they provide a plausible explanation for all the contrasting similarities we find between the *APT* and the *Martyrdom*.

First, it has been noted that the *APT* seems to stress a divide between men and women who are presented as belonging to two opposite sides.[110] This is especially perceivable in the scenes that describe Thecla's trials, where women in the theater express out loud their solidarity with Thecla and condemn the tortures perpetrated by male authorities. The *Martyrdom of Thecla and Her Companions* aligns with this gendered dichotomy by staging two men, an evil king and a wicked priest, putting to death five

---

[106] Ibid. [107] Ibid. [108] See Brock and Harvey (trans.), *Holy Women*, 1998: 79 and 81.
[109] On this reading, see Barrier, *The Acts of Paul and Thecla*, 2009 and the sources therein.
[110] See Kaestli, "Fiction littéraire," 1990: 282.

women. Apart from the possibility of a historical rendering, the opposition and the roles may have been suggested by the *APT*, but further exaggerated and, at the same time, simplified in the *Martyrdom*. Second, and similarly, the Syriac hagiographer may have read some passages of the *APT* as describing Paul's negative behavior toward Thecla and brought them to their extreme conclusions. Scholars have remarked that Paul acts in an unfriendly, if not demeaning, manner toward Thecla in several instances: he prevents her from following him, refuses to baptize her (§ 3.25), and denies knowing her in front of Alexander, which results in a chain reaction of events leading to Thecla's second trial in Antioch (§ 4.1).[111] The author of the *Martyrdom* might have pushed such an attitude to its natural yet harshest conclusion by giving Paul/Pawle the unambiguous role of the evil antagonist. One particular scene in the *Martyrdom* loosely brings to mind one episode among those featuring "Paul's abandonment" of Thecla in the *APT*. It is when, for the first and only time, Thecla and her companions speak to Pawle, who has already lifted up his sword over their heads:

> In unison they cried out, "O base shepherd, are you beginning with your own sheep, slaughtering the lambs of your own flock? In your greed have you turned into a wolf, destroying the lambs in your own sheepfold? Is this the holy and saving Bread that we used to receive at your hands? Is this the life-giving Blood that you offered our mouths?"[112]

The imagery of the lamb and the shepherd borrowed from the Gospels is used here to describe the relationship between the five virgins and the priest, who, before turning into an enemy, was their spiritual guide. The same terminology and the same bond, followed by a similar change (if one accepts this interpretation), recall for us Thecla when she enters the arena in Iconium to be burnt:

> Thecla was as a lamb in the desert looking around for the shepherd, so she sought for Paul. And having looked into the crowd, she saw the Lord sitting as Paul, and she said, "As if I am not enduring, Paul gazes upon me." And she held fast to him, gazing intently, but he went away into the heavens. (*APT* § 3.21)

Jeremy Barrier too seems inclined to read in this passage a sign of Paul's abandonment, contrary to his understanding of other passages in the *APT*:

---

[111] See ibid.: 293–294; Davies, *The Revolt*, 1980: 58–59; and Vorster, "Construction of Culture," 2006: 115. For a different interpretation of these passages, which rather than denoting a malevolent abandonment, would follow the plot and the expectations of a romance novel, see Barrier, *The Acts of Paul and Thecla*, 2009: 9, 117, 123, and 140.

[112] Brock and Harvey (trans.), *Holy Women*, 1998: 80.

> While I think it is important to note that Paul is forced out of Iconium, and does not willingly leave Thecla, the text still seems to imply that there is some degree of abandonment . . . . Thecla has been left by all, so it seems.[113]

The reason is to be found in the text's theological message: "In fact, Thecla has been chosen by God to face these trials alone."[114] This remark echoes Johannes Vorster's interpretation: "Her autonomy is depicted in the absence of any assistance from his [Paul's] side . . . . Yet, in a strange, ironic manner, his actions confirmed her autonomy."[115] We suggest that this reading is significant for understanding the role of Paul/Pawle in our *Martyrdom* too. If Paul becomes here his own extreme alter ego, the Mr. Hyde (a unique, yet famous secondary character) of his apocryphal persona, it is for the purpose of enhancing Thecla's authority and fulfilling her desire to unite with Christ. This sentiment is expressed by the Persian Thecla and her companions: "But now the sword in your hands is indeed our salvation and deliverance: we go now to Jesus, our true possession and eternal inheritance."[116]

Conclusion

This chapter has focused on a form of reception that is less direct and more flexible than the forms that have been identified so far when dealing with Thecla's popularity in Syriac Christianity: it is not concerned with Thecla herself, but with other characters featured by her side. We hope to have illustrated how some prominent secondary characters in a selection of Syriac late antique hagiographical texts are built according to the models offered by the secondary characters of the *Acts of Paul and Thecla*. Whereas the nun Thomais, in the *Martyrdom of Febronia*, acts like a second Tryphaena, and the cruel Abuzard, in the *Martyrdom of Bassus and Susanna*, has the features of the numerous beasts attacking Thecla during her Antiochene trial, John's mother and John's tutor, in the *Life of John of Tella*, are examples of contrasting imitations, as they represent positive versions of Theocleia and Thamyris, inasmuch as Pawle is an extremely negative Paul and the killer of Thecla in the *Martyrdom of Thecla and Her Companions*. The reception of Thecla in these texts goes beyond direct

---

[113] Barrier, *The Acts of Paul and Thecla*, 2009: 123–124.   [114] Ibid.: 124.
[115] Vorster, "Construction of Culture," 2006: 115. Also referred to by Barrier, *The Acts of Paul and Thecla*, 2009: 140.
[116] Brock and Harvey (trans.), *Holy Women*, 1998: 80.

references to the heroine and involves the construction of the narrative in deeper and more structural ways.

Secondary characters have indeed the chief function of highlighting the heroism of the protagonists. In the four case studies presented here, they are characterized in ways that promote the holy main characters as the perfect martyr (Febronia and Bassus and Susanna), the perfect ascetic (John), and those perfectly devoted to Christ (Thecla and her companions). Thus, the story of Thecla not only provides material regarding a saint's pious way of life but also the actions, intentions, and personality to be adopted and/or corrected and even turned upside-down by those close to the saint. The overall effect is to reinforce and guarantee the latter's holiness. The ways in which the hagiographical texts under discussion here portray their secondary characters, whether in line with or in contrast to the secondary characters of the *APT*, strengthen the intertextual connections with the latter, as an important source text. Yet the two variations on imitation may offer important information about the purposes of reception. While the corresponding imitation accentuates the links between the protagonist and Thecla, the contrast serves to either emulate Thecla (surpassing, as in the case of John of Tella) or interpret the *APT* (negatively, as in the case of Pawle).[117] Either way, these connections may be part of a strategy of authentication: the audience is prone to believe more firmly that the protagonist is a saint if he or she assumes the image of Thecla, a link that secondary characters can guarantee further if those gravitating toward the hagiographic protagonists react as or to those featured around Thecla.

Bibliography

Andrade, Nathanael J. "The Syriac *Life of John of Tella* and the Frontier *Politeia*." *Hugoye* 12, no. 2 (2009): 199–234.

Barrier, Jeremy W. *The Acts of Paul and Thecla: A Critical Introduction and Commentary*. WUNT 2.270. Tübingen: Mohr Siebeck, 2009.

Becker, Adam H. "The Invention of the *Persian Martyr Acts*." In *Syriac Christian Culture: Beginnings to Renaissance*, edited by Aaron M. Butts and Robin Darling Young. Washington: Catholic University of America Press, 2020: 113–148.

Bedjan, Paul, ed. *Acta Martyrum et Sanctorum IV*. Leipzig: Otto Harrassowitz, 1894.

---

[117] The cultural and historical reasons for this reception vary from text to text and region to region, but that is an investigation for another time and place.

Acta Martyrum et Sanctorum V. Leipzig: Otto Harrassowitz, 1895.
Binggeli, André. "Les collections de Vies de saints dans les manuscrits syriaques." In *L'hagiographie syriaque*, edited by André Binggeli. Études syriaques 9. Paris: Geuthner, 2012: 49–75.
Brock, Sebastian P. *History of the Holy Mar Maʿin, with a Guide to the Persian Martyr Acts*. Piscataway: Gorgias, 2009.
Brock, Sebastian P., and Susan Ashbrook Harvey, trans. *Holy Women of the Syrian Orient, Updated Edition with a New Preface*. Berkeley: University of California Press, 1998.
Brooks, E. W., ed. "*Vita Iohannis Episcopi Tellae auctore Elia*." In *Vitae Virorum apud Monophysitas Celeberrimorum*. 2 vols. CSCO 111 25, Scr. Syr. 7–8. Paris: E Typographeo Reipublicae, 1907: 1: 31–95 (text); 2: 21–60 (trans.).
Burris, Catherine. "The Reception of the Acts of Thecla in Syriac Christianity: Translation, Collection, and Reception." PhD diss., University of North Carolina, Chapel Hill, 2010.
Burris, Catherine, and Lucas Van Rompay. "Thecla in Syriac Christianity: Preliminary Observations." *Hugoye* 5, no. 2 (2002): 225–236.
"Some Further Notes on Thecla in Syriac Christianity." *Hugoye* 6, no. 2 (2009): 337–342.
Butts, Aaron, and Simcha Gross, eds. and trans. *The History of the "Slave of Christ:" From Jewish Child to Christian Martyr*. Persian Martyr Acts in Syriac: Texts and Translations 6. Piscataway: Gorgias, 2016.
Chabot, Jean-Baptiste, ed. *La légende de Mar Bassus: martyr persan, suivie de l'histoire de la fondation de son couvent à Apamée, d'après un manuscrit de la Bibliothèque nationale*. Paris: E. Leroux, 1893.
Clark, Elisabeth A. *Reading Renunciation: Asceticism and Scripture in Early Christianity*. Princeton: Princeton University Press, 1999.
Cooper, Kate, and James Cork-Webster. "Conversion, Conflict, and the Drama of Social Reproduction: Narratives of Filial Resistance in Early Christianity and Modern Britain." In *Conversion and Initiation in Antiquity: Shifting Identities – Creating Change*, edited by Brigitte Secher Bøgh. Frankfurt am Main; New York: Peter Lang, 2015: 169–183.
Davies, Stevan L. *The Revolt of the Widows: The Social World of the Apocryphal Acts*. Carbondale: Southern Illinois University Press, 1980.
Davis, Stephen J. *The Cult of St. Thecla: A Tradition of Women's Piety in Late Antiquity*. Oxford Early Christian Studies. Oxford; New York: Oxford University Press, 2001.
De Temmerman, Koen. "Noble Slaves: The Rhetoric of Social Status Reversal in the Ancient Greek Novel." In *Slaves and Masters in the Ancient Novel*, edited by Stelios Panayotakis and Michael Paschalis. Ancient Narrative Supplement 23. Groningen: Barkhuis Publishing & Groningen University Library, 2019: 19–35.
Debié, Muriel. "Livres et monastères en Syrie-Mésopotamie d'après les sources syriaques." In *Le monachisme syriaque*, edited by Florence Jullien. Études Syriaques 7. Paris: Geuthner, 2010: 123–168.

Durmaz, Reyhan. "Hearing Sanctity: Oral Performance and Aural Consumption of Hagiographical Stories in the Late Antique and Medieval Syriac Milieu." In *Syriac Hagiography: Texts and Beyond*, edited by Sergey Minov and Flavia Ruani. Texts and Studies in Eastern Christianity 20. Leiden: Brill, 2021: 56–88.

Fiey, Jean Maurice. "Une hymne nestorienne sur les saintes femmes." *Analecta Bollandiana* 84 (1966): 77–110.

Nisibe, métropole syriaque orientale et ses suffragants des origines à nos jours. CSCO 388, Subsidia 54. Louvain: Secrétariat du CSCO, 1977.

Saints syriaques, edited by Lawrence I. Conrad. Princeton: Darwin, 2004.

Ghanem, Joseph Renée. "The Biography of John of Tella by Elias." PhD diss., The University of Wisconsin, 1970.

Graham Brock, Ann. "Political Authority and Cultural Accommodation: Social Diversity in the *Acts of Paul* and the *Acts of Peter*." In *The Apocryphal Acts of the Apostles: Harvard Divinity School Studies*, edited by François Bovon, Ann Graham Brock, and Christopher R. Matthews. Cambridge, MA: Harvard University Press, 1999: 145–169.

Halkin, François. "La passion grecque des saintes Libye, Eutropie et Léonis, martyres à Nisibe." *Analecta Bollandiana* 76 (1958): 293–315.

Harvey, Susan Ashbrook. "Sacred Bonding: Mothers and Daughters in Early Syriac Hagiography." *Journal of Early Christian Studies* 4 (1996): 27–56.

"Revisiting the Daughters of the Covenant: Women's Choirs and Sacred Song in Ancient Syriac Christianity." *Hugoye* 8, no. 2 (2005): 125–149.

Horn, Cornelia B. "Suffering Children, Parental Authority and the Quest for Liberation?: A Tale of Three Girls in the Acts of Paul (and Thecla), the Act(s) of Peter, the Acts of Nerseus and Achilleus, and the Epistle of Pseudo-Titus." In *A Feminist Companion to the New Testament Apocrypha*, edited by Amy-Jill Levine and Maria M. Robbins. London; New York: T&T Clark, 2006: 118–145.

Jullien, Florence. "Le monachisme féminin en milieu syriaque." In *Le monachisme syriaque*, edited by Florence Jullien. Études syriaques 7. Paris: Geuthner, 2010: 65–87.

Kaestli, Jean-Daniel. "Fiction littéraire et réalité sociale: Que peut-on savoir de la place des femmes dans le milieu de production des Actes apocryphes des apôtres?" *Apocrypha* 1 (1990): 279–302.

Kaestli, Jean-Daniel, and Willy Rordorf, eds. and trans. "La fin de la vie de Thècle dans les manuscrits des Actes de Paul et Thècle. Édition des textes additionnels." *Apocrypha* 25 (2014): 9–101.

Kaplan, Michel. "Une hôtesse importante de l'église Saint-Jean-Baptiste de l'Oxeia à Constantinople: Fébronie." In *Byzantine Religious Culture: Studies in Honor of Alice-Mary Talbot*, edited by Denis Sullivan, Elizabeth A. Fisher, and Stratis Papaioannou. The Medieval Mediterranean 92. Leiden: Brill, 2011: 31–52.

McClure, M. L., and Charles Lett Feltoe, eds. and trans. *The Pilgrimage of Etheria*. London: Society for Promoting Christian Knowledge, 1919.

Mellon Saint-Laurent, Jeanne-Nicole, and Kyle Smith, eds. and trans. *The History of Mar Behnam and Sarah: Martyrdom and Monasticism in Medieval Iraq*.

Persian Martyr Acts in Syriac: Texts and Translations 7. Piscataway: Gorgias, 2018.
Menze, Volker. *Justinian and the Making of the Syrian Orthodox Church*. Oxford: Oxford University Press, 2008.
"Yuḥannon of Tella." In *Gorgias Encyclopedic Dictionary of the Syriac Heritage*, edited by Sebastian P. Brock, Aaron M. Butts, G. A. Kiraz, and L. Van Rompay. Piscataway: Gorgias, 2011: 447–448.
Misset-van de Weg, Magda. "A Wealthy Woman Named Tryphaena: Patroness of Thecla of Iconium." In *The Apocryphal Acts of Paul and Thecla*, edited by Jan N. Bremmer. Studies on the Apocryphal Acts of the Apostles 2. Kampen: Kok Pharos, 1996: 16–35.
Monaca, Mariangela. "Tecla e la grotta. Una via di ascesi al femminile." In *Antrum. Riti e simbologie delle grotte nel Mediterraneo antico*, edited by Arduino Maiuri. Quaderni di Studi e Materiali di Storia delle Religioni 16. Brescia: Morcelliana, 2017: 355–372.
Palmer, Andrew. *Monk and Mason on the Tigris Frontier: The Early History of Ṭur ʿAbdin*. Cambridge: Cambridge University Press, 1970.
"Saints' Lives with a Difference: Elijah on John of Tella (d. 538) and Joseph on Theodotos of Amida (d. 698)." In *IV Symposium Syriacum 1984: Literary Genres in Syriac Literature*, edited by René Lavenant, Hans W. J. Drijvers, C. Morgenberg, and G. J. Reinink. Orientalia Christiana Analecta 229. Rome: Pontificium Institutum Studiorum Orientalium, 1987: 203–216.
Saint-Laurent, Jeanne-Nicole. "Images de femmes dans l'hagiographie syriaque." In *L'hagiographie syriaque*, edited by André Binggeli. Études syriaques 9. Paris: Geuthner, 2012: 201–224.
Turner, Peter. *Truthfulness, Realism, Historicity: A Study in Late Antique Spiritual Literature*. Farnham: Ashgate, 2012.
Voicu, Sever J. "Thecla in the Christian East." In *Thecla: Paul's Disciple and Saint in the East and West*, edited by Jeremy W. Barrier, Jan N. Bremmer, T. Niklas, and A. Puig i Tàrrech. Studies on Early Christian Apocrypha 12. Leuven: Peeters, 2017: 47–68.
Vorster, Johannes N. "Construction of Culture through the Construction of Person: The Construction of Thecla in the *Acts of Thecla*." In *A Feminist Companion to the New Testament Apocrypha*, edited by Amy-Jill Levine and Maria M. Robbins. London; New York: T&T Clark, 2006: 98–117.
Vuolanto, Ville. "Choosing Asceticism: Children and Parents, Vows and Conflicts." In *Children in Late Ancient Christianity*, edited by Cornelia B. Horn and Robert R. Phenix. Studien und Texte zu Antike und Christentum 58. Tübingen: Mohr Siebeck, 2009: 255–292.
Children and Asceticism in Late Antiquity: Continuity, Family Dynamics and the Rise of Christianity. Farnham: Ashgate, 2015.
Wright, William, ed. and trans. *Apocryphal Acts of the Apostles Edited from Syriac Manuscripts in the British Museum and Other Libraries*. 2 vols. London: Williams and Norgate, 1871.

CHAPTER 6

Shifting the Poetics of Gender Ambiguity
The Coptic Naturalization of Thecla

Arietta Papaconstantinou

This book, which contains the Holy Scriptures of the Old and the New Testament, we know from tradition that it was written by the hand of Thecla, a noble woman of Egypt, about one thousand three hundred years ago.[1]

When, in 1627, the Patriarch of Constantinople Kyrillos Loukaris (1572–1638) sent the Codex Alexandrinus as a gift to King Charles I (1600–1649), he claimed that it had been written by an Egyptian woman named Thecla who lived at the time of the Council of Nicaea (325). He also stated that, for thirteen hundred years, it had been kept in Alexandria where he found it during his tenure as Patriarch. On his return to Constantinople, Loukaris presumably had brought the precious codex with him. Writing to the Archbishop of Canterbury, the ambassador Sir Thomas Roe (d. 1644), who was charged with the transfer of the Codex, gives more details about the purported scribe:

> He doth testefye vnder his hand, that it was written by the virgin Thekla, daughter of a famous Greeke, called Αργιεριενος,[2] who founded the monestarye in Egypt vpon Pharoas tower, a deuout and learned mayd, who was persecuted in Asya, and to whom Gregorye Nazienzen hath written many epistles. At the end whereof, vnder the same hand, are the epistles of Clement. She dyed not long after the councell of Nice.[3]

---

[1] Liber iste Scriptura Sacra N(ovi) et V(eteris) Testamenti, prout ex traditione habemus, est scriptus manu Theclae, nobilis fœminæ Agyptiæ, ante mile et trecentos annos circiter. See note at the beginning of vol. 1 of the Codex Alexandrinus in Kenyon (ed.), *The Codex Alexandrinus*, 1915.

[2] The name (*Argierienos*) is written in the Greek alphabet by Roe. It corresponds to no known Egyptian or Greek name of the time, which could indicate he only heard it orally and attempted to transcribe it as it sounded.

[3] See Sir Thomas Roe's Letter to George Abbot, February 17/27, 1626, in Roe, *The Negotiations*, 1730: 618. See also Spinka, "Acquisition," 1936.

In an earlier letter to the fourteenth Earl of Arundel (1585–1645), however, Roe had identified Thecla differently. The Codex, he says, was

> an autographall bible intire, written by the hand of Tecla the protomartyr of the Greekes, that liued in the tyme of St. Paul; and he doth auerr yt to be true and authenticall, of his owne writing, and the greatest antiquity of the Greeke church.[4]

However interesting this tradition may be to explore in its own right, I only mention it here to highlight how closely connected Thecla had become with Egypt over the medieval and early modern periods.[5] In his study of the cult of St. Thecla, Stephen Davis showed how the figure of Thecla had become linked with early female asceticism in and around Alexandria with the explicit encouragement of Bishop Athanasius (d. 373).[6] For Davis, that connection fueled the development of her cult. Collecting the evidence for a cult of Thecla in the vicinity of Abu Mina in the Mareotis area, he compellingly demonstrated not only the existence of a cult site but also its integration in the pilgrim route to Abu Mina and its strong relation – at least textually – with female pilgrimage practices.[7] The story of a rich woman who had left home secretly to visit the shrine of St. Menas and who was saved by him from sexual assault near the "martyrium of saint Thecla" is but one of several examples of such a relation.[8] Thecla was styled in the *APT* as an itinerant woman, a "stranger" (ξένη) and therefore in danger of sexual assault – something from which she later protects other traveling women.[9] Her wearing of a male cloak the next time she travels, mentioned almost in passing, can be understood, in the plot of the *APT*, simply as a way to avoid similar episodes as the one in Antioch.[10] Yet it proved foundational for much of the later tradition, as well as for large portions of recent scholarship.

---

[4] See Sir Thomas Roe's Letter to the Earl of Arundel, January 20/30, 1624 in Roe, *The Negotiations*, 1730: 334–335.
[5] A discussion of the attribution of the Alexandrinus to Thecla can be found in Smith, *A Study of the Gospels*, 2014: 32–34.
[6] Davis, *The Cult of St. Thecla*, 2001: 158–159; and Athanasius of Alexandria, *De virginitate* 211–213: Casey, "Der dem Athanasius," 1935: 1034.
[7] Davis, "Pilgrimage and Cult," 1998.
[8] All the relevant evidence is collected by Davis, "Pilgrimage and Cult," 1998; and Davis, *The Cult of St. Thecla*, 2001: 113–136.
[9] Ibid.: 315 and 317–319.
[10] The protective function of male clothing is the central motif in one of the narratives discussed by Marie Delcourt in her early article on transvestite saints. The narrative has attracted no attention because it is Western and dating from the time of the Crusades: the narrative in question revolves around Hildegund of Schönau, whose father had taken her with him on pilgrimage to Jerusalem and dressed her up as a boy and renamed her Joseph. The rest of the story is very different from the

Thecla's story is invoked very explicitly in the story of Eugenia, daughter of the governor of Alexandria under Commodus (161–192), as the reason why the latter refused to marry, left home, and dressed up as a man in order to join a monastery: "She came across the story of the holy Apostle Paul and the virgin Thecla, and reading it secretly she cried at every page, not least because she also had parents who were very committed pagans."[11] Eugenia's story is part of a series of narratives with a similar – if not identical – plot, even though it is the only one that cites the *APT*. It even attributes to Thecla's example her decision to dress up as a man.[12] The intertextual relations between narratives of female cross-dressing saints and the *APT* have been discussed more than once. It has been studied most thoroughly by Davis in an article published after his study on saint Thecla's cult[13] and now in Julie Van Pelt's chapter in this volume (Chapter 7), so I shall leave them aside here.

What has been less discussed, except in 1974 by John Anson, is the connection of many of those narratives with Egypt and more specifically with the monastic literary landscape of Alexandria and its hinterland.[14] When they are not *from* Alexandria, the heroines leave their homes, often in Constantinople, to join monasteries in or around Sketis. This *foisonnement* of transvestite narratives in the area is not unconnected with the popularity of Thecla and her story in the same circles. Already in the fourth century, the injunction by Athanasius (d. 373) to a group of "virgins" to imitate Thecla shows that the character was not only known but uncontroversial – to the controversial bishop, at least – and popular enough to be proposed as a model. Yet Athanasius cast Thecla in a purely ascetic role. In other words, she was to serve as an example of chastity and abstinence for a community of female ascetics, not of a life of adventure and defiance. The element of gender transgression present in the initial legend does not seem to have struck all its readers to the same degree.

Dressing in male clothes, despite its subversive undertones, is not the only device through which gender categories are blurred in those texts.

Byzantine narratives. See Delcourt, "Le complexe de Diane," 1958: 6; and Henschenius and Papebrochius (eds.), *Acta Sanctorum Aprilis II*, 1675: 782–784.

[11] *Life of Eugenia* § 2: Apserou, "Το αγιολογικό dossier," 2017: 291: Ἐνέπεσεν δὲ εἰς τὰς χεῖρας αὐτῆς τοῦ ἁγιωτάτου Ἀποστόλου Παύλου καὶ τῆς παρθένου Θέκλης ἡ ἐξήγησις καὶ ἀναγινώσκουσα λαθραίως ἐδάκρυεν ἐφεκάστης, διὰ τὸ καὶ μάλιστα ἑλληνικωτάτοις αὐτὴν γονεῦσιν ὑπάρχειν.

[12] *Life of Eugenia* § 19: Apserou, "Το αγιολογικό dossier," 2017: 308: "changing her clothes, with the zeal and in imitation of her teacher Thecla" (τὸ σχῆμα μεταβαλοῦσα, ζήλῳ καὶ μιμήσει τῆς διδασκάλου Θέκλης).

[13] Davis, "Crossed Texts, Crossed Sex," 2002.

[14] Anson, "The Female Transvestite," 1974: 12 and *passim*.

A woman traveling alone would also be bending gender rules, and Thecla's characterization as an itinerant stranger but also as well educated, morally sound, and socially prominent, is almost oxymoronic; a woman was either a vagabond following a man outside her home, or she was a well brought-up girl from a good family who did what she was told and did not run the streets. Combining these traits was a male prerogative.

It is not difficult to imagine the attraction of such narratives of reversal among high-status Alexandrian women in late antiquity. They float the themes of independence and free roaming in the perfectly acceptable framework of female Pauline piety. After all, Paul's history of converting women was not limited to Thecla. According to the Acts of the Apostles, in Athens he won over Damaris, about whose identity there was some intrigued discussion in late antiquity.[15] The women portrayed in those stories come mostly from the highest strata of society (daughters of emperors and governors), mirroring Thecla's own high status which is repeatedly stressed in the *APT*. The rich intertextual and citational tradition of that work in the fourth and fifth centuries remains resolutely in the same social circles. And just like Thecla's following of Paul, despite being modeled on the love romance, was not a carnal following but an intellectual one, so the heroines who emulated her were sometimes quite straightforwardly intellectual: at sixteen, for instance, Eugenia "had made such remarkable intellectual progress, being educated to the highest degree in the learning of the Greeks and the Romans, that she was admired even by wise men."[16]

Books, reading, and intellectual reflection were important elements of the forms of female piety constructed in those narratives: an elite woman like Eugenia is converted to the ascetic life after reading about an earlier elite woman who did the same and thinking about that story while traveling in her litter.[17] Like a matryoshka doll, a woman in search of a female model would read a narrative about a woman and her search for a female model by reading another narrative about a woman and her heroic deeds. As Kate Cooper has recently suggested, a female reader would have

---

[15] Acts 17:34. See Childers, "A Reluctant Bride," 2007: 212–221.
[16] *Life of Eugenia* § 1: Apserou, "Το αγιολογικό dossier," 2017: 290: οὕτως ἐξαιρέτως φρονήσει προέκοπτεν ἑλληνικοῖς τε καὶ ῥωμαϊκοῖς εἰς ἄκρον πεπαιδευμένη λόγοις, ὥστε καὶ παρὰ σοφῶν θαυμάζεσθαι.
[17] *Life of Eugenia* § 1: Apserou, "Το αγιολογικό dossier," 2017: 291: "as she was leaving, sitting in her litter, she considered Thecla's story and remembered how she believed what Paul was saying" (ἐν τῷ ἀπιέναι αὐτὴν ἐν τῷ βαστερνίῳ καθεζομένη, ἔνδον διελογίζετο τὰ τῆς Θέκλης καὶ ἐνεθυμεῖτο ὅπως τε ἐπίστευσεν τοῖς ὑπὸ τοῦ Παύλου λεγομένοις).

found a mirror in such a story: Eugenia was a reflection of herself, and the reader might well "identify with Eugenia's own attempt to respond to the challenge posed by a shared heroine, Thecla."[18] The importance of books is not confined to the *Life of Eugenia*; wealthy women projected the image of the assiduous reader by carrying miniature codices around their necks, a habit remarked upon by Isidore of Pelusium (d. c. 449) in Egypt but also by John Chrysostom (d. 407) and Gregory of Tours (538–594).[19] Egeria (fl. fourth century) also mentions reading the *APT* when she visited the saint's shrine in Seleucia.[20] Stephen Davis has noted the small size of some of the earliest surviving manuscripts of the *APT*[21] and has convincingly argued that they point to their use during travel, possibly pilgrimage.[22] I would go further and suggest that exhibiting such conspicuously precious and intellectual objects was part of the construction of a social persona within the female circles of the empire's urban elites, even without actual travel; portability could be useful even for a stroll downtown.

The association of Thecla with the social aspirations of the nerdy bourgeoise seems to have lingered in Alexandrian church lore. At some point between the fifth and the seventeenth century, it also seems to have given rise to the legend Kyrillos Loukaris heard when he came to the city briefly as its patriarch, namely, that after the Council of Nicea (325), a rich Alexandrian woman called Thecla had founded a monastery on Pharos and, presumably, copied the entire Bible in its scriptorium. The popularity of the figure in elite Alexandrian circles eventually trickled down to the urban elites of the Valley, and, by the sixth century at the latest, Coptic translations of the *APT* were being produced.[23]

Until the fifth century, however, the fascination with Thecla was arguably not a cult properly speaking. This changed as the cult of saints developed from the later part of the fifth and especially in the sixth century. A cult figure like Thecla, despite her itinerant identity, started requiring the topographical anchoring of a shrine. This spawned new narratives, attached to competing shrines. Thus, a major rewriting of the section of the *APT* morphed into the *Life and Miracles of Thecla*, which

---

[18] Cooper, "The Bride of Christ," 2013: 539–540.
[19] Isidore of Pelusium, *Epistula* 2.150: *PG* 78.604; and John Chrysostom, *Ad populum Antiochenum* 19.4: *PG* 49.196. See Davis, *The Cult of St. Thecla*, 2001: 145–146, for further discussion and references.
[20] Egeria, *Itinerarium* 23.5.
[21] See, in particular, the papyri from Oxyrhynchus and Antinoopolis: *P.Oxy.* I 6 (5th c.) and *P.Ant.* I 13 (4th c.).
[22] Davis, *The Cult of St. Thecla*, 2001: 146.
[23] Schmidt, *Acta Pauli*, 1904; Kasser and Luisier (eds. and trans.), "Le Bodmer XLI," 2004.

promoted her shrine in Seleucia.[24] Meanwhile, a partial rewriting of the end of the *APT* was carried out in Rome, which states that she had followed Paul there at the end of her life and thus supports a Roman shrine's claim to her relics.[25]

The appearance of a cult spot in the vicinity of Abu Mina in the Mareotis might also have been supported by a now-lost story. The proximity to a shrine of St. Menas, whose intriguing connection with Phrygia in Asia Minor is emphasized in his *passio*, could well not be a coincidence; like with Paul's cult in Rome, Thecla's cult in Egypt could have piggybacked, so to speak, on that of Menas. That shrine devoted to Thecla west of Alexandria does not seem to have had much success, and hardly any memory of it remains apart from a mention in passing in one of Menas' *Miracles* and the ampulla shared with Menas, which was probably produced at Abu Mina.

Davis argues, however, that Thecla's initial popularity was not lost on the Egyptians. In fact, following a well-practiced tradition, they turned her into a recognizably Egyptian martyr through a retelling of her story in the local martyrological idiom.[26] The result was what has come down to us as the *Martyrdom of Paese and Thecla* (henceforth *MPTh*), the story of a brother and a sister from a village called Pousire in Middle Egypt, near Antinoe.[27] Although at first sight the two texts are very different, Davis states, it is possible to discern signs of rewriting of the *APT* in the *MPTh*.

Paese, a rich landowner, and Thecla, the widow of an extremely rich man from whom she has a "small child," are keen, from the very beginning of the persecutions, to visit the prisons to comfort and feed those awaiting martyrdom. Paese has a business partner and friend named Paul, a rich merchant who lived in Shmoun/Hermopolis and bought Paese's flax. On a trip to Alexandria, Paul falls ill and, thinking he is about to die, asks Paese to visit. Once in Alexandria, Paese finds that Paul has recovered but would like Paese to wait until they can travel south together. In Alexandria, too, Paese visits the impending martyrs in prison. One day, he witnesses the trial and torture of the famous martyr from Antioch, Victor the General, at

---

[24] Johnson, *The Life and Miracles*, 2006. [25] Cooper, "A Saint in Exile," 1995.
[26] Davis, *The Cult of St. Thecla*, 2001: 177–190.
[27] Reymond and Barnes (eds. and trans.), *Four Martyrdoms*, 1973: 33–79 (text) and 151–184 (translation). This is a critical edition based on the only complete text, found in the ninth-century codex 591, fol. 49r–88r of the Pierpont Morgan Library, with variants from several fragmentary manuscripts: see ibid.: 20. For an additional fragment, see Browne, "The Martyrdom," 1974. In this chapter, the quotations from this text correspond to the pages of the translation in Reymond and Barnes, where the folio and column of the manuscript are indicated.

the hands of the prefect Armenios. This inspires him to confess his faith, and he ends up in prison where the other "saints" welcome him as one of them. Several very stereotypical scenes of courtroom exchange, torture, miraculous recovery, and imprisonment ensue for two days in a row. Meanwhile, the worried Thecla decides to go and find her brother. She finds a boat docked in Antinoe with two women and a sailor, and they promise to take her along. She does not know at first that these characters are actually Mary and Elizabeth and the archangel Raphael. Later, Mary reveals her identity and anoints Thecla with oil, promising her that Raphael will remain with her throughout her trials-to-come. Having reached Alexandria, she goes to feed the martyrs in prison and to look for Paese. The next day when the court scenes resume, she confesses with her brother. They are both tortured again vainly and sent back to prison at the end of the day. That night an angel comes to Paese and takes him on a tour of heaven, where he shows him his future house, vast and lavish, with three thrones, for him, Thecla, and Paul. Back in prison the next night, after another day of torture and recovery, Thecla writes a parting letter to her son. The next day, the prefect confers with the priests who have realized that the saints are becoming too popular with the inhabitants of the city and decides to pass them on to the duke of the Thebaid, Eutychianos, to whom he had also sent Victor earlier in the narrative. They are finally taken by boat to Tepot, a place in the Antinoite, and beheaded.

Davis argued that the *MPTh* was an offshoot of the *APT*, intended to support a local cult place by capitalizing on Thecla's popularity, and that it recycled several motifs from the original story. More specifically, he pointed to "the three interrelated themes of chastity, itinerant 'strangerhood,' and martyrdom – along with the theme of androgyny," which are essential for the characterization of both Theclas.[28] The Coptic Thecla's chastity is marked by her refusal to remarry after her husband's death; like her namesake, she leaves home to find the male character in a prison and suffers martyrdom in a city where she is a stranger but is saved miraculously by God.

His demonstration did not convince Carolyn Osiek, "for the elements of similarity are common to many romances and martyrdom accounts,"[29] and I suspect that the overall silence of Copticists on the subject reflects their tacit agreement with that verdict. Yet, if the theme of chastity is indeed ever-present in Christian hagiography, it is much less common for

[28] Davis, *The Cult of St. Thecla*, 2001: 183.   [29] Osiek, "Review of *The Cult*," 2003: 423.

female itinerancy to be caused by a strongly expressed yet platonic relation to a male character. The scene where the Coptic Thecla finds Paese in prison is directly inspired by the meeting between Paul and Thecla in the *APT*, and both involve a kiss:[30]

> [Thecla] went in to Paul and, having sat down at his feet, she heard about the magnificent acts of God. And Paul feared nothing, but conducted himself with the boldness of God; and her faith increased as she kissed his fetters. (*APT* § 18)

> She discovered him fettered with the saints – there was great favour upon his face, after the manner of an angel of God. She advanced toward him, and kissed him. (*MPTh* 170)

Davis quotes the two scenes as well as the various moments in the narrative when both Paese and Thecla identify as "strangers" when they are in Alexandria.[31] I would argue that the prison scene itself here is an intertext at least as important as itinerancy, if not more so, as it is a less frequent motif. Prison scenes did become a stock motif in *passiones* in Coptic as well as in Greek and other languages, but they do not usually contain meeting scenes, nor do they concern itinerant women.[32]

As for the theme of martyrdom, the archetypal scenes in the *APT* represent an entire genre in which the impending martyr is saved several times through divine agency, even though Thecla does not succumb to death while protagonists of *passiones* do. In that sense, this motif is perhaps less central in connecting the two narratives as it is more generic. This was recognized by Theofried Baumeister in his study of stock scenes of repeated tortures followed by angel-assisted recoveries in Coptic *passiones*. He characterized texts based on those very standardized scenes as belonging to the "koptischer Konsens."[33] Yet, although Baumeister found that a number of Coptic *passiones* conform almost militantly to the structure he outlined, he did not find this to be the case of the *MPTh*: it is not, he says, a simple reproduction of the usual structure but a "nicely recomposed, individually designed martyr story, almost along the lines of ascetic legends, but interspersed with scenes in the style of the *koptischer Konsens*."[34]

---

[30] All references to the *APT* are drawn from Lipsius (ed.), *Acta apostolorum apocrypha*, 1891: 235–271.
[31] Davis, *The Cult of St. Thecla*, 2001: 184
[32] See now on this motif Papavarnavas, *Gefängnis als Schwellenraum*, 2021.
[33] Baumeister, *Martyr Invictus*, 1972.
[34] Ibid.: 123: "eine schön durchkomponierte, individuell gestaltete Martyrergeschichte etwa in der Art der Mönchslegenden, jedoch durchsetzt mit Szenen im Stil des koptischen Konsenses."

This resemblance to ascetic legends sets the *MPTh* apart from other Coptic martyrologies and reflects its unusual literary origin.

It is possible, I believe, to go even further in examining the relation between the two narratives. A closer reading suggests that even if the author of the *MPTh* did not have a copy of the *APT*, he knew the story and especially that he was conscious of the connotations of gender ambivalence and role reversal that had come to be attached to Thecla's character. Unlike Davis, however, I do not think that this was achieved through a characterization of the Coptic Thecla as slightly androgynous.[35] The ambivalence of the gender roles is rendered in the *MPTh* through a creative game of literary reordering and an expansion of the cast. The resulting work is not merely a transformation of the original one nor even a cultural translation into a new idiom. It is a new, strongly citational work, for which the *APT* is but one of many subtexts. Like the transvestite saints' narratives, it self-consciously situates itself and its heroes in a broader set of narratives that circulated in Egypt, including those of the *koptischer Konsens*.

The characters and their relations are constructed with obvious nods to the *APT*, but along different lines. First, as Davis suggests in passing, Paul is far from being a secondary figure whose only function resides in his name and its reinforcement of the link with the *APT*; he is a central character in the *MPTh*.[36] He is the one who sets the plot into motion since his trip to Alexandria is what brings about the separation of brother and sister. It thus prepares the scene of their reunion in prison – one of the flagship scenes in the *APT*. His place in Paese's universe is at least as large as that of Thecla.

In the *MPTh* narrative, the male character of the *APT* is split, and the romantic, novelistic relations and sub-erotic connotations of the original story are reorganized into a new love triangle. In that way, the author maintains the powerful gender ambiguity associated with Thecla in the literary tradition while, at the same time, entirely subverting the *APT* through the depiction of the male characters. Here, the boundaries are blurred with the initial motifs remixed across genders and across the family/non-family divide. This new take is established from the outset in the presentation of the first character; it is Paese and not Thecla who has "the conversation" with his parents about marriage:

---

[35] Davis, *The Cult of St. Thecla*, 2001: 185–186.   [36] Ibid.: 184 n. 120.

> And his father Elias and his mother Mariam kept urging him, saying, "Let us take a wife for thee, that we may see joy of thee before we die." But he would not endure this at all, saying, "I care not for a wife; for my sister married a husband, and behold, she has become a widow. Now, she has borne a son; he together with her will suffice me." (151)

This passage gives Paese the traditional role of Thecla while, at the same time, setting up his sister symbolically as his wife: she and her son will be his family. Thecla also resists matrimonial advances, but at the same time she is no longer a virgin. Like her namesake, her refusal is accompanied by a preference for prisoners:

> And many rich men of the city urged her, saying "We wish to take thee to wife;" but she was not persuaded, but resolutely devoted herself to the saints, binding up their wounds; to their bodies, subjected to tortures, she applied oil and wine. (153)

Brother and sister share some common characteristics; in particular their wealth and their strong commitment to feeding and comforting "the saints," that is, the victims of the persecutions in the local prisons.[37] After the titular characters, Paul is introduced with at least as much weight:

> There was a man in the city of Shmoun who was a great merchant in his family, being a kinsman of theirs. And this man had much wealth; and it was he who bought the flax fibre of that whole nome; and the name of that man was Paul. And he was a God-fearing man, performing very many charities secretly. And that man was friendly with Paese, since the latter sowed a great plantation of flax. And Paese was noble and rich and famous in that whole nome. He would load the camels for the goods for disposal, and arise and go to the city of Shmoun to Paul the merchant; and Paul was glad whenever he saw Paese and he would keep him with him for a month at a time, while they ate and drank together, rejoicing exceedingly and conversing together upon the word of God. (153)

Already at this point, one of the central themes of the *MPTh* is introduced, namely, the friendship between Paese and Paul. The depth of bond is established immediately, and food, drink, and common prayer and devotion serve as markers of their intimacy. Once the plot is set in motion, however, powerfully emotional language is used to describe their relation. Thus, when Paul falls ill in Alexandria, he writes to his servants back home to come and find him and to tell Paese:

---

[37] The translation "saints" is slightly misleading as the Coptic notes ⲉⲧⲟⲩⲁⲁⲃ, which is rather equivalent to "the holy ones."

> "If thou art willing to come, that I may see thee before I die, then come! Otherwise I bid thee farewell." It befell that when the letter came to the south, Paese was informed. Straightway as soon as Paese heard, his heart was very sorrowful, and he arose and took about the amount of one pound of gold, and goods for disposal, and boarded the boat. (153–154)

On his arrival in Alexandria with Paul's servants, Paese lets them go in and waits outside. Paul's first reaction is to enquire about his friend, thinking he had not come: "Is he well, my friend Paese, and his God-loving sister Thecla?" When the servants let him know that Paese is just outside the door, Paul goes through several emotional phases in quick succession before settling into the usual eating and drinking together:

> They said, "Here is Paese, outside the door." He was angry with his servants, and he arose and came out, and cast himself down on the ground and did him reverence upon his face. And Paese was much moved, and they fell upon each other's necks and wept for a great while. Paul said to Paese, "Come in; why dost thou stand outside? Come in, thou man worthy to be loved by God and men." Paese said, "Verily, my brother, I was glad when I found thee well".... And he took him into his house, and he himself rejoiced with him, and they ate and drank together. (154–155)

Paese makes the best of his time in Alexandria by visiting the prisons. After a couple of weeks of this charitable work, however, he thinks of his sister and wants to go back to the south. Paul pleads with him to wait until they can leave together. He asks, "Why art thou so faint-hearted? Stay for this week, and we will go off together; why shouldst thou go and leave me?" (156).

This moment of emotional weakness marks another turning point in the plot as the following day Paese is witness to the arrest and torture of Victor, which ultimately results in his own arrest and torture. Again, Paul's guilty feelings over this development are conveyed in strong language:

> Paul was in his house, and he did not know what had befallen Paese. But his servant went weeping, and told him what had befallen him. And Paul when he heard this laid hand upon his clothes and rent them, and wept with sore weeping, saying, "O that I had let him go home! For he was distressed, entreating me and saying, 'Let me go away,'" and I did not let him. I would rather have lost twenty pounds of gold today than that this should have happened. What use is wealth of gold and silver to me compared with a friend who is sweet and good?" (160)

Paul visits his friend in prison. When he sees the marks of torture on Paese's body, he weeps and cries out: "The pain of my heart is great today. O my brother; O that I had lost all that I had rather than that this should have befallen thee" (160). Despite the protestations voiced by Paese, who explains that becoming a martyr and being redeemed of his sins is the most joyful outcome he could hope for, Paul goes home and does "not eat or drink for three days and three nights, and he fell sick of bilious humor because of Paese" (160)[38] – just like Thecla when she first heard Paul and stayed at the window for three days without eating or drinking in the *APT*.

These passages characterize the relation between the two characters as powerfully emotional. The body language described at moments of crisis – renting clothes, falling in each other's arms, and weeping – and the cries and lamentations of Paul when he realizes he might lose his friend are used to reinforce this characterization. At the same time, they draw on a gendered repertoire of emotions that is here used against the grain: expressed by a man for another man in a context of male friendship rather than depicting the affection of a mother, a lover, or a servant – the three categories of figures highlighted in the *APT* as afflicted by Thecla's choices.[39]

As the story continues, this aspect becomes more prominent. Instead of the usual rhythm of torture by day and prison by night, the prefect on the following day has Paese put in a furnace and leaves him overnight. This becomes the occasion of a surprising escapade; at midnight, while Paese is praying in the middle of the furnace, an angel comes and takes him to Paul's house. The passage is worth quoting in full:

> Now Paul was sleeping, grieving for Paese, not knowing what had befallen him. And the blessed Apa Paese awakened Paul; and Paul, when he opened his eyes and saw his friend Paese, was amazed, because a bright light was glowing at him within his bedchamber continuously; and since he did not understand the thing which had befallen him, the blessed Apa Paese said to him, "Fear not, my brother; I am Paese." And it befell that when Paul heard the voice of his friend Paese, he arose straightway in haste, and cast himself at his feet, and reverenced him joyfully; and straightway he raised him up, and they both embraced one another. ... And they sat down, and talked together of the great [works] of God, and the miracles which he performs for his saints. ... Paul said to him, "By thy health, my brother, since the time when thou wast taken to the tribunal yesterday, I have neither eaten bread nor drunk water." And straightway he aroused his servants; and when they had seen the blessed Apa Paese they reverenced him, [bowing] down to the ground, and greeted him. And Paul gave orders to his servants and they

---

[38] This echoes Thecla's reaction the first time she heard Paul, when she sat at the window for three days without eating or drinking (*APT* § 8).

[39] "And they wept bitterly, Thamyris for losing a wife, Theocleia a child, the female slaves a mistress" (*APT* § 10).

prepared a table; and they ate and drank together, and they slept until the light spread abroad. (163)

Here the author is venturing into a literally "promiscuous brotherhood"[40] where the ambiguity of the language used is very reminiscent – if on a different register – of that in the *APT* where Thecla is said to be found "bound in affection" with Paul, sparking a scene of jealousy from her aspiring husband.[41] Made up of a recognition scene, a reunion, a declaration of love, and a peaceful night together, the passage plays on a series of stock motifs from romance, repurposed to describe a male spiritual friendship.

The *MPTh* further forces gender categories by applying to Paese the imagery of the Bride of Christ. When for the first time the imprisoned "saints" see him come, not as a visitor but as a tortured fellow martyr, they tell him, "We see thee daily, but today we rejoice the more with thee because thou hast come into the bridechamber of Christ with thy whole heart" (160). Meanwhile, a prisoner back in Antinoe asks Thecla during one of her visits:

> "Why hast thou not gone to the wedding feast of thy brother Paese? For behold, the wedding feast is celebrated with great rejoicing. For it is an angel of the Lord who has said to me: Say to her, 'Go to the wedding feast of thy brother.'" (166)

This fellow sufferer-in-the-making reassures Thecla that her brother is still alive and that many people have "assembled for his wedding," and this is repeated when the passengers of the boat she takes to go north, Mary and Elizabeth, tell her that they are "going to visit Paul the merchant, who holds a marriage feast for a man named Paese, from Pousire" (167–168). As noted above, Mary, after revealing her identity, anoints Thecla with sweet-smelling oil "from the wedding of my son, which I have brought for the wedding of thy brother" (168).

Paese is thus insistently represented as the Bride, while Thecla herself is not once described in this way. The erotic subtext that often accompanies that metaphor in hagiographic texts about women is here not only transferred to a man but inserted in the context of a male-male friendship.[42]

---

[40] Brown, *The Body and Society*, 1989: the expression is the title of ch. 7, 140–159, taken from a passage in Minucius Felix, *Octavius* 9, which takes – or feigns to take – literally the use of para-erotic vocabulary by Christians to describe their relations.
[41] συνδεδεμένην τῇ στοργῇ (*APT* § 19).
[42] For another example, see the discussion of the martyr Bassus by Flavia Ruani in this volume (Chapter 5).

The scene where Paese, sitting in Paul's bedchamber during the night they spend together, tells the latter that Christ has summoned him "to his holy bridechamber" (163) is reminiscent of the chaste marriages so popular in early hagiography in which the metaphoric bedchamber supersedes the material one – a theme that also underpins the plot of the *APT*.

The relation of Paese to Thecla, on the other hand, is less balanced emotionally: the display of emotion comes only from Thecla who goes to her death in Alexandria because she is "very sore at heart for her brother" (166). In the initial parting scene, when Paese leaves to go and find Paul, she tells him:

> "My brother, I know that if thou goest away from me, and I do not come with thee, I shall not be able to endure it because of thee; indeed, in general, if ever I pass a week without seeing thee, I am most afflicted, and I send my son Apollonius to thee in Pousire to bring me news of thee. If thou goest to this distant place and I do not hear news of thee, I shall die because of thee. Thou thyself knowest, my brother, that I have no brother or sister on earth beside thee." He said to her, "Do not be faint-hearted, my sister; but I shall go and satisfy him, for he is my friend; and if it is the will of God, I shall come to thee in peace." Thecla loved him very much. She said to him, "If then this is the way it is, go in peace, and come again in peace, that I may see thee before I die." (154)

Paese's injunction not to be faint-hearted echoes Paul's words to Paese when he wants to leave Alexandria to find Thecla. Indeed, both come at moments when Paese is thinking of *the other person*. Paese is made the center not of an "Apostolic love triangle," as Kate Cooper described the Paul-Thecla-Thamyris complex in the *APT*,[43] but of a partly incestuous, partly homoerotic, and – contrary to the *APT* – entirely spiritual love triangle.

They are also an eschatological love triangle, whose destiny, we are told, is to live together in heaven. Indeed, the angel who takes Paese to show him his future house in heaven tells him, "Thou seest this house: it is thine, and thy sister's and thy friend Paul's. Lo, your three crowns are prepared for you; one for your lot as a stranger, one for your blood which shall be shed for the Name of Christ, and another one because of your chastity. And your bodies shall be in a single shrine on earth" (177).[44] This marks the *MPTh* as more than a simple *passio*; as Baumeister very astutely

---

[43] Cooper, *The Virgin and the Bride*, 1999: 51.
[44] On this passage, and more generally on the motif of multiple crowns, see Łajtar and Wipszycka, "SB IV 7315," 1999; and Łajtar and Wipszycka, "Martyrs Who Received Two Crowns," 2002.

noted, many elements are borrowed from ascetic literature, and the three main characters are recompensed for both these aspects of their lives – as well as their itinerancy.

This "eschatological association of monastic friends," to use Derek Krueger's expression,[45] takes the intertextual nexus of the *MPTh* beyond that of the *APT* and the narratives of the "koptischer Konsens" and into the wider group of texts recounting strong male relationships in monastic contexts. Studied by Krueger, and most recently by Claudia Rapp,[46] the motif seems to have known something of a boom in the seventh century. The stories of male companionship written by the likes of Leontios of Neapolis (fl. seventh century) and Sophronios of Jerusalem (560–638) are replete with the language of brothership, silent understanding, and common prayer. In the *Spiritual Meadow*, the advice given by a hermit to Sophronios and John Moschos (c. 550–619) on how to conduct their partnership in asceticism is to live somewhere "only with vigilance and in tranquility, praying unceasingly."[47] Rapp notes that the motif is especially prominent in a cluster of texts associated with Cyprus; a cluster that, I have argued elsewhere, is also associated with narratives originating from Sketis.[48]

The new literary motif had clearly reached our author who was writing somewhere in the area of Antinoe. Here, however, sobriety has no place: wine and food loom large as rituals of fraternity: from the banquets prepared for the prisoners to the intimate dinners *en tête à tête*, common meals are the marker of friendship and grace. Not eating is a sign of grief. Thus, when Paul stays without food and drink for days because of Paese's imprisonment, it is understood as a pathological situation that has to be treated. But the language of brotherhood and the moments of common prayer and shared meditation remain central in the relationship. After seeing Victor being tortured – a decisive moment in the narrative – Paese goes home:

> As the blessed Apa Paese was saying this in his heart, he came into the house of Paul, and they ate together at noontide. And Paul said to Paese, "My brother, do you see this great man today, how he has endured these great tortures for the Name of Christ?" Paese said to him, "Yes, my brother, I was greatly moved." They continued talking together about his honour. (158)

---

[45] Krueger, "Between Monks," 2011: 58.
[46] Rapp, *Brother-Making*, 2016: esp. chapter 4A, "Seventh-Century Transitions," 180–191.
[47] John Moschos, *Spiritual Meadow* 110: *PG* 87/3.2973. See the comments in Krueger, "Between Monks," 2011: 34.
[48] Papaconstantinou, "Child or Monk?," 2008: 173–176.

Like the fourth- and fifth-century Alexandrian narratives inspired by Thecla, the *MPTh* is also unashamedly a story about the landed and urban elites: A rich landlord in a valley village who befriends a rich merchant in the city and whose sister is the widow of a "very rich man" (152) from another city and is courted by the city's other rich men. Paese leaves for Alexandria with a pound of gold and goods to sell (153). Similarly, Thecla also takes a pound of gold and loads her "baggage upon her servants" to go to the capital (166). Despite spending considerable sums on the prisoners in Alexandria, as they are about to die, there is still some left, and Paese suggests she should send it back to her son (170). For his part, he leaves his belongings to Paul (179).[49]

Of course, this wealth is ostensibly given up by the martyrs for a higher ideal – but not before being shown, in painstaking and voluptuous detail, the form of wealth that awaits them through the looking glass. This description – the tour of heaven – is the only part of the text that, for no apparent reason and without any framing, suddenly switches to a first-person narrator, letting Paese describe his dream. This long passage, which alternates between *ekphrasis* and dialogue with the angel, starts with the description of a richly decorated house "built like a church" (175), that is the house of Victor, "who renounced his dignity and all his possessions" (176) to follow Christ. The angel then shows him the luxurious house he is to share with his sister and Paul:

> And I said to the angel, "My lord, thou hast honoured me exceedingly and beyond measure. But my house is small in comparison with the first one." He answered and said to me, "Dost thou not know that the honour of a king is one thing, and the honour of a magistrate another?" (179)

Thus, the *MPTh* powerfully reaffirms social hierarchies: even in martyrdom, some are more noble than others, and that is measured on how much earthly honor and wealth each of them gave up. Equality before the Lord was clearly not what the author of the *MPTh* had in mind.

Conclusion

There has been a fair amount of discussion on the "domestication" or the "taming" of Thecla in later accounts.[50] Susan E. Hylen, on the other hand, argued that even in the *APT*, there was little about the heroine that was

---

[49] See the discussion on property transmission between male companions in Krueger, "Between Monks," 2011: 46–47.
[50] See Davis, "From Women's Piety," 2015.

subversive.[51] Whatever the case, it is clear that by the late fourth century, the figure had been built up as a model for a number of female literary characters whose non-conventional attitudes were constructed in dialogue with the *APT*. In several of those narratives, the choice of asceticism and chastity against marriage was inextricably linked to literary strategies and the manipulation of a semantic field that dissolved or subverted gender boundaries, even if this did not touch directly on the character of Thecla herself. This is most striking in the case of the *MPTh*. Indeed if, as Davis suggested, it is true that in this story Paese is Thecla's "Paul," arguably he is also Paul's "Thecla." It is when Paul leaves, and Paese follows him, that the narrative is set into motion, and this choice to follow Paul is ultimately the cause of Paese's martyrdom – or, if we prefer, his "wedding." This redoubling of the two main characters of the *APT* made it possible to maintain the blurred gender categories with which it was associated while maintaining Thecla quite firmly within the female sphere – the fact that she showed strength in martyrdom notwithstanding.[52] At the same time, this blurring was inscribed in a literary tradition of chaste male brotherhood that connected it, at least partly, to the textual universe of Alexandrian monasticism. And although this involved a strong reassertion of social hierarchies and elite values, its rather unconventional heavenly ménage à trois also conveys a heightened sense of sexual ambiguity but with Paul rather than Thecla as its epicenter. Ultimately, however, by the time Loukaris arrived in Alexandria, it was the association of Thecla with learning and books that had prevailed, at least within the Patriarchate.

Bibliography

Anson, John. "The Female Transvestite in Early Monasticism: The Origin and Development of a Motif." *Viator* 5 (1974): 1–32.
Apserou, Stephanie. "Το αγιολογικό dossier της Αγίας Ευγενίας (BHG 607w–607z)." PhD diss., University of Ioannina, 2017.

---

[51] Hylen, *A Modest Apostle*, 2015: esp. ch. 4, 71–90.
[52] Davis, *The Cult of St. Thecla*, 2001: 185, signals this in an attempt to find "male" characteristics for the Coptic Thecla. Yet that is something said of every female martyr and, in that sense is, I believe, a very weak marker. Davis also notes that her breasts are slashed off, then stuck back on by an angel. But that is also a stock *topos* for female martyrs and, in another text, even results in the (miraculously restored) breasts squirting milk into the tormentors' faces (*Martyrdom of Shenoufe and His Brethren*: Reymond and Barns (eds. and trans.), *Four Martyrdoms*, 1973: 206–207). I see it more as a theme that points out to the audience that this is a woman since slashing off body parts is one of the most common motifs of those torture scenes, and what one can slash off them defines the gender of the martyr in question.

Baumeister, Theofried. *Martyr Invictus. Der Märtyrer als Sinnbild der Erlösung in der Legende und im Kult der frühen koptischen Kirche.* Münster: Regensberg, 1972.
Brown, Peter. *The Body and Society: Men, Women, and Sexual Renunciation in Early Christianity.* London: Faber & Faber, 1989.
Browne, Gerald M. "The Martyrdom of Paese and Thecla (P. Mich. inv. 548)." *Chronique d'Égypte* 49, no. 97 (1974): 201–205.
Casey, Robert P. "Der dem Athanasius zugeschriebene Traktat Περί παρθενίας." *Sitzungsberichte der Preußischen Akademie der Wissenschaften, phil.-hist. Kl.* 33 (1935): 1022–1045.
Childers, Jeff W. "A Reluctant Bride: Finding a Life for Damaris of Athens (Acts 17:34)." In *Renewing Tradition: Studies in Texts and Contexts in Honor of James W. Thompson*, edited by Mark W. Hamilton, Thomas H. Olbricht, and Jeffrey Peterson. Eugene: Pickwick, 2007: 207–235.
Cooper, Kate. "A Saint in Exile: The Early Medieval Thecla at Rome and Meriamlik." *Hagiographica* 2 (1995): 1–23.
The Virgin and the Bride: Idealized Womanhood in Late Antiquity. Cambridge, MA: Harvard University Press, 1999.
"The Bride of Christ, the 'Male Woman,' and the Female Reader in Late Antiquity." In *The Oxford Handbook of Women and Gender in Medieval Europe*, edited by Judith Bennett and Ruth Karras. Oxford: Oxford University Press, 2013: 529–544.
Davis, Stephen J. "Pilgrimage and the Cult of Saint Thecla in Late Antique Egypt." In *Pilgrimage and Holy Space in Late Antique Egypt*, edited by David Frankfurter. Leiden: Brill, 1998: 303–339.
The Cult of St. Thecla: A Tradition of Women's Piety in Late Antiquity. Oxford; New York: Oxford University Press, 2001.
"Crossed Texts, Crossed Sex: Intertextuality and Gender in Early Christian Legends of Holy Women Disguised as Men." *Journal of Early Christian Studies* 10, no. 1 (2002): 1–36.
"From Women's Piety to Male Devotion: Gender Studies, *The Acts of Paul and Thecla*, and the Evidence of an Arabic manuscript." *Harvard Theological Review* 108, no. 4 (2015): 579–593.
Delcourt, Marie. "Le complexe de Diane dans l'hagiographie chrétienne." *Revue de l'histoire des religions* 153, no. 1 (1958): 1–33.
Henschenius, Godefridus, and Daniel Papebrochius, eds. *Acta Sanctorum Aprilis Tomus II.* Antwerp: Michael Cnobarus, 1675.
Hylen, Susan. *A Modest Apostle: Thecla and the History of Women in the Early Church.* Oxford: Oxford University Press, 2015.
Johnson, Scott F. *The Life and Miracles of Thekla: A Literary Study.* Cambridge, MA: Harvard University Press, 2006.
Kasser, Rodolphe, and Philippe Luisier, eds. and trans. "Le papyrus Bodmer XLI en édition princeps: l'épisode d'Éphèse des Acta Pauli en copte et en traduction." *Le Muséon* 117, nos. 3–4 (2004): 281–384.

Kenyon, Frederic G., ed. *The Codex Alexandrinus (Royal Ms 1 D v–viii) in Reduced Photographic Form, Vol. 1: Old Testament, Part 1, Genesis–Ruth*. London: British Museum, 1915.

Krueger, Derek. "Between Monks: Tales of Companionship in Early Byzantium." *Journal of the History of Sexuality* 20, no. 1 (2011): 28–61.

Łajtar, Adam, and Ewa Wipszycka. "SB IV 7315, texte mentionnant des martyrs qui ont reçu 'deux couronnes:' la plus ancienne inscription chrétienne d'Égypte?" *Journal of Juristic Papyrology* 29 (1999): 67–73.

———. "Martyrs Who Received Two Crowns." *Journal of Juristic Papyrology* 32 (2002): 49–54.

Lipsius, Richard A., ed. *Acta apostolorum apocrypha / 1, Acta Petri, Acta Pauli, Acta Petri et Pauli, Acta Pauli et Theclae, Acta Thaddaei*. Leipzig: Mendelssohn, 1891.

Osiek, Carolyn. "Review of *The Cult of St. Thecla: A Tradition of Women's Piety in Late Antiquity*." *Journal of Early Christian Studies* 11, no. 3 (2003): 422–424.

Papaconstantinou, Arietta. "Child or Monk? An Unpublished Story Attributed to John Moschos in Paris Coislin 257." *Bulletin of the American Society of Papyrologists* 45 (2008): 171–184.

Papavarnavas, Christodoulos. *Gefängnis als Schwellenraum in der byzantinischen Hagiographie: Eine Untersuchung früh- und mittelbyzantinischer Märtyrerakten*. Berlin: De Gruyter, 2021.

Rapp, Claudia. *Brother-Making in Late Antiquity and Byzantium: Monks, Laymen, and Christian Ritual*. Oxford: Oxford University Press, 2016.

Reymond, Eve A. E., and John W. B. Barns, eds. and trans. *Four Martyrdoms from the Pierpont Morgan Coptic Codices*. Oxford: Clarendon, 1973.

Roe, Thomas. *The Negotiations of Sir Thomas Roe in His Embassy to the Ottoman Porte, from the Year 1621 to 1628 Inclusive*. London: Samuel Richardson, 1740.

Schmidt, Carl, ed. and trans. *Acta Pauli aus der Heidelberger koptischen Papyrushandschrift, mit Tafelband*. Leipzig: J. C. Hinrichs, 1904.

Smith, W. Andrew. *A Study of the Gospels in the Codex Alexandrinus: Codicology, Palaeography, and Scribal Hands*. Leiden: Brill, 2014.

Spinka, Matthew. "Acquisition of the Codex Alexandrinus by England." *The Journal of Religion* 16, no. 1 (1936): 10–29.

PART II

An Act to Surpass

CHAPTER 7

Thecla, the First Cross-Dresser?
The Acts of Paul and Thecla *and the Lives of Byzantine Transvestite Saints*

Julie Van Pelt*

The heroine of the late second-century apocryphal *Acts of Paul and Thecla* (hereafter *APT*)[1] says she will cut her hair upon leaving for Antioch (§ 3.25). Toward the end of the narrative, she also wears a garment that she "stitched together into a masculinely fashioned robe" (§ 4.15) before setting out for Myra.[2] Both actions, cutting hair and wearing male clothing, are typically undertaken by later (fourth–tenth century) female transvestite saints at the beginning of their careers as male monks.[3] Based on this premise, scholars have taken to designating Thecla as the "first cross-dresser" of the Christian literary tradition.

Indeed, the connection between Thecla and transvestite saints dates back to *Hippolytus und Thecla*, Ludwig Radermacher's study from 1916.[4] An important landmark in the scholarship on transvestite saints is the article John Anson published in 1974. Anson tracks the development of the cross-dressing motif in early monastic literature and, for the first time, deals with its use and significance across a wide variety of narratives. For instance, in the *APT*, he perceives a link between cross-dressing and baptism; in other words, the act of dressing in male clothes represents communion with Christ. Meanwhile, he explains its function in later Lives from the viewpoint of the male monks who authored these stories and argues that "the fantasy of a holy woman disguised among their number

---

* I would like to thank the editors of this volume for proofreading this chapter and for their invaluable remarks and feedback. This chapter was written as a fellow of the FWO Flanders.
[1] BHG 1710–1716. For the dating, see Johnson, *The Life and Miracles*, 2006: 2 n. 3; and Dagron (ed. and trans.), *Vie et miracles*, 1978: 32.
[2] Translation by Barrier, *The Acts of Paul and Thecla*, 2009. All quotations and translations of the *APT* in this chapter are from this work. All other translations of Greek are my own unless otherwise stated.
[3] I refer to the narratives (primarily composed in Greek and written between the fourth and the seventh centuries, although some occasional later accounts exist) about female saints who pretend to be male monks and which are listed by Patlagean, "L'histoire," 1976, and have been studied by many scholars as one corpus since then.
[4] See n. 95.

represented a psychological opportunity to neutralize the threat of female temptation."[5] Yet, even if he is attentive to the differences, Anson does not question Thecla as the starting point of the later tradition of transvestite saints. According to him, the *APT* represents "the original instance of what subsequently became the dominant motif in the lives of a whole group of saints."[6] Several scholars have perpetuated his views. Evelyne Patlagean, for example, reiterates Anson's conceptualization of the legend of Thecla and notes that the corpus is "enrooted" in the context of the *APT*.[7] Other scholars have described the *APT*'s role as influential for later narratives of cross-dressers,[8] and some consider Thecla simply as "the first transvestite saint."[9] Generally speaking, then, scholars writing about transvestite saints appear eager to claim Thecla as belonging to that tradition. Yet they assume the connection quickly, basing it on rather superficial parallels and hasty assumptions, and treat it as widely accepted.

There are a few exceptions, however, that should be mentioned. First, Marie Delcourt categorizes Thecla's legend with other stories that display "temporary cross-dressing;" she distinguishes stories about heroines who take on male clothing only for a short period of time from the transvestite saints who, by contrast, spend large parts of their L(/l)ives in male disguise.[10] Second, and more recently, Stavroula Constantinou has excluded the *APT* from her discussion on Lives of cross-dressers and likewise states that it is because Thecla cross-dresses only temporarily. By denoting Thecla as a "temporary cross-dresser," Delcourt and Constantinou both indicate that cross-dressing does not impact the development of *APT*'s plot as it does for later Lives of transvestite saints. In addition, Constantinou notes that the function of this motif differs in the

---

[5] Anson, "The Female Transvestite," 1974: 5.
[6] Ibid.: 1. Later, he states that in the *APT* we find "an original form of the female saint in disguise" (6).
[7] Patlagean, "L'histoire," 1976: 608.
[8] Arietta Papaconstantinou and Laurent Capron point to the existence of a shrine dedicated to Thecla in the region of Alexandria to justify their claim that the narrative of Thecla functioned as a model for the author of the *Life of Theodora*. According to Papaconstantinou, "Je suis noire," 2004: 76, "cette sainte a manifestement fourni un modèle aux hagiographes postérieurs." Capron, *Codex hagiographiques*, 2013: 132, speaks of "influence certaine d'un modèle ancien." Lubinsky, *Removing Masculine Layers*, 2013: 99, discusses Thecla among the "influential figures" for the narratives of transvestite saints in her chapter "The Female Monk Intertexts."
[9] For instance, Zlatkova, "Legendary," 2014: 32, who also writes that "St. Thecla became a prototype of many other stories of cross-dressing and change of gender identity" (Ibid.: 37). Delierneux, "Virilité physique," 1997: 191 and 187, writes that "Thècle était la première sainte travestie chrétienne," and considers Thecla as "le prototype des travesties chrétiennes."
[10] Delcourt, "Le complexe de Diane," 1958: 7, in which Delcourt speaks of "travestissement temporaire."

APT and later Lives since it is a means of free travel in the former and a disguise of female gender in the latter.¹¹

As far as I am aware, only one scholar has made an attempt to ground the claim for Thecla as the original instance or influential starting point of the later tradition with in-depth analyses. In two separate publications, Stephen Davis convincingly illustrates that the *APT* functions as an important intertext for the fifth-century *Life and Martyrdom of Eugenia*. This text focuses on a cross-dresser, Eugenia, and contains explicit and implicit references to Thecla: for instance, the saint is said to model her own actions on those of Thecla, and, in certain versions, she explicitly identifies herself with Thecla during the trial that leads to her martyrdom. The problem is that Davis uses the evidence from the *Life and Martyrdom of Eugenia* to assume a meaningful connection between the story of Thecla and *all* Lives of cross-dressers. In the first publication, he writes that "the stories take the life of Thecla as their subtext" and that "the life of Thecla serves as the prototype for this group of legends."¹² In the second publication, he elaborates on the nature of this relationship, relying on poststructuralist intertextuality. Yet, building almost exclusively on the example of Eugenia again, he calls all of the transvestite Lives "hagiographical attempts to reappropriate Thecla's story."¹³ That the *Life and Martyrdom of Eugenia* displays an "explicit reappropriation" of Thecla's tale does not automatically mean, in my view, that there is an "implicit reappropriation" of it in other Lives of cross-dressers, which is what Davis suggests. Only a broader, comparative investigation that takes into account all (or, at least, more of) these tales would be able to justify this claim. Consequently, whether one wants to see Thecla as "one of the cross-dressers" or whether one wants to claim some form of influence of the *APT* on later Lives of transvestite saints, further investigation is needed.

I will contribute to this discussion by examining the narrative parallels between the *APT* and a variety of Greek Lives of cross-dressing saints.¹⁴ My goal is to verify whether other Lives of transvestite saints, apart from the *Life and Martyrdom of Eugenia*, can likewise be regarded as reappropriations of Thecla's story as Davis suggests. Before doing so, however, I will first treat the specific passages in the *APT* that have led to Thecla's qualification as a cross-dresser. In this regard, I argue, following Constantinou, that in the second-century text, the motif of cross-dressing does not represent a means of disguising gender, which is what it represents in later Lives. As such, the basis

---

[11] Constantinou, *Female Corporeal Performances*, 2005: 92. Constantinou devotes only a small paragraph to the differences between Thecla and the transvestite saints. In what follows, I hope to tease out the specifics in depth.
[12] Davis, *The Cult of St. Thecla*, 2001: 141–143.
[13] Davis, "Crossed Texts, Crossed Sex," 2002: 16–19.   [14] The examined corpus is given in n. 54.

for aligning Thecla with later transvestite saints appears thin. However, this did not necessarily impede Thecla and her narrative from becoming models for Lives of transvestite saints as the *Life and Martyrdom of Eugenia* demonstrates. Next, as a way of foregrounding my investigation into narrative parallels, I will examine briefly a few key texts from the Greek hagiographical tradition that are, in various ways, modeled on the account of the *APT* but do not center around cross-dressers. These will serve as a counterweight to the Lives of cross-dressers that will be analyzed afterwards. Though time and space preclude a comprehensive analysis of the wider Greek hagiographical tradition, it is nevertheless important to provide some examples of the various strong echoes of the *APT* that we find in certain Greek hagiographies that are *not* concerned with cross-dressers. For indeed, as I argue next, with the notable exception of the *Life and Martyrdom of Eugenia*, the parallels between the *APT* and Lives of cross-dressers are rather limited, especially when viewed in comparison with the texts that are not concerned with cross-dressers. I therefore conclude that the Lives of transvestite saints do not appear to have been a favored locus for revisiting the *APT* – a text that nonetheless knows a wide legacy in Byzantine hagiographical production.

As the analyses below will illustrate, there is little evidence to confirm the widely held notion that a *direct* line can be sketched from Thecla to the transvestite saints, both as cross-dressers (cross-dressing means something different for each) and as heroines of hagiographical tales (there is no significant literary modeling of the *APT* in the majority of transvestite saints' Lives). The question that follows is how cross-dressing as a motif then traveled from the *APT* until it appeared in later hagiographical accounts. To answer this question, I discuss three texts – the *Acts of Xanthippe and Polyxena*, the *Life and Miracles of Thecla*, and the *Life of Eusebia called Xenê* – which, I argue, are important intermediary steps both in the interpretation of Thecla as a cross-dresser and in the development of this literary theme. As such, these texts help to bridge the gap between the *APT* and later Lives of cross-dressing saints as much as they propel the development of the cross-dressing motif in new ways.

The *APT* Revisited

Is Thecla a cross-dresser?[15] Before we can answer that question, it is crucial to ask what cross-dressing precisely means in the cases of Thecla and the

---

[15] In my readings, I have rarely come across the question itself. It is often taken for granted that she is. Lubinsky, *Removing Masculine Layers*, 2013: 100, for instance, mentions Thecla's "missionary life as a cross-dresser."

Thecla, the First Cross-Dresser? 201

later saints. The basic meaning of "cross-dressing" is to put on clothes that are generally perceived to belong to the opposite sex, and a part of this may be the adoption of a different hairstyle. In this basic sense, then, Thecla is indeed a cross-dresser: she changes her garment into that of a man before she goes to teach (§ 4.15). However, what characterizes Eugenia and other transvestite saints like Theodora, Apolinaria, and Euphrosyne, and, thus, what has led to studying them together as literary heroines, is that they use male clothing to pass as men. Moreover, they all successfully *do* pass as men, and they usually also cut their hair, which further supports the role they take on. Thecla, it is true, says she will cut her hair after she has survived her first trial, an instance that is usually seized on by scholars to associate her with the transvestite saints, but Paul advises against it (§ 3.25).[16] Furthermore, nothing in the text indicates that she *actually* cuts her hair.[17] That the intended effect of this act would be to pass as a man is not supported by the text either, and that she is not perceived as a male de facto is plain and clear from the scene that follows: Alexander is enamored with Thecla and desires her because, as a presumably heteronormative man, he finds her attractive. Paul, who is loaded with gifts and money by Alexander in exchange for her, tells Alexander that he does not know "the *woman* of whom you speak" (§ 4.1).[18] His reply, notorious for its ungentlemanlike lack of support,[19] in fact demonstrates that she is not

---

[16] For this interpretation and an interpretation of the entire passage, see Barrier, *The Acts of Paul and Thecla*, 2009: 135–136. He suggests, however, that Thecla wants to "disguise her figure" (ibid.: 135). As I demonstrate in this chapter, I read the passage in question differently.

[17] I therefore do not agree with Petropoulos, "Transvestite Virgin," 1995: 132, who writes that, when Thecla offers to cut her hair, "the narrative's logic requires her to do so – because she can only travel with Paul disguised as a man." He writes, moreover, that "from the action immediately ensuing it may be securely gathered that she has also donned male clothing" (ibid.), and then, without any additional argumentation, states later on that Thecla "has shaved her hair and donned male attire" (ibid.: 133). Petropoulos is right when he states that such implications are raised and even stated outright in the later fifth-century vita of Thecla (ibid.: 132). (See below for my own analysis of the *Life and Miracles of Thecla* and cross-dressing as a means of safe travel.) However, I do not see any reason that would explain how it is also implied in the original *APT*. It seems that Petropoulos' argument is rather a back-projection. Narro, *El culto*, 2019: 92, similarly assumes that Thecla has actually cut her hair to conceal her beauty, and Hotchkiss, *Clothes Make the Man*, 1996: 22, writes that Thecla cuts her hair and puts on male clothing after her baptism. See also Sowers, "Thecla Desexualized," 2012: 232; and Tommasi, "Cross-dressing as Discourse," 2017: 126, for similar statements.

[18] Emphasis mine.

[19] See, for instance, Davies, *The Revolt of the Widows*, 1980: 58–59; and Burrus, "Mimicking Virgins," 2005: 59. However, Barrier, *The Acts of Paul and Thecla*, 2009: 140 n. 6, comments that this line "has been grossly misinterpreted." He argues that the story pattern followed here is one common in the ancient Greek novels where lovers would come up with false stories to protect their partners in situations like this. In whichever way the line is read, the result remains the same; Alexander clearly

supposed to be perceived as a man. If that were the case, Paul's reply amounts to an even bigger failure.

Compare this to the situation that we find in several Lives of transvestite saints. Unwelcome erotic attention is plentiful here too. Only, in the stories of Theodora, Eugenia, Mary, and Susanna, the sexual predator is a woman. This significantly turns the dynamics around; rather than confirming that the young virgin is being perceived as a woman, erotic tension provides the ultimate proof of the cross-dresser's success as a pretend man. It also leads to a complex intrigue revolving around her assumed male identity, as the cross-dresser is often falsely accused of sexual violence, a crime she could not possibly have committed and for which she can prove her innocence only by revealing her naked body. Thecla's (proposed) haircut, therefore, has a very different and considerably smaller narrative role in comparison to the motif's function in the later Lives of transvestite saints. The same may be stated for Thecla's act of cross-dressing at the end of the *APT*. When she changes her clothing, nothing indicates that she wants to be taken for a man. Moreover, when she arrives in Myra, Paul recognizes her immediately. In the Lives of transvestite saints, on the other hand, such a change of appearance usually leads to false impressions.[20] Generally, in the later stories, the act of cross-dressing comes not at the end, as it does in the *APT*, but in the beginning and kicks off a series of events and (mis)adventures in which the disguised identity of the saint and the misperception of her sex play crucial roles. In the *APT*, cross-dressing does not interfere with the dramatic development of the plot.

What scholars arguably have not stressed enough, then, is that Thecla's cross-dressing is not a disguise. For instance, Anson rightly notes that "by the time she finally does assume male clothing, Thecla not only has been released from legal persecution but is surrounded by a large band of loyal followers who render disguise unnecessary."[21] Yet he still speaks of "Thecla's disguise" at other occasions to refer to her act of cross-dressing. So do other scholars.[22] For Thecla, cross-dressing is not a means to conceal her identity or her sex, whereas this is exactly the point in the Lives of

---

interprets Paul's reply as a free pass to take possession of the woman whom he desires. See also ibid.: 9.

[20] Euphrosyne is not recognized by her father, Theodora and Athanasia not by their husbands, etc.

[21] Anson, "The Female Transvestite," 1974: 3.

[22] Ibid.: 10. Constantinou, *Female Corporeal Performances*, 2005: 92, also refers to Thecla's "male disguise." See also Petropoulos, "Transvestite Virgin," 1995; Hotchkiss, *Clothes Make the Man*, 1996: 21; and Davis, *The Cult of St. Thecla*, 2001: 15 n. 54.

transvestite saints. It is furthermore unclear whether it is a means to conceal her female beauty and thus to enable her safe travels as some have argued.[23] In fact, certain Lives of transvestite saints attest to the various possible meanings that could be attached to the act of cross-dressing. Athanasia is tonsured not in order to appear as a man but to enter a convent (it is only afterwards that she will put on male garments to meet her husband).[24] Her haircut is thus detached from her aspirations to be perceived as a man. Apolinaria, on the other hand, never cuts her hair but loses her female appearance gradually while living in a swamp for years; crucial to her male disguise is not that she cross-dresses but that she assumes a male name.[25] In the *Life of Euphrosyne*, the saint is tonsured and given a monastic cloak, but it is only afterwards that she decides to enter a male monastery and puts on a male garment.[26] As such, her transformation is likewise detached from (and precedes) her decision to disguise herself as a man. These instances suggest that the very act of cutting one's hair or changing one's clothes does not constitute the literary motif that defines the stories of the transvestite saints, assuming a false male identity does. It may not even constitute cross-dressing at all, since women appear to have been tonsured as well upon entering a convent.[27] In short, the act of cross-dressing itself may have various meanings and does not necessarily entail disguise.

In the *APT*, it is unclear whether Thecla offers to cut her hair to dissimulate her beauty out of fear of sexual violence. There are no concrete indications that this is her motivation. Instead, her offer can be interpreted as a sign of her religious aspirations and claims to (male) authority. Paul's response suggests so. He mentions her beauty and that times are bad, yet he also adds: "May another trial (πειρασμὸς) not leave you worse than the first, and you might not endure but you might be cowardly (μὴ ... δειλανδρήσῃς)" (§ 3.25). Using the term δειλανδρήσῃς, which is composed of δειλός (cowardly) and ἀνήρ (man), he responds particularly to her aspired masculinity and suggests that he is not sure whether she is spiritually ready to embrace the typically masculine virtue of religious

---

[23] See n. 17. [24] Alwis, *Celibate Marriages*, 2011: 253, l. 218 and l. 231.
[25] Drescher (ed.), *Three Coptic Legends*, 1947: 157. All other transvestite saints assume a male name as well (on the importance of which see Constantinou, *Female Corporeal Performances*, 2005: 109–111; and Lubinsky, *Removing Masculine Layers*, 2013: 116 and 149–152), but the story of Apolinaria is the only one in which the adoption of a male name assumes such weight; it is what constitutes her male identity.
[26] Boucherie (ed.), "Vita Sanctae Euphrosynae," 1883: 199, ll. 31–32 and 200, ll. 3–4.
[27] Delierneux, "Virilité physique," 1997: 185, notes that the similarity in the male and the female monastic habit undermines the idea of cross-dressing in certain contexts.

authority, lest she proves to be "unmanly" after all in the face of new trials.[28] In this light, it makes sense that he mentions her beauty, namely, to underline the likelihood that Thecla will be tempted again later to forsake her religious aspirations (πειρασμός can mean "trial" but also "temptation"). As we know, the episode in Antioch that follows will prove Paul both right – since Thecla is indeed tortured again after a man sexually assaults her for her beauty – and wrong – since she proves herself to be steadfast enough to withstand these trials and temptations. If we read the passage in this way, the masculinization of Thecla's appearance would not be meant to hide anything so much as it would underscore her transition from a noblewoman to a religious leader and teacher, something that she eventually achieves after her second trial when she finally dons male dress.[29]

In conclusion, if cross-dressing in the *APT* does not represent male disguise, it provides an early account of a female Christian heroine whose claim for authority and independence finds metaphorical and concrete expression in an act of masculinization.[30] As such, her offer to cut her hair and her appropriation of male style at the end may have been perceived as an iconic move in later times. And, indeed, Lives of transvestite saints build on the idea of "the male woman," of which Thecla is a prominent precedent.[31] However, from a narrative point of view, these Lives explore very different waters in their exploitation of the cross-dressing motif. Although this might not have prevented the *APT* from becoming a model

---

[28] Barrier, *The Acts of Paul and Thecla*, 2009: 135, suggests that this is one way in which Paul's response may be interpreted ("Paul is suggesting that the times are shameless and bad, and Thecla would be tempted beyond what she can bear or forced") but continues to defend another interpretation, namely, that Thecla's request is inappropriate. Davis, *The Cult of St. Thecla*, 2001: 6, interprets Thecla's offer as a sign of her religious commitment against the backdrop of her wish to be baptized and her cross-dressing at the end as an androgynous gesture following Galatians 3:28 in the wake of her recent self-baptism (ibid.: 31–32). Thus, he reiterates Anson's view, discussed above. In addition, he suggests that these can be understood in the social-historical context of safe travel for women in antiquity as well (ibid.: 32–34).

[29] I am therefore inclined to agree with McInerney, *Eloquent Virgins*, 2003: 43, who writes that Thecla's "assumption of clothing 'in the fashion of men' has nothing to do with a rejection of femininity; rather, what Thecla is doing is assuming the *tribon*, the mantle of the philosopher." See Ghazzal Dabiri's Introduction for more.

[30] Cox Miller, "Is There a Harlot," 2003: 419, states "'Gender-bending' was a feature of Christian portrayals of ascetic heroes from early on, Thecla being a notable example." See also Aspegren, *The Male Woman*, 1990: *passim*, but especially chapter VII; and Aubin, "Reversing Romance?," 1998: 264–267. See also Klazina Staat's contribution in this volume (Chapter 9) who analyses Eugenia's "manly" aspirations in her rhetorical defense of cross-dressing.

[31] This expression was coined by Kerstin Aspegren in her 1990 study to refer to the use of the metaphor of masculinity for the Christian ideal of virtue. See also Lowerre, *The Cross-Dressing*, 2006: lxxix–xci. Drescher (ed.), *Three Coptic Legends*, 1947: 157, ll. 26–27, offers an example of the relevance of the male woman ideal in the *Life of Apolinaria*.

Thecla, the First Cross-Dresser? 205

for narratives of transvestite saints, it appears that *if* Thecla's narrative was influential (this is investigated below), the conditions of her cross-dressing were not closely mimicked.

Thecla in the Greek Tradition

As a patroness of female agency,[32] Thecla *has* been influential for the development of later Christian female role models. Of course, a wider study needs to be done for a fuller picture.[33] Here, I hope to offer a short indication of Thecla's impact in the Greek tradition by providing a couple of examples of late antique texts that are, in various ways, modeled on the account of the *APT*. As noted above, these serve as an important counterweight to the Lives of cross-dressers. Before delving into the analysis, it should be noted first that it can be difficult to pinpoint exactly how certain themes or motifs found their way into stories, given that hagiographical writing derives from oral traditions of storytelling:[34] Did hagiographers borrow them from other literary texts when composing their own works, or were these transmitted orally, perhaps as part of a common stock of narrative material? Despite this difficulty, there are good reasons, as Ghazzal Dabiri points out in her Introduction to this volume, to assume that hagiographers had access to the *APT*. Moreover, in the following examples, the similarities with the *APT* would at least call to mind the tale or make clear that the texts even explicitly engage with it, so that an intertextual connection is arguably established. It then matters less in what way these similarities originally came into being for our current purposes (as Dabiri also highlights).

For authors of female martyr stories, the legend of Thecla appears to have been fertile ground for the construction of trial scenes. An example is the second *Martyrdom of Lucia*, a ninth-century rewriting of a fifth-century

---

[32] I adopt this expression coined by Kate Cooper who used it in a lecture entitled "Violence and the Early Christian Heroine" (international workshop "God, the Saint and the Text: Hagiographical Studies as an Interdisciplinary Field," November 24, 2017, Oslo University). The idea that Thecla represents female liberation is, however, not uncontested. See Bremmer, "Magic, Martyrdom," 1996, for discussion and further references. In this chapter, I primarily subscribe to the reading of Thecla as a model for women's independence, a model that is overturned in the *Acts of Xanthippe and Polyxena*, as Gorman, "Thinking," 2001, convincingly argues. However, it is fair to say that both currents can be read in the text.

[33] I suspect that Thecla is indeed widely influential; of course, that does not mean that all or even most of the Greek hagiographies engage with her tale, but even if a relatively small percentage of texts reference her, that is quite spectacular and cannot be said of any other female saint.

[34] See, among others, Rapp, "Author, Audience," 2015: 113–115.

narrative about a Syracusan virgin martyr.[35] When the judge orders Lucia to be brought to a brothel, the saint is somehow fixed to the ground like a rock, and it becomes impossible to move her. She is therefore tied to oxen with ropes in the hope that the animals, after being jabbed, would pull her from her spot.[36] The trick with the cattle is ineffective, so the judge sentences her to death by fire. Tied to the pyre, the saint remains unscathed as though she were under a rain shower rather than in a blazing fire.[37] These two scenes parallel images from both of Thecla's trials: Thecla likewise survives her trial by fire thanks to an actual, rather than a metaphorical, rain shower (§ 3.22). And in Antioch, Thecla is sentenced to be gored by bulls to which she is tied with ropes. The bulls rush forward when the executioners "put red-hot irons under their genitals," but a miraculous fire burns the ropes, and she is saved (§ 4.10). Therefore, it is the combination of the two motifs that specifically calls to mind Thecla's legend.[38]

In the *Martyrdom of Christina*,[39] daughter of the eparch of Tyre, the torture of the saint is even more clearly modeled on Thecla's legend. When Christina is about to be burned and prays to God for help, the fire instantly goes out, burning only the bystanders (§ 14.9–10). In the *APT*, the storm that saves Thecla likewise threatens to kill the spectators (§ 3.22). Christina is then thrown in the sea with a stone bound around her neck. Rather than drowning, she walks the waters and calls on the Lord to receive the "bath of immortality." Amidst bands of angels and clouds of sweet fragrances, the Lord appears and baptizes her (§ 15.4–16.11 and in particular 15.8–9). While in the *APT* the Lord appears to Thecla as Paul during her first trial (and before baptism), during her second trial she jumps into the waters "in the name of Jesus Christ" and is baptized (§ 4.9).[40] Apart from the trial scenes, the *Martyrdom of Christina* parallels the *APT* in another scene. It should be recalled that Thecla, who escaped her home at night and bribed her way into Paul's cell, was found listening

---

[35] BHG 995d. See Re, "Italo-Greek Hagiography," 2011: 230.
[36] Costanza (ed.), "Un Martyrion inedito," 1957: 47, ll. 584–591.   [37] Ibid.: 49, l. 618.
[38] On its own, the motif of the fire being ineffective to burn the saint to death is a widespread *topos* in hagiography, appearing also, for instance, in the *Martyrdom of Polycarp*. I thank the anonymous reviewer from Cambridge University Press for pointing this out to me.
[39] BHG 302: Norsa (ed.), *Martiro di Cristina*, 1912. The text is difficult to date but probably belongs to the late antique period.
[40] On Thecla's self-baptism, see Barrier, *The Acts of Paul and Thecla*, 2009: 162 n. 7 and 163–164. Self-baptism and baptism by women were indeed contested after the *APT*, which may explain why Christina is portrayed as being baptized by Christ. The relevant parallel is that both the martyr and the apostle turn their martyrdom by water into a moment of baptism.

to Paul "sitting by his feet" (§ 3.18). Likewise, Christina's mother comes to find her daughter in her prison cell and "curls up at her feet" (§ 11.3).

This prison scene in fact appears in more than one martyrdom account; the *Martyrdom of the Brothers of Lentini* features a side character whose name is, tellingly, Thecla, a rich and pious woman.[41] When the martyrs are being held in prison, this Thecla bribes the guards, enters the cell, and falls at the brothers' feet, just as her namesake had done.[42] In the *Martyrdom of Agatha*,[43] there is a reversal of roles in a very similar jail scene. The virgin martyr from Catania, Agatha, also has a meeting at night with an apostle in prison. However, the saint is the one imprisoned, and it is the apostle Peter who visits her at night.[44] We, nevertheless, are invited to picture the young virgin in Thecla's role. To wit, she even characterizes herself to the judge as a high-born girl from a noble family who, at the same time, also happens to be a slave of Christ.[45] This parallels Thecla's self-characterization as a leading woman of Iconium to Alexander after his assault and then as the handmaid of God to the governor who asks her who she is after she has miraculously survived her trial (§ 4).

The aforementioned examples are accounts of Italo-Greek origin, which prompts further investigation but lies outside the scope of this chapter. Other examples of narratives in the Greek hagiographical tradition that deserve brief mention here are the *Life and Martyrdom of Eudocia* and the *Conversion of Cyprian of Antioch*. The *Life and Matyrdom of Eudocia*[46] features an emblematic, and seemingly recast, episode from the *APT*, namely, the moment of the saint's conversion. The saint from Heliopolis, who is counted among the "holy harlots,"[47] converts, like Thecla, when a holy man, in this case the monk Germanos, comes to

---

[41] *BHG* 57–62. This text probably dates to the end of the eighth or the beginning of the ninth century, see Re, "Italo-Greek Hagiography," 2011: 230–231.

[42] Henschenius, von Papenbroek, and Cnobbaert (eds.), *Acta Sanctorum Maii II*, 1680: 780. Here, like in the *Martyrdom of Christina*, the martyr(s) is/are the imprisoned figure(s), leaving Thecla's role for one of the secondary characters and placing the saint(s) in the role, not of Thecla, but of the apostle Paul. On the role of side characters in the Syriac reception of the *APT*, see the contribution by Flavia Ruani in the present volume (Chapter 5).

[43] *BHG* 37–37d. The text can be dated to a period after the sixth century according to Re, "Italo-Greek Hagiography," 2011: 230.

[44] *PG* 114.1340.   [45] Ibid., 1336.

[46] *BHG* 604. This text has not received much scholarly attention. According to Constantinou, *Female Corporeal Performances*, 2005: 60, it must date between the fifth and seventh centuries.

[47] She undergoes a remarkable conversion from a sinful woman and prostitute to a saint. On this type of narrative, see Ward, *Harlots of the Desert*, 1987; and Constantinou, *Female Corporeal Performances*, 2005: ch. 2.

her city, is hosted in a nearby house and teaches and sings psalms.[48] The *Life of Eudocia*, however, does not mention *how* she hears his words. As one imagines how Germanos' words may have reached the saint, enchanting her to drastically change her life like Thecla, a few possibilities come to mind. One possibility is of course a window that is given symbolic weight in the *APT*.[49] The *Conversion of Cyprian of Antioch*,[50] on the other hand, does not leave that particular detail to the audience's imagination: Justina, the young woman who converts Cyprian the magician, is also a Thecla-like heroine, for she breaks free from her pagan home. She is initially caught up by a religious desire when she hears the teachings of a certain deacon named Praulios "through the nearby window."[51] Moreover, later in the narrative, she is chased by a wealthy young man of noble rank who had fallen in love with her and had asked for her hand in marriage. Upon refusal, he embraces the saint by force, as Alexander does with Thecla. Justina likewise defends herself fervently – she pushes him to the ground: "Destroying his ribs and his face with her fists and tearing apart his tunic, she turned him into a laughingstock (θρίαμβον), following the example of her teacher Thecla."[52]

These are just a few examples among probably many more that may be cited (such as Macrina, who is presented by her hagiographer Gregory of Nyssa as a new Thecla).[53] Such echoes of and parallels with the *APT* found in these texts, which do *not* deal with transvestite saints, give us a brief indication of the literary impact of Thecla as a model for constructing Lives of female (and sometimes male) saints. With these examples in mind,

---

[48] Bollandus, Henschenius, von Papenbroek, and Meursius (eds.), *Acta Sanctorum Martii I*, 1668: 876; *APT* § 3.7.
[49] On the importance of the window in the *APT*, see, for example, Eyl, "Why Thecla Does Not See Paul," 2012: 11–15.
[50] BHG 452.
[51] *Conversion of Cyprian of Antioch*: Radermacher (ed.), *Griechische Quellen*, 1927: 76–78. On the similarities between this narrative and the Thecla-legend, see ibid.: 16–19; and Sowers, "Thecla Desexualized," 2012.
[52] Radermacher (ed.), *Griechische Quellen*, 1927: 84. The corresponding passage in the *APT* (§ 4.1) reads: "And taking hold of Alexander, she tore his cloak and pulled off his crown and made him a laughing-stock (θρίαμβον)." I cite exceptionally here the translation in Cox Miller (ed.), *Women in Early Christianity*, 2005: 162. This translation renders the likeness in the Greek wording more clearly.
[53] Maraval (ed.), *Vie de sainte Macrine*, 1971: 146–149. For a discussion, see Davis, *The Cult of St. Thecla*, 2001: 62–64; and Narro, *El culto*, 2019: 96–98. As I state above, time and space do not allow for comprehensiveness. Yet the examples provided here offer an indication of the importance of the *APT* for later Greek hagiography. Here, I point to three further examples of interest to this discussion: Alwis, *Celibate Marriages*, 2011: 44–45, discusses a connection between the *APT* and the *Martyrdom of Galaktion and Episteme*; Narro, *El culto*, 2019: 79, points out similarities between Thecla and Blandina, and the heroine from the *Martyrdom of Theodora and Didymos* is compared to Thecla (see n. 93).

we may now turn to the Lives of interest to us in this chapter and assess the parallels we find.

Thecla and the Transvestite Saints

Among the Lives of transvestite saints written between the fourth and tenth centuries,[54] the *Life and Martyrdom of Eugenia* is the one text that has been studied thoroughly in relation to the *APT*. This narrative is indeed the only one of the cross-dressers' Lives that *explicitly* engages with the legend of Thecla as Davis notes.[55] In most versions of this legend, the young Eugenia, who is the daughter of a pagan ruler, finds herself reading the *APT*.[56] Moved to tears by the female apostle's example, she is driven to pursue a Christian life.[57] Eugenia is eventually brought to court to be judged by her own father for a crime she did not commit (she has in the meantime joined a male monastery disguised as a man and is falsely accused of sexual harassment by a rich woman named Melanthia whose

---

[54] I will discuss nine narratives; the *Life and Martyrdom of Susanna* (BHG 1673, 4th/5th cent.); the *Life of Pelagia* (BHG 1478, 5th cent.); the *Life of Andronikos and Athanasia* (BHG 120–123 and 123a, 6th cent.); the *Life of Theodora of Alexandria* (BHG 1727, 5th/6th cent.); the *Life of Matrona of Perge* (BHG 1221, 6th cent.); the *Life of Apolinaria* (BHG 148, 6th cent.); the *Life of Euphrosyne of Alexandria* (BHG 625, 6th/7th cent.); the *Life of Mary called Marinos* (BHG 1163, 4th/6th/7th cent. – the dating of this text is contested); and the *Life and Martyrdom of Eugenia* (BHG 607w–608, 5th–10th cent.). This selection follows the same twelve listed by Patlagean, "L'histoire," 1976, and includes the addition of two texts as suggested by Constantinou, *Female Corporeal Performances*, 2005: 92. From this corpus, I exclude the *Lives* of Marina of Scanio and of Euphrosyne the younger (dated to a much later period than the others, namely, eleventh/twelfth and fourteenth century respectively) due to limited space. I also exclude the *Lives* of Anastasia Patrikia, Anna called Euphemianos, and Hilaria because these have either not been transmitted in Greek (Hilaria) or have not been transmitted as full, independent narratives (Anastasia Patrikia and Anna).

[55] Davis, "Crossed Texts, Crossed Sex," 2002: 16.

[56] The *APT* is mentioned in the Syriac and Armenian versions of Eugenia's legend (the Syriac version is edited and translated by Lewis [ed. and trans.], *Select Narratives*, 1900, the Armenian version is edited by Conybeare [ed. and trans.], *The Apology*, 1894). Of the two Latin recensions of the legend, only one mentions the *APT*, whereas the other one mentions the "divine book of the letters of Paul." On the references to Thecla's legend in the Latin versions, see Whatley, "More than a Female Joseph," 2012: 92–93; and Klazina Staat's contribution in this volume (Chapter 9). The explicit references to the Thecla-legend are missing from the Greek Metaphrastic version of the *Life and Martyrdom of Eugenia*, which is the one generally studied; it also mentions the letters of Paul, while Eugenia's self-characterization as Thecla during the trial is missing (see the recent edition and translation by Papaioannou [ed. and trans.], *Christian Novels*, 2017: 189 and 229). However, the original Greek Eugenia-legend, which comes down in two recensions that remain vastly understudied, follows the situation in the Latin tradition: one of these recensions explicitly refers to Thecla, the other one does not. Cf. Apserou, "Το αγιολογικό *dossier*," 2017: 289–370; and Chapter 9. On the interdependence of the Greek and Latin Eugenia-traditions, see Lanéry, "Les Passions latines," 2010: 130, among others.

[57] Apserou, "Το αγιολογικό *dossier*," 2017: 291; and Lewis (ed. and trans.), *Select Narratives*, 1900: 2–3.

advances Eugenia spurns). At the trial, the saint is forced to reveal her sex; in doing so, she explains her own act of cross-dressing as an imitation of her teacher Thecla.[58] In addition to explicit references to Thecla, Davis identifies an intertextual reference to the *APT* in the *Life and Martyrdom of Eugenia*, which is contained in all its versions.[59] Furthermore, the overall legend is modeled on the *APT* in other, implicit ways. Her double trial and torture, for instance, evoke those of Thecla[60] (even if the modeling is here less straightforward than in Lucia's or Christina's cases, discussed above). Davis also sees cultural and iconographic parallels with practices and artifacts connected to Thecla's cult.[61]

However, the question as to whether other Lives of cross-dressers portray implicit parallels with or display similarities to the *APT* still needs to be answered before suggesting that Thecla was a prototype and her life a subtext for these cross-dressers. To begin with, I have not found any striking parallels between the *APT* and the Lives of the cross-dressers in the wording used to express a heroine's act of putting on male clothes other than the frequently resurfacing phrase "male attire" (σχῆμα ἀνδρικόν). However, this short phrase is by far too insufficient to claim a meaningful connection. In what follows, therefore, I will discuss a number of literary motifs that are shared by the *APT* and one or more of the other transvestites' Lives: renunciation of marriage, unwanted erotic attention leading to trial, wild animals, love at first hearing, and *Scheintod*. Then, I will point to two instances of intertextuality.

Firstly, all cross-dressers renounce married life (some of them do so as virgins, e.g., Euphrosyne, Eugenia, Apolinaria, Susanna, and Mary, while others are married women who take leave of their husbands, e.g., Theodora, Matrona, and Athanasia). Thecla's narrative, as we are all by now familiar, revolves primarily around the rejection of social order and marriage, in particular, and the trials the heroine faces and overcomes as a

---

[58] Apserou, "Το αγιολογικό *dossier*," 2017: 308; and Lewis (ed. and trans.), *Select Narratives*, 1900: 20: "I became a man for a short time, being emulous and imitating my teacher Thecla: she who despised and rejected the desires of this world and became worthy of the good things of heaven by means of her chastity and her life." Lewis' translation of the Syriac Life is close to the Greek text (which awaits translation). The passage is, however, slightly ambiguous; does Eugenia mean she is following Thecla's act in her cross-dressing, or rather (and solely) in her choice to remain a virgin? I thank Flavia Ruani for this suggestion.

[59] Davis, "Crossed Texts, Crossed Sex," 2002: 17. See Whatley, "More than a Female Joseph," 2012: 95, on this phrase in the Latin text. I come back to this intertextual reference below.

[60] See Anson, "The Female Transvestite," 1974: 26; and Whatley, "More than a Female Joseph," 2012: 93–94.

[61] Davis, *The Cult of St. Thecla*, 2001: 144–147; and Davis, "Crossed Texts, Crossed Sex," 2002: 19.

consequence.⁶² On the basis of this similarity, Nathalie Delierneux aligns the transvestite saints' Lives with the *APT*.⁶³ However, I would be careful in interpreting this particular parallel as a meaningful connection. In Thecla's case, the renunciation of marriage is dissociated from her crossdressing, unlike in the later Lives of transvestite saints. Renunciation of marriage and, consequently, preservation of virginity or chastity becomes the very motivation for the act of cross-dressing in the case of the transvestite saints and sets the plot in motion.⁶⁴ More importantly, the renunciation of married life is perhaps what aligns almost *all* of the female (and even male) saints in the late antique period. The saintly type of the married woman gains prominence only after the seventh century with Lives like those of Mary the Younger and Thomaïs of Lesbos.⁶⁵ Therefore, the fact that both Thecla and the cross-dressers renounce marriage is hardly an argument for aligning the *APT* specifically with these Lives.

Another story pattern that several of the transvestite saints share with Thecla is that they are exposed to unwanted erotic attention, and rejection of that attention sees them brought before the authorities and often punished. Melanthia, as we have just noted, tries to seduce Eugenia. When Eugenia rebuffs her advances, Melanthia accuses the latter of sexual assault, and Eugenia is brought to trial before the local governor, her father. Susanna finds herself in a similar situation when she is questioned by the local bishop after a woman, who fell in love with her, invented a story about being sexually assaulted by the saint. Theodora, meanwhile, is expelled by the abbot from the monastery in which she has been living after being falsely accused of fathering a child with the daughter of the abbot of another monastery, whose sexual advances she had in fact rejected. Mary is also expelled by the abbot after similar accusations, this time coming from the daughter of an innkeeper.⁶⁶

---

⁶² Delierneux, "Virilité physique," 1997: 191, writes that this aspect of Thecla's tale was particularly influential: "sa légende a[it] servi de critère dans l'hagiographie postérieure."
⁶³ Delierneux, "Virilité physique," 1997: 191.
⁶⁴ Theodora initially flees her husband and takes on male disguise out of shame and guilt after committing adultery, but when the devil, disguised as her husband, tries to win her back, she decidedly renounces married life and chooses asceticism. Cf. Wessely (ed.), "Die Vita S. Theodorae," 1889: 36–37. In the *Life of Susanna*, an explicit explanation for the saint's decision to cross-dress is lacking, but like all the others, her story begins with an overt renunciation of the marriage plans her father has made for her (§ 3): Stiltingus et al. (eds.), *Acta Sanctorum Septembris VI*, 1757: 154.
⁶⁵ On this shift over time, see Talbot, *Holy Women*, 1996: xii–xiii. Translations of both Lives mentioned are found in the same volume.
⁶⁶ Apolinaria, finally, is also falsely accused of fathering a child, but here the dynamics are different; she is not accused because she rejects a sex partner, but because she is the victim of a trick by the devil who makes Apolinaria's sister appear pregnant.

As discussed above, what marks these stories as fundamentally different from the *APT* is that the sexual advances come not from men but from women. Still, to a certain extent, what goes wrong for the cross-dressing saints is not so dissimilar from what goes on in the *APT*. Thecla says she will cut her hair, and we do not know if she actually does, only that Paul replies that "she is beautiful and times are bad" (§ 3.25). Suddenly, Alexander sexually desires her because of her great beauty. If she has cut her hair (and again, we do not have any indication in the text that she does), the act is not successful in safeguarding Thecla from being exposed to sexual violence. The transvestite saints, by contrast, are successful in portraying themselves to the outside world as men, but where it goes wrong is precisely that their male facade does not stop them from being attractive.[67] It is unclear whether we should see this as a deliberate interpretation of the scene from the *APT* or whether the later Lives rather back project this onto the *APT* (an interesting question to which I will have occasion to return). The fact remains that the Lives of these four transvestite saints (three if we exclude Eugenia) indeed share the narrative pattern of unwanted erotic attention followed by trial with the *APT*. But so does, for instance, the *Conversion of Cyprian of Antioch*, which does not belong to the corpus of cross-dressers but in which we perceive a much closer mapping of one particular scene from the *APT* (see discussion above). For the Lives of Mary, Apolinaria, and Susanna, the two narrative motifs just outlined (i.e., rejection of marriage and sexual harassment followed by trial) are the only parallels with the *APT* I could find. This is striking especially with regard to Susanna, who is the only cross-dresser apart from Eugenia to also be a martyr. The *Life of Theodora* offers more promising material in this respect.

Although she is not a martyr as Thecla is portrayed in later texts,[68] Theodora undergoes many trial-like situations that in a way allow her to offer penance for her act of adultery. Several of these episodes involve the motif of the domesticated wild animal: Theodora is sent outside the monastery into the wilderness on three occasions. Each time, wild animals,

---

[67] This is also true for Euphrosyne, whose beauty, even while disguised as a monk, is so extraordinary that it causes trouble for the other monks, which is why she must reside in a separate cell in complete isolation. Cf. Boucherie (ed.), "Vita Sanctae Euphrosynae," 1883: § XI. In her case, however, it does not lead to sexual advances or trial-scenes.

[68] As Davis, *The Cult of St. Thecla*, 2001: 45, demonstrates, Thecla was venerated as a martyr (even if she technically survived her trials). Moreover, as the "first female martyr" she was associated with Stephen, the first male martyr. On Thecla as a martyr in the Ethiopic tradition, see Damien Labadie's contribution in this volume (Chapter 2).

who appear to threaten her life at first, turn out to be agents of God, sparing her and even helping her.[69] This evokes the scene from the *APT* in which the lioness that is brought into the arena to kill the heroine instead defends her against the other beasts (§ 4.8).[70] However, the motif of the wild animals in the *Life of Theodora* (see below) in fact resembles much more a scene from another text, the *Acts of Xanthippe and Polyxena*, which will be discussed in the final section of this chapter.

The *Life of Pelagia* does not display the motifs of renunciation of marriage and sexual violence, but it does have another motif in common with the *APT*: the motif of "love at first hearing."[71] Pelagia is a so-called holy harlot. Like Eudocia, whom I have discussed above, Pelagia converts after she hears the teaching of a prominent religious man, in her case Nonnos, a bishop who is in Antioch for clerical matters. When the latter is preaching in the church while she happens to pass by, she is suddenly "stung with a fear of God."[72] The importance of Thecla's ability to *hear* Paul by the window for the dramatic development of the *APT*'s plot has already been discussed above. Eugenia, too, experiences the urge to convert when she hears Christians chanting.[73] And, in the *Life of Matrona*, the saint's pupil Athanasia, whose story mirrors that of the saint herself, suddenly "heard the sound of psalmody coming from the buildings" and was "struck by the strangeness of the sound."[74] It is in fact Matrona herself who has taken residence inside these buildings and, consequently, who fulfills the role of Nonnos, Germanos, or Paul.[75]

---

[69] Before being admitted into the monastery, the brothers decide to leave her outside for one night to see if the wild animals will attack her. They do not, and this is perceived as a sign that she must be allowed into the monastery. Cf. Wessely (ed.), "Die Vita S. Theodorae," 1889: 28. Another time, she is sent to fetch water from a lake where a man-eating crocodile lives; the beast takes her on his back to the middle of the lake and returns her safely to shore (ibid.: 32). Finally, she is sent to deliver a message by some brothers who are envious and hope she will be eaten alive in the wilderness; a wild animal instead becomes her guide, but it attacks the doorkeeper of the monastery to where she is supposed to deliver the message (ibid.: 32–33).

[70] This is one of the arguments Capron, *Codex hagiographiques*, 2013: 132, uses, along with "la dénonciation calomnieuse et le travestissement," to posit that "on ne peut ignorer que cet ancien récit, lié à un culte local [i.e., that of Thecla], ait pu influencer l'auteur de notre texte [the *Life of Theodora*]."

[71] This expression is used by scholars to refer to a Christian variant on the motif of love at first sight which indicates religious conversion. For a discussion of this motif in the *APT*, see Eyl, "Why Thekla Does Not See Paul," 2012.

[72] The *Life of Pelagia*: Flusin (ed.), "Les textes grecs," 1981: 84, l. 134.

[73] The *Life of Eugenia*: Apserou, "Το αγιολογικό *dossier*," 2017: 291. Cf. Papaioannou (ed. and trans.), *Christian Novels*, 2017: 188, § 8.

[74] I cite the translation by Jeffrey Featherstone in Talbot (ed.), *Holy Women*, 1996: 53.

[75] Eugenia also becomes a teacher later in her Life and resembles Paul when one of her future pupils overhears her teaching. On Eugenia as a teacher and leader, see Ghazzal Dabiri's contribution in this volume (Chapter 10).

In the *APT*, however, the initial element of sound is instantly coupled to a desire for sight (Virginia Burrus remarks that Thecla is sitting by a window, "a place of *viewing*").[76] Indeed, Thecla

> was not turning away from the window, but was being led on in faith with an overabundant joy. But yet seeing many women and virgins going in to Paul, she herself desired to be made worthy to stand in the presence of Paul and to hear the word of Christ, for she had not yet seen the characteristics of Paul, but was only hearing his speech. (§ 3.7)

The verb ἀτενίζω (look intently, gaze earnestly) is peppered throughout the *APT* and describes Thecla's longing for Paul.[77] In the *Lives* of Eudocia and Cyprian and Justina, discussed above, the (imagined) presence of the window makes for a much firmer parallel with the scene from the *APT* (and in the *Conversion of Cyprian of Antioch* this is also followed by a desire to *see* the deacon).[78] Conversely, in the narratives of Pelagia, Matrona, and even Eugenia, we seem to encounter a more general *topos* that deals only with desire triggered by hearing, which is widespread in hagiography.

A final motif that the *APT* has in common with Lives of transvestite saints is the motif of *Scheintod*. In the *Life of Euphrosyne*, Paphnutius, the saint's father, falls to the ground "as if he were dead" right after his daughter dies.[79] Similarly, Tryphaena, who is like a mother to Thecla, faints and even appears to have died when she witnesses the tortures that are meant to kill her "second daughter" (§ 4.11).[80] However, the reason Paphnutius collapses is not so much that Euphrosyne dies but because, right before dying, the saint reveals her identity to her father, who consequently discovers that the monk he has been visiting for years is in fact his long-lost daughter.[81] In such a context, Paphnutius' *Scheintod* rather reminds us of the standard reaction of the heroes and heroines of the pagan love novels of the first centuries. Upon being reunited (which does not occur under the same or similar series of dramatic events that caused Tryphaena's seizure), they usually collapse/faint/are paralyzed and often nearly die, overcome by emotions.[82]

---

[76] Burrus, "Mimicking Virgins," 2005: 57 (her emphasis).
[77] E.g., *APT* § 3.9–10 and 3.20–21. See Barrier, *The Acts of Paul and Thecla*, 2009: 89 n. 9 and 90.
[78] *Conversion of Cyprian of Antioch*: Radermacher (ed.), *Griechische Quellen*, 1927: 78.
[79] Boucherie (ed.), "Vita Sanctae Euphrosynae," 1883: 204, l. 14.
[80] On the character of Tryphaena and her relationship to Thecla, including further references, see Misset-van de Weg, "A Wealthy Woman," 1996.
[81] Boucherie (ed.), "Vita Sanctae Euphrosynae," 1883: 204, l. 13.
[82] I refer to the presence of this motif in the five extant Greek love novels by Chariton: Reardon (ed.), *Charitonis*, 2004; Xenophon of Ephesus: Dalmeyda (ed.), *Xénophon*, 1962; Achilles Tatius: Vilborg (ed.), *Achilles Tatius*, 1955; Longus: Dalmeyda (ed.), *Longus*, 1971; and Heliodorus: Lumb,

The motifs outlined above are shared by the *APT* and one or more Lives of transvestite saints. However, I find that their presence is not convincing enough to perceive a close affinity between the stories of transvestite saints and the *APT*. Where motifs are shared, they are often more general hagiographical themes (e.g., renunciation of marriage, love at first hearing, unwanted erotic attention leading to trial), or their implementation (e.g., wild animals, *Scheintod*) demonstrates stronger affinities with other sources. The presence of intertextual borrowings, on the other hand, could provide more firm evidence that Lives of transvestite saints were modeled after the *APT*.

I know of only two instances of potential intertextual borrowing from the *APT* in Lives of transvestite saints. Firstly, Davis sees an intertextual connection with the *APT* when Matrona's husband interrogates one of her friends about her whereabouts; "the friend answers: 'Who this woman is of whom you speak, I know not ....'" Davis comments: "These words echo the apostle Paul's response when questioned about Thecla in the *Acts*: 'I do not know the woman of whom you speak ....'"[83] Even if they do indeed echo one another, I find the two phrases identified by Davis rather generic in terms of content, such that it is difficult to rule out entirely the possibility that their likeness may be due to coincidence. In other words, rather than a prominent verbal borrowing, we may simply be dealing with a similar narrative situation that calls for a similar response. Moreover, the way the sentence is used in the *APT* is rather different. In both texts, the sentence is uttered against a male aggressor. However, in the *Life of Matrona*, it is a protective measure taken to ensure that Matrona's husband will not be able to find his wife. In the *APT*, it is the opposite – by pretending not to know her, Paul abandons Thecla, exposing her to Alexander's aggression.[84]

If the presence of an intertextual borrowing from the *APT* in the *Life of Matrona* is debatable, one cannot deny that the *Life of Euphrosyne* shares a very particular turn of phrase with the *APT*. The reaction of the saint's family to her disappearance is narrated in the same way as the reaction of those close to Thecla when she stubbornly refuses to eat, drink, speak or

---

Maillon, and Rattenbury (eds.), *Héliodore*, 1960. Examples of the motif in these texts are Char. 8.1.8, Xen. 5.13.3, Ach. Tat. 3.17.7, Long. 2.30.1, Long. 3.7.3, Hld. 2.6.3, and Hld. 7.7.3.

[83] Davis, "Crossed Texts, Crossed Sex," 2002: 30.

[84] But see Barrier, *The Acts of Paul and Thecla*, 2009: 140 n. 6 and 9, who has a different take on this, namely, that the pattern followed here is one from the ancient Greek novels, where lovers would make up false stories to protect each other. Cf. n. 19.

move away from the window through which she can hear Paul.[85] However, the phrase is shared not *only* with the *APT*. In fact, it occurs also in the *Life and Martyrdom of Eugenia*. The intertextual parallel between the *APT* and Eugenia's Life is noted by Davis.[86] However, he does not mention that this particular turn of phrase is found in the *Life of Euphrosyne* as well, where it occurs dissociated from an explicit reference to Thecla. Moreover, I found the same turn of phrase in yet another hagiographical text, the *Life of Theophano*, where it appears dissociated from the context of cross-dressing altogether. This hagiographical narrative about a Byzantine empress, the first wife of Leo VI (886–912), is of a slightly later period than the other texts discussed in this chapter and centers on a very different type of saint.[87] The phrase appears not in reaction to a metaphorical death (Thecla) or a presumed death (Eugenia/Euphrosyne) but to an actual death.[88] Its attestation in the tenth-century *Life of Theophano*, which does not have any other references to Thecla or the *APT*, may indicate that, perhaps, the phrase began to live a life of its own and that the connection with Thecla was lost over time. As such, it is doubtful that its presence in the *Life of Theophano* was meant to invite an intertextual dialogue with the Thecla legend. The question is, of course, whether it does in the *Life of Euphrosyne*. In this text, the phrase pops up in a narrative situation that very clearly parallels the legend of Eugenia (both times to describe reactions to missing girls who fled marriage in male disguise). It may be, therefore, that the phrase in the seventh-century *Life of Euphrosyne* repeats its attestation in the legend of Eugenia without necessarily tracing it back to its original locus. Nonetheless, it also remains possible that individual readers or listeners, familiar with the *APT*, identified this sentence as belonging to it and connected Euphrosyne and Thecla in their minds.

From the *APT* to the Transvestite Saints: New Perspectives

Earlier, we looked at certain Lives of saints *not* dealing with cross-dressers but that are modeled after Thecla and her legend. My analyses above

---

[85] Boucherie (ed.), "Vita Sanctae Euphrosynae," 1883: 201, ll. 28–29: "They wept as if for one dead, her father-in-law for his daughter-in-law, the young man for his fiancé, the servants for their mistress." The corresponding line in the *APT* is found in § 3.10.

[86] Davis, "Crossed Texts, Crossed Sex," 2002: 17.

[87] BHG 1794. The text was composed by an anonymous author in the early tenth century. For further discussion and references, see Efthymiadis, "Hagiography," 2011: 119, especially n. 74.

[88] Kurtz (ed.), "Zwei griechische Texte," 1898: 7, ll. 4–7: When the mother of the emperor Leo dies: "The lord, Basil, lamented for being separated from his wife, the son and very wise emperor Leo was vexed over the loss of his mother, and the young empress and bride [Theophano] mourned the departure of her excellent mother-in-law, [who was like] a second mother to her."

demonstrate that Greek Lives of cross-dressing saints, by contrast, do not appear modeled after Thecla's legend in any specific, much less explicit ways. In fact, the *Life and Martyrdom of Eugenia* turns out to be an exception among cross-dressers' tales in terms of its frequent referencing of the *APT* and evident modeling of Thecla's legend. So why are scholars writing about transvestite saints so keen on citing Thecla as a model? And how did the motif of cross-dressing in early Christian narratives then travel from its first known attestation in the *APT* to its treatment in the Lives of transvestite saints, if the latter apparently are not direct recipients of Thecla's legend? As we will see momentarily, the answer to the first question is related to the second, to which I now turn.

Indeed, in the final section of this chapter, I would like to propose an alternative path for the cross-dressing motif's journey. If contemporary scholarship suggests that Lives of transvestite saints pick up the cross-dressing motif directly from the *APT*, albeit in a new form, I perceive intermediary steps. In addition, if Davis claims that the later Lives were an attempt to reappropriate Thecla,[89] no one seems to have explored the argument's hypothetical converse, namely, that Thecla was reappropriated as a transvestite saint.[90] Three texts provide evidence for this discussion: the *Acts of Xanthippe and Polyxena*, the *Life and Miracles of Thecla*, and the *Life of Eusebia called Xenê*.

The *Acts of Xanthippe and Polyxena* (hereafter *AXP*) is a text that is difficult to pin down in terms of date and generic distinctions. It may have been composed in the middle of the third century[91] and skims along the borders of the Apocryphal Acts of the Apostles, the pagan Greek romances, and hagiography. In any case, there is very little doubt that the *APT* functions as a subtext for this narrative, as scholars have widely acknowledged.[92]

---

[89] Davis, "Crossed Texts, Crossed Sex," 2002: 16.
[90] Turning around the dynamics of appropriation invalidates the question that is posed by Patlagean, "L'histoire," 1976: 609, and which results from viewing Thecla as the first transvestite saint: "Il faut en somme expliquer pourquoi et comment un modèle d'ascèse attesté d'abord dans les marges hétérodoxes de la chrétienté antique conquiert néanmoins une telle place dans l'hagiographie dominante de Byzance." For more on the changing perception of the *APT* and Thecla as models, I refer the reader to Klazina Staat's contribution in this volume (Chapter 9).
[91] *BHG* 1877. James (ed.), *Apocrypha Anecdota*, 1893: 53–54. According to Hunink, "Following Paul," 2015: 148 n. 5, it may have been composed slightly later as well, during the fourth or fifth century, although the sixth century, as argued by Szepessy, "Narrative Model," 2004: 318, seems too late. All translations of this text are taken from Craigie (trans.), "The Acts of Xanthippe and Polyxena," 1980 (references will be made to page numbers, not paragraphs).
[92] The connection between the *APT* and the *AXP* is discussed by James (ed.), *Apocrypha Anecdota*, 1983; Peterson, "Die Acta Xanthippae et Polyxenae," 1947; Dagron (ed. and trans.), *Vie et miracles*, 1978; and Narro, *El culto*, 2019: 98–100.

The story begins when the apostle Paul arrives in Spain and enters the city in which Xanthippe, a married woman and the heroine of the first half of the story, lives. The apostle's presence ignites an all-consuming desire in Xanthippe. Seeing his wife in such an agitated state, Xanthippe's husband Probus, a local official of high rank, sends Paul away and locks up his wife. Not easily deterred, Xanthippe bribes the doorkeeper guarding the gates of her house to visit the apostle while her husband is sleeping. Despite a rocky beginning for Probus, both Xanthippe and her husband are eventually baptized by Paul. After the celebrations, which conclude the first part of the narrative, Xanthippe's younger sister Polyxena is abducted. Thenceforward, the reader follows the trials and travails of this young virgin as she struggles to safeguard her chastity while being exposed to all sorts of dangers during her travels, until she eventually manages to return home and is happily reunited with her family. Not only are there obvious parallels between the fate of the heroines of this tale and Thecla's story, the narrative is presented as taking place within the same storyworld as the *APT*: one of the characters (the son of the prefect who tries to save Polyxena) says he once saw Paul preaching in his city and also heard about his disciple Thecla who was condemned to the wild beasts (83.8–12).

Despite the obvious modeling of the *AXP* on the *APT*, I believe that the Lives of transvestite saints have closer affinities with this third-century interpretation of Thecla's legend than with the *APT* itself. More than in Thecla's story, in the adventures of Polyxena – especially her wanderings in desolate places, her chance meetings with both helpers and opponents, and her circular tale of being separated and reunited with her loved ones – we may recognize the wanderings and adventures of heroines like Theodora, Mary, Apolinaria, Eugenia, Athanasia, Euphrosyne, and Matrona. All these saints' narratives focus on a young heroine who leaves home, enters the wild, and is eventually reunited with her family or husband after a recognition scene. By contrast, the *APT* displaces the structure of departure, adventures, and homecoming/recognition seen in the ancient romances and in the later hagiographies: it focuses on martyr-like trials and ends with Thecla leaving her hometown Iconium for good.

Apart from the general structure of the Lives, some of the motifs they feature resemble motifs from the *AXP*. In fact, wild animals and *Scheintod*, two motifs that the *APT* shares with the Lives of Theodora and Euphrosyne respectively (see above), are found in the *AXP* as well. In both Lives, the way in which the respective motifs are handled resembles more closely its occurrence in the *AXP* than its occurrence in the *APT*. Firstly, the *AXP* features two lioness-episodes, one of which is very explicitly modeled on the *APT* (§ 4.8); both scenes are set in a public arena in which the young heroine is condemned to be devoured by beasts for the entertainment of the public until, unexpectedly, the lioness appears like a domesticated cub at the feet of the virgin (83.28–31). The other time Polyxena meets a friendly lioness is during her wanderings in the wilderness: all alone and completely lost, she encounters the beast, who, rather than eating her, becomes her guide and leads her out of the woods (77.32–78.4). This latter scene, much more than the former or its corresponding episode in the *APT*, is highly reminiscent of the way in which the motif of wild animals plays out in the *Life of Theodora* (in which a wild animal also becomes the saint's guide in the desert). As for the second motif, *Scheintod*, Paphnutius' fainting in the *Life of Euphrosyne* mirrors more closely that of Xanthippe than Tryphaena's fainting. Xanthippe, like Paphnutius, collapses because of the overwhelming emotions that accompany her reunion with her beloved Polyxena at the end of the *AXP* (85.15–16). Moreover, in the *Life of Euphrosyne*, the saint dies immediately after she reveals her identity. Similarly, Xanthippe *actually* dies after fainting, finding peace now that she knows her sister has arrived safely back home, which makes the reunion between the two sisters as short-lived as the reunion between father and daughter in the *Life of Euphrosyne* (86.25–26).

The narrative parallels between the *AXP* and the Lives of transvestite saints once again put into perspective the links between these narratives and Thecla's story. If the Lives of cross-dressers are modeled on early Christian stories featuring young virgins and apostles, it appears to me that the *AXP* is a more likely candidate than the *APT* as a source material. However, we should not forget either that the latter account lives on through the former and that the *AXP*, echoing the *APT*, also features the motif of cross-dressing.

Indeed, any reader familiar with the *APT* may readily trace its storyline almost step by step in the *AXP*. Therefore, when references to cross-dressing surface in the *AXP*, these passages arguably provide a new interpretation to the corresponding events in the *APT*. This is because they are adopted into a new context, but one that is still recognizable as being grafted on Thecla's story. For instance, right before being abducted a second time by the prefect who will condemn her to the wild beasts, Polyxena is advised that it would be in her best interest to adopt male garb. This clearly reiterates Thecla's offer to cut her hair before attacking Alexander in self-defense, for which she is likewise thrown in the arena to face wild beasts. But whereas in the original *APT*, the proposed haircut does not necessarily imply a reference to a male disguise, the corresponding scene in the *AXP* decidedly turns the event into precisely that: rather than saying she will cut her hair, Polyxena is advised by a certain ass-driver, from whom she received help, to "alter her appearance to that of a man, lest," he adds, "for thy beauty's sake someone snatch thee away from me" (81.18–20). However, as in the *APT*, the cross-dressing motif is not developed further and does not impact the course of the narrative. When the maiden is said to be attacked by a presumably heteronormative male suitor, there is no indication that she might have been perceived as a man. Essentially, the idea that Polyxena has undergone any kind of change in appearance has been abandoned. Therefore, it is uncertain whether the heroine *actually* cross-dresses just as much as it is unclear in the corresponding scene in the *APT* whether Thecla cuts her hair. What changes in the *AXP* compared to the *APT* is that the text explicitly refers to the adoption of male dress as a disguise of the heroine's beauty, namely, in order to facilitate her safe travels. Furthermore, just like in the *APT*, there is a second allusion to cross-dressing in the *AXP* when the eparch's son, who wants to help Polyxena escape, tells her to put on his clothes. There is no doubt that the motif of cross-dressing represents disguise related to travel and escape – this time, it is supposed to dissimulate her identity, not just her beauty.[93] However, the motif is, again, not pursued in the narrative: a servant overhears them and alarms the prefect, who, as we know, orders a public trial.

Lives of transvestite saints have elements in common with both the *APT* and the *AXP*, as well as many other variegated sources. Nonetheless, the cross-dressing scenes from the *AXP* emerge as important steps, largely neglected thus far, in the development of the cross-dressing motif within Christian narratives; as reiterations of references to cross-dressing in the *APT*, these instances in the *AXP* develop into moments of disguise related to travel. As such, cross-dressing in the *AXP* also ties in with pagan treatments of this motif of roughly the same period, for instance, the

---

[93] This scene from the *AXP* recalls the story-pattern we find in certain hagiographical texts that are usually not counted among the Lives of transvestite saints because their heroines take on male disguise only temporarily; examples are the *Life of Adrian and Nataly* (BHG 27); the *Martyrdom of Alexander and Antonina* (BHG 50); the *Martyrdom of Theodora and Didumos* (BHG 1742); the legend of the anonymous virgin of Antioch (told by Ambrose in his *De Virginibus* [2.3.22–33] and by Jacobus de Voragine in his *Golden Legend* [ch. 60]). In all these tales, the heroine temporarily takes on male clothing in order to escape imprisonment, usually by switching clothes with her male rescuer. In the *Martyrdom of Theodora and Didumos*, moreover, the heroine is explicitly compared to Thecla.

Greek novels, to which the *AXP* have often been compared.[94] For example, in Xenophon of Ephesus' novel, the old fisherman Aigialeus narrates how he, once upon a time, eloped together with his lover Thelxinoe and how he cut her hair and disguised her as a young man so that she could escape the loveless marriage her parents had arranged for her.[95] Thus, the pagan novel may also play a role in the development of the cross-dressing motif in Christian sources. The point is not to establish direct or definitive links between one corpus of texts and another or between two individual texts. Rather, these motifs traveled widely (as they are also represented in pagan sources) and the reception of texts like the *APT* and the *AXP* (which have indeed been very influential for later hagiography) took place in dynamic and complex ways. More importantly, the *AXP* develops a particular way of dealing with the cross-dressing motif, which seems to be an innovation away from its occurrence in the *APT* and toward the motif's treatment in Lives of transvestite saints. Moreover, by doing so, the *AXP* provides a certain direction for the interpretation and meaning of the cross-dressing motif in the *APT*, and consequently in later narrative reworkings of the *APT*, such as the fifth-century *Life and Miracles of Thecla*, as I will illustrate now.

The *Life and Miracles of Thecla* (hereafter *LM*)[96] was composed in the fifth century by an anonymous author who tied Thecla's narrative more firmly to the city of Seleucia, where a cult for the martyr was in place at the time.[97] The first part, the "Life of Thecla," is an expanded version of the *APT*. As Scott F. Johnson notes, the author uses the technique of literary paraphrase. In the prologue to his work, the author of the *LM* writes: "I followed closely the meaning and chronological order of the events as they were written down in the earlier account but changed their composition and style" (Prol., ll. 15–19).

In general, the author indeed sticks to the contents of the *APT* as a basis for his expansion but, as Johnson demonstrates, also promotes his own

---

[94] Most notably, see Gorman, "Thinking,'" 2001: 418–424 and *passim*, who conducts a thorough comparison of the *AXP* and the Greek novels (Chariton's *Chaereas and Callirhoe* in particular).

[95] Dalmeyda (ed.), *Xénophon*, 1962, book 5, chapter 1. Xenophon's novel is dated to the mid-second century. John Anson refutes the suggestion by Radermacher, *Hippolytos und Thekla*, 1916, that the Thelxinoe-episode served as a source for Thecla's cross-dressing. See Anson, "The Female Transvestite," 1974: 4.

[96] BHG 1717. The text is edited and translated into French by Dagron (ed. and trans.), *Vie et miracles*, 1978. Henceforth, quotations from the *LM* refer to this edition.

[97] Johnson, *The Life and Miracles*, 2006: 5, notes that the *LM* was completed around the year 470. On the cult of St. Thecla, see Davis, *The Cult of St. Thecla*, 2001; Voicu, "Thecla," 2017; and Arbeiter, "El santuario," 2017.

agenda and succeeds in subtly changing the interpretation of certain scenes and phrases.[98] This is particularly evident in the scenes in which Thecla's cross-dressing is suggested. When Thecla says she will cut her hair before leaving for Antioch, in the *LM*, unlike in the *APT*, she explains that this is meant to cover up her beauty (§ 14.12–16). As such, the motivation to cross-dress that is promoted in the *LM*, namely, the disguise of female beauty, is the same as the one found in the *AXP*. In the original *APT*, Thecla's beauty is mentioned by Paul, but, as we saw, her proposed haircut is not (or at least not evidently) presented as a measure against sexual misconduct. The author of the *LM* changes Paul's reply so that it supports the idea of dissimulation of female beauty. It thereby seems to speak in favor of, rather than against the act. Indeed, before speaking about the temptations that might befall the young virgin, he states, "I fear that your beauty and youth is of such a nature that to those who have laid eyes on you it is not possible to restrain themselves, however badly they wanted to" (§ 14.17–19). And this is exactly what happens in the next scene, in which the author of the *LM* takes his interpretations further. When Thecla is approached by Alexander and seeks Paul's assistance, the author of the *LM*, who seems to have an interest in exploring and enhancing the masculine aspects of Thecla's character,[99] adds a small but meaningful phrase to Paul's original reaction: not only does Paul state that he does not know the woman Alexander desires, he also states that he is "not entirely sure whether she is in fact a woman" (§ 15.35).[100] As Johnson indicates, this addition helps to tone down the coarseness of Paul's reply in the corresponding scene in the *APT*, but it also does something else.[101] It provides an interpretation of the scene in the *APT* that aligns Thecla with transvestite saints: it suggests that she did indeed cut her hair,[102] with the purpose of disguising herself for safe travel. As such, the *LM* follows the well-known story pattern of the Lives of the transvestite saints, whose disguises often serve to protect them from pursuers but also sometimes fail

---

[98] On the techniques of rewriting employed by the author of the *LM*, see Johnson, *The Life and Miracles*, 2006: chapter 1. The most notable change to the story is the end: rather than dying, Thecla enters the ground alive, sinking into the earth in Seleucia (on the alternate ending of the Life, see ibid.: 64–66). The second part of the work tells of the many miracles that occurred near Thecla's shrine in Seleucia after her miraculous "death."

[99] For instance, *LM* § 15.59–60 and § 23.2. See also Dagron (ed. and trans.), *Vie et miracles*, 1978: 37–38.

[100] "μηδὲ γὰρ εἰ ἔστι γύναιον ὅλως εἰδέναι σαφῶς." See Johnson, *The Life and Miracles*, 2006: 46–47, on this change.

[101] Ibid.: 47. See n. 19 for a discussion on the meaning of the passage in the original *APT* and for Barrier's reading of this passage, which differs from how most scholars have interpreted it.

[102] As noted by Dagron (ed. and trans.), *Vie et miracles*, 1978: 231 n. 5.

to do so precisely because they can*not* dissimulate their beauty.[103] In the section dealing with Thecla's change of clothes, the author of the *LM* further consolidates the notion that Thecla was in disguise with the addition of the word, "again" (πάλιν) (§ 25.17–18).[104] As Johnson notes, by saying that she "again" dressed in male fashion, the author presents the earlier scene as a real instance of cross-dressing.[105] The narrator repeats, moreover, that this was done "so that she might hide underneath the garment her radiant beauty" (§ 25.18–19), casting the act once again as a disguise, namely, as a disguise of female beauty, in accordance with the *AXP*.

The subtle changes in the *LM* impose a particular interpretation of the events in the *APT*. Specifically, these changes help to explain the references to cross-dressing by offering a more clear-cut reading of the rather obscure original passage. They achieve this in two ways: they reiterate the motivation for cross-dressing found in the *AXP* among other sources (namely, disguise of female beauty to facilitate safe travel) and they consolidate the idea that Thecla indeed cuts her hair and wears male garb as a means of disguising herself. The cross-dressing motif is therefore fully developed here (whereas in the *AXP*, it still remains unclear whether the heroine actually cross-dresses). The literary paraphrast thus indeed becomes an exegete of the second-century text, as Johnson suggests, "confirming its status and explaining its contemporary significance."[106]

I believe the role of cross-dressing in the *LM* has prompted some scholars to compare Thecla to the later transvestite saints and to assume that the latter somehow were modeled after Thecla's example. Furthermore, on the basis of the *LM*, they seem to assume that Thecla cross-dresses to disguise herself in the *APT* as well. They do not sufficiently distinguish between the *APT* and the *LM* when claiming Thecla as a model for cross-dressers.[107] Moreover, by the time the *LM* was composed, the legends of the earliest transvestite saints like Susanna, Pelagia, Eugenia, and Theodora, whose cross-dressing indeed serves as a disguise (and not

---

[103] See Anson, "The Female Transvestite," 1974: 13.

[104] We may note also that the *LM* states that Thecla puts on a new garment (μεταμισχομένη), like the transvestite saints do, whereas in the original *APT* she changes the garment she is already wearing to resemble a man's garment.

[105] Johnson, *The Life and Miracles*, 2006: 61 n. 66.   [106] Ibid.: 10.

[107] Often, scholars who claim Thecla as a model for the transvestite saints do not distinguish between the *APT* and the *LM*, or fail to indicate to which of these sources they are referring (e.g., Delierneux, "Virilité physique," 1997: 187; and Zlatkova, "Legendary," 2014: 32). Petropoulos, "Transvestite Virgin," 1995: 132, distinguishes between the *APT* and the *LM* but sees in the latter only a confirmation of his reading of transvestitism as disguise in the former.

simply of their beauty but, more radically, of their female identity),[108] may have been already in circulation.[109] Rather than thinking of the later Lives of transvestite saints as attempts to adopt Thecla's story, which I hope to have demonstrated they did not entirely do, we may instead shift our focus and think of them as inspirational to the fifth-century author of the *LM*. In looking for a way to deal with the cross-dressing passages from the *APT* in his rewriting, the *LM*'s author may have aligned Thecla's transvestitism with that of transvestite saints. He accomplishes this by making the act of cross-dressing more definitive than in the *APT* and presenting it as a means of disguise for safe travel, as suggested by the *AXP*. Moreover, given that the success of the *LM* was rather limited,[110] I find the converse, namely, that this text was influential for the development of the motif in the Lives of cross-dressers, unlikely. Due to the lack of other evidence, however, this must remain a cautious proposal.

We have examined thus far two later reworkings of the *APT*, each of which look for ways to handle the original references to cross-dressing in that text and may have found their inspiration from different sources (pagan novels, earliest Lives of transvestite saints, etc.). As such, the treatment of the cross-dressing motif in these texts steers toward its treatment in the *Lives* of cross-dressers. Yet the latter precisely do *not* represent cornerstones in the reception of Thecla's story, with the exception of Eugenia's Life, as I have demonstrated above. Therefore, I believe that these two developments – the reception of the *APT* and the development of the cross-dressing motif in Christian narratives – are related but essentially separate processes. In this next section, therefore, I will address another text, the fifth-century *Life of Eusebia called Xenê*, which provides further perspectives on both processes but, at the same time, demonstrates how they must not be confused as one.

The *Life of Eusebia called Xenê*,[111] like the *APT*, is usually discussed in the margins of scholarship on Lives of transvestite saints because its heroine is regarded as a "temporary cross-dresser," like Thecla.[112] Eusebia is a young girl from a noble family in Constantinople who secretly flees overseas because her parents are forcing her to marry, though she prefers to stay true to her heavenly bridegroom, Christ. She convinces two servants to follow her and changes her clothes into male dress. As soon as

---

[108] As explained above in the section entitled "The *APT* Revisited."
[109] If we accept the dates provided above in n. 54.   [110] Johnson, *The Life and Miracles*, 2006: 226.
[111] *BHG* 633. The text is edited by Nissen (ed.), "S. Eusebiae seu Xenae Vita," 1938, and all references to the text henceforth refer to this edition.
[112] See for instance Delcourt, "Le complexe de Diane," 1958 and n. 10.

she reaches less familiar terrain and is no longer afraid of detection, she changes back into female clothes (the cross-dressing episode lasts no more than three paragraphs).

Cross-dressing is here, just as in the *AXP* and *LM*, presented as a means to travel and a way to escape detection. Like the *AXP* and the *LM*, moreover, this narrative also explicitly plays with Thecla's legacy. After her escape, the saint meets a monk and asks him to become her guide and teacher "like the apostle Paul was for the holy Thecla" (109.28–30). When it turns out that this monk is called Paul too, the saint exults, shouting: "Grace to you, God, because you listened to my humble self and sent to me, like to Thecla, [a man named] Paul, so that he may rescue me and my two sisters" (110.23–25).

It is tempting to see Eusebia's cross-dressing as an appropriation of the act by her role model Thecla. However, the function of her male disguise in fact steers away from what cross-dressing means for Thecla in the original *APT* and even in the later interpretations of her legend. For Eusebia, transvestitism is surely not a sign of the heroine's claim to male authority (it must rather keep her from being noticed at all), and even if it is clearly connected to travel, cross-dressing no longer serves to safeguard the heroine's chastity by concealing her feminine beauty. Rather, much like in the other Lives of transvestite saints, the role of the male disguise is to help her escape family members and therefore serves to conceal her identity. Significantly, after she has transformed herself back into a woman, Eusebia adopts a new name, Xenê, in order to make sure that her parents are unable to trace her. Her name, which translates literally to "stranger," symbolizes her new identity as an outcast and wanderer, as one who lives in hiding. While the name itself emphasizes her characterization as a new Thecla, who calls herself ξένη (stranger) in Antioch (§ 4.1),[113] the text, thus, also introduces an element – the adoption of a false name – that is absent from the *APT*, the *AXP*, and the *LM* but that is highly important in the Lives of cross-dressers such as Euphrosyne, Apolinaria, Eugenia, and even Matrona and Theodora (the latter two escaping not their parents but their husbands).[114] Even if Xenê's newly acquired identity is not a male identity – she does not choose a male name unlike the aforementioned heroines – her act of cross-dressing leans much more toward the treatment

---

[113] On the motif of wandering (*xeniteia*) and the term *xenos* (stranger) in the *APT*, see Davis, *The Cult of St. Thecla*, 2001: 22–26.
[114] See n. 25.

of the motif in the Lives of transvestite saints than in the Thecla tradition, even as it explicitly engages with the latter.[115]

The three texts discussed in this section (*LM*, *AXP*, and *Life of Eusebia/ Xenê*) allow us to paint a somewhat revised picture of the development of the cross-dressing motif in early Christian narratives. In the *APT*, the assumption of male clothes is, at best, a "seed" out of which a Christian interest in masculine women may have grown. References to cross-dressing serve to symbolically underline the heroine's claim to male authority. As a motif, it does not expressly represent disguise, and it is only loosely embedded as a means to travel (the references to Thecla's masculine appearance simply precede a change of location in the story and it is even doubtful that the first of these, Thecla's offer to cut her hair, must be read as an actual instance of cross-dressing). It is only in the *AXP* and *LM*, which are to variable and respective extents reworkings of the *APT*, that the motif of cross-dressing becomes a motif of disguise as a means to travel safely. As reworkings, they back project onto the *APT* their interpretations of Thecla as a cross-dresser, specifically one who takes on male disguise to conceal her beauty. The motif's new treatment, moreover, continues to flourish within hagiography. It not only appears in Lives of transvestite saints, where cross-dressing sometimes also serves as a means to facilitate travels, but also in Lives, like those of Indes and Domna, Didumos and Theodora, and Adrian and Nataly, in which the heroine cross-dresses temporarily to escape a difficult situation.[116] It is moreover found in the ancient Greek novel in which cross-dressing fulfills a similar role.

As a means to facilitate safe travel, the cross-dressing motif already receives relatively more weight compared to its usage in the *APT* because it intervenes in the construction of the plot. However, it is in the Lives of transvestite saints that the motif finds its most elaborate treatment, where the entire dramatic action revolves around the concealed identity of the heroine, who successfully passes as a man within her community (often until right before or even after her death). In these tales, the male disguise is often (but not always) connected to traveling and escape. Yet, in addition, and more importantly, "transvestite disguise becomes a source of imaginative interaction rather than simply a more or less elaborate mode

---

[115] The *Life of Eusebia/Xenê* also differs from the aforementioned Lives of heroines because the events after her initial escape do not revolve around the problems and complications that are created by her new identity.

[116] See n. 93.

of escape."¹¹⁷ In the *Life of Eusebia called Xenê*, cross-dressing also serves as an elaborate mode of escape, but it is also combined with the motif of concealed identity. This text dates to the same era as the earliest Lives of transvestite saints and clearly belongs to the same literary pool. What makes it relevant for the current investigation is its prominent appropriation of Thecla's legend. Following in the footsteps of both Thecla and the transvestite saints, Eusebia/Xenê represents a literary encounter between these two narrative spaces but in doing so also constitutes them as two worlds apart.

Conclusion

This chapter has sought to critically examine long-held notions about the motif of cross-dressing in relation to Thecla. In particular, it has reexamined the validity of the idea, widely perpetuated, that Thecla, the first Christian heroine to take on male dress, may be regarded as the forerunner of later transvestite saints and that the second century *APT* is a reference point for their tales (fourth to seventh centuries). Close inspection of the *APT* reveals that it contains only very limited indications of Thecla's cross-dressing and that scholars tend to overstate the role of this motif. They sometimes overinterpret her offer to cut her hair (which in itself, moreover, needs not necessarily indicate cross-dressing as being tonsured is required of men and women embarking upon monastic life). They also note that she disguises herself as a man, something Thecla is not portrayed as doing in the *APT*. It is only in the fifth-century reworking of the *APT*, the *LM*, that this act is explicitly ascribed to Thecla. Based on the date and the limited success of this text, we may conjecture that Thecla's transvestitism there is explained in alignment with existing usages of the motif rather than that it was inspirational for other authors.

Even if we set aside the *LM* and consider that cross-dressing fulfills a very different narrative role in the *APT* than in the stories of the transvestite saints, it remains possible that hagiographers of cross-dressers' Lives were inclined to draw on Thecla's model because they saw, in the (short) references to her assumption of male dress, an opportunity to connect their subjects to the famous female apostle. This is indeed what Eugenia's hagiographer appears to have done. However, an examination of the parallels between the *APT* and a large selection of Lives of transvestite

---

¹¹⁷ Anson, "The Female Transvestite," 1974: 17, notes this with regard to a particular scene from the *Life of Euphrosyne*, but I believe his words apply to the rest of the corpus as well.

saints reveals that hagiographers certainly did not favor cross-dressers' tales for revisiting the legend of Thecla. In fact, the parallels between the *APT* and Lives of transvestite saints, with the exception of Eugenia, are less convincing, in terms of both number and prominence, than those between the *APT* and the Lives *not* dealing with a transvestite saint analyzed here.

These observations destabilize scholars' tendency to see in Thecla a forerunner for later transvestite saints. Moreover, it is surprising that other sources, which may have functioned as important vehicles through which the legend of Thecla was interpreted and made relevant for later literary treatments of cross-dressing, have been overlooked. The *AXP* is an important step both in the development of the cross-dressing motif and in the reception of Thecla's legend, two separate processes that should not be confused. The same may be argued for the *Life of Eusebia called Xenê*, even if its fifth-century date makes it harder to view it as a step in the development *toward* the Lives of transvestite saints. In any case, the majority of the cross-dressers' Lives share much more narrative material with both these texts (*AXP* and *Life of Eusebia/Xenê*) than with the *APT*. Therefore, Thecla's legend was indeed reappropriated by later sources; but contrary to what scholars suggest, I do not see a *direct* reappropriation of the *APT* in the Lives of transvestite saints. The reception of the *APT* occurred gradually, widely, and in different forms. Thecla was a direct model for female saints for many reasons, but as a cross-dresser, her legacy seems to have been adopted indirectly and transformed along the way.

Bibliography

Alwis, Anne. *Celibate Marriages in Late Antique and Byzantine Hagiography: The Lives of Saints Julian and Basilissa, Andronikos and Athanasia and Galaktion and Episteme*. London; New York: Bloomsbury, 2011.

Anson, John. "The Female Transvestite in Early Monasticism: The Origin and Development of a Motif." *Viator* 5 (1974): 1–32.

Apserou, Stephanie. "Το αγιολογικό dossier της Αγίας Ευγενίας (BHG 607w–607z)." PhD diss., University of Ioannina, 2017.

Arbeiter, Achim. "El santuario de Tecla (Ayatekla) en Seleucia." In *Thecla: Paul's Disciple and Saint in the East and West*, edited by Jeremy W. Barrier, Jan N. Bremmer, T. Nicklas, and A. Puig i Tàrrech. Studies in Early Christian Apocrypha 12. Leuven: Peeters, 2017: 152–204.

Aspegren, Kerstin. *The Male Woman: A Feminine Ideal in the Early Church*, edited by René Kieffer. Acta Universitatis Upsaliensis/Uppsala Women's Studies 4. Uppsala; Stockholm: Almqvist and Wiksell International, 1990.

Aubin, Melissa. "Reversing Romance? *The Acts of Thecla* and the Ancient Novel." In *Ancient Fiction and Early Christian Narrative*, edited by Ronald F. Hock, J. Bradley Chance, and Judith Perkins. Society of Biblical Literature Symposium Series 6. Atlanta: Scholars Press, 1998: 257–272.

Barrier, Jeremy W. *The Acts of Paul and Thecla: A Critical Introduction and Commentary*. WUNT 2.270. Tübingen: Mohr Siebeck, 2009.

Bollandus, Ioannes, Godefridus Henschenius, Daniel von Papenbroek, and Jacques Meursius, eds. *Acta Sanctorum Martii Tomus I*. Antwerp: Iacobus Meursius, 1668.

Boucherie, Anatole, ed. "Vita Sanctae Euphrosynae." *Analecta Bollandiana* 2 (1883): 196–205.

Bremmer, Jan N. "Magic, Martyrdom and Women's Liberation in the *Acts of Paul and Thecla*." In *The Apocryphal Acts of Paul and Thecla*, edited by Jan N. Bremmer. Kampen: Kok Pharos, 1996: 36–59.

Burrus, Virginia. "Mimicking Virgins: Colonial Ambivalence and the Ancient Romance." *Arethusa* 38, no. 1 (2005): 49–88.

Capron, Laurent. *Codex hagiographiques du Louvre sur papyrus (P.Louvre Hag.)*. Paris: Presses de l'université Paris-Sorbonne, 2013.

Constantinou, Stavroula. *Female Corporeal Performances: Reading the Body in Byzantine Passions and Lives of Holy Women*. Uppsala: Acta Universitatis Upsaliensis, 2005.

Conybeare, Frederick Cornwallis, ed. and trans. *The Apology and Acts of Apollonius and Other Monuments of Early Christianity*. London: Swan Sonnenschein; New York: Macmillan, 1894.

Costanza, Salvatore, ed. "Un Martyrion inedito di S. Lucia di Siracusa." *Archivio Storico Siracusano* 3 (1957): 5–53.

Cox Miller, Patricia. "Is There a Harlot in This Text? Hagiography and the Grotesque." *Journal of Medieval and Early Modern Studies* 33, no. 3 (2003): 419–435.

———, ed. *Women in Early Christianity: Translations from Greek Texts*. Washington, DC: The Catholic University of America Press, 2005.

Craigie, William Alexander, trans. "The Acts of Xanthippe and Polyxena." In *Ante-Nicene Fathers: Translations of the Writings of the Fathers down to A.D. 325, Vol. X*, edited by Allan Menzies. Grand Rapids: William B. Eerdmans, 1980: 203–217.

Dagron, Gilbert, ed and trans. *Vie et miracles de sainte Thècle. Texte grec, traduction et commentaire*. Subsidia Hagiographica 62. Brussels: Société des Bollandistes, 1978.

Dalmeyda, Georges, ed. *Xénophon d'Éphèse. Les Éphésiaques ou le roman d'Habrocomès et d'Anthia*. 2nd ed. Paris: Les Belles Lettres, 1962. 1st ed., 1926: 3–77.

———, ed. *Longus. Pastorales (Daphnis et Chloé)*. 2nd ed. Paris: Les Belles Lettres, 1971. 1st ed., 1934: 2–106.

Davies, Stevan L. *The Revolt of the Widows: The Social World of the Apocryphal Acts*. London: Feffer & Simons, 1980.

Davis, Stephen J. *The Cult of St. Thecla: A Tradition of Women's Piety in Late Antiquity*. Oxford Early Christian Studies. Oxford; New York: Oxford University Press, 2001.

"Crossed Texts, Crossed Sex: Intertextuality and Gender in Early Christian Legends of Holy Women Disguised as Men." *Journal of Early Christian Studies* 10, no. 1 (2002): 1–36.

Delcourt, Marie. "Le complexe de Diane dans l'hagiographie chrétienne." *Revue de l'histoire des religions* 153, no. 1 (1958): 1–33.

Delierneux, Nathalie. "Virilité physique et sainteté féminine dans l'hagiographie orientale du IVe au VIIe siècle." *Byzantion* 67, no. 1 (1997): 179–243.

Drescher, James, ed. *Three Coptic Legends*. Cairo: Imprimerie de l'Institut Français d'Archéologie Orientale, 1947.

Efthymiadis, Stephanos. "Hagiography from the 'Dark Age' to the Age of Symeon Metaphrastes (Eighth–Tenth Centuries)." In *The Ashgate Research Companion to Byzantine Hagiography, Volume I: Periods and Places*, edited by Stephanos Efthymiadis. Farnham: Ashgate, 2011: 95–144.

Eyl, Jennifer. "Why Thecla Does Not See Paul: Visual Perception and the Displacement of Eros in the *Acts of Paul and Thecla*." In *The Ancient Novel and Early Christian and Jewish Narrative: Fictional Intersections*, edited by Marília P. Futre Pinheiro, Judith Perkins, and Richard Pervo. Groningen: Barkhuis, 2012: 3–20.

Flusin, Bernard, ed. "Les textes grecs." In *Pélagie la Pénitente. Métamorphoses d'une légende. Tome I. Les textes et leur histoire*, edited by Pierre Petitmengin, François Dolbeau, Bernard Flusin, et al. Paris: Études Augustiniennes, 1981: 39–131.

Gorman, Jill. "Thinking with and about 'Same-Sex Desire:' Producing and Policing Female Sexuality in the Acts of Xanthippe and Polyxena." *Journal of the History of Sexuality* 10, nos. 3–4 (2001): 416–441.

Henschenius, Godefridus, Daniel von Papenbroek, and Michel Cnobbaert, eds. *Acta Sanctorum Maii Tomus II*. Antwerp: Michael Cnobarus, 1680.

Hotchkiss, Valerie. *Clothes Make the Man: Female Cross Dressing in Medieval Europe*. New York; London: Garland, 1996.

Hunink, Vincent. "Following Paul: The *Acts of Xanthippe, Polyxena, and Rebecca* as an Ancient Novel." In *Early Christian and Jewish Narrative: The Role of Religion in Shaping Narrative Forms*, edited by Ilaria Ramelli and Judith Perkins. Tübingen: Mohr Siebeck, 2015: 147–159.

James, Montague Rhodes, ed. *Apocrypha Anecdota: A Collection of Thirteen Apocryphal Books and Fragments*. Cambridge: Cambridge University Press, 1893.

Johnson, Scott F. *The Life and Miracles of Thekla: A Literary Study*. Washington, DC: Center for Hellenic Studies, 2006.

Kurtz, Eduard, ed. "Zwei griechische Texte über die hl. Theophano, die Gemahlin Kaisers Leo VI." *Mém. Acad. Imp. Pétersbourg, classe historico-philologique* 3, no. 2 (1898) 1–24.

Lanéry, Cécile. "Les Passions latines composées en Italie." In *Hagiographies: Histoire internationale de la littérature hagiographique latine et vernaculaire en Occident des origines à 1500*, edited by Guy Philippart. Vol. 5. Turnhout: Brepols, 2010: 15–369.

Lewis, Agnes Smith, ed. and trans. *Select Narratives of Holy Women: from the Syro-Antiochene or Sinai Palimpsest: As Written Above the Old Syriac Gospel by John*

the Stylite or Beth Manri-Qanūn in A.D. 778. 2 vols. Studia Sinaitica 9–10. London: C. J. Clay and Sons, 1900.
Lowerre, Sandra. *The Cross-Dressing Female Saints in Wynkyn de Worde's 1495 Edition of the Vitas Patrum*. Frankfurt: Peter Lang, 2006.
Lubinsky, Crystal Lynn. *Removing Masculine Layers to Reveal a Holy Womanhood: The Female Transvestite Monks of Late Antique Eastern Christianity*. Turnhout: Brepols, 2013.
Lumb, Thomas Wallace, Jean Maillon, and Robert Mantle Rattenbury, eds. *Héliodore. Les Éthiopiques (Théagène et Chariclée)*. Paris: Les Belles Lettres, 1960: vol. 1, 2–124; vol. 2, 2–164; vol. 3, 2–126.
Maraval, Pierre, ed. *Vie de Sainte Macrine [par] Grégoire de Nysse: Introduction, texte critique, traduction, notes et index*. Sources chrétiennes 178. Paris: Éditions du Cerf, 1971.
McInerney, Maud Burnett. *Eloquent Virgins: From Thecla to Joan of Arc*. New York: Palgrave Macmillan, 2003.
Misset-van de Weg, Magda. "A Wealthy Woman Named Tryphaena: Patroness of Thecla in Iconium." In *The Apocryphal Acts of Paul and Thecla*, edited by Jan N. Bremmer. Kampen: Kok Pharos, 1996: 16–35.
Narro, Ángel. *El culto a las santas y los santos en la antigüedad tardía y la época bizantina*. Madrid: Editorial Sintesis, 2019.
Nissen, Theodorus, ed. "S. Eusebiae seu Xenae Vita." *Analecta Bollandiana* 56 (1938): 106–111.
Norsa, Medea, ed. "Martiro di Cristina nel Cod. Messin. 27." *Studi italiani di filologia classica* 19 (1912): 316–327.
Papaconstantinou, Arietta. "'Je suis noire, mais belle': le double langage de la Vie de Théodora d'Alexandrie, alias abba Théodore." *Lalies* 24, no.1 (2004): 63–86.
Papaioannou, Stratis, ed. and trans. *Christian Novels from the Menologion of Symeon Metaphrastes*. Dumbarton Oaks Medieval Library 45. Cambridge, MA: Harvard University Press, 2017.
Patlagean, Evelyne. "L'histoire de la femme déguisée en moine et l'évolution de la sainteté féminine à Byzance." *Studi Medievali* 3, no. 17 (1976): 597–623.
Peterson, Erik. "Die Acta Xanthippae et Polyxenae und die Paulus-Akten." *Analecta Bollandiana* 65 (1947): 57–60.
Petropoulos, John. "Transvestite Virgin with a Cause: The *Acta Pauli and Thecla* and Late Antique Proto-'feminism.'" In *Greece and Gender*, edited by Brit Berggreen and Nanno Marinatos. Bergen: Norwegian Institute at Athens, 1995: 125–139.
Radermacher, Ludwig. *Hippolytos und Thekla. Studien zur Geschichte von Legende und Kultus*. Kais. Akademie der Wissenschaften in Wien, Philosophisch-historische Klasse 182.3. Vienna: A. Hölder, 1916.
———, ed. *Griechische Quellen zur Faustsage. Der Zauberer Cyprianus, Die Erzählung des Helladius, Theophilus*. Vienna; Leipzig: Akademie der Wissenschaften in Wien, 1927.
Rapp, Claudia. "Author, Audience, Text and Saint: Two Modes of Early Byzantine Hagiography." *Scandinavian Journal of Byzantine and Modern Greek Studies* 1 (2015): 111–129.

Re, Mario. "Italo-Greek Hagiography." In *The Ashgate Research Companion to Byzantine Hagiography, Volume I: Periods and Places*, edited by Stephanos Efthymiadis. Farhnham: Ashgate, 2011: 227–258.

Reardon, Bryan Peter, ed. *Charitonis Aphrodisiensis de Callirhoe narrationes amatoriae. Bibliotheca scriptorum Graecorum et Romanorum Teubneriana (BT)*. Munich; Leipzig: K. G. Saur, 2004: 1–147.

Sowers, Brian. "Thecla Desexualized: The Saint Justina Legend and the Reception of the Christian Apocrypha in Late Antiquity." In *"Non-Canonical" Religious Texts in Early Judaism and Early Christianity*, edited by James H. Charlesworth and Lee M. McDonald. New York: T&T Clark International, 2012: 222–234.

Stiltingus, Joannes, Constantinus Suyskenus, J. Perierus, and J. Cleus, eds. *Acta Sanctorum Septembris Tomus VI*. Antwerp: Bernardus Albertus Vander Plassche, 1757.

Szepessy, Tibor. "Narrative Model of the *Acta Xanthippae et Polyxenae*." *Acta antiqua Academiae scientiarum Hungaricae* 44 (2004): 317–340.

Talbot, Alice-Mary, ed. *Holy Women of Byzantium: Ten Saints' Lives in English Translation*. Washington, DC: Dumbarton Oaks, 1996.

Tommasi, Chiara O. "Cross-dressing as Discourse and Symbol in Late Antique Religion and Literature." In *TransAntiquity: Cross-dressing and Transgender Dynamics in the Ancient World*, edited by Domitilla Campanile, Filippo Carlà-Uhink, and Margherita Facella. New York; London: Routledge, 2017: 121–134.

Vilborg, Ebbe, ed. *Achilles Tatius: Leucippe and Clitophon*. Stockholm: Almqvist & Wiksell, 1955: 1–161.

Voicu, Sever J. "Thecla in the Christian East." In *Thecla: Paul's Disciple and Saint in the East and West*, edited by Jeremy W. Barrier, Jan N. Bremmer, T. Nicklas, and A. Puig i Tàrrech. Studies in Early Christian Apocrypha 12. Leuven: Peeters, 2017: 47–68.

Ward, Benedicta. *Harlots of the Desert: A Study of Repentance in Early Monastic Sources*. London: Mowbray, 1987.

Whatley, E. Gordon. "More than a Female Joseph: The Sources of the Late-Fifth-Century *Passio Sanctae Eugeniae*." In *Saints and Scholars: New Perspectives on Anglo-Saxon Literature and Culture*, edited by Stuart McWilliams. Cambridge: D. S. Brewer, 2012: 87–111.

Wessely, Karl, ed. "Die Vita S. Theodorae." In *Fünfzehnter Jahresbericht des K. K. Staatsgymnasiums in Hernals*, edited by Georg Kotek. Vienna: Verlag des K. K. Staatsgymnasiums in Hernals, 1889: 24–48.

Zlatkova, Julia. "Legendary and Semi-legendary Female Characters in Late Antique Hagiography: Repentant Harlots, Cross-Dressing Ascetics and Holy Fools." *Initial: A Review of Medieval Studies* 2 (2014): 31–45.

CHAPTER 8

From Diotima to Thecla and Beyond
Virginal Voice in the Lives of Helia and Constantina

Virginia Burrus*

Do not force the stranger! Do not force the servant of God.
(Acts of Thecla § 4.1)[1]

Allow me to enjoy the spouse whom I desire. Allow me to have as husband the one whom I myself will choose.
(Life of Helia § 3.34–35)[2]

Virginity that is sure of the state of its own soundness obtains the highest good.
(Life of Constantina § 1.12)[3]

The first of these statements comes to us in the voice of Paul's virginal disciple, featured in the second-century novella known as the *Acts of Thecla*. The second and third statements derive from later, fifth- or sixth-century hagiographical novels – the *Life of Helia* and the *Life of Constantina* – and are voiced by their respective heroines. Speaking out in a moment of crisis, Thecla adopts a tone that is demanding, even

---

* This chapter emerges from a process of thought that began in 2010 when, at the invitation of Marco Conti, I first started working on the *Life of Helia*, and has extended to my recent and ongoing work on the *Life of Constantina*, also undertaken in collaboration with Marco, as well as Dennis Trout. A very early version of the argument about virginal voice (lacking Constantina) was drafted for a lecture that I was graciously invited to offer in October of 2011 at the Oxford Center for Late Antiquity, in coordination with the Corpus Christi Classical Seminar titled "God's Sophists." I am particularly grateful for conversations with Averil Cameron, Neil McLynn, and Tim Whitmarsh on that occasion. I subsequently tried out that same argument with audiences at LeMoyne College, Washington University in St. Louis, Yale Divinity School, and the University of Texas at Austin, and I am grateful for the sharp and helpful responses I received in all of those contexts as well. Finally, I thank the editors of this volume for inviting me to think about Thecla yet again and thus for attuning me to her voice as it echoes through both prior and later texts.

[1] For the *Acts of Thecla*, I follow the Greek edition and English translation of Barrier, *The Acts of Paul and Thecla*, 2009.
[2] For the *Life of Helia*, I follow the Latin edition and translation of Burrus and Conti (eds. and trans.), *The Life of Saint Helia*, 2014.
[3] For the *Life of Constantina*, I follow the Latin edition and translation of Conti, Burrus, and Trout (eds. and trans.), *The Lives of Saint Constantina*, 2020.

233

commanding. However, she is more often silent than talkative in the *Acts*, which records that Thecla "enlightened many with the word of God" (§ 4.18), yet rarely lets us hear her doing so. Like Thecla, Helia and Constantina both speak with authority. Like Thecla, they speak their desire, and they speak of desire, in tones passionate and measured in turn. But these are virgins much more voluble than the Thecla of the *Acts*. They speak seemingly without restraint – excessively even. You can hardly shut them up.

How is it that female figures – though whether they are *properly* female is debatable – *come to voice* in Christian texts of late antiquity? How, in particular, do their voices enter into debates about desire, traditionally the province of masculine speech? And what do these virginal voices *sound* like? Are they distinct and recognizable to our reading ears? There is a story to be told, it seems to me, and it starts with Thecla. Every Christian virgin who arrogates voice in some sense *follows Thecla*, speaking her desire in speech that both is and is not her own. Thecla, in other words, both inaugurates and serves as a figure for virginal voice in its startling, inbreaking forcefulness. But Thecla, however definitively novel, *follows others* as well, as we shall see.

Shane Butler has recently argued that ancient literature is "phonographic," that is, it aims "to capture the voice precisely as something conceptually distinct from language."[4] He has also argued, taking Augustine (354–430) as his example, that Christian writing breaks with this phonographic tradition: now "meaning is everything," and the distinctive sonority of Ciceronian Latin gives way to "one reshaped by and even stitched together from scripture."[5] But perhaps this scriptural writing does not so much break away from voice as introduce a new kind of voice. Butler himself acknowledges the sonic dimension of Augustine's *Confessions*, which he describes as "relentlessly noisy."[6] One might say the same of the Lives of Helia and Constantina: they are noisy texts, not least because their heroines are so persistently, performatively vocal. To a great extent, it is scripture that provides their scripts. But it is Thecla, we might say, who lends them the audacity of virginal voice.

Originally a Greek speaker, the Thecla of the *Acts* travels widely, and her story is familiar and frequently referenced. Most remarkably, perhaps, Thecla appears in Methodius of Olympus' (250–311) late third-century *Symposium*, a Greek dialogue modeled on Plato's work of the same title, featuring ten rhetorically proficient young women offering speeches in

---

[4] Butler, *The Ancient Phonograph*, 2015: 12. [5] Ibid.: 191–192. [6] Ibid.: 193.

praise not of *eros* (as in Plato's text) but of virginity. The voices of the Latin-speaking Helia and Constantina are, by contrast, unfamiliar to most and are preserved exclusively in a few tenth-century northern Spanish manuscripts. Three of these transmit an anthology of late ancient female hagiographies, which include (in this order) the Lives of Constantina, Helia, Melania, Castissima (Greek: Euphrosyne), an anonymous virgin, Egeria, Pelagia, and Mary of Egypt. A fourth manuscript includes only the Lives of Constantina and Melania, the most monastic of the saints.[7]

The *Life of Saint Helia* (*BHL* 3798) tells the tale of a young girl who dedicates herself to virginity in defiance of her mother's will and is subsequently brought to trial for her disobedience and her refusal to marry. Thecla is not named, but it is clear that her story serves as a narrative template for Helia's. The *Life* is generically eclectic, with the bulk of the text in dialogue format. Two of its three books are dominated by an extended debate between the young Helia and her mother regarding the relative merits of virginity and marriage, followed by briefer exchanges between the two women and a bishop; a third book records a debate between Helia and a judge, in which most of the talking is done by the vociferous virgin. All the speeches are generously laced with biblical citations, enhancing the air of self-conscious rhetorical virtuosity that pervades the Life.

The *Life of Saint Constantina* (*BHL* 1927), in turn, relates the story of a beautiful and learned young queen – the emperor Constantine's (d. 337) daughter, no less – who is miraculously healed of leprosy by a vision of the virgin martyr Agnes. Thereby converted to Christianity, she dedicates herself to a life of celibacy and transforms her palace into a convent of virgins. This *Life* incorporates a text associated with the Roman *Gesta martyrum* – the *Passion of Gallicanus, John, and Paul* (*BHL* 3237, 3239). It also references the legend of Constantina's healing narrated at greater length in the *Passion of Agnes* (*BHL* 0156). Focusing on the figure of Constantina, the *Life* extends and elaborates the earlier textual traditions, in which she is a secondary character, supplementing those traditions with new narrative materials, fictive letters, and a sprawling dialogue in which twelve virgins deliver prepared speeches on the "highest good" and "ultimate evil," to each of which Constantina responds with a speech of her own. Initially brief, the queen's speeches become increasingly expansive,

---

[7] The anthology and manuscript tradition are discussed by Salisbury, *Church Fathers*, 1991; Burrus and Conti (eds. and trans.), *The Life of Saint Helia*, 2015: 2–15; and most recently Conti, Burrus, and Trout (eds. and trans.), *The Lives of Saint Constantina*, 2020: 5–6, 41–48.

demonstrating her exegetical and theological facility. Her voice dominates those of the other speakers, positioning her as not only their loving patron and teacher but also their victor in rhetorical contest. Here, too, Thecla goes unmentioned. Nonetheless, the dialogue is strikingly reminiscent of Methodius' restaging of Plato's *Symposium*, featuring ten declaiming virgins, among whom Thecla is declared the winner. It is impossible to know whether the author of the *Life of Constantina* was familiar with Methodius' dialogue, and I am not making claims for direct influence. However, it also seems impossible not to count Methodius' work as a forerunner of sorts.

This chapter will initially backtrack briefly to consider the articulation of virginal voice in two non-Christian texts, Plato's dialogical *Symposium* and Achilles Tatius' *Leucippe and Clitophon*, a second-century romance whose heroine exhibits particular affinities with the Thecla of the *Acts*. Then, we shall consider the Thecla tradition as it emerges in both novelistic and dialogue formats, before turning to the *Life of Helia* and the *Life of Constantina*. If the former reflects the novelistic and the latter the dialogical Thecla traditions, both converge in their emphasis on virginal eloquence and desire.

Before Thecla: Diotima and Leucippe

Public speaking in antiquity was marked as a quintessentially masculine practice. Rhetorical training was crucial to the pedagogical formation that aimed to make men out of boys, and public oratory (particularly in the Roman period) constituted a culturally central enactment of elite manhood, played out on a tensely competitive stage.[8] At least two factors nonetheless complicate our assessment of the gendering of rhetoric in the literary tradition. First, from the vantage point of a Platonic discourse that continued to exert considerable influence in later antiquity, rhetoric was typically degraded as superficial, deceptive, and effeminate, aligned with the realm of mere becoming, in contrast to the profundity and truthfulness of philosophy, aligned with the realm of being.[9] Second, and, paradoxically, the works of that same philosophical tradition famously position two women, Aspasia and Diotima, as skilled rhetoricians who tutor none other than Socrates – and Socrates is, for Plato at least, the philosopher par excellence.[10] That is to say, the Platonic corpus itself both asserts and deconstructs the binaries of philosophy versus rhetoric, masculine versus

---

[8] Gleason, *Making Men*, 1995. [9] Jarratt, *Rereading the Sophists*, 1998: 63–79.
[10] Jarratt and Ong, "Aspasia," 1995: 9–24; and Swearingen, "A Lover's Discourse," 1995: 25–51.

feminine speech, presenting us with a paradox. Women do not have voice when the philosophers speak, yet they teach the philosopher to speak well. Rhetoric is a possibly effeminate art, yet only men practice it.

Here Plato's *Symposium* must draw our initial attention. This well-known dialogue text purports to represent a series of competing speeches in praise of Eros, delivered by and to a group of unusually abstemious male symposiasts: we are told that the flute-girl engaged to entertain the diners is dismissed, along with the wine. This is not, however, an altogether sober symposium, nor is it an exclusively masculine one. Both the flute girl and the wine return in the end, as it happens. Moreover, a dialogue between Socrates and a foreign woman, the prophetess Diotima, is nested within one of the supposedly sober speeches of the Athenian men. Indeed, it is Diotima's discourse on Love, as reported by Socrates, that is often considered to be the heart of the entire text, representing Plato's "real" views on the topic of sublime Eros. The gist of her speech is familiar to many:

> [love] is begetting on a beautiful thing, by means of both the body and the soul .... But there are persons ... who in their souls still more than in their bodies ... conceive those things which are proper for the soul to conceive and bring forth; and what are those things? Prudence and virtue in general .... Everyone would choose to have got children such as these rather than the human sort.[11] (206b–209c)

To be sure, Diotima – who is described by Socrates as speaking "like the accomplished sophists" (208c) – is absent from the actual scene of Plato's dialogue, her polished rhetorical voice appropriated by the male philosopher. So too are Socrates and the other male speakers absent, in a sense: the entire account of the evening and its speeches is nested within another dialogue, a conversation between two men who were not present but who are discussing the event, many years after the fact. Yet, Plato appears to have granted the greatest authority and vividness to the rhetorical performance that is the most mediated – Apollodorus' revoicing of Aristodemus' revoicing of Socrates' revoicing of Diotima's speech. Indeed, Diotima's alien voice is arguably the most generative of all as it reverberates in the voices of all these Athenian men, and more.

David Halperin has framed the question memorably: "Why is Diotima a woman? Why did Plato select a woman to initiate Socrates into the mysteries of a male homoerotic desire?"[12] Halperin argues that Diotima's

---

[11] For Plato's *Symposium*, I follow the Greek edition and English translation of Lamb (ed. and trans.), *Plato*, 1925.
[12] Halperin, "Why Is Diotima a Woman?," 1990: 114.

femininity conveys a desire that is both excessive and procreative, characteristics that Plato turns to the service of a revised theory of male erotics, advocating the sublimated procreative potentialities of mutual and reciprocal love between men. In the end, then, the absent and possibly fictive figure of Diotima functions to erase the feminine via its masculine appropriation, Halperin suggests.[13] More recently, Daniel Boyarin has proposed that "Diotima has to be a woman ... in order to negate Aspasia and all that she means," that is to say, in order that philosophy should negate rhetoric, as embodied by the apparently more historically grounded figure of Aspasia, who is represented as Socrates' rhetoric teacher in the dialogue *Menexenus*.[14] On this reading – which seems to beg the question of why *Aspasia* is a woman (for Plato is no slave to historical "fact"), as well as why it takes a woman to negate a woman – Socrates' description of Diotima as a sophist is deemed either ironic or mistaken.[15] These two arguments – Halperin's and Boyarin's – are not necessarily incompatible. Yet, even in combination, they seem to me insufficient to explain Diotima's gender, either the why or the what of it.

Luce Irigaray is a reader particularly attuned to the distinctive tones of Diotima's voice, even as they are, to her ear, partly muffled by Socrates' own tones. Repeatedly, Diotima's voice, marking a sexual difference, "disappears" and "returns" in Socrates' speech, she suggests.[16] She notes explicitly that Diotima speaks "through her style, which *entwines* with what she says without *tying the knot*."[17] Style and meaning are in the closest relation, then, but they are not fused; together, they distinguish Diotima's voice. Irigaray herself revoices Diotima's speech: "Everything is always in movement, in a state of becoming. And the mediator of all of this is, among other things or exemplarily, *love*. Never fulfilled, always becoming."[18] This is recognizably Irigaray's voice, and it is also Diotima's: Diotima lends Irigaray her voice. Or is it the other way round? Yet Diotima has already lent Socrates her voice, and he hers; the two voices remain themselves entwined in any subsequent revoicing. Irigaray acknowledges as much as she closes her reading of the *Symposium*. Having distinguished between an initial Diotiman voice and a subsequent shift in tone toward the masculinist discourse of metaphysics in which transcendence is always the victor, she suddenly considers another possibility: "Unless what she [Diotima] proposes to contemplate, beauty itself, is seen as that which confounds the opposition between immanence and

---

[13] Ibid. [14] Boyarin, *Socrates*, 2009: 308. [15] Ibid.: 301. [16] Irigaray, *An Ethics*, 1993: 28.
[17] Ibid. [18] Ibid.: 21.

transcendence."[19] Here Socrates' and Diotima's voices become indistinguishable, though not identical. Or rather, voice itself emerges in the very transit across difference that also unsettles identity. "Everything is always in movement, in a state of becoming," as Irigaray has written. And as Mary Bloodsworth-Lugo points out, this movement between is mediated not only by Eros but also by Diotima herself. Specifically, "Diotima resides in-between male and female bodies and positions."[20]

Whether Socrates' ventriloquistic revoicing of Diotima's speech wins the day remains an open question, in the end, moreover. For just as he concludes his seemingly sober and ascetical discourse, a drunken and amorous Alcibiades crashes the party, dragging the flute-girl back in with him and bringing the wine as well; he delivers his own encomium not to Eros but to the ever-alluring Socrates – or, rather, to Socrates as Eros. Thus, Plato's dialogue finally both raises and leaves artfully suspended the question of the status of Diotima's discourse: it remains unclear how seriously we are to take *either* the argument for a purely sublimated desire *or* its attribution to a woman. Yet such sustained ambiguity itself conveys a message, namely, that talk about desire is necessarily disrupted by otherness, haunted by belatedness, and shadowed by the possibility of duplicity. Perhaps *that* is why Diotima is, if not precisely a woman, crucially also not exactly a man. In the speaking of desire, the voice of Socrates' prophetess, unstable and indeterminate in its gender and tone, is at once utterly distinct and eminently appropriable.

Centuries later, Plato's *Symposium* proved a generative work for the writers of the early Roman imperial period. Plutarch's (46–c. 119) *Erotic Dialogue* (c. 100), the *Dialogue on Loves* attributed (falsely) to Lucian (probably late second century), and Achilles Tatius' novel *Leucippe and Clitophon* (probably second century)[21] all restage the Platonic dinner party, even as they both adapt its genre and refocus its agenda. Neither women nor marriage figure significantly in Plato's *Symposium*, except in relation to the "pregnancy" that is merely "of the body" and thus to be transcended in an all-male love, according to the ambiguously female Diotima. However, in these later works, women are notable both for their *presence* as contested

---

[19] Ibid.: 33. [20] Bloodsworth-Lugo, *In-Between Bodies*, 2007: 34.
[21] The dating of Achilles Tatius' novel rests on papyrological evidence that indicates it was in circulation by the second century, perhaps by the early second century. See Henrichs, "Missing Pages," 2011: 302–322, especially 306–312. Thus, the novel may predate the *Acts of Thecla*, which was in circulation by the end of the second century; however, this is not crucial to my argument. There is general agreement that the *Acts of Thecla* plays with the conventions of romantic novels, of which Achilles Tatius' novel is one example.

objects of discourse and desire – do women or boys make better lovers? being the key question – and for their continuing *absence* as speakers. In Achilles Tatius' novel – "a Platonic pastiche," as Helen Morales names it[22] – the debate about love is enacted on a ship's deck over a breakfast shared among newly made acquaintances, all men. As the youthful narrator Clitophon relates: "I struck up a conversation aimed at erotic entertainment" (§ 2.35). He goes on immediately to remark, with regard to his girlfriend: "Leucippe was not, of course, present: she was sleeping below deck" (§ 2.35).[23] Clitophon's subsequent spirited defense of the love of women, as opposed to that of boys, reflects a level of sexual experience and explicitness in the telling that surprises even his male companions: "A woman's body is doughy when you embrace it, her lips soft when you kiss them. That is why she can hold her companion's body perfectly enfolded in her embraces, in her very flesh, and he is enveloped by pleasure," he recounts knowingly (§ 2.37). Clitophon's defense also raises serious questions as to the truthfulness of his prior claims of virginal fidelity in relation to Leucippe. Thus, Leucippe's sleeping ear is scarcely irrelevant to the reader's experience of the irony of this scene – nor is her potentially outraged voice.

Later in the novel, the girl will repeatedly defend her own virginity against increasingly violent attacks, demonstrating no lack of rhetorical skill or boldness. Given the choice of submitting to sexual violation or to torture, she declares:

> Prepare the tortures! Someone bring in the wheel and stretch my hands: here they are! Someone bring in the whips, too, and beat my back: here it is! Someone bring in fire and burn my body: here it is! Someone bring in a blade and slice up my skin: here it is! You will behold a novel kind of contest: one woman competes against all your tortures, and conquers them all! (§ 6.21)

The interplay between the framing narrative that focuses on Leucippe's vociferous defiance in the face of her many persecutions, on the one hand, and the embedded debate about desire from which she is excluded, on the other, raises questions not only about whether *masculine desire* can ultimately be harnessed to marriage (be it desire for women or for boys) but also about whether *female chastity* can. This latter question does not only arise from the acknowledgement that female chastity may *fall short* (Leucippe herself appears to have every intention of losing her virginity at the beginning of the novel, so here too there is irony). It arises as well from

---

[22] Morales, "Introduction," 2001: xx–xxi.
[23] For this novel, I follow the English translation of Whitmarsh (trans.), *Achilles Tatius*, 2001; and the Greek edition of Gaselee (ed. and trans.), *Achilles Tatius*, 1969.

the reader's growing suspicion that it may also *overshoot its mark*. When a girl's parentally guarded chastity becomes her own passionately defended virginity, it arguably begins to exceed the bounds, as well as the bonds, of patriarchal marriage. Indeed, virginity seems to open the possibility for the voicing of an active female desire – something representable in the men's breakfast symposium as no more than a titillating gasp. That desire begins (and may also end) as a desire for virginity itself. Leucippe addresses a would-be rapist passionately: "I am unarmed, alone, a woman: freedom is my only weapon, but it will not be battered by your blows, nor cut up by your knife, nor scorched by your fire. My freedom I will never renounce – not I! Even if you set it ablaze, you will find the fire is not hot enough" (§ 6.22).

Like Diotima's, Leucippe's voice necessarily emerges outside the framework of the debate about love. Does she not instruct the men, nonetheless, by her exemplary chastity, as Diotima once did? When Leucippe accuses Clitophon of infidelity, he protests (seemingly with only slight hypocrisy), "I have imitated your virginity, if there be a male equivalent of virginity" (§ 5.20); still later (and with increasing hypocrisy, since he has just consummated a sexual affair with the voluptuous Melite), he repeats, "If there be such a thing as virginity in a man, I have retained it up to the present day, as far as Leucippe is concerned" (§ 8.5). *Is* there such a thing as male virginity? *Can* a youth mimic the example of a maid? We rather suspect that the answer is no, not least because we, unlike Leucippe, have been able to listen in on the men's symposium. Yet a "straight" reading of the hetero-erotic plot of the novel, not unlike a monologic and Diotima-centered reading of Plato's symposium, seems to depend on the possibility that there *is* such a thing as male virginity, that the man *can* mimic the maid – and also (in the case of Tatius' novel) that the maid *will* marry. Here the destabilizing question is not only "Why is the central figure of the novel a woman?" but also "Why is that woman, Leucippe, (still) a virgin?" Of course, Leucippe does eventually marry, yet here as in other ancient novels, interest in the heroine's fiercely defended virginity eclipses interest in her status as bride.

Thecla: Acts and Dialogue

Thecla is Leucippe's Christian double.[24] Like Leucippe, she falls in love (with the apostle Paul) and leaves home with her beloved but is separated

---

[24] I explore parallels in Burrus, "Mimicking Virgins," 2005: 54–68.

and experiences persecutions, only ultimately to reunite with her beloved (at least briefly) and to return home (to preach the word of God). Crucial for our interests, Thecla, like Leucippe, finds her voice in confronting the threat of sexual violence. That voice does not emerge immediately, however. In the *Acts of Thecla*, we initially encounter the protagonist sitting silently in a window, listening raptly to Paul preaching. She ignores the pointed questions directed to her by her mother, her fiancé, and even the provincial governor: Why do you sit like this? Why will you not marry? Deaf to their threats and stubbornly mute as well, Thecla has ears for Paul alone and words for no one, it seems. It is only when she has been condemned to be burned at the stake that she finally speaks from the stage of the theater in Iconium. Her words remain oddly detached in relation to any possible audience, despite the public context: she seems almost to be speaking to herself, as she marvels, upon seeing Paul (or rather, one she takes to be Paul): "As if I am not enduring, Paul gazes upon me" (§ 3.21).

Subsequently, Thecla's voice begins to gain strength and force, however. Saved by a miracle, she addresses her god: "I thank you because you saved me, in order that I might see Paul" (§ 3.24). Taking matters into her own hands, or very nearly so, she tracks Paul down, announces her eschewal of feminine guise, and implores him to baptize her: "I will cut my hair and follow you wherever you should go .... Only give to me the seal in the Lord" (§ 3.25). Paul demurs, and Thecla subsequently claims the performative power of ritual speech for herself, in the midst of an arena where she is besieged by wild beasts. Leaping into a pool of water, she cries out: "In the name of Jesus Christ I baptize myself for the last day" (§ 4.9). Earlier she has confronted a would-be rapist. "Do not force the stranger! Do not force the servant of God. I am a leading woman of the Iconians" (§ 4.1). It is this vigorous resistance to sexual threat that causes her to be arrested and ultimately sentenced to the beasts. But she continues to speak with confident authority. Twice she beseeches her god on behalf of her patron Tryphaena, who has protected her virginity while she awaits trial: "Give to her according to her wish, in order that her daughter Falconilla might live forever" (§ 4.4). "Reward Tryphaena, the one who has sympathized with your slave" (§ 4.6). Her lengthiest and most powerful speech is delivered shortly after her self-baptism, when she has been released. Standing naked in front of the governor, who asks her why none of the beasts have harmed her, she declares: "I am a slave of the living God ... I have placed my trust in the one whom God blessed, namely, his son; on account of which not one of the beasts touched me" (§ 4.12). Thecla's is by now a recognizable voice, a voice that says "I am" – a voice that others will read and write.[25]

It may be this distinctive voice, together with her fame as a virgin and a disciple of Paul, that induces Methodius to give Thecla pride of place in his *Symposium*, a work modeled closely on its Platonic original.[26] Strikingly, Methodius feminizes the entire cast of characters, from the interlocutors in the framing dialogue, to the intermediary narrators, the hostess of the dinner party, and the ten maidens who present speeches in praise not of eros but of virginity – or rather of virginal eros. The transgendering of this symposium, although both an obvious feature and one commonly noted, seems to demand more extensive discussion than it has hitherto received. As Jason König has shown, Methodius deliberately mobilizes the agonistic potential of the dialogue form, using athletic imagery to call attention to the aspect of debate or controversy, while ultimately focusing attention on the internal struggle of the Christian against desire's temptation.[27] König acknowledges a degree of playfulness in Methodius' text. Yet, he does not address the potential irony that inheres in the fact that the athleticized rhetorical contenders that he notes Methodius deliberately mobilizes are here female. Adapting Halperin's question, we might ask, "why are Methodius' symposiasts *all* women, *nothing but* Diotimas, and, lacking, moreover, the fuller veiling of reported speech?"

The prologue mimics Plato's by featuring two characters, one of whom requests from the other an account of a symposium at which neither was present. However, there are significant divergences from the Platonic text as well. Intriguingly, Methodius seems to have cast himself as the virgin Eubolion, a feminine variation on the name "Eubolius" that he adopts elsewhere.[28] Whereas the interlocutors of Plato's *Symposium* meet on the road, Methodius' interlocutors converse in a domestic setting.

The questions debated by the virgins at Methodius' symposium both are and are not Plato's. Is an earthly or a heavenly spouse more desirable? Earthly or spiritual progeny? Is it better never to have felt physical desire or to have experienced it and transcended it? The first, and eldest, speaker is

---

[25] See Butler, *The Ancient Phonograph*, 2015: 37, 194–195, on voice as the call "I am."
[26] There is no sign that our author is familiar with other sympotic literature; see Bril, "Plato and the Sympotic Form," 2006: 280.
[27] König, "Sympotic Dialogue," 2008.
[28] I.e., in the treatise *On the Resurrection*. Epiphanius, *Panarion* 64.63, also reports that Methodius was "otherwise known as Eubolius." The manuscript tradition for the *Symposium* wobbles on the gender of Eubolion, introducing masculine adjectives and participles. It seems most likely that this is the result of attempts to "correct" Methodius' gender in the text. See Musurillo (trans.), *St. Methodius*, 1963: 3, 7, and 184.

Marcella, who asserts that virginity supersedes marriage in the providential history of salvation, elaborating a progression from sibling marriage, to exogamous polygamy, to adulterous monogamy, to chaste monogamy, to the purity of virginity. She associates the last with a state of physical incorruptibility, comparing it to salted, versus wormy and putrefying, meat. It is the incarnate Christ who inaugurates the age of virginity, as she explains. Marcella graciously cedes the floor to the next speaker, Theophila, who suggests, less graciously, that Marcella's argument needs not only completing but also correcting: "Her suggestion that henceforth humans are not to procreate is not well stated" (§ 2.1).[29] Theophila proceeds to argue at some length that procreative marriage remains a good thing, even if less good than virginity. She cites the example of Adam's ecstatic "birthing" of Eve from his side, recorded in the second chapter of Genesis, to argue that sexual desire and pleasure are God-given manifestations of the drive to conceive new life; indeed, she describes Adam's ecstasy in very explicit physiological terms as orgasmic:

> For under the stimulation of intercourse, the body's harmony... is greatly disturbed, and all the marrow-like generative part of the blood, which is liquid bone, gathers from all parts of the body, curdled and worked into a foam, and then rushes through the generative organs into the living soil of the woman.... For man made one with woman in the embrace of love is overcome by a desire for children and completely forgets everything else. (§ 2.2)

This might seem a curious discourse, placed in the mouth of a virginal woman, its matter-of-fact biologism notwithstanding, but Theophila explains herself: "So we are told by those who have consummated the rites of marriage" (§ 2.2). Even the children of adulterous unions are providentially conceived, since all procreation is the work of God, Theophila suggests further. At this point, an outraged Marcella interrupts her, but Theophila rallies to defend herself. As Methodius describes the agonistic moment: "Now Theophila, although grasped around the waist by a sturdy opponent in the arena, began to grow dizzy, and recovering herself with great difficulty she spoke" (§ 2.4). A third virgin, Thalia, subsequently questions Theophila's argument in support of marriage on different grounds, suggesting that Theophila has interpreted scripture in too strictly a literal sense: Adam is also, and indeed more properly, to be understood as a figure for Christ, his sexual ecstasy a figure for the ecstasy of Christ's

---

[29] For Methodius' *Symposium*, I follow the English translation of Musurillo (trans.), *St. Methodius: The Symposium*, 1958; and the Greek edition of Musurillo and Debidour (eds.), *Méthode d'Olympe*, 1963.

passion, in which he empties himself, sowing spiritual seed in his holy spouse, the Church, that collectivity of virgins who have received Christ's seminal Word, experienced his ecstasy, and given birth to his children. Images of ejaculatory climax merge with those of child-birth and are sublimated, much as in Diotima's speech; also similar to Diotima's speech, these are centered on the fecundity of *male* desire, albeit a desire that must be taught by a woman.[30] Or rather, by three women, in this case, yet not because they are all teaching the same thing. Here, the doctrine of virginity emerges both exegetically and agonistically as the product of mutually contested interpretive positions, and it remains therefore at least somewhat unstable. The symposiastic discourses that follow these are less explicitly contentious; however, they continue to expand and complicate the understanding of virginal eroticism.[31]

Thecla's speech, the eighth, opens with the virgin's declaration that she is "like a cithara inwardly attuned and prepared to speak with care and with grace and dignity" (§ 8.prol.). The cithara classically evokes poetic inspiration; it may stand in for soul or voice, understood as an instrument played by the god. Thecla understands herself to be a medium of divine voice, then. In closing her lengthy speech, she offers Arete "these gifts of mine woven as they are from god's own words" (§ 8.17); the shift to a textile metaphor now suggests that the divine words are scriptural ones. The god speaks through her because she revoices the divine word of scripture. And indeed, her discourse, like those of the other virgins, is highly citational and exegetical. Opening with a distinctly Platonic invocation of the winged soul, ascending toward the heavens, Thecla transitions smoothly to an extended reading of the heavenly woman depicted in Apocalypse 12:1–6, "a woman clothed with the sun, and the moon under her feet, and on her head a crown of twelve stars." Despite the fact that the woman gives birth to a son, Thecla identifies her as a virgin while also insisting that she is not Mary but the Church. "It is the Church that is in labor, and it is those who are washed in baptism who are brought forth" (§ 8.7). The Church may be a virgin but she can still be compared to a woman who "receives the unformed seed of her husband and after a period of time brings forth a perfect human being" (§ 8.6). Is Christ the husband, as in Thalia's speech? The sixth and seventh speeches, delivered by Agatha

---

[30] Ralph Norman, "Methodius and Methodologies," 2006, explores the centrality of male sexuality in Methodius' erotic imaginary.
[31] I here diverge from readers who see Methodius promoting a particular ascetic orthodoxy at the expense of other positions, e.g., "Encratism;" see Aspegren, *The Male Woman*, 1990: 144–164.

and Procilla, have also introduced bridal themes, exegetically grounded in the parable of the wise and foolish virgins (Matt 25:1–13) and the Song of Songs, respectively. Thecla, however, initially identifies Christ not as bridegroom or husband but as the collectivity of the Church's children. "And so it is that the Church is with child and labors until Christ is formed and born within us, so that each of the saints by sharing in Christ is born again as Christ" (§ 8.8). Perhaps Christ is the husband, as well, however. Thecla, for her part, is drawn to his virginal spouse. She depicts the Church as "the bride of the Word," nourished in "the lovely place of Virtue" (Arete) that is "difficult of access and hard for the majority to pass through." As such, the Church is a model for the virgins who gather flowers and weave a crown for their "queen" (§ 8.11) and "mother," with whom they will "enter joyously … into the bridal chamber" (§ 8.12).

Arete, who hosts the symposium, has already introduced Thecla as "second to none in [her] grasp of philosophy and universal culture" (§ 8. prol.); she later pronounces her the winner in the "contest of words." All ten virgins receive victory crowns, but Thecla receives a larger one, "for she has been [their] leader and has shone more magnificently than the rest" (§ 11). At Arete's prompting, Thecla continues to lead the virgins, now in song. While Arete stands on her right, the other virgins circle her, their queen and mother, joining as a chorus in singing a refrain that ends with the line: "My spouse, I go forth to meet you." The refrain is repeated twenty-five times, as the virgins performatively appropriate the voice of Thecla, bride of Christ.

An Act to Follow Thecla's: Helia

Like Methodius' work, the *Life of Helia*, whose date and place of composition are unknown,[32] offers a rare instance of a full-scale dialogue staging a Christian debate about desire: Is marriage or virginity better? An earthly or a heavenly lover? Also, like Methodius' work, it does so in the voices of women. However, far more than Methodius' *Symposium*, the *Life of Helia* is a controversial or polemical dialogue, set within a novelistic narrative in which Helia's virginity is under attack. More a Leucippe than a Diotima, Helia takes the witness stand in passionately defiant defense of her virginity. Here, the *Life* leans heavily on the narrative structure of the *Acts of Thecla* to position and frame Helia's voice.

---

[32] Perhaps fifth-century Spain? See Burrus and Conti (eds. and trans.), *The Life of Saint Helia*, 2014: 15–46.

The rhetorical character of the work is emphasized from the first sentence, as the prologue opens with a nod to pedagogical tradition: "In former times it was the custom of teachers first to establish the boys' talents through exercises in rhetorical narration, so that they might later be able to defend the interests of their clients more skillfully" (prol.2–4). The author of the Life is still learning basic skills, like a boy in a rhetorician's classroom, he thereby implies. However, rather than a mock role play, as would have been appropriate, he has been assigned a serious defense: "You entrust the narration of spiritual achievements to one whose inexperience you would not have put to the test even while in playful studies!" he protests to his addressee, the priest Macedonius (prol.5–8). Thus, the line is both drawn and blurred between a rhetorical exercise involving the recitation of a possibly fictional tale, expanded with plausible dialogue, and the requested composition of "the life of Helia, the most blessed virgin of Christ, arranging from the beginning in an orderly sequence," a task imbued with the full gravity of forensic oratory (prol.9–10). The burden of the prologue is the author's argument for his abject inadequacy as the narrator of Helia's *Life*, a problem resolved through expressions of filial piety: his "father" has asked this of him, and a child owes obedience to a parent who has long prepared him for just such a moment and who will continue to encourage his effort. Having been called upon to perform, despite his reluctance, our narrator will now obediently unfold his plot; he will place speeches in the mouths of his characters.

That plot follows the *Acts of Thecla* at crucial points, while adapting the narrative to a different context.[33] Helia, who is both beautiful and nobly born, develops a passion for ascetic life but is left to struggle with her passions on her own, lacking the guidance of text or teacher. By providential design, an itinerant ascetic presbyter arrives and begins to lecture publicly on the scriptures. Hearing him through a window, as Thecla hears the apostle Paul, Helia approaches the presbyter for instruction, and, under his direction, her ascetic practice flourishes – as does, apparently, her scriptural acumen. Her mother, like Thecla's, is displeased, to put it mildly. "Inflamed by the torches of rage, she abused the girl with thunderous words: 'Why,' she asked, 'do you oppose the doctrine of your fathers and follow a new superstition?'" (§ 1.88–89). This is the opening salvo in the debate between the girl and her mother, which takes up more than half of the *Life*. At the end of that lengthy exchange, the mother is described as abusing the girl physically as well as verbally, beating her

[33] As discussed by Burrus and Conti (eds. and trans.), *The Life of Saint Helia*, 2014: 49–53.

mercilessly and depriving her of warm clothes in the winter, hoping to cool her ardor. At the urging of the presbyter, Helia flees from her mother's house, dressed like a man (here too imitating Thecla's example),[34] having bribed the portress (just as Thecla bribed a porter). Seeking support from the local bishop, she gives a rousing speech that wins her the sympathy of her audience. However, when the bishop attempts to intervene with the mother on behalf of the girl, the mother is unpersuaded, demanding that her daughter be brought before a judge to declare publicly what is in her vows – the implication being that these vows will be found unlawful. The plot thickens: first Helia's mother lays plans for the judge to abduct the girl and force her to marry him when she is summoned to the tribunal; then her paternal aunt, learning of those plans, gathers a peasant army to intimidate the judge and prevent the abduction. The judge, thus partly thwarted, subjects the girl to an extremely hostile interrogation, nonetheless. She easily holds her own in this public contest of oratory in which the *Life of Helia* remains suspended. The dialogue concludes with Helia pronouncing "Amen" to her own speech on the witness stand. Her exultant testimony thus finally undoes the linearity of plot. It also dissolves the distancing framework insinuated by the prologue. By this point, the obediently confabulating boy in the rhetorician's classroom has very nearly fused his voice with that of the defiant girl.

The initial debate between mother and daughter is structured in two parts: the first is a battle of scriptural *exempla*, the second a series of arguments about scriptural commands. From the beginning, the mother attempts to position her daughter as a sophist, in the most pejorative sense: "It is far from surprising," she notes, addressing Helia,

> if the evasiveness of your arguments and the tortuous circumlocution of your words should cause contradictions of truth and present questions more deceptively, since the order of the discussion has been destroyed. One must make one's case in a few words and speak with extreme brevity, so that the cunning subtlety of disputation, established by its very groundlessness, cannot wander about, fleeing here and there. Respond if you can to challenges made quickly and briefly. You will either support marriage or condemn it. (§ 1.131–136)

Repeatedly, the mother accuses Helia of evasiveness, duplicity, and empty verbosity. Repeatedly, she tries to shift the terms of the debate by simplifying or restricting the subject matter. Near the end of their lengthy

---

[34] See Julie Van Pelt's contribution in this volume (Chapter 7) for more.

exchange, she states: "Since I am insufficiently educated in the words of the *lectio divina* and cannot recount the narrative of holy scripture, I will cite only one example, so that all the keenness of your rapid style may be weakened .... 'Children, obey your parents' [Eph. 6:1]" (§ 2.190–194). To this, Helia replies condescendingly: "Any aspect of the reading, when it is not recapitulated in its entirety, confounds and fogs the intellect. Since the sharpness of your mind is blunted, your incomplete argument augments the shadows of your depraved intelligence. For when the apostle said, 'Children, obey your parents,' he added, 'in the Lord' [Eph. 6:1], which you have omitted." Proceeding to explain the passage in context, Helia concludes her rejoinder with a citational flourish: "'Those who said to their father and mother, we do not know you, these have observed your commands' [Deut. 33:9]" (§ 2.196–204). Typically, Helia appeals not merely to the authority of the Bible but also to the authority of biblical scholarship. As the debate progresses, the girl's tone becomes ever more confident and patronizing, as she practices what she preaches with regard to hermeneutics, delivering one inventively intertextual exegetical discourse after another, with scarcely a pause for breath.

The question of whether virginity or marriage is to be preferred is pursued with focused passion throughout the mother-daughter debate. It reaches a certain peak of intensity in a discourse delivered by Helia, in which she elaborates a supersessionist salvation history already familiar to us in basic outline from Methodius but with emphasis not on development but on contrast:

> Marriage is made known in Adam, virginity in Christ. Marriage generated a murderer, virginity a Savior. Marriage gave birth in pain; virginity brought forth the Redeemer in blessing. Eve generates amidst thorns, Mary in the house of bread... Eve gives birth in low places, Mary on the mountains [cf. Ps. 71(72):16] .... In Eve's childbirth, pains and groans are increased; in the Virgin's childbirth, the hosts of the angels are gathered. There groans; here joy .... There the earth brought forth brambles; here it produces the Savior. There the condemnation of the entire world occurred, but in the childbirth of the Virgin there is redemption for the whole world. Eve is frightened by the flaming sword; Mary is protected by the coming of the Holy Spirit. Adam endures thorns; the Lord Jesus Christ is flower and lily [cf. Song 2:1–2]. Then it was said: "It is not good that humans should be so" [Gen 2:18], now it is said: "It is good for humans to be so" [1 Cor 7:26]. (§ 2.137–150)

Helia's positive understanding of virginal eroticism unfolds most richly, however, in her self-defense before the judge, when the threat of violence is even more intense. Now, having been commanded to marry, she refuses the binary of marriage and virginity, instead emphasizing virginity as a marital erotic choice. "Allow me to have as a husband the one whom I myself will choose," she demands of the judge, citing a Pauline dictum (§ 3.34–35; cf. 1 Cor 7:39). Indeed, she insists that she already has a husband and that she not only has children but that she gives birth every day, without pain and torment, lengthy pregnancy, or the squalling of infants. With regard to her virginal body, she proclaims to the judge, "And may you be amazed that, as much as it remains whole to the touch, so abundantly does it bring forth multitudes of spiritual children" (§ 3.108–110). Who will touch that wholeness? Her spouse Christ and none other. "Who does not desire to hang on *his* kisses?" she demands. "Who does not strive to cling to *his* embraces?" (§ 3.113–114). She goes on to describe her husband's many attractions (he is beautiful, wealthy, wise, humble – and very strong), concluding: "If anyone described such a man to women, I believe that they would abandon their husbands and desire eagerly to live with him! But what those women would get to enjoy illegally, I already possess lawfully." She insinuates that her auditors are envious of her: "Do you perhaps want to become his spouses too?" (§ 3.122–125). Her own imagined erotic body merges with the natural world. Artfully weaving together imagery from the Song of Songs and the gospel parable of the sower (cf. Matt 13:1–23), Helia describes her virginity as the flowering of a meadow that returns a hundredfold. Her body is a field set high in the soaring mountains "where the Lord our God always visits" (Deut 11:11–12), fruitful beyond imagination, neither sown nor irrigated by mortal men but touched only by the dew of heaven. "Why do you want to make me an exile from that soil?" she demands (§ 3.194). "Why do you hold me off from Christ's embraces?" (§ 3.234).

Faced with such poetic overflow of scriptural imagery, the judge continues to respond with stern brevity. When Paul said that "a woman is only saved through the generation of children," he meant just that, he insists (§ 3.274–275; cf. 1 Tim 2:15). Helia merely sighs at his limited hermeneutical capacities. The apostle references Eve in the same passage; yet everyone knows that child-bearing does not save Eve but rather comes as a curse, she patiently explains. The scripture thus cannot be interpreted literally. Moreover, Paul only says that a woman will be saved by the generation of children "if she remains in faith and devotion and holiness with sobriety" (§ 3.302–304; cf. 1 Tim 2:15). Clearly, here, woman is a figure for the soul, as is often the case in scripture. Souls will be saved when all their fruits are steady in faith and devotion: that is the meaning of the passage, Helia states firmly. And at this point, having expanded the figure of female virginity to include all the faithful, she proclaims her "Amen!"

A Speech to Follow Thecla's: Constantina

Like the *Life of Helia*, the *Life of Constantina* (whose provenance is also unknown)[35] is a generically hybrid text that features an extended dialogue. The narrative focuses not on a mother-daughter relationship but on a father-daughter one, and that relationship is loving rather than hostile. Yet, here, too, the daughter has the upper hand even as she faces adversity. The threat to her virginity comes in the guise of a powerful suitor whom Constantine hesitates to refuse, although he acknowledges that his daughter would rather die than marry. The tense situation never reaches a crisis, however. Like the Thecla of the *Acts*, Constantina prays to her god for deliverance. In the end, it is as much through her own cleverness as through divine intervention that her virginity is preserved. By the time she faces Gallicanus, her erstwhile fiancé has converted to a life of Christian asceticism under the influence of servants whom she has placed in his retinue, and she has turned her house into a convent of virgins among whom Gallicanus' own daughters number. Thus, although the plot of the *Life* initially turns on virginity endangered and defended, Constantina does not ultimately find her voice in defiant resistance to rape or torture. Rather, she emerges as a speaker in the competitive give and take of a banquet of words. In this she follows Methodius' Thecla. At the same time, Constantina's voice arguably claims an even more singular authority than that of her predecessor, in part due to the hagiographical tendency to focus on a single figure, and in this case an imperial one. She does not merely deliver the winning speech on the virtues of virginity. She also hosts the party, playing Thecla and Arete at once.

Staging speeches on virginal love, Constantina's symposium also embodies such love. As we have seen, Methodius' Thecla rushes toward her heavenly groom in the company of nine other virgins who encircle her like bridesmaids, joining their voices to hers. Constantina's erotic orientation is even queerer than that. Plato's Socrates may play it cool with Alcibiades, but Constantina does not suppress the heat of her passion for

---

[35] Given its dependence on the *Acts of Roman Martyrs* (*Gesta martyrum romanorum*), among other factors, a mid-sixth-century date seems plausible; given its downplaying of distinctly Roman elements, together with its interest in monastic life, a female monastic setting outside of Rome, perhaps in Gaul, seems plausible. See Conti, Burrus, and Trout (eds. and trans.), *The Lives of Saint Constantina*, 2020: 16–25.

her virginal disciples. She desires their bodily presence, and she desires their words; she wants to give them voice. But they also give her voice. Their speech provides the pretext for her own.

Methodius' Arete gazes upon her guests "with great joy as though she were a mother seeing her children after a long separation" (prol.). She embraces and kisses each one in greeting. Once they have eaten, she asks: "What do you suppose I wish and look forward to? That each of you deliver a panegyric on virginity" (prol.). As we have seen, the ten virgins then speak obediently, with Arete responding at the end and declaring Thecla, the eighth speaker, the victor among victors. Constantina, for her part, gathers not just ten but "a multitude of virgins," numbering roughly 120, we are told, and she hosts them for three full days, wooing them with gifts and the intimacy of shared meals, conversation, and affection, and "kissing them as her sisters" (§ 1.9). The girls are said to be "so intimate with her that they were like her *cubiculariae*," that is, the slaves who attend her in her bedroom (§ 1.10). At the end of the three days, she sends them home with an assignment, namely, to "write down their personal opinions about 'the highest good' and 'the ultimate evil'" and present these views to her as a gift in five days (§ 1.9). While the virgins are away, they are overwhelmed with desire, and the period of waiting seems like a year. When they return, "united ... in their love for the Augusta," 12 of the 120 are called upon to deliver their prepared speeches (§ 1.10). At the request of the first speaker, Constantina responds to each of them in turn, so that they may more fully understand what they themselves have written, as the girl explains it. Constantina amplifies the virgins' voices, then, bringing them to mature expression. In this manner, the girls' brief speeches, interspersed with Constantina's increasingly lengthy responses, stretch out across two days. And regardless of how her charges state their opinions on the highest good (*summum bonum*) – law, life, a good conscience, peace, knowledge, simplicity – Constantina's interpretative responses demonstrate conclusively that the highest good is always identical with virginity.

Among the differences that emerge when we compare the dialogues of Methodius' *Symposium* and of the *Life of Constantina* is the shift from oral to written discourse, albeit one orally performed. The virgins are initially asked to write their statements (*sententiae*), and we are repeatedly reminded that they are not only speaking but also reading. Constantina extemporizes but she does so exegetically, in relation to written texts, both the virgins' own and the Christian scripture. Citation allows her to appropriate other voices, then, voices that echo through hers. With respect to scripture, this is also the case for Methodius' virgins, as for Helia, of course. Another shift is from a maternal to a sisterly intimacy, conjoined with a heightened eroticism in the relationship of the hostess to her guests – guests who in Constantina's case will, in the end, have committed to a permanent sleep-over. Arete is hostess, teacher, and mother. Constantina is hostess, teacher, and lover. She is also, like Methodius' Thecla, the winning voice in the rhetorical contest: when she finishes her closing discourse, following the twelfth virgin's statement, "a shout of acclamation rang out and with spiritual joy they decreed the full completion of her victory" (§ 1.25). The virgins, it seems, *want* Constantina to dominate the symposium, as indeed she has. But all of them have found their voices.

Girls with No Doors on Their Mouths

From an ancient perspective, rationally articulated speech or *logos* distinguishes the human from the nonhuman; tellingly, it also separates real men from others. Women make *sounds*, often wild and uncontrolled – they shriek, weep, or wail, for example – but they do not make *sense*. They are unable to guard their tongues any more than they can guard their chastity. Noisy but not articulate, incapable of self-regulation, they are vocal but lack full voice. In *Philoctetes*, Sophocles refers to the nymph Echo as "the girl with no door on her mouth."[36] "Putting a door on the female mouth has been an important project of patriarchal culture from antiquity to the present day," observes Anne Carson, in an essay entitled "The Gender of Sound."[37]

What, then, are we to make of the voluble virgins of late antiquity and beyond – Thecla and those who follow her? Helia and Constantina, for example. How does the virgin come to voice? What does that voice sound like? What is the gender of its sound? Virginal speech, I have suggested, emerges under duress, in the face of violent threat. It emerges in crisis, a crisis that is both ameliorated and intensified by the impossible event of a girl claiming voice in debates about desire. But it also emerges, therefore, in the give and take of dialogue. Virginal voice is, moreover, a voice always becoming, always a surprise, always in transition, always *in-between* – animal-human, child-adult, divine-creaturely, female-male. It is both sound – shrieking, weeping, or wailing, for example – and sense, both emotion and reason, excessive and measured at once. It is written and it is read and thus also spoken – ever ready to be re-voiced.

[36] Sophocles, *Philoctetes* 188. [37] Carson, "The Gender of Sound," 1995: 121.

Indeed, any reader can hope to appropriate the voice of the virgin, borrowing its impossible fecundity; yet the virgin's voice may also prove to be precisely the one that cannot simply be mimicked or borrowed. When the virgin speaks, it is always a new beginning, something utterly singular. Then again, the virgin has always been speaking, at least since Diotima. Her speech is an echoing chorus. *It is all the voices.*

Bibliography

Aspegren, Kerstin. *The Male Woman: A Feminine Ideal in the Early Church*. Acta Universitatis Upsaliensis/Uppsala Women's Studies 4. Uppsala; Stockholm: Almqvist and Wiksell International, 1990.

Barrier, Jeremy W. *The Acts of Paul and Thecla: A Critical Introduction and Commentary*. WUNT 2.270. Tübingen: Mohr Siebeck, 2009.

Bloodsworth-Lugo, Mary K. *In-Between Bodies: Sexual Difference, Race, and Sexuality*. Albany: State University of New York Press, 2007.

Boyarin, Daniel. *Socrates and the Fat Rabbis*. Chicago: University of Chicago Press, 2009.

Bril, Alexander. "Plato and the Sympotic Form in the *Symposium* of St. Methodius of Olympus." *Zeitschrift für Antike und Christentum* 9 (2006): 279–302.

Burrus, Virginia. "Mimicking Virgins: Colonial Ambivalence and the Ancient Romance." *Arethusa* 38, no. 1 (2005): 49–88.

Burrus, Virginia, and Marco Conti, eds. and trans. *The Life of Saint Helia: Edition, Translation, Introduction, and Commentary*. Oxford: Oxford University Press, 2014.

Butler, Shane. *The Ancient Phonograph*. Brooklyn: Zone Books, 2015.

Carson, Anne. "The Gender of Sound." In *Glass, Irony, and God*. New York: New Directions, 1995: 119–142.

Conti, Marco, Virginia Burrus, and Dennis Trout, eds. and trans. *The Lives of Constantina*. Oxford: Oxford University Press, 2020.

Gaselee, Stephen, trans. *Achilles Tatius: Leucippe and Clitophon*. Loeb Classical Library. Cambridge, MA: Harvard University Press, 1969.

Gleason, Maud W. *Making Men: Sophists and Self-Presentation in Ancient Rome*. Princeton: Princeton University Press, 1995.

Halperin, David M. "Why Is Diotima a Woman? Platonic Ερως and the Figuration of Gender." In *Before Sexuality: The Construction of Erotic Experience in the Ancient Greek World*, edited by David Halperin, Jack Winkler, and Froma Zeitlin. Princeton: Princeton University Press, 1990: 257–308.

Henrichs, Albert. "Missing Pages: Papyrology, Genre, and the Greek novel." In *Culture in Pieces: Essays on Ancient Texts in Honour of Peter Parsons*, edited by Dirk Obbink and Richard Rutherford. Oxford: Oxford University Press, 2011: 302–322.

Irigaray, Luce. *An Ethics of Sexual Difference*. Translated by Carolyn Burke and Gillian C. Gill. Ithaca: Cornell University Press, 1993.
Jarratt, Susan. *Rereading the Sophists: Classical Rhetoric Refigured*. Carbondale: Southern Illinois University Press, 1998.
Jarratt, Susan, and Rory Ong. "Aspasia: Rhetoric, Gender, and Colonial Ideology." In *Reclaiming Rhetorica: Women in the Rhetorical Tradition*, edited by Andrea A. Lunsford. Pittsburgh: University of Pittsburgh Press, 1995: 9–24.
König, Jason. "Sympotic Dialogue in the First to Fifth Centuries C.E." In *The End of Dialogue in Antiquity*, edited by Simon Goldhill. Cambridge: Cambridge University Press, 2008: 85–113.
Lamb, Walter R. M., ed. and trans. *Plato: Lysis, Symposium, Gorgias*. Loeb Classical Library. Cambridge, MA: Harvard University Press, 1925.
Morales, Helen. "Introduction." In *Achilles Tatius: Leucippe and Clitophon*, translated by Tim Whitmarsh. Oxford: Oxford University Press, 2001: vii–xxxv.
Musurillo, Herbert, trans. *St. Methodius: The Symposium: A Treatise on Chastity*. Ancient Christian Writers 27. London: Longmans, Green and Co., 1958.
Musurillo, Herbert, and Victor-Henry Debidour, eds. *Méthode d'Olympe: Le Banquet*. Sources Chrétiennes 95. Paris: Les Éditions du Cerf, 1963.
Norman, Ralph. "Methodius and Methodologies: Ways of Reading Third-Century Christian Sexual Symbolism." *Theology and Sexuality* 13, no. 1 (2006): 79–100.
Salisbury, Joyce. *Church Fathers, Independent Virgins*. London: Verso, 1991.
Swearingen, C. Jan. "A Lover's Discourse: Diotima, Logos, and Desire." In *Reclaiming Rhetorica: Women in the Rhetorical Tradition*, edited by Andrea A. Lunsford. Pittsburgh: University of Pittsburgh Press, 1995: 25–51.
Whitmarsh, Tim, trans. *Achilles Tatius: Clitophon and Leucippe*. Oxford: Oxford University Press, 2001.

CHAPTER 9

Reception and Rejection
Thecla and the Acts of Paul and Thecla in the Passion of Eugenia and Other Latin Texts

*Klazina Staat**

Introduction

How is Thecla received in late antique and early medieval Latin hagiography?[1] The question may be answered only partially since there are numerous texts that still await detailed scholarly analyses and from different perspectives. My contribution to this volume and, thus, to the field of Latin literature will be to examine the reception of Thecla and the Latin translation of the apocryphal *Acts of Paul and Thecla* (henceforth *APT*) in two Latin versions of the *Passion of Eugenia*. The first version of the *Passion* is *BHL* 2667, also called "M" after Bonino Mombritius' early edition of the text. It was probably composed in Rome in the second half of the fifth century and seems to lie at the basis of the Greek translation (*BHG* 607w, 608b).[2] The second is the later rewriting, *BHL* 2666 or "R," which was

---

* This chapter was written at Ghent University with the support of the ERC Starting Grant *Novel Saints: Ancient Novelistic Heroism in the Hagiography of Late Antiquity and the Early Middle Ages* (Grant Agreement 337344) and a junior postdoctoral grant by the Flemish Research Council-FWO (Grant Agreement 1232820N). I thank the editors of this volume for their insightful comments and suggestions.

[1] Several publications focus on the reception of Thecla in early Christian literature. The most comprehensive overview of this topic can be found in Tommasi Moreschini, "Thecla in the Latin Sources," 2017. For Latin and Greek sources, see Hayne, "Thecla and the Church Fathers," 1994; Pesthy, "Thecla among the Church Fathers," 1996; Castelli, *Martyrdom and Memory*, 2004: 143–146; and Hylen, *A Modest Apostle*, 2015: 91–113, including a useful bibliography in nn. 1–4 on pp. 146–147.

[2] There is still no other edition of the text than Mombritius' fifteenth-century one, which is reprinted in Mombritius (ed.), "Passio Eugeniae," 1910 and is used in this chapter. The translation is taken from Lapidge (trans.), *The Roman Martyrs*, 2018: 233–249 (which also provides the paragraph subdivision followed in this article). Lapidge gives further discussion on the *Passion* on pp. 228–232. See Whatley, "Eugenia before Ælfric," 2008; and "Textual Hybrids," 2011, for variant readings in the various manuscripts of the *Passion* and Lanéry, "Les Passions latines," 2010: 134–135, for its dating. The interconnection between the Latin and Greek versions has been the topic of scholarly debate, which has now been settled in favor of the former: see Lanéry, "Les Passions latines," 2010: 130–132, for further references. Nevertheless, the Latin variant may not be the first version of the *Passion* ever written. According to Apserou, "Το αγιολογικό dossier," 2017: 124–125, both the Greek and Latin variants go back to another source, perhaps in Syriac (i.e., *BHO* 282).

first edited in Heribert Rosweyde's *Vitae Patrum* and probably appeared after the M version in the sixth or seventh century.[3] As earlier scholarship has noted, these texts are insightful for the reception of Thecla in Latin hagiography since they are inspired by the *APT* in terms of theme, story line, and language. However, the two versions of the *Passion* are remarkably different in their use of the *APT*.[4] In the first *Passion*, Eugenia is converted after she has read a copy of one of the letters of Paul as well as the *APT*:

> When through her devotion to chastity she had resisted many others seeking her hand, there came into her hands a copy of the letter of St Paul and the story of the virgin Thecla (*peruenit ad manus eius beati Pauli Apostoli epistola et uirginis Teclae historia*); reading it secretly every day, she wept; and although she was the child of purely pagan parents, she began to become Christian in her heart. And when she had daily turned over in her mind by what means she might gain access to Christian teaching, she sought permission from her parents to depart from the city for their country villa.[5]

During her journey, the hagiographer states that Eugenia "was turning over in her mind the story of Thecla (*eventum Teclae uirginis*), which she was reading in the sedan chair."[6] The rewritten version, meanwhile, omits these explicit references to the *APT*. In fact, the rewritten version states that Eugenia is converted after reading "the doctrine of the blessed apostle Paul."[7] It also removes the description of Eugenia reading Thecla's story in the sedan chair after her escape from home.

Generally, scholarship has mainly focused on the function of Thecla as a model of virtue in late antique and medieval literature.[8] Following the

---

[3] Rosweyde, *Vitae Patrum*, 1615: 340–349, reprinted in *PL* 21.1105–1122 and *PL* 73.605–624. I use the edition in *PL* 73, which according to Whatley, "Textual Hybrids," 2011: 33 n. 4, contains less errors. The translations are my own. For the interconnections between the M and R versions of the *Passion*, see Delehaye, *Étude*, 1936: 177–180; Whatley, "Eugenia before Ælfric," 2008; and Whatley, "Textual Hybrids," 2011; and Lanéry, "Les Passions latines," 2010: 132–135. Scholars now agree that M is the older version of the *Passion*. See Delehaye, *Étude*, 1936: 177–180; and Lanéry, "Les Passions latines," 2010: 132–135. For the dating of M, see Lanéry "Les Passions latines," 2010: 135.

[4] Delehaye, *Étude*, 1936: 175–178. For later discussions, see Whatley, "Textual Hybrids," 2011; Cooper, "Virgin as Social Icon," 2005: 19, following the unpublished master's thesis of Jones, *The Passio of Eugenia*, 1998; and Apserou, "Το αγιολογικό dossier," 2017: 228–244.

[5] *Passion* M § 1: Lapidge (trans.), *The Roman Martyrs*, 2018: 233–234; and Mombritius (ed.), "Passio Eugeniae," 1910: 391, 41–46.

[6] *Passion* M § 2: Lapidge (trans.), *The Roman Martyrs*, 2018: 234; and Mombritius (ed.), "Passio Eugeniae," 1910: 391, 46–47.

[7] *Passion* R § 2: *PL* 73.607B.

[8] Cooper, "Virgin as Social Icon," 2005: 19; and Hylen, *A Modest Apostle*, 2015: 91–113, for example, note the lasting importance of Thecla as an exemplary model in late antique Christian literature. Castelli, *Martyrdom and Memory*, 2004: 144, argues that the figure of Thecla is "domesticated" in literature after the *APT* in order to make her more orthodox and a morally acceptable example of

work of Hannah Jones, Kate Cooper takes the issue a step further to argue that the explanation for the changing reception of the *APT* in the later *Passion* should be sought in the figure of Thecla, who

> was a controversial figure in the early Church, because at the end of the tale, the Apostle exhorts her to "go and preach the word of God," thus obviating his own injunction, in 1 Corinthians 11.2–16, that women should not teach, but should remain silent in the churches.[9]

Cooper continues by noting that the omitted references to the *APT* is "presumably on account of the fluctuating esteem in which the text was held."[10] She refers to the fact that a second-century group of religious women used the text to legitimate their right to teach and baptize, which Tertullian (b. c. 155) criticized in his *On Baptism* (c. 203):

> But if certain *Acts of Paul*, which are falsely so named, claim the example of Thecla for allowing women to teach and to baptize, let men know that in Asia the presbyter who compiled that document, thinking to add of his own to Paul's reputation, was found out, and though he professed he had done it for love of Paul, was deposed from his position. How could we believe that Paul should give a female power to teach and to baptize, when he did not allow a woman even to learn by her own right? Let them keep silence, he says, and ask their husbands at home.[11]

Even though the clash between Tertullian and the women, who were teaching and baptizing, may explain the "fluctuating esteem" of the *APT*, it did not prevent Thecla from becoming a model of virtue in late antique Christianity as Cooper argues:

> Clear historical evidence attests that from the fourth century at the latest, historical women were being advised to study the example of Thecla, and to model their own spiritual lives accordingly.[12]

She uses Eugenia, as she is portrayed in *BHL* 2667, as an example of such a woman who models her life on Thecla.[13] In other words, thus, what is at

---

virtue. See also Hayne, "Thecla and the Church Fathers," 1994; and Pesthy, "Thecla among the Church Fathers," 1996: 168, 175–177, who argue that later writings on Thecla increase her orthodoxy. Hylen, *A Modest Apostle*, 2015: 91–92, gives a general overview and critical evaluation of these trends in scholarship, which was prevalent in feminist studies in particular. Barrier, *The Acts of Paul and Thecla*, 2009: 45–47, provides a discussion of feminist criticisms of the *Acts of Paul and Thecla*.

[9] Cooper, "Virgin as Social Icon," 2005: 19.   [10] Ibid.
[11] Tertullian, *de Baptismo* 17: Evans (ed. and trans.), *Tertullian's Homily*, 1964: 37. On this passage, see also Jeremy Barrier's contribution in this volume (Chapter 1).
[12] Cooper, "Virgin as Social Icon," 2005: 19.   [13] Ibid.: 18–23.

stake is not the problematic authority of Thecla as a figure but rather the authority of the *APT* as a text.

Expanding on Cooper's work and to provide wider context for the changing reception of the *APT* in the Passions, I first will retrace the reception of Thecla and the rejection of the *APT* in a few key Latin texts written by prominent Christian authors that are exemplary of this paradoxical attitude. From this position, I then extrapolate the debates in the early Church concerning the status of the *APT*, which were officially condemned (together with many other Acts of the Apostles) as apocryphal in the sixth-century *Pseudo-Gelasian Decree*. Subsequently, I turn to the two versions of the *Passion* to explore their creative engagement with Thecla as a figure and the *APT* as a text, specifically through rhetoric. By focusing on rhetoric, I hope to illustrate the Passions' creative reception of Thecla as a model: the Passions do not simply imitate and take Thecla as an exemplar for Eugenia, they also *emulate* (surpass) Thecla. Furthermore, I illustrate that even if the later *Passion* does not mention Thecla or the *APT* directly as the earlier version does, nevertheless, it indirectly evokes Thecla as an ideal model. In the analysis, I will turn to materials related to Thecla's cult and prayers invoking the heroine, which corroborate the extents to which the later *Passion* engages with the heroic figure even while it simultaneously attempts to obliterate the *APT* as an intertext.[14]

Thecla as an Accepted Model and the *APT* as a Problematic Text

Early Christian Latin literature conveys a paradox: Thecla is presented as a symbol and model of virtue, while the *APT* is rejected – sometimes by the same author. To be sure, this is not the case for Tertullian, the earliest author writing in Latin that we know of who mentions the *APT* and who famously disapproves of it. Tertullian uses the problematic authority of the *APT* as the argument to discard Thecla as a role model for women.[15] Accordingly, the problem is that it is written by an author who was not

---

[14] I will use the Latin translation of the *APT*, which, according to Willy Rordorf, "Sainte Thècle," 1986: 439–441, was perhaps already extant in the West in the fourth century and thus may have been known to the author of the Latin *Passion of Eugenia*. The Latin *APT* was transmitted in various versions, some of which have been edited in von Gebhardt (ed.), *Passio S. Theclae Virginis*, 1902. Much work still needs to be done to consider their interconnections and dates of composition. I use the A version of the Latin *APT* as it was recently edited in Kaestli and Poupon (eds.), "Les Actes de Paul et Thècle," 2016: 28–109. Scholars usually focus on the Greek *APT*, but this may change now that the edition by Kaestli and Poupon has recently appeared. Translations of the *APT* are my own.

[15] For more on the reception of Thecla and the *APT* in Tertullian, see Jeremy Barrier's contribution in this volume (Chapter 1). See also Tommasi Moreschini, "Thecla in the Latin Sources," 2017: 78.

allowed to write such a text. This point of view may be seen as part of a wider tendency in the gradual constitution of the biblical canon to discard some texts that recount the adventures of the apostles as "apocryphal" due to their supposedly uncertain authorship or to the fact that their contents are claimed as containing lies and falsehoods or that they were used in schismatic and heretic circles.[16]

While Tertullian's claim about the problematic canonicity of the *APT* reappears in later literature, it seems that he stands alone in his criticism of Thecla *as a model*. At the end of the fourth century, for instance, Jerome (d. 420) adopts Tertullian's claim about the dubious authority of the *APT* but adduces a much more positive role to Thecla as a model of virtue. In his *On Illustrious Men* 7 (written between 392–393), he rejects the story of the baptized lion in the *Acts of Paul* – the larger text to which the *APT* belongs – on the basis of its contents, stating that it is a "fable" (*fabula*) of the class of "apocryphal writings" (*scriptura apocrypha*). He further substantiates his claim by referring to Tertullian:

> He mentions a certain presbyter in Asia, an adherent of the apostle Paul, who was convicted by John of having been the author of the book, and who, confessing that he did this for love of Paul, resigned his office of presbyter.[17]

However, in his earlier *Letter to Eustochium* (c. 383–384), Jerome presents Thecla as a model of virginity for his youthful addressee, stating that the saint will joyfully embrace the virgin upon her entrance in heaven.[18] Elsewhere, Jerome indicates that Thecla served as a model of virtue for aristocratic women. For instance, under the lemma of the year 374 in his *Chronicles* (written in 381), he writes about the noblewoman Melania who was called "Thecla" because of her ascetic virtue and humility.[19]

A similar dynamic characterizes Augustine's (354–430) treatment of Thecla and the *APT*. In his early fifth-century *City of God*, Augustine summons his reader to reconsider the apocryphal texts in general:

---

[16] See Rose, *Ritual Memory*, 2009: 42–77, for further discussions of late antique and medieval views on the authority of the Apocryphal Acts of the Apostles and the sources therein.

[17] Halton (trans.), *On Illustrious Men*, 1999: 16; Ceresa-Gastaldo (ed.), *Gli uomini illustri*, 1998: 88. See also Hayne, "Thecla and the Church Fathers," 1994: 211; and Tommasi Moreschini, "Thecla in the Latin Sources," 2017: 78–80, for Jerome's references to Thecla.

[18] Jerome, *Epistolae* 22.41: Fremantle (trans.), *St. Jerome*, 1893: 41: "Then shall Thecla fly with joy to embrace you."

[19] See also Davis, *The Cult of St. Thecla*, 2001: appendix B, for the dissemination of the name "Thecla."

[L]et us then pass over the tales of those writings (*scripturarum fabulas*) which are called apocrypha (*apocryphae*) because their origin was hidden and uncertain to the fathers, from whom the authority of the true Scriptures (*auctoritas veracium scripturarum*) has come down to us by a very sure and well-known line of transmission.[20]

In his refutation of the apocryphal story about Enoch, Augustine uses (1) the argument of the doubtful authorship of texts, like Tertullian, and another common argument, namely, (2) that apocryphal stories were used in schismatic and heretic circles:

> For they were judged of dubious authenticity (*suspectae fidei*) because of their age. It was also impossible to ascertain whether they were what Enoch had written (*ille scripsisset poterat inveniri*) since they were not presented by men who were found to have kept them with proper ceremony through successive generations. Hence discerning authorities are right in their judgement that the writings presented under Enoch's name with those tales (*fabulas*) about giants not having human fathers should not be attributed to him. In like manner, many writings are presented by heretics (*haereticis*) under the names of other prophets or, if they are later, under the names of the apostles, but all these too have been excluded after careful examination from canonical authority (*ab auctoritate canonica*) and go under the name of apocrypha (*nomine apocryphorum*).[21]

To be sure, Augustine does not explicitly mention the *APT* but refers to the apocryphal texts in general. Nevertheless, in his almost contemporary treatise on virginity, Augustine refers to Thecla as an example of a virgin who is willing to preserve her virginity by choosing an ascetic life or even undergoing martyrdom.[22]

The writings of Augustine and Jerome reflect an opposite dynamic: while there is an increase in negative terms in the appraisal of apocryphal writings as the biblical canon is being established (not in the least through Jerome and Augustine), the opposite trajectory is taken for Thecla, as both authors present her as a model of virtue. This cannot be seen apart from the increasing anxiety about the authority of the *APT*, which finally resulted in its rejection in the sixth-century *Pseudo-Gelasian Decree*.[23] In line with Augustine's argument, the decree defines the *APT* together with many other Acts of the Apostles as "apocryphal," stating that they "cannot

---

[20] Augustine, *De civitate Dei* 15.23.4: Levine (ed. and trans.), *City of God*, 1966: 557.   [21] Ibid.
[22] See Augustine, *De sancta virginitate* 1.44–45: McQuade (trans.), "Holy Virginity," 1955: 199, following the edition of Saint-Martin (ed.), *L'ascétisme chrétien*, 1949.
[23] See Rose, *Ritual Memory*, 2009: 24–77; and Pervo (trans.), *The Acts of Paul*, 2014: 54, for the rejection of the work as apocryphal in the *Pseudo-Gelasian Decree*.

in any case be considered as acceptable" since they are "written or predicated by heretic or schismatic people."[24]

It is clear that the theological debate concerning the value of the *APT* did not prevent Thecla from remaining a symbol and model of virtue in the late antique and the early medieval Latin West. In fact, it appears that the figure of Thecla is more important than the story behind the figure. As Léonie Hayne notes, "in the West, the adulation can almost be regarded as perfunctory. Thecla is a name rather than a person."[25] This is also visible in the way Thecla is treated in other media. These provide what could be called "iconic" images of the saint that focus on one or a few characteristics of which Thecla becomes a symbol. Examples are the early Christian pilgrim flasks with images of the saint, which were related to Thecla's cult in Egypt but were widespread in the late antique Mediterranean.[26] The images allow the spectator to witness Thecla's virtues at a glance. Thecla is depicted with naked breasts, which recalls how Thecla preserved her modesty even while she was stripped naked in the first and second trial scenes (§ 22 and § 33–38). She also stands as an *orans* between two bulls, a bear, and a lion that sometimes licks her feet, which demonstrates her power over animals and her steadfastness during her trials in the second court scene (§ 33). As I will explore later, the iconic representation of Thecla as a model and symbol is important for the portrayal of Eugenia in both versions of her *Passion*.

Another factor may be the Christian prayer for the dead in Western ritual, the so-called *Commendation of the Soul* (*Commendatio Animae*). This prayer, which was known already from the fourth century and probably goes back to earlier Jewish prayers, presents an "iconic" image of the saint, including Thecla as a symbol of God's salvation:

> And as you have liberated your holy virgin and martyr Thecla from the three horrible torments, deem it worthy to also liberate the soul of your servant and make him enjoy the celestial goods with you.[27]

---

[24] *Pseudo-Gelasian Decree* 354: Denzinger and Hünemann (eds.), *Enchiridion Symbolorum*, 2014: 152; the translation is my own. See Vouaux (ed. and trans.), *Les Actes*, 1913: 53–58; and Pervo (trans.), *The Acts of Paul*, 2014: 54, for further discussion on the increasingly problematic status of the apocryphal Acts in the late antique West.
[25] Hayne, "Thecla and the Church Fathers," 1994: 210.
[26] For images of these pilgrim flasks, see Davis, *The Cult of St. Thecla*, 2001: figs. 8, 10, and 11.
[27] *Commendation of the Soul* 13. I henceforth use the edition in Brown Tkacz (ed.), *The Key*, 2002: 109–130. Translation is mine. For a general description of the prayer, see Brown Tkacz, "Commendatio Animae," 1991. For its dating, see von Severus, "Gebet I," 1972: 1255–1256.

Each of the other invocations in the prayer convey the same pattern, starting with the opening formula "Liberate, Lord, the soul of your servant, as you have liberated... (*Libera, Domine, animam servi tui, sicut liberasti...*)." The prayer seems to have had an influence on late antique Latin hagiography.[28] For instance, in the anonymous fourth-century *Passion of Cyriacus and Paula* (*BHL* 2066t), the young Cyriacus mentions Thecla as one of the examples of steadfastness during trials in his exhortation to the virgin Paula:

> Let us strengthen our hearths and bodies in order to sustain us during torture. Other martyrs have set for us an example (*exemplum*), who have already suffered for Christ and were liberated (*liverati sunt*) from the impious. Daniel, who loved the Lord, was liberated from the mouth of the lion; Ananias, Azaria, and Misael were snatched away from the furnace, the holy virgin Thecla was saved from all the wild animals in the amphitheater (*Tecla virgo sancta salvata est ab omnibus feris in anfiteatro*).[29] (§ 6.3)

It is unlikely that the reference to Thecla in this passage indicates an intertextual connection with the *APT*; this *Passion* contains no other direct or indirect references to the text, nor structural similarities. The passage rather reflects in language and content the *Commendation of the Soul*, alluding to the opening formula of the invocations, while the examples of Daniel, the friends – Ananias, Azarias, and Misael – and Thecla are three of the thirteen paradigms of divine deliverance enumerated in the prayer.[30] Interestingly, this *Passion* does not distinguish between the different figures: while Thecla is an example taken from a biblical book that was ultimately considered as non-canonical, Daniel and the three Hebrews originate from a canonical one. This reflects the *Commendation of the Soul*, which places the examples from non-canonical texts (Thecla and Susanna) on a par with the figures from the canonical books of Scripture. This may point to another type of treatment of apocryphal texts in late antique hagiography: while a text such as the R version of the *Passion of Eugenia* removes the explicit references to the *APT*, the *Passion of Cyriacus and Paula* includes Thecla among heroes from the canonical

---

[28] For its influence on medieval Irish hagiography, see Caitríona Ó Dochartaigh's contribution in this volume (Chapter 3).

[29] I follow the edition by De Gaiffier (ed.), "Cyriaque et Paule," 1942: 12–13. Translation is mine. The information concerning the dating of the *Passion* is taken from Saxer, "Afrique latine," 1995: 52–53; the text is briefly discussed on pp. 58–59 of the same work.

[30] *Commendation of the Soul*, 9, 10, and 13: "Liberate, Lord, his soul, as you have liberated Daniel from the lion's den. Liberate, Lord, his soul, as you have liberated the three youth from the fiery furnace, and from the hand of the inimical king. ... And as you have liberated your holy virgin and martyr Thecla from the three horrible torments, deem it worthy to also liberate the soul of your servant and make him enjoy the celestial goods with you."

books of the Old Testament. In any case, the *Passion of Cyriacus and Paula* demonstrates the lasting importance of Thecla as a symbol of divine deliverance. What is more, Cyriacus presents her as a model of virtue, explicitly calling the saint an "example," teaching them to "strengthen the heart" and to "sustain themselves during the various trials" (§ 6.3).

Other Latin sources refer to Thecla in a similarly iconic way, presenting her as a model of virtue. Thecla usually appears among other female virgins and without much reference to her story, which suggests that the references are topical rather than inspired by any particulars of the *APT*.[31] An example can be found in Venantius Fortunatus' (c. 530–c. 600) *Carmina*. In the first poem of book 8, which was written for the queen of the Franks, Radegund (520–587), the poet claims that the queen imitates Melania in her keenness while she equals Eugenia in her vigils and Thecla in her ascetic suffering.[32] In a later poem, addressed this time to the virgins who remain after Radegund's death, Venantius presents Thecla and Eugenia as models of chastity alongside other celibate virgins.[33] He may have been inspired by Sulpicius Severus (363–425) who, in his *Dialogues* (c. 404), lets his spokesperson Gallus say that Antony is frequently visited by Agnes, Thecla, and Mary in his nightly visions.[34] In addition, there is the highly interesting reference to Thecla by a non-Christian author, namely, Claudian (c. 370–c. 404) in his *Carmina Minora* 51 (written at the beginning of the fifth century). The poet ironically criticizes the Christian cult of saints and Christian belief in miracles, especially with regards to the question of whether saints can help cities during battles. For example, after a pseudo-laudatory list of other saints and their miracles, Claudian praises Thecla for her martial qualities as she "guides the armies of Rome."[35] Claudian's ironical treatment of the saint illustrates her broad

---

[31] The examples that follow have been listed by Tommasi Moreschini, "Thecla in the Latin Sources," 2017: 81–86. The analyses are mine.

[32] Venantius Fortunatus, *Carmina* 8.1.46: "In her vigils she wants to be like Eugenia, and like Thecla [she wants to be] in her suffering." For Venantius' poems, I henceforth use the edition of Reydellet (ed.), *Venance Fortunat*, 1994. The translation of the passage at present is taken from Tommasi Moreschini, "Thecla in the Latin Sources," 2017: 92. See the latter for further discussion. See also Smith, "Radegundis Peccatrix," 2009: 311–312.

[33] Venantius Fortunatus, *Carmina* 8.4.13–14: "We encourage you, sweet virgins, to seek after those things that Christ granted Eugenia and gentle Thecla." Translation is mine. See also Tommasi Moreschini, "Thecla in the Latin Sources," 2017: 81.

[34] Sulpicius Severus, *Dialogues* 2.13.5: Fontaine and Dupré (eds. and trans.), *Sulpice Sévère*, 2006: 278–279. Cf. Tommasi Moreschini, "Thecla in the Latin Sources," 2017: 81.

[35] Claudian, *Carmina Minora* 51: Platnauer (ed. and trans.), *Claudian*, 1922: 279. See Tommasi Moreschini, "Thecla in the Latin Sources," 2017: 84–86, for further discussion of the figure of Thecla in the poem.

status as a model of virtue in late antiquity. Claudian may have known Thecla from the *APT* or from her titular church in Rome, which was refurbished around 400 when Claudian worked in the city.[36] He was, perhaps, also inspired by his contemporary, Niceta of Remesiana (335–414), who refers to Thecla in his *On the Fall of Susanna*. In response to the fallen virgin Susanna, who stated that she could not resist her suitor because her flesh was fragile, Thecla and her "innumerable companions" say, "we are clothed with the same flesh, and yet, the fragility of our flesh could not mutilate our full intention, nor could the fury of tyrants destroy it with various torments."[37] Thus, not only does Thecla appear here as a model of chastity, there is also a heroic dimension to her portrayal that Claudian likely capitalized on.

Evidently, the reception of Thecla and the *APT* in the wider Latin literature of late antiquity and the early middle ages indicates that Thecla was a notable symbol and model. As we have seen, she is presented as an "icon" of virtue in artifacts as well as in later texts, despite the rejection of the *APT* as "apocryphal." As noted above, this rejection often came from the very same authors who present Thecla as an exemplary model. This type of "contradictory" reception, as I call it, contextualizes the ways in which both passions of Eugenia engage with the figure of Thecla in the representation of Eugenia.

Reception and Rejection: Thecla and the *APT* in the Passions of Eugenia

Let us now turn to Eugenia as she appears in the two versions of her *Passion*. As Stephen Davis highlights, the various thematic and linguistic parallels suggest that the *APT* inspired the construction of the *Passion* and that Thecla was used as a model for Eugenia's actions.[38] However, comparing the two versions of the Latin *Passion*, we can observe the same tendency toward the contradictory reception of Thecla in the wider realm of late antique Latin literature as Jones and Cooper have highlighted: Thecla is and remains an exemplary model in a time in which there was a growing debate about the apocryphal status of the *APT*. This is particularly evident in the later *Passion*; while it does not mention directly

---

[36] Vanderspoel, "Claudian, Christ," 1986: 251.
[37] Niceta, *De lapsu virginis consecratae* 11: Gamber (ed.), *Niceta de Remesiana*, 1969: 27. Translation is mine. See also Tommasi Moreschini, "Thecla in the Latin Sources," 2017: 86.
[38] Davis, *The Cult of St. Thecla*, 2001; and Davis, "Crossed Texts, Crossed Sex," 2002.

Thecla or the *APT* as the earlier version does, nevertheless, it indirectly evokes Thecla as an ideal model. In both versions of the *Passion*, however, Eugenia does not straightforwardly imitate Thecla but emulates her, especially through her rhetorical skills.

Here, I will provide a brief overview of the well-known similarities between the two tales to highlight how Thecla inspires Eugenia's actions and character, which will aid in our investigations into rhetoric further on.[39] While Thecla is born to a rich and noble family in Iconium, Eugenia is of a similarly high social standing: she is the daughter of the prefect of Alexandria. Mirroring Thecla, who is converted when she hears Paul's teaching, Eugenia accepts the Christian faith after she reads a copy of one of Paul's letters and the *APT* in M, but the apostle's "doctrine" in R. Similar to Thecla, Eugenia escapes from home after her conversion. Eugenia then decides to enter a male monastery with her two now-freed eunuch servants, Prothus and Hyacinthus, in tow. Toward that aim, she disguises herself as a man by changing her clothes and cutting her hair, which echoes Thecla's proposal to shave her head in order to accompany Paul on his travels and her donning a male cloak when she inevitably sets out on her own. Meanwhile, great distress befalls Eugenia's family upon discovery of the heroine's escape, which closely follows the lament of Thecla's household when Thecla rejects her impending marriage to her fiancé, Thamyris. As scholars have noted previously, the passage describing the distress of Eugenia's family (which is more or less similar in both versions of the *Passion*) is even intertextually connected to the scene in the *APT*:[40]

> Accordingly, there was immense wailing of unimaginable lamentation. Everyone was in mourning: the parents for their daughter, the brothers for their sister, the slaves for their mistress; and sadness and infinite distress possessed everyone.[41]

The passage in the APT runs as follows:

> Everybody in the house wept: Thamyris for his lost fiancée, Theoclia for her daughter, the female servants for their mistress. There was much confusion and weeping in the house. (§ 10.5–7)

---

[39] Many of the similarities between Thecla and Eugenia have already been noted in Whatley, "More than a Female Joseph," 2012: 92–98.

[40] For instance, Davis, "Crossed Texts, Crossed Sex," 2002: 17; and Whatley, "More than a Female Joseph," 2012: 95.

[41] *Passion* M § 7: Lapidge (trans.), *The Roman Martyrs*, 2018: 237; and Mombritius (ed.), "Passio Eugeniae," 1910: 393, 31–33. *Passion* R § 8: *PL* 73.610D–611A.

Other parallels with Thecla's tale are as follows: Eugenia obtains a leading position as the abbot in the monastery, which parallels Thecla's role as teacher and leader.[42] After Eugenia is falsely accused of sexual abuse by Melanthia, who is unaware that "Eugenius" is actually a woman, Eugenia is taken to court. This resembles the moment when Thecla is taken to court after her encounters with Thamyris and Alexander, whom she rejects. Though the details are not exactly the same, rejection and, consequently, violence underlie all three episodes. Moreover, after the death of her father and brothers, Eugenia travels with her mother to Rome, where she converts Basilla and persuades her to break up with her fiancé, as Thecla did with Thamyris. And, similarly to Thecla, Basilla and Eugenia are taken to court by the former's disappointed fiancé. Although unlike Thecla, Eugenia is put to death in this instance.

One important parallel occurs in Alexandria when Eugenia discloses her identity as a woman at court to counter Melanthia's charge. The recognition also engenders Eugenia's reunion with her family, as the prefect recognizes her as his daughter. The R version states that Eugenia "appears as a woman" after she has ripped apart her clothes.[43] The corresponding M version is more elaborate and reads as follows:

> She tore from her head the dress she was wearing (*scidit a capite tunicam*); and she appeared (before them) attractive in appearance with beautiful breasts; and immediately covering herself up, although her clothing was torn, she said to the prefect: "You are my father in the flesh; Claudia is my mother; these (men) who are with you now are my brothers, Avitus and Sergius. I am your daughter, Eugenia, who rejected the world with its delights for the love of Christ."[44]

As mentioned above, Davis argues that this scene in both Passions is inspired by the iconography of late antique pilgrim flasks and oil lamps depicting Thecla.[45] He notes that artifacts linked to Thecla's cult in Egypt and throughout the Mediterranean portray Thecla with naked breasts and a dress that is ripped open to the girdle, much like Eugenia is described as tearing apart her dress and showing her breasts. However, as Whatley

---

[42] For more on this theme, see Ghazzal Dabiri's contribution in this volume (Chapter 10).
[43] *Passion* R § 15: *PL* 73.614D: "And while she said this, she tore her dress, in which she was clothed, from her head (*scidit a capite tunicam*) and appeared as a woman. And she said immediately to the prefect: 'You are my father according to the flesh, Claudia is my mother, and these two brothers who are sitting with you are Avitus and Sergius. I am your daughter Eugenia, who rejected this whole world with its delicacies as dung for the love of Christ.'"
[44] *Passion* M § 13: Lapidge (trans.), *The Roman Martyrs*, 2018: 241–242; and Mombritius (ed.), "Passio Eugeniae," 1910: 395, 23–27.
[45] Davis, "Crossed Texts, Crossed Sex" 2002: 18–19.

notes, an intertextual link can be noted, as well, with the scene in the *APT* in which Thecla attacks Alexander:⁴⁶

> While she seized him, she tore his cloak (*scidit clamidem*) and threw away the crown from his head (*a capite*), and so she conquered him in the middle of the street. (§ 26.12–13)

Thus, despite the difference in their details, the passages in *both* Passions may be inspired by the *APT* in a more direct way.⁴⁷ However, the passages can be seen as an instance of *contrast* imitation,⁴⁸ in which intertextual references are used to simultaneously express a contrast between the source text and the target text: while Thecla strips Alexander of his clothes, Eugenia tears her own dress so that she appears naked. Even still, the effect is the same; both heroines establish their control over their suitors by ripping apart clothing and averting danger—Eugenia undoes Melanthia's charge, and Thecla obviates the threat of sexual abuse by Alexander.

Having now gone through some of the parallels between the two Passions and the *APT*, here we turn our attention to Eugenia who surpasses her model Thecla. However, we should first take a closer look at Thecla's rhetoric, her vocality, to provide the appropriate context.⁴⁹ To start, Thecla is not verbose, much less rhetorically accomplished, at the beginning of the Latin *APT*.⁵⁰ It is a skill that she gradually develops as her circumstances grow increasingly dire with each new trial as she remains firm in her encratic beliefs. Conversely, other figures appear quite talkative as soon as the opening scenes. For instance, Paul preaches the Gospel for three whole days and nights, while Thecla listens rapturously by her window. Her mother Theoclia complains that Thecla, who is now converted and wishes to pursue a life of chastity, is changed by the apostle's preaching. In addition, her fiancé Thamyris uses sweet words to try and win back her affections after her conversion: "Thecla, my beloved, what thing possesses your will? Return to your Thamyris" (§ 10.2–3). However, Thecla does not respond to either of them. Instead, the author characterizes her as "seeing" through a remarkable instance of synesthesia: "She gazed (*intuebatur*) at the words of Paul" (§ 10.8).

---

⁴⁶ Whatley, "More than a Female Joseph," 2012: 95–96.
⁴⁷ Below we will discuss whether the *APT* would have been perceived as a model by the historical readers of the R version too.
⁴⁸ On the conceptualization of contrast imitation, see Thraede, "Epos," 1963: 1039.
⁴⁹ On Thecla's vocality, see Virginia Burrus' contribution in this volume (Chapter 8).
⁵⁰ On Thecla's silence, see also Hylen, *A Modest Apostle*, 2015: 75–78.

Things only change when Thecla is put to trial at her own mother's request, following Paul's trial. At the arena, she has a vision in which she sees the Lord sitting in attendance among the spectators and in the appearance of the apostle. Thecla now finds her voice, saying, "How impatient am I, now Paul comes to look at me" (§ 21.7–8). Still, Thecla's rhetorical requests to Paul after she survives her first trial remain brief and are even quickly rejected by him. For instance, she states, "I shave myself and follow you wherever you go" (§ 25.4–5). Yet she does not seem to have shaved herself after all.[51] Paul rejects her by putting her off, telling her that her time will come. Thecla responds by asking him to baptize her, which he also refuses (§ 25). However, at the end of the story, when Thecla has returned to Paul after her second trial, she finally has gained full rhetorical agency, which she demonstrates by initiating a conversation with him (before she never initiated any conversations). She also guarantees her role as a servant of God. Upon seeing her, Paul erroneously "thinks" (*aestimans*) that she has come to seduce him (§ 40.6). Strikingly, no direct speech is quoted by Paul before Thecla speaks. Thecla corrects Paul, declaring, "Paul, I have accepted the baptism. He, who worked through you in the Gospel, has worked through me in the baptism" (§ 40.8–9). She continues by unfolding her plan: "I go to Iconium" (§ 41.5). It is only then that Paul confirms her vocation and sends her as an apostle to the gentiles and, thus, supports her role as God's servant: "Go, my daughter, teach the word of God" (§ 41.5–6).

Clearly, Thecla has found her voice and takes the opportunity to pursue her own goals. The story ends with the moving scene in which Thecla tries to convert her mother through her speech:

> Theoclia, mother, you can believe that God lives, and all who believe in him will not be deserted. If you desire money, God will give it through me, if you desire your daughter, look I'm here. (§ 43.2–5)

Nevertheless, although "she spoke a lot and often with her mother," the narrator states that the mother "did not respond" and "kept silent" (§ 43.5–7).[52] The circle has closed – the silent Thecla, who did not respond to her mother in the beginning, has become verbose in the end but encounters a silent mother. Although this may account for one of her rare rhetorical "failures," it actually allows Thecla to become an apostle:

---

[51] See Julie Van Pelt's contribution in this volume (Chapter 7) for further discussion on this topic.
[52] This phrase is absent in the Greek *APT* (§ 4.18): Pervo (trans.), *The Acts of Paul*, 2014: 183–184, which only represents Thecla's command to convert but not Theoclia's reaction.

realizing that it no longer makes sense to speak with her mother because she does not listen, Thecla departs for Seleucia, where she "illuminates many people" (§ 43.8).

Eugenia, meanwhile, is rhetorically skilled from the beginning. It is even considered her most remarkable character trait in the two Passions.[53] Upon her introduction in the story, both hagiographers state that she was perfectly trained in the liberal arts and instructed in Greek and Latin rhetoric.[54] As Cooper notes, it was not uncommon for girls to receive philosophical training as part of their education in fifth- and sixth-century aristocratic families. Eugenia's rhetoric thus has its basis in family life.[55] Interestingly, however, Eugenia first employs her skill to subvert traditional family values. For instance, in M, it is Eugenia's discovery of Thecla's story that sets the plot into motion while it also inspires the heroine to display her rhetorical skills. When we actually hear Eugenia, she uses her voice to reject her parents' proposal for her to marry a man of equal noble standing: "A husband is chosen more for his probity than for his lineage; we should consider his morals, not his social class."[56] Subsequently, she devises a ruse to escape from the marriage: she asks her parents for permission to depart for a holiday to hide the fact that she actually wants to escape from home and be educated in the Christian faith. Eugenia's actions may be seen as another sign of her imitation of Thecla, who also rejects marriage to a wealthy Thamyris and escapes from home. Even still, it may be a remarkable move for a girl who is only sixteen years old, especially when we consider this in conjunction with Thecla's initial silence at the beginning of the *APT* and the latter's very quiet departure from her home to visit Paul.

Far from her parents now, Eugenia constantly turns over in her mind the story of Thecla in the sedan chair. Inspired by a second reading of the

---

[53] As Annelies Bossu, Koen De Temmerman, and Danny Praet indicate, the focus on rhetorically skilled heroines is a more general feature of late antique Latin hagiographical stories. See Bossu, "An Entertaining Martyr," 2015; Bossu et al., "Erotic Persuasion and Characterization," 2015; and Bossu et al., "The Saint as a Cunning Heroine," 2016.
[54] *Passion* M § 1: Lapidge (trans.), *The Roman Martyrs*, 2018: 233; and Mombritius (ed.), "Passio Eugeniae," 1910: 391, 35–38. *Passion* R § 2: *PL* 73.607A.
[55] See Cooper, "Virgin as Social Icon," 2005: 22–23. In Cooper and Corke-Webster, "Conversion, Conflict, and the Drama," 2015, the authors draw attention to the contrast between Thecla's silence and her mother's attempts to persuade her daughter to marry in the beginning of the *APT*. They interpret this as a sign of the conflict between the mother, who wants to assure her social security as a single woman through the procreation of her family, and Thecla, who rejects marriage.
[56] *Passion* M § 1: Lapidge (trans.), *The Roman Martyrs*, 2018: 233; and Mombritius (ed.), "Passio Eugeniae," 1910: 391, 39–41. *Passion* R § 2: *PL* 73.607B.

APT, she bursts out into her first long speech and addresses Prothus and Hyacinthus who have accompanied her:

> It is not unknown to you (*nec lateat*), who have been my learned companions during my literary studies, what great (*quanta*) fictions are contrived by the poets concerning God, and what great (*quanta*) things the philosophers contemplate and perceive. But can you hear anything greater and truer concerning God than what is said in these acta (*actibus*) [of Paul and Thecla]? Is not this form of worship – to believe that God is a stone and to call upon a wooden image for assistance – absurd and disgraceful?[57]

Eugenia not only highlights her philosophical education in this speech, she also demonstrates her rhetorical skills, employing various rhetorical tropes such as euphemism and litotes (*nec lateat*), repetition (*quanta . . . quanta*), and the rhetorical question. Finally, she administers the traditional argument against paganism when she states that the ancient gods are unworthy of belief in them because they are only made of wood.[58] Although it is not stated explicitly, Eugenia's skillful and willful display of her rhetorical skills right after her discovery of the *APT* may be understood by the historical reader as an indication that she felt inspired by the example of Thecla.

Here, it may behoove us to note that as R omits all explicit references to the *APT*, it is less obvious whether historical readers considered its heroine as dependent on Thecla as a model for imitation as much as it seems likely that they would have for the M version. However, it is important to emphasize that the intertextual references to the *APT* (noted above and below) are maintained in R. On the one hand, the occurrence of these intertextual references may indicate that they were no longer recognized as such and had escaped omission during the process of rewriting. On the other hand, it is possible that the historical reader of the R version, one who was also familiar with the *APT*, would have recognized the references, especially because their language is, using Michael Riffaterre's term, "ungrammatical," that is, differing in style, syntax, and vocabulary from the rest of the text.[59] Such an informed reader also may have recognized the similarities between the stories of Thecla and Eugenia and considered the first virgin as the model for the second, even if the overt references to the *APT* are omitted in the later *Passion*.

Turning our attention back to the texts, Eugenia's early demonstration of her rhetorical skill is an instance of her *emulation* of Thecla. She is

---

[57] *Passion* M § 2: Lapidge (trans.), *The Roman Martyrs*, 2018: 234; and Mombritius (ed.), "Passio Eugeniae," 1910: 391, 47–51.
[58] Is 37:19; Dan 5:23; Rev 9:20.   [59] Riffaterre, *Semiotics*, 1978: 1–6.

further distinguished from Thecla by the refinement and effectiveness of her speech. We just had occasion to note how Eugenia convinces her parents to let her leave for holiday after an important conversation about marriage. Almost immediately after she "confesses" her religious leanings to her servants, Eugenia hears some singing Christian monks and decides to join them in the monastery dressed as a man. She then delivers a similarly rhetorically and theologically refined speech to convince her servants to accompany her:

> Human foolhardiness made me your mistress (*dominam*), but wisdom (made me) your sister (*sororem*). Let us be brothers in spirit, harmony, determination, and wisdom (*animo concordia uoto atque prudentia*), and, abandoning all trace of human dignity (*omnem humanae dignitatis gloriam*), let us hasten in an orderly manner to the men of God. But so that we do not become separated through some mischance, begin first by shaving off my hair. But tomorrow, let our passage to the men of God take place; and with you two on my right and left next to the sedan chair, let us all three, in male attire, make haste to join the men of God.[60]

One may observe various rhetorical tropes such as: antithesis (*dominam . . . sororem*), *copia verborum* (*animo concordia uoto atque prudentia*), and hyperbaton (*omnem humanae dignitatis gloriam*). In addition, Eugenia demonstrates that she is well-versed in Christian literature. The passage alludes to the idea expressed in the Pauline letters that there is no difference between the genders among those who believe in God, as it is expressed in, for instance, Gal 3:26–28:

> So in Christ Jesus you are all children of God through faith, for all of you who were baptized into Christ have clothed yourselves with Christ. There is neither Jew nor Gentile, neither slave nor free, nor is there male and female, for you are all one in Christ Jesus.[61]

Even though the passage in R is different, Eugenia appears as similarly rhetorically skilled, using antithesis to define her relationship with the eunuchs: "Usurped power made me your mistress (*dominam*), but wisdom made me your sister (*sororem*)."[62] She also employs an argument of authority, stating: "Divine wisdom commands that we should be brothers."[63] In both passages, Eugenia addresses her servants as their mistress while promising them freedom from servitude and being equal

---

[60] *Passion* M § 3: Lapidge (trans.), *The Roman Martyrs*, 2018: 234; and Mombritius (ed.), "Passio Eugeniae," 1910: 392, 8–13.
[61] The translations of biblical passages are from the *New International Version*.
[62] *Passion* R § 3: *PL* 73.607D.   [63] Ibid.

to their mistress. Not unexpectedly, the eunuchs obey the orders of their mistress. In both Passions, then, Eugenia uses rhetoric more effectively than Thecla, who simply asks Paul for permission to shave herself, albeit in vain, while Eugenia convinces her servants to take the tonsure to enter a monastery, altering their lives permanently in various ways.

Another example of Eugenia's rhetorical refinement is her speech to her father just before she reveals herself to him as his daughter. Above, we noted how Thecla, upon her final reunion with Paul, addresses him with short sentences in which she informs him about her baptism and plan to go to Iconium. Upon her reunion with her father, however, Eugenia gives a long speech in which she expresses a rather refined view on the topic of chastity in rhetorically and biblically stylized language. In M, after having expressed her regret that she is taken to court, Eugenia includes a gnome about the power of chastity: "True chastity cannot be frightened: whatever worldly opinion thinks of it will pass away with the world itself."[64] She then includes a comparison: "Modesty is not directed by wise persons at the approbation of men, but at the glory of God; (likewise) is purity preserved, chastity retained."[65] Finally, Eugenia wonders whether it is morally acceptable for her to dress as a man. She does so sophisticatedly, justifying her decision to cross-dress by making her argument in syllogistic manner:

> *First premise:* . . . **because the Christian spirit acts manfully for the love of God, I did not wish my faith to be of a feminine nature.** I reflected on the false pretense [of the cross-dressing], inimical to all honesty, by which a woman imitates a man. If for love of vice a man touches a woman, this is punished by the law;
> *Second premise:* but if for love of virtue the weaker sex imitates masculine behavior, this ought to be praised by the law.
> *Conclusion:* I, therefore, inspired by the love of divine religion, adopted male behavior and acted as a "perfect" man, thus vigorously preserving my virginity for Christ.[66]

Not only is Eugenia capable of constructing a rhetorical argument, she also displays her knowledge of Scripture, alluding to Paul's Letter to the Ephesians (4:13), in which he states that the faithful are built up "until

---

[64] *Passion* M § 13: Lapidge (trans.), *The Roman Martyrs*, 2018: 241; and Mombritius (ed.), "Passio Eugeniae," 1910: 395, 14–15.
[65] *Passion* M § 13: Lapidge (trans.), *The Roman Martyrs*, 2018: 241, slightly adapted; and Mombritius (ed.), "Passio Eugeniae," 1910: 395, 15–17.
[66] *Passion* M § 13: Lapidge (trans.), *The Roman Martyrs*, 2018: 241; and Mombritius (ed.), "Passio Eugeniae," 1910: 395, 17–23. Emphasis mine.

we all reach unity in the faith and in the knowledge of the Son of God and become mature (Vulgate: "a perfect man," *virum perfectum*), attaining to the whole measure of the fullness of Christ."[67] In R, Eugenia distinguishes herself further through her use of Scripture. She starts with an allusion to Eccl. 3:7: "It is time to speak; the time of remaining silent has passed." At the end of her speech, she quotes Paul's Letter to the Galatians (3:28) to justify her decision to disguise herself as a man:

> The virtue of Christ's name is so large that even women standing in fear of it obtain male dignity. No diversity of the sex can be considered superior in faith because the holy apostle Paul, the teacher of all Christians (*beatus Paulus apostolus, magister omnium Christianorum*), says that there is no distinction between men and women with the Lord because we are all one in Christ. I fervently embraced his standard in my mind and, in faith in Christ, I did not want to be a woman but was fully intended in my mind to preserve my virginity, and resolutely acted as a man for Christ.[68]

The biblical quotations are another instance of Eugenia's rhetorical and theological refinement. Eugenia concludes in a highly rhetorical fashion, arguing that she never lost her female dignity: "Acting as a woman in masculine fashion (*femina viriliter*), I behaved like a man (*virum*), powerfully (*fortiter*) embracing my virginity (*virginitatem*) that is in Christ."[69] One may further observe the figures of speech Eugenia employs in this instance as well: antithesis (*femina viriliter*) and assonance (*femina viriliter ... virum ... fortiter ... virginitatem*). In both passions, then, Eugenia appears as more rhetorically skilled than Thecla and even overtly displays her knowledge of biblical literature and Christian exegesis when Thecla never does.

Thecla's importance as a model for imitation and emulation may have implications also for understanding the remarkable difference between the two versions of the *Passion*, namely, the omission of the references to the *APT* in R. The omission seems not so much related to the importance of Thecla as a model for imitation and the basis of emulation – evidently, this remains the same in the two versions of the *Passion*. As noted above, it may be inspired by the status of the *APT* itself as a text of problematic authority. It is significant, in this respect, that R includes texts of a less problematic nature as sources of reference, most importantly, the canonical letters of Paul. The R version even contains references to Paul's writings

---

[67] The reference and the quotation to the Vulgate are noted by Lapidge (trans.), *Roman Martyrs*, 2018: 241 n. 46.
[68] *Passion* R § 15: *PL* 73.614C.   [69] Ibid.: 614D.

which are lacking in M. I already have had occasion to mention Eugenia's reference to Paul's Letter to the Galatians by which she justifies her cross-dressing in her speech to her father. Another example is the digression into the tale of Helenus, the bishop of Eugenia's monastery, and his contest and victory over the magician Zareas by a trial by fire. This episode is significant, for, as the hagiographer indicates, the bishop deems the ordeal necessary because he is unable to persuade the magician by words:

> And turning to Zareas, he entered into a debate with him. But because the magician was very clever, and he could not persuade him with rational words, Helenus considered that the people perhaps would be hurt because Zareas was superior in speech. He made a sign of silence and said to the people: "Everybody should keep to the warnings of the apostle Paul (*Pauli apostoli*) in this part; for he says to his disciple Timothy: 'Keep away from quarreling in words, because it is of no value, and only subverts those who listen' (2 Tim 2:14)."[70]

The bishop's rhetorical (in)ability is in remarkable contrast with Eugenia's: whereas she is able to convert her eunuchs through her speech, the bishop explicitly acknowledges that he cannot rhetorically convince Zareas, and an ordeal is needed to prove that the latter's beliefs are false.[71] Eugenia is definitely much more powerful than the bishop, who not only fails in persuading his opponent but goes a step further by trying to justify why it is better *not* to debate after losing the speech contest. However, what is important now is the explicit mention of the apostle Paul in the passage, as well as the quotation of his second Letter to Timothy: both are lacking in M. On the one hand, the quotation has a rhetorical function in Helenus' speech at the story level, increasing the rhetorical force and authority of his speech to his interlocutors. At the discourse level, moreover, the reader may perceive the quotation as reinforcing the distance with respect to the *APT* already created by the omission of its reference as the hypotext in the beginning of the *Passion*. The newly inserted quotations from the Pauline letters may fill in the empty space created by the deletion of the references to the *APT*. While the *APT* is decreased in importance as a text of authoritative status, Paul's letters thus retain their value and even become a more significant intertext.

---

[70] Ibid.: col. 609A.
[71] See above where Eugenia uses her rhetorical ability as a mistress. The same pertains to the other version, cf. *Passion* M § 4: Lapidge (trans.), *The Roman Martyrs*, 2018: 235; and Mombritius (ed.), "Passio Eugeniae," 1910: 392, 31–32.

The underlying reason may be the growing uncertainty regarding the authority of the *APT* as outlined above. Significantly, the quoted letters of Paul were seen as canonical. This is in contrast to the status of the *APT*, which was problematic already before it was rejected as apocryphal in the sixth century. The increased importance of Paul's writings, together with the removal of the explicit references to the *APT* in R, can be considered as a form of "normalization," so to speak, of the story of Eugenia. As the canonical status of the *APT* was already a topic of debate at least from the time of Tertullian at the start of the third century, the explicit reference to the work in M may have been strange and objectionable for its historical readers in late antiquity. Actually, M goes against the tendency I outlined in the other Latin sources as it both uses Thecla as a model *and* accepts the *APT* as a source of inspiration. The R version conveys a multifaceted strategy of rewriting, removing the explicit references to the *APT* and replacing its importance with that of Paul's writings, all while keeping Thecla as a model. In this way, the second *Passion* "normalizes" the story of Eugenia and aligns it with the common tendency in late antique Latin literature.

Concluding Remarks

In this chapter, I have traced in detail the reception of Thecla in two hagiographical texts and provided additional context with regard to the reception of Thecla in late antique and early medieval Latin hagiography and other literature. We can observe a remarkable disjunction between text and character. The reception of Thecla *as a figure* is coherent and long-lasting as a model, whereas *her tale* is not. Instances of this "contradictory reception" can be found in the wider Latin late antique and early medieval literature, in which the *APT* is dismissed for its dubious origins, falsehoods, and use in schismatic and heretic circles, whereas Thecla continues to be praised as an "icon" of virtue.

Similarly, in the two versions of the *Passion*, Thecla is the paradigm for many aspects of Eugenia's character and life: her decision to escape home, to shave her head (to enter the monastery), tearing her clothes and demonstrating her nakedness during the recognition scene, her trials, and most importantly her speech. While Eugenia imitates the model in most of these aspects, she emulates Thecla in her rhetorical skills and, by extension, her theological and exegetical qualities. This does not change in the later R version of the *Passion* in which Thecla remains the model to be imitated and emulated. However, while Thecla continues to be important as a model for imitation and emulation, this later *Passion* does not convey the same attitude toward the *APT* since it omits the explicit references to the text. This probably reflects the growing concern about the authority of the hypotext. In addition, it may betray the intention to "normalize" the story of Eugenia itself, aligning it with the common tendency in late antique Latin literature that upholds Thecla as a model but dismisses the *APT*.

However, an important distinction needs to be made. As problematic as the *APT* had become, it is nevertheless treated in an ambiguous way in the Passions as the analyses above highlight; it is indeed used as a model text for *both* versions (otherwise we would have a different story) even while the later one omits any mention of it. This duality seems to be par for the course. Apostles such as Paul and Peter and figures such as Mary, the mother of Jesus, were revered in the literature of the authoritative writers of the Church and depictions of their "apocryphal" Acts occur in the visual arts, even though these texts were officially rejected.[72]

It seems that these writings constituted another category of writings besides the officially accepted "canonical" and rejected "apocryphal" writings: a category of texts that François Bovon called "useful for the soul," which continued to inspire the private piety, education, and edification of the audience, even if they were officially and sometimes simultaneously condemned as apocryphal.[73] As my analysis suggests, the *APT* was also "useful" in a different way; it offers Thecla as an *exemplum* to be imitated and emulated by new heroines, while providing a literary model for the writing of new hagiographical narratives.

Bibliography

Apserou, Stephanie. "Το αγιολογικό dossier της Αγίας Ευγενίας (BHG 607w–607z)." PhD diss., University of Ioannina, 2017. https://olympias.lib.uoi.gr/jspui/bitstream/123456789/28903/1/Δ.Δ.%20ΑΨΕΡΟΥ%20ΣΤΕΦΑΝΗ%202017.pdf.

---

[72] See Cartlidge and Elliott, *Art and the Christian Apocrypha*, 2001: 134–171, for Thecla, Paul, and Peter in the visual art of late antiquity and beyond; and Jensen, "The Apocryphal Mary," 2015, for depictions of the apocryphal Mary in early Christian art. For the reception of the apostles Peter and Paul in late antique Christian literature, see the overviews of Ehrmann, *Peter, Paul, and Mary Magdalene*, 2006; and Eastman, *The Ancient Martyrdom Accounts*, 2015.

[73] Bovon, "'Useful for the Soul,'" 2015. See also Nicklas, "Neutestamentlicher Kanon," 2016: 608–609, in which he argues that the apocryphal writings were "useful" ("wertvoll") for the identity construction of the early Church and particular groups of early Christians.

Barrier, Jeremy W. *The Acts of Paul and Thecla: A Critical Introduction and Commentary*. WUNT 2.270. Tübingen: Mohr Siebeck, 2009.

Bossu, Annelies. "An Entertaining Martyr: Characterization in the Latin *Passio Agnetis (BHL* 156)." *Vetera Christianorum* 51 (2015): 89–114.

Bossu, Annelies, Danny Praet, and Koen De Temmerman. "Erotic Persuasion and Characterization in Late Antique Hagiography: The *Passio Caeciliae* and the *Passio Susannae*." *Latomus* 74, no. 4 (2015): 1059–1072.

Bossu, Annelies, Koen De Temmerman, and Danny Praet. "The Saint as a Cunning Heroine: Rhetoric and Characterization in the *Passio Caeciliae*." *Mnemosyne* 69, no. 3 (2016): 433–452.

Bovon, François. "'Useful for the Soul:' Christian Apocrypha and Christian Spirituality." In *The Oxford Handbook of Early Christian Apocrypha*, edited by Andrew Gregory, Christopher M. Tuckett, T. Nicklas, and J. Verheyden. Oxford: Oxford University Press, 2015: 185–195.

Brown Tkacz, Catherine. *The Key to the Brescia Casket: Typology and the Early Christian Imagination*. Notre Dame: University of Notre Dame Press, 2002.

"Commendatio Animae." In *The Oxford Dictionary of Byzantium*, edited by Alexander P. Kazhdan. Oxford: Oxford University Press, 1991. www.oxfordreference.com/view/10.1093/acref/9780195046526.001.0001/acref-9780195046526-e-1177.

Cartlidge, David R., and J. Keith Elliott. *Art and the Christian Apocrypha*. London; New York: Routledge, 2001.

Castelli, Elizabeth. *Martyrdom and Memory: Early Christian Culture Making*. New York: Columbia University Press, 2004.

Ceresa-Gastaldo, Aldo, ed. *Gli uomini illustri. De Viris Illustribus*. Florence: Nardini, 1988.

Cooper, Kate. "The Virgin as Social Icon." In *Saints, Scholars and Politicians: Gender as a Tool in Medieval Studies*, edited by Mathilde van Dijk and Renée Nip. Turnhout: Brepols, 2005: 9–24.

Cooper, Kate, and James Corke-Webster. "Conversion, Drama, and the Conflict of Social Reproduction: Narratives of Filial Resistance in Early Christianity and Modern Britain." In *Conversion and Initiation in Antiquity: Shifting Identities-Creating Change*, edited by Birgitte Secher Bøch. Frankfurt am Mainz; New York: Peter Lang, 2015: 167–183

Davis, Stephen J. *The Cult of St. Thecla: A Tradition of Women's Piety in Late Antiquity*. Oxford: Oxford University Press, 2001.

"Crossed Texts, Crossed Sex: Intertextuality and Gender in Early Christian Legends of Holy Women Disguised as Men." *Journal of Early Christian Studies* 10 (2002): 1–36.

Delehaye, Hippolyte. *Étude sur le légendier romain*. Brussels: Société des Bollandistes, 1936.

Denzinger, Heinrich J. D., and Peter Hünemann, eds. *Enchiridion symbolorum definitionum et declarationum de rebus fidei et morum: Kompendium der Glaubensbekenntnisse und kirchlichen Lehrentscheidungen. Lateinisch – Deutsch*. 44th ed. Freiburg; Basel; Vienna: Herder, 2014.

Eastman, David L. *The Ancient Martyrdom Accounts of Peter and Paul: Translated with an Introduction and Notes*. Atlanta: SBL Press, 2015.
Ehrman, Bart D. *Peter, Paul, and Mary Magdalene: The Followers of Jesus in History and Legend*. Oxford: Oxford University Press, 2006.
Evans, Ernest, ed. and trans. *Tertullian's Homily on Baptism: The Text Edited with an Introduction, Translation, and Commentary*. Eugene: Wipf and Stock, 1964.
Fontaine, Jacques, and Nicole Dupré, eds. and trans. *Sulpice Sévère, Gallus: dialogues sur les "vertus" de saint Martin*. Sources chrétiennes 510. Paris: Les Éditions du Cerf, 2006.
Fremantle, William H., trans. *St. Jerome: Letters and Select Works*. Nicene and Post-Nicene Fathers 2. Vol. 6. Oxford: James Parker; New York: The Christian Literature Company, 1893.
De Gaiffier, Baudouin, ed. "La Passion des SS. Cyriaque et Paule." *Analecta Bollandiana* 60 (1942): 1–15.
Gamber, Klaus, ed. *Niceta de Remesiana. De lapsu Susannae*. Regensburg: Pustet, 1969.
Gebhardt, Otto von, ed. *Passio S. Theclae Virginis. Die lateinischen Übersetzungen der Acta Pauli et Theclae*. Leipzig: Hinrichs, 1902.
Halton, Thomas P., trans. *St. Jerome: On Illustrious Men*. Washington, DC: The Catholic University of America Press, 1999.
Hayne, Léonie. "Thecla and the Church Fathers." *Vigiliae Christianae* 48 (1994): 209–218.
Hylen, Susan E. *A Modest Apostle: Thecla and the History of Women in the Early Church*. Oxford: Oxford University Press, 2015.
Jensen, Robin M. "The Apocryphal Mary in Early Christian Art." In *The Oxford Handbook of Early Christian Apocrypha*, edited by Andrew Gregory, Christopher Tuckett, T. Nicklas, and J. Verheyden. Oxford: Oxford University Press, 2015: 289–305.
Jones, Hannah. "The Passio of Eugenia and the Passio of Agnes." MA thesis, University of Manchester, 1998.
Kaestli, Jean-Daniel, and Gérard Poupon, eds. "Les Actes de Paul et Thècle latins. Édition de la version A et de sa réécriture dans le manuscrit de Dublin, Trinity College, 174." *Apocrypha* 27 (2016): 9–110.
Lanéry, Cécile. "Les Passions latines composées en Italie." In *Hagiographies: Histoire internationale de la littérature hagiographique latine et vernaculaire en Occident des origines à 1550*, edited by Guy Philippart. Vol. 5. Turnhout: Brepols, 2010: 15–369.
Lapidge, Michael, trans. *The Roman Martyrs: Introduction, Translations, and Commentary*. Oxford: Oxford University Press, 2018.
Levine, Philip, ed. and trans. *Augustine: City of God, LCL volume IV: Books 12–15*. Cambridge, MA; London: Harvard University Press, 1966.
McQuade, John, trans. "Holy Virginity (De sancta virginitate)." In *Writings of St. Augustine, V. 15, Treatises on Marriage and Other Subjects: Fathers of the*

Church, a New Translation, V. 27, edited by Roy J. Deferrari. Washington, DC: The Catholic University of America Press, 1955: 133–213.

Mombritius, Bonino, ed. "Passio Eugeniae." In *Sanctuarium seu Vitae Sanctorum II*. Paris: Fontemoin, 1910: 391–397.

Nicklas, Tobias. "Neutestamentlicher Kanon, christliche Apokryphen und antikchristliche 'Erinnerungskulturen,'" *New Testament Studies* 62 (2016): 588–609.

Pervo, Richard I., trans. *The Acts of Paul: A New Translation with Introduction and Commentary*. Eugene: Wipf & Stock, 2014.

Pesthy, Monika. "Thecla among the Church Fathers." In *The Apocryphal Acts of Paul and Thecla*, edited by Jan N. Bremmer. Kampen: Kok Pharos, 1996: 164–178.

Platnauer, Maurice, ed. and trans. *Claudian: On Stilicho's Consulship 2–3. Panegyric on the Sixth Consulship of Honorius. The Gothic War. Shorter Poems. Rape of Proserpina*. Cambridge, MA; London: Harvard University Press, 1922.

Reydellet, Marc, ed. *Venance Fortunat: Poèmes*. Paris: Belles Lettres, 1994.

Riffaterre, Michael. *Semiotics of Poetry*. Bloomington: Indiana University Press, 1978.

Rordorf, Willy. "Sainte Thècle dans la tradition hagiographique occidentale." In *Liturgie, foi et vie des premiers chrétiens: études patristiques*. Nouvelle édition revue et corrigée. Paris: Beauchesne, 1986: 435–443. Reprint of Rordorf, Willy, "Sainte Thècle dans la tradition hagiographique occidentale." *Augustinianum* 24, nos. 1–2 (1984): 73–82.

Rose, Els. *Ritual Memory: The Apocryphal Acts and Liturgical Commemoration in the Early Medieval West (c. 500–1215)*. Leiden; Boston: Brill, 2009.

Rosweyde, Heribert, ed. *Vitae Patrum*. Antwerp: Plantin, 1615.

Saint-Martin, Jules, ed. *Augustin d'Hippone. L'ascétisme chrétien: De continentia, De sancta virginitate, De bono viduitatis, De opere monachorum*. 2. éd., rev. et cor. Paris: Desclée de Brouwer, 1949.

Saxer, Victor. "Afrique latine." In *Hagiographies: Histoire internationale de la littérature hagiographique latine et vernaculaire en Occident des origines à 1550*, edited by Guy Philippart. Vol. 1. Turnhout: Brepols, 1994: 25–95.

Severus, Emmanuel von. "Gebet I." In *Reallexikon für Antike und Christentum*. Vol. 8. Stuttgart: Anton Hiersemann Verlag, 1972: 1255–1256.

Shepard Kraemer, Ross. *Her Share of the Blessings: Women's Religions among Pagans, Jews, and Christians in the Greco-Roman world*. New York; Oxford: Oxford University Press, 1992.

Smith, Julia M. H. "Radegundis Peccatrix: Authorizations of Virginity in Late Antique Gaul." In *Transformations of Late Antiquity: Essays for Peter Brown*, edited by Philip Rousseau and Manolis Papoutsakis. Farnham; Burlington: Ashgate, 2009: 303–326.

Thraede, Klaus. "Epos." In *Reallexikon für Antike und Christentum*. Vol. 5. Stuttgart: Anton Hiersemann Verlag, 1962: 1034–1041.

Tommasi Moreschini, Chiara O. "Thecla in the Latin Sources." In *Thecla: Paul's Disciple and Saint in the East and West*, edited by Jeremy W. Barrier, Jan N. Bremmer, T. Nicklas, and A. Puig i Tàrrech. Studies on Early Christian Apocrypha 12. Leuven: Peeters, 2017: 69–105.

Vanderspoel, John. "Claudian, Christ and the Cult of the Saints." *Classical Quarterly* 36, no. 1 (1986): 244–255.

Vouaux, Léon, ed. and trans. *Les Actes de Paul et ses Lettres apocryphes. Introduction, textes, traduction et commentaire*. Paris: Letouzey et Ané, 1913.

Whatley, E. Gordon. "Eugenia before Ælfric: A Preliminary Report on the Transmission of an Early Medieval Legend." In *Intertexts: Studies in Anglo-Saxon Culture Presented to Paul E. Szarmach*, edited by Virginia Blanton and Helen Scheck. Tempe: Arizona Center for Medieval and Renaissance Studies, 2008: 350–367.

"Textual Hybrids in the Transmission of the 'Passio S. Eugeniae' (*BHL* 2666, 2667)." *Hagiographica* 18 (2011): 31–66.

"More than a Female Joseph: The Sources of the Late-Fifth-Century *Passio Sanctae Eugeniae*." In *Saints and Scholars: New Perspectives on Anglo-Saxon Literature and Culture*, edited by Stuart McWilliams. Cambridge: D. S. Brewer, 2012: 87–111.

CHAPTER 10

A Medieval Sufi Thecla?
Female Civic and Spiritual Leadership in ʿAttār's "Tale of the Virtuous Woman" and the Life and Passion of Eugenia

Ghazzal Dabiri

Introduction: The "Tale of the Virtuous Woman" and Christian Lives of Female Saints

Farīd al-Dīn ʿAttār (c. 1145–c. 1220), a prolific Sufi poet and hagiographer,[1] wrote a peculiar tale that centers around a beautiful, holy woman. Known as the "Tale of the Virtuous Woman" (henceforth TVW), it details the trials and travails of an anonymous woman who attains prominence as a spiritual leader and civic authority figure in a land far from her home through her deeply ascetic choices. The tale's peculiarity is marked along several fronts. First, the story stands at the head of and sets the tone for ʿAttār's *Ilāhīnāmah* (*Book of the Divine*), a collection of stories bound by a frame tale that centers on *male* rulers who, unlike the virtuous woman, struggle in their path toward spirituality. Indeed, the frame tale is about a caliph who gathers his six sons, consummate kings in their own rights, to ask them about their goals and aims. Nearly each son desires some manifestation of worldly power such as complete knowledge of alchemy, thaumaturgy, Solomon's signet, Jamshīd's world-seeing chalice,[2] and Alexander the Great's water of life. When the caliph tells them that their desires are superficially motivated, the sons, each in their turn, defend their choices. In response, the caliph narrates a series of tales that supports his teachings.

These tales, which largely focus on male protagonists too, are drawn from the rich well of Islamicate literature to illustrate the Sufi way of being

---

[1] Sufism is the most popular form of Islamic mysticism. For an introduction, see Chittick, *Sufism*, 2000. In this chapter, I have adopted yet simplified the Library of Congress System of Romanization for Persian such that only long vowels are marked with diacritics. The exceptions are words such as Sufi/Sufism which are common in English. An early version of this chapter was written at Ghent University and funded by a European Research Council Grant (no. 337344)

[2] Jamshīd is an ambiguous figure in the Avesta (the holy book of Zoroastrians) and the later Iranian epic cycles: he is the most emblematic king but also loses the kingship three times due to his vanity. In coded Sufi terminology, Jamshīd's world-seeing chalice is also a mirror that reflects the world and the self.

in the world. The stories are lively, comical, and sometimes dramatic accounts of episodes from the lives of famous kings, biblical prophets and heroes, early Islamic theologians and judges, as well as Sufi saints, or stock-character types who come from every walk of life across confessions. Throughout the *masnavī* (long narrative poem), the caliph reinforces the idea that the ultimate source of power is the divine and that his sons' desires are the binary opposite of what they actually need.[3] He encourages them to nurture their souls and to become self-aware (in a manner similar to the famed exclamation "know thy self!") to cultivate an awareness of the divine. In the Sufi context, knowing oneself and cultivating an awareness of the divine are the first steps in the arduous, self-effacing path of love toward the ultimate and nigh unattainable goal, namely, union with the divine in this world – the illusive death-before-death (*fanā' billāh*).[4]

Surprisingly, the first son does not want any well-known trinkets or manifestations of worldly power. Rather, he has heard of the magnificent beauty of a fairy princess and wants her hand in marriage. The father, recognizing that at the heart of his desire is love's binary opposite, namely, lust, admonishes him:

> any man who is entrapped by his lust / depletes the stores of his soul[5]

But he does not altogether crush his son's aspirations. He tells him, instead, that the ideal woman is one who, if she is like a man in conduct, is a complete stranger to lust.[6] And then as an example of such a woman, he dives into the TVW, the story of an incomparably beautiful and virtuous woman whose conduct, it turns out, is vastly superior to the

---

[3] For instance, when the second son claims that he wants magic to reach the apex of love, he does so after his father has admonished him twice for wanting magic for the wrong reasons. But, of course, his sincerity also comes into question since the process is supposed to be arduous and strenuous. There are no easy shortcuts in achieving the near impossible, union with the divine. 'Attār, *Ilāhīnāmah*, Discourse 5: Shaff'ī-Kadkanī (ed.), *Ilāhīnāmah*, 2013: 177; and Discourse 7: ibid.: 198. Translations of the *Ilāhīnāmah* are mine.

[4] *Fanā' billāh* (lit. annihilation in God), the soul's return to its ultimate source, the divine. Sufi masters have claimed to have achieved near union with the divine in this world through their all-consummate love of and devotion to the divine. Sufis lose consciousness for days at a time, and when they come to, they retell all that they have witnessed to their devotees and/or family members. These retellings are prominently featured moments in medieval Sufi autobiographies and hagiographies. An illuminating and early example comes from Rūzbihān Baqlī's (1128–1209) autobiography. See Ernst (trans.), *Rūzbihān Baqlī*, 1996. It should be noted though that while experiencing the death-before-death, they never come in direct contact with the divine since human senses are unable to withstand any direct interaction. Instead, they come into contact with angels and past prophets who are sent by God.

[5] 'Attār, *Ilāhīnāmah*, Discourse 1: Shaff'ī-Kadkanī (ed.), *Ilāhīnāmah*, 2013: 131, l. 481.

[6] 'Attār, *Ilāhīnāmah*, Discourse 1.

men around her. For that matter, her conduct is far superior to that of the caliph's sons for whom she is presented as an ideal type of wife and queen consort. For, when separated from her husband, who has gone on pilgrimage, she remains steadfast in her virtue against all odds: beginning with her brother-in-law, she rebuffs the sexual advances of all the men who find themselves unable to resist her beauty and who threaten her with (sexual) violence when she rejects them. In each encounter, she rhetorically defends her chastity. After a series of harrowing escapes, including a shipwreck, she lands on the shore of a kingdom where she disguises herself as a man, becomes an ascetic, and is appointed by the king as his heir-apparent. After a great reveal of her gender and identity, she then becomes "a leader among men at God's court"[7] and a kingmaker when she refuses the throne to spend her time in prayers. She, instead, appoints her long-lost husband to rule after their happy reunion.

As such, the TVW also stands distinctly apart from the tales of other women within the *Ilāhīnāmah*. This holds even as we consider that all the women in the *Ilāhīnāmah*, like the virtuous woman, are on par with paradigmatic figures, such as Moses and Jesus, for they are rarely fallible and teach by example or through speeches (unlike men, including male saints, who are quite often fallible). Among the features that distinguish the majority of the women in the *Ilāhīnāmah* from the virtuous woman, the most striking is that by and large, they are the poor, old, grandmother with bent-back types. The dangers and obstacles they face, moreover, are lack of social and economic justice rather than lustful men. Although, these women too, like their biblical counterparts and the virtuous woman, are quite rhetorically proficient in their ability to bring (wayward) kings to tears in reminding them of their duty to the people, which is inseparable from their responsibility toward God.[8] Meanwhile, the few tales that do focus on young, beautiful women differ from the plot of the TVW. We may mention first the tale of a princess of extraordinary beauty and a palace servant who fall in love with each other. Incidentally, this tale is also quite unique in terms of its plot – tragic romance – and its commentary on love – the relationship between the ruling elites and serving class should

---

[7] 'Attār, *Ilāhīnāmah*, Discourse 1: Shafī'ī-Kadkanī (ed.), *Ilāhīnāmah*, 2013: 131, l. 483. This line does not appear in ms. S, which is the basis of the edition by Muhammad Riżā Shafī'ī-Kadkanī (ed.), *Ilāhīnāmah*, 2013: 452. It does appear in mss. A F I B G H U Q D the first of which is the basis of Hellmut Ritter's edition of the *Ilāhīnāmah*, on which, see Ritter (ed.), *Ilahi-nama*, 1989.

[8] See 'Attār, *Ilāhīnāmah*, Discourse 9, story 1; Discourse 14, story 22; and Discourse 15, story 1, for instance.

mirror God's love for humankind and the care given to one's own soul.[9] Then there are the handful of short tales, in which young, beautiful women are imbued with the ideal characteristics of Sufis; they are lovers consumed with an unrequited love for the beloved (the divine)[10] to the point of madness; lovers who are best exemplified by the more famous Potiphar's wife,[11] Rābi'ah of Basra (d. 801),[12] Farhād,[13] and Majnūn (fl. seventh century),[14] all of whom also appear across a wide variety of other Sufi texts.[15] This leads us to the third point; the TVW certainly makes use of a number of motifs popular in the tales of the prophets (*qiṣaṣ al-anbiyā'*)[16] and Sufi saints. But the TVW markedly differs even from the vast majority of these, irrespective of the gender and historicity of the protagonists.[17]

The peculiarity of the TVW led two scholars to cast their nets wider than Sufi popular tales in an attempt to better understand its underlying sociocultural context. As Ulrich Marzolph has noted, there are, in fact,

---

[9] See Dabiri, "When a Lion Is Chided," 2019: 71–72 and *passim* for a general discussion.

[10] The divine is usually symbolized as a beautiful and cruel beloved. All beauty in the world emanates from the divine so the beautiful beloved (oftentimes described semi-erotically) is both the manifestation of and symbol for the divine. On this in terms of the TVW, see below. The beloved is cruel since the love of the Sufi will always be unrequited in this world as true union with the divine is unachievable in the corporeal world.

[11] See 'Aṭṭār, *Ilāhīnāmah*, Discourse 8, story 7 and Discourse 20, story 7. Potiphar's wife is known as Zulaykhā in the Islamic tradition.

[12] On Rābi'ah, see Cornell, *Rabi'a*, 2019 and n. 30.

[13] According to the medieval Persian epic tradition, Farhād, whose historicity is unlikely, enters into a love triangle with Khosro II (d. 628), the king of the Sasanian empire, and his beloved and wife, Shīrīn, a Christian from Khuzistan, Iran (though in the epic tradition she is an Armenian princess). According to the popular version by Niẓāmī Ganjavī (1141–1209), when Khosro enters into a political marriage with the daughter of the Byzantine emperor, Maurice (r. 582–602), Shīrīn is left jilted. Khosrow hires the most skilled artisan, Farhād, to carve a waterway from the mountains to her remote castle as a way to appease her. Farhād falls hopelessly in love with her. Khosrow is enraged with jealousy and plots to separate the two. He summons Farhād to court and then tells him that while he was traveling to court, Shīrīn died. In his grief, Farhād throws himself off a mountainside and dies.

[14] Majnūn (meaning "mad" in Arabic) is the pen name of a seventh century Arabian poet who bemoaned the separation he and his cousin and beloved Laylá endured because their families disapproved their union. His individual poems were gathered together and translated into Persian as a long narrative poem (*masnavī*) by Niẓāmī Ganjavī.

[15] The tales of these figures became popular metonyms for the nigh improbability of achieving union with the divine in the corporeal world. The exception is Saint Rābi'ah whose love of the divine was all-consuming and well-known.

[16] In the Islamic context, many biblical heroes, such as Adam, Abraham, Isaac, and Joseph are considered prophets, while Moses, Jesus, and Muhammad are known as messengers. Among the biblical tales and motifs that the TVW plays on, we may mention briefly Jonah's tale (Jonah prays to God while he is on a ship to save him from impending physical violence by the men on board with him, which results in a terrible storm delivering Jonah from the attack).

[17] See below for more.

numerous versions of the tale circulating throughout Eurasia.[18] However, the vast majority of these are much later than ʿAṭṭār's version, and the few that predate it or are nearly contemporaneous hardly represent Sufi ideals, much less of good leadership (discussed further below). Interestingly, Dick Davis noted that the plot and structure of the TVW resembles that of ancient romances, specifically ancient Greek novels, in which beautiful women, separated from their fiancés, try to dissuade men from their unwanted advances using their rhetorical skills before finally escaping, which leads them to travel across the Mediterranean world – which includes sometimes a shipwreck – until they are reunited with their beloveds.[19] I have argued elsewhere that upon closer inspection, TVW's structure and plot actually resemble those of Christian Lives of female saints and protagonists, which engage with the motifs and plots also found in ancient romances, to promote their own religio-spiritual aims.[20] The most pertinent and famous examples of such texts that the TVW evokes in this regard are (1) the second-century *Acts of Paul and Thecla* (henceforth *APT*) and the fifth-century *Life and Miracles of Thecla*, (2) the second- or third-century Pseudo-Clementine *Recognitions*, and (3) the fourth-century *Life and Passion of Eugenia* (henceforth *Life of Eugenia*).[21]

We may notice several important clusters of motifs these texts and the TVW share in common. For instance, Thecla's beauty causes her to be accosted by a nobleman, Alexander, and when she rebuffs his advances, he demands she be put to trial for violently rejecting him. Nevertheless, she miraculously survives. This is similar to the virtuous woman who miraculously survives a trial by stoning after she steadfastly refuses the advances of her brother-in-law who then brings her up on false charges of adultery. In order to remain in the presence of an authoritative male figure/benefactor, the apostle Paul, Thecla offers to cut her hair presumably to disguise her beauty/identity,[22] while the virtuous woman disguises her identity completely to gain the protection of a king.

---

[18] See Marzolph, "Crescentia's Oriental Relatives," 2008, which traces the various versions of the tale in pre-modern Arabic, Persian, and Hebrew texts. I would like to thank D. Gershon Lewental for bringing a reference to this article to my attention. How it was brought to his attention resembles the travels of the itinerant stories under discussion here. That, however, is a tale for a different time.

[19] Davis, *Panthea's Children*, 2002: 105–109.

[20] Dabiri, "Reading the *Elāhīnāma*," 2018. On the adoption of common motifs for religio-spiritual aims in hagiography, see, for instance, Perkins, *The Suffering Self*, 1995: 15–40 and 200–214; Cooper, *The Virgin and the Bride*, 1996: 20–44; Aubin, "Reversing Romance?," 1998; and Barrier, *The Acts of Paul and Thecla*, 2009: 1–30.

[21] For the editions used here, see below.

[22] There is some ambiguity in the passage: Thecla does not state why she offers to cut her hair. We only have Paul's response, that she is beautiful. From that we may interpret it as an offer to dissimulate her beauty or, more drastically, pass as a man. While at the end of the tale she sews and

Both, moreover, are offered God's protection by or in spite of fire: For instance, when Thecla is ordered to be burned at the stake during her first trial, the fire does not touch her because God sends down a cloud full of rain and hail that kills many but not Thecla. During her second trial, Thecla, desiring baptism, in the name of Jesus Christ jumps into a pool of seals brought out to attack her. As she does, fiery flashes of lightning appear over the pool, and the seals float up dead while a cloud of fire envelops her so that none can touch or see her. And finally, in a last-ditch attempt, her persecutors let loose bulls whose genitals they had first inflamed. Instead of Thecla being burned or gored in a sexually sadistic manner, the fire from the bulls' genitals jump and burn through the ropes that had bound her, leaving her unscathed by either the fire or the bulls. The virtuous woman, meanwhile, when cornered on a ship by her would-be rapists, declares that she is a stranger and a free woman as Thecla does with Alexander.[23] When they do not heed her pleas, the virtuous woman prays fervently to God for death, for she would rather die than be deprived of her (bodily) virtue. God, instead, sends a terrible hell-fire storm that instantaneously burns the sailors to ashes. Knocked unconscious throughout the ordeal, she eventually arrives safely and unscathed on shore. While she is unconscious, she presumably experiences the rare death-before-death because she wakes up able to perform healing miracles. Thus, in their respective close encounters with fire, nearly everything in their vicinity is destroyed, but they remain protected. More specifically, it is at the exact moment when they face inescapable sexual violence that Thecla and the virtuous woman, surrounded by protective fire, undergo baptism – receive divine assistance and are saved physically and spiritually with or near water, respectively – echoing the older Indo-European fire-in-water motif.[24]

---

dons a male cloak, she does not do so to disguise herself. See n. 31. For more on the topic of cross-dressing saints in relation to the *APT* and the ambiguity of the passage, see Julie Van Pelt's contribution in this volume (Chapter 7).

[23] She had been sold into slavery by the man she had freed from torture by buying off his debts. She was bought by a merchant who takes her to his ship. On the ship, when the men succumb to their lust, she asserts that she is a stranger and a free woman. As noted above, this is similar to Thecla's own assertion that she is a foreigner and a leading woman of Iconium to Alexander when he lays hands on her (§ 4.1). Thecla as a stranger is discussed throughout the volume. The virtuous woman of course notes that, in addition to being a free woman, she is a married woman also. Thecla, meanwhile, informs her accoster, Alexander, that she was cast out for not wanting to marry her fiancé. It is not an uncommon trope for free women sold into slavery to declare that they are free-born women. What is striking here is that the motif occurs in a cluster of other similar motifs at similar moments. All references to the *APT* are taken from Barrier, *The Acts of Paul and Thecla*, 2009.

[24] Puhvel, *Comparative Mythology*, 1987: 277.

Moreover, both, after their grueling ordeals, gain the protection and enter the ranks of the ruling elite (on which see below). They also end up in secluded spots, where a shrine is built for them that becomes a place where they perform miracles (*Life and Miracle of Thecla*).

Finally, there is the theme of forgiveness that is deployed similarly at like points in their stories: the virtuous woman forgives, heals, and bequeaths wealth to the men, including her brother-in-law, who had been maimed in divine punishment for bringing harm to her, even though they first presented themselves as allies. In the final moments of the *APT*, Thecla seeks out her mother, though the latter had insisted that Thecla be burned at the stake for refusing marriage, and similarly offers her wealth and herself as her daughter again.[25]

As for Pseudo-Clementine *Recognitions*, the similarities are likewise readily apparent: a beautiful woman, Mattidia, is separated from her husband, flees the unwanted advances of her brother-in-law, and after a series of travel misadventures and a shipwreck that leads her to a foreign land where she resides for years, she holds onto her virtue until she is eventually reunited with her long-lost husband and son in a rather engineered recognition scene by the apostle Peter who then baptizes the whole family.[26] In Eugenia's tale, we find a female saint living in disguise in a monastery, who resembles the virtuous woman living in disguise in her sanctuary. Significantly for our purposes, the virtuous woman is designated by the king of the realm her ship lands on as his heir-apparent and then as kingmaker by the community when she turns down the appointment. Likewise, Eugenia becomes not just a "manly woman"[27] or a woman who

---

[25] Since a later reworking of Thecla's tale, the *Life and Miracles of Thecla*, is discussed here, it may be of interest to note that in the Ethiopic *Book of Thecla* the two governors who persecute Thecla are maimed by divine punishment. After she survives her trials, they ask her to help heal them. She asks for Paul to be brought to her. Paul arrives and heals them, and the governors live the rest of their lives in faith. On the Ethiopic *Book of Thecla*, see Damien Labadie's contribution to this volume (Chapter 2).

[26] It should be mentioned here that recognition scenes are frequently deployed in medieval Arabic and Persian literature. The salient point here is the cluster of motifs (love triangle between husband, wife, and brother-in-law) and the ordering of plot (unwanted advances, flight, shipwreck, eventual recognition scene in foreign land) that leads to conversion of confession in Pseudo-Clementine *Recognitions* and spiritual conversion in TVW. See below for more on this latter point.

[27] For more on the concept of the "manly woman," in other words, the rejection of female identity through the appropriation of male style and dress and renunciation/asceticism in Roman and Byzantine hagiography, see Aspegren, *The Male Woman*, 1990; Burrus, "Reading Agnes," 1995; and Cooper, "The Bride of Christ,'" 2013 (especially 538–540 for the *Life of Eugenia*). For an interesting look at how sermons and hagiographies were written for imperial women, imputing to them the deeds of earlier saints while dealing with the issue of gendered power, see Bartolini, "Manlier Than Many Men," 2016.

is "like a man in conduct" but "a leader among men at God's court" when she is chosen by her brothers-in-faith to be the leader of the monastery even though she, too, at first refuses the appointment. Both women also undergo two reveals – first of gender (in the monastery/sanctuary) and later one of identity (to their respective families): when the virtuous woman refuses the appointment as heir-apparent, she reveals her gender to a group of women she has asked to bear witness. Then, when her long-lost husband finds his way to his wife's shrine, she disguises herself for a second time, and, then, in a reveal of her identity, the couple is happily reunited and become co-rulers of sorts. Eugenia, disguised as Eugenius, enters the monastery where she is to be elected leader. Later brought to the arena on false charges of sexual assault, she happily reunites with her family, the ruling elite of Alexandria, when she too finally reveals her gender and identity and then enters into a type of co-rulership, but with her father. And finally, as in the TVW, in which the virtuous woman's husband and community (including the men who had previously sought to harm her) experience a spiritual conversion, Eugenia's recognition and reunion with her family leads the family and the entire city to convert to Christianity.[28] Here too, then, the affinities between Pseudo-Clementine *Recognitions*, the *Life of Eugenia*, and the TVW are palpable when we look at the rippling effects of individual conversion on family and community.

A quick glance at the summary outlines of the *APT*, *Life of Eugenia*, and TVW illustrates that these tales are intimately connected not just at the level of story and plot but more importantly in terms of the commentary the texts offer on female spiritual and earthly leadership and its relationship to the body politic. When we follow the story arc of Thecla, Eugenia, and the virtuous woman, we see noble women become strangers after a spiritual awakening and then enter the ranks of the ruling elite.[29] Of particular interest to us here is that the tales of Eugenia and the virtuous woman explore positive instances of independently attained female leadership[30] and familial-to-communal conversion at the moment when

---

[28] Lipsett, *Desiring Conversion*, 2011: 6–17, offers a concise overview of conversion as (1) professing a new faith toward a "prophetic religion" or (2) a change from "laxity to intense observance" for Judaism and Christianity. This is also applicable broadly speaking for conversion to Islam (1) and what Sufi practitioners seek for themselves and the laity (2).

[29] While Eugenia always belonged to this group as the daughter of the eparch, her *return* to the ruling elite happens on more equal terms with her father. For the many-layered relationship between the *Life of Eugenia* and the *APT*, see Davis, "Crossed Texts, Crossed Sex," 2002; Cooper, "The Virgin as Social Icon," 2005; and Klazina Staat's contribution in this volume (Chapter 9).

[30] Here, I am marking the difference between Eugenia and the virtuous woman who become authority figures in well-established androcentric arenas (court/monastery) independently of any familial

Thecla in the *APT* has attained leadership[31] but fails to convert her mother, and the story ends. Thecla's leadership has been studied through the lens of modesty and the *civitas*.[32] For my contribution to this volume, therefore, I will focus on the depiction of independently attained female civic and spiritual leadership and its relationship to the social body in the *APT*, *Life of Eugenia*, and TVW.[33] This may help us paint a more detailed and nuanced picture of late antique and medieval attitudes toward female leadership across confessions and geographical boundaries, which, as far as I am aware, remain little studied.

It is important to note here that in addition to the compartmentalization of various fields of study, this lacuna may stem from the very texts we have in hand. In a significant number of Christian hagiographies, and this is especially true for martyr acts, rulers are male and are oppositional figures; they generally only vary from one another by the degree to which they make life, or dying as it were, difficult for our saints. Nevertheless, there are three major types of women in positions of power and authority[34] who are the subjects of hagiographies and who have received scholarly

---

connections or familial wealth. This is in stark contrast to those such as Melania the Elder (c. 350–c. 410), Melania the Younger (c. 385–439), and Macrina (324–379), the older sister of the Cappadocian Christian authors Basil of Caesarea (330–379) and Gregory of Nyssa (d. 395), who use familial name and wealth to establish and then lead convents and monasteries or who with their daughters and/or mothers turn familial compounds into convents. For more on this latter topic, see Talbot, "The Byzantine Family," 1990. For a brief overview of powerful female Sufi teachers and similar types of patronage, namely, women instituting Sufi *khānaqāhs* (orders), including places of retirement, see Schimmel, "Women in Mystical Islam," 1982. The wildly popular medieval female Muslim ascetic, Rābiʿah partially fits into our category; she was born into poverty before being abducted and sold into slavery. She was apparently released because of her piety, and she soon amassed a gathering, befriended the most famous Sufis and ascetics, became a teacher, and, according to many sources, performed miracles. On Rābiʿah and the development of her myth, see Cornell, *Rabiʿa*, 2019.

[31] McInerney, *Eloquent Virgins*, 2003: 41–43, sees, in light of antique practices, the acclamation Thecla receives in the arena and Queen Tryphaena's patronage as markers of civic recognition. Furthermore, she understands the wearing of the male cloak as a marker of the philosopher's cloak and as suitable for the virgin-apostle.

[32] Hylen, *A Modest Apostle*, 2015: ch. 4 (especially pp. 81–85).

[33] Since Mattidia does not hold any positions, Pseudo-Clementine *Recognitions* is excluded from the remainder of the discussion. For a discussion on Mattidia as a precursor to later medieval European tales of women who escape unwanted advances of a relative and their successive misfortunes and adventures, see Archibald, "The Flight from Incest," 1986.

[34] Byzantine hagiographies tend to deal with noble women, to the near exclusion of women from lower social classes. There are, however, the tales of female slaves and captives, for instance, who convert entire kingdoms. See Sterk, "Mission from Below," 2010. Albeit, the most famous of these captives, Rhipsime (Arm. Hṙipʿsimē), who is credited with the conversion of the Armenians through her martyrdom, is a noble woman. On Rhipsime, see Valentina Calzolari's contribution in this volume (Chapter 4) and the sources therein.

attention: saint-empresses such as Saint Helena and Saint Irene,[35] noble women, such as Melania the Elder who founded and led convents,[36] and, predominantly, historical and fictional noble women who are presented as models of continence and asceticism.

In the Islamic and specifically Sufi contexts, the saints are also by and large male and so, too, are the rulers.[37] There are certainly female saints and Sufi masters. However, nearly all but a few derive their status through familial bonds – their husbands, fathers, brothers, or sons are Sufi masters or saints. They are rarely ever rulers, though the most prominent ones are highly revered teachers,[38] become leaders of Sufi orders (sing. *khānqāh*) through death of a male relation,[39] or become the patron saints of cities.[40] This type of male-dependent female leadership and holiness, apparently, is not unfamiliar territory in the Byzantine context either. As Stavroula Constantinou notes "the sanctity of the large majority of women commemorated in Byzantine hagiography is associated with a man who makes female holiness possible either as a torturer or as a spiritual father."[41]

---

[35] As of yet, Saint Ilaria and Saint Onesima have not received proper attention. Meanwhile, the popularly studied Saint Helena (c. 250–c. 330) is largely treated in her role as holy woman and less so as Augusta (empress). This is largely due to the fact that the primary sources are later hagiographical works that focus on her holy deeds. On this, see, for instance, Harbus, *Helena of Britain*, 2002: 9–27; and Drijvers, *Helena Augusta*, 1992: 1–19. If one turns to Roman and Byzantine empresses in general, we are on slightly more solid ground. Despite the generally androcentric and (sometimes even hostile) primary sources, we know from various cultural materials (such as coins, inscriptions, friezes, and sculptures) that empresses wielded considerable power and authority in a variety of ideological and religious ways, even if different from their husbands, the emperors. And, of course, there are those who did rule independently (as regent upon the death of husband/emperor or when their sons were too young to rule) and enjoyed impressive military and political successes in addition to embodying the religious ideologies of the state. For more, see James, *Empress and Power*, 2001 and the notes and sources therein. See Kruk, *The Warrior Women*, 2014: 175–186, for an analysis of warrior-queens in medieval Arabic tales.

[36] However, the focus of scholarly attention has been on the historical information about the convents and familial relationships. See Yarbrough, "Christianization," 1976. On the study of these ascetic women's lives for social history rather than for their "literariness," see Clark, "Holy Women, Holy Words," 1998.

[37] Sufi saints' relationships with rulers are, comparatively, more nuanced since, in the hagiographies and historiographies we have in hand, they often enter into symbiotic relationships with rulers. Even in moments when saints are at odds with rulers, the stakes are never as dramatic or pressing as their early Christian counterparts who must face a hardened pagan ruler whose duty it is to enforce the pagan laws of the empire.

[38] See Cornell (ed. and trans.), *Early Sufi Women*, 1999, which is a translation of Sulamī's seminal biography of prominent female saints, for examples. On Sulamī, see below.

[39] For more, see Bashir, *Sufi Bodies*, 2011: 135–163.

[40] See Kugle, *Sufis and Saints' Bodies*, 2007: 81–122, for an example of a female patron saint in pre-modern Morocco.

[41] Constantinou, "Performing Gender," 2014: 32.

As just noted, women did exercise power and authority in Roman, Byzantine, and Islamicate societies and are represented as such in hagiographies, even if the converse (focus on male power and authority) is more common.[42] The *Life of Eugenia* and TVW, however, offer an opportunity to study female power but from a different perspective, as they depict women in positions of leadership in ways that are atypical. For instance, like Thecla and numerous other women in saints Lives, Eugenia is from a noble family – she is actually of the ruling elite since her father is the eparch of Alexandria – just as she is noble in spirit as the narrator consistently points out.[43] Similarly, the virtuous woman comes from a wealthy background since her husband is able to undertake the costly and lengthy pilgrimage to Mecca and leave her in the care of family. Nevertheless, Eugenia and the virtuous woman, like Thecla, attain prominent leadership positions among their newly adopted communities, independently of any familial connections. Significantly, they are elected to those positions by communities who know absolutely nothing about their true identities, respective families, or their previous positions in society. Furthermore, they confer spiritual and civic authority onto their male relations and then enter into a type of co-rulership with them. In order to highlight these shared aspects and to set the stage for analysis, it would behoove us to first address Farīd al-Dīn ʿAṭṭār's circumstances and the pressing question of the possible circulation of the *APT* and *Life of Eugenia* within and without the Iranian world.[44] Next, I will offer a summary of ideal leadership according to the *Ilāhīnāmah* and the ways in which the first tale, TVW, sets the tone for the work as a whole. Finally, I will highlight how the *APT*, *Life of Eugenia*, and TVW converge and diverge on the point of female leadership before offering a few concluding remarks.

---

[42] Taking her cue from recent cultural theorists working on women's lives, Susan E. Hylen, *A Modest Apostle*, 2015: 13, notes that "even when male status is universally constructed as higher than female status, women may in practice exercise various forms of power." See also Kugle, *Sufis and Saints' Bodies*, 2007, on such instances in the pre-modern Muslim world and Hill, "'All Women Are Guides," 2010, for a discussion of Senegalese Sufi women leaders in the context of chastity. See, also, the collected essays in Hambly (ed.), *Women*, 1998.

[43] The name Eugenia is related to the Greek word, *genos* (gene/family), and entails nobility (*eugenos*: well-born). See also Clark, *Ascetic Piety*, 1981, for a general discussion of this topic beyond the *APT*.

[44] It may be of interest to note here that there is a marked difference between Byzantine and Eastern Christian hagiographies that were composed during the Sasanian period and are famously known altogether as the Persian Martyr Acts. The latter demonstrate a familiarity with the Sasanian epic tradition, which, in addition to their attempts to undermine Zoroastrian doctrine, they employ to subvert the authority of the kings. See Walker, *The Legend of Mar Qardagh*, 2006, for more.

ʿAttār and the Various Versions of the "Tale of the Virtuous Woman"

Farīd al-Dīn ʿAttār is counted among the most important and popular medieval Sufi poets and hagiographers. He lived in the ancient city of Nishapur, which is in the northeast of modern-day Iran and which was an important stop along the Silk Road. The latter part of his pen name, ʿattār, means that he was an apothecary, which is confirmed by a handful of lines, peppered throughout his works, regarding his personal circumstances. His trade as the city's apothecary means that he was able to and did work, as far as we know, independently of courts. While ʿAttār's famous contemporary poets, scholars, Sufis, and hagiographers lived and worked in other cities, Nishapur, in the century leading up to ʿAttār's time, boasted an active scholarly life, which attracted prominent scholars who visited the city. Nishapur was also the home of Sulamī (d. 1020), the seminal hagiographer who, in addition to his seminal biography of male saints, compiled a book of the most prominent female Sufi saints, many of whom lived in Nishapur.[45] The city was also the home of a number of prominent polymaths, such as Thaʿālibī (961–1038) and Thaʿlabī (d. 1035), who were avidly interested in biblical, Islamic, and/or Iranian history and tales and compiled important works of their own. ʿAttār, following in the same vein as his illustrious predecessors, was an ardent collector and author of numerous stories of historical (and fictional) saints, which are featured in his most popular and popularly studied prose hagiographical text, *Tazkirat al-awliyaʾ* (*Memorial of God's Friends*),[46] and in his *masnavī*s.

The earliest known version of the story of the virtuous woman in the Islamicate world is by the prominent ninth–tenth century Shiʿite *hadith* scholar Kulaynī (d. 941) who hailed from the ancient city of Ray (located in northern Iran).[47] Given ʿAttār's collecting habits and Nishapur's reputation as a scholarly city, it is possible (even probable) that the base of

---

[45] See Cornell (ed. and trans.), *Early Sufi Women*, 1999.
[46] The *Ilāhīnāmah* is not generally considered a hagiography. However, as I have argued elsewhere, specifically in Dabiri, "'When a Lion Is Chided,'" 2019, and offer a brief synopsis of this below, the *Ilāhīnāmah* does adopt the generic stance of hagiographies to create (momentary) saints out of every social type.
[47] In his article, Marzolph, "Crescentia's Oriental Relatives," 2008: 252–253 and 255, notes that the possible source of a late thirteenth-century Hebrew version might be an "assumedly tenth century compilation from Iran" but that the tale may have been added in later. In Kulaynī's version, the men who sought to harm the virtuous woman all come to a tragic end (the brother refuses to allow his perfidious brother to be cured, the servant who killed a boy and blamed it on the virtuous woman is killed by the boy's father).

'Attār's version of the TVW is drawn from Kulaynī's version. However, Kulaynī's much shorter version differs markedly from 'Attār's in the details in which we are most interested and in their underlying meaning, namely, the intricate relationship between spirituality, corporeality, and leadership (which will be addressed further below). The major points of divergence, in the version that has come down to us, begin once Kulaynī's virtuous woman boards the ship.[48] For instance, when the sailors, who only ever had ill intentions,[49] make their move to forcefully take the virtuous woman, God simply knows she is in trouble. He sends a (regular) rainstorm to drown the sailors and delivers her safely to an island. Then he calls on one of his prophets to bring his people and their king to an island where they are to encounter a holy person who will forgive them their sins.[50] Among the company are the men who had harmed the virtuous woman previously, including her brother-in-law and the king who had ordered her to be stoned. When they arrive, they notice that the holy person is a woman, and after they each tell her their story, she forgives them.

In this version, then, none of the men are maimed, the virtuous woman does not use rhetoric to stave off unwanted advances, she does not pray for deliverance, she is not knocked unconscious to wake up to healing powers, nor does fire-in-water play a protective role as it does for Thecla and 'Attār's virtuous woman. Moreover, she does not disguise herself as a man in any instance (rather her husband and brother-in-law simply fail to recognize her, and she has to tell them who she is). Nor is she appointed heir-apparent, which means she is not later elected kingmaker by the people. She even trades the wealth of the sailors for a place of worship like 'Attār's virtuous woman does. Except, instead of giving it to the king as the latter does, Kulaynī's virtuous woman gives it to her husband in exchange for being left alone on the island to worship God. And her husband readily agrees. He immediately leaves with the company, unlike the husband in 'Attār's TVW who is happy to see his wife again, remains with her, and becomes a co-ruler with her.[51]

---

[48] Interestingly, this virtuous woman is a mother of prophets. See ibid.
[49] In 'Attār's version, there is more tension. The sailors first fall in love with her and are moved to compassion when she first entreats them not to make advances toward her. They eventually succumb to their misplaced desire and lust. On this, see below.
[50] This version is similar to the dramatic conclusion of Pseudo-Clementine *Recognitions* since God, like Peter, engineers a recognition scene, except with a twist. It is not a happy family reunion in Kulaynī's version.
[51] There are other interesting differences in addition to the fact that she is the mother of prophets. Kulaynī's virtuous woman is married to the brother of a king's judge. Interestingly, when she

A Medieval Sufi Thecla? 295

Another version of the tale is, interestingly, by ʿAṭṭār's younger contemporary, ʿAwfī (1171–1242), who hailed from Bukhara (in modern-day Uzbekistan) and died in India. Albeit considerably shorter, ʿAwfī's version runs remarkably close to ʿAṭṭār's, with two major exceptions: the virtuous woman is not knocked unconscious[52] and, more importantly, she never becomes a leader.[53] The significance of the virtuous woman being knocked unconscious when she prays for death and wakes up to healing powers is that experiencing the rare death-before-death and receiving healing powers evokes the hagiographies and autobiographies of (historical and fictional, usually, male) Sufi masters who have similar experiences and powers.[54] More significantly, while ʿAwfī's virtuous woman (1171–1242) does perform healing miracles, she is not recognized as a figure of authority or as attaining temporal power as ʿAṭṭār's virtuous woman.[55] ʿAṭṭār's virtuous woman is, then, unique for being recognized as both a spiritual and civic leader within a Sufi context. Thus, further examination is warranted given these differences and the affinities of ʿAṭṭār's TVW to the *APT* and *Life of Eugenia* in the way that it (1) adapts certain popular motifs, actions, and

---

survives the stoning, she becomes a teacher. But even in this capacity she is a private tutor: after her stoning, she finds her way to a monastery where a monk takes her in (instead of the Bedouin in ʿAṭṭār's version), and he asks her to teach his son when she is set upon by another man. The remaining tales of escape are similar to ʿAṭṭār's version until she meets the sailors. For more, see Kulaynī's version in Sarwar (ed. and trans.), *al-Kāfī*, 2013: vol. 5, ch. 9; and Marzolph, "Crescentia's Oriental Relatives," 2008: 300–302.

[52] Her husband instead is knocked unconscious when she comes out of hiding to be reunited with him.

[53] ʿAwfī's version, however, includes the prayer by the virtuous woman on the ship because of which God sends a fire that engulfs everyone on the ship except our heroine. See Marzolph, "Crescentia's Oriental Relatives," 2008: 303–305.

[54] Sufi masters need not necessarily experience the death-before-death, nor do they all by necessity perform healing miracles. These are presented here as popular features of hagiographies and autobiographies of Sufi masters.

[55] The question that cannot be answered here is how familiar ʿAwfī and ʿAṭṭār were with each other's respective works. It could be that ʿAwfī, nearly thirty years ʿAṭṭār's junior, picked up ʿAṭṭār's version and merely recorded its outline. Or the converse, that ʿAwfī's version is the one that ʿAṭṭār picked up and expanded on its plot for his own purposes. We do know that ʿAwfī, who was also an avid collector of stories, resided for some time in Nishapur around 1202. The text in which ʿAwfī's version of the tale appears was completed in 1228 in Delhi, sometime after ʿAṭṭār's death, which occurred at some point between 1215 and 1220. ʿAwfī's text, *Jawāmiʿ al-ḥikāyāt wa lawāmiʿ al-riwāyāt*, began as a translation into Persian of stories by Qāẓī Abū ʿAlī Muḥāssin Tanūkhī (939–994) before he began to expand it by including more tales he had collected along his many travels. (For more on this text, its compilation, circulation, and modern editions, see Kargar, "Jawāmeʿ al-Ḥikāyāt," 2008.) Tanūkhī's most famous work, *al-Faraj baʿd al-shiddah* (*Deliverance after Stress*), is a collection of tales of people who faced incredible hardships and were saved by God or Muhammad. As the number of digitized manuscripts increases, perhaps other earlier versions of the tale may come to light and help us paint a more detailed picture of the itinerary of the tale and its development and the uniqueness (or not) of ʿAṭṭār's version.

behaviors towards religio-spiritual aims and (2) articulates female spiritual and civic leadership. Below, I will outline the possible circulation of the *APT* and the *Life of Eugenia* in the Iranian world before turning to our analyses.[56]

The Circulation of the *APT* and *Life of Eugenia* across the Iranian World

It hardly needs mentioning here that the apocryphal *Acts of Paul*, in which the *Acts of Thecla* appears, is one of the foundational texts for Christianity throughout the pre-modern world, even while its status as an authoritative text changed over time.[57] Thecla, indeed, is one of the most popular models of female sanctity and chastity, and her story is one of the earliest of Christian saints to spread rapidly across east and west.[58] In late antiquity, the *Acts of Thecla* was in wide circulation within and without the Iranian political and cultural sphere, and we may name Asia Minor, where the tale takes place, Sasanian Mesopotamia, Egypt, Georgia, and Armenia, the latter two of which boasted strong historical, dynastic, and religious ties with the Parthians (247 BCE–224 CE) and Sasanians (224–651).

As for the possible circulation of Thecla's tale across the Iranian world, we should consider two routes. First, the importance of the Church of the East, which covers much of the late antique Iranian world, should be stressed along with their various interactions with their brethren in Armenia and Georgia. Generally speaking, moreover, Christian communities flourished in the late Sasanian empire.[59] In fact, by the sixth century, the largest number of Christians lived within its territories. Christians continued to have a strong presence in the Islamicate world and, especially for our purposes, twelfth–thirteenth century Nishapur. Archaeological and textual evidence suggests that inasmuch as Christians, Jews, Buddhists, and Muslims had their places of worship located in separate quarters, eastern medieval Iranian cities were nevertheless teeming melting pots, and

---

[56] Much of what follows is published in Dabiri, "Reading the *Elāhināma*," 2018: 49–51. I would like to thank the editor, Saïd Amir Arjomand, for permission to reprint.
[57] On which, see Barrier, *The Acts of Paul and Thecla*, 2009: 25–30; and Klazina Staat's contribution in the present volume (Chapter 9).
[58] For more, see the collected papers in Barrier et al. (eds.), *Thecla*, 2017.
[59] It is a well-known fact that Christians from the Roman empire were brought and resettled in Iranian cities after the Sasanians won several decisive victories over the Romans. It is conceivable that they would have brought their stories with them considering other artistic exchanges. For more on this latter point, see Canepa, *The Two Eyes*, 2009.

A Medieval Sufi Thecla?

inter-confessional interactions were frequent. And, here, it may be of interest to us to mention the medieval translations of the *Acts of Thecla* into Arabic.[60]

Second, a recent discovery of a manuscript in Kocho, Turfan, where there was a large community of Manichaeans, as attested by the thousands of manuscript fragments found there, contains some lines from the *Acts of Thecla*.[61] Thus, we turn briefly to the Manichaeans who are a fruitful avenue to pursue for the circulation of the *Acts of Thecla*. For, indeed, the Manichaeans, whose founder, Mani (d. c. 277), hailed from southwest Iran, flourished in late antiquity, and their missionary work took them to various cities throughout the Iranian and Byzantine worlds. Though they were persecuted by the early ʿAbbasids (750–1258), they nevertheless "persistently survived, clandestinely perpetuating their teachings."[62] In their missionary work, Manichaeans set about translating not only the works of Mani himself but also of the Apocryphal Acts.[63] Focusing his attention on Manichaeans and the circulation of the *Acts of Thecla* in Egypt, Stephen Davis makes the astute observation that the Manichaeans were also actively disseminating the *Acts of Thecla* and "considered her the paradigmatic virgin exemplar for women."[64] Of great significance also is the relationship between the development of Islamic mysticism and the establishment of Sufi orders[65] to post-Islamic Manichaean developments

---

[60] The Arabic *Acts of Thecla* are housed in St. Catherine's Monastery in the Sinai. Of the medieval manuscripts, there is one tenth-century manuscript (ms. 513) and one twelfth-century manuscript (ms. 534). They currently remain unedited: Davis (ed. and trans.), "An Arabic *Acts*," 2017: 106–109.

[61] Voicu, "Thecla," 2017: 67.   [62] Reeves, *Prolegomena*, 2011: 281.

[63] For more on this, see Kaestli, "L'utilisation," 1977.

[64] Davis, *The Cult of St. Thecla*, 2001: 101. The following is an excerpt from the fourth-century Manichaean Coptic *Psalms of the Wanderers*: "Peter the Apostle, who was crucified upside down ... Andrew the apostle – they set fire to the house beneath him ... John the Virgin, he also was made to drink the cup ... And James also, he was stoned and killed .... The same things also did Thomas endure in his cross ... Paul the Apostle – they went against him that they might kill him ... Thecla, the lover of God, who was made to go up on the fire. She received the sign of the cross, she walked into the fire rejoicing. Yet was she not ashamed, naked in the midst of the crowd. She was thrown to the bears, the lions were let loose to her. She was bound to the bulls, the seals were let loose to her. All these things that she suffered, she did not flinch .... The blessed Drusiane also, she also suffered the same, fourteen days imprisoned like her master, her Apostle. Maximilla and Aristobula – on them was great torture inflicted. What need for them to suffer these things? It is purity for which they fight:" Allberry (ed. and trans.), *A Manichaean Psalm-Book*, 1938: 142, l. 18–143, l. 14. I thank Flavia Ruani for the reference.

[65] Sufism by the medieval period, and especially in ʿAttār's city and region, had become a broad social-based movement, and Sufi *khānaqāhs* (orders) were centers of learning that also provided lodging for travelers.

in Greater Khorasan,[66] a region to which Nishapur belongs, where Thecla's tale, thus, may have been transmitted.

Eugenia's tale too is popularly attested, appearing in Latin, Greek, Armenian, and Syriac. It, moreover, circulated throughout Eurasia and North Africa, perhaps along the same routes as, if not with, the *APT* throughout Iranian Christendom. Finally, in terms of the Mattidia narrative,[67] it should be mentioned here that Pseudo-Clementine *Recognitions*, "an enigmatic corpus of writings whose affinities with important streams of Palestinian and Syro-Mesopotamian religious communities,"[68] displays a quasi religio-political interest in Iranian history and genealogy as it relates to Judeo-Christian history.[69]

Given the strong affinities between ʿAṭṭār's TVW and the aforementioned tales, the question that one may ask is this: However exciting the prospect, did ʿAṭṭār actually have access to the *APT* or the *Life of Eugenia*? Based on the evidence we have in hand, we can only state that this is possible given the wide circulation of these tales throughout the Iranian world and, with them, many others. Its probability, however, remains an open question. An alternate scenario, or more aptly hypothesis, may be proposed as well, namely, the reconstitution of tales and motifs. Put in another way, inasmuch as the itineraries of the tales of our specific itinerant female saints are significant so too are the ways in which narratives, in general, were reconstituted, adopted, and adapted along the way both orally and in written texts toward various aims. ʿAṭṭār certainly adopted and adapted genres (see below) and tales to suit his purposes. Thus, rather than access to specific texts, we may hypothesize that circulating widely were a series of motifs that were tightly bound together through ordering and that clustered around tales of holy women, in which some wield both power and authority.[70] Whatever the case may prove to be, the remarkably

---

[66] This area covered much of the northeastern territories of modern-day Iran as well as parts of modern-day Afghanistan, Turkmenistan, Tajikistan, and Uzbekistan. For the connections between the *khānaqāhs* and post-Islamic Manichaeism, see Böwering and Melvin-Koushki, "*Ḵānaqāh*," 2010.

[67] Though Mattidia's story is not analyzed in this chapter, nonetheless, for our purposes it is important to note here.

[68] Reeves, "Jacob of Edessa?," 2016: 204.

[69] A number of paragraphs are dedicated to an exposition of the genealogical tables in the Old Testament. These passages consider the origins of Zoroastrianism through the biblical figure, Nimrod, and the origins of the "Persians" through Abraham. See Smith, "Recognitions of Clement," 1886: book I, chapter 30 and 33, respectively.

[70] For which we then must suppose that there were other similar texts (oral and written) to which we no longer have access. Further comment on this as it relates to the motifs and themes discussed here and medieval Iranian (oral) storytelling and Persian hagiography would lead us down a rabbit hole of speculation, a topic that lies well beyond the scope and interests of this chapter. Instead, I refer the reader to scholarship on the possible oral background of the *APT* and women as storytellers in

A Medieval Sufi Thecla? 299

strong affinities between the texts under discussion here are certainly worth noting. What may prove a more rewarding avenue to pursue henceforward, however, is the representation and promotion of and, thus, possible attitudes toward independent female leadership in our three texts. Here, now, we turn to ʿAttār's ideals of rulership as prescribed by the *Ilāhīnāmah* and TVW.

The *Ilāhīnāmah* and the Ideal Sufi King

Before turning to a comparison of Eugenia and the virtuous woman as spiritual and civic leaders who surpass Thecla, it may behoove us to first provide some additional context about the *Ilāhīnāmah* since it frames the TVW and especially since, despite ʿAttār's overwhelming popularity, the *Ilāhīnāmah* remains one of his least studied works, undeservedly so.

As noted above, the *Ilāhīnāmah* features a wide variety of historical and fictional characters from every cross-section of life. Each tale finds these characters in situations in which exemplary living is stressed but not always by saints: while fictional bakers and street-sweepers are sometimes taught invaluable life lessons from historical saints, feckless judges are admonished by fictional poor farmers, and anonymous Zoroastrians claim spiritual superiority to impious, yet famous, historical Muslim rulers. Even the saints sometimes find themselves in awkward situations of their own making, and their mistakes gently corrected, sometimes by other saints and sometimes by the laity. As the caliph puts it:

> How often those who have submitted to the religion / learn the most from the least of God's servants.[71]

Moreover, each tale, beginning with the TVW, is suffused with the spirit of Sufism. As such, the *Ilāhīnāmah* is ontological; it offers examples of holy, exemplary living from the mundane (what to do if a dog wanders into a mosque) to the extraordinary (what to do if you are a princess and fall in love with the palace servant) according to the tenets of Sufism. In this way, the *Ilāhīnāmah* appropriates the generic stance of hagiographies, as portraits of exemplary living for a non-specialist audience. Conversely, the *Ilāhīnāmah* targets and invites a broad, non-specialist audience to live

---

the late antique Byzantine world. For an overview of the sources and main arguments, see Davis, *The Cult of St. Thecla*, 2001: 8–18. See, also, Burrus, *Chastity as Autonomy*, 1987: 34–35, for a list of motifs several hagiographies of female saints share in common and that, thus, suggest an oral background. Barrier, *The Acts of Paul and Thecla*, 2009: 30–47, sees a weaker link between the oral tradition and the *APT*.

[71] ʿAttār, *Ilāhīnāmah*, Discourse 11, story 7: Shafīʿī-Kadkanī (ed.), *Ilāhīnāmah*, 2013: 250, l. 3117.

moral, holy lives, by representing them as exemplary protagonists.[72] With its focus on kings receiving lessons (frame and individual tales), however, the *Ilāhīnāmah* also adopts the generic stance of mirrors-for-princes that overlap hagiographies in their formal aspects, namely, entertaining tales of memorable characters in easily accessible language to convey the philosophical or theological, respectively, underpinnings of a just and moral society.[73]

Certainly, mirrors-for-princes are concerned with good governance and civic duty. In fact, by and large, mirrors focus on kings (1) as the most important members to whom their respective societies owe their obedience and loyalty and, in circular fashion, (2) as the head of the body politic who ensures, through his own conduct and governance, the well-being of the populace and, thus, is deserving of that loyalty and obedience. Accordingly, then, when a king is just, society prospers. When unjust, rebellions proliferate, and society falls to ruin. The *Ilāhīnāmah* adopts the structure and style of mirrors while disrupting them at the level of meaning, however, to illustrate exemplary *holy* living for kings and everyday folk *alike*. Indeed, similar to practical ethics and mirrors, the *Ilāhīnāmah* is concerned with good governance and civic duty. However, while practical ethics and mirrors usually place the focus of tales on kings and their responsibilities, in the *Ilāhīnāmah*, regular folks, saints, *and* kings are equal in their responsibility toward the divine, religion, and each other. The *Ilāhīnāmah*, thus, places its primary emphasis on love of the divine and spiritual awareness for the proper functioning of society.

Significantly, by offering portraits of everyday folk who sometimes one-up those saints and kings who momentarily have forgotten the meaning and basis of their ranks, it creates momentary saints and ideal leaders, broadly defined, out of each community member. In other words, anyone can be in a position of power and authority, not just kings, and every moment in life is an opportunity to exemplify holy living when wielding power and authority, which helps create an ideal state. This is exemplified in various moments of the TVW: the virtuous woman's speech to the king about life's priorities (see below), when she forgives and heals the repentant men, who previously had harmed her, and when she brings them into the fold of a community who, in their election of her as king and then kingmaker, recognize the importance of holy, exemplary living in a ruler.

---

[72] For more on audience and the *Ilāhīnāmah*, see Dabiri, "Reading the *Elāhīnāmah*," 2018: 30–43; and Dabiri, "'When a Lion Is Chided,'" 2019: 66–67 and 79.

[73] One important aspect that should be mentioned as well is that they reject esoteric concepts.

A Medieval Sufi Thecla? 301

Thus, instead of the ideal philosopher king of practical ethics and mirrors, it is the ideal Sufi king that the *Ilāhīnāmah* promotes as well as everyday folk as exemplars on par with even saints.

According to the *Ilāhīnāmah*, from the beggar to the king, Christians, Jews, Muslims, and Zoroastrians alike must be actively engaged in cultivating their souls, their *bātin* (interior) over their *zāhir* (exterior), as the first and most difficult step in taking responsibility. In its promotion of the interior, where the heart – the most perceptive organ that can sense the divine – resides, the *Ilāhīnāmah* makes immaterial several socially important aspects of the exterior, namely, class, gender, and confessional divides, an aspect put on full display in the TVW.[74] For indeed, even though the virtuous woman turns down the kingship when she is appointed by the king as his heir, the tale nevertheless subverts the principle of the right of the first-born son or agnatic succession by the very offer.[75] And, it is the community who insists that she, despite her refusal on the grounds that she is a woman, rule like a man[76] or, as heir-apparent, select someone she deems worthy to rule instead. The significance is that the community recognizes her religious and civic authority, as noted above. However, it is worth stressing that they do so regardless of her gender and the fact that she is not from among the ruling elite, much less family, or even the region (she is a complete stranger!) and selects her anyway.[77]

The *Ilāhīnāmah*, thus, highlights its three main concerns, namely, the individual, the community, and state, all of which are to mirror God's love and his kingdom. This is especially salient in the conversations the caliph has with his sons and in the supporting tales he narrates. As noted above, the caliph's concern is immediately his sons and their souls. However, as kings, they, like the virtuous woman, are the heads of the body politic and are society's premier exemplars, or at least they *should* be. Therefore, their shortcomings extend to the general populace as, according to practical ethics, the king's deeds determine whether or not society is calm and

---

[74] This aspect of the *Ilāhīnāmah* is an argument against all the intra-confessional divides among Sufis as well as society as a whole. See Dabiri, "'When a Lion Is Chided,'" 2019.
[75] In selecting the wisest and most religious as heir-apparent, the *Ilāhīnāmah* follows a number of medieval practical ethics that advocate for selecting the best to rule. This is a theme that is also found in the ancient Iranian religious and later epic traditions as it is related in the story of King Firaydūn who must decide how to divide the world between his three sons. He chooses his youngest and wisest son, Īraj, to rule over the best part of the world, Iran, which incurs the wrath of his older brothers who devise and successfully execute a plot to kill their younger brother.
[76] For she had been living as a male ascetic until her reveal.
[77] This hearkens to early Islamic versions of the ancient Iranian narratives of kingship whereby the community plays an active role in selecting rightful leaders and in measuring them up.

prosperous or chaotic and rebellious. For instance, though the sons are kings and their desires are traditionally associated with that of rulers, they nonetheless are all too familiar. Who has not dreamt of changing their lives with magic, with a wish or a power-granting talisman? (Hollywood producers have built veritable empires on such desires, and it seems our medieval counterparts were no less susceptible to such fantasies.) Thus, when the sons respond, the caliph recognizes a disruption, a disconnect between the body and the soul, or more aptly, the embodiment of the soul – a disconnect that is a common ailment in society.[78] It is, essentially, a lack of control over the interior, which leads to the corruption of the exterior.

The caliph in his attempt to teach his sons these important lessons, turns his sons, the kings, into Sufi disciples (just as the *Ilāhīnāmah* does with the audience it invites). Much like the caliph who wears both a king's robe and a Sufi's, so too does the virtuous woman. In these terms, then, the virtuous woman embodies the responsibility to the community and the divine in her tripartite role as a member of the populace (wife of a wealthy husband), a holy woman, and a leader, thus one-upping even the caliph who only embodies two roles. One of the most important aspects of the virtuous woman's tripartite role is in the control she exerts over her virtue, which she extends to her husband and society as their spiritual leader. We can extrapolate this not just from the underlying principles of practical ethics and mirrors-for-princes outlined above but from the way in which two prominent dual motifs in Sufism are deployed in the tale, that is the dual motif of love (of the divine) and beauty (manifestations of the divine) that is intertwined with the interior-exterior dual motif. For instance, the virtuous woman's beauty propels her into different situations in different locales, like many a heroine in Byzantine hagiography and ancient romances. The difference between the latter (with the exception of Eugenia) and the virtuous woman lies in the fact that the control she exerts over her interior *and* exterior allows her to become a holy woman *and* a leader. The men in the tale are like the caliph's sons, they are like (wayward) Sufi adepts and are, thus, in need of instruction. They have not yet learned to truly love. By allowing their physical desires to guide their actions, the men's violent attempts to take the virtuous woman by force means they have not nurtured their interiors (souls/hearts). The disconnect between their souls and bodies – their incorrect understanding of

---

[78] For more on the relationship between embodiment, the body, and the body politic especially in terms of a hagiography of a female saint, see Kugle, *Sufis and Saints' Bodies*, 2007.

and wrong response to beauty, which is but one manifestation of the divine – sets them on a terrible path that leads to physical disability and distress. In Sufi coded terminology, then, in addition to the benefits of self-awareness and love of the divine, nurturing one's interior also helps keep one's physical exterior intact. For indeed, it is only when the men repent and are open to cultivating their souls – when they recognize the virtuous woman's spirituality and value it and God's love over her physical beauty – are their exteriors miraculously healed through the virtuous woman's exertion of her divinely given spiritual power.

Taking this an extra step further, the TVW depicts the intimate relationship between kingship, religion, and society in the form of a celibate marriage. Though the text does not mention if the virtuous woman and her pious husband resume marital relations, we can presume that they did not because she continues to devote her life to worship. The holy woman has not only selected her pious husband as king but, by default, has made him a virtuous (celibate) king. The kingmaker has installed her male equivalent on the throne. Yet religious authority remains in her domain. She, thus, confers on him both temporal and religious authority while safeguarding the realm as its spiritual and as its moral leader. Significantly, she engenders a spiritual conversion at the individual, communal, and state levels. The kingdom prospers with the control she exerts not just over her body but over the bodies of the men and the new king, her husband, and, thus, over the body politic.[79] She "lays the happy foundation" of society.[80] And, thus, the tale upends not only practical ethics in general but also the gendered terms of the Sufi master (male/authority)-disciple (female/submissive) relationship.[81]

Having now discussed some of the general points about gender, leadership, the body, and body politic in 'Aṭṭār's *Ilāhīnāmah* and TVW, we now turn to the ways in which TVW and *Life of Eugenia* explore independently attained female leadership with Thecla as a forerunner.

---

[79] In reading the *APT* in terms of desire, Lipsett, *Desiring Conversion*, 2011: 85, notes something similar transpires: "Desire takes a destructive force in certain characters, and Thecla is never so autonomous as to be unaffected. Yet desire is destabilizing in ways that propel conversion – social re-identification, ritual act, changes in language, changes in the self."
[80] 'Aṭṭār, *Ilāhīnāmah*, Discourse 1, story 1: Shafīʿī-Kadkanī (ed.), *Ilāhīnāmah*, 2013: 144, l. 792.
[81] See Malamud, "Gender," 1996: 112, for examples of this engendered language that depicts the "unequal relations between men and between women and men who were intimately linked in an entire social system. The medieval Islamic social order was made up of a complex web of personally contracted relationships which were nearly always asymmetrical." It is worth noting that included in this is the image of the master as mother and nurturer and the disciple as the babe suckling at the master's breasts.

Female Leadership, Independently Attained

Though the reasons for which the author of the *Life and Miracles of Thecla* composed his work are manifold,[82] one can imagine that like many a reader of the *APT*, he was perhaps left unsatisfied by the story's abrupt end. In any case, the *Life and Miracles of Thecla* is an extensive elaboration of Thecla's life – her teaching, evangelizing, and performance of miracles – after her last trial, baptism, and farewell with Paul and her mother. Similarly, it seems as if the *Life of Eugenia*[83] and TVW zoom in on the theme of independently attained female authority and expand and elaborate upon it, albeit in ways different from the *Life and Miracles of Thecla*.[84]

To begin with, Thecla's story ends abruptly, as just noted, fairly soon after she receives baptism. Before her final departure from Paul and then her mother, however, she forms a bond and solidifies an alliance with Queen Tryphaena. Tryphaena, it should be recalled here, is a cousin of the emperor.[85] She becomes Thecla's benefactor and provides her with the emotional and financial support Thecla loses when she is rejected by her mother for her choices and again by the apostle Paul, the inspiration for those choices. Tryphaena, thus, supplants her mother *and* Paul, who by the end (rather begrudgingly) gives Thecla permission to teach after the fact – as he witnesses her growing following and, thus, her development into a successful teacher and evangelizer without his assistance. But it is worth stressing that Thecla first becomes teacher and evangelizer immediately after her baptism at her trial. She teaches first the governor of Antioch who is overseeing the trial, she converts some of the people in attendance at the arena, and she teaches and converts Tryphaena and her household afterwards. This group in turn grows as they follow Thecla out of Antioch. Likewise, it is precisely the moment when they are baptized that the virtuous woman and Eugenia also become leaders, teachers, and

---

[82] See, for instance, Johnson, *The Life and Miracles*, 2006: 6–14; Hylen, *A Modest Apostle*, 2015: 109–111; and Wood, "The Invention of History," 2009: 132–134.
[83] This is the case with the Latin version of the *Life of Eugenia*. Even if a later version "erases" all references to the *APT*, it nevertheless engages with both Thecla and her tale in other ways. See Klazina Staat's contribution in this volume (Chapter 9) for more.
[84] Though, of course, Thecla is a teacher in the *Life and Miracles of Thecla*. As the leader of and teacher at her own sanctuary, her authority and leadership here may fall more along the lines of hagiographies of saints such as Melania the Elder.
[85] On the identity of Queen Tryphaena as the first cousin of the Emperor Claudius, see Barrier, *The Acts of Paul and Thecla*, 2009: 145.

evangelizers (although there is a lengthier process for Eugenia in the Syriac version).[86]

Even as significant as the baptism is for the conversion of these women into leaders and evangelizers, so to speak, the women are at earlier points in the narrative marked as special. Much like Thecla, during her first trial in Iconium, Eugenia and the virtuous woman are immediately recognized for their rather miraculous power and authority by male leaders. In the *APT*, the proconsul at her trial "wept and marveled at the power in her" (§ 3.22). When the virtuous woman arrives on shore, she tells her tale to the king and his ministers, and after they witness her miraculous powers, they immediately obey her commands, which includes building a shrine where she may devote her time to worshipping God. In Eugenia's case, she is a precocious child[87] who, before any encounter with the *APT* or Paul's teachings,[88] is predisposed toward a life of continence. Later, she is recognized as a woman by the abbot of the monastery she wishes to enter despite her disguise (he tells her that her gender was revealed to him in a dream). Despite her gender and contrary to many hagiographies, she is allowed entry into the monastery, albeit in the guise of a man. During her time at the monastery, she proves herself to be superior in every way, but it is her humility and service to the monastery and her brothers-in-faith that set her apart.

Eugenia's and the virtuous woman's power and authority, their conduct, make it clear to their respective new communities that they are most suited to lead: when the abbot of the monastery dies, the monks hold elections, and they unanimously elect Eugenia. In the case of the TVW, when the king is at his deathbed, he summons his ministers and his army to inform them that he has selected the virtuous woman as his heir-apparent, a proclamation to which they all immediately agree. Neither the virtuous woman nor Eugenia are particularly overjoyed by the respective turn of events, as they would rather continue in their daily worships. As noted above, both reject the position on account of being women, but this rejection spurs the men on. The men remain unpersuaded by their arguments. Both tales, thus, offer a stunning reversal of the typical motif of rejection and rhetoric used to maintain female chastity.

---

[86] In the Metaphrastic version, Eugenia is immediately baptized, while in the Syriac version she is baptized within three months. See Papaioannou (ed. and trans.), "Life, Conduct, and Passion," 2017: 207; and Lewis (trans.), "Eugenia," 1900: 11.

[87] A common trope of hagiographies of male saints is the precocious child.

[88] Some versions of the *Life of Eugenia* note Paul's teachings or the *APT*.

Indeed, in the TVW, the ministers and army insist that she, as the king's designated heir, lead them as a man (presumably as she has lived her life as a male holy saint thus far) or select someone she finds suitable. In her desire to continue her devotions, she chooses someone to reign while she continues to worship God. Similarly, when Eugenia turns to the Bible for guidance, she happens on the passage:

> Ye know that the chiefs of the nations are their lords, and their great men ruler over them. It shall not be so among you, but whosoever among you wishes to be the chief, let him be the servant and minister of every man.[89]

After reading this passage, she turns to her brethren and says, "since ye have made known that this is your wish, it is incumbent upon us that we fulfill the commandments of the Christ" and accepts only the title of abbot to not vex them. Her compromise does not persuade them as they demand that she, who unbeknownst to them is the daughter of the pagan eparch, be the head of the monastery:

> She yielded to them also in this ... and the things which the last ought to do to the first in the service of the saints, she in her eagerness and in her humility used to do."[90]

In other words, she continues to clean and sweep the floors as she used to. (While she has taken the guidance of the Bible to heart, an egalitarian, just streak was already running through Eugenia: when she first decided to become a Christian, she freed her servants and proclaimed them her equals in their new confession, though they still obeyed their former mistress in everything.)

Following the vein of rhetoric, interestingly, as kingmaker and the kingdom's spiritual leader, the virtuous woman never directly addresses the public. There is one moment, however, when the virtuous woman speaks to a larger audience that resembles the *APT* in certain respects. When the governor of Antioch calls a halt to Thecla's sadistic, yet quite unsuccessful, trial he asks the simple question: "Who are you?" to which Thecla gives the powerful response, "I am the servant of God" (§ 4.12). Emboldened by the fact that she has been baptized by her own initiative, she arrogates to herself the authority to teach and informs the governor (and all within earshot at the theater) that God offers salvation and eternal life to those who place their trust in him (§ 4.12). Meanwhile, the virtuous woman tells her story, including her harrowing escape from her would-be

---

[89] Lewis (trans.), "Eugenia," 1900: 14.   [90] Ibid.

rapists on the ship, to the king and all his men as a lesson to the king and his army about God's power and the futility of worldly pursuits.

When Eugenia is falsely accused of sexually assaulting Melanthia, a noble woman, the proconsul, Philip, asks if this (sexual assault) is what Christianity teaches.[91] In the Armenian and Syriac versions, Eugenia informs him that Christianity teaches exactly the opposite. She elaborates further by offering a defense of herself in her choice to live chastely. Only then does she reveal her identity to Philip to prove that she is incapable of attacking Melanthia in the way that the latter and her maid have claimed. In the Metaphrastic version, she also takes a moment to flex her rhetorical[92] abilities and offers Philip an invaluable lesson on just rule:

> Indeed, you should have neither given credence to my accusers so easily nor passed sentence so readily and precipitously; you ought instead to have first listened to both sides then made a decision. If it should become apparent I did such things, I should be rightfully punished. But if these accusations should prove to be false and an obvious slander, I ask one favor above all: that nothing terrible befall this woman ... for this is the command of our law, and we are persuaded that we should not repay evil with evil under any circumstance, but rather with good.[93]

Philip and Eugenia have had ample time to develop their abilities as leaders over the years. Philip was nominated by the emperor in Rome to be the eparch of Alexandria and ruled for a time. Eugenia, meanwhile, was unanimously elected by her brethren to be leader of the monastery and led in that capacity for a number of years. Yet, despite the difference in age between them and the fact that Philip has been a civic leader, it is Eugenia who is the teacher of civic and religious laws and holds moral authority in their exchange. Just as the virtuous woman's lesson on the meaninglessness of wealth leads to her being selected as heir-apparent, the younger Thecla teaches the proconsul and the older Queen Tyrphaena and her household, and the young Eugenia teaches her father (and later his household and city).

Philip, as noted above, cannot accept at first that a Christian of low birth could be telling him the truth, much less be able to give lessons on proper justice. Then, she reveals herself to be a woman and his daughter.

---

[91] For the Syriac version, see ibid., 20. For the Greek version see, Papaioannou (ed. and trans.), "Life, Conduct, and Passion," 2017: 222–223; and for the Armenian, see Conybeare (ed. and trans.), "The Acts of Saint Eugenia," 1896: 175.
[92] On rhetoric in the Latin passions of Eugenia, see Klazina Staat's contribution in this volume (Chapter 9).
[93] Papaioannou (ed. and trans.), "Life, Conduct, and Passion," 2017: 227.

The reveal is perceived as a miracle by all in attendance, but especially by her father, which leads to the conversion of her family. However, on a first reading of this episode, there seems to be a reversal of the *APT* and TVW in the *Life of Eugenia*. In his joy at discovering that his long-lost daughter is standing before him, Philip places a robe embroidered with gold on her and lifts her onto his throne. Philip's move signals a return to membership of the family and the ruling elite. The converse of this occurs in the *APT* when (1) Thecla trades her gold bracelets for access to Paul, (2) abandons her mother, and her mother in turn later ignores her, and (3) again when Thecla knocks Alexander's crown off his head when he sexually accosts her – which symbolizes a loss of divinity, "the inferiority of the 'leading man' to the Christ."[94] But in fact when she is adopted by Queen Tryphaena, she gains membership into a more powerful, elite social circle than the one she was already a member of as Alexander quickly discovers when she proclaims, "I am a leading woman of the Iconians" (§ 4.1). Much like the virtuous woman, who when she first lands on shore, gains the protection of the king and becomes a member of the ruling elite.

Furthermore, like the changing opinions of the spectators at Thecla's trial and her growing number of followers, Philip and the rest of the family convert to Christianity. So too does the entire arena of spectators, who were until that moment against Eugenia. Eventually, the entire city converts as the happy news spreads that the leader of a monastery is in fact the eparch's missing daughter, and he has converted. For indeed, Eugenia was beloved, from an early age, by the city, and her loss was deeply felt – she was mourned by all.[95] She is, thus, at the very heart of the conversion of the entire city of Alexandria, the body politic, when she reveals her body and, thus, her identity and belonging to the family who stands at the head of the body politic. Much like the virtuous woman, Eugenia goes back to her ascetic life. Nevertheless, through her familial association, Philip's rulership takes a new turn, and the city enters into a new state of religiosity. Though the text does not explicitly state this, it does imply that father and daughter enter into a type of co-rulership, with Eugenia as its spiritual leader and Philip as its civic leader, at least until later when he is named bishop. And, thus, similar to the virtuous woman's role as kingmaker, Eugenia becomes a bishop-maker of sorts. In any case, until Philip's appointment as bishop, Eugenia lends the eparch moral and religious authority as the leader of the monastery just as she was

---

[94] Barrier, *The Acts of Paul and Thecla*, 2009: 141.
[95] Papaioannou (ed. and trans.), "Life, Conduct, and Passion," 2017: 209–211.

instrumental in teaching the eparch about just rule. Thus, while we may know that Tryphaena, together with her household, follows Thecla, in the *APT* we are left to imagine what such a powerful relationship might entail once the trials are over, apart from the fact that we are told she illuminated many (§ 4.18). The *Life of Eugenia* takes the time to explore this story line. But it is significant that the latter swaps the adoptive mother-queen and daughter relationship for a father-eparch and daughter relationship. This androcentric shift will be discussed momentarily.

The ramifications of the reveal for leadership and the body politic is similar to that noted above for the virtuous woman. It should be recalled here that when the virtuous woman reveals her identity (which happens semi-privately in her sanctuary with her husband and the men who had previously attacked her), she heals the men of their disabilities. She also bequeaths unto them wealth, putting them to shame. Then, she makes her husband the king and the one man who aided her during her travails, a Bedouin, his minister. Even if there is no conversion *of confession* as in the *APT* and the *Life of Eugenia*, there is a *spiritual* conversion. The bodies of the men and the body politic are made whole by her and through her co-rulership with her husband.[96]

For all these similarities, we must also acknowledge that the *Life of Eugenia* is certainly more androcentric and maintains a stricter social order than the *APT* and TVW. In addition to the Tryphaena-Thecla, Philip-Eugenia relationships noted above, the crowd that Thecla first attracts in the arena at her first trial is mixed gendered and some are for and some are against her. In her second trial, the spectators are all women who cry out as one that "a profane judgement has come to this city" (§ 4.3).[97] Eugenia, meanwhile, faces spectators of both genders, who are all resolutely against her since she is up against one of their own. It is only after their recognition that she too is one of their own, that she is able to effect

---

[96] 'Aṭṭār, in his other works, deals with both spiritual conversion and conversion across confession using the so-called other (Christians and Zoroastrians) as a springboard. In many tales, when a Sufi master converts a Zoroastrian to Islam, it is considered a miracle and spurs others to renew their faith. For more on this, see Dabiri, "Who's the Authority?," 2021. For the theme of conversion in tales featuring Christians in 'Aṭṭār's works, see Lewis, "Sexual Occidentation," 2009.

[97] Later, during the trial, when the crowd's gender is mixed, the audience's reaction is also mixed, with some crying out against "'the Sacrilegious One,' while others were saying, 'May the city be wiped out concerning this unlawful act. Wipe us all out Proconsul. A bitter spectacle, evil judgement'" (§ 4.7). Later, when Thecla survives the gruesome trial unscathed, and she is released, the women call out "in a great voice and as out of one voice they gave thanks to God saying, 'One is God who has saved Thecla,' so that the whole city was shaken by the sound" (§ 4.13). Though there is no conversion of the whole city, it parallels the moment when spectators in the arena and later the whole city are converted after Eugenia's trial.

change. (There is one caveat, though. Elite women seem to have a powerful voice in government as demonstrated by the ease with which Melanthia is able to bring Eugenia to court in Alexandria; an action for which she is similar to Thecla's mother in the *APT*.) The second half of the *Life of Eugenia*, however, becomes quite drastically androcentric in its move to Rome. With Philip beheaded in Alexandria by a rival, Eugenia and her mother and brothers flee to Rome where they take up their former lives as nobles. While her brothers are offered positions as leaders in the empire (in certain versions, at least), Eugenia relinquishes her leadership role. At least she does so in the public domain: Eugenia is demoted, so to speak, to a private life of evangelization among an inner circle of elite women, which takes place often in the sanctuary of their homes (and here she is more like Paul at the beginning of the *APT* than Thecla).

In Rome, Eugenia and her mother and brothers are in a place where their new religion is not represented (see below). Nevertheless, and this is important, being Christians does not prevent the family from retaining their social status or the comforts and privileges it affords them. Her brothers, it should be stressed, are even given leadership roles. This easy integration into the nobility lasts until Eugenia threatens the social order: she convinces the noble women in her circle to become the brides of Christ. And in this, the *Life of Eugenia* and TVW diverge dramatically. The difference lies in the rhetoric of early Christian texts and Islamic views on marriage and ascetic practice. For the latter, the practice of both had their respective places. Early Christians, on the other hand, used self-mastery as Christianity's claim to moral superiority – the ascetic teacher represents a challenge to the status quo, namely, the single body integrated into a single household, into the (reproductive) body social.[98]

The androcentrism and restricted social order in relation to the *APT* and TVW becomes dramatically clear when Eugenia takes on a disciple, Basilla, and convinces her to renounce marriage. Basilla's fiancé takes the matter to the emperor and argues his case against Eugenia. The fiancé maps the familial (lack of heir) onto the communal and political: he asks the emperor first what will happen to the homeland and population of Rome if everyone were to remain virgins and, second (perhaps more importantly), what would happen to the numbers of the emperor's army without those sons being born.[99] The first question is one the first son also poses to his father, the caliph, after the virtuous woman's story comes to an

---

[98] Cooper, *The Virgin and the Bride*, 1999: 57–58.
[99] Papaioannou (ed. and trans.), "Life, Conduct, and Passion," 2017: 249–251.

end.[100] The caliph follows up with a tale that depicts the eventual happy union between a lover (a presumably low-ranking woman) and her aloof beloved (a prince) when she demonstrates to the king the true meaning of love, and he sends her to be with his son.[101] The latter question, meanwhile, seems to motivate the emperor, and Eugenia is ordered to be executed. In the *APT*, it is Thecla's mother who demands that her daughter be punished for upsetting the social order. For when Thecla rejects her fiancé, Thamyris, she seems to threaten her *mother's* source of income and also to reject her reproductive choices and values.[102]

So, what are we to make of the differences between the first and second halves of the *Life of Eugenia*? In the first half, we have a tale that builds on independently attained female leadership, whereas the second half undercuts what it built, much like Eugenia and her father who are unceremoniously beheaded, effectively cutting off the heads of the civic and religious body politic. Should we understand the text as ultimately policing the extents to which women could attain such positions of leadership and authority, or more simply as part of the ambivalent attitudes toward women prevalent in Byzantine hagiographies?[103] And we must acknowledge that though Eugenia becomes bishop-maker, so to speak, and demonstrates her aptitude for just, moral leadership and confers that authority on her father, she never actually becomes a civic leader.

Though reading for the complex ways in which pain and suffering were articulated across the Greek-speaking world and what this meant for the growth of Christianity, Judith Perkins' assertions about representation may help shed some light.[104] Indeed, her point that "textual representations do not just reflect, in some unproblematic way, reality and social institutions, but, rather, help to create and maintain them"[105] is particularly helpful. Reading the *Life of Eugenia* in terms of representation, it seems to me that the second half is more a damning castigation of what the hagiographer thought Rome, the center of power, could envision in terms of Christianity *and* female ascetic practice, leadership, and/or authority.

---

[100] The father's response is that carnal desire, when directed properly, may give way to passionate love and eventually to spiritual love until annihilation in the divine. Among his responses though, the father asks the son, when it is possible to be in the company of Jesus, why would anyone choose to be in the presence of an ass? See ʿAttār, *Ilāhīnāmah*, Discourse 2: Shafiʿī-Kadkanī (ed.), *Ilāhīnāmah*, 2013: 144, l. 793–145, l. 814.
[101] ʿAttār, *Ilāhīnāmah*, Discourse 2, story 1.
[102] For more on this, see Cooper and Corke-Webster, "Conversion, Conflict," 2014.
[103] For more, see Davis, "Crossed Texts, Crossed Sex," 2002.
[104] Perkins, *The Suffering Self*, 1995.   [105] Ibid.: 12.

This holds even with the understanding that the individual was often subordinated to the familial and social in the Greco-Roman world.[106]

For indeed, as we have seen, on the peripheries of empire the differences are vast. In the first half of the *Life of Eugenia*, Christians in Alexandria lead a very *public* life: Eugenia hears them singing as they parade about on the streets, they are a community that can defeat so-called magicians publicly by a trial by fire, their church has infrastructure (they have bishops, abbots, and monasteries), and they have easy access to the foundational texts of Christianity as we learn through Eugenia. It, thus, complements what we know of women's lives in North Africa, from the popularity of the *APT* among Christian men and women and the fact that women were teaching and preaching as Tertullian's (b. c. 155) *de Baptismo* (*On Baptism*) informs us.[107]

In the second half, which takes place in Rome, gone are the bishops and monasteries. More significantly, gone are the moments when active, public Christian life is on full display. And while we are told that the brothers are given leadership roles, these are elsewhere, and we hear nothing more about them. The *Life of Eugenia*, in its two halves, represents two vastly different worlds within a single empire; its commentary on female leadership and the happy Christian family and, thus, community in the periphery versus the center offers us another window unto the complexities of reality and representation and the social worlds from which these texts emerge. Rather than seeing the *Life of Eugenia* as policing female boundaries, I understand the text as one that takes a decidedly anti-Roman, anti-androcentric, pro-Alexandrian, pro-female stance in imagining the possibilities each city affords Christians and specifically Christian women to partake in public life.[108]

---

[106] For more on human agency, see Hylen, *A Modest Apostle*, 2015: 7–17 and especially 10, for her insightful statement that "[c]ultures provide an array of social roles, values, and ways of making meaning, which actors employ, depending on the resources and power available to them. The dispositions of culture shape human action, but they allow for multiple expressions of the same values and even, to some extent, choice between the values expressed."

[107] See Jeremy Barrier's and Damien Labadie's respective contributions in this volume (Chapters 1 and 2) for more.

[108] The *Life of Eugenia* may even be said to repurpose the happy ending and integration into family and society on the periphery of empire in the ancient novels in its first half and, in its second half, to reenact the Apocryphal Acts at the center of power. See Cooper, *The Virgin and the Bride*, 1999: 66–67, in which she sums up the differences between the ancient romances and the Apocryphal Acts along these lines: essentially the ancient romances "written by and for provincial families" lured "readers toward the duty of procreation" by redistributing wealth more evenly whereas the Apocryphal Acts promoted active resentment of the politically powerful in the city.

A Medieval Sufi Thecla? 313

'Aṭṭār's views on leadership are more egalitarian even if there is a power differential in terms of position, namely, caliph versus king and, more so drastically, kingmaker. Both the TVW and the first half of the *Life of Eugenia* imagine and present women who have awe-inspiring inner power but also modesty that allows them to exert not just spiritual authority as women did throughout the Roman, Byzantine, and Muslim world in variegated ways,[109] but they also imagine women attaining true leadership, as strangers no less, thus disrupting the strict social hierarchies of monasteries and kingdoms in a unique way. Ultimately, however, Eugenia's and the virtuous woman's reluctance to lead mark them as starkly different from Thecla. Thecla, it should be recalled, asks for baptism and, when denied, claims it for herself and immediately becomes a teacher and leader. Here, then, we have one other shift in attitude toward female leadership; according to the *Life of Eugenia* and TVW, it is best held in the hands of the chaste, yet reluctant woman.

Conclusion

Whether there may be direct links or ties between 'Aṭṭār's TVW and the *APT*, the *Life of Eugenia*, and Pseudo-Clementine *Recognitions* or not, we do know that certain types of tales traveled frequently on a transregional circuitry covering vast distances in time and space. At each destination certain plots, themes, and motifs like recombinant DNA were attached and reattached and adopted and reshuffled. Careful readings of the similarities and differences across a variety of texts that make use of the same narrative types and cluster of motifs may help shed light on certain attitudes and help us paint ever more detailed pictures of late antique and medieval thought-worlds in different regions and under different religio-political and cultural circumstances. Essentially, these are tales that held widespread appeal and were retold for maximum affect for Muslim and Christian audiences with as many aims as there were hagiographers. Here, I hope to have demonstrated the strong affinities between the *APT*, the *Life of Eugenia*, and the TVW in terms of their adoption of popular motifs toward not only religio-spiritual aims but also independently attained female leadership. Ultimately, I hope to have shown that the

---

[109] See above.

Life of Eugenia and TVW offer a unique opportunity to address how two hagiographers separated by time, culture, religion, and space similarly imagined and represented positively attained female leadership with plots, motifs, and themes popularly found in a wide variety of literatures in the east and west, and especially in the *APT* as an earlier instance.

Bibliography

Allberry, Charles R. C., ed. and trans. *A Manichaean Psalm-Book, Part II*. Stuttgart: Kohlhammer, 1938.

Archibald, Elizabeth. "The Flight from Incest: Two Late Classical Precursors of the Constance Theme." *The Chaucer Review* 20, no. 4 (1986): 259–272.

Aspegren, Kerstin. *The Male Woman: A Feminine Ideal in the Early Church*. Acta Universitatis Upsaliensis/Uppsala Women's Studies 4. Uppsala; Stockholm: Almqvist and Wiksell International, 1990.

Aubin, Melissa. "Reversing Romance? *The Acts of Thecla* and the Ancient Novel." In *Ancient Fiction and Early Christian Narrative*, edited by Ronald F. Hock, J. Bradley Chance, and Judith Perkins. Society of Biblical Literature Symposium Series 6. Atlanta: Scholars Press, 1998: 257–272.

Barrier, Jeremy W. *The Acts of Paul and Thecla: A Critical Introduction and Commentary*. WUNT 2.270. Tübingen: Mohr Siebeck, 2009.

Barrier, Jeremy W., Jan N. Bremmer, T. Niklas, and A. Puig i Tàrrech, eds. *Thecla: Paul's Disciple and Saint in the East and West*. Studies in Early Christian Apocrypha 12. Leuven: Peeters, 2017.

Bartolini, Maria Grazia. "'Manlier Than Many Men:' Images of Female Sanctity in Simeon Polockij's Court Sermons." *Studi Slavistici* XIII (2016): 59–88.

Bashir, Shahzad. *Sufi Bodies: Religion and Society in Medieval Islam*. New York: Columbia University Press, 2011.

Böwering, Gerhard, and Matthew Melvin-Koushki. "Kānaqāh." *Encyclopædia Iranica*, 2010. www.iranicaonline.org/articles/kanaqah.

Burrus, Virginia. *Chastity as Autonomy: Women in the Stories of the Apocryphal Acts*. Studies in Women and Religion 23. Lewiston; Queenston: Edwin Mellon, 1987.

——— "Reading Agnes: The Rhetoric of Gender in Ambrose and Prudentius." *Journal of Early Christian Studies* 3, no. 1 (Spring 1995): 25–46.

Canepa, Matthew. *The Two Eyes of the Earth: Art and Ritual of Kingship between Rome and Sasanian Iran*. Berkeley; Los Angeles: University of California Press, 2009.

Chittick, William C. *Sufism: An Introduction*. Oxford: One World, 2005.

Clark, Elizabeth A. "Holy Women, Holy Words: Early Christian Women, Social History, and the 'Linguistic Turn.'" *Journal of Early Christian Studies* 6, no. 3 (Fall 1998): 413–430.

Constantinou, Stavroula. "Performing Gender in Lay Saints' Lives." *Byzantine and Modern Greek Studies* 38, no. 1 (2014): 24–32.

Conybeare, Frederick Cornwallis, ed. and trans. "The Acts of Saint Eugenia." In *The Apology and Acts of Apollonius and Other Monuments of Early Christianity: Edited [and Translated] with a General Preface, Introductions, Notes, etc., by F. C. Conybeare*. London; New York: Swan Sonnenschein & Co.; Macmillan & Co., 1896: 147–160.

Cooper, Kate. *The Virgin and the Bride: Idealized Womanhood in Late Antiquity*. Cambridge, MA: Harvard University Press, 1996.

——— "The Virgin as Social Icon." In *Saints, Scholars, and Politicians: Gender as a Tool in Medieval Studies*, edited by Mathilde van Dijk and Renée Nip. Medieval Church Studies 15. Turnhout: Brepols, 2005: 9–24.

——— "The Bride of Christ, the 'Male Woman,' and the Female Reader in Late Antiquity." In *The Oxford Handbook of Women and Gender in Medieval Europe*. Oxford: Oxford University Press, 2013: 529–544.

Cooper, Kate, and James Corke-Webster. "Conversion, Conflict, and the Drama of Social Reproduction: Narratives of Filial Resistance in Early Christianity and Modern Britain." In *Conversion and Initiation in Antiquity: Shifting Identities-Creating Change*, edited by Birgitte Secher Bøgh. Frankfurt am Main; New York: Peter Lang, 2014: 169–183.

Cornell, Rkia E. "Introduction." In *Early Sufi Women: Dhikr an-niswa al-muta'abbidāt aṣ-ṣūfiyyāt, Abū 'Abd ar-Raḥmān ās-Sulamī*, translated by Rkia E. Cornell. Louisville: Fons Vitae, 1999: 15–79.

——— trans. *Early Sufi Women: Dhikr an-niswa al-muta'abbidāt aṣ-ṣūfiyyāt, Abū 'Abd ar-Raḥmān ās-Sulamī*. Louisville: Fons Vitae, 1999.

——— *Rabi'a from Narrative to Myth: The Many Faces of Islam's Most Famous Saint, Rabi'a al-'Adawiyya*. London: Oneworld, 2019.

Dabiri, Ghazzal. "Reading the *Elāhināma* as Sufi Practical Ethics: Between Reception, Genre, and Muslim and Christian Audiences." *Journal of Persianate Societies* 11, no. 1 (2018): 29–55.

——— "'When a Lion Is Chided by an Ant:' Everyday Saints and the Making of Sufi Kings in 'Attār's *Elāhināma*." *Journal of Persianate Societies* 12, no. 1 (2019): 62–102.

——— "Who's the Authority around Here? Zoroastrians as Sites of Negotiation in 'Aṭṭār's *Tazkirat al-awliyā'* and *Ilāhināmah*." In *Narrating Power and Authority in Late Antique and Medieval Hagiography across East and West*, edited by Ghazzal Dabiri. Fabulae 1. Turnhout: Brepols, 2021: 103-118.

Davis, Dick. *Panthea's Children: Hellenistic Novels and Medieval Persian Romances*. Biennial Ehsan Yarshater Lecture Series. New York: Bibliotheca Persica, 2002.

Davis, Stephen J. *The Cult of St. Thecla: A Tradition of Women's Piety in Late Antiquity*. Oxford Early Christian Studies. Oxford; New York: Oxford University Press, 2001.

——— "Crossed Texts, Crossed Sex: Intertextuality and Gender in Early Christian Legends of Holy Women Disguised as Men." *Journal of Early Christian Studies* 10, no. 1 (2002): 1–36.

Davis, Stephen J., ed. and trans. "An Arabic *Acts of Paul and Thecla*: Text and Translation, with Introduction and Critical Commentary." In *Thecla: Paul's Disciple and Saint in the East and West*, edited by Jeremy W. Barrier, Jan N. Bremmer, T. Niklas, and A. Puig i Tàrrech. Studies in Early Christian Apocrypha 12. Leuven: Peeters, 2017: 106–151.

Drijvers, Jan Willem. *Helena Augusta: The Mother of Constantine the Great and the Legend of Her Finding of the True Cross*. Leiden: Brill, 1992.

Ernst, Carl W., trans. *Rūzbihān Baqlī: Mysticism and the Rhetoric of Sainthood in Persian Sufism*. London; New York: Routledge, 1996.

Hambly, Gavin R., ed. *Women in the Medieval Islamic World: Power, Patronage and Piety*. New York: St. Martin's Press, 1998.

Harbus, Antonina. *Helena of Britain in Medieval Legend*. Suffolk; Rochester: D. S. Brewer, 2002.

Hill, Joseph. "'All Women Are Guides:' Sufi Leadership and Womanhood among Taalibe Baay in Senegal." *Journal of Religion in Africa* 40 (2010): 375–412.

Hylen, Susan E. *A Modest Apostle: Thecla and the History of Women in the Early Church*. New York: Oxford University Press, 2015.

James, Liz. *Empress and Power in Early Byzantium*. London; New York: Leicester University Press, 2001.

Johnson, Scott F. *The Life and Miracles of Thekla: A Literary Study*. Washington, DC: Center for Hellenic Studies, Trustees for Harvard University, 2006.

Kaestli, Jean-Daniel. "L'utilisation des Actes Apocryphes des Apôtres dans le Manichéisme." In *Gnosis and Gnosticism*, edited by M. Krause. Nag Hammadi Studies 8. Leiden: Brill, 1977: 373–395.

Kargar, Dariush. "Jawāmeʿ al-Ḥikāyāt." *Encyclopædia Iranica*, 2008. www.iranicaonline.org/articles/jawame-al-hekayat.

Kruk, Remke. *The Warrior Women of Islam: Female Empowerment in Arabic Popular Literature*. London; New York: I. B. Tauris, 2014.

Kugle, Scott A. *Sufis and Saints' Bodies: Mysticism, Corporeality, and Sacred Power in Islam*. Islamic Civilization and Muslim Networks. Chapel Hill: University of North Carolina Press, 2012.

Lewis, Agnes Smith, trans. "Eugenia." In *Select Narratives of Holy Women from the Syro-Antiochene or Sinai Palimpsest: As Written Above the Old Syriac Gospel by John the Stylite or Beth Manri-Qanūn in A.D. 778*. 2 vols. Studia Sinaitica 9. London: C. J. Clay and Sons, 1900: vol. 2, 1–35.

Lewis, Franklin D. "Sexual Occidentation: The Politics of Conversion, Christian-love and Boy-love in ʿAṭṭār." *Iranian Studies* 42, no. 5 (2009): 693–723.

Lipsett, B. Diane. *Desiring Conversion: Hermas, Thecla, Asenneth*. Oxford: Oxford University Press, 2011.

Malamud, Margaret. "Gender and Spiritual Self-Fashioning: The Master-Disciple Relationship in Classical Sufism." *Journal of the American Academy of Religion* 64, no. 1 (Spring 1996): 89–117.

Marzolph, Ulrich. "Crescentia's Oriental Relatives: The 'Tale of the Pious Man and His Chaste Wife' in the Arabian Nights and the Sources of Crescentia in Near Eastern Narrative Tradition." *Marvels and Tales* 22, no. 2 (2008): 240–258.

"Crescentia's Oriental Relatives: Four Translations." *Marvels and Tales* 22, no. 2 (2008): 299–311.
McInerney, Maud Burnett. *Eloquent Virgins: From Thecla to Joan of Arc.* The New Middle Ages. New York: Palgrave Macmillan, 2003.
Papaioannou, Stratis, ed. and trans. "Life, Conduct, and Passion of the Holy Martyr of Christ Saint Eugenia and Her Parents." In *Christian Novels from the Menologion of Symeon Metaphrastes.* Dumbarton Oaks Medieval Library 45. Cambridge, MA: Harvard University Press, 2017: 183–261.
Perkins, Judith. *The Suffering Self: Pain and Narrative Representation in the Early Christian Era.* London: Routledge, 1995.
Puhvel, Jaan. *Comparative Mythology.* Baltimore: The Johns Hopkins University Press, 1987.
Reeves, John C. *Prolegomena to a History of Islamicate Manichaeism.* London; Oakville: Equinox, 2011.
———. "Jacob of Edessa and the Manichaean Book of Giants?" In *Ancient Tales of Giants from Qumran and Turfan: Contexts, Traditions, and Influences*, edited by Matthew Goff, Loren T. Stuckenbruck, and Enrico Morano. Tübingen: Mohr Siebeck, 2016: 199–211.
Ritter, Hellmut, ed. *Ilahi-Name: Die Gespräche des Königs mit seinen sechs Söhnen: Eine Mystische Dichtung.* Bibliotheca Islamica. Leipzig: Brockhaus, 1940.
Sarwar, Muhammad, ed. and trans. *al-Kafi: Arabic Text and Translation.* New York: The Islamic Seminary, 2013.
Shafiʿī-Kadkanī, Muhammad Rizā, ed. *Ilāhīnāmah-i Farīd al-Dīn ʿAttār.* 3rd ed. Tehran: Intishārāt-i Sukhan, 2013.
Smith, Thomas. "Recognitions of Clement." In *From Ante-Nicene Fathers, Book 8*, edited by Alexander Roberts, James Donaldson, and Cleveland Coxe. Buffalo: Christian Literature, 1886. www.newadvent.org/fathers/0804.htm.
Sterk, Andrea. "Mission from Below: Captive Women and Conversion on the East Roman Frontiers." *Church History* 79, no. 1 (March 2010): 1–39.
Talbot, Alice-Mary. "The Byzantine Family and the Monastery." *Dumbarton Oaks Papers* 44 (1990): 119–129.
Voicu, Sever J. "Thecla in the Christian East." In *Thecla: Paul's Disciple and Saint in the East and West*, edited by Jeremy W. Barrier, Jan N. Bremmer, T. Nicklas, and A. Puig i Tàrrech. Studies in Early Christian Apocrypha 12. Leuven: Peeters, 2017: 47–68.
Walker, Joel Thomas. *The Legend of Mar Qardagh: Narrative and Christian Heroism in Late Antique Iraq.* Berkeley; Los Angeles; London: University of California Press, 2006.
Wood, Philip. "The Invention of History in the Later Roman World: The Conversion of Isauria in 'The Life of Conan.'" *Anatolian Studies* 59 (2009): 129–138.
Yarbrough, Anne. "Christianization in the Fourth Century: The Example of Roman Women." *Church History* 45 (January 1976): 149–165.

Afterword
Thecla and the Power of an Open Story
Kate Cooper*

> And while Paul was thus speaking in the midst of the assembly in the house of Onesiphoros, a virgin (named) Thecla – her mother was Theocleia – who was betrothed to a man (named) Thamyris, sat at a near-by window and listened night and day to the word of the virgin life as it was spoken by Paul; and she did not turn away from the window, but pressed on in the faith ... when she saw many women and virgins going in to Paul she desired to be counted worthy herself to stand in Paul's presence and hear the word of Christ; for she had not yet seen Paul in person.[1]
>
> (APT § 7)

Our story begins with a young woman listening to words that will change her life. She is, of course, Thecla, Virgin of Iconium, one of the most popular but also one of the most elusive figures in early Christian literature. Thecla was a valuable commodity in the Christian communities of the Roman provinces and the post-Roman kingdoms of late antiquity, and her story was told and re-told across the centuries, possibly within the living memory of those who had known Paul during his travels in Asia Minor in the '50s of the first century[2] and certainly ever since.

Perhaps more than most ancient traditions, Thecla's has been characterized by controversy, beginning within the text itself and culminating at the turn of the third century, with Tertullian's (b. c. 155) account of a debate over whether Thecla's example was a precedent for women to preach and baptize. Apart from a shared interest in the teachings of Paul,

---

* I am grateful to Hildelith Leyser for inspiring discussion of more than one early version of this chapter.
[1] Schneemelcher and Kasser (eds.), "*The Acts of Paul*," 1992: 240.
[2] Hilhorst, "Tertullian on the *Acts of Paul*," 1996, notes that Jerome's (d. 420) *De Viris Illustribus* 7 places Tertullian's story (*de Baptismo* 17.5) that a presbyter was convicted of having compiled the *Acts of Paul* and resigned his post, in the apostolic period.

there is no single common denominator uniting the individuals and communities that remembered Thecla with reverence.

Over the half-century since John Anson published his surprising article on the value of the "female transvestite" motif in Greek hagiography to all-male ascetic communities, it has been clear that no one understanding of the Thecla tradition could account for all of the readers and listeners who invested in her story.[3] Still, as interest in the Apocryphal Acts gained momentum in the early 1980s, a lively debate emerged over the pastoral needs that had given rise to her tradition, building on the idea common to biblical studies that a narrative retains traces of "the type of situation where it is being used ... the *Sitz im Leben*."[4]

In 1980, Ross Kraemer and Stevan Davies explored how the Apocryphal Acts addressed the concerns of early Christian women. Kraemer underlined the centrality of sexually continent women in the narratives,[5] while Davies' provocative monograph, *The Revolt of the Widows*, put forward the then unexpected thesis that the Apocryphal Acts had been created to serve the needs of – and perhaps had been written by – such women themselves.[6] Not long afterward, Dennis MacDonald's *The Legend and the Apostle* took the question of female involvement in the genesis of the narratives a step further, arguing that oral traditions steered by female storytellers had served as the basis from which the traditions had been gathered into written form.[7] Finally, Virginia Burrus made the case that the rhetoric of virginity and sexual continence was intended not only to defend ascetic practice but to secure its place as a platform for female autonomy.[8]

During the same years, a new impetus was arriving from the study of the Greek novel, where the idea that the Apocryphal Acts should be read alongside the non-Christian romances had long held sway. The *Acts of Paul and Thecla* takes pride of place in Tomas Hägg's chapter on "The New Heroes: Apostles, Martyrs and Saints" in *The Novel in Antiquity*,[9] and his renewal of the comparative approach found support from both classicists and historians of early Christianity.[10] Especially influential was Judith

---

[3] Anson, "The Female Transvestite," 1974.   [4] Tuckett, *Reading the New Testament*, 1987: 95.
[5] Kraemer, "The Conversion of Women," 1980.   [6] Davies, *The Revolt of the Widows*, 1980.
[7] MacDonald, *The Legend and the Apostle*, 1983.
[8] Burrus, *Chastity as Autonomy*, 1987. Important as a context for Burrus' central contention are Kraemer, "The Conversion of Women," 1980; and Clark, "Ascetic Renunciation and Feminine Advancement," 1981.
[9] Hägg, *The Novel in Antiquity*, 1983.
[10] Holzberg, *Der antike Roman*, 1986. David Konstan should also be mentioned here; although his *Sexual Symmetry*, 1994, does not develop the comparison, his dialogue with scholars of early

Perkins' *The Suffering Self*, which argued that the Apocryphal Acts and the ancient novel emerged simultaneously as parallel responses to the same cultural challenges faced by Greek speakers in the Mediterranean of the first to third centuries.[11]

My own *The Virgin and the Bride* raised an alternative approach to the function of the heroines in these texts, suggesting that whether or not the stories reach back to an early, female-centric oral tradition, the versions that survive in writing reflect a process of shaping and pruning by literate people, almost certainly men, whose use of a heroine's narrative magnetism did not necessarily reflect an interest in female autonomy.[12] In other words, the voice of early storytellers, if it can indeed be traced, is distorted by the layering of other, later voices in the text. Some scholars have taken this approach to imply that the female storytellers could not have existed,[13] but this was not my argument; rather, it was that while the evidence for an oral phase behind the surviving Apocryphal Acts is inconclusive, the later phase of transmission, that of the surviving texts, merits discussion in its own right.[14] In more recent work, I have explored the role household-based storytelling may have played in the earliest Christian communities, since this question remains important. (Modern scholarship on high-growth religious movements suggests that their message tends to travel through friendship and family networks, and this lends support to the possibility that such networks played an important role in the transmission of the early Christian message.)[15]

Shelley Matthews' illuminating review of the historiography of gender in the Apocryphal Acts in the last two decades of the twentieth century called attention to the urgency of continuing to seek after the histories of real historical women, warning that rhetorical criticism of early Christian narrative can play into the hands of conservative interpreters who wish to silence the voices of women in both history and scholarship.[16] This said, I would dissent from her view of rhetorical criticism as suggesting that

---

Christianity was influential before he began publishing on this theme (see, e.g., Konstan, "Acts of Love," 1998.)

[11] Perkins, *The Suffering Self*, 1995.   [12] Cooper, *The Virgin and the Bride*, 1996.
[13] Including the otherwise remarkably astute Kraemer, *Unreliable Witnesses*, 2011: 127–133.
[14] While Matthews, "Thinking of Thecla," 2001, gives it only limited attention, a distinct but extremely important view of related questions is outlined by Clark, "The Lady Vanishes," 1998; Clark, "Holy Women, Holy Words," 1998; and Clark, *History, Theory, Text*, 1998. Later, but worthy of attention, is the review of the latter by Burrus, Haines-Eitzen, Lim, and Vessey, "Reviewed Work," 2005, including contributions by the editors and a response by Clark.
[15] Cooper, *Band of Angels*, 2013, with Stark, *The Rise of Christianity*, 1996.
[16] Matthews, "Thinking of Thecla," 2001.

"each woman becomes a sign, a means of communication between men, but serves no other possible function."[17] Recognizing that a woman "becomes a sign" is not the same as saying that she "serves no other possible function." In other words, writers not committed to female autonomy may have had reasons for exploiting the magnetism of virginal heroines, but this does not mean that real historical women could not have told stories about them, nor, for that matter, does it mean that the heroines could not have existed as real historical people.

Reception and reuse can take stories in new directions. As I put it then:

> The *Apocryphal Acts* are insecurely dated . . . and relatively little is known of the circumstances of their production. But we do know that the episodes about the preaching of continence were influential models for female piety in the centuries that followed. This means that an understanding of how the episodes functioned rhetorically might prepare the ground for a clearer understanding of the later texts that drew on them.[18]

If heroines are "good to think with,"[19] they are also a source of narrative power that can be borrowed for many uses.

If we recognize the Apocryphal Acts as layered stories that were the object of lively reframing and contestation in the early centuries, attention to the problems raised by rhetorical criticism is a necessity. The aims of later writers who received, reframed, and redirected early traditions differed – sometimes dramatically – from those of their predecessors, and the meanings that listeners found in – or "read into" – the narratives may have been different yet again.[20]

David Konstan's study of the *Alexander Romance* makes a case that certain narratives from the ancient world should be understood as "open texts" in counterpoint to the "well-constructed pattern" of the ideal version of the Greek novel. Konstan describes the "episodic character" and "loose principle of organization" of these narratives: "The story of an individual's life serves as the pole on which to hang an indefinite string of adventures and encounters."[21] These are texts that found themselves constantly being

---

[17] Ibid.: 50.   [18] Cooper, *The Virgin and the Bride*, 1996: 46.
[19] The phrase is of course Lévi-Strauss'; see Matthews, "Thinking of Thecla," 2001: 47, citing Brown, *The Body and* Society, 1988: 153.
[20] Esch-Wemeling, *Thekla – Paulusschülerin wider Willen?*, 2008, has argued, for example, that within the surviving *Acts of Thecla* earlier story elements are reframed by a later redactional layer in a way that tends to compromise and diminish Thecla's agency. On "reading into" heroines, see Cooper, "The Bride of Christ," 2013.
[21] Konstan, "The Alexander Romance," 1998: 124. See also Hägg, "Orality, Literacy, and the 'Readership' of the Early Greek Novel," 1994: 47–81.

rewritten: "The effort to retrieve an original form is not only futile but detrimental."[22] This has important questions for how we should understand questions of authorship and authorial voice: "By their nature they admit a degree of variation or indeterminacy that is incompatible with authorial control."[23]

Writing in the same year and explicitly in dialogue with Konstan, Christine M. Thomas' "Stories without Texts and without Authors" of the same year addressed the "problem of fluidity" in the Apocryphal Acts.[24] Thomas suggests that too much emphasis has been directed at establishing stable original versions of ancient sources, observing that continuous reinvention reflected the investment of listeners in beloved narratives:

> The impulse to create a new version of the story with each retelling of it has more affinity with oral habits of performance than with the modern print-conditioned tendency toward exact reproduction of texts . . . . The written text at times served chiefly as a resource for later retellings.[25]

Thomas noted further that part of the value of these texts to their audiences was in their fluidity: "These documents, as demonstrated by their variegated transmission, had an ongoing life in their communities."[26]

This way of framing the relationship of "living" texts to their communities offers an important complement to Stock's influential idea of "textual communities." Stock's initial study, *The Implications of Literacy*, focused specifically on eleventh- and twelfth-century monastic communities and how the shift from oral to literate institutional cultures changed their experience of the interaction between text, symbol, and ritual. However, his conceptual framework captures something of the centrality of narrative to ancient and medieval communities that is relevant to the more variegated and chaotic landscape of late antiquity.[27]

In turning to think about Thecla, we want to ask, what was it about Thecla and her story that made it such a fertile platform for investment and reinvention? What was it that invited so many different textual communities to invest in her so extravagantly – as we have seen attested

---

[22] Konstan, "The Alexander Romance," 1998: 126.   [23] Ibid.: 127.
[24] Thomas, "Stories without Texts and without Authors," 1998. This collection also includes a valuable detailed study of the *Acts of Thecla*, Melissa Aubin, "Reversing Romance?," 1998, to which we will return below.
[25] Thomas, "Stories without Texts and without Authors," 1998: 289.   [26] Ibid.: 290.
[27] Note that Stock himself believed the concept could be modified to be useful to understanding ancient readers: Heath, "'Textual Communities,'" 2019, with Stock, *The Implications of Literacy*, 1983; and Stock, *Listening for the Text*, 1990.

so vividly in the present volume – even when it was impossible to claim her definitively?

It will come as no surprise that Thecla's love for Paul stands at the center of the enigma. In what follows, I want to return to the proposition that the narrative form of the Apocryphal Acts presented an inverted form of the "marriage plot" of the ancient romance in which the virginal heroine's desire to follow the apostle disrupts the closure offered by the expected marriage.

The Thecla cycle, I will argue, creates a distinctive type of "open story," one in which the disruption of genre conventions is made more powerful through the ambiguous or indeterminate qualities of the heroine. Recent scholarly work has offered exciting (and sometimes troubling) insights to support this reading. B. Diane Lipsett's *Desiring Conversion: Hermas, Thecla, Aseneth* argues for a productive ambiguity in the characterization of Thecla and other figures in her story cycle. Building on Aubin's suggestion that, as Thecla becomes progressively "masculine" in the *Acts of Paul and Thecla*, Paul becomes progressively "feminine,"[28] Lipsett emphasizes the tension between Thecla as a desiring subject – who yearns to follow Paul and to reach union with God – and as desired object – the woman whom successive male antagonists pursue sexually – observing that Thecla's story illustrates perfectly Judith Butler's observation that "the subject is constituted in the dislocation of desire."[29]

But there are other kinds of desire at work in the narrative. Commenting on the proliferation of maternal figures in the *Acts of Paul and Thecla*, Lipsett invokes Kristeva's binary view of maternal love. If it is characterized by "serenity . . . the 'object' of satisfaction is transformed into an 'other' – to care for, to nourish . . . which defers eroticism into tenderness"[30] – here we think of Queen Tryphaena and the generous lioness of Antioch – it is also characterized by "the tendency to annex the cherished other, to project herself onto it, to monopolize it, to dominate it, to suffocate it"[31] – here we can only think of Thecla's biological mother, Theocleia, who hands over her daughter to the authorities for execution the moment the child becomes disobedient. For Lipsett,

---

[28] Aubin, "Reversing Romance?," 1998: 266–267.
[29] B. Diane Lipsett's *Desiring Conversion*, 2010: 56, citing Judith Butler, "Desire," 1995: 380–381.
[30] Clément and Kristeva, *The Feminine and the Sacred*, 2001: 56–57, cited in Lipsett, *Desiring Conversion*, 2010: 57.
[31] Clément and Kristeva, *The Feminine and the Sacred*, 2001: 57, cited in Lipsett, *Desiring Conversion*, 2010: 57.

it is the ambiguity of Thecla as both male and female, both desired and desiring, that secures her unusual value as a protagonist.

More recently still, J. D. McLarty has explored the *Acts of Paul and Thecla* as a narrative that reveals its ideology through its form. While others have seen the *Acts* as offering a form of narrative closure characterized by situational irony,[32] specifically inverting the wedding-as-happy-ending of the canonical romances,[33] McLarty sees Thecla's disruption of expectations as forestalling narrative closure and calling into question the narrative contract. For McLarty, the story ends not with Thecla's commission to preach – a moment of recognition – but rather with the fact of her wandering: "For the story to end with an unmarried girl travelling along (instead of returning to home and family) is a startling departure from the romantic plot."[34] On this reading, the bride neither marries her groom nor settles into a stable niche in the social order but departs to live the life of a wandering she-apostle. Like Paul's preaching, Thecla's story is an invitation to break free of the bounds of society, to find an identity keyed to an eschatological frame. McLarty takes the narratological approach into the realm of affect, tracing how the narrative guides the reader's emotions toward a heightened ability to perceive the eschatological imperative signaled in the text by the preaching of Paul. (While McLarty's analysis is framed in terms of "readers" rather than "listeners," I believe her suggestions are equally relevant, if not more so, to understanding the experience of audiences who heard the story read or told aloud.)

McLarty's reading offers a new path to understanding why Thecla is so successful as a figure to anchor an open story: while she possesses the characteristics of beauty and good birth, we are told almost nothing about her character:

> The author gives greater depth to the emotional life of the surrounding characters than to that of Thecla herself. After the reader's initial encounter with Thecla, when in narrator text [*sic*] we are told of her longing to sit at Paul's feet, her actions are portrayed "from the outside;" her thoughts are not recounted at any length. By contrast, immense power and vividness is given to the reactions of Theocleia and Tryphaina by the use of extended

---

[32] Aubin, "Reversing Romance?," 1998: 266.
[33] Thomas, "Stories without Texts and without Authors," 1998: 278: "Instead of marriage, which Thekla has rejected at the outset in her pursuit of holiness, she is confirmed into another stable social role: she is commissioned to preach the gospel as her model does."
[34] McLarty, *Thecla's Devotion*, 2018: 3.

direct speech, access to the inner thoughts of the characters and narratorial commentary on their emotions. Thecla is the object rather than the subject of the larger part of the narrative.[35]

Yet for McLarty this strategy of distance does not prohibit the audience from becoming emotionally involved with Thecla; to the contrary, there are multiple anchoring-points for emotional involvement. Again and again, we find onlookers reacting to Thecla's trials with concern: spectators in the arena, a lioness, a childless mother. It is with these onlookers that the audience is invited to identify: "The fascination of Paul and Thecla in the narrative is their aberrant nature, their 'otherness' ... Paul and Thecla are viewed from the perspective of the settled believer whose identity is located within household and family."[36] On this reading, the distance imposed between the audience and its heroine does not undermine their investment in her. Rather, the distance becomes a space of possibility.

Rosie Andrious offers further insight into how the *Acts of Paul and Thecla* establish distance between its audience and its heroine. The ordeals Thecla is repeatedly subjected to create a cycle of anxiety, humiliation, indignation, and revulsion that heighten the audience's emotional involvement in the story. But Andrious observes that paradoxically, the sexualized and dehumanizing quality of the ordeals also enhances the audience's ability to hold Thecla at a distance: "She becomes available to the audience as an alluring object ... stripped not only of clothing but also of subjectivity and personhood."[37] Again, it is the heroine's indeterminate quality that sets her apart. "Despite the focus on Thecla's body and beauty, and in contrast to Paul, we are never given a description of her ... [and this] helps audiences to distance themselves."[38] Thecla's indeterminacy contributes to her ability to remain powerful in the face of torture and degradation: "No physical or psychological effects of the traumas or ordeals she experiences are ever hinted at, let alone narrated."[39]

To conclude, Thecla is an ambiguous heroine in an unstable story. The harder we try to capture her, the more decisively she eludes us. And yet, as they wrestled with diverse challenges and burdens, successive writers and preachers turned to Thecla's story, developing the elements that spoke to their own requirements, and then handing it on. In the end, Thecla's

---

[35] Ibid.: 190. [36] Ibid.: 226. [37] Andrious, *Saint Thecla*, 2020: 114. [38] Ibid.: 124.
[39] Ibid.

indeterminacy may have been what made her so valuable. Her mentor Paul is remembered as having claimed to "become all things to all people, so that by all possible means I might save some" (1 Cor 9:22). Thecla, too, had a way of being all things to all people – and this made her indispensable.

Bibliography

Andrious, Rosie. *Saint Thecla: Body Politics and Masculine Rhetoric*. London: Bloomsbury, 2020.

Anson, John. "The Female Transvestite in Early Monasticism: The Origin and Development of a Motif." *Viator* 5 (1974): 1–32.

Aubin, Melissa. "Reversing Romance? *The Acts of Thecla* and the Ancient Novel." In *Ancient Fiction and Early Christian Narrative*, edited by Ronald F. Hock, J. Bradley Chance, and Judith Perkins. Society of Biblical Literature Symposium Series 6. Atlanta: Scholars Press, 1998: 257–272.

Brown, Peter. *The Body and Society: Men, Women and Sexual Renunciation in Early Christianity*. New York: Columbia University Press, 1988.

Burrus, Virginia. *Chastity as Autonomy: Women in the Stories of the Apocryphal Acts*. Studies in Women and Religion 23. Lewiston; Queenston: Edwin Mellon, 1987.

Burrus, Virginia, Kim Haines-Eitzen, Richard Lim, and Mark Vessey. "Reviewed Work: *History, Theory, Text: Historians and the Linguistic Turn* by Elizabeth A. Clark." *Church History* 74, no. 4 (2005): 812–836.

Butler, Judith. "Desire." In *Critical Terms for Literary Study*, edited by Frank Lentricchia and Thomas McLaughlin. Chicago: University of Chicago Press, 1995: 369–386.

Clark, Elizabeth A. "Ascetic Renunciation and Feminine Advancement: A Paradox of Late Ancient Christianity." *Anglican Theological Review* 6 (1981): 240–257.

History, Theory, Text: Historians and the Linguistic Turn. Cambridge, MA: Harvard University Press, 1998.

"Holy Women, Holy Words: Early Christian Women, Social History, and the 'Linguistic Turn' (A Feminist Historian Questions the Objectivity of 'Male Knowledge' Regarding Verified Representations of Female Ascetics of the Fourth- and Fifth-Century)." *Journal of Early Christian Studies* 6, no. 3 (1998): 413–430.

"The Lady Vanishes: Dilemmas of a Feminist Historian after the 'Linguistic Turn.'" *Church History* 67 (1998): 1–31.

Clément, Catherine, and Julia Kristeva. *The Feminine and the Sacred*, translated by Jane Marie Todd. New York: Columbia University Press, 2001.

Cooper, Kate. *The Virgin and the Bride: Idealized Womanhood in Late Antiquity*. Cambridge, MA: Harvard University Press, 1996.

Band of Angels: The Forgotten World of Early Christian Women. London: Atlantic, 2013.

"The Bride of Christ, the Male Woman, and the Female Reader." In *Oxford Handbook of Women and Gender in Medieval Europe*, edited by Judith Bennett and Ruth Karras. Oxford: Oxford University Press, 2013: 529–544.

Davies, Stevan L. *The Revolt of the Widows: The Social World of the Apocryphal Acts.* Carbondale: Southern Illinois University Press, 1980.

Esch-Wemeling, Elisabeth. *Thekla – Paulusschülerin wider Willen?* Münster: Aschendorff 2008.

Hägg, Tomas. *The Novel in Antiquity.* Berkeley: University of California Press, 1983.

"Orality, Literacy, and the 'Readership' of the Early Greek Novel." In *Contexts of Pre-Novel Narrative: The European Tradition*, edited by Roy Eriksen. Berlin: De Gruyter, 1994: 47–81.

Heath, Jane. "'Textual Communities:' Brian Stock's Concept and Recent Scholarship on Antiquity." In *Scriptural Interpretation at the Interface between Education and Religion: In Memory of Hans Conzelmann*, edited by Florian Wilk. Leiden; Boston: Brill, 2019: 5–35.

Hilhorst, Anthony. "Tertullian on the *Acts of Paul*." In *The Apocryphal Acts of Paul*, edited by Jan N. Bremmer. Kampen: Kok Pharos, 1996: 150–163.

Holzberg, Niklas. *Der antike Roman. Eine Einführung.* Munich; Zurich: Artemis, 1986.

Konstan, David. *Sexual Symmetry: Love in the Ancient Novel and Related Genres.* Princeton: Princeton University Press, 1994.

"Acts of Love: A Narrative Pattern in the Apocryphal Acts." *Journal of Early Christian Studies* 6 (1998): 15–36.

"The Alexander Romance: The Cunning of the Open Text." *Lexis* 16 (1998): 123–138.

Kraemer, Ross S. "The Conversion of Women to Ascetic Forms of Christianity." *Signs* 6 (1980): 298–307.

Unreliable Witnesses: Religion, Gender, and History in the Greco-Roman Mediterranean. New York: Oxford University Press, 2011.

Lipsett, B. Diane. *Desiring Conversion: Hermas, Thecla, Aseneth.* Oxford: Oxford University Press, 2010.

MacDonald, Dennis R. *The Legend and the Apostle: The Battle for Paul in Story and Canon.* Philadelphia: Westminster, 1983.

Matthews, Shelly. "Thinking of Thecla: Issues in Feminist Historiography." *Journal of Feminist Studies in Religion* 17, no. 2 (2001): 39–55.

McLarty, Jane D. *Thecla's Devotion: Narrative, Emotion and Identity in the Acts of Paul and Thecla.* Cambridge, James Clarke & Co., 2018.

Perkins, Judith. *The Suffering Self: Pain and Narrative Representation in the Early Christian Era.* London: Routledge, 1995.

Schneemelcher, Wilhem, and Rodolphe Kasser, eds., "*The Acts of Paul.*" In *New Testament Apochrypha*, edited by Edgar Hennecke and Wilhelm

Schneemelcher, English translation edited by Robert McLachlan. Revised ed. Cambridge: James Clark & Co., 1992: 213–272.

Stark, Rodney. *The Rise of Christianity: A Sociologist Reconsiders History*. Princeton: Princeton University Press, 1996.

Stock, Brian. *The Implications of Literacy: Written Language and Models of Interpretation in the Eleventh and Twelfth Centuries*. Princeton: Princeton University Press, 1983.

Listening for the Text: On the Uses of the Past. Philadelphia: University of Pennsylvania Press, 1990.

Thomas, Christine M. "Stories without Texts and without Authors: The Problem of Fluidity in Ancient Novelistic Texts and Early Christian Literature." In *Ancient Fiction and Early Christian Narrative*, edited by Ronald F. Hock, J. Bradley Chance, and Judith Perkins. Society of Biblical Literature Symposium Series 6. Atlanta: Scholars Press, 1998: 273–291.

Tuckett, Christopher M. *Reading the New Testament: Methods of Interpretation*. London: SPCK, 1987.

APPENDIX

Summaries of Texts

Provided below are summaries of the major texts dealt with in each chapter (arranged in chronological order). Several texts, such *de Baptismo* (*On Baptism*), *Life and Passion of Eugenia*, *Symposium* by Methodius of Olympus, and the *Life and Miracles of Thecla*, are mentioned frequently throughout the volume. For the *Acts of Paul and Thecla* (*BHG* 1710 and *CANT* 211.III), see the Introduction.

1 Jeremy W. Barrier, "A Cainite Invocation of Thecla? The Reception of the *Acts of Paul* in North Africa as Exemplified in Tertullian's *de Baptismo*"

Gospel of Judas, anonymous, second century, Coptic. The Gospel of Judas is a brief Gospel that was written sometime during the middle of the second century. It was brought to light in 2006 and made available to the general public at this time by the National Geographic Society. It is a Gnostic, Christian text in which Jesus offers up his teachings to his disciples just prior to eating the Passover feast with them and just a few days prior to his death. Most notable is that Jesus gives a special revelation to Judas – a hidden, Gnostic cosmology.

Against the Heresies (*CPG* 1306), Irenaeus, late second century, Greek, Lyon, France. Irenaeus was a Christian bishop who authored a five-volume work entitled *Against the Heresies* to (1) confront many of the heresies he knew about that he perceived to be a threat to true, Apostolic tradition stemming from Jesus and to (2) present an overview of the "orthodox" faith. He wrote the work while living in Lyon, France in his later years, but the text survives in a complete form only in its Latin translation.

On Baptism (*CPL* 8), Tertullian, third century, Latin, Carthage, North Africa. Tertullian was a Christian writer from Carthage who wrote an extensive corpus of Latin writings. He wrote *On Baptism* sometime at the turn of the third century in order to combat others in North Africa who were teaching that baptism was not a necessary Christian ritual.

2   Damien Labadie, "Saint Thecla in Geʿez Hagiographical Literature: From Confessor to Martyr"

Martyrdom of Cyrus and John (BHG 469–471), anonymous, seventh century, Greek, Egypt. This hagiographical text, originally written in Greek but also preserved in Latin, Coptic, and Arabic as well as Geʿez, relates the martyrdom of a group of Alexandrian Christians under Diocletian's (244–311) imperial rule. Living in Antioch but hailing from Alexandria, these Christians are arrested by Diocletian, who then sends them to Alexandria so that they may be judged and sentenced by the local governor. After their brutal deaths, their relics were kept hidden in Alexandria until the bishop Cyril (412–444) transferred the holy remains to a new sanctuary in Menuthis (today Abukir in northern Egypt).

Gadla samāʿtāt (*The Contendings of the Martyrs*), anonymous, thirteenth century, Geʿez, Ethiopia. This text is a Geʿez hagiographical collection of Lives, Acts, Passions, martyrdoms, collections of miracles, and homilies dealing with biblical, Eastern, and Egyptian martyrs.

Maṣḥafa Ṭēqalā (*Book of Thecla*), anonymous, thirteenth (?) century, Geʿez, Ethiopia. This is a Geʿez version of the *Acts of Paul and Thecla* transmitted in the Ethiopic hagiographical collection of the *Gadla samāʿtāt* (*The Contendings of the Martyrs*). Though much shorter than the other versions (Greek, Latin, Syriac, Latin, and Coptic), the *Maṣḥafa Ṭēqalā* offers some interesting variants and additions.

Epistle of Pelagia (BHO 890), anonymous, thirteenth (?) century, Geʿez, Ethiopia. The *Epistle* is a hagiographical text transmitted in the Ethiopic hagiographical collection, the *Gadla samāʿtāt* (*The Contendings of the Martyrs*). It narrates the events surrounding the apostle Paul's visit to Caesarea in Palestine to preach the Gospel there. After baptizing a huge lion, he converts a noble woman, Pelagia, who, following Paul's exhortation, renounces marriage. She is sentenced to death and cast into a burning brazen cow. But suddenly a pouring rain extinguishes the fire. Nevertheless, Pelagia still decides to go in, and her husband, appalled by this, commits suicide. This story is based on several previous accounts, including the *Passion of Pelagia of Tarsus*, the *Acts of Paul and Thecla* (in a form that cannot be determined accurately), and the Coptic *Acts of Paul* in Ephesus, especially the episode regarding the lion's baptism.

Senkessār (Ethiopic *Synaxarium*), anonymous, fifteenth and sixteenth centuries, Geʿez, Ethiopia. The *Senkessār* is a collection of hagiographical notices designed for a liturgical reading and organized according to the liturgical calendar of the whole year. Translated from the Arabic *Synaxarium* of the Coptic Church, it also contains material concerning Ethiopian saints.

3   Caitríona Ó Dochartaigh, "Versified Martyrs: The Reception of Thecla from the Latin West to Medieval Ireland"

Félire Óengusso (*The Calendar of Oengus*), Óengus mac Óengobann, ninth century, Old Irish, Leinster, Ireland. The *Félire Óengusso* is believed to be the work of Óengus mac Óengobann, a monk, hermit, and bishop who was most active in the first quarter of the ninth century. Óengus is also credited with the compilation of the Latin *Martyrology of Tallaght*, from which a great deal of the material in *Félire Óengusso* is drawn. The work on both martyrologies was most likely completed at the Monastery of Tallaght, now a suburb of Dublin but in the early Middle Ages an important monastic center in northern Leinster. *Félire Óengusso* is the earliest metrical martyrology in the vernacular in Europe; however, its structure is not typical of such saints' calendars. In addition to 365 verses, one for each day of the year – commemorating both Irish and Continental saints, including a number of references to Thecla – the work also contains an extensive prologue and epilogue.

Saltair na Rann (*The Psalter of the Stanzas*), anonymous, tenth-eleventh century, Middle Irish, Ireland. The *Saltair na Rann* was traditionally held to be the work of the same Óengus who composed *Félire Óengusso*. The supposed ascription was due to line 8009 in poem 152 where the author identifies himself as one "Óengus Céile Dé." However, the language of *Saltair na Rann* is late tenth- or early eleventh-century Middle Irish, whereas the original Óengus mac Óengobann lived in the ninth century. The name of the text derives from its deliberate adoption of a Psalter-like structure, that is, the main body of the work consists of 150 poems, with 12 additional poems appended. The subject of the work as a whole is biblical history from the creation of the world and its cosmology through the Old Testament and New Testament narratives until Doomsday and Judgment Day. However, the poems often deviate from the narrative of the Vulgate and include a great deal of apocryphal material, including a brief reference to Thecla's trials.

4 Valentina Calzolari, "The Reception of the *Acts of Thecla* in Armenia: Thecla as a Model of Representation for Holy Women in Ancient Armenian Literature"

History of Armenia, Agathangelos, second half of the fifth century, Armenian. The *History of Armenia* is a history of the conversion of Armenia at the beginning of the fourth century under the rule of the Armenian king Tiridates the Great (250–330). This *History* is the result of a compilation comprising different sections, in which it is difficult to distinguish between oral and/or written sources and the work of the editor whose identity remains unknown. Agathangelos ("the one who announces the good," "the good messenger") is indeed a fictitious name of Greek origin that was chosen by the Armenian compiler. At the heart of the country's conversion, as Agathangelos describes it, are two holy figures: Gregory, the Illuminator of Armenia (257–331), and Saint Hṙipʻsimē, the main figure among a group of Roman virgins, whose martyrdom is considered fundamental for the conversion of the Armenians. The figure of Saint Hṙipʻsimē has been inspired by the portrait of Thecla as a holy virgin and martyr.

Martyrdom of Thaddaeus and Sanduxt (*BHO* 1145), anonymous, fifth century, Armenian. The *Martyrdom of Thaddaeus and Sanduxt* is an apocryphal Armenian text that describes the circumstances surrounding the preaching and martyrdom of Thaddaeus (presented as an apostolic figure) in Armenia. The origin of the text is controversial. Scholars have hesitated between the hypothesis of a translation (from Greek or Syriac) and the hypothesis of a text written directly in Armenian; we concur with the latter assessment. The author knew earlier apocryphal sources, which he used in his account, and knew especially the Syriac *Teaching of Addai*, which relates the journey of Thaddaeus to Edessa to the court of King Abgar (fl. first century). After his stay in Osrohene (frontier of modern-day Syria and Turkey), the text describes the apostle's arrival in Armenia, where he evangelizes many, including Saint Sanduxt, the daughter of the Armenian king Sanatruk. Sanduxt and the apostle are condemned to death by the king. Before dying, Sanduxt participates in the conversion of Armenians through her speeches and charitable works. Several passages allow us to suppose that the author of this *Martyrdom* knew the *Acts of Thecla* and that he was inspired to draw the portrait of Thaddaeus' young disciple, Sanduxt.

History of Armenia (also *Buzandaran Patmutʻiwnkʻ*), Faustus of Byzantium, second half of the fifth century, Armenian. This text deals with Armenian history in the fourth century. It is centered around three narrative veins devoted respectively to (a) the organization of the primitive Church of Armenia and the history of its first patriarchs, especially the patriarch Nersēs the Great (353–373), (b) the history of the Armenian Arsacid kings (12–428), and (c) the history of the noble Armenian family, the Mamikonians. In this period, the Armenian Church was confronted with questions about religious orthodoxy that agitated the Christian East, especially after the Council of Nicaea (325), whose canons it had adopted. The religious policy of the kingdom was conditioned inter alia by the requirement of loyalty that the kings of Armenia necessarily owed to the Roman emperors. This question became complex when the emperors followed Arian tendencies, which the Armenian Church had always condemned strongly. Thecla is depicted as a patroness of Nicene orthodoxy, most likely on the basis of the role she has in the *Miracles of Thecla* by pseudo-Basil.

Martyrdom of Saint Photine (*BHO* 992), anonymous, not dated by the editor, Armenian – probably an Armenian translation of a Greek text. The Armenian *Martyrdom of the Holy Samaritan Woman Photine, Which Is Something Luminous* tells the story of the Samaritan woman who believed in the Messiah and, by her example and preaching of the Gospel, converted other Samaritans in her city (cf. Jn 4:39–42). The Armenian *Martyrdom* states that Christ himself sent Photine as a female apostle, before the apostles, to preach his coming. After receiving baptism and taking the name of Photine, the Samaritan woman, described as "follower of apostles," became one of Peter's and Paul's disciples and accompanied them to Rome where she continued to teach. Like them, she too was condemned to martyrdom by the emperor Nero (r. 54–68). The date of redaction is not known, and extensive studies to clarify its origins have not been done. Despite these unresolved issues, its existence in Armenian remains an interesting testimony to the reception of Thecla in Armenia. Indeed, this text contains several details that explicitly establish unique connections between Thecla and Photine.

5 Flavia Ruani, "Thecla Beyond Thecla: Secondary Characters in Syriac Hagiography"

Martyrdom of Thecla and Her Companions (*BHO* 1157), anonymous, between the fifth and the seventh century, Syriac. This very short text is part of the "corpus" of the Persian Martyr Acts. The story takes place in the year 346, during the reign of the Sasanian king Shapur II (309–379), in Adiabene, a region near the present-day borders of Iraq, Iran, and Turkey. Five pure, consecrated women, "daughters of the covenant" (i.e., who belong to the Syriac urban ascetical movement), are killed by their priest Pawle. Pawle, whose wealth and livelihood are threatened by the Zoroastrian governor, apostatizes and consents to behead his religious sisters on the orders of the governor before he is hung like Judas Iscariot. It is striking that the names of the two protagonists, Thecla and Pawle, are the same as the apostolic heroes.

Life of John of Tella (*BHO* 524), composed by the monk Elias, mid-sixth century, Syriac. The text is framed as a letter that Elias writes in reply to a request by two spiritual brothers. In this letter, he presents himself as an eyewitness to the vicissitudes of John's life. John is a historical figure; between 483 and 519, he was the Syrian Orthodox bishop of Tella, a city not far from Callinicus (present-day Raqqah), Syria. The narrative is composed of two major parts and includes a long preface. In the first part, Elias describes John's early life and how he discovered his ascetic vocation and became a monk before being elected as bishop. The second focuses on the upheavals of his episcopal career, which is marked by his teachings, debates with religious opponents, and ordinations in Syria and Persia until his incarceration and death. Promised to a brilliant career in the Byzantine administration, John decides to abandon a worldly life in favor of a Christian radical asceticism after reading the story of Thecla.

Martyrdom of Febronia (*BHO* 302), anonymous, late sixth-early seventh century, Syriac. A notice at the end of the text states that the author of the martyrdom is Thomais, a nun, who is herself a character in the story. Very popular in Greek and Latin as well, the story takes place in Nisibis (modern-day Nusaybin, Turkey) during the reign of the emperor Diocletian (r. 284–305). The tale is about Febronia, a girl of astonishing beauty, who lives in a convent where, under the guidance of the abbess Bryene, she distinguishes herself as a wise disciple and a gifted teacher and for her knowledge of the Scriptures. One day, the Roman army enters Nisibis with the purpose of persecuting the Christians and takes hold of Febronia. She is then put to public trial and, upon refusing the pagan judge's offer for her to marry his nephew and commander in chief, she is repeatedly and cruelly tortured and mutilated until she is beheaded. Miracles and healings occur at the site in which her body is interred at the convent. Before Febronia enters the arena for her trial, Bryene encourages her to remain steadfast under torture and to remain a virgin like Thecla did before her.

Martyrdom of Bassus and Susanna (*BHO* 174), anonymous, probably composed after the middle of the seventh century, Syriac. This text, in metrical prose (*memra*), consists of 741 verses and also belongs to the so-called collection of "Persian Martyr Acts" since it describes the martyrdom of Christians living in the Persian Empire under Zoroastrian rule. It narrates the conversion to Christianity of two teenaged twins, Bassus and Susanna, by the captive Stephen and the solitary Longinus. The twins are the children of a Zoroastrian who was a renowned official during the reign of Shapur II (309–379). The father, upon discovering their conversion, persecutes his children together with Stephen and Longinus: he follows them through valleys and mountains and kills them all, one after the other, with his sword before dying himself by divine punishment. The narrator praises Susanna, a moment before her martyrdom, as a virgin who is as courageous as Thecla and Febronia.

6 Arietta Papaconstantinou, "Shifting the Poetics of Gender Ambiguity: The Coptic Naturalization of Thecla"

The Martyrdom of Paese and Thecla, anonymous, seventh or eighth century, Coptic, Middle Egypt. This tale recounts the events leading to the martyrdom of Paese, a rich landowner, and his sister Thecla, a widow with a small child. A third character, Paul, is a close friend of Paese's and plays an important role in the narrative. Although the text conforms to some extent to a common model of Coptic martyr stories, it also borrows elements from other types of texts and is a more original composition than some of the more stereotypical martyrologies.

7 Julie Van Pelt, "Thecla, the First Cross-Dresser? The *Acts of Paul and Thecla* and the Lives of Byzantine Transvestite Saints"

The Acts of Xanthippe and Polyxena (*BHG* 1877), anonymous, third century, Greek. The story begins when the apostle Paul arrives in Spain. He enters the city in which Xanthippe, a married woman and the heroine of the first half of the story, lives. The apostle's presence ignites an all-consuming desire in Xanthippe. Seeing his wife in such an agitated state, Xanthippe's husband Probus, a local official of high rank, is overcome by grief and acts against the apostle. In the end, however, he is baptized by Paul along with his wife. After the celebrations, which conclude the first part of the narrative, Xanthippe's younger sister Polyxena is abducted. The young virgin struggles to safeguard her chastity while being exposed to all sorts of dangers throughout her travels, until she eventually manages to return home.

The Life and Miracles of Thecla (*BHG* 1717), anonymous, fifth century, Greek. This text was composed by an author who must have lived in the region of Seleucia (modern-day Sifilike, Turkey). The first part of this long text tells of the life, trials, and death of the virgin Thecla. Similar to the second century *Acts of Paul and Thecla*, it tells of how the young virgin is enchanted upon hearing the apostle Paul's preaching and is consequently condemned to be burned for rejecting her fiancé. After she is miraculously saved and follows Paul, she is condemned a second time when she defends her chastity against Alexander, an important man of high standing who assaults her. Finally, after being released once again, Thecla enters the ground alive, sinking into the earth in Seleucia, where a shrine is built for her. The second part of the work narrates the many miracles that occurred near Thecla's shrine in Seleucia.

The Life of Eusebia called Xenê (*BHG* 633), anonymous, fifth century, Greek. This hagiographical narrative is about Eusebia, a young girl from a noble family in Constantinople who secretly flees overseas because her parents are forcing her to marry, though she prefers to stay true to her heavenly bridegroom, Christ. She convinces two servants to follow her and exchanges her clothes for male garb. As soon as she reaches less familiar terrain and is no longer afraid of detection, she changes back into female clothes. However, she does change her name; she calls herself Xenê (stranger). She enters a convent and becomes a model of piety for all in her immediate environment.

8 Virginia Burrus, "From Diotima to Thecla and Beyond: Virginal Voice in the Lives of Helia and Constantina"

Symposium, Plato, fourth century BCE, Greek, Athens. This famous dialogue features a series of seven speeches in praise of Eros or Love, said to have been delivered at a banquet. Although the speakers are all male, Socrates' discourse recounts an exchange he once had with the prophetess Diotima, and it is Diotima's reported words that are typically held to prevail in what amounts to a debate on the true nature of Eros.

Leucippe and Clitophon, Achilles Tatius, second century, Greek. This romantic novel relates the adventures of Leucippe and Clitophon, told in the voice of the latter. The two well-born cousins meet and fall in love when Leucippe visits Tyre, where Clitiphon resides. Fearing opposition to their marriage, they leave Tyre secretly and face a series of dangers and challenges as they travel through the eastern Mediterranean, including shipwreck, capture by bandits, abduction, apparent deaths, attempted rapes, actual infidelities, and more. Eventually they are reunited and marry in Byzantium, Leucippe's home.

Symposium (*CPG* 1810), Methodius of Olympus, third century, Greek. This dialogue, modeled on Plato's text of the same name, features a series of ten speeches in praise of virginity, said to have been delivered at a banquet hosted by Arete, or Virtue. All of the speakers are virginal women, and the winning discourse is delivered by Thecla.

Life of Saint Helia (*BHL* 3798), anonymous, possibly fifth century, Latin. This hagiographical novel tells the tale of a young girl who dedicates herself to virginity in defiance of her mother's will and is subsequently brought to trial for her disobedience and her refusal to marry. The story of Thecla, who is not named, serves as a narrative template for Helia's, but the bulk of the text is not in narrative but in dialogue format. Two of its three books are dominated by an extended debate between the young Helia and her mother regarding the relative merits of virginity and marriage, followed by briefer exchanges between the two women and a bishop; a third book records a debate between Helia and a judge, in which most of the talking is done by the vociferous virgin. All of the speeches are generously laced with biblical citations, enhancing the air of self-conscious rhetorical virtuosity that pervades the *Life*.

Life of Saint Constantina (*BHL* 1927), anonymous, possibly sixth century, Latin. This hagiographical novel relates the story of the emperor Constantine's daughter, who is said to be miraculously healed of leprosy by a vision of the virgin martyr Agnes. Thereby converted to Christianity, she dedicates herself to a life of celibacy and transforms her palace into a convent of virgins. This *Life* incorporates two prior texts that are associated with the Roman *Gesta martyrum* – the *Passion of Gallicanu*s and the *Passion of John and Paul*. It also references the legend of Constantina's healing narrated at greater length in the *Passion of Agnes*. Focusing on the figure of Constantina, the *Life* extends and elaborates on the earlier textual traditions, in which she is a secondary character, supplementing those traditions with new narrative materials, fictive letters, and a sprawling dialogue in which twelve virgins deliver prepared speeches on the "highest good" and "worst evil," to each of which Constantina responds with a speech of her own. Initially brief, the queen's speeches become increasingly expansive, demonstrating her exegetical and theological facility. Her voice dominates those of the other speakers, positioning her as not only their loving patron and teacher but also their victor in rhetorical contest.

9   Klazina Staat, "Reception and Rejection: Thecla and the *Acts of Paul and Thecla* in the *Passion of Eugenia* and Other Latin Texts"

The Life and Passion of Eugenia (BHL 2667 and 2666), anonymous, second half of the fifth to early sixth century (first recension) and sixth or seventh century (second recension), Latin, Rome. Eugenia is the daughter of a Roman prefect in Egypt who converts to Christianity after she has read a copy of the *Acts of Paul and Thecla* and/or a letter by the apostle Paul. She decides to escape from home with her eunuchs Prothus and Hyacinthus. They enter a male monastery with Eugenia disguised as a man. Eugenia (now Eugenius) is later elected the leader of the monastery. After she is falsely accused of sexual abuse by the noble woman, Melanthia, she is taken to court in Alexandria, which is presided over by her father Philip. Eugenia proves her innocence by revealing her identity as the prefect's daughter. She is reunited with her mother and brothers. The family and the city convert to Christianity. Philip becomes the bishop of Alexandria but is martyred (and in the Latin versions, with his sons. In the Armenian, Greek, and Syriac versions they return to Rome and are selected to govern other provinces). Eugenia and her mother return to Rome, where they convert other noble women. Eugenia dies as a martyr together with Basilla who is converted by the saint and persuaded to renounce marriage. After Eugenia is buried by her mother Claudia, she appears to her in a dream, predicting their reunion in heaven. Claudia dies soon after and is buried with her daughter. Much like the other versions that exist in other languages, the earlier Latin version (*BHL* 2667) has explicit references to the *Acts of Paul and Thecla* while the later version (*BHL* 2666) does not.

10   Ghazzal Dabiri, "A Medieval Sufi Thecla? Female Civic and Spiritual Leadership in ʿAttār's "The Tale of a Virtuous Woman" and *The Life and Passion of Eugenia*

The Tale of the Virtuous Woman, Farīd al-Dīn ʿAttār, mid-twelfth to early thirteenth century, Persian, Nishapur, Iran. The tale appears as the first story in ʿAttār's *Ilāhīnāmah* (*Book of the Divine*), a long narrative poem (*masnavī*) that is more accurately a collection of versified tales bound by a frame tale. While many later versions proliferated, only two other early versions of this tale are known; one is dated to the late ninth–early tenth century and is written in Arabic and another, in Persian, is contemporaneous to ʿAttār's version. In ʿAttār's version, an incomparably beautiful, virtuous woman, whose husband has left for pilgrimage, is left in the care of her brother-in-law. Soon, the brother-in-law falls in love with the virtuous woman and makes unwanted advances toward her. She refuses him and in his bitter disappointment brings her before judges on false charges of adultery. Her miraculous survival of a trial by stoning is the catalyst for her travels and misadventures. During her travels, she encounters several men who try to have their way with her, including sailors who at first had wished to aid her. When their kindness turns to lust, and she faces physical/sexual assault, she prays to God for deliverance, preferring death over defilement. Instead of death, she is knocked unconscious as God unleashes a firestorm that devours the men, turning them to ash. Later, she comes to and sees she has reached shore safely and is sitting atop the sailors' riches. Before anyone can see her, she disguises herself as a man. Later, when she is found, she states she will only speak to the king of the realm. When he comes, she relates her travails and offers him the riches in exchange for a place nearby where she can be free to pray to God in peace. Awed by her, the king acquiesces. Sometime later, when the king is on his death bed, he appoints the virtuous woman as his heir. She reveals herself to be a woman and refuses the throne on account of her gender. The king's army and viziers partially reject her refusal. They offer her the choice to either rule as a man or to select someone from among them she deems worthy to rule in her stead. She agrees to the latter and returns to her prayers and performs healing miracles. One day, the husband returns home to find his wife gone and his brother blind and paralyzed. He tells his brother that he has heard of someone in a different land who has the power to heal. The brothers agree to visit the holy person, and on their way, they encounter other maimed men who are traveling to visit the holy person also. Unbeknownst to the husband, his new traveling companions are the very men who previously had harmed his wife and were maimed by divine punishment. When he arrives at her shrine, she immediately recognizes her husband but disguises herself once more when she sees his companions. They each come forward and ask to be healed; she grants them their wish on the condition that they confess the sins that had led them to such misery. They each confess, including her brother-in-law, and when she sees their repentance is sincere, she heals each of them. Then she reveals herself to her husband and the other men, who are simultaneously ashamed and overjoyed when they recognize her. Having forgiven each of them, the virtuous woman and her husband enjoy a happy reunion before she appoints him as king of the realm and selects the only man, a Bedouin, who aided her during her trials as his vizier.

Index

3 Corinthians, 37

'Abbasids (750–1258), 297
abduction. *See* motifs
Abgar (fl. first century), king, 123
Abu Mina, Egypt, 176, 180
Abuzard, 153, 157–158, 170
Achilles Tatius (fl. 2nd century), 236, 239
   Leucippe and Clitophon, 15, 214, 236, 239
Acts of Andrew, 126
Acts of Cyrus and John, 79–80
Acts of Paul, 1, 7, 9, 35, 37–38, 40–41, 44, 48–51, 54–56, 105, 112, 258, 260, 296, 318. *See also Acts of Paul and Thecla*
Acts of Paul and Thecla, 1–2, 4, 7, 9–10, 13, 15, 18–19, 26, 36, 38, 41, 50, 52, 55, 64, 66–67, 72–73, 75, 80–81, 97, 100, 105, 111, 113–115, 119, 122–125, 130, 142, 144, 155, 168, 182, 197, 210, 216, 218, 220, 225, 228, 242, 246, 256–257, 259–260, 263, 265–266, 268, 274, 276–277, 286, 288, 290, 292, 296–298, 304–306, 308–310, 312, 319, 321, 323, 325
Acts of Peter, 126
Acts of Philip, 126
Acts of the Apostles, 41, 94, 105, 112, 178, 217, 259, 261
Acts of Thecla. *See Acts of Paul and Thecla*
Acts of Thomas, 126
Acts of Xanthippe and Polyxena, 16, 200, 217–218, 220–223, 225, 228
Adrianople, 131
adventure. *See* motifs
Aethelthryth (636–679), Abbess of Ely, 98
Agathangelos, 13, 110, 112, 115–116, 119, 121–122
   History, 13, 111–112, 115, 119–121
Aldhelm (639–709), Abbot of Malmesbury, 89, 98, 104
   De virginitate, 98

Alexander, 5, 7, 13, 64, 72, 119, 159, 201, 207, 212, 219, 222, 267–268, 286, 308
Alexander Romance, 321
Alexandria, 61, 78, 175–177, 180, 182–183, 185, 188, 190–191, 266–267, 289, 292, 307–308, 310, 312
Ambrose of Milan (d. 397), bishop, 96–97
   Ad Simplicianum, 96
   Ad Vercellensem ecclesiam, 96
   De virginibus, 96
Amra Choluim Chille, 85
Antioch, 2, 5, 64, 72, 78, 88–89, 91, 93, 103, 119, 156, 159, 169, 176, 197, 204, 206, 213, 222, 225, 304
Apocalypse of Adam, 40
Apocalypse of Paul, 45
Apocryphal Acts, 319–321, 323
Apocryphon of John, 40, 46
Apolinaria, 201, 203, 212
APT. *See Acts of Paul and Thecla*
Apuleius (c. 125–170), 48
   Florida, 48
   Metamorphoses, 120
Arete, 95, 245–246, 251, 253
Arsacids
   of Armenia (12–428), 130
assault. *See* motifs
Athanasius of Alexandria (d. 373), bishop, 36, 176–177
   De virginitate, 176
   Life of Antony, 36
'Aṭṭār. *See* Farīd al-Dīn 'Aṭṭār (c. 1145–c. 1220)
Augustine of Hippo (354–430), bishop, 98, 234, 260–261
   Confessions, 234
   De civitate Dei, 261
   De haeresibus ad Quodvultdeum, 39
   De sancta virginitate, 98, 261
autonomy, 113
   female, 8, 170, 319–320

Index

'Awfi (1171–1242), 295
  Tale of the Virtuous Woman, 295
AXP. *See Acts of Xanthippe and Polyxena*

baptism, 1, 6, 9, 12, 14, 35, 39, 41, 43–44,
    46–47, 49–53, 55, 74, 76, 121, 123,
    126, 129, 197, 206, 242, 245, 269, 273,
    287, 304, 313
Basil of Ancyra (d. c. 364), bishop
  On Virginity, 118
Basil of Caesarea (330-379), bishop, 96–97
Basil of Seleucia (d. c. 468), bishop, 110. *See also*
  Life and Miracles of Thecla
Basilla, 267, 310
Bassus, 153, 156–159, 171
beauty. *See* motifs
Bede (d. 735), 91, 98
  Historia ecclesiastica, 98
  Martyrology, 99
Book of Thecla, 62–63, 67, 69, 72–73
Book of Women, 112, 143
Brigit bé bithmaith, 85
Brigit, saint, 85
Bryene, 146, 148–149, 151, 153
Bukhara, 295

Caena Cypriani, 104
Caesarea, 74–75, 77
Cain, 42–43, 48
Cainites, 38–40, 42–44, 48, 55
calendars, 64, 67, 90
  Menologia, 15, 20
Carthage, 35, 48
Chalcedonians, 159
Chariton, 221
  Chaereas and Callirhoe, 214, 221
Charles I (1600–1649), king, 175
chastity, 95–96, 98, 105, 113, 115, 117, 126,
    156, 177, 181, 190, 218, 225, 240, 264,
    268, 273, 296, 305
  defense of, 113, 119, 122
  preservation of, 9, 16, 95, 150, 211, 262
  valorization of, 115
Christ, 25, 35, 40, 47, 51, 70, 72, 79, 92–93, 95,
    117, 128–129, 131, 133, 147, 152, 155,
    160, 170–171, 188, 190, 197, 206, 214,
    242, 244, 246–247, 249, 263, 267, 272,
    274, 287, 306, 308
  Bride of, 61, 158, 187, 246, 310
  as Bridegroom, 1, 95–96, 118, 150, 187, 224,
    245, 250, 273
  Handmaiden of, 156
  Slave of, 156, 207
Christianity
  Armenian, 13, 110, 133

  early, 7, 24, 320–321
  Eastern, 16
  establishment of, 8
  growth of, 10
  Syriac, 143, 167, 170
  Western, 16
Christina, 206–207, 210
Church
  Alexandrian, 179
  Armenian, 110, 130, 133
  Coptic, 64
  Ethiopian, 67
  Great, 44, 47
  Greek, 111, 176
  North African, 14, 37, 39, 56
  of the East, 2, 296
  proto-Orthodox, 47
  Syrian Orthodox, 111, 159
Claudian (c. 370–c. 404), 264
  Carmina Minora, 51, 264
Clement of Alexandria (150–215), 38
  Stromata, 38
Clitophon, 240
Colum Cille (d. 597), saint, 85
Commendatio animae. *See Commendation of the Soul*
Commendation of the Soul, 99, 101, 262–263
Commodian (fl. 3rd century)
  Carmen Apologeticum, 75
Constantina, 234–235, 251–253
Contra Celsum. *See* Origen (d. 254): *Against Celsus*
conversion, 12–13, 18, 71, 110, 112, 115–116,
    122–123, 126, 129, 162, 165, 207, 266,
    268, 289, 305, 308
  spiritual, 13, 289, 303, 309
Conversion of Cyprian of Antioch, 207–208, 212, 214
Council
  of Nicaea (325), 130, 175, 179
  Vatican
    Second, 99
cross-dressing. *See* motifs
Cynics, 48
Cyprian of Antioch (d. 304), saint, 102, 104
Cyprian of Carthage (d. 258), bishop, 102
Cyril of Alexandria (412–444), bishop, 78
Cyrus (Alexandrian martyr), 79–80

Daniel, 120, 161, 263
death-before-death. *See Fanā' billāh*
desire. *See* motifs
Diocletian (r. 284–305), Roman emperor, 36, 146
Diotima, 236–239, 241, 245–246, 254
disguise. *See* motifs
Dublin, 91

East Africa, 3
Egeria (fl. 4th century), 152, 179, 235
　Itinerarium, 179
Egypt, 66, 175, 177, 179–180, 183, 262, 267, 297
　Lower, 61, 65
　Middle, 180
Elias (fl. 6th century), 159, 162, 166
　Life of John of Tella, 14, 142, 145, 159, 165, 170
Epiphanius of Salamis (d. 403), bishop
　Panarion, 38, 45, 243
Epistle of Pelagia, 14, 74–75, 77–78, 81
eros, 95, 237, 239
Ethiopia, 26, 62
Eudocia, 213
Eugenia, 15, 160, 177–178, 201, 209, 211–213, 216, 228, 257, 265, 267–268, 270, 272, 275, 288, 292, 304–305, 307–309, 311–312
Euphrosyne, 201, 214
Eusebia, 224–225, 227
Eusebius of Caesarea (d. 339), bishop
　An Assembly of Ancient Martyrs, 36
　Ecclesiastical History, 117, 123
Eusebius of Emesa (d. c. 359), bishop
　Homily 6 On the Martyrs, 118
　On Virginity, 118
'Ēzānā (d. 356), ruler of Ethiopia, 63

Falconilla, 3, 5, 100, 242
Fanā' billāh, 283, 287, 295
Farīd al-Dīn 'Attār (c. 1145–c. 1220), 282, 292–293, 298, 313
　Ilāhīnāmah, 282, 284, 292, 299–301
　Tale of the Virtuous Woman, 282–285, 289, 292, 294, 298–301, 303–305, 309–310, 313
　Tazkirat al-awliya', 293
Faustus of Byzantium (fl. 5th century)
　History of Armenia, 110, 130, 133
Febronia, 14, 146–148, 150, 152–156, 158
Feqerta Krestos, 63
fidelity. See motifs
Filaster of Brescia (330–397), bishop
　Diversarum Hereseon Liber, 39

Gadla samā'tāt, 64, 67–68, 73, 80
Gadla Ṭēqalā, 61
Gaul, 42, 102–103
Gelasian Sacramentary, 101
Gellone Sacramentary, 102
Génair Pátraic, 85
Gnosticism, 38, 46, 49
Gnostics, 43, 45–46, 49–50, 55

Gospel of Judas, 39–40, 42–45, 47, 50, 55
Gospel of the Egyptians, 40
Goths, 131
Gregory of Nazianzus (d. 390), archbishop, 2, 96
　Contra Julianum, 96
　Poemata Moralia, 96, 100
Gregory of Nyssa (d. 378), archbishop, 114, 208
　Life of Macrina, 114
Gregory of Tours (538–594), bishop, 179

Hagia Thecla, 2
Handmaiden of God, 3, 6. See also Christ, Handmaiden of
harlots
　holy, 207
Helia, 234, 246, 248–249, 251, 253
Heliodorus (fl. 4th century)
　Aethiopica, 214
Hildelith, abbess, 98
Hippolytus of Rome (d. 236)
　In Danielem, 75
Holy Book of the Great Invisible Spirit. See Gospel of the Egyptians
homilies, 16, 112
Hṙipʿsimē. See Rhipsime
Hymn On the Saintly Women, 155

Iconium, 2, 4, 6, 11, 64, 80, 122, 162, 218, 242, 269, 273, 305
intertextuality, 23–24, 132, 146, 199, 210
Iran, 2, 292, 296–298
Ireland, 2, 26, 85, 89–90
Irenaeus of Lyon (130–202), bishop, 42, 44, 49
　Adversus Haereses, 38–39, 42, 44, 49
Isaac, 88
Isidore of Pelusium (d. c. 449), 179
'Iyasus Mo'a (1214–1294), 62

Jacob, 88
Jacobus de Voragine (1228–1298), archbishop, 220
　Golden Legend, 220
Jerome of Stridon (d. 420), 49, 96, 260–261
　Adversus Vigilantium, 48–49
　Chronicles, 260
　De Viris Illustribus, 75, 96, 318
　Epistle 82, 48
　Indiculus de haeresibus, 39
　Letter to Eustochium, 114, 260
John (Alexandrian martyr), 79–80
John Chrysostom (d. 407), archbishop, 179
　Ad populum Antiochenum, 179
　De Virginitate, 115
John Moschos (c. 550–619), 189
　Spiritual Meadow, 189

Index   343

John of Tella (d. 538), bishop, 159, 161–162, 164–166, 170
John, apostle, 88, 94
Judas Iscariot, apostle, 40, 43, 47, 168
Julian the Apostate (331–363), Byzantine emperor, 131

Karlsruhe Calendar, 89, 91
Koutloumous
    Imperial Menology, 129
Krestos Śemrā (fl. 15th century), 63
Kulaynī (d. 941), 293–294
Kyrillos Loukaris (1572–1638), patriarch, 175

Leo VI (886–912), Byzantine emperor, 216
Leucippe, 240–241, 246
Libelli precum, 104
Life and Martyrdom of Eudocia, 207–208
Life and Martyrdom of Eugenia. See *Life of Eugenia*
Life and Martyrdom of Susanna, 209
Life and Miracles of Thecla, 13, 16, 110, 131, 179, 200, 221–223, 225–227, 286, 304
Life and Passion of Eugenia. See *Life of Eugenia*
Life of Adrian and Nataly, 220
Life of Andronikos and Athanasia, 209
Life of Apolinaria, 209
Life of Constantina, 15, 233, 236, 251–252
Life of Eudocia. See *Life and Martyrdom of Eudocia*
Life of Eugenia, 13, 15, 27, 145, 179, 199, 209–210, 216–217, 257, 263, 265, 268, 271, 274, 276, 286, 289, 292, 298, 304, 308–313
Life of Euphrosyne of Alexandria, 203, 209, 214–216, 219
Life of Eusebia called Xenê, 16, 200, 217, 224, 226–228
Life of Helia, 15, 233, 236, 246, 248, 251
Life of Mary called Marinos, 209
Life of Matrona of Perge, 209, 213, 215
Life of Melania, 118
Life of Pelagia, 213
Life of Theodora of Alexandria, 212, 219
Life of Theophano, 216
lions. See motifs
LM. See *Life and Miracles of Thecla*
Longus (fl. 2nd century)
    Daphnis and Chloe, 214
love. See motifs
Lucia, 206, 210

Macedonia, 68, 75
Majnūn (fl. 7th century), 285
Mani (d. c. 277), 297

Manichaeans, 297
marriage, 9, 11, 48, 69, 156, 183, 191, 208, 210, 221, 235, 239–240, 244, 246, 249, 272, 283, 310
    celibate, 188, 303
    eschatological, 95, 158, 187
    renunciation of, 74, 210–213, 216, 266, 270, 288, 310, 323–324
Martyrdom of ʿAbda da-Mšiḥa, 154
Martyrdom of Agatha, 207
Martyrdom of Alexander and Antonina, 220
Martyrdom of Badmo, 167
Martyrdom of Bassus and Susanna, 14, 142, 145, 153, 155, 170
Martyrdom of Behnam and Sarah, 154
Martyrdom of Christina, 206
Martyrdom of Cyrus and John. See *Acts of Cyrus and John*
Martyrdom of Febronia, 14, 23, 142, 145–146, 149, 152, 161, 170
Martyrdom of Galaktion and Episteme, 208
Martyrdom of Lucia, 205
Martyrdom of Matthew, 124
Martyrdom of Narsai, 167
Martyrdom of Paese and Thecla, 14, 16, 26, 180–182, 187–188, 190
Martyrdom of Paul, 112
Martyrdom of Polycarp, 206
Martyrdom of Saba Pirguśnasp, 154
Martyrdom of Shenoufe and His Brethren, 191
Martyrdom of Thaddaeus and Sanduxt, 110, 122–123
Martyrdom of the Brothers of Lentini, 207
Martyrdom of the Holy Samaritan Woman Photine, 128
Martyrdom of Thecla and Her Companions, 142, 146, 167–168, 170. See also *Gadla Ṭēqalā*
Martyrdom of Theodora and Didumos, 220
Martyrologium Hieronymianum, 88, 91
Martyrology of Tallaght, 91, 104
Mary Magdalene, 94
Mary, Virgin, Mother of the Lord, 90, 97–98, 181, 187, 249, 277
Maṣḥafa Ṭēqalā. See *Book of Thecla*
Maštocʿ (d. 439), 111
Matrona, 213, 215
Mattidia, 288, 298
Maximus of Turin (b. 380), bishop, 90
    Sermon for St. Agnes, 90
Mazdeism
    Armenian, 120
Mediterranean, 3, 91, 103, 262, 267, 286, 320
Melanthia, 211, 267–268, 307, 310
Menas, saint, 176, 180

Menologia. See Calendars
Methodius of Olympus (250–311), bishop, 15, 95, 105, 114, 234, 236, 243–244, 246, 249, 251–252
  Symposium, 15, 95, 105, 234, 243, 246, 252
Milan, 97
Minucius Felix (d. 260)
  Octavius, 187
Miracles of Thecla. See Life and Miracles of Thecla
motifs
  abduction, 218–219, 248
  adventure, 10, 41, 202, 218, 260, 288
  assault, 1, 9, 95, 119, 176, 204, 207, 211, 289, 307
  beauty, 5, 77, 118, 162, 203, 212, 220, 222–223, 283–284, 286, 302, 324
    contemplation of, 238
    dissimulation of, 203, 222–223, 225–226, 286
    manifestation of the divine, 302
    wrong response to, 303
  clothes
    tearing of, 5, 186, 267–268, 276
  cross-dressing, 16, 26, 177, 197–200, 202–203, 210–211, 217, 219–220, 223, 225–227, 273, 275
    temporary, 198
  desire, 7–9, 15, 27, 170, 201, 208, 212, 214, 218, 222, 234, 236, 238–240, 243, 245–246, 250, 252–253, 282–283, 302, 306, 323
  disguise, 16, 149, 198, 202, 204, 216, 220, 222–223, 225–226, 266, 274, 284, 286, 288, 294, 305
  fidelity, 10, 240
  fire-in-water, 287
  hair, cutting of, 5, 71, 197, 201, 203–204, 212, 219, 221–223, 226–227, 266, 286
  lions, 65, 71, 74–76, 93, 125, 159, 325
  love, 1, 6, 64, 118–119, 187, 211, 237–238, 240–241, 284, 299, 311, 323
    at first hearing, 210, 213, 215
    at first sight, 10, 208
    brotherly, 14
    commentary on, 284
    debate on, 241
    eschatological, 14, 26, 188
    of the divine, 283, 300, 302
    of God for humanity, 285, 301, 303
    paternal, 127
    transcendental, 1
    triangle, 183
    unrequited, 285
    virginal, 251
  prison, 182, 184, 186
  devotion to teacher at, 5, 164, 207
  reunion in, 183
  teaching in, 64, 144
  visiting, 180, 185
  Scheintod, 210, 214, 218
  shipwreck, 284, 286, 288
  storms, 75, 206, 287, 294
  stranger, 100, 178, 181, 188, 225, 242, 301
  torture, 1, 6, 66, 70, 73, 75, 79, 81, 129, 147, 149–150, 153, 155, 181, 185–186, 189, 204, 206, 210, 214, 240
  travel, 9–11, 41, 176, 178–180, 199, 203, 218, 220, 222–224, 226, 266, 286, 288, 318, 320, 324
MPTh. See Martyrdom of Paese and Thecla
Muhammad al-Afšīn (d. 901), emir of Azerbaijan, 133

Nebuchadnezzar (605–562 BCE), 120
Nersēs (353–373), Armenian Catholicos, 130
Ní car Brigit búadach bith, 86
Nicephoros Callistos (1256–1335), 75
  Historia ecclesiastica, 75
Niceta of Remesiana (335–414), bishop
  On the Fall of Susanna, 265
Nishapur, 293, 296, 298
Novels, ancient Greek. *See* Romances, ancient

Oengus (d. 824), bishop, 87
  Félire Óengusso, 86, 88–91, 93–94, 99, 102, 104–105
Ophites, 38, 40, 44, 49
Orationes Cypriani, 102, 104
Origen (d. 254)
  Against Celsus, 38, 117
Ovid (43 BCE–17/18 CE), 120
  Metamorphoses, 120

Paese, 14, 180, 182–183, 185, 187, 189, 191
Palestine, 74
Parthians (247 BCE–224 CE), 296
Passion of Agnes, 235
Passion of Cyriacus and Paula, 263
Passion of Eugenia. See Life of Eugenia
Passion of Gallicanus, John, and Paul, 235
Passion of Pelagia of Tarsus, 74, 76
Paul (Egyptian martyr), 14, 180, 183–185, 188–189, 191
Paul, apostle, 1–6, 9, 11–13, 15, 51–55, 61, 64–65, 67–69, 71, 73–76, 80, 88, 94, 102–103, 105, 122, 129, 147, 164, 168–170, 176–177, 180, 182, 187–188, 201–202, 204, 206, 213, 215, 218, 222, 225, 233, 242–243, 247, 250, 257, 266,

268, 273, 275, 277, 286, 304–305, 308, 318, 323–324, 326
Pawle, 167, 169–170
Pelagia (holy harlot), 213
Pelagia (martyr), 74, 76, 78, 81
Persian Empire. *See* Sasanian Empire (242–651)
Persian Martyr Acts, 154, 167
Peter, apostle, 88, 94, 102–103, 129, 207, 277, 288
Philip, 307–309
Photine, 129
Plato (d. 347 BCE)
  Symposium, 15, 236, 238–239, 241, 243
Plutarch (46–c. 119)
  Erotic Dialogue, 239
Polyxena, 218–220
prison. *See* motifs
Prodigies of Thecla, 111
Prothus and Hyacinthus, 266, 271
Psalms of the Wanderers, 297
Pseudo-Alcuin
  Officia per ferias, 104
Pseudo-Athanasius
  Life of Saint Syncletica, 114
Pseudo-Basil
  On Virginity, 118
Pseudo-Clement
  Recognitions, 286, 288–289, 298
Pseudo-Gelasian Decree, 259, 261
Pseudo-Hippolytus
  Refutatio omnium haeresium, 38
Pseudo-Lucian
  Dialogue on Loves, 239
Pseudo-Tertullian
  Adversus omnes haereses, 38

Rābiʿah of Basra (d. 801), saint, 285
Radegund (520–587), queen of the Franks, 264
reception, 13, 15, 19, 22, 24, 27, 35–36, 38, 40, 63, 111, 129, 132, 143, 159, 170, 221, 224, 228, 256, 258–260, 276
Rheinau Sacramentary, 100, 102, 104
Rhipsime, 13, 63, 112, 115–116, 118–119, 121
Roman Empire, 131, 146, 153
Romances, ancient, 1, 9–10, 156, 178, 214, 218, 286, 302, 319, 321, 323–324
Rome, 117, 129, 180, 256, 265, 267, 307, 310, 312

Saklas, 47
Salām, 65–66, 81
Saltair na Rann, 91, 93, 99, 102, 104–105
Sanduxt, 122–123, 125–128
Sasanian Empire (242–651), 153, 296
Scheintod. *See* motifs

Seleucia, 2, 6, 122, 132, 157, 179–180, 221, 270
Senkessār. *See* Synaxarium
Seth, 40, 45
Sethianism, 46
Severus of Antioch (d. 538), patriarch, 159
Shapur II (309–379), Sasanian king, 153, 167
shipwreck. *See* motifs
Socrates (c. 470–399 BCE), 114, 236–237, 239, 251
  Menexenus, 238
  Philoctetes, 253
Sophronius of Jerusalem (550–638), bishop
  Miracles of Cyrus and John, 78
storms. *See* motifs
storytellers, 320
  female, 152, 319–320
stranger. *See* motifs. *See also* Thecla of Iconium
Sufis, 282, 285, 291, 293, 295, 303
Sufism, 299, 302
Sulamī (d. 1020), 293
Sulpicius Severus (363–425), 264
  Dialogues, 90, 264
Susanna, 153–154, 156–157, 159
Symposios (c. 370-380), Arian bishop, 132
Synaxarium, 61, 63, 65–66, 73–74, 78, 80

Tʿovma Arcruni (fl. 9th–10th century)
  History of Arcruni, 133
Takla Hāymānot (b. 1215), 62
Tale of the Virtuous Woman. *See* Farīd al-Dīn ʿAṭṭār (c. 1145–c. 1220)
Tallaght, 91, 104
Teaching of Addai, 123
Tertullian (b. c. 155), 12, 14, 17, 20, 26, 35–36, 38, 40–46, 48–55, 258–260, 276, 312, 318
  de Baptismo, 20, 26, 35, 39–40, 44, 48, 51–53, 55–56, 258, 312, 318
Thaddaeus, apostle, 13
Thamyris, 3–4, 163–164, 170, 266–268, 270, 311
Thaʿālibī (961–1038), 293
Thaʿlabī (d. 1035), 293
Thecla (Egyptian martyr), 14, 180, 182–183, 187, 190
Thecla (Persian martyr), 62, 155, 167, 170
Thecla of Iconium, 62, 167, 186–187, 190, 318, 322–325
  as apostle, 26, 62, 64–65, 79, 94, 128, 324
  as ascetic, 176, 264
  as confessor, 14, 66
  as evangelizer, 124, 304
  as healer, 93
  as intercessor, 99–100, 262, 264
  as leader, 267, 292

Thecla of Iconium (cont.)
　as apostle, 110, 128
　as model, 4, 16–17, 25, 39, 56, 117, 121, 126, 133, 144–145, 147, 163, 177, 208, 210, 225, 258–260, 264, 266, 268, 271, 274, 276, 296
　　for baptisms, 14, 17
　　of chastity, 96
　　of forbearance, 14, 21, 153
　　proto-martyr, 81
　　teacher, 14, 17
　　virgin, 15, 95, 261
　as proto-martyr, 14, 73, 78, 80, 90, 98
　as stranger, 176
　as teacher, 37, 122, 267, 304, 307
　as virgin, 112, 177, 246
　cult of, 8, 89, 132, 176–177, 210, 262, 267
　performance of miracles, 132
Theocleia, 3–4, 163–164, 170, 323
Theodora, 211–212
Theodoret of Cyrrhus (d. 457), bishop
　Haereticarum fabularum Compendium, 39
Theophila, 244
Thomais, 146, 148–150, 153, 170
Thomas Roe (d. 1644), sir, ambassador, 175
Tiridates IV (298–330), king of Armenia, 115
torture. *See* motifs
transvestism. *See* motifs: cross-dressing
travel. *See* motifs
Trimorphic Protennoia, 40

Tryphaena, 3, 5, 14, 72, 100, 124, 149–150, 153, 170, 214, 219, 242, 304, 308–309, 323
TVW. *See* Farīd al-Dīn ʿAttār: Tale of the Virtuous Woman

Vahagn, God of War, 120
Valens (328-378), Arian emperor, 130–131
Venantius Fortunatus (530–609), bishop
　Carmina, 264
virginity, 8, 37, 95, 98, 114, 156, 235, 241, 246, 249–252, 274, 319
　defense of, 115, 117, 119, 240, 242, 246
　doctrine of, 245
　in praise of, 94, 96, 98, 235, 243, 252
　model of, 97, 260
　preservation of, 118, 211, 251, 261. *See also* chastity

Walatta Ṗēṭros (1592–1642), 63
wedding, 118, 158, 187, 191. *See also* marriage

Xanthippe, 218–219
Xenê. *See* Eusebia
Xenophon of Ephesus, 221
　Ephesian Tale, 214, 221

Zarmanduxt, 13, 124
Zeno the Isaurian (d. 491), Byzantine emperor, 2
Zostrianos, 40

For EU product safety concerns, contact us at Calle de José Abascal, 56–1°,
28003 Madrid, Spain or eugpsr@cambridge.org.

www.ingramcontent.com/pod-product-compliance
Lightning Source LLC
LaVergne TN
LVHW011758060526
838200LV00053B/3624